Routledge Handbook on the Governance of Religious Diversity

This book critically reviews state-religion models and the ways in which different countries manage religious diversity, illuminating different responses to the challenges encountered in accommodating both majorities and minorities. The country cases encompass eight world regions and 23 countries, offering a wealth of research material suitable to support comparative research. Each case is analysed in depth looking at historical trends, current practices, policies, legal norms and institutions.

By looking into state-religion relations and governance of religious diversity in regions beyond Europe, we gain insights into predominantly Muslim countries (Egypt, Morocco, Tunisia, Turkey, Indonesia, Malaysia), countries with pronounced historical religious diversity (India and Lebanon) and into a predominantly migrant pluralist nation (Australia). These insights can provide a basis for re-thinking European models and learning from experiences of governing religious diversity in other socio-economic and geopolitical contexts. Key analytical and comparative reflections inform the introduction and concluding chapters.

This volume offers a research and study companion to better understand the connection between state-religion relations and the governance of religious diversity in order to inform both policy and research efforts in accommodating religious diversity. Given its accessible language and further readings provided in each chapter, the volume is ideally suited for undergraduate and graduate students. It will also be a valuable resource for researchers working in the wider field of ethnic, migration, religion and citizenship studies.

Anna Triandafyllidou holds the Canada Excellence Research Chair in Migration and Integration at Ryerson University, Toronto. She was previously based at the European University Institute (EUI) where she held a Robert Schuman Chair on Cultural Pluralism in the EUI's Global Governance Programme. She is Editor of the *Journal of Immigrant and Refugee Studies*.

Tina Magazzini is a Research Associate at the Robert Schuman Centre for Advanced Studies of the European University Institute, in Florence, where she researches different models of religious diversity governance. She holds a PhD in Human Rights and a MA in International Relations, and prior to joining the EUI worked with different research institutes and international organizations in the US, Belgium, Hungary, Spain and Zimbabwe.

Routledge International Handbooks

Routledge Handbook of Bounded Rationality
Edited by Riccardo Viale

Routledge International Handbook of Charisma
Edited by José Pedro Zúquete

Routledge International Handbook of Working-Class Studies
Edited by Michele Fazio, Christie Launius, and Tim Strangleman

Routledge Handbook of Digital Media and Communication
Edited by Leah A. Lievrouw and Brian D. Loader

Routledge International Handbook of Religion in Global Society
Edited by Jayeel Cornelio, François Gauthier, Tuomas Martikainen and Linda Woodhead

The Routledge Handbook on the International Dimension of Brexit
Edited by Juan Santos Vara and Ramses A. Wessel; Assistant Editor, and Polly R. Polak

Routledge Handbook of Critical Finance Studies
Edited by Christian Borch and Robert Wosnitzer

Routledge Handbook on the Governance of Religious Diversity
Edited by Anna Triandafyllidou and Tina Magazzini

The Routledge Handbook of Critical European Studies
Edited by Didier Bigo, Thomas Diez, Evangelos Fanoulis, Ben Rosamond and Yannis A. Stivachtis

Handbook on Arctic Indigenous Peoples in the Arctic
Edited by Timo Koivurova, Else Grete Broderstad, Dorothée Cambou, Dalee Dorough and Florian Stammler

For more information about this series, please visit: https://www.routledge.com/Routledge-International-Handbooks/book-series/RIHAND

Routledge Handbook on the Governance of Religious Diversity

Edited by Anna Triandafyllidou and Tina Magazzini

LONDON AND NEW YORK

First published 2021
by Routledge
2 Park Square, Milton Park, Abingdon, Oxon OX14 4RN

and by Routledge
52 Vanderbilt Avenue, New York, NY 10017

Routledge is an imprint of the Taylor & Francis Group, an informa business

© 2021 selection and editorial matter, Anna Triandafyllidou and Tina Magazzini; individual chapters, the contributors

The right of Anna Triandafyllidou and Tina Magazzini to be identified as the authors of the editorial material, and of the authors for their individual chapters, has been asserted in accordance with sections 77 and 78 of the Copyright, Designs and Patents Act 1988.

All rights reserved. No part of this book may be reprinted or reproduced or utilised in any form or by any electronic, mechanical, or other means, now known or hereafter invented, including photocopying and recording, or in any information storage or retrieval system, without permission in writing from the publishers.

Trademark notice: Product or corporate names may be trademarks or registered trademarks, and are used only for identification and explanation without intent to infringe.

British Library Cataloguing-in-Publication Data
A catalogue record for this book is available from the British Library

Library of Congress Cataloging-in-Publication Data
A catalog record has been requested for this book

ISBN: 978-0-367-53826-2 (hbk)
ISBN: 978-1-003-08340-5 (ebk)

Typeset in Bembo
by codeMantra

The sole responsibility of this publication lies with the authors.
The European Union is not responsible for any use that may be made of
the information contained therein.

Any enquiries regarding this publication should be sent to us at:
anna.triandafyllidou@ryerson.ca

This publication has received funding from the
European Union's Horizon 2020 research and innovation
programme under grant agreement number 770640.

Contents

List of figures   *x*
List of tables   *xi*
Notes on the contributors   *xiii*
Acknowledgements   *xix*

1 The governance of religious diversity: challenges and responses   1
Anna Triandafyllidou and Tina Magazzini

PART I
Western Europe   **11**

2 Belgium: devolved federalism   13
Thomas Sealy and Tariq Modood

3 France: from *laïcité* to *laicism*?   24
Thomas Sealy and Tariq Modood

4 Germany: federal corporatism   35
Thomas Sealy

5 The United Kingdom: weak establishment and pragmatic pluralism   46
Thomas Sealy and Tariq Modood

PART II
Southern Europe   **57**

6 The Italian case: 'baptised *laicità*' and a changing demographic   59
Tina Magazzini

7 Spain: all religions are equal, but some are more equal than others   74
Tina Magazzini

Contents

  8 Greece: the 'prevailing religion' and the governance of diversity   88
      Eda Gemi

PART III
Central Eastern Europe and Russia   99

  9 Hungary: religion as the government's political tool   101
      Dániel Vékony

10 Lithuania: the predicament of the segregation of religions   111
      Egdūnas Račius

11 Slovakia: fear of new religious minorities   121
      Egdūnas Račius

12 Russia: governance of religion – what, how, and why   131
      Marat Iliyasov

PART IV
South-Eastern Europe   147

13 Bulgaria: strong cultural legacies, weak institutions, and political instrumentalisation of religion   149
      Mila Mancheva

14 Albania: legacy of shared culture and history for religious tolerance   162
      Liliya Yakova and Leda Kuneva

15 Bosnia and Herzegovina: persisting ethno-religious divide   176
      Gergana Tzvetkova and Rosalina Todorova

PART V
The MENA region   191

16 Turkey: whither secularism?   193
      Haldun Gülalp

17 Lebanon: confessionalism and the problem of divided loyalties   206
      Yüksel Taşkın

18 Egypt: religious diversity in an age of securitisation   217
      H.A. Hellyer

19 Tunisia: governing the religious sphere after 2011   228
    Georges Fahmi

20 Morocco: governing religious diversity   238
    Mehdi Lahlou and Mounir Zouiten

PART VI
South and Southeast Asia and the Asia Pacific   **253**

21 India: the challenge of being plural and multicultural   255
    Gurpreet Mahajan

22 Indonesia: a complex experience of religious diversity governance   267
    Pradana Boy Zulian and Hasnan Bachtiar

23 Malaysia: a secular constitution under siege?   282
    Zawawi Ibrahim and Imran Mohd Rasid

24 Australia: diversity, neutrality, and exceptionalism   296
    Michele Grossman, Vivian Gerrand and Anna Halafoff

25 Governing religious diversity across the world: comparative insights   309
    Anna Triandafyllidou and Tina Magazzini

Index   *321*

Figures

6.1	Income tax form: options for 0.08 per cent 'donation'	63
6.2	Number of religious weddings and civil weddings, 1948 to 2017	64
7.1	The Worship Places Directory compiled by the Observatory of Religious Pluralism.	77
7.2	List of worship places by confession (excluded Catholic churches) in Spain in 2019	77
7.3	Number of foreign citizens residing in Spain grouped by country of origin in 2016	78
12.1	'Muslim' regions in the Russian Federation	134
12.2	The North Caucasus	135
13.1	Map of Bulgaria	150
15.1	Map of Bosnia and Herzegovina	181

Tables

2.1	Belgian population, by religious affiliation	14
3.1	French population, by religious affiliation	25
4.1	German population, by religious affiliation	36
5.1	UK population, by religious affiliation	47
6.1	Changes in total population and percentage of foreign residents in Italy (2004–2019)	61
6.2	Citizenship of foreigners residing in Italy (2019)	62
6.3	Changes in people self-identifying as Catholic, non-believers, or believers in another (non-Catholic) faith (2007–2017)	63
6.4	Religious affiliation of immigrants residing in Italy (2018)	65
6.5	Italy's multi-tier system of legal recognition for different confessions	67
7.1	Religious self-identification in Spain (1965–2019)	75
7.2	Changes in total population and percentage of foreign residents in Spain (1991–2018)	76
7.3	Spain's multi-tier system of legal recognition for different confessions	83
9.1	Breakdown of religious affiliation in Hungary based on the 2011 census	103
9.2	Levels of recognition of churches and religious communities	105
10.1	Main ethnic groups in Lithuania (percentage)	112
10.2	Faith groups in Lithuania (percentage)	113
11.1	Main ethnic groups in Slovakia (percentage)	122
11.2	Religious affiliation of Slovak population (percentage)	123
12.1	The largest ethnic groups of the Russian Federation and their 'ethnic religions'	133
12.2	Religious identity of the Russia's inhabitants as declared (2011)	134
13.2	Population of Bulgaria by denomination in 2011	151
13.1	Population of Bulgaria by ethnicity in 2011	151
13.3	Distribution of religious affiliations among self-identifying Roma	152
13.4	Newly registered third-country nationals, by year	152
13.5	Education levels by ethnicity (percentage)	153
13.6	Population of Bulgaria by denomination: 1992, 2001, 2011	154
14.1	Constitutional provisions on the issue of religion, religious freedoms, state-religion relations, and religious governance	163
15.1	Population of BiH by ethnic/national affiliation, Census Results 2013	180
15.2	Population of BiH according to ethnicity and religious affiliation	182
17.1	Percentage of Christian and Muslim Sects: 1913–2011	209
17.2	Sectarian composition of post-Taif Parliament	212

Tables

20.1	Evolution of the (legal) Moroccan population by area of residence, 1960–2019 (millions)	240
21.1	Population by religious affiliation	257
24.1	Religion in Australia: 2016 Census data summary	298
25.1	Relations between the nation and religion	312
25.2	Religious homogeneity of the resident population	314
25.3	Presence of minority groups who declare themselves as non-believers, atheists, or humanists	315
25.4	Regimes of accommodation of religion and religious diversity	317

Contributors

Hasnan Bachtiar is a member of the Muhammadiyah Young Intellectual Network (JIMM). Currently, Bachtiar works as a Research Fellow at the Center for Islamic Studies and Philosophy (PSIF) and also at the Center for the Study of Religion and Multiculturalism (PUSAM), at the Graduate School of the University of Mukammadiyah Malang. In the past he has worked as a researcher in the field of social theology at the National University of Singapore (NUS) with Muslim intellectuals in Singapore.

Georges Fahmi is a research fellow at the Middle East Directions Programme of the Robert Schuman Centre for Advanced Studies, European University Institute (EUI) in Fiesole, Italy. Previously, Fahmi was a non-resident scholar at the Carnegie Middle East Centre in Beirut, Lebanon. His research focusses on religious actors in democratic transition in the Middle East, the interplay between state and religion in Egypt and Tunisia, and religious minorities and citizenship in Egypt and Syria.

Eda Gemi is specialised in the governance of migration and integration. She is a Senior Lecturer of Political Sociology at the University of New York Tirana. Since 2010, she is a Research Fellow (project-based) at the Robert Schuman Centre for Advanced Studies of the European University Institute. In the period 2018–2019 she was Visiting Researcher at the ISR – Institute for Urban and Regional Research of the Austrian Academy of Sciences in Vienna. A Research Fellow at the Hellenic Foundation for European and Foreign Policy in the period 2012–2016, she headed the migration research team and conducted research on migration and integration. Gemi has authored three books on migration, integration, and transnationalism, and the EU-Western Balkan migration system. She co-authored with Anna Triandafyllidou a monograph titled *Rethinking Migration and Return in Southeastern Europe: Albanian Mobilities to and from Italy and Greece* (Routledge, 2020). She has published extensively in refereed journals, edited volumes, and media.

Vivian Gerrand is a Research Fellow at the Alfred Deakin Research Institute for Citizenship and Globalisation, Deakin University. She coordinates the Addressing Violent Extremism and Radicalisation to Terrorism (AVERT) Research Network. She is also a co-investigator of the EUI-led Horizon 2020 Building Resilience to Violent Extremism and Polarisation (BRaVE) Coordination and Support Action (2019–2021). Her research interests lie in the areas of belonging and migration, image-making and representation, re-imagined citizenship and resilience to violence and violent extremism. In 2017–2018 Vivian was a Max Weber Fellow in the Global Governance Programme, Robert Schuman Centre for Advanced Studies, at the European University Institute. Vivian completed her PhD at the

University of Melbourne on representations of Somali belonging in Italy and Australia. She is the author of *Possible Spaces of Somali Belonging* (Melbourne University Press, 2016).

Michele Grossman is Professor of Cultural Studies and Research Chair in Diversity and Resilience at the Alfred Deakin Institute for Citizenship and Globalisation at Deakin University. She is also the Convenor of the Australian-based AVERT (Addressing Violent Extremism and Radicalisation to Terrorism) Research Network and Director of the Centre for Resilient and Inclusive Societies (CRIS). Michele's expertise and publications lie in addressing and countering violent extremism within communities and understanding terrorism in diverse gender and cultural contexts. She holds research grants from a wide range of funding agencies including National Institute of Justice (USA), Public Safety Canada, the Centre for Research and Evidence on Security Threats (ESRC-CREST, UK), Australia-New Zealand Counter-Terrorism Committee (ANZCTC) and Department of Home Affairs (Australia), and others. She serves on several advisory boards and groups focussed on preventing violent extremism, including the Commonwealth CVE Cadre of Experts, the Canadian International Consensus Guidelines Committee for the Prevention of Violent Radicalization and Extremist Violence, and the Horizon 2020 BRaVE (Building Resilience Against Violent Extremism) project.

Haldun Gülalp recently retired as Professor of Political Science at Yıldız Technical University and currently chairs the Global Studies and Class Strategies (GSCS) Research Group in Istanbul, Turkey. Previously, he taught sociology at Hamilton College (New York) and Boğaziçi University (Istanbul). Currently affiliated with the Turkish Economic and Social Studies Foundation, he has held visiting professorships at George Washington University, Northwestern University, and the University of California, Los Angeles (UCLA) and research fellowships at the Woodrow Wilson International Center for Scholars and Oxford University. He has published widely in the fields of political sociology, sociology of religion, secularism, and citizenship.

Anna Halafoff is a Senior Lecturer in Sociology and a member of the Alfred Deakin Institute for Citizenship and Globalisation at Deakin University. She is also a Research Associate of the UNESCO Chair in Interreligious and Intercultural Relations – Asia Pacific at Monash University and of Canada's Religion and Diversity Project. In 2011, she was named a United Nations Alliance of Civilizations' Global Expert in the fields of multifaith relations, and religion and peacebuilding. Her current research interests include: religious diversity; cosmopolitanism and anti-cosmopolitanism; interreligious relations; countering violent extremism; education about religions and worldviews; Buddhism and gender; and Buddhism in Australia. Previously, she was a lecturer at the School of Political and Social Inquiry, and a researcher for the Global Terrorism Research Centre, at Monash University (2005–2012).

H.A. Hellyer is Senior Associate Fellow at the Royal United Services Institute (London) and at the Carnegie Endowment for International Peace (DC). A scholar and author in politics, international studies, and religion, particularly in the West and the Arab world, he is also a Professorial Fellow at Cambridge Muslim College and visiting Professor at the University of Technology's Centre for Advanced Studies on Islam, Science and Civilisation in Malaysia. The author of various books, chapters and articles in his subject, his published works include "Muslims of Europe: the 'Other' Europeans" (Edinburgh Edinburgh University Press), "Engagement with the Muslim Community & Counter-Terrorism: British Lessons for the West" (Brookings Institution Press), and "A Revolution Undone: Egypt's Road Beyond Revolt" (Oxford University Press). Widely published in various international media outlets, his work in public policy included an appointment as Deputy Convenor of the UK Government's Taskforce on tackling radicalisation, as an independent and critical subject matter expert, following the 2005 London bombings.

Zawawi Ibrahim is affiliated with Malaysia's Strategic Information and Research Development Center and is currently working as Professor of Anthropology in the Faculty of Arts & Social Sciences and the Institute of Asian Studies at University Brunei Darussalam (UBD). A Malaysian citizen, Zawawi earned his PhD in Social Anthropology from Monash University, Melbourne, Australia.

Marat Iliyasov is a Researcher at Vytautas Magnus University and a Research Associate at the University of St. Andrews, where he obtained his PhD. His work is situated at the crossroad of several disciplines, among which are International Relations, Ethnography, and Political Demography. Iliyasov is an author of several publications that analyse Chechen identity and demography in regard to the last Russo-Chechen wars. He also explores the possible vectors of post-war developments in Russia and Chechnya and Chechen policies of remembering and forgetting. He is a regular contributor to online journal *Osservatorio Balcani e Caucaso* and holds a position of Associate Editor in the *Journal of Ethnogeopolitics*. His latest project focusses on the radicalisation in Russia and the state's methods in fighting and preventing it.

Leda Kuneva is a Programmes and Projects Expert at the Centre for the Study of Democracy (CSD). Her previous endeavours include standing on the executive boards of the GLOW Association in Bulgaria as a Programming Manager, and the University of London Student Central in London, UK, as an Advisory Committee Primary Officer. She has interned for the Sub-Saharan Africa department of the Bilateral Relations Directorate at the Ministry of Foreign Affairs of the Republic of Bulgaria, working on food security and humanitarian aid. In 2018 she graduated with a joint Honors degree in International Relations and Law from the School of Oriental and African Studies (SOAS), University of London, receiving the School of Law's Award for Best Performance in Public International Law. Her areas of interest include women's and children's rights, international humanitarian law, anti-discrimination, Global South development and human security, radicalisation, and organic forms of democracy.

Mehdi Lahlou is Professor of Economics at the National Institute of Statistics and Applied Economics (INSEA) in Rabat, Morocco, and an associated professor at University Mohammed V (Rabat). He holds a PhD in Economics from Université Paris 1, Panthéon-Sorbonne. He has authored several contributions and reports on the topics of education, poverty, professional training and employment, emigration/immigration and its socio-economic consequences, sustainable development (mainly in Africa), as well as economic and socio-political dynamics in Morocco. Lahlou oversaw a Values Interuniversity project on 'Migration/Integration, health and culture' between 2013 and 2016. He is a member of the Moroccan association of economic studies, member of the International Union of Scientific Study of Population and President of ACME-Morocco (Association for a World Contract on water). He is also co-founder of the 'Common good University' (Brussels, 2002), co-founder of the World Alternative Forum on Water, and founder of the Open University on 'Migration, human rights and development' (2006).

Gurpreet Mahajan is Professor at the Centre for Political Studies, School of Social Sciences, Jawaharlal Nehru University. She has written extensively on issues of multiculturalism, minority rights, secularism, and civil society. She is the author of *Explanation and Understanding in the Human Sciences* (OUP 1992, 1997, 2011), *Identities and Rights: Aspects of*

Contributors

Liberal Democracy in India (OUP 1998), *The Multicultural Path: Issues of Diversity and Discrimination in Democracy* (Sage 2002) and *India: Political Ideas and the Making of a Democratic Discourse* (Zed Books 2013). Her other recent publications include *Religion, Community and Development: Changing Contours of Politics and Policy in India* (Routledge 2010) and *Accommodating Diversity: Ideas and Institutional Practices* (OUP 2011).

Mila Mancheva is Director of the Sociological Programme of the Center for the Study of Democracy (CSD). Previously she worked for the Sofia Mission of the International Organization for Migration in the spheres of counter-trafficking, border management and migrant rights (2001–5). She was also Alexander von Humboldt Fellow in migration studies at the Institute for East European Studies, Free University, Berlin (2005–2006). Mancheva received her PhD in history from the Central European University in Budapest. Her main areas of research include migration, asylum and integration, inter-ethnic relations, and radicalisation. Over the past 15 years she has co-ordinated and participated in over 20 projects funded by DG-Just, DG-Home, and DG-Research and Innovation. Mila Mancheva represents CSD at EASO's Consultative Forum and at the Radicalisation Awareness Network (RAN) and she is a member of the European Expert Network on Terrorism Issues (EENeT).

Tariq Modood is Professor of Sociology, Politics and Public Policy and the founding Director of the Centre for the Study of Ethnicity and Citizenship at the University of Bristol. He has held over 40 grants and consultancies, has over 35 (co-)authored and (co-)edited books and reports and over 200 articles and chapters. He was awarded an MBE for services to social sciences and ethnic relations in 2001, made a Fellow of the Academy of Social Sciences in 2004 and elected a Fellow of the British Academy in 2017. He served on the Commission on the Future of Multi-Ethnic Britain, the National Equality Panel, and the Commission on Religion and Belief in British Public Life. His key books include *Multiculturalism: A Civic Idea* (2007, Polity Press); *European Multiculturalisms: Cultural, Religious and Ethnic Challenges* (with Triandafyllidou and Meer, 2011 Edinburgh University Press), *Secularism, Religion and Multicultural Citizenship* (with G. Levey, 2009, University Press), and his latest book *Essays on Secularism and Multiculturalism* (2019, Rowman & Littlefield).

Egdūnas Račius holds a PhD in Arabic and Islamic Studies (University of Helsinki, 2004) and is Professor of Middle Eastern and Islamic studies at Vytautas Magnus University (Kaunas, Lithuania). He is the Reviews Editor of the *Journal of Muslims in Europe* and a co-editor of the *Yearbook of Muslims in Europe* (both by Brill). His research interests encompass Eastern European Muslim communities and governance of religion (particularly Islam) in post-communist Europe. Račius is a co-editor (together with Antonina Zhelyazkova) of *Islamic Leadership in the European Lands of the Former Ottoman and Russian Empires Legacy, Challenges and Change* (Brill, 2018) and the author of *Muslims in Eastern Europe* (Edinburgh University Press, 2018).

Imran Mohd Rasid is a graduate student and a Research Fellow at Strategic Information & Research Development Centre, Malaysia. His area of research includes critical theory, Malaysian political history, global political economy, and the phenomenon of transnational and translocal religious-political movements. He formerly served as Research Analyst for Islamic Renaissance Front, an Islamic Think Tank that works to promote progressive Islamic discourses in Malaysia. His research has been presented in several academic conferences, and some were published as book chapters. He has also co-founded an organisation called Imagined Malaysia, a research group that strive to push for greater historical literacy in Malaysia.

Contributors

Thomas Sealy holds an MA in Sociology (Citizenship & Rights), an MSc in Social Science Research Methods, and a PhD in Sociology. He is currently a Research Associate on the Horizon 2020 project *GREASE: Radicalisation, Secularism and the Governance of Religion* at the School of Sociology, Politics and International Studies at the University of Bristol. His research interests are in the areas of multiculturalism, religious identity, religious conversion, Georg Simmel, and religion, politics, and secularism.

Yüksel Taşkın is a researcher affiliated with TÜSES Foundation (Social, Economic and Political Research Foundation of Turkey). Between 2002 and 2017 he was a full-time faculty member at the Department of Political Science and International Relations, Marmara University, Istanbul. He was a visitor scholar at the Center for Near Eastern Studies, New York University in 1998–1999. He carried out his post-doctoral studies at ISIM (International Institute for the Study of Islam in the Modern World), Netherlands in 2006. He was also a visiting professor at the Buffet Center for International and Comparative Studies, Northwestern University in 2011. His academic interests are political and intellectual history of Turkey, Nationalism, Conservatism and Islamism, Society and Politics in the Middle East, Youth, and Politics.

Rosalina Todorova is Junior Analyst at the Sociological Programme of the Center for the Study of Democracy (CSD). She received her Master's Degree in Sociology (Marginality and Exclusion) from the University of Cambridge, UK. Her published academic works concern topics such as The Cosmopolitan Perspective to the Sociological Analysis of Brexit and Homeownership in the Context of De-industrialization and Depopulation. Rosalina has experience with academic and non-academic research, focussing on areas such as the ethnography of the small town in post-socialist contexts, archival research of homelessness, and co-operative practices in the interwar period, the mapping of rural shrinkage tendencies and the lived experiences of demographic crises. Her areas of interest include inequality, marginalisation, post-socialist strategies and trends of societal development, and ideologies of nationalism.

Gergana Tzvetkova is an Analyst at the Center for the Study of Democracy (CSD). She is a Senior Editor of *Politikon*, the journal of the International Association for Political Science Students (IAPSS) and for two years chaired the Research Committee on International Relations Theory at IAPSS. Previously, Gergana worked in the NGO sector as an Associate Manager of the World Stroke Organization (Switzerland) and as a Program Coordinator at the Free and Democratic Bulgaria Foundation (Bulgaria). She received her PhD in Politics, Human Rights and Sustainability from Sant'Anna School of Advanced Studies, Pisa, Italy. Her areas of interest include human rights, foreign policy, radicalisation, transitional justice, and democratisation. Gergana has published a number of papers on these topics and has presented her work at several international conferences such as the *ECPR General Conference*, the *ECPR Joint Sessions* and the *Convention of the Italian Political Science Association*.

Dániel Vékony is a Researcher at the Vytautas Magnus University, Kaunas, Lithuania and a Senior Lecturer at the Corvinus University of Budapest, Hungary. His main research interests include European Muslims and the prospects of multiculturalism as a political theory and a model of cohabitation. Recently, he focussed his attention of the collective memory narratives about Islam and Muslims in British and Hungarian societies. His other professional interest is the field of international relations between Hungary and the Middle East during the Cold War.

Contributors

Liliya Yakova is Research Fellow at the Center for the Study of Democracy (CSD). Previously she held the position of Associate Director of Operations for the Purdue Peace Project (USA), a violence prevention initiative active in West Africa and Central America. She has done research for the Hudson Institute (USA) and worked in the NGO sector as Manager of International Relations, Products and Services for the International Council for Cultural Centers (Bulgaria). She received her PhD in Organizational Communication and Policy from Purdue University, USA. Her areas of interest include marginalised populations, social justice, communication and policy for social change, peacebuilding, and organisational policy. Her work has been published by outlets such as *The International Journal of Communication, Journal of Applied Communication Research, The International Encyclopedia of Organizational Communication, the Diplomatic Courier,* and the *G20 Executive Talk Series Magazine.*

Mounir Zouiten is a professor of Urban and Regional Studies at Mohammed V University – Rabat with over 30 years of teaching, research, and consulting experience in Urban and Regional Development in Morocco. He holds a dual PhD in Regional Development (University of Montreal, Canada) and Development Economics (University of Grenoble, France). He has served as a consultant for numerous international organisations including the United Nations Development Programme, the German Technical Cooperation Agency (GTZ), the Friedrich Ebert Foundation, and the European Union. His consulting activities have included the conduct of satisfaction surveys for social programmes, capacity-building for national and local urban development groups, and coalition-building to improve urban living conditions in poor neighbourhoods. Dr. Zouiten was instrumental in the creation of the World Bank-funded Social Development Agency. As a consultant to this agency, he provided guidance in national-level programme administration and travelled extensively in Morocco to help local associations navigate the grant-writing and programme implementation process. His commitment to improved local governance and equitable development is further reflected in his volunteer activities to empower both homeowners' associations in beach communities and the impoverished residents of a former urban slum area.

Pradana Boy Zulian is a Lecturer in Islamic Legal Studies at the Faculty of Islamic Studies, University of Muhammadiyah Malang, Indonesia. From 2015 to 2018 he led the Center for the Study of Islam and Philosophy (Pusat Studi Islam dan Filsafat) at the same university. He was trained as an Islamic legal scholar at the University of Muhammadiyah Malang, where he received his degree in Islamic Legal Studies (2000). In 2007 he obtained a Master of Arts in Asian Studies from Australian National University (ANU), Canberra, writing a thesis discussing the contestation of progressive and conservative groups within Muhammadiyah, an Islamic movement known for its modern ideology. He pursued his PhD at the Department of Malay Studies, National University of Singapore and completed in 2015 after successfully defending his thesis on fatwa in Indonesia. This thesis was published as the monograph *Fatwa in Indonesia: An Analysis of Dominant Legal Ideas and Modes of Thought of Fatwa-Making Agencies and Their Implications in the Post-New Order Period* (Amsterdam University Press, 2018).

Acknowledgements

This edited volume is the outcome of research conducted under the auspices of the project Radicalisation, Secularism and the Governance of Religion: Bringing together European and Asian Perspectives (acronym: GREASE) funded by the Horizon2020 programme of the European Commission, for the period 2019–2022 (grant agreement 770640). The GREASE project investigates how religious diversity is governed in 23 countries – those that are also included in this volume – bringing together researchers and eminent scholars from Europe, South and Southeast Asia, Asia Pacific, and the MENA region. Comparing norms, laws, and practices, the GREASE project just like this Handbook sheds light on different societal approaches to accommodating religious minorities and migrants.

This Handbook brings together all our colleagues involved in the project and has benefitted from not just the project funding but also sustained exchange at project meetings and via email with researchers from these different world regions, which have helped us open up our comparative horizons to countries and issues that are less known in the European context. Thanks to the project, this Handbook has a truly global ambition and inter-continental perspective that we hope will benefit researchers, graduate students but also practitioners or media professionals in the quest for understanding how we can best accommodate different religious beliefs, needs, and claims in inclusive ways.

Our special thanks go to all our fellow contributors in this volume for completing their work in the middle of other ongoing research obligations related to the project, to Diane Shugart for carefully copyediting the manuscript and always raising pertinent clarification questions, and to Routledge for having embraced and supported this book project from the start. This book would not have been possible without the support of the Horizon2020 programme.

8 June 2020
Anna Triandafyllidou, Toronto, Canada
Tina Magazzini, Florence, Italy

1
The governance of religious diversity
Challenges and responses

Anna Triandafyllidou and Tina Magazzini

Introduction

According to the Pew Research Centre 2015s *The Future of World Religions: Population Growth Projections,* the role of religion in contemporary societies is all but declining, with global trends pointing at a shrinking percentage of atheists and agnostics. Such predictions are largely based on demographic trends, which see religious families having a higher fertility rate than non-religious ones.[1] In particular, while over the next decades Christians (currently representing almost one-third of the global population) are expected to remain the largest religious group – growing 35 per cent, about the same rate as the global population overall – Muslim communities are projected to grow faster than any other major religion.

Against this backdrop, this Handbook responds to the need for critically investigating how religion and religious diversity is governed today in different world regions, looking at historical trends, current practices, norms, and institutions, and assessing the different ways in which religious minorities and majorities can have their needs and requests satisfied while safeguarding social cohesion.[2]

Europe represents an exception compared to much of the world, including other parts of the 'West' such as the US, since European societies have undergone a long process of secularisation, reflected in the fact that participation in religious activities, including private prayer, has become a minority pursuit, particularly in Western Europe (Berger, 1999; Berger et al., 2008). While Europe is not the only part of the world to have undergone secularisation, it is the only place where this has not resulted from state ideology or coercion but from social and economic change, education, political argument, and the working of liberal democracy (Casanova, 1994). But both religion and religious intolerance are returning to European society and politics through multiple channels. These channels include the dynamics of international migration and the 'new' religions – notably Islam, even though there is a long pedigree of that faith and its adherents in Europe going back many centuries – that accompany such migration. They are also returning through the fervent religious practice of native minorities (for example, Evangelists and other Protestant groups), and the social and political antipathies this has generated among more secularly inclined social majorities. Last but not least, religion is returning to Europe through international relations. Religion in the early twenty-first century has become an important dimension structuring global governance through perceived hierarchies of 'good', 'bad', 'modern', 'advanced', and 'backward' cultures. Islam has been largely stigmatised in the public arena by the West, with a warped reading that provides part of the rationale for terrorist violence perpetrated a decade ago by Al Qaeda and its related affiliates. Today the stigmatisation of Islam is being violently exploited by insurgent extremist Islamist groups like the Islamic State of Iraq and the Levant (ISIS).

Since the Iranian Revolution in 1979, the contrast and confrontation between an essentialised 'West' and even more essentialised 'Islam' has acquired a global dimension. Symbolically, politically, and militarily this confrontation has continued to grow, gaining strength after the fall of the Berlin Wall in 1989 and particularly after 9/11. In the absence of Communism and the Soviet threat, the West has found in Islam and Muslims a contemporary 'Other' against which to affirm the superiority of its cultural and political model (Triandafyllidou, 2001, 2017). At the same time, disenchanted or marginalised or both youth both within Europe and in Middle Eastern, African, and Asian countries have found in extremist interpretations of religion and religiously contextualised terrorist violence a way to express their frustration, disenfranchisement, and struggle for change.

The international confrontation between 'the West' and 'Islam' also finds local expression in Europe. Local integration challenges are interpreted within the global context, with Muslims being stigmatised as 'alien' and 'unfit' for European liberal democracies (Lindekilde et al., 2009; Mouritsen & Olsen, 2013; Triandafyllidou & Kouki, 2013). Some scholars have called this the rise of 'liberal intolerance' (Lindekilde, 2014) or the 'end of tolerance' (Hervick, 2012). In some ways Western European polities have developed forms of moderate secularism – supporting organised religion without an historic national identity controlling or being subordinated by it – which have fostered social cohesion, democracy, and freedom of religion. Yet this has historically been achieved in the context of the presence of a single religion, Christianity. The growing public salience of religion and of religiously inspired radicalisation and violence, and the related 'failure of integration', raise questions about whether models of moderate secularism can further adapt to multi-religious diversity, and what form that adaptation should take.

This Handbook covers different countries in Europe, the Middle East and North Africa (MENA), South and Southeast Asia, and Australia to enquire in the historical trends, policies, and practices in these regions and compare with each other and with European approaches. The book thus seeks to highlight the rich experiences outside Europe in places where religion is closely related to politics and occupies an important position in public life.

Beyond secularism or adopting multiple secularisms?

This Handbook offers a sociological reflection on what can be viable forms of governing religion and religious diversity in a large variety of countries and world regions. This country-specific and comparative (in the last chapter) discussion of how different countries seek to govern religion and accommodate religious diversity feeds into an analytical reflection on what is the normative basis for state-religion relations (see also Modood & Sealy, 2019, GREASE concept paper 1.1). The case studies provided in this Handbook lend themselves to an analytical discussion that is also iterative with a view of identifying appropriate versions or models of secularism that can function in a variety of contexts (Modood & Thompson, 2018).

The analytical and normative debate on how to govern religion and religious diversity in Europe has been dominated by the notion of political secularism. The core idea of political secularism is the idea of political autonomy, namely, that politics or the state has a *raison d'être* of its own and should not be subordinated to religious authority, religious purposes, or religious reasons. This is a one-way type of autonomy. Secularism may also involve a two-way autonomy, where there is some government control of religion, some interference in religion, some support for religion, and some cooperation with (selected) religious organisations and religious purposes. Such state control and support, though, must not compromise the autonomy of politics. In other words, it must be largely justifiable in political terms, not just religious reasons, and it must not restrict (but may support) political authority and state action (Modood, 2012).

Political secularism is not necessarily democratic (see also Bader, 2007). In the West it has largely been conjoined with liberal democracy (but not necessarily, as the USSR illustrates), and it has been linked to a two-way mutual autonomy written into relevant constitutional arrangements so that both state and religion enjoy their independence. This mutual autonomy is what Alfred Stepan (2000) calls 'twin tolerations'. Mutual autonomy – but not strict separation – has historically emerged as the liberal democratic version of secularism and is the one that is most widespread today. For such secularists, religious freedom is one of the most essential and cherished political values. It must be noted though that in Muslim majority countries such as Turkey, Algeria, or Egypt secularism often has an anti-democratic, anti-popular character, but may be cast as more accommodating of minorities than alternatives in order to promote support for secularism.

Taylor (2010, also 2014 discussed by Bilgrami, 2014) has suggested that secularism is, at its core, really about 'managing diversity'. While the importance of secularism for managing religious diversity should not be under-appreciated, it should be noted that even if there was no religious diversity in a country or in the world, if only one religion was present, there would still be a question about the relationship between religion and politics, and 'political autonomy' would still be a suitable answer. Moreover, secularism is not an answer to questions about *any* kind of diversity; it arises specifically in relation to the power and authority of religion, and the challenge it may pose to political rule or to, for instance, equality among citizens (Bilgrami, 2014).

Indeed, one can go further and say that secularism and religion are correlative concepts. If there was no religion in the world, not merely that it had passed away, but if it had never existed in the first place, so that there was no concept of religion, then secularism would have no reference point and there would be no concept of political secularism. In that sense, secularism is a secondary concept, dependent on the concept of religion. However, once there is a concept of secularism – with advocates, promoters, or indeed critiques – then it engages into a dialectical relationship with religion. In other words, secularism also intellectually and politically redefines religion to suit secularist values and purposes (Asad, 2003). What we regard today as religion (an 'inner life', a 'belief', a private matter) in secularist countries is a much more socially restricted set of activities, relationships, and forms of authority than was the case before secularism's widespread adoption, or than what prevails in non-secularist countries today.

The political secularism adopted in the majority of European countries is a moderate one (Modood, 2010, 2019) which allows for privileged state-religion relations in line with the history and contemporary experience of each of these countries. Thus, for instance, in Germany, the Catholic and Protestant Churches are constitutionally recognised corporations, on whose behalf the federal government collects voluntary taxes and grants large amounts of additional public money. In Belgium, a number of religions have constitutional entitlements and a national Council of Religions enjoys the support of the monarch. Norway, Denmark, and England each have an 'established' Church; Sweden had one until 2000, and Finland has two (Stepan, 2011; cf. Koenig, 2009). The UK also has two state recognised national churches, the Church of England and the Church of Scotland, but the latter is independent of the UK state, including of the Scottish state in which it plays no formal role. Yet, it would be difficult to dispute that these countries are not among the leading secular states in the world. They adopt, however, a moderate or flexible form of secularism.

The question arises as to whether frameworks of secularism, both 'rigid' secularism (Bouchard & Taylor, 2008) such as that adopted by France in the form of *laïcité* and 'moderate' secularism (Modood, 2010) such as that of most of the European countries reviewed in this volume, are adequate for addressing the issues raised by religious minorities. The challenge is that these secularism models invariably adopt the liberal language of choice. While they help to secure freedom of belief and conscience for all, their attitude towards religious practices of minorities is often ambiguous, if not outrightly hostile. Secular states can be particularly reluctant to change existing public norms to accommodate the practices of post-migration minorities, and even when they have done so, they have considered them as if they were a set of lifestyle preferences or freely chosen beliefs. In this way, they have tended to ignore that religious observances are closely tied to a person's inner sense of dignity and respect, a constitutive element of their very self, and hence experienced as something more than merely a question of freedom of 'choice' (Mahajan, 2017).

To underscore this point, we will take an example from India (Mahajan, 2017). In Jawaharlal Nehru University (like many other public institutions) there are no separate prayer rooms. This does not mean that there are no devout religious believers at the university. Religious believers who wish to offer prayers during the day assemble (among other places) on the sixth floor of the university library. Administrations have changed and so have librarians, but the practice of keeping a little space clear and clean for offering prayers is a practice that has continued. While there is no formal notification for this, the concerned authorities understand that several Muslim students would need to offer prayers at specific times during the day. They also recognise that not accommodating this need for religious worship is likely to be read, by both those wishing to offer prayers and those who do not observe the fast, as hostility to the community as a whole. For this reason, practice-related needs are often accommodated. The fact that this is a practice involving, by and large, worship in accordance with religious norms means an extra effort is made to accommodate the concerns of the devout.

Similar accommodation is not made, however, for 'choice-driven' activities. It is highly unlikely that space would be provided in the library for, say, table tennis players who have no other place to practise and are strongly committed to winning the upcoming tournament. The point is that matters of religion are often treated differently from other kinds of actions in India. To some extent this is because religion continues to play an important role in individual and social life, but also because religious and cultural diversity are values recognised and inscribed in the Constitution. The framers of the Indian Constitution did not merely envision a 'secular' polity, where the state would not be aligned with any religion and everyone would enjoy freedom of conscience and belief; rather they conceived of a state where different religious and cultural communities would, to a considerable extent, be able to live in accordance with their beliefs and practices. It is this commitment to diversity that has made the crucial difference and encouraged greater willingness to accommodate religious practices of the minorities as well as of the majority. In the chapters of this book we can find similar considerations in Indonesia and Malaysia where the primacy of religion is recognised to the extent that one cannot not have a religion. Indeed, non-European countries draw our attention to the importance of religion and religious diversity as a socio-cultural asset (Mahajan, 2017).

The variety of country perspectives and approaches reviewed in this Handbook allows us also to appreciate that secularism can only be highly contextual. It takes a different shape depending on the state traditions and political culture of a society as well as of which religion or religions it is contoured around – secular and religion being correlative, mutually informing concepts and mutually shaping each other in varied permutations. This means that we are talking of 'multiple secularisms' (Taylor, 1998; Casanova, 2009; Stepan, 2010; Calhoun et al., 2011).

Taking this point further, we recognise that multiple secularisms are an aspect of the wider theoretical and sociological understanding that the very phenomenon of modernity has to be understood in terms of 'multiple modernities' (Eisenstadt, 2000). This approach rejects the association of modernisation with Westernisation, that to become modern all societies must follow the path of the West and become like the West. Eisenstadt recognises that Western modes of modernity continue to 'enjoy historical precedence' and serve as 'a basic reference point for others', but the last half-century has made plain that 'Western patterns of modernity are not the only "authentic" modernities' available for concrete societal expression (ibid.). Rather, different parts of the world are modernising in their own ways and this refers not least to developments concerning religion, secularity, diversity, and governance.

In probing different models of governing religion and accommodating religious diversity in the different world regions and country cases analysed in this volume, we question whether secularism should be seen as a complete (or less complete) form of separation of religious institutions and state or as a form of reciprocal toleration and reciprocal autonomy and enquire into what could be alternative models for a smooth governance of religious diversity within liberal democracies where both majority and minority religions share a sense of legitimacy.

This volume aims at bringing together a multi-disciplinary and innovative perspective on religious diversity governance. The role that religion plays in the public space has been a key issue in contemporary European cohesion policies for some time, and its relevance has increased with recent migratory flows that bring with them the need to accommodate new forms of religious diversity (Bramadat & Koenig, 2009). However, because of their multifaceted and complex dynamics, relations between the state and religious institutions have been studied mainly at a national or sub-national level rather than as part of an effort to understand what similarities and differences exist among various countries and world regions.

This has prevented a comprehensive understanding of current trends for action in the challenging processes of religious diversity management. This book's perspective is that there is a need to transcend the current conception of Europe an insular space in favour of an understanding of religious diversity governance as a nodal point in multi-level and transnational exchanges. The key objective of the volume is therefore to analyse the dissonances, overlaps, and synergies that characterise the design and implementation of policies aimed at religious communities above and beyond the European sphere or Australia, looking at under-studied models both in Eastern Europe (Leustean, 2014) and most importantly in South Asia, Southeast Asia, and the MENA region (Triandafyllidou & Modood, 2017).

While building on recent research on religion and politics (Haynes, 2009; Muck et al., 2014) and on the governance of religious diversity (Triandafyllidou & Modood, 2017; Furseth, 2018) this Handbook provides for a wider overview of different approaches to state-religion relations. The chapters included in this volume also investigate how religion relates to national or ethnic identity both historically in terms of nation/state formation and symbolically as one of the quintessential elements for identifying with (or against) the nation.

Anna Triandafyllidou and Tina Magazzini

The contents of this volume

Our analytical and empirical work for each chapter starts with a thorough desk research and analysis of secondary data: related studies, legal texts, policy documents/grey materials, statistical data on economics and demographics, and political statements and interviews of key leading personalities including politicians, religious leaders, civil society stakeholders, minority representatives, journalists, and academics, as quoted in the media or available through their own web sites. In some countries selected stakeholders have been interviewed to further enrich and assess the secondary materials analysed. This was particularly the case in countries where secondary materials were scant. Each chapter includes both qualitative and quantitative data and brings together different disciplinary approaches, notably political theory, international relations, sociology, ethnic studies, and economics.

While addressing very different contexts, populations, and processes, all chapters follow a similar outline, which allows for comparability. Each chapter starts by presenting the socio-demographic profiles of the population and particularly the existence of different religious groups and the extent to which this is a result of recent immigration or a long-standing historical presence of such minorities. This is by itself no small challenge as most countries do not keep official records of religious affiliation data in order to protect the privacy of their citizens and residents. The second section in each chapter investigates the legal and institutional regulatory framework concerning religion in each country, looking notably at the place that religion is given in the Constitution as well as at the major laws and policies regarding religious matters and regulating state-religion relations. Attention is paid to both the letter of the law and its implementation. Thus, our focus is to uncover not only what is officially foreseen in each country but also what happens in reality, whether minorities have access to their rights or what hurdles they face in doing so. Each chapter then provides a brief history of the role of religion in the specific state and nation formation, and how religious minorities-majority relations evolved and how the specific framework of governance was formed. This gives us the opportunity to highlight which laws and policies are actually an expansion of the religious majority rights to those of minorities or whether new policies have been developed in recognition of the changing demographics of a given country. The concluding comparative chapter offers an overview of how the different chapters speak to each other, comparing the different factors that are at play in state-religion relations and the governance of religious diversity among and within the different world regions.

The book is organised in six parts corresponding to the world regions covered: Europe (subdivided into western, southern, south-eastern, and eastern Europe/Russia), the MENA region, South and Southeast Asia and the Asia Pacific.

We have selected to cover different macro-regions within Europe with a view of going beyond the usual focus on Western European countries (for example, France, Germany, or the UK) that are characterised by the highest levels of post-migration diversity, related conflicts, and, of course, public policies to address these issues. Our aim thus is to highlight and compare the experiences of Western Europe – which are already quite varied in terms of state-religion relations, degree of secularism, and type of support to majority and minority religions – with those of southern Europe (the countries that have become immigration hosts during the last 25 years and where religion played an important role in defining national identity) and with the different sets of post-Communist countries – those in south-eastern Europe with relatively large native Muslim and minority Christian populations – and those in central-eastern Europe with a largely secular or religiously indifferent approach and a dominant nominally Christian majority. With the aim of considering the post-Communist legacy in Europe's easternmost corner, we also include Russia, which is a global player and has dealt with radicalisation and violence in its war against Chechnya and the related terrorist attempts.

Our coverage expands also to the south and east to include the historical and political experience of the MENA region, notably Turkey, Lebanon, Egypt, Tunisia, and Morocco. These are all predominantly Muslim countries with different degrees of religious rule/moderate secularism. These countries have been characterised by important socio-political upheavals related to what is known as the Arab Spring, albeit in different directions. Thus while Turkey has been verging towards authoritarianism and a further instrumentalisation of religion in the public sphere by the political leadership, Tunisia and Morocco have followed the opposite path of democratisation and moderate secularism; in Egypt, the overthrow of Islamist president Mohammed Morsi ended the 2011–2013 experiment which was characterised by far more pluralism than hitherto or hence. Lebanon retains its multi-communal arrangements, albeit faced with many challenges and political instability. In addition, four out of the five countries presented have been faced with increased radicalisation and ethno-religious violence both against Muslims and Christians of different denominations and have reacted with different degrees of state radicalisation and violence. The four eastern and the four southern EU neighbours allow us to put the EU countries' experience in its historical and geopolitical context (that is inseparable from these two regions).

We then introduce in the regions covered, a fourth 'double' region, notably South Asia and Southeast Asia. The reason for including South Asia and Southeast Asia is to investigate state-religion relations and models of secularism as well as trends of radicalisation in countries with a Muslim majority population, like Indonesia and Malaysia, and in a country of Hindu majority with a large Muslim population (India) with a view to exploring how they have organised their state-religion relations beyond European models of secularism and in view of a deep respect for the role that religion plays in people's lives. We also find this region particularly important as it has also experienced important religious violence events including both bomb explosions and public riots against religious minorities.

Last but not least, we have included Australia because it is an immigrant nation and as such different from all European countries, while at the same time sharing a lot in common with Western European countries as regards a common perception of belonging to the 'West' as well as the close ties between Australia and the UK.

Contributions to this book are organised in 23 country-specific chapters that are historically contextualised by taking into account national and macro-regional frameworks. We critically review the models of state-religion relations and governance of cultural diversity in four macro-regions within Europe.

By looking into state-religion relations and governance of religion/religious diversity in these regions beyond Europe, we gain insights into predominantly Muslim countries (Egypt, Morocco, Tunisia, Turkey, Indonesia, Malaysia), countries with pronounced historical religious diversity (India and Lebanon), and into a predominantly migrant pluralist nation (Australia). These insights will provide a basis for re-thinking European models and learning from the experiences of governing religious diversity in other socio-economic and geopolitical contexts – contexts shaped by the Christian tradition (such as Australia) as well as non-Christian majority traditions (for example, in MENA or South and Southeast Asia).

Building on the unique variety and complexity of the 23 country chapters in this book, the concluding chapter offers a comparative overview of their approaches to state-religion relations. We look at the different factors at play in state-religion relations and the governance of religious diversity in different countries, comparing among and within the different world regions. First of all, we look at the socio-demographic profile of the different countries assessing the size and complexity of the challenge as levels of religious diversity vary greatly from a largely mono-religious Lithuania, for instance, to the world's largest and most diverse democracy, notably India. We discuss the relationship between religion and state formation and the national self-concept to asses to what extent religious minorities are included in the national narrative or are excluded from it. Based on the analysis presented in the country chapters, we discuss the institutional make up and compare among countries as to their main principles and practices for regulating religion. We look at whether a country privileges mainly freedom of or freedom from religion and, in the case of the former, the extent to which religious minorities suffer discrimination or disadvantage. Last but not least, we compare the politics of governing religious diversity in different countries and look at how politicised religion is.

Notes

1 The complete report is available at https://www.pewforum.org/2015/04/02/religious-projections-2010-2050/
2 This book is based on analytical and empirical research conducted within the framework of the EU-funded Horizon 2020 project: **GREASE** – Radicalisation, Secularism and the Governance of Religion: Bringing together European and Asian Perspectives (http://grease.eui.eu, contract no.770640).

References

Asad, T. (2003). *Formations of the Secular. Christianity, Islam, Modernity*. Stanford, CA: Stanford University Press.
Bader, V. (ed.). (2007). *Secularism or Democracy? Associational Governance of Religious Diversity*. Amsterdam: Amsterdam University Press.
Berger, P. L. (1999). *The Desecularization of the World: Resurgent Religion and World Politics*. Washington, DC: Etehics and Public Policy Center.
Berger, P., Davie, G., & Fokas, E. (2008). *Religious America, Secular Europe? A Theme and Variations* (pp. 9–21). Aldershot: Ashgate.
Bilgrami, A. (2014). Secularism: Its Content and Context. In A. Stepan & C. Taylor (eds.), *Boundaries of Toleration* (pp. 79–129). New York: Columbia University Press.
Bouchard, G. & Taylor, C. (2008). *Building the Future: A Time for Reconciliation*. Consultation Commission on Accommodation Practices Related to Cultural Differences, Montreal: Government of Quebec.
Bramadat, P. & Koenig, M. (eds.). (2009). *International Migration and the Governance of Religious Diversity*. Montreal and Kingston: McGill-Queen's University Press.
Calhoun, C., Juergensmeyer, M., & VanAntwerpen, J. (2011). *Rethinking Secularism*. Oxford and New York: Oxford University Press.
Casanova, J. (1994). *Public Religions in the Modern World*. Chicago: University of Chicago Press.
Casanova, J. (2009). The secular and secularisms. *Social Research*, 76(4): 1049–1066.
Eisenstadt, S. N. (2000). Multiple modernities. *Daedalus*, 129(1): 1–29.
Furseth, I. (2018). *Religious Complexity in the Public Sphere: Comparing Nordic Countries*. London: Palgrave Macmillan.
Haynes, J. (ed.). (2009). *Routledge Handbook of Religion and Politics*. London: Routledge.
Hervick, P. (2012). Ending tolerance as a solution to incompatibility: The Danish 'crisis of multiculturalism'. *European Journal of Cultural Studies*, 15: 211–225.
Koenig, M. (2009). How Nations-States Respond to Religious Diversity. In P. Bramadat & M. Koenig (eds.), *International Migration and the Governance of Religious Diversity* (pp. 293–322). Ontario: School of Policy Studies, Queens University.
Leustean, L. N. (2014). *Eastern Christianity and Politics in the Twenty-First Century*. Abingdon: Routledge.

Lindekilde, L. (2014). The mainstreaming of far-right discourse in Denmark. *Journal of Immigrant & Refugee Studies*, 12: 363–382.

Lindekilde, L., Mouritsen, P., & Zapata-Barrero, R. (2009). The Muhammad cartoons controversy in comparative perspective. *Ethnicities*, 9(3): 291–313.

Mahajan, G. (2017). Living with Religious Diversity: The Limits of the Secular Paradigm. In A. Triandafyllidou & T. Modood (eds.), *The Problem of Religious Diversity: European Challenges, Asian Approaches* (pp. 75–92). Edinburgh: Edinburgh University Press.

Modood, T. (2010). Moderate secularism, religion as identity and respect for religion. *Political Quarterly*, 81(1): 4–14.

Modood, T. (2012). Is there a crisis of secularism in Western Europe? *Sociology of Religion*, 72(2): 130–149.

Modood, T. (2019). *Essays on Secularism and Multiculturalism*. London: Rowman-Littlefield and European Consortium of Political Science.

Modood, T. & Sealy, T. (2019). Secularism and the governance of religious diversity. GREASE Concept paper, May 2019, available at http://grease.eui.eu/publications/concept-papers/.

Modood, T. & Thompson, S. (2018). Revisiting contextualism in political theory: Putting principles into context. *Res Publica*, 24(3): 339–357, available at https://www.springer.com/journal/11158.

Mouritsen, P. & Olsen, T. V. (2013). Denmark between liberalism and nationalism. *Ethnic and Racial Studies*, 36(4): 691–710.

Muck, T., Netland, H., & McDermott, G. (eds.). (2014). *Handbook of Religion: A Christian Engagement with Traditions, Teachings, and Practices*. Grand Rapids, MI: Baker Academic.

Stepan, A. (2000). Religion, democracy, and the 'twin tolerations'. *Journal of Democracy*, 11(4): 37–57.

Stepan, A. (2010). The multiple secularisms of modern democratic and non-democratic regimes. In *APSA 2010 Annual Meeting Paper*, available at SSRN: https://ssrn.com/abstract=1643701.

Stepan, A. (2011). The Multiple Secularisms of Modern Democratic and Non-Democratic Regimes. In C. Calhoun, M. Juergensmeyer, & J. Van Antwerpen (eds.), *Rethinking Secularism* (pp. 114–144). Oxford: Oxford University Press.

Taylor, C. (1998). Modes of Secularism. In R. Bhargava (ed.), *Secularism and Its Critics* (pp. 31–53). New Delhi: Oxford University Press.

Taylor, C. (2010). The meaning of secularism. *The Hedgehog Review*, 12(3): 23–34.

Taylor, C. (2014). How to Define Secularism. In A. Stepan & C. Taylor (eds.), *Boundaries of Toleration* (pp. 79–129). New York: Columbia University Press.

Triandafyllidou, A. (2001). *Immigrants and National Identity in Europe*. London: Routledge.

Triandafyllidou, A. (2017). Nation and religion: Dangerous liaisons. In A. Triandafyllidou & T. Modood (eds.), *The Problem of Religious Diversity: European Challenges, Asian Approaches* (pp. 1–26). Edinburgh: Edinburgh University Press.

Triandafyllidou, A. & Kouki, H. (2013). Muslim immigrants and the Greek nation: The emergence of nationalist intolerance. *Ethnicities*, 13(6): 709–728.

Triandafyllidou, A. & Modood, T. (2017). *The Problem of Religious Diversity. European Challenges, Asian Approaches*. Edinburgh: Edinburgh University Press.

Part I
Western Europe

2

Belgium
Devolved federalism

Thomas Sealy and Tariq Modood

Introduction

In Western Europe, two approaches to the governance of religious diversity that are often contrasted are the 'radical' secularism of France and the 'moderate' secularisms of the UK and Germany (see chapters in this volume). While these kinds of comparisons are usually made *between* countries, owing to its federal structure, in Belgium we find such variance *within* the same country.

Belgium is a federal parliamentary constitutional monarchy and has a complex institutional organization comprising three territorial regions – Wallonia, Flanders, and the Brussels–Capital region – and three linguistic communities, French, Dutch, and German – all of which have devolved areas of competency. As a result, within one overarching national framework, there are also two distinct models of governance of religious diversity: the more radical form of secularism in the francophone region of Wallonia and a multicultural form in the Dutch-speaking region of Flanders. As well as this structure providing an interesting case for analysing Belgium's model(s) of governance of religion, it is also from this that key challenges arise. As with a number of Western European countries, these challenges have emerged and been particularly important in recent decades with regard to a growing Muslim population.

Socio-demographic context

Belgium's three regions and three communities each have different demographic characteristics. The regions are organized territorially and along linguistic lines. Belgium thus comprises Dutch-speaking Flanders, French-speaking Wallonia, and the bilingual Brussels–Capital region. The three communities are organized along linguistic lines: Dutch, French, and German. There are also bilingual municipalities within the regions.

According to official figures Belgium's total population stood at 11,431,406 as of 1 January 2019. The Flemish region is the largest by population, at 57.5 per cent of the total population, the Walloon region follows at 32 per cent, and the Brussels–Capital region with 10.5 per cent. The growth rate of the population is 0.5 per cent, with 82 per cent of this a result of net migration. A higher proportion of people migrate to the Flemish region in comparison to Wallonia or Brussels-Capital. In Brussels a large part of the population, well over one-third, is of non-Belgian origin, considerably more than the regions, with figures around 10 per cent in Wallonia and 5 per cent in Flanders. Belgium is in the top ten destination countries for Muslim migrants in Europe (Pew, 2017); of 230,000 migrants coming to Belgium between 2010 and 2016, it is estimated that 57 per cent were Muslim.

Belgium's economy, as measured by GDP per capita, has been rising since 2015, with Flanders providing the largest share (58 per cent). Employment rates vary between the regions: Flanders has an employment rate above that of the Belgian average, whereas Wallonia and Brussels-Capital both have unemployment rates above the national average. Overall, as of the second quarter of 2019, the employment rate stood at an all-time high of 70.1 per cent. Although this trend is consistent across the regions, figures are also different between them: 76 per cent in Flanders, 65.2 per cent in Wallonia, and 61.7 per cent in Brussels.

Despite these positive trends, in its cities Belgium has one of the highest risks of urban poverty and social exclusion of EU member states. There is also a much larger unemployment rate among non-EU-born residents. The National Register in Belgium does not provide data on migration background, and so reliable data is difficult to attain, particularly when it comes to second- and third-generations (Bovenkerk, 2017). Nevertheless, research generally points to ethnic and religious minority groups being considerably disadvantaged and facing higher rates of poverty, lower educational attainment, and higher unemployment figures, while also being more concentrated in lower skilled employment sectors and also reporting higher levels of discrimination than the national average (see Bovenkerk, 2017; Costa and de Valk, 2018).

There is also no religion question in official Belgian demographic statistics, thus accurate figures are difficult to come by. Yet, for Belgium, Christianity remains overwhelmingly the dominant religion in the country in terms of identification. Those who are unaffiliated to any religious tradition form the second largest group, with Islam being Belgium's 'second religion'. Notably, while the number of those identifying as Christian is steadily declining, for Muslims this number is rising. Table 2.1 captures these trends.

In terms of religion in politics, Christian political parties have been a steady part of Belgium's political scene since its inception. In recent decades, however, the previously strong Catholic identity of these has shifted to a more generically and nominally Christian discourse. Various attempts at founding a specifically and self-defined Islamic political party have been

Table 2.1 Belgian population, by religious affiliation

	2010	%	2020 (projected)	%
Christian	6,880,000	64.2	6,590,000	60.5
Muslim	630,000	5.9	810,000	7.5
Unaffiliated	3,110,000	29	3,370,000	31
Hindu	<10,000	<0.1	10,000	<0.1
Buddhist	30,000	0.2	40,000	0.3
Folk religions	20,000	0.2	30,000	0.2
Other	10,000	<0.1	10,000	0.1
Jews	30,000	0.3	30,000	0.3

Source: Pew (from https://www.pewforum.org/2015/04/02/religious-projection-table/2050/number/Europe/).

made since the early 1990s, although none have enjoyed any real success (Koutroubas et al., 2009). Muslim candidates have served in the national and European parliaments, however.

Main trends and challenges

Belgium has been a country of immigration from the early to mid-twentieth century, although it was slow to acknowledge and respond to this status as a consequence of originally encouraging labour migrants on a temporary 'guest worker' basis with the assumption that these migrants would return to their countries of origin, a policy which ended in 1974 (Loobuyk and Jacobs, 2006). While in the early part of the twentieth century these migrants were predominantly from other European countries (notably Italy from the 1920s), since the 1960s there have been increasing groups of migrants, from Turkey and Morocco most notably, and since the 1990s from Belgium's former non-European colonies, Democratic Republic of the Congo and the territory of Ruanda-Burundi, as well as from France and the Netherlands. Settlement patterns in these successive migrations have generally followed labour market trends at the time, and immigrants have tended to become concentrated in particular municipalities (Bovenkerk, 2017; Imeraj et al., 2018).

As a result of these migration patterns, and in parallel with a number of Western European countries, Belgium has undergone increased ethnic and religious pluralization. This is most notable in relation to Islam and Muslims who now form the second largest and most culturally and politically significant religious minority in Belgium. The differences in organizational and institutional structures between the regions, as well as the politico-ideological difference in inclusion which underpins them, present considerable challenges as different regions pursue different modes for the governance of religious diversity.

Following the federalization of the country, competencies over significant legislative and policy areas were devolved to the regions. Political competencies are shared between the federal government (with jurisdiction over matters such as defence, finance, social security, and justice), the regions (territorial issues, employment, economic development, environmental, and housing issues), and the communities (culture, education, media, and some social services) (Adam and Jacobs, 2014; Jacobs, 2004). One result of this is that there are few unified policies or data measures.

In addition, there are a few notable characteristics of Belgium's federal composition that bear on the different governance structures between the regions and mean that the challenges faced also manifest in distinct ways. The structure of the federation limits intergovernmental cooperation and since the late 1970s political parties have been regionalized into two distinct party systems between the regions along linguistic lines (Billiet, 2006). There are, therefore, no country-wide political parties or a 'genuine country-wide public sphere' (Loobuyck and Sinardet, 2017: 394).

Rates of racial or ethnic discrimination in Belgium have often been high in relation to other EU countries. Explanations for this vary between the regions, with the Flemings tending to emphasize issues around perceptions of cultural threat in relation to immigrants and Walloons' perceptions of an economic threat (Billiet, 2006). Such feelings of threat in Flanders declined through the second half of the 1990s, with economic recovery and low unemployment, but increased again in the early 2000s, when Belgium experienced a significant rise in net migration from between 15,000 and 20,000 to 27,790 in 2003 (Loobuyk and Jacobs, 2006), during which time there was a concomitant drop in the percentage of people evaluating multiculturalism positively (Billiet, 2006). A recent report has found that Islamophobia in Belgium has steadily increased across a number of areas, including the media, education, and employment (Easat-Daas, 2019). Moreover, minorities face forms of institutional discrimination; they are more likely to be stopped and arrested by police, detained in custody, and given longer prison sentences as relations with police can be 'dismal' (Bovenkerk, 2017: 62). Further indications are that second generations are proving more successful than their parents, but, notwithstanding differences between and within ethnic groups, still tend to concentrate in certain labour market sectors and do not perform as well in school as non-immigrant Belgians (Bovenkerk, 2017). It also seems to be the case that second generations exhibit higher rates of crime than the first, especially among those who are socio-economically disadvantaged (ibid.).

Migrants' electoral and civil society participation has been increasing since the mid-1990s and particularly since the mid-2000s, albeit in patchy fashion. To a large extent, this has been a result of institutional arrangements such as proportional representation in Brussels that have facilitated an openness to minorities' inclusion (Zapata-Barrero and Gropas, 2012). Overall, Belgians of immigrant background tend to identify with a Belgian national identity or with a city more than with one of the regional or community identities (Loobuyck and Sinardet, 2017: 398). Young Muslims, however, return lower levels of national identification than the majority as well as other minorities, and, moreover, religious importance is a key explanatory factor for this negative effect on national identification of being Muslim (Fleischmann and Phalet, 2018: 51, 53, 56). A recent study, however, has found that there is no evidence to support a reactive Muslim religiosity in relation to a negative discursive climate or political opportunity structure (Torrekens and Jacobs, 2016).

Devolved federalism and the place of religion

Belgium's particular model of federalization is rooted in historic conflicts along linguistic lines between the Flemish nationalist movement and francophone responses to it. Belgium became independent in 1830, at which time it was a unitary state. However, it embarked upon a series of constitutional reforms towards federalism beginning in 1970 and was officially transformed into a federal state in 1993 (Jacobs, 2004), although the linguistic borderline became fixed in 1963 (Loobuyck and Sinardet, 2017: 392).

Belgian politics and policies are often analysed with reference to three cleavages. The first is a religious cleavage between Catholics and non-believers, the second a linguistic cleavage between Francophones and Dutch-speakers, and the third a socioeconomic cleavage, which opposes employers and workers (Adam and Torrekens, 2015). Along the third, Wallonia industrialized early in the nineteenth century, while Flanders remained more agricultural and poorer for longer. It is the first two of these that are particularly and directly pertinent for the considerations of this chapter.

It is perhaps the linguistic cleavage that without which 'Belgium would not be Belgium' (Adam and Torrekens, 2015) and which led to the unilingualism of each region, and eventually the bilingualism of the Brussels-Capital region. Relations between a Belgian identity and regional identities represent a form of 'nested nationalities' (Billiet, 2006; Loobuyck and Sinardet, 2017) that may also be conducive to a multiculturalist identification (Modood, 2017: 22). Moreover, trends seem to suggest that the stronger an identification with a Belgian national identity, the more positive the attitude towards foreigners (Billiet, 2006; Loobuyck and Sinardet, 2017; Maddens et al., 2000). Furthermore, although not yet common and standard practice, politicians and media are increasingly crossing the language border and addressing the different communities (Loobuyck and Sinardet, 2017: 396).

Along the religious cleavage, Belgium has historically been a Catholic country, Catholicism being the inherited state religion from pre-independent Belgium. This meant a cultural monopoly for the Church, socialization in Catholic culture being legally imposed (Dobbelaere, 2010: 284; Dobbelaere and Voyé, 1990). Following the French Revolution, at the end of the eighteenth century this alliance between Church and State came to an end (Dobbelaere, 2010). The Church retained dominant significant influence, however. Belgium inherited the French Concordat, under which the Catholic Church gave up its direct political role for state recognition of its significance (Adam and Torrekens, 2015). Notwithstanding methodological and interpretive cautions, in the census of 1846, 99.8 per cent of the population was registered as Catholic (Billiet, 2006: 919; Dobbelaere and Voyé, 1990). Historically, nevertheless, the Flemish are more Catholic and the Walloons more anti-clerical. Arrangements between the state and other religious faiths have followed the model inherited from this historical arrangement. In addition to the Catholic Church, Judaism was recognized in 1832, Protestantism and Anglicanism in 1870.

During the early period of independent Belgium, the state was organized jointly between Liberals and Catholics. This period of Unionism shifted, however, and from the second half of the nineteenth century radical liberals gained greater control and, along with the socialist party, set about implementing secularist policies (Dobbelaere, 2010: 284). This political shift resulted in one of the most significant areas in which the religious cleavage has played out: through the so-called 'school wars' over the role of the Church in education. The first of these occurred between 1879 and 1884, when the state established its own school system (Dobbelaere and Voyé, 1990) and pillarization, the system of vertical pluralism and a form of segmented differentiation, emerged as an outcome of the first school war. The Catholic pillar formed one of three pillars, the other two being a socialist pillar and a smaller liberal pillar, each with their own systems of schools, hospitals, and so on. The Catholic pillar expanded to include schools from kindergartens to universities, youth and adult organizations, cultural organizations, media, hospitals, trade unions, banks, and more (Dobbelaere, 2010). In 1921 the Catholic pillar was institutionalized with the Catholic Union party representing its political channel (Dobbelaere, 2010: 287).

The second school war occurred in the 1950s, when the Catholic pillar was at its apex and the socialist-liberal government began restricting the subsidies allowed to the Church. The 'School-Pact-Law' of 1959 sealed a compromise, establishing basic principles later (in 1988) brought in as constitutional revisions (through Article 24). This constitutionally guaranteed freedom of religion – in part to meet the religious and non-religious plurality of students – also resulted in support for faith-based schools and the possibility of education in the recognized religions or non-confessional ethics, although Catholic schools have maintained their prominent position in Belgium's education system (Franken, 2016a, 2016b). There is regional variance here; the role of the Church has been defended more in Flanders than in Wallonia, which can be seen translated into the preference for Catholic schools in Flanders and for state schools in Wallonia. The outcome of this period was also a notable shift from a Catholic pillar to a Christian pillar, with many of the organizations and even the political party switching from the former to the latter term.

Billiet notes that the traditional depiction of 'Flanders is Catholic and Christian democrat, Wallonia unbelieving and socialist, and Brussels liberal and free-thinking' has been steadily eroding, the differences between the regions shrinking (2006: 913). In numerous indicators, a gradual decline of religion's place in social and political life can be seen from the 1960s to the present day, with a steady decline in those identifying as Catholic, Church affiliation, involvement and attendance, and organization membership (Billiet, 2006; also Dobbelaere,

2010: 288; Dobbelaere and Voyé, 1990; Franken, 2016a). Overall, religious affiliation is also proving a weaker indicator of voting behaviour than previously, a process which itself seems to be occurring more gradually in Flanders (Billiet, 2006; Dobbelaere and Voyé, 1990), where the Flemish Christian pillar remains institutionalized (Dobbelaere, 2010: 294).

Whether or not this represents a process of de-pillarization is a matter of interpretation. The Catholic/Christian pillar, which has proven able to adapt its 'collective consciousness' to the changing social and cultural process of secularization, now perhaps increasingly represents a 'socio-cultural Christianity' with 'soft' values that are more characterized by *bricolage* in contrast to Orthodoxy (Dobbelaere, 2010; Dobbelaere and Voyé, 1990). Franken suggests that this might represent a form of 'mental depillarisation' (2016a: 312). Indeed, it may be for this reason that it is argued that 'religion has definitively been bypassed by the linguistic and territorial divide as the strongest impulse behind the identity struggles in Belgium' (Foret and Riva, 2010: 806). In relation to education and the continued dominance of Christian schools, Franken notes how often these are now chosen for practical rather than confessional reasons, including by those of other faiths (Franken, 2016a, 2017). In terms of state support for religions more generally, a small majority of the population is in favour as long as subsidies are fairly distributed, compared to about one-quarter who are not in favour and one-fifth who are indifferent to state support for religion (Franken, 2016b).

Struggles over recognition

The separation of church and state in Belgium is not explicitly mentioned in the Constitution and Belgium may be considered a form of moderate secularism (Franken, 2016b: 149; Franken and Loobuyck, 2012; Modood, 2017). The federal state formally recognizes certain religions, and this brings support and financial benefits (Adam and Torrekens, 2015; Franken, 2015, 2016b).

Articles 19 and 20 of the Constitution fix the positive freedom and negative freedom of religion respectively (Franken, 2015: 66) and state support as found in Art.181, for instance, has the purpose of guaranteeing these religious freedoms (Franken, 2016b: 150). The state pays the salaries and pensions of the 'ministers of religion' (Art. 181), and Article 24 stipulates that 'all pupils of school age have the right to moral or religious education at the community's expense' (Franken, 2016a: 309). Article 21 prohibits the state from 'interven[ing] either in the appointment or in the installation of ministers of any religion whatsoever'. Furthermore, there is an annual general assembly of the National Ecumenical Commission to discuss various religious themes at a national level.

Catholicism retains its central position in public life; on the King's birthday and national holidays, for instance, the Catholic Church performs civil-religious rituals (Dobbelaere, 1995: 171). The Catholic Church plays a leading role in national and local level religious affairs between religious organizations and with the state, helping maintain inter-faith dialogue and promote tolerance among all religious groups. Roman Catholicism is also favoured when it comes to financial support (Franken, 2016b: 155n; also Dobbelaere, 1995; Franken and Loobuyck, 2012: 491).

In the second half of the twentieth century further religions have gained official state recognition in addition to the Catholic and Protestant Churches and Jewish Consistory: Islam was recognized in 1974, Orthodox Christianity in 1985, non-confessional free-thinkers in 1993, and Buddhism in 2008 (Adam and Torrekens, 2015), while a union of Hindu associations and the Syrian Orthodox Church have requested recognition (Franken, 2016b). Recognition is conditional and reflects the inheritance and importance of the Catholic Church model. In order to be recognized, a religious faith must organize according to this model: requiring a nationally representative institution, they must bring together 'several tens of thousands' of adherents, have been present in Belgium for a fairly long period, be of social benefit, and not contravene public order in their activities (Franken, 2015: 67, 2016b; Franken and Loobuyck, 2012).

These requirements have often meant that more recent minority religions have faced difficulties in gaining official recognition. Islam provides a good example, especially pertaining to the institutional requirement of a nationally representative Islamic council. The main interlocuter for the Belgian state until 1990 was the Islamic and Cultural Centre (*Centre Islamic et Culturel* [CIC]), although not seen as representative this was not officially recognized by the Belgian state (Çitak, 2010). It wasn't until 1999 that the Belgian Muslim Executive (*Exécutif des Musulmans de Belgique*, BME) was established, although, beset with debates about legitimacy, the implementation of recognition was delayed further until the early 2000s.[1] This is a result of several factors: Islam does not traditionally organize in hierarchical ways similar to that of Catholicism; disagreements between different ethnic and sectarian groups; and, issues over government interference in elections of the body. Particularly important for the BME have been Turkish groups, these being dominated by religious rather than national groups such as Milli Görüş in the BME's early incarnation, and by the Turkish *Diyanet* since the mid-2000s. This itself has meant a tension between Belgium's institutionalization of a 'Belgian Islam' and the *Diyanet*'s emphasis on retaining a Turkish cultural character (Çitak, 2010).

In terms of Belgian government interference, in a social and political context marked by fears of religious radicalization and terrorism, the government stipulated further interventions for the recognition of Islam and greater scrutiny of Muslim organizations. These included government-organized elections for representative candidates and screening of these candidates. As a result of these kinds of issues, the BME has had an erratic institutional relationship with the state that has slowed the development of Islamic organizational structures (Fleischmann and Phalet, 2018: 48).

Incorporation of minorities: regional variation

A significant development for minority incorporation began in 1974 when competence over the 'welcoming policy for migrant workers' was devolved to the regions, setting the conditions for regional variation in this area (Adam, 2013). In 1980, integration policy was transferred from the regions to the communities (ibid.), coinciding with immigration and integration first becoming prominent on the agenda in Belgium (Loobuyck and Jacobs, 2010). Following this devolvement and beginning in the mid-1980s, what can be observed when it comes to the incorporation of minority populations and integration policies is a move away from an initial convergence and towards greater divergence between the regions. Two further events also brought immigrant integration to the foreground: the creation of the Brussels-Capital region in 1989 and the electoral success in Flanders in 2004 of the right-wing populist Vlaams Blok party,[2] gaining almost one-quarter of the vote (Adam, 2013: 553). Jacobs has in fact suggested ethnocentrism/multiculturalism represents a new political cleavage in Belgian politics (2004).

Since the mid-1980s the regions have pursued quite different strategies of inclusion of minority faiths based on different conceptions of citizenship (Adam and Jacobs, 2014). There is thus not one Belgian model but a combination of a central immigration policy with divergent migrant integration policies between the regions. Wallonia's approach can be characterized as *laissez-faire* assimilationist and adopts more radically secular and colour-blind policy approaches (Jacobs, 2004; Loobuyck and Jacobs, 2010). Approaches to integration in Flanders can be characterized as multiculturalist and more interventionist than the path pursued in Wallonia, with far more resources allocated to integration measures; perhaps representing a parallel to the UK approach (Modood, 2017). Notable policy measures include establishing regional organizations (VOCOM, *Vlaams Overleg Comité Opbouwwerk Migratie*, Minorities Forum) to co-ordinate the activities of minority organizations; public financing of grassroots ethnic minority organizations; incorporating diversity concerns into most policy sectors; and, renaming 'immigrants' 'ethno-cultural minorities' (Adam, 2013; Jacobs, 2004; Loobuyck and Sinardet, 2017).

Nevertheless, increasingly both regions mix assimilationist as well as multiculturalist policy measures, with the significant difference between the two being one of the balance of emphasis between cultural homogeneity and cultural diversity, and between the degree of interventionism each considers necessary for integration (Adam, 2013; Bousetta and Jacobs, 2006). Wallonia has shifted to a policy frame that is slightly more interventionist-assimilationist (Adam, 2013). For example, minority language courses are supported by the state through the education system (Adam and Torrekens, 2015; Loobuyck and Sinardet, 2017). In Flanders, especially following the electoral success of the Flemish Liberals (*Open Vlaamse Liberalen en Democraten*, VLD), a hybridic approach at once multiculturalist and assimilationist has emerged more explicitly. In 2003 a compulsory civic integration policy was introduced, bringing in Dutch-language courses and courses on Flemish social norms and values. Yet these more assimilationist measures reinforced the existing multiculturalist policies as well as introduced new multiculturalist measures; for example, legitimate absence from school on religious festival days for all recognized religious denominations (Adam, 2013; Jacobs, 2004).

Incorporation of minorities: religious accommodations

For the incorporation of religious diversity more specifically, under Belgian law there is no general duty for public or private institutions to grant forms of reasonable accommodation on grounds of religion. In 2008 this issue was taken up by the Centre for Equal Opportunities and Opposition to Racism. The Centre has highlighted 'pragmatic creativity' rather than general principles as 'the Belgian way' (Bousetta and Jacobs, 2006; Bribosia et al., 2011: 107). In fact, the concept of reasonable accommodation for religious diversity was absent from Belgian public discourse until 2009 (Bribosia et al., 2011). There is provision for religious worship in the 1978 Act on employment contracts, coming under an earlier Act from 1900, which imposes the obligation 'to grant the employee the necessary time to fulfil his religious obligations as well as the civil obligations imposed by the law' (ibid.). General employment law though has largely left matters of religious accommodations to *ad hoc* measures, and the granting of accommodations remains contingent on a variety of localized factors (ibid.).

Demands on grounds of reasonable accommodation have been made, although not always granted, in relation to areas including dress, diet, prayer space, and holidays for religious celebrations. Despite the lack of a general law, various exemptions and accommodations have been enacted, albeit with regional, sector, and institution specific variation. Flemish authorities have developed lines of case law interpreting and adapting the definition of reasonable accommodation from the Employment Equality Directive, dealing with disability discrimination, to include other forms of discrimination, including religion (Bribosia et al., 2011). Although there is no provision for halal or kosher meat, school children can get meals which take their religious faith into account. Also, school children may take days off school to celebrate 'in conformity with the pupil's philosophical beliefs as recognised by the Constitution' (Bribosia et al., 2011). In contrast, in the French-speaking community no similar provision exists and pupils must rely on more *ad hoc* measures.

As in a number of Western European countries, Belgium has been concerned with issues around religious signs and symbols stimulated by the presence and politicization of Islam and Muslims in the public sphere, and again, regional approaches to these vary. While both regions have followed similar policies and discourse around the language of 'neutrality', in Wallonia justifications have relied on arguments based in anti-clerical secularism, a feature not found in Flanders (Adam and Torrekens, 2015).

Two areas of note relate to places of worship and to religious signs and symbols in the public sphere. Notably, these measures apply only to Islam and Muslims. In regard to the first of these, in Flanders, for instance, in order to be recognized, mosques must have written documents stating and proving their commitment to a) their use of Dutch as their *lingua operandi* (with the exception of the *Khutba*), b) their respect for the Constitution and basic rights and liberties, and c) their not being involved in terrorist activities (ibid.). These sorts of interventionist policies are more absent in Wallonia, where only administrative conditions have been introduced to fulfil requirements for recognition (ibid.).

With regard to religious signs and symbols, this can be seen by considering the Islamic headscarf, which in common with several other European countries has proved controversial. Belgium has introduced a criminal ban on face-covering in the public sphere (since 2011), provoked by the desire to outlaw the wearing of the *niqab*. No general ban on head covering exists but such bans have appeared in both regions *ad hoc*, stimulated by concerns over the headscarf. Public schools run by the Flemish community have prohibited the wearing of religious signs for both teachers and pupils, teachers of religious education classes excepted, despite the Council of State (Belgium's highest administrative court) declaring headscarf bans in Flemish public schools discriminatory (Adam and Torrekens, 2015; Brems et al., 2017). For Flemish private schools, as for both public and private schools in francophone Belgium, the decision is left to the discretion of the individual school authorities, resulting, nevertheless, in *de facto* bans. A Constitutional Court ruling in June 2020 declared that a ban on religious symbols (centred around the headscarf) in higher education would be permissible, although most universities have assured that they will not be imposing such bans. Similarly, bans have also been introduced for employees of the French Community Parliament and some other local municipalities when in contact with the public. There have also been several cases where women wearing *hijab* have been refused access to goods or services; for example, in gyms, restaurants, and the housing market, and headscarf discrimination has become more common in workplaces and courtrooms (Brems et al., 2017: 895). In addition to these *hijab* bans, 'burkinis' have also been banned by a number of municipal swimming pools (Brems et al., 2018). Bans have also been introduced for ritual slaughter as of January and September 2019 in Flanders and Wallonia respectively (Easat-Daas, 2019).

Concluding remarks

Belgium presents an interesting case of variance in approach to the governance of religious diversity based on its model of devolved federalism. Belgium has an overarching framework in which freedom of religion is constitutionally guaranteed and in which religions can gain recognition affording them significant levels of support financially as well as in their operation in the public sphere. This recognition is conditional, however, and its shape and conception reflect the inheritance of the dominant historical position of the Catholic Church.

Moreover, within this framework, different regions pursue distinct, albeit in many ways overlapping, policies that are, furthermore, underpinned by distinct philosophies with regard to the public place and role of religion. In a context marked by fears of religiously inspired radicalization, Islam and Muslims have been at the forefront of debates and policies addressing in recent years the governance of public religious minorities, which have seen increasing conditions, restrictions, and requirements placed upon Muslims and Muslim organizations in particular.

Notes

1 Technically recognition was gained in 1998, although for various reasons and disagreements recognition can be said to have occurred in 2003, although this was not the end of controversy, see http://www.euro-islam.info/country-profiles/belgium/. Also, Çitak (2010).
2 Later changed to Vlaams Belang following a conviction for racist propaganda.

References

Adam, I. (2013). Immigrant Integration Policies of the Belgian Regions: Substate Nationalism and Policy Divergence after Devolution. *Regional & Federal Studies*, 23(5): 547–569.

Adam, I. & Jacobs, D. (2014). Divided on Immigration, Two Models for Integration. The Multilevel Governance of Immigration and Integration in Belgium. In E. Hepburn & R. Zapata-Barrero (eds), *The Politics of Immigration in Multi-Level States: Governance and Political Parties* (pp. 65–85). Basingstoke: Palgrave Macmillan.

Adam, I. & Torrekens, C. (2015). Different Regional Approaches to Immigration Related Cultural Diversity: Interpreting the Belgian cultural diversity policy paradox. *Régionalimse et Fédéralisme*, 15.

Billiet, J. (2006). Attitudes towards Ethnic Minorities in Flanders. In L. d'Haenens, M. Hooghe, D. Vanheule, & H. Gezduci (eds), *'New' Citizens, New Policies? Developments in Diversity Policy in Canada and Flanders* (pp. 35–56). Gent: Academia Press.

Bousetta, H. & Jacobs, D. (2006). Multiculturalism, Citizenship and Islam in Problematic Encounters in Belgium'. In T. Modood, A. Triandafyllidou, & R. Zapata-Barrero (eds), *Multiculturalism, Muslims and Citizenship* (pp. 23–36). Abingdon: Routledge.

Bovenkerk, F. (2017). Understanding Crime and Delinquency in a Multicultural Society. In T. Modood & F. Bovenkerk (eds), *Multiculturalism – How Can Society Deal with It? A Thinking Exercise in Flanders* (pp. 43–70). Brussels: KVAB Standpunt 51.

Brems, E., Chaib, S. O., & Vanhees, K. (2018). 'Burkini' Bans in Belgian Municipal Swimming Pools: Banning as a Default Option. *Netherlands Quarterly of Human Rights*, 36(4): 270–289.

Brems, E., Heri, C., Chaib, S. O., & Verdonck, L. (2017). Head-Covering Bans in Belgian Courtrooms and Beyond: Headscarf Persecution and the Complicity of Supranational Courts. *Human Rights Quarterly*, 39(4): 882–909.

Bribosia, E., Rea, A., Ringelheim, J., & Rorive, I. (2011). Reasonable Accommodation of Religious Diversity in Europe and in Belgium: Law and Practice. In A. Rea, S. Bonjour, & D. Jacobs (eds), *The Others in Europe: Legal and Social Categorization in Context* (pp. 91–116). Brussels: PUB.

Çitak, Z. (2010). Religion, Ethnicity and Transnationalism: Turkish Islam in Belgium. *Journal of Church and State*, 53(2): 222–242.

Costa, R. & de Valk, H. A. G. (2018). Ethnic and Socioeconomic Segregation in Belgium: A multiscalar approach using individualised neighbourhoods. *European Journal of Population*, 34(2): 225–250.

Dobbelaere, K. (1995). The Surviving Dominant Catholic Church in Belgium: A Consequence of Its Popular Religious Practice? In W. C. Roof, J. W. Carroll, & D. A. Roozen (eds), *The Post-War Generation and Establishment Religion: Cross-Cultural Perspectives* (pp. 171–190). Oxford: Westview Press.

Dobbelaere, K. (2010). Religion and Politics in Belgium: From an institutionalised manifest Catholic to a latent Christian pillar. *Politics and Religion*, 4(2): 283–296.

Dobbelaere, K. & Voyé, L. (1990). From Pillar to Postmodernity: The changing situation of religion in Belgium. *Sociological Analysis*, 51(S): S1–S13.

Easat-Daas, A. (2019). Belgium. In E. Bayakli & F. Hafez (eds), *European Islamophobia Report 2018* (pp. 141–166). Istanbul: SETA.

Fleischmann, F. & Phalet, K. (2018). Religion and National Identification in Europe: Comparing Muslim youth in Belgium, England, Germany, the Netherlands, and Sweden. *Journal of Cross-Cultural Psychology*, 49(1): 44–61.

Foret, F. & Riva, V. (2010). Religion between Nation and Europe: The French and Belgian 'No' to the Christian heritage of Europe. *West European Politics*, 33(4): 791–809.

Franken, L. (2015). State Support for Religion in Belgium: A critical evaluation. *Journal of Church and State*, 59(1): 59–80.

Franken, L. (2016a). The Freedom of Religion and the Freedom of Education in Twenty-first-century Belgium: A critical approach. *British Journal of Religious Education*, 38(3): 308–324.

Franken, L. (2016b). *Liberal Neutrality and State Support for Religion*. Cham: Springer.

Franken, L. (2017). Islamic Education in Belgium: Past, present, and future. *Religious Education*, 112(5): 491–503.

Franken, L. & Loobuyck, P. (2012). Is Active State Support for Religions and Worldviews Compatible with the Liberal Idea of State Neutrality? A critical analysis of the Belgian case. *Journal of Church and State*, 55(3): 478–497.

Imeraj, L., Willaert, D., & de Valk, H. A. G. (2018). A Comparative Approach towards Ethnic Segregation Patterns in Belgian Cities Using Multiscalar Individualized Neighborhoods. *Urban Geography*, 39(8): 1221–1246.

Jacobs, D. (2004). Alive and Kicking? Multiculturalism in Flanders. *International Journal on Multicultural Societies*, 6(2): 280–299.

Koutroubas, T., Vloeberghs, W., & Yanasmayan, Z. (2009). Political, Religious and Ethnic Radicalisation among Muslims in Belgium. MICROCON Policy Working Paper 5.

Loobuyck, P. & Jacobs, D. (2006). The Flemish Immigration Society Political Challenges on Different Levels. In L. d'Haenens, M. Hooghe, D. Vanheule, & H. Gezduci (eds), *'New' Citizens, New Policies? Developments in Diversity Policy in Canada and Flanders* (pp. 105–123). Gent: Academia Press.

Loobuyck, P. & Jacobs, D. (2010). Nationalism, Multiculturalism and Integration Policy in Belgium and Flanders. *Canadian Journal for Social Research*, 3(1): 29–40.

Loobuyck, P. & Sinardet, P. (2017). A Hard Case for Liberal Nationalism? In K. Banting & W. Kymlicka (eds), *The Strains of Commitment: The Political Sources of Solidarity in Diverse Societies* (pp. 289–419). Oxford: Oxford University Press.

Maddens, B., Billiet, J., & Beerten, R. (2000). National Identity and the Attitude towards Foreigners in Multi-National States: The case of Belgium. *Journal of Ethnic and Migration Studies*, 26(1): 45–60.

Modood, T. (2017). Multicultural Nationalism, Political Secularism and Religious Education. In T. Modood & F. Bovenkerk (eds), *Multiculturalism – How Can Society Deal with It? A Thinking Exercise in Flanders* (pp. 13–42). Brussels: KVAB Standpunt 51.

Pew. (2017). *Europe's Growing Muslim Population*. Pew Research Center, Nov. 29, 2017.

Torrekens, C. & Jacobs, D. (2016). Muslims' Religiosity and Views on Religion in Six Western European Countries: Does national context matter? *Journal of Ethnic and Migration Studies*, 42(2): 325–340.

Zapata-Barrero, R. & Gropas, R. (2012). Active Immigrants in Multicultural Contexts: Democratic challenges in Europe. In A. Trandafyllidou, T. Modood, & N. Meer N. (eds), *European Multiculturalisms: Cultural, Religious and Ethnic Challenges* (pp. 167–191). Edinburgh: Edinburgh University Press.

3

France

From *laïcité* to *laicism*?

Thomas Sealy and Tariq Modood

Introduction

France's mode of separation between church and state is something of an exception in Western Europe. It is in fact, along with Turkey, the only European nation described as secular in its Constitution. The French model emphasises social cohesion founded in a civic nationhood, where recognising group 'difference' is seen as antithetical to citizenship and the state is officially colour and ethnicity 'blind'. This is based on a form of republican egalitarian individualism which the granting of group rights is seen to undermine, and religious difference is therefore restricted to the private sphere.

Fundamental to understanding the French model, its historical emergence as well as pertinent contemporary debates is the principle of *laïcité*. Commentators have pointed to two different trends and emphases, emerging from an historical 'two Frances', when it comes to understanding *laïcité* and the debates surrounding it (Jansen, 2013; Kuru, 2009). One is a combative, strict, closed or assertive *laïcité*, which is anti-clerical and republican. Historically, the second France was clerical and monarchist. Today, however, France's second face is characterised by a pluralistic, soft, open or passive *laïcité*. Indeed, it is worth noting that *laïcité* was from its inception a principle supported by people with a variety of metaphysical beliefs and ideas about the proper role of religion in its relation to politics. What may perhaps be just as significant are the 'cultural layers of laicism', where *laïcism* is understood to refer to a recent hardening of a cultural discourse of *laïcité* with ideological underlying presuppositions of assimilationism and the disappearance of religion (Jansen, 2013).

Socio-demographic overview

France's population stands at 66.99 million according to official statistics (as of November 2019). Ethnic and religious statistics are highly controversial as they are thought to foster racism and French law forbids distinguishing citizens by their race or faith; official statistics are generally restricted to national origin. In 2004, it was estimated that 85 per cent of the population of Metropolitan France was white or of European origin, with 10 per cent from North Africa, 3.5 per cent Black and 1.5 per cent Asian. The net migration rate has been stable over the last few years and comparatively low for Western European countries. As a colonial power, France ruled several Muslim territories between the mid-nineteenth and mid-twentieth centuries, notably Algeria, Morocco, and Tunisia, thus France's current ethnic and religious diversity owes much to its colonial history.

Whereas prior to the 1950s immigration to France was mainly from majority Catholic European countries, since the period following the Second World War the Muslim population of mainland France grew more rapidly as France became the first European country that actively recruited labour migrants as a matter of policy to fill the labour shortage, predominantly from Tunisia, Algeria, and Morocco (Bowen, 2009). Following the oil crisis in the 1970s and resulting recession and higher unemployment, however, the French government successively sought to halt this recruitment of foreign-born labour migrants and reduce immigration overall. The unintended consequence of this was that these migrants who had seen themselves as 'temporary' came to settle in France and bring their families over. With the population growth so too has grown the visibility of Islam and Muslims. Muslims in France constitute the largest Muslim population in Europe and comprise about 7–8 per cent of the population, making Islam the second largest religious group (Ajrouch, 2007; Amghar, 2009). It is the increasing presence of Islam and Muslims that gives rise to the most significant contemporary challenges France faces as a result of religious diversity. Cesari (2002) has in fact argued that it is this Muslim settlement in France that has unsettled the 'uneasy peace' that had gradually taken hold between France's religious communities and *laïcité* since the 1905 law on church-state separation. Kastoryano (2004) further suggests that it is the religion of Islam itself more than the presence of immigrants that is the source of the 'disquiet'. It is also important to note though that although only 0.5 per cent of the population, France's Jewish population represents the highest number of Jews outside of Israel and the U.S. Table 3.1 shows the estimates of the religious composition of France.

France has one of the lowest levels of religiosity in Europe and one of the highest levels of negative views towards public religion (Pew Research Center, 2019; Religion Monitor, 2017). Overall patterns and trends of religious practice show a decline, although these vary among different religious groups. According to official statistics, while 45 per cent of citizens of metropolitan France aged between 18 and 50 say they are agnostic or atheist, approximately 75 per cent of Muslims and Jews say that religion plays an important role in their lives. Weekly attendance at a place of worship or frequency of prayer is less than 10 per cent (Pickel, 2013), although some suggest figures for mosque attendance is notably higher (El Karoui,

Table 3.1 French population, by religious affiliation

	2010	%	2020	%
Christian	39,560,000	63	37,940,000	58.1
Muslim	4,710,000	7.5	5,430,000	8.3
Buddhists	280,000	0.5	310,000	0.5
Jews	310,000	0.5	340,000	0.5
Folk Religions	220,000	0.3	250,000	0.4
Hindu	30,000	<0.1	40,000	<0.1
Unaffiliated	17,580,000	28	20,830,000	31.9
Other	100,000	0.2	110,000	0.2

Source: Adapted from Pew (https://www.pewforum.org/2015/04/02/religious-projection-table/2010/number/Europe/).

2016). In a Gallup poll 40 per cent of the French public said that being less expressive of one's religion was important for integration compared to half that figure for Muslim respondents (Cesari, 2013).

France also has particularly negative attitudes towards its Muslims: 35 per cent of French respondents to the same Gallup survey expressed reservations about the loyalty to France of French Muslims (Cesari, 2013: 13). A Pew survey found that more than two-thirds of people were worried about Islamic extremists in France (ibid.: 17). A Religion Monitor report (Pickel, 2013) found that 55 per cent of respondents felt Islam was not compatible with the West. Polls have also shown that a majority believe that French Muslims are not integrated into society and, moreover that this failure is a result of Muslims' refusal to integrate (Cesari, 2013).

France's unemployment rate has been declining over the last few years and currently is 8.7 per cent, yet there is significant disparity along lines of ethnic origin. OECD data show that those with Muslim ancestry in France have significantly lower educational attainment levels than the national average (Cesari, 2010: 19) and are over-represented in low-skilled occupations and unemployment despite high levels of fluency in French (El Karoui, 2016; Religion Monitor, 2017). A 2016 report found that the probability of being called to an interview was 30 per cent higher for Catholics than for Jews and twice as likely as for Muslims, with Muslim men especially facing high levels of discrimination (Valfort, 2015). People of immigrant backgrounds from Algeria, Tunisia, Morocco, and Turkey are also far more likely to be concentrated in social housing in urban areas and are more likely to be living in poverty than the national average.

In politics, minorities have been underrepresented in the French Parliament. This has improved in the last few years, although representatives with a Muslim background are few.

Establishing *laïcité*

France is a historically Catholic country and significant for its mode of governance of religious diversity is the long process of 'the state's defiant slippage from its traditional Catholic moorings' that broke Roman Catholic dominance and privilege and brought the Church more firmly under the auspices of the French state (Englund, 1992).

Fundamental to understanding France's approach is *laïcité*. Indeed, *laïcité* is so frequently referred to by politicians (and often rather poetically) and held to be so important that it has for some been called a 'state religion' and may at least be considered the Republic's founding principle (Kastoryano, 2006). *Laïcité* is often rendered in English as 'secular' or 'secularism', yet it is important to appreciate that *laïcité* came to connote a particular anti-clerical attitude and policies (Gunn, 2004), where France is seen to represent an approach based on freedom *from* religion, with the state's role one of protecting citizens in this regard (Gunn, 2009). It is for these reasons that French *laïcité* stands out in Western Europe and is not neutral with regard to religion (cf. Joppke, 2007).

What Gunn (2004) has referred to as the first phase of *laïcité* began with the Revolution of 1789, which abolished the monarchy, breaking the close tie between church and state, and subordinated the Church to the political sphere. Revolutionaries destroyed or appropriated Church land and property, banned religious services, withdrew state subsidies, and guillotined priests (Gunn, 2004, 2009; Kuru, 2009). However, in 1801, Napoleon Bonaparte signed a Concordat with Pope Pius VII that recognised Catholicism as 'the religion of the great majority of the French people' but maintained state authority over the clergy. At this time the Organic Laws, which regulated the state's relations with Protestants (in 1802) and Jews (in 1808), were also issued (Kuru, 2009).

The second phase of *laïcité* (Gunn, 2004) occurred during the period of the Third Republic (1875–1905), when an anti-clerical secularism re-emerged as the dominant ideological force. During this period, a number of secularisation laws were passed, including for schools (under the so-called Ferry Law) and hospitals, the abolishment of prayers in parliamentary sessions, prohibition of religious symbols in public buildings, banning of state funding of religion, appropriation of religious property, and the requirement that all religious associations were authorised by the state.

The law that enshrined *laïcité* as a fundamental principle of the Republic was the law of 1905, which formally separated church and state. Article 1 of the law states 'The Republic assures freedom of conscience. It guarantees the free exercise of religious worship, limited only by the exceptions enumerated below in the interest of public order' (Kastoryano, 2006: 61). Furthermore, Article 2 states that 'The Republic does not recognize, finance, or subsidize any religious group' (Gunn, 2009: 955).

There are exceptions to the dominance of state *laïcité*. The region of Alsace-Moselle recognises Catholicism, Lutheranism, Calvinism, and Judaism; the state pays the salaries of the clergy of these religions and religious instruction is taught in schools (Gunn, 2009). This exception is a result of the region being part of Germany when the secularisation laws were applied, and thus it was agreed when the region became a part of France again following the First World War to base its legal framework on the Concordat of 1801 and Organic Laws of 1802–1808 and not the law of 1905. Based on related historical reasoning, some of France's overseas *départements* have also not had the secularisation laws imposed on them, as is the case in French Guiana, for instance (ibid.).

Struggles over *laïcité*

The 1905 law is enshrined in the current Constitution (1958), which states 'France is an indivisible, secular [laic], democratic and social Republic. It ensures the equality before the law of all its citizens, without distinction as to origin, race, or religion. It respects all beliefs' (Article 2) (Gunn, 2009: 953–954). Gunn comments that the 1905 law has the status of a cultural icon, approaching an importance on a level with the Constitution itself (2009: 954). In fact, such is the importance of *laïcité* that most Christians, Jews, and Muslims as well as secularists justify their positions by appealing to some version of it and can support and defend it as long as basic freedoms of religion, guaranteed by the Constitution, are not violated (El Karoui, 2016).

Despite a vision of *laïcité* as strict separation, there are several ways in which church and state are related owing to the state's regulatory role. Official affairs to do with religion are the responsibility of the Bureau of Religious Affairs (*Bureau des Cultes*), an office within the Ministry of the Interior. This office is responsible for deciding which religious associations are officially recognised as 'religions', and receive the benefits of this status, rather than just as 'associations'. Obtaining the status of 'religion' is difficult and requires the state undertake 'a substantive review' of its purposes and practices (Gunn, 2009: 978). This includes consideration by the State Council of several factors, including: coming together in formal ceremonies; how long the group has existed; if beliefs contain universal religious principles; and, ensuring that the group's activities do not threaten public order (Bowen, 2009). Moreover, the state maintains a high degree of interference. For example, prior to papal appointment the Minister checks that the values of nominees for Bishops are not incompatible with those of the Republic (Troper, 2016). It is also heavily involved in making decisions about employees and the curriculum in state-funded religious schools (see below).

In line with the constitutional provision of religious freedom, the state does undertake certain measures to help support the position of religions in French society. Legal institutional status was granted to representative bodies for Catholics, Protestants, and Jews, represented by the Council of Bishops, Protestant Federation, and Central Consistory respectively. This recognition comes with tax exemptions and assistance in access to public spaces and building places of worship. These bodies consult with the state on the management and regulation of religious life, the presence of chaplains in public services and bodies, and the organisation of holidays among other matters. There are state-paid chaplains who operate in public schools, prisons, hospitals, and the military (Kuru, 2009). Faith-based hospitals and institutions for care can also get state funding in recognition of their *utilité publique*, providing they meet appropriate criteria (Franken, 2016). An anomaly emerging from the state historically taking ownership of religious property is that it now owns and pays significant subsidies towards the maintenance of the majority of Catholic churches, around half of Protestant churches, and one-tenth of synagogues (Gunn, 2009; Kuru, 2009).

Historically inherited privilege for Catholicism also continues. Fish is generally served in schools on Fridays for Catholics but, while non-pork options are usually provided, no provision is made for halal meat, for instance. Moreover, historical precedence also means that schools' 'neutrality' is more accommodative of Christianity through, for instance, the acceptance of religious holidays and Sundays and Wednesdays as days free from school. The state also observes Christian calendar holidays such as Easter and Christmas (Gunn, 2009).

France has been highly restrictive of religious associations, particularly New Religious Movements (NRMs) not officially recognised by the Bureau of Religious Affairs as 'religions', perceiving them as partaking in psychological manipulation, fraud, exploitation, and anti-democratic activities, and has actively pursued their suppression (Beckford, 2004; Duvert, 2004; Franken, 2016; Luca, 2004). One high-profile incident was when the Jehovah's Witnesses were ordered to pay millions of dollars in taxes and fined for publishing religious material, following which the European Court of Human Rights (ECtHR) found France in violation of Article 9 of the European Convention on Human Rights (ECHR). Further examples of unrecognised sects are the Baptists and Opus Dei (Gunn, 2009: 983).

Towards the end the 1990s religion and particularly Islam became more prominent in media discourses and in the early 2000s issues about Muslims became more prominent on the French political agenda. Stemming from the recognition of the problematic position of Muslims and Islam in France, a desire to reduce the foreign influence over France's Muslim population (through, for example, funding for buildings and foreign-born and educated imams), and from demands of Muslims for recognition themselves, attempts to institutionalise Islam in France through establishing a representative body for Muslims similar to those of other faiths have been made (Kastoryano, 2004, 2006; see Bowen, 2009).

In 1990, the Council of Reflection on Islam in France (CORIF) was created. It comprised representatives from major Islamic associations, under the supervision of the Interior Minister, although this was permanently suspended due to infighting (Cesari, 2002). In April 2003 the *Conseil Français du Culte Musulman* (CFCM) was established to be the official consultative body and coordinator with the state on a range of matters, including mosque building, halal meat, cemeteries, Muslim chaplains, and training imams. The CFCM was made up of several Muslim associations representing different national origins of France's Muslim population, including the Paris mosque (originally sponsored by Morocco but switched to Algeria by the French Foreign Minister in 1957); the Union of Islamic Organisations of France (UIOF); the Federation National of Muslims of France (FNMF), with links to Morocco; and the Turkish Islamic Union for Religious Affairs (DITIB), the European division of Turkey's Diyanet.

The goal, frequently made by successive senior French political figures, was to shift from Islam *in* France to an Islam *of* France, or French Islam. In fact, Muslims themselves are refashioning norms, forms of reasoning, and institutions, also constructing a French Islam (see Bowen, 2009). As a result of this approach, questions around the legitimacy and representativeness of these bodies have been raised as well as of greater state interference.

Issues around ethnic, racial, and religious discrimination have received greater attention in the last couple of decades, with patterns of systematic discrimination against people of North African descent emerging. This is often directed at Muslim women who wear the *hijab*, and who 'have [illegally] been prohibited from celebrating marriages in the local municipality, attending naturalization ceremonies, entering public buildings, consulting a doctor, going to a bank agency, participating in outdoor school activities, etc.' (Cesari, 2012: 444). There were also large spikes in anti-Muslim incidents, such as hate speech, vandalism, and violence against individuals, following the 2015 attacks in Paris, with France's Interior Ministry reporting they had more than tripled (Pew Research Center, 2017).

The French imaginary of Islam and Muslims is intimately tied up with the legacy of colonialism (Kuru, 2009) and its 'continual weight' (Bowen, 2009: 2). The Algerian War of independence[1] has left particularly 'searing effects … on the psyches' of ethnic Europeans, Arabs, and Berbers in France (Fetzer and Soper, 2005: 63). It is in the context and scope of this imaginary that it is perhaps necessary to understand, if not to justify, France's '*ordre public*' arguments. France's Muslim immigrants have been viewed by many as 'unassimilable', something attested to by the relative successes of the Front National Party. This, however, runs counter to repeated survey results that show that Muslims want to be able to pursue upward social mobility as part of society (Body-Gendrot, 2007: 302).

These perceptions have, moreover, been compounded in a post-9/11 context, where France has faced some of the most high-profile attacks associated with Islamic extremism. This has also involved a more practical approach towards recognising ethnic and religious differences, developing Islamic institutions as well as consultative bodies for governing religious diversity, which have increasingly taken on a local, civil shape (Martínez-Ariño, 2019). Moreover, there has also been an emphasis on collaborating with foreign governments (such as Morocco, Turkey, and Algeria), who are able to have an influence on the religion's development through their policies towards diasporas (Bruce, 2018). The practicalities of this approach, however, are still seen within the scope of *laïcité* and the national retains its emphasis – Muslim associations, for instance, are required to sign a declaration of adherence to its principles under the Constitution (Cesari, 2002: 341) as part of the goal of domesticating Islam. France's approach has thus increasingly taken on more explicit local, national, and transnational features.

As well as this focus on France's Muslim population and issues of Islamophobia, there have been several high-profile anti-Semitic attacks in recent years. While historically France's relations with its Jews have been highly controversial (the Dreyfus affair around the turn of the twentieth century and their treatment under the Vichy regime of the Second World War being prominent examples), today, on the whole, public attitudes data suggest Jews are well-regarded in France, especially in relation to other minorities, although long-standing prejudices and suspicions of communitarianism and loyalty to Israel over France persist. Moreover, following the Second World War, the state sought to protect Jews and suppress anti-Semitism. Yet in the 2000s there has been a notable increase in anti-Semitic attacks. Both anti-Semitic attacks and harassment peaked in 2014, before dropping sharply, reported to be a result of protective security measures enacted by public authorities (CNCDH, 2017). Nevertheless, they have risen again in 2018, with the Interior Minister announcing a 74 per cent increase in anti-Semitic attacks (FRA, 2019). Although anti-Semitism stems from far left and far right circles (as it has historically), according to official statistics most high-profile incidents have been related to Islamist extremism and the Israel-Palestine conflict, with targeted deadly attacks having occurred at a Jewish school (2012), supermarket (2015), museum (2014), and memorial (2019). The government has sought to crack down on hate speech, including adopting a controversial bill to expand the definition of anti-Semitism and a focus on online hate speech.

Laïcité and schools

Ferrari speaks of a 'narrative secularism' as well as a 'legal secularism' (2009) and this can be seen in the high-profile debates concerning *laïcité* and state schools, which are one of the most important sites for French Republicanism as 'French national identity is inseparable from its schools' (Minister Bayrou from 1994, quoted in Kastoryano, 2006: 61). Schools, according to the assertive strain of *laïcité*, are a place of 'emancipation' and *mise à distance* where community identities and ties are left at the door (Jansen, 2013; Kuru, 2009) and students 'become future autonomous citizens (in their minds and their bodies) with the capacity to live together and share common principles within a larger political body' (Body-Gendrot, 2007: 292).

Of particular contemporary prominence for *laïcité* have been *les affaires du foulard* of the last few decades, which have led to extensive public and political debates around the principles of the Republic, of *laïcité*, and of French national identity. In this vein the initial *affaire du foulard* in 1989 gained a social and political significance disproportionate with the actual presence of the headscarf – becoming 'one of the biggest political debates in France since the Dreyfus affair' (Kuru, 2009: 20, citing Kepel, 1994; also Gunn, 2004).

It is important to understand the precise historical moment in 1989. As Bowen points out, Muslim girls had been wearing headscarves to schools without fuss for years, either wearing them throughout the day or removing them for classes as was the general rule. Indeed, the same middle school that triggered the debates in 1989 had an earlier class photo of a girl in a headscarf as a display of the cultural diversity at the school (2009: 83). In 1989, however, political forms of Islam were emerging onto the international scene. The Rushdie affair earlier the same year in the UK,[2] and the birth of the Islamic Salvation Front (FIS) in France's former colony of Algeria, for instance, meant that a perception of a growing and threatening political Islam served to train an acute focus and emphasis on visible forms of Muslim religious identity in France (Bowen, 2009), resulting in a gradual hardening of discourses on *laïcité*.

Les affaires involve a series of cases brought before the French courts, beginning in 1989 when three schoolgirls were expelled for wearing headscarves in class at their public school in Creil, in the north of Paris. The then-Minister of Education, Lionel Jospin, having first stressed dialogue between the schools and students and parents, referred the matter to France's highest administrative court, the State Council (*Conseil d'État*), following a barrage of criticism of his more open stance. The State Council also adopted an accommodative stance, ruling that the wearing of the headscarf did not contravene *laïcité*, emphasising the pupils' right to 'express and manifest their religious beliefs within public institutions with respect for pluralism' (Kastoryano, 2006: 59). Between 1992 and 1999 the State Council ruled on 49 cases of similar expulsions on a case-by-case basis, emphasising pupils' freedom of religion, and overturning 41 of the expulsions (Kuru, 2009: 104, 127; see also Bowen, 2009). When the headscarf in schools became a public and political issue again in 1994, the (new) Minister of Education issued a directive to public schools forbidding any conspicuous religious signs

(Kastoryano, 2006). The ban on religious signs was opposed by Muslim associations as well as the French Catholic Church and Chief Rabbi of France.

In 2003 the then-President, Jacques Chirac, appointed a commission to reassess *laïcité* and consider the issue of religious signs in schools. The Stasi commission, so called after its chair Bernard Stasi, delivered its report the same year and legislation banning conspicuous religious signs in public schools was introduced in early 2004 (Gunn, 2004; Kuru, 2009). Although the legislation was indiscriminate between religions – Sikh students wearing turbans, the Jewish yarmulke, and Christians wearing 'big' crosses have also been expelled under it – it has disproportionately affected Muslims and commentators both for and against widely agree that the legislation and the mission of the commission itself targeted Muslims and the headscarf (see Bowen, 2009; Cesari, 2012; Gunn, 2009). The focus on the headscarf was based on it being viewed as a binding into an immigrant culture against the emancipatory role of the public school, and a tool of female subordination (support for its banning has been high among French feminists).

To grasp, again if not justify, the rationale, it is important to understand that the French state, on its own understanding, saw its role as protecting the positive liberty of the girls, and moreover, positively protecting the girls from themselves, protecting their 'real' liberty and autonomous selves based on a universalist metaphysics going back to the Revolution (Tourkochoriti, 2012: 825–826). As the Debré report, a parallel parliamentary commission to the Stasi commission, stated it, 'Students are not simple users of public services but individuals-in-the-making within an institution whose mission is to form them' (in Joppke, 2007: 322). Indeed, Tourkochoriti argues that 'For the French, the rights of society are the ones by which the rights of the individual exist and not the other way around' (also Bowen, 2009; Troper, 2016). This position made no attempt to quantify the supposed problem and paid no attention to those who argued that the headscarf may in fact indicate a break with immigrant culture and an assertion of being Muslim and French. Although positions on the headscarf among Muslims were mixed (Ajrouch, 2007; Gunn, 2004), it was those in favour of the ban whose voices were heard in public debate. In the years following the 2004 law, veiled women and girls have been forbidden access from a host of public and semi-public spaces, including universities, swimming pools, and public transport.

In 2010 another ban was introduced, coming into effect in April 2011, this time banning clothing that concealed one's face in public places and spaces. This became known as the 'burqa ban' as the targets of law and subject of debates leading up to it were the burqa and niqab (Lægaard, 2015). Women in breach of the ban have been fined, received warnings, and been made to attend citizenship courses (Cesari, 2012). It in fact was to a large extent these cases that meant that France was one of two countries in Europe to have over 200 cases of government force against religious groups in 2014 and 2015 (the other being Russia) (Pew Research Center, 2017). When the case *S.A.S. v France* was brought before the ECtHR to challenge the ban, the state's defence was based on such coverings being 'incompatible with the fundamental requirements of living together in French society' (quoted in Lægaard, 2015: 204). The ECtHR found in favour of the French state, deferring to the margin of appreciation in regard to the conception of religious liberty in a particular state (Tourkochoriti, 2012).

Private schools, in contrast to the public schools discussed above, maintain more freedom when it comes to the manifestation of religion and have existed since the mid-nineteenth century. State-funded private schools now account for around 13.5 per cent of schools, around 90 per cent of which are Catholic, and educating some 17 per cent of students (Franken, 2016). These schools receive public funds subsidising the majority of the schools' budgets under the Debré law of 1959, reinforced by the Guermuer Law of 1977, providing certain conditions are met, including: functioning for at least five years; well-qualified teachers, a relatively large number of students, clean facilities, non-discriminatory admissions criteria, voluntary religious instruction, and the general curriculum would have to be followed (Fetzer and Soper, 2005; Troper, 2016). It is possible to run a private school not so regulated, but these receive no state funding and are far less numerous. By 2012, in part a consequence of the ban on headscarves, there were 29 Islamic private schools (Cesari, 2013: 100). The Debré law provided a compromise position emerging from conflict between leftist secularists on the one hand and rightist politicians and the Catholic Church on the other (Kuru, 2009), demonstrating again the tensions between assertive and open strands in *laïcité* and a further exception to a supposed strict separation between state and religion.

Concluding remarks

France serves as an important comparative case – an example of what has been called 'radical secularism', captured in the principle of *laïcité*, in contrast to the more moderately secular paths trod by other European countries. While it is important to maintain this distinction, it is also easy to mischaracterise France's model in too strict terms. There are a number of ways in which the state and religion are closely connected through historical anomalies and struggles. France has increasingly developed more moderate features in its state-religion relations, and there have been shifts in the assertiveness with which *laïcité* has been understood and applied. Moreover, there is also notable regional variance in how *laïcité* and resulting restrictions on religious freedoms have been applied. Some regions have adopted a more accommodationist approach, whereas others have been more combatively secular; as has been the case in relation to mosque building, the headscarf and meal provision in schools, for instance. There are also the regions where the 1905 law doesn't apply for historical reasons and connexions between state and religious institutions. There is then a simultaneous hardening of a discursive cultural secularism, or an ideological *laicism*, alongside some (and this shouldn't be overstated) more pragmatic moves.

Notes

1 Algeria gained independence in 1962.
2 For a discussion of the Rushdie Affair and *l'affaire de foulard* being two simultaneous pivotal events in 1988–1989, the responses to which were, respectively, illustrative of multiculturalism and radical secularism, see Modood (2019: chapter 9).

References

Ajrouch, K. J. (2007). Global contexts and the veil: Muslim integration in the United States and France. *Sociology of Religion*, 68(3): 321–325.
Amghar, S. (2009). Ideological and theological foundations of Muslim radicalism in France. In M. Emerson (ed.), *Ethno-Religious Conflict in Europe: Typologies of Radicalisation in Europe's Muslim Communities* (pp. 27–50). Brussels: Centre for European Policy Studies.
Beckford, J. A. (2004). 'Laicite', 'dystopia', and the reaction to New Religious Movements in France. In J. T. Richardson (ed.), *Regulating Religion: Case Studies from Around the Globe* (pp. 27–40). New York: Springer.
Body-Gendrot, S. (2007). France upside down over a head scarf? *Sociology of Religion*, 68(3): 289–304.
Bowen, J. R. (2009). *Can Islam Be French? Pluralism and Pragmatism in a Secularist State*. Oxford: Princeton University Press.
Bruce, B. (2018). Transnational religious governance as diaspora politics: Reforming the Moroccan religious field abroad. *Mashriq & Mahjar*, 5(1): 36–70.

Cesari, J. (2002). Islam in France: The shaping of a religious minority. In Y. Haddad-Yazbek (ed.), *Muslims in the West, from Sojourners to Citizens* (pp. 36–51). Oxford: Oxford University Press.

Cesari, J. (2010). Sharia and the future of secular Europe. In J. Cesari (ed.), *Muslims in the West after 9/11: Religion, Politics, and Law* (pp. 145–175). Abingdon: Routledge.

Cesari, J. (2012). Securitization of Islam in Europe. *Die Welt des Islams*, 52(3/4): 430–449.

Cesari, J. (2013). *Why the West Fears Islam: An Exploration of Muslims in Liberal Democracies*. Basingstoke: Palgrave Macmillan.

CNCDH, Commission nationale consultative des droits de l'homme. (2017). *Report on the Fight against Racism, Antisemitism and Xenophobia*. Available at https://www.cncdh.fr/sites/default/files/essentiels_anglais_rapport_racisme_2017.pdf. Accessed 20/12/2019.

Duvert, C. (2004). Anti-cultism in the French Parliament: Desperate last stand or an opportune leap forward? A critical analysis of the 12 June 2001 Act. In J. T. Richardson (ed.), *Regulating Religion: Case Studies from Around the Globe* (pp. 41–52). New York: Springer.

El Karoui, H. (2016). *A French Islam Is Possible*. Institut Montaigne. Available at https://www.institutmontaigne.org/en/publications/french-islam-possible. Accessed 20/12/2019.

Englund, S. (1992). Church and state in France since the revolution. *Journal of Church and State*, 34(2): 325–361.

Ferrari, A. (2009). De la politique à la technique: laïcité narrative et laïcité du droit. Pour une comparaison France/Italie. In B. Basdevant-Gaudemet, J. P. Delannoy & F. Jankowiak (eds.), *Le droit ecclésiastique en Europe et à ses marges (XVIIIe-XXe siècles): actes du colloque du Centre Droit et Sociétés Religieuses* (pp. 333–344). Paris: Peeters.

Fetzer, J. S. & Soper, J. C. (2005). *Muslims and the State in Britain, France, and Germany*. Cambridge: Cambridge University Press.

FRA, European Agency for Fundamental Rights. (2019). *Antisemitism*. Available at https://fra.europa.eu/sites/default/files/fra_uploads/fra-antisemitism-overview-2008-2018_en.pdf. Accessed 20/12/2019.

Franken, L. (2016). *Liberal Neutrality and State Support for Religion*. Cham: Springer.

Gunn, T. J. (2004). Under God but not the scarf: The founding myths of religious freedom in the United States and laïcité in France. *Journal of Church and State*, 46(1): 7–24.

Gunn, T. J. (2009). Religion and law in France: Secularism, separation, and state intervention. *Drake Law Review*, 57: 949–984.

Jansen, Y. (2013). *Secularism, Assimilation and the Crisis of Multiculturalism: French Modernist Legacies*. Amsterdam: Amsterdam University Press.

Joppke, C. (2007). State neutrality and Islamic headscarf laws in France and Germany. *Theory & Society*, 36(4): 313–342.

Kastoryano, R. (2004). Religion and incorporation: Islam in France and Germany. *The International Migration Review*, 38(3): 1234–1255.

Kastoryano, R. (2006). French secularism and Islam: France's headscarf affair. In T. Modood, A. Triandafyllidou, & R. Zapata-Barrero (eds), *Multiculturalism, Muslims and Citizenship: A European Approach* (pp. 57–69). Abingdon: Routledge.

Kuru, A. T. (2009). *Secularism and State Policies toward Religion: The United States, France, and Turkey*. Cambridge: Cambridge University Press.

Lægaard, S. (2015). Burqa ban, freedom of religion and 'living together'. *Human Rights Review*, 16: 203–219.

Luca, N. (2004). Is there a unique French policy of cults? A European perspective. In J. T. Richardson (ed.), *Regulating Religion: Case Studies from Around the Globe* (pp. 53–72). New York: Springer.

Martínez-Ariño, J. (2019). Governing Islam in French cities: Defining 'acceptable' public religiosity through municipal consultative bodies. *Religion, State & Society*, 47(4–5): 423–439.

Pew Research Center. (April 11, 2017). *Global Restrictions on Religion Rise Modesty in 2015, Reversing Downward Trend*. Available at https://www.pewforum.org/2017/04/11/global-restrictions-on-religion-rise-modestly-in-2015-reversing-downward-trend/. Accessed 21/05/2019.

Pew Research Center. (April 2019). *A Changing World: Global Views on Diversity, Gender Equality, Family Life and the Importance of Religion*. Available at https://www.pewglobal.org/2019/04/22/a-changing-world-global-views-on-diversity-gender-equality-family-life-and-the-importance-of-religion/. Accessed 01/05/2019.

Pickel, G. (2013). *Understanding Common Ground: An International Comparison of Religious Belief*. Religion Monitor, Bertelsmann Foundation. Available at https://www.bertelsmann-stiftung.de/fileadmin/

files/BSt/Publikationen/GrauePublikationen/Studie_LW_Religionsmonitor_Internationaler_Vergleich_2014.pdf. Accessed 30/04/2019.

Religion Monitor. (2017). *Muslims in Europe Integrated but Not Accepted?* Bertelsmann Stiftung. Available at https://www.bertelsmann-stiftung.de/en/publications/publication/did/results-and-country-profiles-muslims-in-europe/. Accessed 30/04/2019.

Tourkochoriti, I. (2012). The burka ban: Divergent approaches to freedom of religion in France and in the U.S.A. *William & Mary Bill of Rights Journal*, 20(79): 791–852.

Troper, M. (2016). Republicanism and freedom of religion in France. In J. L. Cohen & C. Laborde (eds), *Religion, Secularism, and Constitutional Democracy* (pp. 316–337). Chichester: Columbia University Press.

Valfort, M.-A. (2015). *Religious Discrimination in Access to Employment: A Reality*. Institut Montaigne. Available at https://www.institutmontaigne.org/en/publications/religious-discrimination-access-employment-reality. Accessed 20/12/2019.

4

Germany
Federal corporatism

Thomas Sealy

Introduction

Germany presents a compelling comparative case for several reasons. One is that it has historically had a mixed confessional character with two dominant and recognised churches, Protestant and Catholic. Today these still maintain close connections between state and religion through public corporation status, and thus Germany represents a case of moderate secularism, which has provided a significant mode for how Germany has managed its relations with its religious minorities and contemporary religious diversity. Moreover, through the processes of division and reunification in the twentieth century, Germany has been made and remade in a way, giving it a unique religious profile within Western Europe. There is, for instance, a marked difference between East and West when it comes to religion stemming from Germany's division throughout much of the latter half of the twentieth century.

In addition, Germany is a federal state with 16 regions, or *Länder*, each with their own governmental structures. There is thus variation in the application and interpretation of federal laws pertaining to religion between the regions owing to historical and demographic reasons. This means that within an overarching federal framework, there can be significant regional variation, further serving to make Germany an interesting case.

This chapter begins by outlining the socio-demographic composition of Germany, paying particular attention to religion, and identifies some general trends. An historical overview is then provided, showing how Germany's current framework and arrangements for state-religion connections have developed. The contemporary picture is then discussed in detail, outlining legal and policy measures for incorporating and accommodating religion, with special attention given to the religion and education.

Socio-demographic overview

According to official figures Germany's population currently stands at approximately 83 million people (as of November 2019), making it the most populous country in Europe; recent annual population rises are largely owing to positive net migration. Germany has the second lowest unemployment rate in the EU after the Czech Republic, 3.4 per cent according to

OECD figures, reaching its highest rate of employment since reunification in 1991. Its economy has also seen year-on-year growth for the past nine years. On a number of well-being indicators Germany performs (often comfortably) above the average for OECD countries, including in education and skills, work-life balance, employment, income and wealth, environmental quality, social connections, health, civic engagement, and housing, along with personal security and subjective well-being.

Official integration indicators suggest that German is the language spoken in most households where at least one person has an immigrant background, with the most common languages after German being (in descending order) Turkish, Russian, Polish, and then Arabic. In terms of labour market participation, education, and income, people of a migrant background perform poorly compared to the national average and, moreover, there is little sign of improvement in these areas as the difference has not changed since 2005, according to official figures.

In 1970 almost 95 per cent of the population were members of one of the two dominant churches (Catholic and Protestant), 1.3 per cent Muslim, and just 3.9 per cent confession free. By the late 1980s this had shifted to 83.5 per cent, 2.7 per cent and 11.4 per cent respectively. By 2003, those identified as confession free were as high as 31.8 per cent. In 2010, those formerly affiliated with either the Protestant or Catholic Churches had dropped to 58.5 per cent while those of no confession had risen to 37.2 per cent (Großbölting, 2017: 207). Catholics report higher regular church attendance than Protestants, 10.2 per cent compared to 3.5 per cent. A Pew report provides an estimate of religion statistics and is shown in Table 4.1.

Within Christianity the major split is between members of the Roman Catholic Church, at 23.76 million, and members of the Protestant Church, at 22.27 million, according to official figures, with smaller numbers of non-denominational and Orthodox members. Islam now constitutes Germany's second religion after Christianity in terms of population size. The majority of Germany's Muslims are Sunni and of Turkish origin. Jews also have gradually re-established communities in Germany, significantly bolstered by immigrants from Eastern Europe. There are now more than 100 Jewish congregations (Großbölting, 2017: 251).

There is a significant difference between East and West in terms of both religiosity and religious diversity. East Germany today is one of the most secularised societies in the world, reflecting its years of ideologically atheist socialist rule (Müller et al., 2012). Muslims in Germany are concentrated in the West of the country to a much higher degree than the East, which is also reflected in the large disparity between numbers of mosques and inter-faith dialogue events between the two (Körs, 2017). Muslims in Germany report higher levels

Table 4.1 German population, by religious affiliation

	2010	%	2020	%
Christian	56,540,000	68.7	53,190,000	66
Muslim	4,760,000	5.8	5,530,000	6.9
Buddhists	210,000	0.3	230,000	0.3
Jews	230,000	0.3	220,000	0.3
Folk Religions	40,000	<0.1	40,000	<0.1
Hindu	80,000	<0.1	80,000	<0.1
Unaffiliated	20,350,000	24.7	21,150,000	26.3
Other	100,000	0.1	100,000	0.1

Source: Pew (from https://www.pewforum.org/2015/04/02/religious-projection-table/2010/percent/Europe/).

of religiosity than those of other faiths despite age variations: 57 per cent of Sunni Muslims between the ages of 16 and 30, 63 per cent of those aged 31–40, 49 per cent of 41–50-year-olds, and 20 per cent over the age of 50 identify as highly religious according to a Religion Monitor report (2015). By comparison, 29 per cent of all Catholics in Germany and only 13 per cent of those between the ages of 16 and 30 are highly religious. While older Christians say they are more religious, the reverse is true of Muslims, fitting in with general trends of decreasing levels of Christian religiosity and higher levels reported by Muslims across generations – a trend found in other European countries also.

The same report also found that Muslims in Germany feel closely connected to the state and society, and a poll in 2009 indicated that levels of trust in governmental institutions were slightly higher among Muslims than the average population (Cesari, 2013: 68). The figures are fairly evenly split between those who oppose an increased role for religion in society (35 per cent) and those who favour it (34 per cent) (Pew Research Center, 2019a). Yet, Muslims in particular are increasingly seen to pose a threat by a large proportion of the population; in western Germany 55 per cent and in eastern Germany 66 per cent of non-Muslims said that they saw Islam as a threat and a failure of Muslims to integrate (see also, Cesari, 2013). A general scepticism towards Islam and Muslims is apparent across political parties and the majority churches also (ibid.: 245). This might suggest that while diversity more broadly can be viewed more positively, when the focus is Islam and Muslims, people are more sceptical. These views do vary on various factors, however. In a Pew survey, 29 per cent of Christians scored highly on anti-immigrant and anti-religious minority attitudes, compared to 18 per cent of the religiously unaffiliated; among these Catholics are more likely than Protestants to profess these attitudes (Pew Research Center, 2019c). Young people and states with broader experience of immigration are generally more open to diversity (Religion Monitor, 2018). In fact, it seems that Germans' relations with non-Christian religions, including although not only Islam, is notably worse than other parts of Western Europe (Großbölting, 2017: 240).

Unification and reunification: divisions between states and churches

Prior to unification in 1870–1871, Germany had been made up of a number of states, each with a different state religion – Catholic, Lutheran or Calvinist – under the terms of the Treaty of Westphalia. Upon unification, however, Protestants became a majority and Roman Catholics a minority (Hatfield, 1981).

In the late nineteenth century, the *Kulturkampf* (cultural struggle) aimed to limit Catholic and Protestant influence over politics, although it was particularly focussed on the institutional power of the Roman Catholic Church (Großbölting, 2017; Hatfield, 1981; Henkel, 2006). Yet Articles 15, 16, and 18 of the Prussian Constitution also guaranteed the religious freedoms and autonomy of the Catholic Church as well as of the more privileged Protestant Evangelical Church. With this separation the Protestant churches kept alive their public and political force through the notion of the *Volkskirche*, binding it to the idea of the nation.

A national framework for the recognition of religions, which can still be seen today, came into place during the inter-war period of the Weimar Republic (1919–1933) (Hofhansel, 2013). The Weimar Constitution adopted the principle of separation between church and state as well as protecting religious freedoms. Article 137, paragraph 1 stated 'there shall be no state church' and Article 136 that, 'civil and political rights and duties shall be neither dependent on nor restricted by the exercise of religious freedom'. Yet this was not an absolute separation as the Constitution retained subsidies and privileges for the Protestant and Catholic churches, codifying cooperation between church and state, especially on matters of education and welfare. The Constitution guaranteed the status of corporation under public law (*Körperschaft des öffentlichen Rechts*) to the Protestant and Catholic Churches and also left this open to other religious associations, although in practice *Länder* governments were restrictive of granting minorities this status (Hofhansel, 2013: 106–107).

Despite initial support of Hitler's rise on behalf of some church leaders, the period of the Third Reich saw significant changes in Germany's governance of religion with public corporation rights all but ended. Hitler enacted a church constitution for a unified, pro-Nazi German Evangelical Church, within which a group known as the German Christians (*Deutsche Christen*) supported the Nazi regime (Helmreich, 1970). Splits soon emerged in the Protestant Church over its position vis-à-vis the Nazi party and its policies. This led to the rise of the Confessing Church (*Bekennende Kirche*), a conglomeration of churches which had a more antagonistic although not wholly separate relationship to the regime, and which in 1934 issued the *Barmer Theologische Erklärung* (Barmen Declaration) rejecting the totalitarian claim of the Nazi state and German Christians (Helmreich, 1970; Henkel, 2006).

With regard to the Catholic Church, a Concordat had been signed between Hitler and the Vatican within months and the Church was on the whole more compromising with regard to the regime, only objecting when its position was directly threatened (Ramet, 2000).

Other religious groups suffered greatly during the Nazi period. Prior to the Second World War, Jews had formed the third largest religious group in Germany, but the Nazi period saw the systematic destruction of the Jewish population of Germany and in the territories it gained control over. Religious sects were also targeted: the harassment and surveillance of Jehovah's Witnesses stepped up, for instance (Besier and Besier, 2001), and they also were imprisoned and sent to Concentration Camps. As for Muslims, they were not systematically persecuted, although were certainly repressed if in violation of the 'race laws' of the period. In fact, the Islamic Central Institute in Berlin (*Islamisches Zentral-Institut*) sought to build ideological bridges with the National Socialists (Großbölting, 2017: 231).

In many ways the Christian churches emerged from the period of Nazi rule, 'damaged but still alive' (Obermayer, 1975: 100). The Confessing Church in some respects appeared as the only social organisation that withstood the Nazi policies of *Gleichshaltung*[1] (Conway, 1992; Großbölting, 2017). Comparatively less tarnished than other institutions, they thus found themselves in the position of being well-placed to provide social and political resources for a post-Nazi era Germany (Conway, 1992: 830; Gabriel, 1995). Moreover, the Protestant churches were able to begin their own as well as Germany's recovery from the horrors of Nazism through public acts of repentance. In October 1945, for instance, the Council of the Evangelical Church in Germany (*Evangelischen Kirche in Deutschland*, EKD) issued the Stuttgart Declaration of Guilt, which acknowledged the church's complicity in not effectively combatting the Nazi state and set up a period of greater political involvement of the Protestant churches (Conway, 1992; Ramet, 2000). The Catholic Church would not make a similar declaration until 1995 (Ramet, 2000: 137).

The period following the Second World War during which Germany was split between East and West saw two very different forms of governance of religion.

In the Western Federal Republic of Germany (est. 1949) the church-state arrangements from the Weimar republic were reinstated (Henkel, 2006). The two major confessions attained a privileged position with considerable financial support and a strong role in education and welfare for the churches as well as a lack of interference in church affairs (such as the appointment of Bishops) from the state. In the 'long' 1960s, however, the churches' continued position in politics would undergo a series of pragmatic compromises both internally and in relation to the state (Großbölting, 2017). A further notable feature of this period was a decline in a confessional mindset when it came to party politics. The Christian Democratic Union (CDU), which emerged from a Catholic base, integrated different Christian confessions, for instance (Großbölting, 2017: 66–71, 135–136).

In the Eastern German Democratic Republic (GDR) the staunchly atheistic Marxist-Leninist Socialist Unity Party sought to suppress the churches and erode the idea and the role of the Church in public life (see Großbölting, 2017). One way it sought to do this was to replace the traditional rites of passage managed through the churches with socialist equivalents; the *Jugendweihe*, a declaration made to the socialist state at age 14, was designed to replace Christian confirmation, for instance[2] (Barker, 2000; Henkel, 2006). Religious sects particularly suffered under the GDR, which, for example, banned and persecuted Jehovah's Witnesses from 1950 (Besier and Besier, 2001; Henkel, 2006).

During this period the two dominant churches again trod quite different paths, with the Catholic Church proving more compromising under an authoritarian regime (Ramet, 2000). Although relations between the Nazi regime and the Evangelical Church settled, the Church played a dissident role. The state did exert a level of control of and interference in Church affairs, and its deliberate politicisation of the Church was part of a strategy of containment and control of its activities (Burgess, 1990), but the Church had some success in representing an ideological and political alternative to the communist state (Burgess, 1990; Conway, 1992). It, moreover, played a significant role in the peaceful revolution, the regime's overthrow, and in subsequent East-West relations (Burgess, 1990; Großbölting, 2017). Following the fall of the socialist government and the Berlin Wall, after the unification of East and West Germany in 1990, the church quickly found itself on the margins as membership that had been substantially dropping for decades did not recover.

Contemporary extra-Christian religious diversity has been particularly focussed on Muslims and Islam. Prior to the 1960s, numbers of Muslims were low, reaching only around 16,000 during the 1960s (Großbölting, 2017: 231). Since the 1960s there has been a significant increase in Germany's Muslim population – by 1972 the numbers had grown to around half a million (ibid.), the majority from Turkey as part of guest worker agreements it signed with a number of countries beginning in the 1950s (see Großbölting, 2017: 231–232; Jonker, 2005). In the post-war period Germany was struggling to integrate large numbers of German refugees and the prospect of visible and cultural 'foreigners' was even harder to accept (Jonker, 2005). Along with the workers themselves, Islam was seen as a 'guest religion' and thus efforts at its accommodation and recognition had also not been undertaken; the German government had left the religious needs of its Turkish population to the Turkish government. Indeed, it is only much more recently that religious policy as an independent policy area has begun to develop (Körs, 2017).

Contemporary corporatism

Reaffirming principles from the Weimar Constitution, the German Basic Law (*Grundgesetz*) establishes a formal separation between church and state, but at the same time the Constitution secures cooperation between the two institutions in areas such as education and social welfare. Pastoral work in public services such as the army, prisons, and hospitals is also guaranteed by Article 141. Furthermore, other institutional and informal channels are also available. To this end Article 140 re-established articles from the earlier constitution outlining the partnership between churches and state in key policy areas and their status as public corporations, which also preserves and has in fact enhanced their legal autonomy (Hofhansel, 2013; Kastoryano, 2004). In addition to the right to belief, Article 140 also protects the right to *exercise* religious freedom, which is given additional meaning by Article 4 guaranteeing 'the undisturbed practice of religion'. These freedoms and protections have generally meant the privileging of a Christian worldview on the basis of historical inheritance; publicly recognised religious holidays (as stipulated in Art.139 of the Constitution), and family law, for example, reflect this.

These arrangements offer minorities a route to recognition and accommodations. Article 140 also provides that 'Other religious communities shall be granted like rights upon application where their constitution and the number of their members offer an assurance of their permanency'. The granting of this status is devolved to each *Land*, which determines applications within its jurisdiction, resulting in some variation in this process (Hofhansel, 2013). The conditions in this part of Article 140 are generally interpreted as requiring a group make up at least 0.1 per cent of the *Land* population and to have been in existence for at least 30 years, as well as satisfying the government that they respect the law (Henkel, 2006: 310). Public corporation status has been granted to an estimated 400 groups in total, with variation in numbers between *Länder*. Minority faiths have also been able to gain some exemptions and accommodations in relation to general laws that indirectly discriminate against members' ability to fulfil aspects of the faith.

One of the particular features of public corporation status is the arrangement for the collection of a 'church tax' (*Kirchensteuer*). This arrangement, established in the Basic Law, means the government levies tax directly from the income of members on the behalf of the churches, typically 8–9 per cent, which is then used for the religious, education, and social welfare work that the churches provide; a local community tax (*Kirchgeld*) is also collected (Barker, 2000). The *Kirchensteuer* is collected from members of the Protestant and Catholic churches as well as some Jewish and Humanist groups. This is voluntary but is automatically collected unless an individual formally leaves membership of the church to which they are registered. It is currently paid by about a quarter of the population and makes up about 50 per cent of the churches' total revenue (Pew Research Center, 2019b). In fact, of the public money that the state distributes to semi-public organisations to provide welfare on its behalf, the churches, taken together, are the largest recipients of public money and providers of welfare services (Barker, 2000; Großbölting, 2017: 80; Lewicki, 2014). A number of minority religious associations, including Muslim groups, have, however, declined for the state to collect taxes on their behalf (Henkel, 2006: 310). In addition to tax revenue, the churches are also major property holders, owning tens of thousands of buildings in addition to the some 14,000+ Protestant churches and around 11,000 Catholic churches. They, furthermore, continue to receive compensation from the state for historical property losses dating back to the early nineteenth century, totalling close to €500 million by some estimates.

Accommodation and exemption

Religious associations that do not have public corporation status are registered under private rather than public law. It is under this status that many Muslim organisations have separate agreements and contracts with the regional governments as well as granting them some tax relief. Thus, absent formal recognition, they have found other ways of working within the existing structure of church-state relations and put in place *ad hoc* agreements with regional governments over, for example, education (see below) (Körs, 2017). On the whole, recognised religious minorities have been reasonably successful in gaining rights and accommodations from the courts. In 2002, Muslims won the right to perform ritual slaughter and in 2012, Muslim and Jewish groups won the right to circumcision (Cesari, 2013: xiv).

Decisions around the greater presence and visibility of religious minorities have at times proven controversial, however. An issue of contention marked by at times bitter disputes has been the building of mosques, which did not begin to make their mark on the cityscape until the 1980s and 1990s (Großbölting, 2017: 231). In fact, Germany's first anti-Islamic party was launched on an anti-mosque platform in Cologne (Cesari, 2013: 97; 2012). There are large mosques in traditional styles in some cities (Berlin, Köln, and Frankfurt, for example), mosques restricted to industrial and lower-income residential areas in others (Bremen and Munich, for example), and plans have been blocked elsewhere (for instance, Stuttgart). Notable here is the importance of inter-faith relations in addition to relations with local governments, where Christian and Catholic churches have at times supported Muslims' desire to build places of worship, for instance, in Mannheim in 1995. There are currently somewhere around 2,600 mosques throughout Germany (Großbölting, 2017: 234).

For other groups, far greater restrictions have been imposed. During the 1990s a number of sects gained attention and were seen as such political threats that government campaigns targeted them and a special commission, the Enquete Commission, was established to focus on New Religious Movements (Seiwert, 2004). The Jehovah's Witnesses, for example, continued to face suspicion and criticism and were for a long time denied public corporation status, eventually granted in 2009 in various *Länder*.

Muslim groups have routinely had their applications for public corporation status denied; Muslim organisations represent under 2 per cent of the total groups with this status despite being the third-largest religious group after Protestantism and Catholicism. One reason for this is that Muslim organisations do not conform to the inherited model on which granting such status is based; some nearly 3,000 Muslim communities in Germany, with affiliations to different Muslim majority countries, often struggle to come together into larger umbrella organisations, regionally or nationally. In fact, it should be noted that while some Muslim organisations have been and are keen to gain public corporation status, others prefer to work separately at local levels rather than unified at the national level, or are cautious over the benefits of this structure (Barker, 2000; Großbölting, 2017: 237; Seiwert, 2004). The first Muslim group to obtain public corporation status was Ahmadiyya Muslim Jamaat in Frankfurt by The Culture Ministry in the state of Hesse in 2012. An Ahmadi group has also attained this status in Hamburg (Körs, 2017, 2019). These were the only two Muslim groups to have attained public corporation status by 2018, although other talks are ongoing.

Germany's 'moral panic' when it comes to Muslims and Islam needs to also be put into the context of the changing citizenship status of Germany's Turkish population. Minorities have frequently been treated as the objects of politics rather than participators, and although not exclusive to Muslims, has affected them particularly (Peter, 2010; Schiffauer, 2006: 96; see also Jonker, 2005: 121). In addition, much mainstream political and media discourse has routinely linked Muslims with security issues, continuing to position them as other, as foreign, and as a threat (Cesari, 2013: 10). An example of Muslims as the objects of German politics is in the distinction between 'real Islam' (as religion and law abiding) and 'Islamism' (as ideology that wants to change state and society through violent means), which is made primarily by German politicians and the *Verfassungsschutz* (The Federal Office for the Protection of the Constitution – Germany's domestic security agency), with only Muslim partners who accept this definition allowed to participate in the debate (Schiffauer, 2006: 99). Under this distinction, Milli Görüş, for example, have come under suspicion (ibid.) and there has been a focus on Salafist movements. Some secular Turkish organisations have also squarely pointed the finger at their more pious countrymen (Choudhury, 2009).

Following recognition of the problems with integrating Muslim organisations into the country's institutional and political structures, in more recent years Germany has sought to institutionalise its relations with its Muslim communities through using the key instrument of the annual German Islam Conferences (*Deutsche Islam Konferenz*, DIK), the first of which took place in 2006. Various representatives from public offices and from Muslim communities and associations are invited to a national discussion covering various issues relating to Muslims in Germany and were pitched by Wolfgang Schäuble, the then-Home Secretary who launched the initiative, in his inaugural opening speech as 'about a genuine dialogue with Muslims in Germany, who no longer are a foreign population, but who have become an integral part of our society' (quoted in Lewicki, 2014: 64). Yet, the issue of representation has been a matter of controversy and debate (Großbölting, 2017: 237) as are approaches to the 'integration' of Germany's Muslim population and the focus on the issue of promoting a 'German Islam'.

Education

When it comes to the key area of education, Article 7 of the Basic Law stipulates that religious instruction (*Religionsunterricht*) is provided as part of the core curriculum in state schools for recognised communities and is the only subject to enjoy this status. Those groups who are not recognised receive only secularised religious education (*Religiöse Unterweisung* or *Religionskunde*). The requirement and application of this constitutional provision varies between *Länder*, the governments of which (*Bundesländer*) are responsible for educational policy. Thus, Germany's federal system means that there can be considerable regional variation in what and how religion is taught in state schools (Franken, 2016: 176; Körs, 2017). In some regions Islamic religious classes take place in public schools despite not having achieved public corporation status, such as in Berlin since 2001 and in Bavaria since the 1980s. The Berlin Buddhist Society also offers religious education in public schools – these schools receiving the majority of their funding from the state (see Körs, 2017: 448).

In terms of religious signs and symbols in schools, in 1995 the Federal Constitutional Court's (*Bundesverfassungsgericht*, FCC) controversial (and fairly ineffective) 'Crucifix decision' found Bavaria's regulation that classrooms in public schools had to display a crucifix in violation of the Basic Law's article on freedom of religion, which the Court declared included the freedom not to have a religion and not to be exposed to specific religious symbols in classrooms (Henkel, 2006: 313; Ramet, 2000: 140–141). The Court did not, however, order that crosses be removed, stipulating that schools obtain unanimous parental consent, thus providing for leeway in the interpretation of the ruling (Ramet, 2000). As a result, in Bavaria crosses continue to be displayed in schools and courtrooms, and the state government has also more recently expanded the requirement to include the entrances of all state administrative buildings, where the cross serves as an expression of cultural identity (Hendon and Prather, 2018).

When it comes to religious clothing, unlike in France there has been no restriction on students wearing *hijab* and there have also generally been pragmatic compromises when it comes to accommodating requirements such as provision of halal meat in schools and exemption from certain co-ed activities such as swimming, sports lessons, and school trips. For teachers, however, the situation has been different; and again, there has been significant variation between *Länder*. In an important case brought before the FCC in 2003, an Afghan-born naturalised German Muslim teacher, Fereshta Ludin, from a small town in Baden-Württemberg, contested her denial of a teaching position because she wore the headscarf. The legal debate revolved around freedom of religion and the understanding of a teacher as a *Beamter* and therefore a neutral public servant and representative of the state (Schiffauer, 2006: 104). The political and public debate revolved around the perception of the headscarf as a symbol of inequality and intolerance – the supposed opposite of German politics and morals. The FCC ruled that there wasn't sufficient provision under current law for a ban (Schiffauer, 2006: 102–103) and in 2015 again ruled against a blanket ban on the headscarf. This did not prevent some *Länder* from instituting bans, at times in contravention and disregard of the FCC stipulation. Notably, the variation between them follows political lines of the *Länder* governments, with those on the left favouring general bans, and those on the right selectively targeting the Islamic headscarf, distinguishing it from Christian symbols on the basis of the former's supposed political content and the latter's more cultural and historical (Joppke, 2007: 330–331). Similar variation is also the case with regard to full-face coverings, where there is no general ban but in July 2020 Baden-Württemberg banned them in schools targeting the *niqab* and *burqa*.

When it comes to private schools, again there is constitutional provision and as long as certain conditions are met they are supported by the state, although such schools are only attended by a minority of the population. Article 7 of the Basic Law provides for the right to operate private schools, with the approval of the relevant *Land*, and numbers vary between *Länder*. Most of these schools are Catholic or Protestant but such schools have been approved for Jews, Hindus, and Muslims (Franken, 2016: 172).

Concluding remarks

Germany has a complex history when it comes to state-religion connexions, although overall relations have been close and Germany reflects a good example of what has been termed 'moderate secularism' (Modood, 2017). The churches' political position has weakened as secularisation has taken hold, yet both the Protestant and Catholic churches continue to occupy significant roles in relation to public services and the public good, working in partnership with the state, and to lesser and more restricted degrees minority faith groups are also a feature of this. Significantly though, there is variation between the regions when it comes to managing religious diversity, such as the granting of public corporation status, along with political differences.

As with other countries in Western Europe, the constitutional provisions and protections along with the historically inherited structures and arrangements between state and religion provide both opportunities and difficulties for minority faiths; Islam and Muslims in particular have found it extremely difficult to secure the same status and role. There are various factors that contribute to this. One is how the faith itself is organised in a way unlike Christian churches. Another factor is the general suspicion around Muslim communities and the view of them as 'other' and foreign. Germany has particularly high levels of suspicion of Muslim communities in Western Europe, creating a situation in which Muslims struggle to penetrate mainstream consciousness as those who belong and can play a public role.

Notes

1 Literally 'coordination', refers to the process of Nazification of state and society, that is, establishing totalitarian control.
2 And which still enjoys considerable popularity, albeit shorn of its previous ideological content.

References

Barker, C. R. (2000). Church and state relationships in German 'Public Benefit' law. *The International Journal of Not-for-Profit Law*, 3(2). Available at http://www.icnl.org/research/journal/vol3iss2/art_1.htm. Accessed 28/06/2019.

Besier, G. & Besier, R.-M. (2001). Jehovah's Witnesses' request for recognition as a corporation under Public Law in Germany: Background, current status, and empirical aspects. *Journal of Church and State*, 43(1): 35–48.

Burgess, J. P. (1990). Church-State relations in East Germany: The Church as a 'religious' and 'political' force. *Journal of Church and State*, 32(1): 17–35.

Cesari, J. (2013). *Why the West Fears Islam: An Exploration of Muslims in Liberal Democracies*. Basingstoke: Palgrave Macmillan.

Choudhury, T. (2009). Muslims and discrimination. In S. Amghar, A. Boubecker, & M. Emerson (eds), *European Islam: Challenges for Public Policy and Society* (pp. 77–106). Brussels: Centre for European Policy Studies.

Conway, J. S. (1992). The political role of German Protestantism, 1870–1990. *Journal of Church and State*, 34(4): 819–842.

Franken, L. (2016). *Liberal Neutrality and State Support for Religion*. Cham: Springer.

Gabriel, K. (1995). The post-war generations and institutional religion in Germany. In W. C. Roof, J. W. Carroll, & D. A. Rozen (eds), *The Post-War Generation and Establishment Religion: Cross-Cultural Perspectives* (pp. 113–130). Oxford: Westview Press.

Großbölting, T. (2017 [2013]). *Losing Heaven: Religion in Germany Since 1945* (A. Skinner, Trans.). Oxford: Berghahn.

Hatfield, D. W. (1981). Kulturkampf: The relationship of Church and State and the failure of German political reform. *Journal of Church and State*, 23(3): 465–484.

Helmreich, E. C. (1970). The nature and structure of the Confessing Church in Germany under Hitler. *Journal of Church and State*, 12(3): 405–420.

Hendon, D. W. & Prather, S. (2018). Notes on Church-State affairs. *Journal of Church and State*, 60(4): 771–783.

Henkel, R. (2006). State–church relationships in Germany: past and present. *GeoJournal*, 67: 307–316.

Hofhansel, C. (2013). Recognition regimes for religious minorities in Europe: Institutional change and reproduction. *Journal of Church and State*, 57(1): 90–118.

Jonker, G. (2005). From 'foreign workers' to 'sleepers': The churches, the state and Germany's 'discovery' of its Muslim population. In J. Cesari & S. McLoughlin (eds), *European Muslims and the Secular State* (pp. 113–126). Abingdon: Routledge.

Joppke, C. (2007). State neutrality and Islamic headscarf laws in France and Germany. *Theory & Society*, 36(4): 313–342.

Kastoryano, R. (2004). Religion and incorporation: Islam in France and Germany. *The International Migration Review*, 38(3): 1234–1255.

Körs, A. (2017). The plurality of Peter Berger's 'two pluralisms' in Germany. *Society*, 54(5): 445–453.

Körs, A. (2019). Contract governance of religious diversity in a German city-state and its ambivalences. *Religion, State & Society*, 47(4–5): 456–473.

Lewicki, A. (2014). *Social Justice Through Citizenship? The Politics of Muslim Integration in Germany and Great Britain*. Basingstoke: Palgrave Macmillan.

Modood, T. (2017). Multiculturalism and moderate secularism. In A. Triandafyllidou & T. Modood (eds), *The Problem of Religious Diversity: European Challenges, Asian Approaches* (pp. 52–74). Edinburgh: Edinburgh University Press.

Müller, O., Pollack, D., & Pickel, G. (2012). The religious landscape in Germany: Secularizing west – Secularized east. In D. Pollack, O. Müller, & G. Pickel (eds), *The Social Significance of Religion in the Enlarged Europe: Secularization, Individualization and Pluralization* (pp. 95–120). Farnham: Ashgate.

Obermayer, C. (1975). State and religion in the Federal Republic of Germany. *Journal of Church and State*, 17(1): 97–111.

Peter, F. (2010). Welcoming Muslims into the nation: Tolerance, politics and integration in Germany. In J. Cesari (ed.), *Muslims in the West after 9/11: Religion, Politics, and Law* (pp. 119–144). Abingdon: Routledge.

Pew Research Center. (2019a). *A Changing World: Global Views on Diversity, Gender Equality, Family Life and the Importance of Religion*, April 2019. Available at https://www.pewglobal.org/2019/04/22/a-changing-world-global-views-on-diversity-gender-equality-family-life-and-the-importance-of-religion/. Accessed 01/05/2019.

Pew Research Center. (2019b). *In Western European Countries with Church Taxes, Support for the Tradition Remains Strong*, April 30, 2019. Available at https://www.pewforum.org/2019/04/30/

in-western-european-countries-with-church-taxes-support-for-the-tradition-remains-strong/. Accessed 29/04/2020.

Pew Research Center. (2019c). *Once a Majority, Protestants Now Account for Fewer than a Third of Germans*, February 2019. Available at https://www.pewresearch.org/fact-tank/2019/02/12/once-a-majority-protestants-now-account-for-fewer-than-a-third-of-germans/. Accessed 01/05/2019.

Ramet, S. P. (2000). Religion and politics in Germany since 1945: The evangelical and catholic churches. *Journal of Church and State*, 42(1): 115–145.

Religion Monitor. (2015). *Understanding Common Ground: Special Study of Islam, 2015. An Overview of the Most Important Findings*. Gütersloh: Bertelsmann Stiftung.

Religion Monitor. (2018). *Living in Cultural Diversity: Views and Preferences in Germany*. Gütersloh: Bertelsmann Stiftung.

Schiffauer, W. (2006). Enemies within the gates: The debate about the citizenship of Muslims in Germany. In T. Modood, A. Triandafyllidou, & R. Zapata-Barrero (eds), *Multiculturalism, Muslims and Citizenship: A European Approach* (pp. 94–116). Abingdon: Routledge.

Seiwert, H. (2004). The German Enquete commission on sects: Political conflicts and compromises. In J. T. Richardson (ed.), *Regulating Religion: Case Studies from Around the Globe* (pp. 85–102). New York: Springer.

5

The United Kingdom

Weak establishment and pragmatic pluralism

Thomas Sealy and Tariq Modood

Introduction

The United Kingdom forms an interesting country case for several reasons related to the need to consider it across three interrelated dimensions: secular, Christian, and plural (Weller, 2009). It is one of few European states, along with, for instance Denmark, to retain an established church. The United Kingdom bears some distinctive features as a result of this arrangement, although strictly speaking it is only in England that this arrangement persists. Yet, despite this prominent position for the Protestant Anglican Church, establishment in the United Kingdom can be considered 'weak', following a long period of historical pluralisation and secularisation. Religious diversity has been further expanded since the mid-twentieth century from post-Second World War migration patterns; given the locations and extent of Britain's former empire, this has resulted in the United Kingdom having a profile of religious diversity different from other Western European states.

In terms of state-religion connexions, the United Kingdom represents a mode of moderate secularism, and also provides examples of what has been called a *multiculturalised secularism* (Modood, 2019a). This is in part owing to its general approach to religious diversity being one of pragmatic accommodation, for which, nevertheless, historical inheritance and the position of the established Anglican Church provide important sites of reference.

This chapter begins by outlining the socio-demographic composition of the United Kingdom, paying particular attention to religion. It identifies some general trends as well as variance in profile between the four nations that comprise the United Kingdom. An historical overview is then provided, showing how the United Kingdom's current framework and arrangements for state-religion connections have developed through its shifting relations with Christianity. The contemporary picture is then discussed in detail, outlining legal and policy measures for incorporating and accommodating religion, and resulting in an overall pragmatic pluralism.

Socio-demographic overview

The United Kingdom of Great Britain and Northern Ireland is a union comprised of England, Scotland, and Wales, which together make up Great Britain, and Northern Ireland. Each (except England) has a devolved government with degrees of autonomy. At last census the population of the United Kingdom was 63,182,178 (2011) and was estimated to be 66,435,600 as of June 2018 according to figures from the Office for National Statistics; being 55,977,200 in England, 3,138,600 in Wales, 5,438,100 in Scotland, and 1,881,600 in Northern Ireland. The United Kingdom is a parliamentary democracy and a constitutional monarchy. In 2016 the United Kingdom voted to leave the EU in a national referendum, albeit with significant differences in voting patterns among its constituent nations.

From 2001 a voluntary question on religion has been included in the census for England and Wales. The census for Scotland and Northern Ireland also collects religious affiliation data. Table 5.1 shows census data for the United Kingdom as a whole.

Overall, Christianity remains the majority religion. However, those identifying with Christianity have declined along with a similar increase in those choosing 'no religion', which is comfortably second looking in both directions. Religious membership and attendance have gradually dropped since the 1960s as has the use of the church for traditional rites of passage such as marriage, baptism, and funerals (CofE, 2018). Some smaller Christian churches such as Evangelical, Pentecostal, and so-called fresh expressions congregations have grown in recent years, largely as a result of immigration. Nevertheless, these patterns of growth do not offset the general pattern of decline. Minority faiths all show small increases, with Muslims increasing by the largest figure and constituting the largest non-Christian faith group. Muslims are diverse in their origins (50+ nationalities), with just over half coming from Pakistan and Bangladesh (MCB, 2015), although this ratio is decreasing.

There are also significant differences. Scotland's 'no religion' population is noticeably higher than elsewhere. The dominance of Christianity and extremely low numbers of minority faiths stands out for Northern Ireland.

Attitudes towards public religion are increasingly negative compared to 1998 figures (BSA 36). Less than half (46 per cent) have confidence in religious institutions, down from 54 per cent; over one-third (35 per cent) say they think religious organisations have too much power, up by 15 per cent; and almost two-thirds (63 per cent) say they agree that religion brings more conflict than peace, although this figure has decreased from 75 per cent in 1998 (ibid.). Attitudes towards those who are religiously different are contrastingly tolerant with largely indifferent or positive attitudes towards people of other faiths reported, although people felt least positive towards Muslims. Opinion polls have routinely found that over half

Table 5.1 UK population, by religious affiliation

United Kingdom	2001 %	2011 No.	2011 %
Christian	71.6	37,583,962	59.5
Buddhist	0.3	261,584	0.4
Hindu	1.0	835,394	1.3
Jewish	0.3	269,568	0.4
Muslim	2.7	2,786,635	4.4
Sikh	0.6	432,429	0.7
Other religion	0.3	262,774	0.4
No religion	14.8	16,221,509	25.7
No answer	7.7	4,528,323	7.2

Source: Office for National Statistics

think Islam is not compatible with 'British values', in stark contrast to over 90 per cent of Muslims reporting a strong sense of belonging to Britain (Ipsos Mori, 2018). Whereas overall trends of racism and religious discrimination may show a decline (Weller et al., 2015), the trend for discrimination against Muslims shows the reverse (Modood, 2019b). While controversies and challenges in recent decades have arisen in relation to accommodating a number of faiths in relation to contemporary religious diversity in the United Kingdom, Muslims and Islam have attracted particular attention.

Economy, employment, and education

Government departments, local authorities, and public services have faced deep budget cuts as part of austerity measures following the 2008 financial crisis. The economy gradually recovered, GDP rising until 2014, although it has been dropping since and the impacts of Brexit are yet to fully materialise.

The unemployment rate is estimated at 3.8 per cent (as of May 2019), its lowest level since 1974; the employment rate is 76 per cent and has been steadily rising over the last five years. For religious minorities, the picture is intersectionally complex, but scholars have pointed to a 'religion penalty' that particularly affects Muslims (especially Muslim women), who have rates of unemployment at more than double the national average in addition to lower occupational status in comparison to other religious groups as well as to the national average (Khattab and Modood, 2015; Modood, 2019b). By contrast, Jews rank above the national average and Hindus seem to do equally as well as the national average.

Patterns in education are similarly intersectionally complex and vary at different educational levels. Muslims have tended to record comparatively lower attainment levels, whereas Hindus and Jews are above the national average (Khattab, 2009), but Muslims now seem to be performing at the national average (Khattab and Modood, 2018). Yet, while nearly all ethnic minorities have proportionally higher levels of participation in higher education than whites (Modood, 2004), nearly all have worse degree results and lower levels of post-graduation 'sustained employment'.

Numbers of ethnic minority MPs were limited to a few figures until 1987, since when numbers have increased, although remaining disproportionately low. The 2017 general election led to 52 ethnic minority MPs in the House of Commons (out of 650), and following the December 2019 general election this has risen to 1 in 10 MPs. The Johnson cabinet is also proportionally the most ethnically diverse so far in not just the United Kingdom but in the EU.

From established entanglement to secularisation and diversity

The United Kingdom as a whole does not have an established church, as relations are and have been different for each constituent nation. There are in fact two established churches, the Church of England and the Church of Scotland; those in Ireland and Wales having disestablished in 1871 and 1920 respectively. The monarch is the 'Supreme Governor' of the established Church of England (CofE) and also the 'Defender of the Faith'. The Church of Scotland is characterised as 'separate and distinct' from the state, or 'national and free', in a way that the CofE is not (Morris, 2009: 78, 84). The following sections thus concentrate on the Church of England.

Establishment and accommodations

The establishment of the Church of England is in many ways a muddled arrangement defined by various statutes and conventions. The establishment of the Church of England came through the First and Second Acts of Supremacy in 1534 and 1559, under which the monarch became 'supreme Head on earth of the Church of England',[1] a result of Henry VIII's break with Rome in 1533 prompted by his desire to have his marriage to Catherine of Aragon annulled and the Pope's refusal. This marked the beginning of the English Reformation. Following the Reformation, religious minorities, Protestant non-Conformists and Dissenters, Catholics, and Jews (who had been expelled in the thirteenth century) were frequently persecuted and under legal disabilities. The 1689 settlement following the English Civil War, however, is most significant for the Church's current constitutional basis and the privileging of Anglican Protestantism. From the second half of the seventeenth century 'old' religious minorities gradually came to be accommodated, the Toleration Act 1689 being notable, Protestantism pluralised, and Jews were readmitted.

The nineteenth century represents an important turning point. Early in the century there was mutual entanglement of State and Church: Parliament was wholly Protestant and predominantly Anglican, Anglican bishops sat in the House of Lords, Parliament legislated on both secular and ecclesiastical affairs, the monarch could not be or marry a Roman Catholic (this was repealed in 2013 although the monarch still cannot be Catholic), Anglican bishops, and Archbishops were appointed by the state, and the Anglican Church received financial support in the forms of tithe and church rates, which everyone had to pay no matter their faith. Furthermore, following a low period in the eighteenth century, church attendance picked up.

At mid-century, however, the religious census (1851) showed that nearly half the population did not attend church, the results weakening the claim on privileges enjoyed by the Anglican Church. As the century progressed the rights of Dissenters and Non-Conformists, Catholics, and Jews were increasingly recognised; the church tax was abolished in 1868, the tithe phased out before being abolished in 1936, and other forms of financial gifts and grants ceased from 1828. The state expanded into and took over various civil functions previously dominated by the Church, such as marriages and divorces, and education and welfare provision. As a result of the disentangling process begun in this period, the Church reinstituted separate bodies, including its own legislative body; the General Synod (founded in 1970) is the body that currently fulfils this function.

The loosening of ties towards a 'weak' establishment has continued and the Church has also gained greater autonomy in its own affairs, although erastianism would become apparent in 1927–1928 when Parliament refused to pass measures for a revised prayer book, and also on the issue of the ordination of women priests in the early 1990s and late 2000s (see Maltby, 2011). Yet, from 1976 the Church could nominate candidates for the appointment of bishops (submitting two names for the prime minister to choose from) and since 2007 the Prime Minister no longer plays an active role in Church appointments.

Secularisation and 'new' diversity

The 1960s were a pivotal decade in the decline of relevance of the Church and of Christianity as significant for people's self-conceptions (Brown, 2009), although it should be noted that secularisation discourses emanated from within British Christianity (at least) as much as from without.

There was also increasing recognition of Britain as a multi-religious country. Prior to post-Second World War migration patterns, religious minorities were largely absent from public awareness, despite a longer history of more limited settlement owing to Britain's colonial relations. This changed from the 1950s, since when Britain has seen a growth in Christian denominations as well as non-Christian religions, notably Muslims, Hindus, and Sikhs. An important reason for these immigration flows was economic; there was a labour demand for the post-war rebuilding effort, which migrant labour from the Commonwealth countries went a long way to filling, direct recruitment was even used for some industry gaps.

Under the terms of the 1948 British Nationality Act, Commonwealth immigrants, in theory at least, had access to all rights and privileges under the expansive category of Citizenship of the United Kingdom and Colonies (CUKC). The utilisation of this by migrants from the 'new Commonwealth' (the West Indies and Indian sub-continent) and subsequent immigration flows had been unanticipated, however, and resulted in successive citizenship legislation becoming more restrictive under the Commonwealth Immigrants Act 1962 and Immigration Act 1971 (Karatani, 2003). The British Nationality Act 1981 established British citizenship and created differentiated statuses, limiting those in the former colonies without the requisite ancestral connection to British Overseas Citizenship or British Dependent Territories Citizenship, while simultaneously maintaining a fairly liberal naturalisation process for those already residing in the United Kingdom. This had its own unintended consequence in further increasing immigration as people already settled in Britain brought their families over. As a result, the ethnic minority population in Britain grew rapidly, from 1 per cent in 1968 (<500,000) to 5.5 per cent (3 million) in 1991, 7.1 per cent (4.5 million) in 2001, and was 14 per cent (8 million) in the 2011 census.

Recognition and state-religion connexions: issues and accommodations

Britain does not have a formal written constitution, and a more pragmatic and tangled relationship between the state and various religious bodies has developed across different areas.

Freedom of religion is guaranteed under the Equality Act 2010, with freedom of conscience an absolute right and freedom to manifest a religion or belief a qualified right. The Act consolidated and simplified a diverse variety of separate equality and anti-discrimination regulations into one as well as supplementing the 1998 Human Rights Act, which had incorporated the European Convention on Human Rights into domestic law. It designates nine 'protected characteristics', of which religion is one (the others being age, disability, gender reassignment, marriage and civil partnership, pregnancy and maternity, race and sex). For a religion or belief to be recognised under the Act, it must be cogent, serious, cohesive, compatible with human dignity, and widely recognised in the United Kingdom (Hunt, 2012: 704–705). Faith traditions recognised as such include Christianity (and denominations within), Bahai, Buddhism, Hinduism, Islam, Jainism, Judaism, Paganism, Rastafarianism, Sikhism, and Zoroastrianism.

In balancing the protected characteristics 'religious clauses' were included, as they had been in previous equality acts, granting exemptions to religious bodies to be able to discriminate on certain grounds according to religious conscience. Sexuality, or non-heterosexuality, was a particular concern for many religious groups, and has proven especially controversial, including from groups and individuals within faiths.

The Church of England continues to play a significant role in the life of the nation and retains certain privileges; it is often still relied upon at times of national celebration or crisis and presides over national rites and ceremonies such as state weddings and funerals, and the coronation of the monarch. Also, reserved seats in the House of Lords for 26 bishops remain. The United Kingdom is the only country in Europe to have such an arrangement for explicit religious representation (Morris, 2009: 45).

Minority faiths have gradually been making claims for their role as part of a multi-faith Britain (Modood, 1994, 1997, 2019a). Moreover, the religious establishment has generally helped with their institutional access and claims for recognition.

Religion reemergent

In political discourse and policy, a shift has occurred over recent decades when it comes to minorities in Britain, from 'race' in the 1950s and 1960s to ethnicity in the 1980s and 1990s, and since the turn of the century groups have come to be defined more and more through 'religion'. Earlier exemptions and accommodations for Jews and Sikhs were on the basis of them being an ethnic rather than religious group; for example, the exemption for turbaned Sikhs from wearing a motorcycle helmet in 1976 and allowances of the Sikh kirpan worn under clothing for Khalsa-baptised and observant Sikhs in schools (see, for example, *Mandla v Dowell-Lee* (1982)), hospitals, and public places. The absence of religion from early discrimination legislation and accommodation was commented on by Muslims (Nielsen, 2009), who also felt that anti-racism movements did not offer adequate protection from religious discrimination. Emerging from these concerns the term 'Islamophobia' came to conceptualise the discrimination faced by Muslims, gaining popular currency following the publication in 1997 of the Runnymede Trust's landmark report *Islamophobia: A Challenge for Us All*. In 2001 a religion question was included in the England and Wales census for the first time in 150 years, largely a result of lobbying on the part of British Muslim organisations (Sherif, 2011).

If the shift to religion in political discourse, along with a focus on Muslims, can be traced back to a particular event, the Rushdie Affair in 1989 was undoubtedly pivotal. The protests that followed the publication of Salman Rushdie's *The Satanic Verses*, citing its blasphemy against the Prophet Muhammad, along with the ensuing *fatwa* issued by Ayatollah Khomeini (then leader of Iran) calling for Rushdie's death, announced Muslims and their religion in the public sphere. This became further amplified following urban riots in Oldham, Burnley, and Bradford in 2001.

The re-emergence of public religion and controversies over religious diversity, therefore, have occurred in a context of growing concern over social and cultural integration of minority communities, with a particular emphasis on the 'otherness' of Muslims. In the last few years instances of Islamophobia have risen and in 2017 the Runnymede Trust marked the twentieth anniversary of its original report with a follow up report titled *Islamophobia: Still a Challenge for Us All*. According to official statistics there was an overall rise of 17 per cent from 2016/2017 to 2017/2018, including a 40 per cent rise in religion-specific cases and 50 per cent rise in vandalism, although TellMAMA, an NGO that works to combat anti-Muslim hatred, reports a slight fall in 2018. Islamophobia, moreover, represented over half of all religiously motivated hate crime offences. Also noteworthy is that some forms of discrimination 'spike' in particular social and political circumstances, highlighting the importance of social and political context; instances of Islamophobia, for example, increase following reports of terror-related attacks, and also rose following the referendum as part of assertive ethno-nationalist discourses.

While instances of Islamophobia both online and on the street have risen, it has also proven politically controversial. To address the issue of Islamophobia in 2017 the All-Party Parliamentary Group on British Muslims (APPGBM) launched an enquiry into a working definition of Islamophobia. While this definition has been adopted by other major political parties – including Labour, the Liberal Democrats, the Scottish Conservatives, the Scottish National Party (SNP), Plaid Cymru, as well as the Mayor of London, Sadiq Khan – the Conservative government has rejected it. In fact, the Prime Minister, Boris Johnson, has himself been embroiled in a controversy surrounding comments he made in a newspaper article in 2018 when he was Foreign Secretary, where he compares Muslim women who wear the *niqab* or *burqa* to bank robbers and letterboxes. Indeed, this caused its own 'spike' with a 375 per cent increase in Islamophobic incidents in the week following the article's publication.

Indications also suggest that anti-Semitism has risen in the last couple of years, up by 16 per cent in 2018, and the Labour Party with Jeremy Corbyn as leader faced serious accusations of anti-Semitism within the party.

Institutionalisation

Since the years of New Labour (1997–2010), the government has partnered with and supported faith-based organisations more systematically, although, with the exception of the Greater London Authority, there is no statutory requirement for local authorities to do so. Currently, responsibility for relations with faith communities lies with the Department for Communities and Local Government (DCLG), although a number of government departments consult with faith groups and inter-faith networks on policies.

Although local faith organisations have been around for decades, for minority faiths this has made necessary the creation of an organisational infrastructure and bodies to serve as representative interlocutors and participate in national and local forms of governance. Important national umbrella organisations include the Hindu Council UK, National Council of Hindu Temples, and The Hindu Forum of Britain; the Network of Sikh Organisations and Sikh Federation; The Buddhist Society and the Network of Buddhist Organisations; the Board of Deputies of British Jews, the Office of the Chief Rabbi, and the Jewish Leadership Council. For Muslims, the fallout from the Rushdie affair eventually led to the creation of the Muslim Council of Britain (MCB) in 1997 (McLoughlin, 2005) and since the 7/7 bombings in 2005 the government has increasingly recognised as well as had a strong hand in creating a more diversified 'democratic constellation' of Muslim consultative bodies (Modood, 2013[2007]).

As well as umbrella organisations for different faiths, there are also interfaith bodies; the Inter Faith Network (IFN) being one of the most important of these. The IFN, established in 1987, has been a key organisation in engaging with government and public bodies as well as instrumental in bringing together other faith organisations. More recently there has been a large growth in interfaith organisations, including bilateral (Jewish-Muslim, Christian-Muslim, for example) and regional organisations as well as organisations that operate internationally. A result of this growth is that interfaith cooperation and engagement has developed more rapidly in the United Kingdom in contrast to many other countries (Pearce, 2012).

Public religion and society

The 'advancement of religion' is recognised as a charitable purpose under the Charities Act 2011, and it is from gaining charitable status that financial benefit in terms of tax reliefs are open to religious bodies. Indeed, the vast majority of religious organisations and churches are charity organisations, mostly overseen by the Charity Commission. The Church of England must fund its own running costs but does receive larger subsidies and grants for some religious buildings, although this is based on their heritage value rather than it being religious per se.

Since the 1980s socio-economic restructuring, faith-based organisations have played an increasing role in welfare provision as part of the growing plurality and competition among service providers in the 'third sector'. This gained prominence in the 2000s under New Labour and then the so-called Big Society under the Coalition government. A national review of faith organisations in 2007 identified 48 categories of community activities and thousands of projects in each region across the country (Dinham, 2007, 2009).

Chaplains' salaries are paid for in the armed forces, education and healthcare institutions, and prisons, although it is the state that provides for these services and salaries come from the requisite budgets.

Establishing religious buildings has been, on the whole, comparatively less controversial than elsewhere, although doing so either through a new building or repurposing an existing building has not always been easy. Restrictions and delays in the planning permission process tend to revolve around existing laws of building use and concerns around access and parking. The ISKCON Temple at Bhaktivedanta Manor provides a prominent example. In this case Hare Krishnas fought a long-running battle in the 1980s and 1990s with the local planning authority to repurpose an old manor house for religious worship (Nye, 1998).

Further exemptions and accommodations to meet religious practice requirements also exist; for halal and kosher slaughter of animals, for open-air funeral pyres, and for circumcision of infants, for instance. On the whole, pragmatic accommodations have generally won out on an *ad hoc* approach rather than blanket legislation and legal provision (Malik, 2008).

A few important cases related to accommodations at work were taken to the European Court of Human Rights under *Eweida and Others v United Kingdom*. For *Eweida*, suspended for wearing a visible cross by British Airways, the court upheld her complaint. The three other cases were *Chaplin*, *Ladele*, and *MacFarlane*. Chaplin was prevented from wearing a crucifix on a necklace as a nurse, which was in contravention of the hospital's uniform policy disallowing necklaces. Ladele, who worked as a registrar, had refused to perform civil partnership ceremonies for same sex couples. MacFarlane had refused to offer counselling services to same sex couples and was dismissed. The claims for these three were dismissed on the basis that other considerations – health and safety in the case of *Chaplin*, and the balance against the rights of others in *Ladele* and *MacFarlane* – outweighed any infringement on religious freedom (see Cranmer, 2013; Maher, 2014). There have been no serious political moves to ban clothing that covers the head or face in the United Kingdom.

Church of England ecclesiastical courts are recognised as part of state law and have certain jurisdictional autonomy in church affairs, such as over discipline of the clergy. While minority faiths do not have their own courts with a similar legal status, Catholics, Jews, and Muslims do have bodies that adjudicate on areas mainly to do with family law as part of what has been termed 'minority legal orders' that interpret and apply religious and cultural norms according to the faith community (Malik, 2014, 2012). For Jews, the London Beth Din is the oldest and largest authority, and Muslims are served by sharia councils, of which there are many across different communities without a centralised structure. These are subordinate to state law and decisions made do not have the same legal status. Sharia councils in particular have attracted attention and controversy (see, for example, discussion in Modood, 2019a: ch. 7), and in 2018 a government-commissioned independent review into their operation submitted its report.

Among the recommendations were that examples of best practice be shared and the relation between rulings in these councils and state law be clarified for those who use them.

Faith and education

Religious education is stipulated for state schools in the Education Act 1944, which also included a stipulation for an act of worship. In the Education Reform Act 1988 it was further stated that the act of worship 'shall be wholly or mainly of a broadly Christian character', although exceptions to the character of worship are permitted 'as may be appropriate having regard to any relevant considerations relating to the pupils concerned'. The syllabus for religious education likewise 'shall reflect the fact that the religious traditions in Great Britain are in the main Christian whilst taking account of the teaching and practices of the other principal religions represented in Great Britain'. As such the religious make-up of the school is taken into consideration.

There is a variety of types of school, which include faith schools, each with slightly different arrangements when it comes to the provision of religious education, worship, and involvement of, for example, churches. Broadly speaking, having faith school status, of whatever kind, means that schools may have different admissions criteria and staffing policies, to varying degrees according to school type, and are to an extent permitted to discriminate along religious lines if they are oversubscribed, an exception provided for under the Equality Act 2010.

The first state-funded Muslim primary schools were opened under New Labour in the late 1990s, which also saw a more general expansion of faith school provision for minority faiths, and included Sikh, Seventh-Day Adventist, Greek Orthodox, and Hindu schools – an expansion in part further encouraged by the Education Act 2005.

Muslim schools have been particularly controversial in recent years, highlighted by the 'Trojan Horse' affair beginning in 2014, in which it was asserted that there was a conspiracy over an alleged 'Islamisation' of some schools in Birmingham. The initial government response banned a number of teachers and prompted extra inspections of certain schools by the government's education inspectorate (Ofsted), although these were later overturned by the courts and the whole affair was shown to be unfounded (see Holmwood and O'Toole, 2017).

Religious signs and symbols in schools have also been debated. The accommodation of religious difference in school uniform policy is left to individual schools, in consultation with parents. A high-profile case, *Shabina Begum v Denbigh High School*, concerned Islamic clothing when Shabina Begum, who started wearing the *jilbab*, was told she could not wear this to school. The school was 79 per cent Muslim and had designed its uniform policy in consultation with parents and mosques, providing a *shalwar kameez* and *hijab* as an alternative to the standard uniform for those who preferred. The case went to the High Court, which upheld the school's position. The Court of Appeal, after Shabina had since left the school and was 17, overruled this decision in 2005, before the House of Lords reversed the decision again in 2006.

Securitisation

A final aspect of governance in recent years, and which has focussed on Muslims, is the government's counter-radicalisation strategy *Prevent*, which has proved especially controversial. *Prevent* represents 'soft' measures or the 'hearts and minds' approach to addressing the social, cultural, and ideological aspects of (de)radicalisation, along with promoting 'moderate' Islam, challenging extremist ideologies, and helping develop a British Islam. Commentators have generally criticised its near-exclusive emphasis on Muslims and positioning of Muslims as a 'suspect community', and thereby as representing an instance of structural and institutional Islamophobia. Indeed, the lack of a formal recognition status for religious organisations in the United Kingdom has meant that 'state patronage' can be easily removed, as highlighted by the MCB falling out of favour with the New Labour government when it failed to support the war in Afghanistan in 2001 (see McLoughlin, 2005).

Concluding remarks

Britain is an example of a moderately secular country, well along the road of secularisation in many respects but also encompassing the historical inheritance of dominant Christianity, into which religious diversity and pluralism has been finding a home.

There are clear areas in which the historical inheritance and legacy of Anglican dominance can be seen. Yet, there is also no clear Anglican versus non-Anglican or even Christian versus non-Christian divide that fits the whole picture. What is found in general terms are forms of tolerant pragmatism with space within the existing state-religion framework. While there is an on-going decline in Christianity, religion has become a highly visible, if controversial, feature. With regard to this, however, it is important to make more explicit an important qualification which has been perhaps more implicit in the summary discussions above; that is that these accommodations have often been hard fought and hard won by minorities themselves, and Muslims have often been at the forefront of claims-making for religion's role in the public sphere (Modood, 2005, 2019a). The focus on Muslims, however, continues to put this tolerant pragmatism under strain, with, at least as far as Islam is concerned, a trend towards the securitisation.

Note

1 Changed to 'Supreme Governor' under Elizabeth I.

References

British Social Attitudes (BSA) 36, *Religion*, by D. Voas & S. Bruce. The National Centre for Social Research. Available at http://www.bsa.natcen.ac.uk/media/39293/1_bsa36_religion.pdf. Accessed 08/08/2019.
Brown, C. (2009). *The Death of Christian Britain: Understanding Secularisation 1800–2000* (2nd ed.). Abingdon: Routledge.
Church of England (CofE). (2018). *Statistics for Mission 2017*. London: Research and Statistics. Available at https://www.churchofengland.org/sites/default/files/2018-11/2017StatisticsForMission.pdf. Accessed 08/08/2019.
Cranmer, F. (2013). Accommodating religion in the workplace – Or maybe not: A note on Chaplin, Eweida, Ladela and McFarlane. *Law & Justice – The Christian Law Review*, 170: 67–76.
Dinham, A. (2007). Priceless, unmeasureable? Faiths and community development in 21st century England. Available at http://www.fbrn.org.uk/files/Priceless.pdf. Accessed 27/08/2019.
Dinham, A. (2009). *Faiths, Public Policy and Civil Society: Problems, Policies, Controversies*. Basingstoke: Palgrave Macmillan.
Holmwood, J. & O'Toole, T. (2017). *Countering Extremism in British Schools? The Truth about the Birmingham Trojan Horse Affair*. Bristol: Bristol University Press.
Hunt, S. (2012). Negotiating equality in the Equality Act 2010 (United Kingdom): Church-state relations in a post-Christian society. *Journal of Church and State*, 55(4): 690–711.
Ipsos Mori. (2018). *A Review of Survey Research on Muslims in Britain*, February 2018. Available at https://www.ipsos.com/sites/default/files/ct/publication/documents/2018-03/a-review-of-survey-research-on-muslims-in-great-britain-ipsos-mori_0.pdf. Accessed 27/08/2019.
Karatani, R. (2003). *Defining British Citizenship: Empire, Commonwealth and Modern Britain*. London: Frank Cass.

Khattab, N. (2009). Ethno-religious background as a determinant of educational and occupational attainment in Britain. *Sociology*, 43(2): 304–322.

Khattab, N. & Modood, T. (2015). Both ethnic and religious: Explaining employment penalties across 14 ethno-religious groups in the United Kingdom. *Journal for the Scientific Study of Religion*, 54(3): 501–522.

Khattab, N. & Modood, T. (2018). Accounting for British Muslim's educational attainment: Gender differences and the impact of expectations. *British Journal of Sociology of Education*, 39(2): 242–259.

Maher, J. (2014). Eweida and others: A new era for Article 9? *International & Comparative Law Quarterly*, 63(1): 213–233.

Malik, M. (2008). Religious freedom and multiculturalism: R (Shabina Begum) v Denbigh High School. *King's Law Journal*, 19(2): 377–390.

Malik, M. (2012). *Minority Legal Orders in the UK: Minorities, Pluralism and the Law*. The London: The British Academy.

Malik, M. (2014). Minorities and law: Past and present. *Current Legal Problems*, 67: 67–98.

Maltby, J. (2011). Gender and establishment: Parliament, 'erastianism' and the ordination of women 1993–2010. In M. Chapman, J. Maltby, & W. Whyte (eds), *The Established Church: Past, Present and Future* (pp. 98–123). London: T & T International.

McLoughlin, S. (2005). The state, 'new' Muslim leaderships and Islam as a 'resource' for engagement in Britain. In J. Cesari & S. McLoughlin (eds), *European Muslims and the Secular State* (pp. 55–69). Aldershot: Ashgate.

Modood, T. (1994). Establishment, multiculturalism and British citizenship. *The Political Quarterly*, 65(1): 53–73.

Modood, T. (ed.). (1997). *Church, State and Religious Minorities*. London: Policy Studies Institute.

Modood, T. (2004). Capitals, ethnic identity and educational qualifications. *Cultural Trends*, 13(2): 87–105.

Modood, T. (2005). *Multicultural Politics: Racism, Ethnicity, and Muslims in Britain*. Edinburgh: Edinburgh University Press.

Modood, T. (2013[2007]). *Multiculturalism: A Civic Idea* (2nd ed.). Cambridge: Polity Books.

Modood, T. (2019a). *Essays on Secularism and Multiculturalism*. London: Rowman & Littlefield.

Modood, T. (2019b). Oral evidence: Islamophobia, HC 1828, Home Affairs Committee, 25 June 2019. Available at http://data.parliament.uk/writtenevidence/committeeevidence.svc/evidencedocument/home-affairs-committee/islamophobia/oral/103379.html. Accessed 27/08/2019.

Morris, R. M. (2009). *Church and State in 21st Century Britain: The Future of Church Establishment*. Basingstoke: Palgrave Macmillan.

Muslim Council of Britain (MCB). (2015). *British Muslims in Numbers*. Available at http://www.mcb.org.uk/wp-content/uploads/2015/02/MCBCensusReport_2015.pdf. Accessed 08/08/2019.

Nielsen, J. S. (2009). Religion, Muslims, and the state in Britain and France: From Westphalia to 9/11. In A. H. Sinno (ed.), *Muslims in Western Politics* (pp. 50–66). Bloomington, IN: Indiana University Press.

Nye, M. (1998). Minority religious groups and religious freedom in England: The ISKCON Temple at Bhaktivedanta Manor. *Journal of Church and State*, 40(2): 411–436.

Pearce, B. (2012). The Inter Faith Network and the development of inter faith relations in Britain. In L. Woodhead & R. Catto (eds), *Religion and Change in Modern Britain* (pp. 150–155). Abingdon: Routledge.

Sherif, J. (2011). A Census chronicle–reflections on the campaign for a religion question in the 2001 Census for England and Wales. *Journal of Beliefs & Values*, 32(1): 1–18.

Weller, P. (2009). Religions and governance in the United Kingdom: Religious diversity, established religion, and emergent alternatives. In P. Bramadat & M. Koenig (eds), *International Migration and the Governance of Religious Diversity* (pp. 161–194). Montreal: McGill-Queen's University Press.

Weller, P., Purdam, K., Ghanea, N., & Cheruvallil-Contractor, S. (2015). *Religion or Belief, Discrimination and Equality: Britain in Global Contexts*. London: Bloomsbury.

Part II
Southern Europe

6

The Italian case

'Baptised *laicità*' and a changing demographic

Tina Magazzini

Introduction

Italy represents a peculiar case with respect to the governance of religion, in that it could be said that church-state relations are older than the state itself. An article in the *New York Times* once labelled Italy as 'the European nation where religion and state have mingled most', claiming that

> the debate over church and state has not stopped for 1,700 years, in this nation with a public Christian heritage stretching back to the Emperor Constantine's conversion early in the fourth century, where a neighbourhood in Rome is its own country and seat of the Roman Catholic Church. Those years seem to have lent enough time and hard experience for church and state to settle into an almost indistinct whole, where the very real secularization in Italy in the last few decades is balanced by its history, culture, architecture and, even though church attendance has declined significantly, faith.
>
> (Fisher, 2004)

Indeed, the history of the Italian institutions and of the Catholic Church are deeply intertwined, to the point that Catholicism influences the very notion of Italian *laicità*, which scholars have singled out as being distinct from the French *laïcité* (Ercolessi, 2009) and which represents a principle that does not only refer to state-church relations, but is considered to be 'a synthesis of the values and duties of the contemporary plural and democratic state in which religion plays a full role, like each other component of a civil society' (Ferrari & Ferrari, 2010: 433).

Yet, Italy has been a unified nation-state for less than 160 years. The city of Rome only became part of Italy in 1870, and the country's unification was not really completed until after the First World War, when, in 1918, the territories of Venezia Giulia and Trentino (previously belonging to the Austro-Hungarian Empire) were annexed.

In line with this volume's aim to highlight how countries govern and address religion – and particularly religious minorities – this chapter focusses on religious diversity governance in contemporary Italy, the existing official recognition of (and lack thereof) religious groups, and the regulations between the state and the different confessions practised by various religious communities, old and new.

In the following sections I will first provide an overview of the current challenges and opportunities in the field of religious diversity governance. These are the country's demographics and the population's changing composition, mostly due to an ageing population, recent migration (of both Italian youth leaving the country and immigrant flows arriving from EU recent member states as well as from Africa, Asia, and South America) and the significant economic, political and cultural regional differences that characterise the country. It would however be difficult to make sense of Italy's current institutional asset and religious governance without considering the central role that the Catholic Church and the Vatican State have played over the centuries, particularly in Italy's nation-building and state-building process.

Therefore, the following section provides a historical background of state-organised religion relations and analyses the current institutional framework that governs religions and religious diversity today.

Finally, I will look at how the legal and institutional frameworks for managing religious diversity play out in practice since legal provisions do not necessarily apply uniformly to all minorities, legal voids tend to favour customary traditions, and the interpretation of the courts of what constitutes an 'active' or 'passive' religious symbol plays an important role in everyday religious diversity governance.

The conclusions aim at briefly summarising the various sections and providing pointers regarding possible avenues for future research and for meaningful comparisons.

Socio-demographic context, main trends, and challenges

Italy's population, according to the last official census (January 2020), is of slightly over 60 million inhabitants, which places it roughly in same group as France and the UK. What is noteworthy of Italy's demographics, however, is that while in the 1980s its population (at 56.5 million) was slightly larger than the populations of France and Britain, it has practically stagnated since, and has actually been steadily declining in the last decade, while both France and the UK now count around 67 million residents.

While the overall size of Italy's population has remained fairly stable over the past decades, its composition has not. From being a large-scale emigration country in the nineteenth and twentieth centuries,[1] it has in the past few decades become a destination country for migrants coming from Central and Eastern Europe (CEE) countries, North Africa, and Latin America. As Simon McMahon pointed out, in Italy the underground labour markets have provided employment opportunities for immigrants (albeit often in precarious, irregular, and temporary conditions) regardless of their legal status, fostering high levels of undocumented migrants that have been addressed through *ad hoc*, but fairly regular, amnesties (in 1986, 1990, 1995, 1998, 2002 and 2009) (Ambrosini, 2013, 2014; McMahon, 2015: 6).

Arguably immigration is, together with a low birth rate, the defining characteristic of Italy's population shift in the twenty-first century. It is a trend that holds great promise, as most migrants are younger than the average Italian population and immigrant families tend to have a higher birth rate than the average Italian family. But this shift also holds challenges, particularly in terms of administrative regularisations and access to citizenship. As of 2021, Italy's citizenship legislation remains slightly more restrictive than in other EU-15 countries (ISMU, 2018). Despite the increasing importance of citizenship in Italy's public discourse and multiple attempts to introduce new bills to Parliament, the current citizenship law has not changed significantly since 1992 and there is no provision for acquiring citizenship through *ius solis*[2] (ibid.).

Overall, while the reality of majority-minority relations in Italy varies across regions and minority groups, and a number of successful integration practices exist, over the past decade there has been a rising number of racist attacks (Giuffrida, 2019), and migration has become one of the main polarising themes in national politics, with much of the attention focussed on the phenomenon of a Muslim migration possessing specific identity and cultural claims[3] (Chiodelli & Moroni, 2017; Russo Spena, 2010) (Table 6.1).

Table 6.1 Changes in total population and percentage of foreign residents in Italy (2004–2019)

Year	Total population	Foreign residents	%
2004	58,462,375	1,990,159	3.4
2005	58,462,375	2,402,157	4.1
2006	59,131,287	2,670,514	4.5
2007	59,619,290	2,938,922	5
2008	60,045,068	3,432,651	5.8
2009	60,340,328	3,891,295	6.5
2010	60,626,442	4,235,059	7
2011	59,394,207	4,570,317	7.5
2012	59,685,227	4,052,081	6.8
2013	60,782,668	4,387,721	7.4
2014	60,795,612	4,922,085	8.1
2015	60,665,551	5,014,437	8.2
2016	60,589,445	5,026,124	8.3
2017	60,483,973	5,047,028	8.3
2018	60,359,546	5,144,440	8.5
2019	60,238,522	5,255,503	8.7

Source: Data based on the Italian Statistical Office (Instituto Nazionale di Statistica. ISTAT). Available at http://www4.istat it/

The composition of migrants based on country of origin, as of 2019, is as follows (Table 6.2):

Table 6.2 Citizenship of foreigners residing in Italy (2019)

Country of citizenship	Residents in Italy	% of total foreign residents in Italy
Romania	1,206,938	22.97
Albania	441,027	8.39
Morocco	422,980	8.05
China	299,823	5.70
Ukraine	239,424	4.56
Philippines	168,292	3.20
India	157,965	3.01
Bangladesh	139,953	2.66
Moldavia	128,979	2.45
Egypt	126,733	2.41
Pakistan	122,308	2.33
Nigeria	117,358	2.23
Sri Lanka	111,056	2.11
Senegal	110,242	2.10
Peru	97,128	1.85
Tunisia	95,071	1.81
Poland	94,200	1.79
Equador	79,249	1.51
North Macedonia	63,561	1.21
Bulgaria	60,129	1.14

Source: Data based on the Italian Statistical Office (Instituto Nazionale di Statistica. ISTAT). Available at http://www4.istat it/

Note: The table does not include those migrants who either were never able to register as residents or who lost their residency status following the Decree no. 113 of October 4, 2018. The number of unregistered migrants currently residing in Italy is estimated by the National Office of Statistics to be around 600,000, and in May 2020 the Minister of Agriculture put forward a proposal to regularise them, citing the fact that many irregular migrants are exploited in the agriculture industry and the health emergency and hazard that, in the context of a pandemic, half a million people without access to health services represent (Casadio, 2020).

The data regarding religious identification are neither systematically collected nor easily available. The national census includes no question aimed at collecting data on religious affiliation, and even though a number of surveys have been conducted by the Pew Research Center – as well as by Ipsos, Eurispes, and the Eurobarometer in recent years – they all use different questions, samples, and methodologies thus making comparisons unreliable. Additionally, as pointed out by Alessandro and Silvio Ferrari, the available figures often present contradictory findings: in 2010, around 90 per cent of the population was baptised and a similar percentage of students was enrolled in Catholic religious education classes (which are not compulsory, but are offered in public schools as optional classes), but fewer than 40 per cent of taxpayers that same year chose to allot to the Catholic Church the part of income tax (0.8 per cent, more on this below) which is earmarked for religious denominations or welfare institutions (Ferrari & Ferrari, 2010: 431) (See Figure 6.1). Even though Italy, according to the Pew Research Center, is one of just two countries in Western Europe – the other is Portugal – in which church-attending Christians are more numerous than non-church-attending Christians, the shares of highly observant people (27 per cent) do not reach one-third of the overall population (Pew Research Center, 2018: 95).

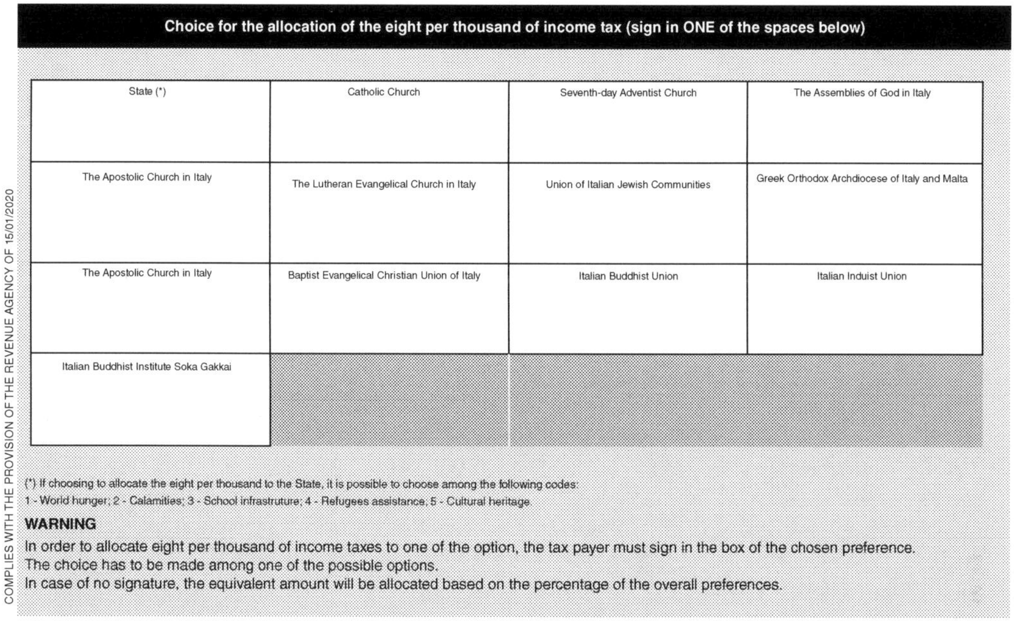

Choice for the allocation of the eight per thousand of income tax (sign in ONE of the spaces below)

State (*)	Catholic Church	Seventh-day Adventist Church	The Assemblies of God in Italy
The Apostolic Church in Italy	The Lutheran Evangelical Church in Italy	Union of Italian Jewish Communities	Greek Orthodox Archdiocese of Italy and Malta
The Apostolic Church in Italy	Baptist Evangelical Christian Union of Italy	Italian Buddhist Union	Italian Induist Union
Italian Buddhist Institute Soka Gakkai			

(*) If choosing to allocate the eight per thousand to the State, it is possible to choose among the following codes:
1 - World hunger; 2 - Calamities; 3 - School infrastruture; 4 - Refugees assistance; 5 - Cultural heritage

WARNING

In order to allocate eight per thousand of income taxes to one of the option, the tax payer must sign in the box of the chosen preference.
The choice has to be made among one of the possible options.
In case of no signature, the equivalent amount will be allocated based on the percentage of the overall preferences.

COMPLIES WITH THE PROVISION OF THE REVENUE AGENCY OF 15/01/2020

Figure 6.1 Income tax form: options for 0.08 per cent 'donation'.

Despite the lack of comprehensive data, in terms of general trends some overall cues can be taken from looking at the changes in the responses to the surveys conducted over the years: all surveys show a decline in the percentage of those who declare themselves Catholic, and the most comprehensive study (Ipsos), which is conducted yearly and based on a sample of 60,000 interviews, has documented over the last decade three parallel phenomena: (1) a rise of about 10 per cent in the number of people who identify as non-religious; (2) a decrease in those who declare themselves Catholic – also about 10 per cent, matching with the increase of those who identify as non-religious; and (3) an increase of religious affiliations other than Catholic, from 1.6 to 3 per cent (Table 6.3).

Table 6.3 Changes in people self-identifying as Catholic, non-believers, or believers in another (non-Catholic) faith (2007–2017)

Year	*Catholics (%)*	*Non-believers/atheists (%)*	*Other religions (%)*
2007	85.4	13	1.6
2008	87	11.4	1.6
2009	84	14.2	1.8
2010	83.2	14.5	2.3
2011	81.9	15.6	2.5
2012	80.7	16.8	2.5
2013	81	16.5	2.5
2014	80.2	17.2	2.6
2015	78.4	18.9	2.7
2016	77	20.1	2.9
2017	74.4	22.6	3.0

Source: Data collected by Ipsos and presented at Italy's Parliament on November 15, 2007. Presentation titled "I cattolici tra presenza nel sociale e nuove domande alla politica" and available on Ipsos' website.

Tina Magazzini

Of those who self-identify as Catholic, most claim to go to Church 'occasionally' (35 per cent of the overall population in 2017), while approximately 27 per cent of the total population declared to be a frequent church-goer or to be actively involved in church activities in 2017. Regarding how and to what extent church attendance has varied in Italy over the past decades, Vezzoni and Biolcati-Rinaldi pooled, in 2015, multiple cross-section surveys, showing that the trend of attendance at Mass in Italy has decreased since the 1960s (Vezzoni & Biolcati-Rinaldi, 2015). According to their analysis, the decline was sharpest in the 1970s and slowed in the 1980s, but has been on a steady pace from the second half of the 1990s onward and offers solid evidence refuting the thesis of a religious revival in Italy put forward by some scholars in the early 2000s (Diotallevi, 2002; Introvigne & Stark, 2005).

Other than the above-mentioned surveys and studies, one available indicator of the role that religiosity plays in contemporary Italian society is the number of religious weddings versus the number of civil weddings. According to the Italian National Institute of Statistics (ISTAT), the proportion of religious weddings shrank from 98.34 per cent in 1948 to 50.49 per cent in 2017, when 49.51 per cent of Italians marrying opted for a civil ceremony. More noteworthy than the shift from religious to civil weddings however is that the overall number of weddings has decreased significantly, with more couples choosing not to get married at all (Figure 6.2).

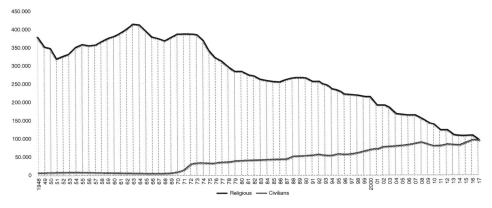

Figure 6.2 Number of religious weddings and civil weddings, 1948 to 2017.
Source: Data based on ISTAT figures.

Regarding the religiosity of foreign residents, in absence of surveys or census data on religious affiliation for migrant individuals, the percentages in Table 6.4 were calculated on the basis of the prevalent religion in the migrants' country of origin.

Table 6.4 Religious affiliation of immigrants residing in Italy (2018)

Religion	Members	%
Muslims	1,682,600	32.7
Orthodox	1,523,300	29.6
Catholics	918,100	17.8
Atheists	241,700	4.7
Protestants	224,400	4.4
Other Christian denominations	39,900	0.8
Hinduists	152,500	3
Buddhists	117,200	2.3
Other	90,700	1.7
Other East Asian religions	83,700	1.6
Tradition religions	65,300	1.3
Jews	4,600	0.1

Source: Data based on the Statistical Dossier on Immigration of 2018. Available at https://www.dossierimmigrazione.it/

While Catholicism remains the most widespread and well-established majority religion in the country – to the point that the historian Paul Ginsborg has defined Italy as a country characterised by a feeling of 'widespread religion' [*religione diffusa*] (Ginsborg, 2006) – the percentage of Italians who identify as Catholics has been slowly but steadily declining, as is the case in most Western European countries. Of these, even less self-identify as 'practicing Catholics'.

It can therefore be said that, with secularisation as a backdrop, immigration to Italy increases the percentage of religious members of the population since estimates from 2017 and 2018 see only 4.7 per cent of foreigners residing in Italy identifying as 'atheists or agnostic' against a 22.6 per cent of Italian citizens who declare themselves as non-religious.

If, until the late 1990s, the main challenges related to religious governance in Italy had to do with the obstacles in advancing civil rights opposed by the Catholic Church (such as abortion rights, LGBT equal rights, and so on) and protecting the freedom of the non-religious minority *from* Catholic religion (more on this below, see the *Lautsi v. Italy* case), the country now faces a dual challenge.

While the threat of majority religious norms being imposed on atheists or agnostics persists – for instance, while accessing legal abortions is a right according to Law no. 194 of 22 May 1978, the right of doctors to opt out from providing them based on their religious conscience effectively renders the norm void in certain regions – the discrimination in treatment between different religions has also become a serious issue. Given that Italy's population is expected to continue becoming increasingly more diverse – religiously, ethnically, linguistically – (ISTAT, 2018), the inequalities in recognition between different minority religions will become increasingly salient, unless the institutional framework on which such disparities are based is reformed. In order to understand how the state-religion relationship came to evolve into the current institutional framework, it is useful to look at the historical foundations and developments of the institutional setting.

Tina Magazzini

Historical background of state-church relations and current institutional framework

The Catholic Church in Italy has always been, above and beyond a religious institution, a political one. One of the most powerful entities in the peninsula, the Papal States controlled most of what is now considered central Italy for about a millennium[4] and played a crucial role in the formation of the Italian state. After Italy was unified in 1861, when King Vittorio Emanuele II of Sardinia was proclaimed King of Italy, Rome and the whole region of Lazio remained in the hands of the Pope, and hence Turin was temporarily declared Italy's capital.

The Kingdom of Sardinia, which already in 1848 had recognised equal civil and political rights to Jews and Waldesians, favoured a separation of state and religion, despite many of the political leaders of the Italian Risorgimento being religious (and often Catholics) in their private lives. Even though the 1848 Albertine Statute – the constitution of the former Kingdom of Sardinia, which was adopted by the Kingdom of Italy in 1861 – recognised Catholicism as the state's official religion, it also adopted a regime of separation between church and state based on the principle of individual freedom and declared the toleration of 'other currently existing confessions'.[5]

When Italian troops conquered Rome in 1870, putting an end to the temporal power of the Pope, the so-called *legge delle guarentigie* [statute of the guaranties] was declared by the Italian government to ensure the independence and diplomatic status of the Holy See. However, the then-Pope Pius IX retreated to the Vatican, where he declared himself a 'prisoner', excommunicated the king and the leaders of the Italian government, and ordered 'good Catholics' not to recognise its legitimacy and abstain from participation in Italian political life and parliamentary elections (*non expedit* policy) (Ercolessi, 2009; Kertzer, 2015). This meant that the first half century of the Italian state was characterised by the absence of Catholic factions in politics since the *non expedit* was only definitely revoked in 1918, even though in 1905 Pope Pius X had modified it so that the bishops could ask for a suspension of the rule in case of the need to prevent the election of a 'subversive' candidate.

A Catholic party, the *Partito Popolare*, participated in the general elections of 1919, winning approximately 20 per cent of the votes, but was abolished in 1929 – along with all other parties – by the Fascist dictatorship. That very same year, however, the Holy See and the Italian Kingdom signed the Lateran Treaty, which created the Vatican City State and restored many of the prerogatives of the church, to the point that Pope Pius XI referred to Mussolini as the man of providence (Kertzer, 2015).

Following the end of the Second World War, the transition to democracy and to a Republican form of government, Italy's governance of religion shifted, but the fundamental regulatory framework remained that of 1929. The Lateran Concordat was incorporated into Italy's Constitution in Article 7, which reads 'The State and the Catholic Church are independent and sovereign, each within its own sphere. Their relations are regulated by the Lateran pacts. Amendments to such Pacts which are accepted by both parties shall not require the procedure of constitutional amendments'. The Pacts were replaced in 1984 by the Agreement of Villa Madama, which eliminated some outdated provisions, such as those forbidding a referendum on divorce (which was held in 1974, confirming Law 898 of 1970 which allowed for divorce) and the now-obsolete rules on the governmental approval of ecclesiastical appointments.

The most important change, however, was the abolition of the clause that recognised the status of 'state religion' to Catholicism and the consequent abolition of both the obligation to teach Catholic religion in public schools (the classes remained, but became optional) and of the *Congrua* – the salary of Catholic priests, which until then had been fully paid by the state. To replace the Congrua, the 0.8 per cent financing system was introduced with Law 222 of May 1985; the so-called eight per thousand is an income-based tax that is still in force and which the taxpayers can choose to allocate to either the Catholic Church, to the state, or to another religious denomination among those recognised by the state.

This 1984 reform also initiated a more effective recognition of the other religions professed on the national territory. This was based on Article 8 of the Constitution that 'All religious denominations shall be equally free before the law. Denominations other than Catholicism shall have the right to self-organisation according to their own statutes, provided these do not conflict with Italian law'. However, while from the mid-1980s some religious minorities started being recognised through *ad hoc* agreements that provide a certain degree of legal protection, these are not comparable to the relations between the State and the Catholic Church, which continue to be regulated by the Concordat, albeit renewed.

Regarding non-Catholic denominations, the path of *ad hoc* agreements between minority confessions and the Italian state hinge on the political will on behalf of the state, as well as on the capacity of minority religions to speak with a single voice. This has translated into the fact that Muslims, who are divided between various religious associations, have not yet obtained an official recognition as a religion by the Italian state despite representing the largest religious minority of approximately 1.5 million (3.3 per cent of the population). The differentiation among denominations based on the 'tiered' system of agreements is summarised in Table 6.5.

Table 6.5 Italy's multi-tier system of legal recognition for different confessions

Level of recognition	Legal basis for different treatment	Confession and year of legal agreement	Legal status of the relationship
1	Constitution, Art. 7: specific reference	Catholics (1929, 1985)	Agreement of Villa Madama (international treaty) + numerous other regulations (ordinary laws)
2	Recognised denominations which have no characteristics incompatible with Italian law + Agreement with the State	Valdensians (1984, 1993, 2009) Seventh-Day Adventists (1988, 1996, 2009) Pentecostal (1988) Union of Jewish communities (1989, 1996) Christian Evangelical-Baptist Union (1995) Lutheran Church (1995) The Greek Orthodox Archdiocese (2012) Mormon Church (2012) Apostolic Church (2012) Italian Buddhist Union (2012) Italian Hinduist Union (2012) Soka Gakkai Buddhist Institute (2016)	*Ad hoc* Agreements which allow them to enjoy tax reductions; participating in the 0.8%, tax exemption from donations, etc.
3	Recognised denominations which have no characteristics incompatible with Italian law (without Agreement)	Jehova's witnesses Church of England (agreement signed in 2019 but not yet approved by the state)	Law 1159 of 1929, which allows tax reductions and the possibility, under some conditions, of places of worship and presence in hospitals, schools, prisons and the army.
4	No recognition. Characterised as being in more or less open conflict with 'public order'	Muslims Sikh Scientologists All others	Governed by the general laws on associations/ private groups, excluded by all taxation benefits, religious education and pastoral care

As the table shows, the type of state support and state recognition of a certain denomination is the aspect in which the inequality between different religious communities is the most prominent. While increasing religious diversity is becoming a normal feature of Italian society, particularly in large cities where globalisation and migration's effects are more visible, one telling indicator of the differential treatment still rooted in the current regulatory framework is that the Central Directorate for Religious Affairs – the institute in charge of religious affairs, including the key role of stipulating agreements between the Italian state and religious groups – is divided into two branches: Catholic affairs and non-Catholic affairs.

Only the Catholic Church belongs to the 'first tier': the 1929 Lateran Treaty and the 1985 agreement between the Italian state and the Catholic church ensure 'the full freedom of the Church to develop its pastoral, educational, and charitable mission, of evangelization and sanctification' (Agreement Between the Italian Republic and the Holy See, 1985, Art. 2) with vast privileges that range from military to tax exemptions, to the civil effects of marriages contracted by canon law, to the recognition on behalf of the Italian state of the 'particular significance that Rome has to Catholicism' (ivi), to a special joint Commission to be appointed by the Holy See and the Italian state in case of controversy on the interpretation and application of provisions.

All non-Catholic religions are grouped together under the Central Directorate for Religious Affairs (which is placed under the Ministry of Interior), and while Article 8 of the 1948 Constitution does envision the possibility for non-Catholic religious groups to enter into an agreement (*Intesa*) with the Italian state, this ultimately depends on the discretion of the Directorate for Religious Affairs. Thus far agreements between the state and the government – which in any case are far from resembling the kind of privileges afforded to the Catholic Church – have been stipulated with the Valdensian Evangelical Church, the Evangelical Christian Churches Assemblies of God in Italy, the Seventh-day Adventist Church, the Union of Italian Jewish Communities (UCEI), the Baptist Evangelical Christian Union of Italy, the Evangelical Lutheran Church, the Greek Orthodox Archdiocese, the Church of Jesus Christ of Latter-day Saints, the Apostolic Church, the Italian Buddhist Union, the Italian Hinduist Union, and the Soka Gakkai Italian Buddhist Institute (IBISG).[6] These belong to what can be therefore qualified as a 'second tier': religious denominations that have an agreement with the Italian state that is regulated by ordinary law and 'are guaranteed a position equivalent, although not equal, to that of the Catholic Church' (Ferrari & Ferrari, 2010: 441) regarding tax exemptions and the 0.8 per cent system, but they lose the right to self-organisation in case of practices in conflict with Italian law.

A third tier is constituted by those religions such as the Church of England and Jehovah's Witnesses that are regulated by the so-called 'norm on the admitted cults' under Law 1159 approved on 24 June 1929 by the Fascist dictatorship. Such legislation allows, under certain conditions, for the faith communities recognised by it to have a presence in hospitals, prisons, schools, and the army, as well as for tax reductions on certain activities. The bottom tier, despite including Italy's largest religious minority (Muslims), is characterised as faiths presenting aspects that are fundamentally at odds with public safety and security (such as the kirpan for Sikhs, for example[7]), and follow the same general disposition as any cultural or private association.

In the case of Islam, a series of attempts were made on behalf of different Muslim groups in the 1990s to gain recognition as a religious minority, but none succeeded[8] (Morucci, 2018). In 2005, the Ministry of Interior created a 'Consulting body for an Italian Islam' to which individuals considered to be authoritative representatives of the Muslim world in Italy were appointed. This body was charged by a subsequent government with the drafting of a 'Charter of citizenship and integration values'. In 2010, the Interior Ministry created a 'Committee for Italian Islam', largely holding the same aims of improving Muslim communities' social inclusion and integration into Italian society; the Committee had the same consultative status as the previous Consulting body. The most recent advisory body, created in 2016 (again by the Interior Ministry), is the 'Council for relations with Islam', which like the previous bodies was charged with the task of providing opinions and formulating proposals on integration issues. In February 2017 a 'National Pact' was signed between the Ministry of Interior and the Council, which includes among its points the possibility of initiating 'negotiations aimed at reaching agreements pursuant to art. 8, paragraph 3, of the Constitution' (ibid.). Despite the Pact being an important development since it predisposes the signatory parties to a path leading to one or more agreements, the recognition of the legal status of Muslims as a religious minority seems to have suffered a setback since 2017, having completely disappeared from the governmental agenda if not in terms of security threat (Zaccaria et al., 2020).

Religious diversity, its accommodation, and politicisation

Beyond Article 8 of the Constitution, matters of religious freedom are to be found in constitutional articles 2, 3, 19, and 20, which read:

> 2: The Republic shall recognise and protect the inviolable rights of the person, both as an individual and in the social groups where *human personality is expressed*. [...]
> 3: All citizens shall have equal social dignity and shall be *equal before the law, without distinction of* gender, race, language, *religion*, political opinion, personal and social conditions. [...]
> 19: Everyone shall be entitled to *profess freely their religious beliefs* in any form, individually or with others, and to promote such beliefs and celebrate rites in public or in private, provided they are not offensive to public morality.
> 20: No special limitation or tax burden shall be imposed on the establishment, legal capacity or activities of any organisation on the *ground of its religious nature* or its religious or confessional goals.

Despite such provisions, in practice, the lack of a formal agreement on the behalf of a religious group with the Italian government translates into significant difficulties since it creates obstacles in accessing places of worship and cemeteries, as well as a lack of recognition for religious festivities, dietary requirements, and so on.[9] For members of religious minorities, the lack of recognition also risks translating into the feeling of being faced with an impossible choice between one's faith and one's national identity.

Nadia Bouzekri, a Milanese business analyst and vice president of the Italian Union of Muslim Communities (*Unione delle Comunità Islamiche d'Italia*, UCOII), stated:

> Being Muslim in Italy is currently quite difficult. By this I don't mean at a social level, but particularly at an institutional level. I'm often asked whether I am Italian or Muslim, whether I choose the Constitution or the Quran…We are now a third generation [of migrants of Muslim faith] in Italy, we cannot continue to talk about a 'foreign' community anymore. We can only think of it as a religious minority.
> *(May 2019, video interview for the GREASE documentary film Religion and Society)*

On the one hand, the mostly public and inclusive Italian school and health care systems ensure that social and public services are affordable and tend to foster mixity. On the other, the economic sector and employment opportunities are still strongly segregated along ethnic and religious lines (which often overlap), on top of class and gender ones. This situation is rendered more complicated for non-European citizens by the fact that Italy's naturalisation law is among the most restrictive in Europe for those who cannot acquire it via *ius sanguinis*, but who are born and raised in Italy. As Bouzekri pointed out:

> As a young Italian with parents of migrant background, you often realize that you do not have Italian citizenship when you are denied the visa to go on a school trip with your classmates, when you cannot apply for a grant. I have friends who graduated from law school, went on to became lawyers, and yet they are often mistaken for the interpreter or the translator, sometimes for the cleaning lady. And this just because in Italy it is still so incredibly difficult to imagine a lawyer wearing a headscarf!
>
> *(Ibid.)*

If we look at the presence of religion in society and politics more broadly, Alessandro Ferrari coined the term of 'baptised *laicità*' to capture the contradictions and idiosyncrasies present in Italy between juridical and 'narrative' *laicità* (Ferrari, 2009): from a juridical point of view, Italian *laicità*

> can be assimilated neither to laicism (if this word is intended to be synonymous with anti-religiousness) nor to secularism (if this word is intended to be synonymous with the invisibility of religious in the public sphere). *Laicità* supposes the existence of a plurality of value systems, it entails equal protection for religious and non religious beliefs, and it requires State neutrality regarding both of them.
>
> *(Ferrari & Ferrari, 2010: 433)*

Yet, Italy's political, economic, social, and cultural life remains strongly permeated by Catholicism, which has come to be considered 'a cultural expression of the core national heritage' rather than a religion on equal footing as other value systems (ivi).

Despite the absence of restrictions on religiously based political parties, the only ones to have ever participated in elections, in political life, or indeed to exist, have been Catholic or Catholic-inspired. In particular, the Christian Democracy (a Catholic-inspired centrist party) was the largest party in Parliament from 1946 to 1994. As of 2021, three of the seven main political parties sitting in Parliament include explicit references to their Christian identity in their manifesto, and during the pandemic that hit Italy particularly hard in March and April 2020, one of the most prominent right-wing political leaders (the head of the Northern League) used a live interview on television to recite the Catholic prayer Eternal Rest for those who died from the pandemic, while also asking for churches to be kept open for Easter mass (contrary to government decrees and social distancing).

With regard to finances and taxation, as previously mentioned, the 1985 Agreements between the Holy See and the Italian State grant the Catholic Church special social security benefits, while until 1986 the state paid a monthly salary to the Catholic clergymen. Such 'allowance' was replaced by the so-called 'eight per thousand' in the late 1980s: nowadays, taxpayers devolve a compulsory 0.08 per cent of their annual income to an organised religion recognised by Italy. While in 1986 this percentage went directly to the Catholic Church, over the years the number of options for taxpayers to choose other recognised religions has broadened to include the 12 possibilities shown in Figure 6.2. There is, however, no Muslim option since Islam is not a recognised religion in Italy. In addition to the 12 religious denominations, the *Stato* (state) option offers the possibility to choose between (1) fight against world hunger, (2) emergencies, (3) school infrastructure, (4) refugee assistance, and (5) cultural heritage.

In terms of social and cultural life, how people dress has not come under the same kind of scrutiny as in other European countries, but this does not mean that the display of religious symbols – particularly in educational settings and public offices – has not caused controversy. Debate on the issue of the Catholic religion's role and presence in public schools, in particular, has been heated for decades (Pollard, 2008).

One telling controversy that provides a good example of the kind of public discourse still ongoing in Italy regarding freedom of religion in society is the *Lautsi v. Italy* case. The case was raised by Mrs. Lautsi, who complained about her children having to be exposed to the Catholic crucifix in class while attending public school, which is supposed to be non-confessional, and asked for it to be removed from the classrooms. When the school in question decided not to do so, the case went first to the regional administrative court of Veneto, then to the supreme administrative court, and finally to the European Court of Human Rights. The final decision was that the presence of crucifixes in public schools did not violate the principle of secularism, so Mrs. Lautsi lost the case (Panara, 2011). What is noteworthy, however, is the reasoning based on which the Italian government defended the presence of crucifixes in public schools, claiming that the crucifix symbolised not a religious confession but rather Italian civilisation, its historical roots and 'universal values'. In a different case also involving a crucifix – that of a judge who refused to hold hearings in a courtroom displaying a crucifix – the High Council of the Judiciary expelled Luigi Tosti, the judge in question, in 2010 (European Court of Human Rights, 2011; Morondo Taramundi, 2015). As Ferrari and Ferrari noted, 'What the history of the crucifix issue seems to say is that a particular interpretation of national identity prevails on both neutrality of institutions and individual rights' (Ferrari & Ferrari, 2010: 448).

Concluding remarks

While Catholicism remains the most widespread and well-established majority religion in the country – to the point that the historian Paul Ginsborg has defined Italy as a country characterised by a feeling of 'widespread religion', and a particular brand of laicism, 'baptised *laicità*', is used in reference to state-church relations – the percentage of Italians who identify as Catholics has been slowly but steadily declining, as is the case in most Western European countries. Of those who identify as Catholic, less than one-third self-identify as 'practicing Catholics'.

With secularisation as a backdrop, immigration to Italy increases the percentage of religious members of the population. The novelty and perceived threat on behalf of the majority, however, has little to do with whether immigrants are religious or not, as the concern is squarely with migrants from Muslim majority countries.

The current Italian Constitution, which entered into force in 1948 reinstating democracy after two decades of fascist dictatorship, incorporated the Lateran Treaty in Art. 7, acknowledging both the political treaty that recognises the full sovereignty of the Holy See in the State of Vatican City and the 'Concordat' regulating state-church relations. While the Constitution also guarantees the right of freedom of religion, in recent years a number of legal cases have highlighted the difficulty of disentangling religious and state matters.

Overall, Italy's current religious diversity management approach reflects an underlying framework according to which minority religions are only relevant to the specific minorities, but Catholicism is seen as holding a universal cultural value, which, in turn, can become problematic not only for minority religions but also for an increasing non-religious minority.

In this respect, Italy presents clear similarities to other European states that have been referred to as the 'majority Catholic South' (Sealy, Magazzini, Modood, & Triandafyllidou, Forthcoming 2021), yet it also offers some insights for those countries in which a majority religion risks being exploited and politised for electoral ends. It could therefore be useful to compare the evolution of Christian narratives and state-religion relations in EU member states of recent immigration in which the societal and political factions that profess to defend a certain brand of 'national' religiosity are also those who have had the strongest disagreements with the current Catholic Pope Francis.

Notes

1 An estimated 13 million Italians emigrated and permanently settled in their host countries between 1880 and 1976 (Ben-Ghiat & Hom, 2016) and by the late 1970s an estimated 25 million Italians were residing abroad (King, 1978), even though a Registry of Italians Resident Abroad (A.I.R.E.) was not created until 1988, now counting approximately 5 million registrations.
2 Children born to foreign parents who have been resident in Italy for a period of time need to wait until they are 18 to apply for citizenship, unless the parents acquire it meanwhile, in which case they can naturalise through the parents.
3 According to a survey conducted in 2017 by the Pew Research Centre, 53 per cent of respondents in Italy claimed that Islam is fundamentally incompatible with Italy's culture and values (Pew Research Center, 2018).
4 Beyond the Lazio region, the Papal States controlled the Marche, Umbria, and most of Emilia-Romagna.
5 Such 'toleration' was eroded and eventually completely done away with under fascism, despite an initial formal window-dressing with the so-called Law on allowed worships (Law 11593/1929) passed in the same year as the Lateran Treaty.
6 See the official governmental webpage 'Service for relations with religious denominations and institutional relations', accessible at http://presidenza.governo.it/USRI/confessioni/intese_indice.html
7 See the sentence n. 24084, 15 May 2017, Corte di Cassazione.
8 Draft proposals for an official agreement with the Italian government were put forward by the Union of Muslim Communities and Organizations in Italy (UCOII) in 1992, by the Association of Italian Muslims (AMI) in 1994, and by the Italian Muslim Religious Community (Coreis) in 1998.
9 In Italy, currently fewer than 10 out of 1,300 Muslim places of worship are officially recognised as mosques, and all are funded by the communities themselves.

References

Ambrosini, M. (2013). *Irregular Migration and Invisible Welfare*. London: Palgrave Macmillan UK. https://doi.org/10.1057/9781137314321

Ambrosini, M. (2014). Italy. In A. Triandafyllidou & R. Gropas (Eds.), *European Immigration: A Sourcebook* (pp. 200–210). Ashgate: Aldershot.

Ben-Ghiat, R., & Hom, S. (Eds.). (2016). *Italian Mobilities*. London and New York: Routledge.

Casadio, G. (2020, May 13). Governo, ecco la bozza sulla regolarizzazione dei migranti che arriva in Consiglio dei Ministri. La Repubblica. Retrieved from https://www.repubblica.it/politica/2020/05/13/news/decreto_bozza_migranti-256494579

Chiodelli, F., & Moroni, S. (2017). Planning, pluralism and religious diversity: Critically reconsidering the spatial regulation of mosques in Italy starting from a much-debated law in the Lombardy region. *Cities, 62*, 62–70.

Diotallevi, L. (2002). Internal Competition in a National Religious Monopoly: The Catholic Effect and the Italian Case. *Sociology of Religion, 63*(2), 137–155.

Ercolessi, G. (2009). Italy: The Contemporary Condition of Italian Laicità. In B. A. Kosmin & A. Keysar (Eds.), *Secularism, Women & The State: The Mediterranean World in the 21st Century* (pp. 9–28). Hartford, CT: Institute for the Study of Secularism in Society and Culture.

European Court of Human Rights. (2011). *Case of Lautsi and Others v. Italy*. Strasbourg. Retrieved from hudoc.echr.coe.int › app › conversion › pdf

Ferrari, A. (2009). De la politique à la technique: laïcité narrative et laïcité du droit. Pour une comparaison France/Italie. In B. Basdevant Gaudemet & F. Jankowiak (Eds.), *Le droit ecclésiastique en Europe et à ses marges (XVIII-XX siècles)* (pp. 333–345). Leuven: Peeters.

Ferrari, A., & Ferrari, S. (2010). Religion and the Secular State: The Italian Case. *Italian National Reports, Law and Religion*, (16), 363–364. Retrieved from https://classic.iclrs.org/content/blurb/files/Italy.pdf

Fisher, I. (2004, December 1). Italy's Church and State: A Mostly Happy Union. *The New York Times*. Retrieved from https://www.nytimes.com/2004/12/01/world/europe/italys-church-and-state-a-mostly-happy-union.html

Ginsborg, P. (2006). *Storia d'Italia dal dopoguerra a oggi*. Torino: Giulio Einaudi Editore.

Giuffrida, A. (2019, November 12). More than half of Italians in polls say racist acts are justifiable. *The Guardian*. Retrieved from https://www.theguardian.com/world/2019/nov/12/more-than-half-of-italians-in-poll-say-racism-is-justifiable

Introvigne, M., & Stark, R. (2005). Religious Competition and Revival in Italy : Exploring European Exceptionalism. *Interdisciplinary Journal of Research on Religion*, 1, 1–20.

ISTAT. (2018). *Il futuro demografico del paese. Previsioni regionali della popolazione residente al 2065 (base 1.1.2017)*. Retrieved from https://www.istat.it/it/files//2018/05/previsioni_demografiche.pdf

Kertzer, D. I. (2015). *The Pope and Mussolini: The Secret History of Pius XI and the Rise of Fascism in Europe*. Oxford: Oxford University Press.

King, R. (1978). Report : The Italian Diaspora. *The Royal Geographical Society (with the Institute of British Geographers)*, 10(5), 386.

McMahon, S. (2015). *Immigration and Citizenship in an Enlarged European Union. The Political Dynamics of Intra-EU Mobility* (Palgrave S). London: Palgrave Macmillan.

Morondo Taramundi, D. (2015). *Ripensando alle sentenze Lautsi c. Italia: la libertà religiosa, l'eguaglianza e l'art. 14 della Convenzione*. Bilbao. Unpublished paper kindly provided by the author.

Morucci, C. (2018). I rapporti con l'Islam italiano: dalle proposte d'intesa al Patto nazionale. *Stato, Chiese e Pluralismo Confessionale*, 38, 1–32. Retrieved from https://www.statoechiese.it/images/uploads/articoli_pdf/Morucci.M_I_rapporti.pdf?pdf=i-rapporti-con-lislam-italiano-dalle-proposte-dintesa-al-patto-nazionale

Panara, C. (2011). Lautsi v. Italy: The Display of Religious Symbols by the State. *European Public Law*, 17(1), 139–168.

Pew Research Center. (2018). *Being Christian in Western Europe*. Retrieved from https://www.pewforum.org/2018/05/29/being-christian-in-western-europe/

Pollard, J. (2008). *Catholicism in Modern Italy: Religion, Society and Politics Since 1861*. London and New York: Routledge.

Russo Spena, M. (2010). Muslims in Italy: Models of Integration and New Citizenship. In A. Triandafyllidou (Ed.), *Muslims in 21st Century Europe: Structural and Cultural Perspectives* (pp. 256–287). London: Routledge.

Sealy, T., Magazzini, T., Modood, T., & Triandafyllidou, A. (Forthcoming 2021). Managing Religious Diversity in Europe. In G. Davie & L. Leustan (Eds.), *The Oxford Handbook of Religion in Europe*. Oxford: Oxford University Press.

The Migration Policy Group in coordination with Iniziative e studi sulla multietnicità (ISMU). (2018). *Access to Citizenship and Its Impact on Immigrant Integration. Handbook for Italy*. Retrieved from https://cadmus.eui.eu/bitstream/handle/1814/32271/ACIT_Handbook_Italy_ENGLISH_.pdf?sequence=2&isAllowed=y

Vezzoni, C., & Biolcati-Rinaldi, F. (2015). Church Attendance and Religious Change in Italy, 1968–2010: A Multilevel Analysis of Pooled Datasets. *Journal for the Scientific Study of Religion*, 54(July 2011), 100–118.

Zaccaria, R., Domianello, S., Ferrari, A., Floris, P., & Mazzola, R. (Eds.). (2020). *La legge che non c'è. Proposta per una legge sulla libertà religiosa in Italia*. Bologna: Il Mulino.

7
Spain
All religions are equal, but some are more equal than others

Tina Magazzini

Introduction

Spain constitutes one of Europe's oldest states, yet one that has always been strongly characterized by its multinational, multilinguistic, and multicultural population. It has therefore struggled to reconcile centralization tendencies with the need to recognize and accommodate multiple belongings and overlapping identities and loyalties within one political unit.

It is also a country of recent immigration, which has seen a rapid growth in its Muslim population over the past few decades. Having been heavily hit by the 2008 economic crisis, Spain can offer some pointers and insights to Eastern European states that are currently struggling both with a weaker economy than their Western neighbours, and with immigration as a new phenomenon to be managed.

Despite having witnessed Europe's deadliest terrorist attack in Madrid in 2004 and another attack claimed by the Islamic State of Iraq and Syria (ISIS) in Barcelona in 2017, anti-Muslim sentiment has not found widespread representation in Spanish political parties (Lahnait 2018). Even though a fragmentation of the party system over the past years has made it more difficult to form a stable government, the general elections of 2019 (of both April and November) saw a strong turnout in favour of the socialist party, and while an extreme right-wing party entered Parliament for the first time, it did so by focussing on territorial and gender issues more than on religious or ethnic diversity.

Bearing in mind these issues, the chapter is organized in the following manner: the first section provides the socio-demographic context, followed by an overview of the most pressing challenges regarding religious diversity governance in contemporary Spain. The third section briefly traces the historical developments of Church-State relations in Spain in order to understand the current constitutional and institutional framework. Finally, the conclusions summarize and reflect upon the state of play of Spain's handling of religious diversity, looking at how it has shifted and been addressed differently with respect to different religious minorities.

Socio-demographic context

Emerging from 40 years of dictatorship in 1975, Spain developed plural liberal institutions and joined the European Union one decade later. In parallel with the juridical and political changes, over the past decades the country has also seen important sociological changes in terms of the weakening of religion as a widely shared identity marker, new immigration fluxes arriving from outside the country, and the demographic composition of its population.

Regarding the role of religion in society, in line with Article 16.2 of the Constitution – which postulates that no individual may be compelled to answer questions regarding religion or religious beliefs – no religious affiliation indicator has ever been included in the national census, and therefore no official comprehensive data on religiosity exists. However, the public Spanish Centre for Sociological Research (*Centro de Investigaciones Sociologicas*, henceforth CIS) has been conducting periodic surveys that include a question on religious self-identification since the 1960s.[1] The results of such surveys over the years provide a clear picture of the overall and ongoing process of secularization of Spanish society, even though the question on religiosity was dropped by the CIS for some years during the 1990s (during which one can assume that the trend remained the same, even though, unfortunately, we have no data).

What we can observe from Table 7.1 is that, as is the case in many other Western European countries, religion has significantly declined in terms of the relevance it holds in individuals' daily lives over the past few decades (Pew Research Center 2015, 2018a, 2018b, Magazzini 2021). Despite two-thirds of the Spanish population still identifying as Catholic (if asked to choose between the options in the table), CIS has estimated that of those who self-identify as Catholic, less than 15 per cent attend mass regularly (there is however no systematic data collected on this issue, see Urrutia Asua 2016:124).

Table 7.1 Religious self-identification in Spain (1965–2019)

Year	Catholics (%)	Other religions (%)	Non-believers/atheists (%)	No answer (%)
1965	98	0	2	0
1975	88	0.2	2	4
1985	87	1	11	2
2000	83	2.5	13	1.5
2005	79	2	17	2
2006	77.3	1.7	19.4	1.6
2007	76.7	1.5	19.7	2.1
2008	77.4	1.6	19.3	1.7
2009	77.4	1.7	19	1.8
2010	76.4	1.5	20.2	1.9
2011	74.3	2.6	21.7	1.4
2012	72	2.8	23.3	1.9
2013	72.4	2.3	23.8	1.5
2014	71.5	2.4	24.7	1.3
2015	69.3	1.9	26.3	2.5
2016	71.8	2.5	23.8	2.4
2017	69.8	2.6	25.2	2.4
2018	68.5	2.6	26.4	2.6
2019	67.5	2.9	26.8	2.7

Source: Table based on data available at the CIS open database (http://www.cis.es/cis/opencms/EN/index.html) and in Urrutia Asua (2016, p. 122).

Along with the decline in self-identified Catholics – which almost perfectly matches the increase in those who identify as non-believers or atheists – we observe a slow but steady rise, over the past decades, in those who identify with another (non-Catholic) religion. Such trend is strongly linked to a shift from Spain being mainly a country of emigration to its current status as a country of both emigration and immigration, with the percentage of immigrants residing in Spain growing from under 1 per cent in 1991 to approximately 10 per cent in 2018. Since immigration was virtually an irrelevant issue before the 1990s, the collection of systematic data on foreign residents in Spain is only reliable since then, as it was facilitated by the creation of a 'Foreign Resident ID' official document in 1992 (*Numero de Identificación de Extranjero*, N.I.E.).

The number of Muslims in Spain as of 2020 is estimated at 2,100,000, according to the Islamic Commission of Spain (CIE): 42 per cent have Spanish nationality, 39 per cent are Moroccan nationals, while the rest are migrants from other African countries (Algeria, Senegal, Nigeria, Mali) and from Pakistan and Bangladesh. These percentages are approximations based on the number of foreign nationals residing in Spain and the number of naturalizations of foreign nationals from predominantly Muslim countries over the past 20 years (*Unión de Comunidades Islámicas de España* (UCIDE) 2020) (Table 7.2).

Table 7.2 Changes in total population and percentage of foreign residents in Spain (1991–2018)

Year	Total population	Foreign residents	%
1991	38,872,268	360,655	0.9
1996	39,878,880	542,314	1.4
1998	40,303,568	637,086	1.6
2000	40,499,790	923,879	2.3
2002	41,837,894	1,977,947	4.73
2004	42,372,689	2,963,838	7.02
2006	43,516,505	4,012,765	9.27
2008	44,723,411	5,063,755	11.4
2010	45,283,064	5,440,232	12.2
2012	47,265,321	5,736,258	12.1
2014	47,171,105	5,023,487	10.7
2016	46,347,576	4,618,581	9.9
2017	46,354,321	4,572,807	9.8
2018	46,397,452	4,734,691	9.9

Source: Data based on the Spanish Statistical Office (Instituto Nacional de Estadistica, INE), available at https://www.ine.es/

While no disaggregated data exists with regard to the differences in religious affiliation between nationals and non-nationals, some cues can be taken by looking at the main countries of origin of immigrants and the distribution and development of places of worship in the Spanish territory over the past years.[2] The 'Worship places directory' compiled by the Observatory of Religious Pluralism, lists 7,248 places of worship,[3] most of which are situated in large urban settings (Barcelona, Madrid, Valencia) (Figure 7.1).

It is interesting to note how the number of places of worship present on the territory does not necessarily reflect the legal status or recognition of the confession in the Spanish system: for instance, while very few synagogues (39) are registered, the Spanish Federation of Jewish Communities is among the few to have a legal agreement with the State (Law 25/1992, more on this below) (Figure 7.2).

Spain

Figure 7.1 The Worship Places Directory compiled by the Observatory of Religious Pluralism.
Source: The Directory is a tool for the identification and spatial location of the places of worship of the different religious confessions in the Spain. The data is gathered from three sources: the Registry of Religious Entities of the Ministry of Justice; researched carried out by the Pluralism and Coexistence Foundation; and requests for registration, cancellation or modification of data communicated by representatives of religious communities. Available at http://www.observatorioreligion.es/directorio-lugares-de-culto/

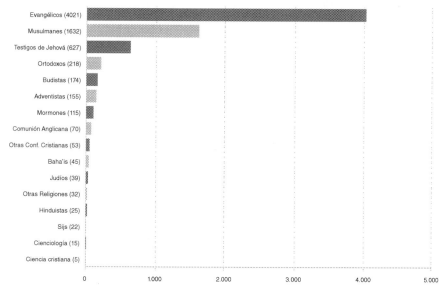

Figure 7.2 List of worship places by confession (excluded Catholic churches) in Spain in 2019.
Source: Data collected by the Observatory for Religious Pluralism. Available at: http://www.observatorioreligion.es/directorio-lugares-de-culto/index_graficos.php

Regarding the main countries of origin of migrant communities residing in Spain, most newcomers have arrived from other European member states, North Africa, and Latin America. It should, however, be noted that migrants from Latin America can access Spanish citizenship after two years of continuous residence (while naturalization otherwise takes ten years), and once they naturalize, they disappear from the statistics on migration. Therefore, while according to the Spanish Statistical Office the main countries of origin of immigrants to Spain over the past years have been Morocco and Romania, followed by Colombia, the UK and Italy, Latin American communities are significantly underrepresented in the statistics; if it weren't for the naturalization rate (Marín et al. 2015:19), Colombia would lead the statistics (Figure 7.3).

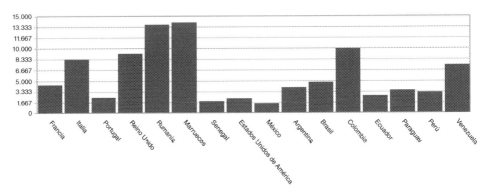

Figure 7.3 Number of foreign citizens residing in Spain grouped by country of origin in 2016.

Main trends and challenges

Regardless of the specific numbers, which are difficult to capture given the lack of religious indicators in the census, the diversification of the Spanish population as the result of immigration has brought with it both a revival of Catholicism from Latin American migrants (García 2005:232–37) and the need to recognize and accommodate 'new' religious practices and beliefs, particularly Islam, practised by migrants coming from North Africa, in an increasingly secularized society. Although it can be said that, in general terms, Spain allows anyone to freely exercise any religion, the main challenges in terms of respect for religious freedom existing in the country nowadays have to do with the practice of religion by – generally migrant – minority groups. These consist, in practical terms, of obstacles in accessing public spaces faced by minority groups and in the unequal application of legal rights: as a number of scholars and stakeholders have noted, there are significant incoherencies and regional variations in the allocation of places of worship, of public lots for religious cemeteries, in the recognition of religious public demonstrations, and in the accommodation of religious claims in hospitals and prisons (Griera and Martínez-Ariño 2017; Ruiz Vieytez 2019; interview, Religious Pluralism Observatory, April 2019). For instance, despite the equality principle enshrined in Article 14 of the Constitution, several Spanish cities have witnessed, over the past years, conflicts over the construction of mosques. In many instances local politicians have struggled to manage and appease the hostility of some of their constituencies over the construction of non-Catholic places of worship, resulting in controversies and discriminatory practices; difficulties encountered in opening or maintaining religion centres or places of worship is currently the most widespread complaint from minority religious communities in terms of exercising their right to religious freedom in Spain (Estruch et al. 2007; Moreras 2017; Urrutia Asua 2016). On top of the issues related to gaining access to real estate in an often hostile market, many religious communities have denounced administrative regulations and practices that have had the effect of significantly hindering the right to establish places of worship for members of any religious community.[4]

Regulations on this matter have somewhat improved after the reforms introduced through Law 27/2013, on the Streamlining and Sustainability of Local Administration, which, in line with the Services Directive (2006/123/EC), eliminated the need to obtain a licence in order to establish a new centre of worship. Despite this improvement, administrative practices at the municipal level continue to change between cities and regions, with different (and at times contradictory) interpretations being put forward, thus generating legal insecurity.

Another serious issue is that of discriminatory treatment by the State towards clerics of confessions other than the Catholic Church with respect to the access to social security and to retirement benefits. In practice, priests and clerics of the Catholic Church are ensured retirement benefits and access to social security, which is paid for by the government, but the same is not true for other confessions. The European Court of Human Rights established that this is tantamount to discriminatory treatment of clerics of confessions other than the Catholic Church since it is not objectively or reasonably justified[5] (Moreras 2017; Ruiz Vieytez 2012).

Moreover, due to the lack of institutional and social norms and practices properly adapted from the Catholic Church model to other religious institutions and communities, people belonging to minority religious groups often lack information and access to procedures such as the regional ombudsman and the judicial system. For this reason, the relatively low number of complaints or judicial cases regarding discrimination based on religious grounds should not be interpreted as a sign that there are no problems in the implementation of the right to religious liberty.

Regarding the wearing of religious symbols in public spaces (such as the *hijab* or the *kippah*), an issue that has been highly visible and contentious in some other European countries, in Spain the educational institutions have the authority to decide on dress code. This is due to a legal vacuum on this issue which has left the matter to the arbitrariness of each institute (Ruiz Vieytez 2019:19; Unión de Comunidades Islámicas de España (UCIDE) 2013). However, in cases in which female students dropped out of school because of the school's ban on wearing the headscarf, the authorities have demanded their readmission based on the reasoning that the constitutional right to education supercedes the internal school regulations.

An historical overview of religious governance: a multi-tier system

The developments in Spain's constitutional history and in Spanish society more broadly are strongly intertwined with the history of the relationship between the Catholic Church and the State.

From its state-building process until recently, Spain has been a confessional state with Catholicism as the state religion. Born out of religious struggles mainly between Catholicism and Islam, the first written mention of the 'Spanish nation' is to be found in Alonso de Santa Cruz's *Crónica de los Reyes Católicos* (1491–1516). The Spanish Inquisition, under direct control of the Spanish monarchy,[6] was voted down by the Cortes of Cadiz in 1812, and only completely abolished in 1834. The 1812 'Constitution of Cadiz' was the first Spanish legislature that issued a liberal Constitution but asserted Roman Catholicism as the only official legal religion in Spain and outlawed all the others. Subsequent Constitutions (1837, 1845,

1876) followed in the same footsteps, maintaining no separation between State and Catholic Church; in 1851, the Spanish government signed a Concordat with the Holy See through which Catholicism was asserted as the state religion. The Concordat – which committed Spain to pay the salaries of the clergy as well as other expenses of the Catholic Church – was renounced in 1931 by the Second Spanish Republic with its secular Constitution. This was the first measure to ever establish a strict separation between religious and government affairs in Spain, and even though the 1931 Constitution accorded broad civil liberties, it was criticized as anticlerical and oppressive by the Catholic Church. The political polarization and the Civil War that ensued became strongly entrenched along religious lines, with the Catholic Church supporting the uprising of Francisco Franco in 1936 (Urrutia Asua 2016), which was presented as necessary to preserve the role of the Catholic Church (Pérez-Díaz 1993:162–68; Suárez Pertierra 2006:18–22; Urrutia Asua 2016:118).

Under Franco's dictatorship (1939–1975), 'National Catholicism' (*Nacional-catolicismo*) represented one on the main tenets of the government's ideological identity. This not only meant that the Catholic Church's privileges – state subsidies, tax exemptions, censorship of materials deemed as offensive – were restored and that Catholicism was re-established yet again as the only religion with legal status, but also that the role of the church in both private and public life reached its peak, with compulsory Catholic instruction in public schools, restriction of sexual rights, and so on, sanctioned by the 1953 new Concordat.[7]

Francoist Spain's National Catholicism has been described in these terms:

> A Catholic state is the same as a confessional state. A confessional state does not mean that the instruments of government should be absorbed by religion, or that the state will be run by the clergy and the positions of the civil servants taken by priests. It basically means that the state as such, its codes, laws and institutions abide by God's commandments and the laws of the Church, so that she can dedicate to spread the reign of God on Earth. A confessional state means having the cross and receiving religious education at school; it means recognizing the sacred nature of marriage between Catholics, and the religious status of the cemeteries.
>
> *(Colom González 2017:84)*

While the 1960s saw some slight openings with the Second Vatican Council of 1965, it was not until Franco's death in 1975 that a gradual separation between the Catholic Church and the Spanish State could be agreed upon in a new treaty.

Since 1978, with the current democratic Constitution, Spain is a secular but not secularist state, meaning that while public authorities are expected to be independent of ecclesiastical structures, they are however mandated to ensure that religious freedom is achieved, including the freedom to express and exercise one's faith publicly. The only restrictions that may be adopted regarding the right to religious freedom relate to public security and with the principle of no harm to others.[8]

The principles of freedom of religion and of a secular state are enshrined in Article 16 of the Constitution, which reads:

> 16.1: Freedom of ideology, religion and worship is guaranteed to individuals and communities, with no other restriction on their expression than may be necessary to maintain public order as protected by law.
> 16.2: No one may be compelled to make statements regarding his or her ideology, religion or beliefs.

16.3: There shall be no State religion. The public authorities shall take the religious beliefs of Spanish society into account and shall consequently maintain appropriate cooperation with the Catholic Church and the other confessions.

(Boletín Oficial del Estado (BOE) 1978)

The regulations that operationalize such principles are contained in the Spanish Organic Law 7/1980 on Religious Freedom and in the Cooperation Agreements stipulated between the Spanish State and specific confessional institutions which will be detailed below.

In addition, Article 9.2 of the Spanish Constitution entrusts public authorities with the responsibility to promote conditions 'ensuring that freedom and equality of individuals and of the groups to which they belong are real and effective, to remove the obstacles preventing or hindering their full enjoyment, and to facilitate the participation of all citizens in political, economic, cultural and social life'; and Article 14 prohibits discrimination based on ideological or religious grounds.

Current regulatory and constitutional framework

The main feature of the current regulatory framework concerns the fact that the Spanish legal system provides different types of recognition and collaboration agreements with different religions.

Spain's shift to a governance model with no state religion attempted to reconcile the Catholic Church's traditional privileges with secular and democratic constitutional principles. This resulted in a special treatment that is made explicit in Article 16.3 of the 1978 Constitution, which singles out the Catholic Church by requiring the State to cooperate with it (Souto Paz 2001). Such cooperation is regulated by four Agreements signed in 1979 between the Spanish State and the Holy See, and which replaced the 1953 Concordat. The agreements cover (a) legal matters; (b) educational and cultural matters; (c) economic matters; and (d) religious assistance in the armed forces and the military service of the clergy, and were incorporated into Spanish law as international treaties.[9]

The same constitutional provision, Article 16.3, also establishes that '[T]he public authorities shall take the religious beliefs of Spanish society into account and shall consequently maintain appropriate cooperation with the Catholic Church *and the other confessions*'. It has been argued that, by grouping all 'other confessions', the very system established to govern religious diversity and allow for a plurality of beliefs in the public sphere is at the basis of inequality between religious groups (Ruiz Vieytez 2019).

In regulatory terms, given that the Catholic Church had already signed the Agreements with the State as a privileged interlocutor in 1979, the 1980 Organic Law on Religious Freedom – which implements the constitutional provision for freedom of religion – focussed on other religious groups. Such law establishes the right to (a) profess any religious belief; (b) take part in the liturgy in one's own faith, celebrate religious festivities, hold marriage ceremonies, and receive decent burial; (c) choose religious and moral education in keeping with one's own convictions; and (d) assemble publicly for religious purposes and form associations to undertake religious activities (Article 2, Law 24/1992, 10 November 1992).

In implementing these rights, the Organic Law established a legal regime and certain privileges for religious organizations. The enjoyment of the benefits of this regime, however, is conditional (based on Article 7) upon religious organizations being entered in the Register of Religious Entities maintained by the General Directorate of Religious Affairs of the Ministry of Justice.[10]

In addition to being included in the General Directorate of Religious Affairs, cooperation agreements with the State require that a confession be deemed as being 'socially rooted' or 'clearly established' in the Spanish territory (*notorio arraigo* in Spanish),[11] which is defined as having 'influence in Spanish society, due to their domain or number of followers' (Article 7, Organic Law 7/1980).

Based on this principle, three cooperation agreements between the State and other confessions – namely, the Spanish Federation of Religious Evangelical Entities (FEREDE), the Spanish Federation of Jewish Communities (FJCE), and the Spanish Islamic Commission (CIE) – were reached and approved one decade later. They were codified in laws 24/1992 (Evangelical federation), 25/1992 (Jewish federation), and 26/1992 (Muslim federation) respectively, all passed on 10 November 1992.

These three agreements are treated as ordinary positive law emanating from the Parliament and entail a wide-range series of religious accommodation practices. While still not having the same privileges granted to the Catholic Church (which does not need to be registered in the General Directorate of Religious Affairs of the Ministry of Justice; enjoys a more favourable economic regime, and benefits from long-established institutions),[12] these provisions marked a significant improvement for members of Evangelical, Muslim, and Jewish communities in 1992.

It should however be noted that the fact that the three Agreements present uniform standards in their scope, content, and wording constitutes a limitation and shows that the degree of participation on behalf of the religious minorities in shaping such agreements was, in fact, restricted. While all religious groups share certain necessities with respect to the freedom to practise their belief in the public space, different religious beliefs face different problems and require different solutions. The standardized approach to all non-Catholic religious communities suggests therefore that the government opted for granting generic rights, rather than seriously engaging in negotiation processes that would have led to differentiated bilateral agreements. Such an interpretation is coherent with the fact that in the early 1990s, when the State concluded these three Cooperation Agreements, there was significant institutional pressure to avoid signing multiple and different legal commitments specific to each religious community (Relaño Pastor 2016). The Spanish government therefore opted to engage in fewer agreements with broader federations of denominations rather than a larger number of agreements with individual religious groups. This has the advantage, from the state's perspective, of reducing the number of interlocutors and thus the number of administrative, legal, and political issues to accommodate. However, it does not take into account the different needs and agendas of the diverse groups within the large federations that legally comprise one denomination.[13]

Beyond the Jewish, Muslim, and Evangelical communities, another four religious groups have been acknowledged to date as 'clearly established' in the country, which allows them to participate in the Advisory Commission on Religious Freedom.[14] These are the Church of Jesus Christ of Latter-day Saints (2003), Christian Jehovah's Witnesses (2006), the Federation of Buddhist Entities of Spain (2007), and the Orthodox Church (2010). Such recognition does not automatically entitle them to enter an agreement with the State that would afford them similar rights, economic or otherwise, to those confessions who already have one – but it is a step in that direction.

Beyond specific agreements with individual religious communities, a number of laws apply to all religions: these are the 1980 Organic Law on Religious Freedom; the Royal Decree 932/2013, through which the Commission on Religious Freedom is regulated; and the Royal Decree 593/2015, which regulates the principle of 'social rootedness'. The 1980

Religious Freedom Law Act provided an important legal basis leading to a period of significant expansion of religious minority rights in the 1980s and 1990s; however, this framework has not been revised to keep up with the changes of an increasingly diverse society, nor has there been a reckoning about the privileges afforded to the Catholic religious tradition (Camarero Suárez 2006). The differential treatment provided by institutional arrangements to the Catholic majority, to religious minorities and to a growing non-religious population, continues therefore to pose issues that have to do with equality of recognition and access to the public arena:

> This operates at several levels that affect the recognition of the various religious denominations and their funding. But it also poses some problems in the exercise of freedom of conscience by non-believers when their public processions or demonstrations are unreasonably and disproportionately banned in comparison with those of the Catholic tradition. The same can be said about the symbols that still persist in many public institutions in various spheres. […] [T]he question of discrimination based on religious parameters remains open and becomes more substantial as Spanish society is also increasingly diverse in this area. It seems clear that the conditions for the exercise of this fundamental right are substantially different by virtue of this unequal public treatment which does not always appear to be entirely based on sociological or legal grounds.
>
> *(Ruiz Vieytez 2019:13–14)*

The recognition of the various religious groups by the State and the positionality in five different levels of the various religious communities within the current Spanish system can be defined as a multi-tiered system and is summarized in Table 7.3.

Table 7.3 Spain's multi-tier system of legal recognition for different confessions

Level of recognition	Legal basis for different treatment	Confession	Legal status of the relationship	Church/body engaging in dialogue
1	Constitution, Art. 16.3: specific reference	Catholics	international treaties	Roman Catholic Church
2	Clearly well-established (socially rooted) + Agreement with the State	Muslims Jews Evangelicals	Agreements + Laws	CIE (Muslim) FJCE (Jewish) FEREDE (Evangelical)
3	Clearly well-established (socially rooted) (without Agreement)	Mormons Jehova's witnesses Buddhists Orthodox	Recognition of being well-established/ socially rooted	Respective federations
4	Official Registration	Many	Register of Religious Entities[15]	Each registered community
5	No registration	Rest of communities	–	–

Source: Table in Ruiz Vieytez, E. (2019), The Spanish Observatory of Religious Pluralism: the challenge of fostering accommodation through information, dissemination and research activities, p. 12 (unpublished paper provided by the author).

With respect to issues of religious presence and assistance in the armed forces, hospitals, and prisons, the legal system's transformations often have not been accompanied by corresponding changes in public policies (Griera and Martinez-Arino 2017:256–57). In practical terms, despite the legal recognition of the right of religious minorities to religious assistance in public institutions, no policy measure was taken to operationalize such right for over a decade.

A positive change in this direction was marked by the creation, in 2004, of the Pluralism and Coexistence Foundation (*Fundacion Pluralismo y Convivencia*) under the Ministry of Justice, to promote religious freedom and the inclusion of religious practices in the agenda of diversity management. Beyond offering economic and logistical support to officially recognized denominations, the Foundation set up the Observatory of Religious Pluralism in 2011 to study and share best practices in religious accommodation. Through information, research, and the development of guidelines and technical advice, the Foundation provides guidance to public administrations in the implementation of management models consistent with the constitutional principles and regulatory framework that govern the exercise of the right to religious freedom in Spain. Yet, as noted by the Vice-Director of the Foundation (who is also Technical Director of the Observatory of Religious Pluralism):

> [D]espite this legal system being fairly inclusive with minorities, the mechanisms adopted for ensuring its implementation were extremely weak. The Spanish legal framework was originally designed in a top-down manner and left little room for the participation of other actors, making its implementation quite difficult. One of the biggest difficulties is that, ultimately, it is the local and municipal administrations who are charged with the responsibility of accommodating minorities; and yet, they are provided no budget by the government for it.
> *(Interview, Pluralism and Coexistence Foundation, April 2019)*

Concluding remarks

Since the democratic transition, the institutionalized pattern of Church-State relations in Spain has evolved significantly. In 1980, the Religious Freedom Act was passed, codifying freedom of thought and religion and defining the procedures by which the State might protect the individual and collective rights of religious minorities (Boletín Oficial del Estado (BOE) 1980). Four decades later, the main challenge is that despite this legal system being fairly inclusive with minorities, the mechanisms adopted for ensuring its implementation have been extremely weak. This results in a significant differentiation in the right that different religious communities can exercise in practice. Such differences between religions are rooted in historical legacies, and even though Spain maintains a neutral position in religious matters (there is no official state religion), the official state neutrality is challenged by the practice of a disproportionately privileged treatment in favour of the Catholic Church.

As noted by Ruiz Vieytez (2019), among others, society's increasing secularization and the rise of religious diversity as a result of migration flows make the issue of a fair religious diversity governance increasingly salient. The contemporary Spanish legal system provides a relatively strong guarantee of freedom of religion; yet, the main limitations and unsatisfied demands regarding religious minorities often perceived them as 'foreign' or 'non-national'. Despite demographic evolutions (that is, a notable increase in Spain's Muslim population) the Catholic Church still occupies a powerful position as the majority religion: disentangling national identity from that of Catholicism remains a work in progress.

Notes

1 The question asked by the CIS surveys on religious self-identification does not offer respondents the possibility of specifying an alternative religious community with which they may identify. The question has not changed over the years, and remains the following: 'How do you define yourself in religious matters: Catholic, believer of another religion (other than Catholicism), non-believer or atheist?' (in Spanish '¿*Cómo se define Ud. en materia religiosa: católico/a, creyente de otra religión, no creyente o ateo/a?*')
2 The Observatory of Religious Pluralism, a research institute and knowledge transfer tool for the public management of religious diversity created in 2011 by a public foundation called Pluralism and Coexistence (*Pluralismo y Convivencia*), has developed a 'Worship place directory' where it is possible to map all existing and registered worship places by confession and by region in the country. The directory is available at http://www.observatorioreligion.es/directorio-lugares-de-culto/
3 Catholic Churches are not included in the map as there are so many of them that it would render the rest of the data impossible to read.
4 For instance, the 2012 urban planning for the city of Bilbao (*Plan General de Ordenación Urbana*) forbade the establishment of any new non-Catholic worship sites in residential buildings to avoid conflicts with residents who had complained about mosques generating noise or disturbance. Such Plan was revoked in November 2014 as the result of an appeal to the Court of Justice but is far from being an isolated case. To date, the most progressive regional autonomy is Catalunya, which has seen both the most progressive implementation of religious accommodation and the most legal cases being brought against the establishment of mosques (Relaño Pastor 2016; interview, Religious Pluralism Observatory, April 2019).
5 See ECHR, Judgement of 3 April 2013, *Manzanas Marin vs. Spain*, Application no. 17966/10.
6 While Catholicism represented a main pillar of Spain's colonial empire during its so-called Golden Age, the Spanish monarchy insisted on its independence from the Pope. Bishops in the Spanish domains were forbidden to report to the Pope except through the Spanish crown, and in 1767 Carlos III expelled the Jesuits from their Spanish empire, accusing the congregation of having promoted the Esquilache Riots of 1766.
7 Based on the 1953 Concordat, Franco secured the right to appoint bishops in Spain.
8 Even when such limitations are called into cause, the Spanish system requires public authorities to evaluate each specific case following the principle of proportionality (since only minimal restrictions can be imposed on fundamental freedoms).
9 The agreements that currently regulate the relationship of the State with the Catholic Church are, in addition to the Agreements of 1979, the Agreement of 1976 between the Holy See and the Spanish State and the Agreement of 1994 between the Holy See and the Kingdom of Spain on matters of common interest in the Holy Land (see https://www.religlaw.org/content/religlaw/documents/agrsphs1976.htm).
10 The register, established in 1981, is updated regularly, and the norm that regulates its entries was updated in 2015 with Law 594 of 3 July 2015 (available here: https://www.boe.es/diario_boe/txt.php?id=BOE-A-2015-8643).
11 Being considered 'socially rooted' in Spanish society is an indispensable prerequisite for any religious group to reach an agreement of cooperation with the State. The definition of the requirements and the procedure for the obtaining of the '*notorio arraigo*' is regulated by Royal Decree 593/2015. The requirements that the confession must meet are:
   (a) To be registered in the Registry of Religious Entities for 30 years;
   (b) Demonstrate a presence in at least ten Autonomous Communities or the Cities of Ceuta and Melilla;
   (c) One hundred entities and/or places of worship registered in the Registry of Religious Entities;
   (d) Possess an adequate structure and representation;
   (e) Presence and active participation in Spanish society.
12 For instance, the government income tax form includes a box that allows taxpayers to assign 0.5 per cent of their taxes to the Catholic Church. A taxpayer who chooses not to assign a share of his or her taxes to the Catholic Church can only choose 'social associations' as an alternative.
13 The Islamic Commission of Spain (CIE) is made up of two federations of Muslim communities, both of which have 50 per cent representation. Because the CIE is the organ that interacts with the State, the lack of understanding between these two federations has resulted in significant obstacles to the implementation of the 1992 agreement.
14 Article 8 of the Organic Law of Religious Freedom established the creation of the Religious Freedom Advisory Commission under the Ministry of Justice. The Commission has the powers to

study, report, and propose on any issue related to the application of the Organic Law 7/1980. It also has competence over the preparation of cooperation agreements with other religious Confessions on which it can express a binding opinion; additionally, at the justice ministry's request, it can advocate for the registration of Religious Entities in the official State Registry.
15 The registration of a Religious Entity into the Directory of Religious Entities maintained by the Spanish Ministry of Justice carries no legal consequence, in that it affords the registered religion no preferencial treatment nor access to those rights afforded to those religions that are deemed '-well-established'. Registration into the government's Directory is however a prerequisite to access the status of 'well-established', together with the need to prove the religion's 'rootedness' in the territory (by number of followers over the years).

References

Boletín Oficial del Estado (BOE). 1978. *Constitución Española*. Madrid.
Boletín Oficial del Estado (BOE). 1980. *Ley Organica 7/1980, de 5 de Julio, de Libertad Religiosa*. Madrid.
Camarero Suárez, Marita. 2006. "La Comisión Asesora de Libertad Religiosas." Pp. 233–45 in *La libertad religiosa en España: XXV años de vigencia de la Ley Orgánica 7/1980, de 5 de julio*, edited by A. C. Álvarez Cortina and M. Rodríguez Blanco. Madrid: Comares.
Colom González, Francisco. 2017. "Political Catholicism and the Secular State: A Spanish Predicament." Pp. 77–91 in *Multireligious Society: Dealing with Religious Diversity in Theory and Practice*. London/New York: Routledge, Taylor & Francis Group.
Estruch, Joan, Joan Gómez i Segalà, Maria del Mar Griera, and Agustí Iglesias. 2007. *Las Otras Religiones. Minorías Religiosas En Cataluña*. 2nd ed. Barcelona: Icaria Editorial. Pluralismo y convivencia.
García, Paola. 2005. "La Inmigración: Un Nuevo Reto Para La Iglesia Católica Española." *Anuario Americanista Europeo* 3(La migración transatlántica. Fuentes, fondos y colecciones):225–59.
Griera, Mar and Julia Martínez-Ariño. 2017. "The Accommodation of Religious Diversity in Prisons and Hospitals in Spain." Pp. 251–66 in *Multireligious Society: Dealing with Religious Diversity in Theory and Practice*, edited by F. Colom Gonzalez and G. D'Amato. London/New York: Routledge, Taylor & Francis Group.
Lahnait, Fatima. 2018. "Preventing Violent Extremism to Counter Home-Grown Jihadism: Learning by Doing." Pp. 41–53 in *Revisiting the Barcelona Attacks: Reaction, Explanations and Pending Discussions*, edited by M. Bourekba. London: CIDOB Report, no. 2.
Magazzini, T. 2021. "The Italian case. 'Baptised laicità' and a changing demographic." Pp. 59-73 in Routledge Handbook on the Governance of Religious Diversity, edited by A. Triandafyllidou and T. Magazzini. London/New York: Routledge, Taylor & Francis Group.
Marín, Ruth Rubio, Irene Sobrino, Alberto Martín Pérez, and Francisco Javier Moreno Fuentes. 2015. *Country Report on Citizenship Law: Spain*. Florence: EUDO Citizenship Observatory. https://cadmus.eui.eu/bitstream/handle/1814/34480/EUDO_CIT_2015_04-Spain.pdf;sequence=1
Moreras, Jordi. 2017. *La Gobernanza de Conflictos Relacionados Con La Pluralidad Religiosa*. Madrid: Observatorio del Pluralismo Religioso en España.
Pérez-Díaz, Victor M. 1993. *The Return of Civil Society: The Emergence of Democratic Spain*. Cambridge, MA: Harvard University Press.
Pew Research Center. 2015. *The Future of World Religions: Population Growth Projections, 2010–2050*. https://assets.pewresearch.org/wp-content/uploads/sites/11/2015/03/PF_15.04.02_ProjectionsFullReport.pdf
Pew Research Center. 2018a. *Being Christian in Western Europe*. https://assets.pewresearch.org/wp-content/uploads/sites/11/2015/03/PF_15.04.02_ProjectionsFullReport.pdf
Pew Research Center. 2018b. *Eastern and Western Europeans Differ on Importance of Religion, Views of Minorities, and Key Social Issues*. https://assets.pewresearch.org/wp-content/uploads/sites/11/2015/03/PF_15.04.02_ProjectionsFullReport.pdf
Relaño Pastor, Eugenia. 2016. *Religious Diversity in Spain*. Unpublished paper kindly provided by the author.
Ruiz Vieytez, Eduardo Javier. 2012. *Las Prácticas de Armonización Como Instrumento de Gestión Pública de La Diversidad Religiosa*. Madrid: Observatorio del Pluralismo Religioso en España. Available at http://www.observatorioreligion.es/upload/56/11/Las_practicas_de_armonizacion.pdf.
Ruiz Vieytez, Eduardo Javier. 2019. "The Spanish Observatory of Religious Pluralism: The Challenge of Fostering Accommodation through Information, Dissemination and Research Activities." Pp. 1–38. Unpublished paper kindly provided by the author.

Souto Paz, José Antonio. 2001. "La Laicidad En La Constitución de 1978." Pp. 215–28 in *Estado y religión. Proceso de secularización y laicidad. Homenaje de don Fernando de los Ríos*, edited by Ó. Celador Angón. Madrid: Universidad Carlos III.

Suárez Pertierra, Gustavo. 2006. "La Ley Orgánica de Libertad Religiosa, 25 Años Después." Pp. 45–58 in *La nueva realidad religiosa española: 25 años de la Ley orgánica de libertad religiosa*. Madrid: Ministerio de Justicia.

Unión de Comunidades Islámicas de España (UCIDE). 2013. *Informe Especial 2012. Istitución Para La Observación y Seguimiento de La Situación Del Ciudadano Musulmán y La Islamofobia En España*. Madrid.

Unión de Comunidades Islámicas de España (UCIDE). 2020. *Estudio Demográfico de La Población Musulmana. Explotación Estadistica Del Censo de Ciudadanos Musulmanes En España Referido a Fecha 31/12/2019*. Madrid.

Urrutia Asua, Gorka. 2016. *Minorías Religiosas y Derechos Humanos. Reconocimiento Social y Gestión Pública Del Pluralismo Religioso En El País Vasco*. Madrid: Ediciones Akal.

8

Greece

The 'prevailing religion' and the governance of diversity

Eda Gemi

Introduction

For Greeks religion plays a fundamental role in defining the national identity. In historical terms, national ideology and Orthodoxy (alongside language and ancestry) shaped what is known as membership in the Greek nation (Tsitselikis, 2012: 8). What is more, the attachment to Orthodoxy as the key element of the national identity formation makes it difficult to draw a distinction between Greek ethnicity and religiosity (Halikiopoulou, 2011). Such historical and political contingencies have forged a genuine model of religious governance whereby Orthodoxy has an especially prominent place in the public sphere and in dominant citizenship discourse (Fokas, 2012: 403).

In addition, the historical legacy linked to the nature of nation formation in the Balkans that has generated the dominant nationalistic discourse, coupled with the extremely strained relations with neighbouring countries and the co-existence with ethnic minorities on either side of the borders, has diachronically shaped the Greek approach to ethnic and religious differences. Apparently, the 'historical anxiety' of the Greek state fuelled by traditional tensions in the Balkans led to the gradual minoritization and nationalization of the 'Other' (Baltsiotis, 2011:18) – a process that resulted in either its compulsory assimilation or its exclusion from the Greek nation-state and its political community. In this context, Greek national identity has been historically constructed in opposition to a religious 'Other' and the Muslim one in particular. Hence, Muslim populations belonging either to 'Old Islam' (the Muslim minority living in Thrace) or 'New Islam' (recent migrants) have been historically identified with Turkey and the Turks (Hatziprokopiou and Evergeti, 2014).

However, while the Orthodox Church is viewed as tolerant towards diversity, it persistently retains its privileged position as a national church which is clearly embedded in the legal order. Interestingly, despite the fact that religious freedom is safeguarded by the Constitution, Orthodoxy remains the 'prevailing' religion in Greece. This privileged position of the Church of Greece gives it the right to have a say in the activities of all 'known religions' and other state affairs such as the curriculum and textbooks for religious education in the school curriculum and morning prayer in Greek schools.

Although Greece has a long experience in managing the Islamic religious institutions due to the historical presence of 'Old Islam', it has been very reluctant to provide equal religious rights to the 'New Islam'. The reason appears to lie in the strong view of Greece as a Christian Orthodox nation, where the presence of Islam is perceived as a rival cultural element that could potentially threaten and destabilize the homogeneity of the Greek 'ethnos' (Skoulariki, 2010: 302). It is not coincidental that a recent survey by the Pew Research Center (2018) found that three-quarters of Greeks consider being Orthodox Christian important to being truly Greek, while almost 90 percent of respondents said Greek culture was superior to other cultures (2018: 6).

Co-ethnics from the former Soviet Union and Albania along with immigrants coming mostly from Islamic countries (that is, Pakistan) account for more than 9 percent of the total resident population (MIP, 2019). A notable increase since 2015 in asylum seeker and undocumented migrant arrivals from the Middle East, Asia, and Africa via Turkey coincided with the economic recession and political crisis, and rise of extreme right political forces. The rejection of the religious 'other' is at the core of the racist ideology articulated by the neo-Nazi Golden Dawn party. Meanwhile, the increase in racist attacks against refugees and migrants recorded in 2018 denotes that intolerance in Greece is on the rise (RVRN, 2019).

This chapter provides for a critical overview of Greek state-religion relations and the prevalent approach to governing religious diversity in Greece. It is based on both desk research and field work conducted between February and March 2019. This involved interviews with seven key informants, including experts and representatives of the three largest Muslim associations operating in Greater Athens.

This chapter is organized in three sections. It begins with a brief overview of the country's profile in terms of the human geography of religious communities in Greece. The second section elaborates on the historical background of state-organized religion relations while examining how the governance of religious diversity and tolerance has shaped the legal and institutional framework in Greece. The final section discusses the regulation of religious courses in the public education system and overall religious affairs.

Human geography of religion communities

Greece is considered a demographically homogeneous country. The two fundamental elements that support the fabric of ethnic homogeneity are found in the population's common language and religion (Greek Orthodox) (Anagnostopoulos, 2017). As the 'prevailing religion' by virtue of Article 3 of the Constitution, the Eastern Orthodox Church of Christ is a legal entity of public law. In demographic terms, it is estimated that the population of 10.8 million is 81–90 percent Greek Orthodox, 2 percent Muslim, 4 percent atheist, and 0.7 percent other religions (U.S. Department of State, 2019b: 3). Among the religious communities, Muslims are the largest, followed by Roman Catholics and the Jewish community.

The Muslim population consists of two legal categories. The first is Greek citizens and belongs to a traditional religious minority while enjoying special legal status on the basis of an 'historical settlement' ('Old Islam') (Tsitselikis, 2012: 535). The second includes foreigners who are not Greek citizens and have the legal status of aliens (αλλοδαπός) ('New Islam'). The two groups represent diametrically different cases that make Greece perhaps the only European Union member state where Islam is configured in these two forms (Tsitselikis, 2012: 19).

Greece's Muslim minority, 'Old Islam', is protected under the Treaty of Athens (1913), the Treaty of Sevres (1920), and the Treaty of Lausanne (1923). It embraces a number of distinct communities, including some 100,000–120,000 individuals living in Thrace and descending from the Muslim minority officially recognized by the Lausanne treaty: 50 percent are of Turkish origin, 35 percent Pomak, and 15 percent Roma (Anagnostopoulos, 2017: 104). Each group has its own unique cultural background – for instance, Pomaks are mostly Sunni Muslims and are considered slavophone Islamized Greeks – with religion the only common element.

The Muslim minority of Western Thrace has its own religious institutions, including approximately 290 mosques and minority schools (both regulated by the Greek state), several associations and unions, and full civil and political rights. These are, however, territorially confined to the Thrace region which means that when members of Thracian Muslim minority move to Athens (or elsewhere) they lose the legal access to provisions and rights attached to their status. Muslims also enjoy a judicial system known as 'sharia law', which has created controversies with the constitutional law because of its conflicting interpretation in relation to gender equality and other provisions and conventions on human rights (Anagnostopoulos, 2017: 114).

With respect to 'New Islam', according to the Ministry of Immigration Policy statistics (MIP, 2019), migrants from South and Southeast Asia, the Middle East, and North Africa represent 10 percent of the total immigrant population in Greece. They are mostly staying in the country as immigrants and asylum seekers, while living in clustered ethnic communities in either urban centres or reception facilities (U.S. Department of State, 2019a: 3). According to interviewees, some 150,000–200,000 Muslim migrants from South Asia, Southeast Asia, the Middle East, and North Africa reside mostly in the Greater Athens area and its western suburbs. Their number has been swelled by the refugee crisis in the mid-2010s, with Asylum Service data (March 2019) recording 62,418 asylum seekers, mainly from Muslim countries.

Meanwhile, migrants from South Asia, particularly Pakistan and Bangladesh, constitute the largest Muslim community of 'New Islam'. They are predominantly employed in the low skill sectors of the economy: agriculture, construction, textiles, services, and trade (Gemi, 2018). Albanians, who constitute 66 percent of Greece's immigrants and who theoretically come from a neighbouring country with a predominantly (70 percent) Muslim population, appear to be either converting to Orthodoxy or not practising Islam at all.

According to the key informants, there are 100 mosques (mostly makeshift prayer rooms); only three are officially registered while the rest operate unofficially under the label of cultural associations. Of those, 97 mosques belong to Sunni Islam and three to the Shia denomination (Interviews 2 and 6).[1]

After years of political controversy over the establishment of a mosque in Athens, one was recently inaugurated in the neighbourhood of Eleonas, not very far from central Athens. However, there is no Islamic cemetery in Athens, and Muslim immigrants are thus forced to use the cemeteries in Western Thrace for their funerals or to cover the cost of repatriating the bodies to the place of origin.

The religious community of Greek Catholics numbers about 50,000 members (0.5 percent of the population).[2] Apart from the permanent residents, there is a considerable 'temporary presence' of other Catholics who arrived in Greece as economic or political refugees. According to the official data published at the website of the Catholic Church in Greece, the total population of 'old' and 'new' Catholics is estimated at 350,000; the majority is established in Athens, while a large number of Catholics live in the Cyclades, mainly on the islands of Syros (8,000) and Tinos (3,000). There are also sizeable communities of Polish and Filipino migrants, with some 80,000 and 40,000 members respectively.

The size of the Jewish community is estimated at 5,000 individuals (U.S. Department of State, 2019a: 23). Today, there are nine Jewish Communities located in Athens, Thessaloniki, Larissa, Chalkis, Volos, Corfu, Trikala, Ioannina, and Rhodes (KIS, 2019). Local Jewish communities are represented by the Central Jewish Coordination and Consultation Council. The Chief Rabbi is chosen by the Jewish community, but his appointment requires the approval of the Greek Minister of Education and Religious Affairs (Anagnostopoulos, 2017: 110). Under Law 2456/1920, the Jewish Community has the right to establish itself as a legal entity, provided that there are more than 20 Jewish families in a certain locality. It also enjoys the right to establish educational institutions and their curricula, as long as this does not impinge on national legislation and ensures sufficient training in the Greek language.[3]

In total, there are about 80 religious entities formally registered with the General Secretariat for Religious Affairs of the Ministry of Education. Among them the Greek Orthodox Church, the Jewish community, and the Muslim minority of Thrace have the status of official religious legal entities as 'Legal Body under State Law' under the jurisdiction of the Ministry of Education and Religious Affairs. Additionally, the Greek Orthodox Church, Muslim minority of Thrace, Jewish community, and Roman Catholic Church receive government benefits that are not available to other religious communities (U.S. Department of State, 2019b: 1).

Meanwhile, the Anglican Church, Evangelical Christian groups, and Ethiopian, Coptic, Armenian Apostolic, and Assyrian Orthodox Churches acquired the status of religious legal entities under Law 4301/2014[4] 'Organization of the Legal Form of Religious Communities and their organizations in Greece'. The status of the religious group allows for them to administer houses of prayer and worship, private schools, charitable institutions, and other non-profit entities (Article 7).

Legal and institutional framework governing religion and diversity

The Constitution recognizes Orthodoxy as the 'prevailing religion' under Article 3. Article 13 states that freedom of religious conscience is inviolable and provides for the enjoyment of civil rights and liberties that do not depend on the individual's religious beliefs. The Constitution further provides that freedom of worship shall be performed 'unhindered and under the protection of the law'. It prohibits proselytizing and allows for the prosecution of publications that offend Christianity or other 'known religions' (Article 14), while under Article 13 no rite of worship is allowed to 'offend public order or the good usages (χρηστά ήθη)'.[5] Also under Article 13, 'the ministers of all known religions being subject to the same supervision by the State and to the same obligations toward it as those of the Greek Orthodox religion'. It further stipulates that individuals shall not be exempted from their obligations to the state or from compliance with the law because of their religious convictions.

The Greek state provides direct support to the Greek Orthodox Church, including funding for clerics' salaries, religious and vocational training of clergy, and religious instruction in schools. Similarly, the government-appointed muftis and imams in Thrace are paid directly from the state budget as civil servants. In November 2018, under an agreement reached between the then-Prime Minister, Alexis Tsipras, and Archbishop Ieronymos of the Church of Greece, the state will in the future transfer an annual subsidy of around 200 million euros to a special church fund for the payment of priests' salaries, who will no longer be classed as civil servants and be paid directly by the church (AMNA, 2018). The agreement also foresees a settlement to a decades-old dispute over church property between the Greek state and the Church, which is one of the country's largest real estate owners (Reuters, 2018).

On 14 February 2019, Parliament held the first vote on the constitutional amendments to be submitted for parliamentary revision to the Parliament that emerged from the June 2019 general election. In this context, the Parliament approved by a one-vote majority the then-leftist government's proposal to amend Article 3 so as to explicitly establish the religious neutrality of the state (To Vima, 2019). However, within his first days in office, the new Prime Minister, Kyriakos Mitsotakis, overturned the above decision; on 16 July 2019, following a meeting with Archbishop Ieronymos, he declared that his government will not push through changes in Articles 3 and 13 of the Constitution on relations between church and state (Kathimerini, 2019b).

The introduction of Law 4301/2014 'Organization of the Legal Form of Religious Communities and their organizations in Greece' provides for religious groups to become recognized as 'religious legal entities' under civil law. The same law established the registry of clergy and other staff of 'known religions' and religious legal entities, while exempting from the requirement the Greek Orthodox priests, imams in Thrace, and Jewish rabbis. A new law passed in August 2018 (Law 4559/2018) extended the application of the former law (2014) to all religious officials including the Greek Orthodox Church, the Muftiates of Thrace, and Jewish communities, requiring that they register within a year in the electronic database of the Ministry of Education and Religious Affairs.

The granting of permits for a temple of worship is regulated under Circular 128231/2016.[6] The planning authorities are authorized to issue a permit to construct a temple or place of worship of any religious community (except for those within the ecclesiastical jurisdiction of the Eastern Orthodox Church of Christ), provided that it has been first approved by the Ministry of Education and Religious Affairs. Another Circular[7] (118939/2016) provides for the Ministerial decision that shall be issued following verification that the three conditions laid down in Article 13, par. 2 of the Constitution are fulfilled, namely, that it is a 'known religion' without secret dogmas; that proselytism is not carried out; and that the practice of rites of worship is in conformity with public order or good usage.

Despite the positive steps taken by the Greek state to give permits for worship sites and modernize the legal context regulating religious affairs, many undocumented mosques continue to operate. According to a key informant, the procedure for obtaining a permit is extremely expensive (about 5,000 euros) and time-consuming.

The controversy over the mosque

One of the most controversial issues has been the much-debated issue of the construction of a mosque in Athens. It is, indeed, an oxymoron that while there are about 300 mosques in Western Thrace and the islands of Rhodes and Kos, there was until recently no mosque in Athens to serve the religious needs of Muslims. Contentious political issues with regard to constructing a public place of prayer for Muslims have been addressed by Law 3512/2006 'Construction of mosque in Athens and other provisions'[8] and Article 29 of Law 4014/2011.[9] Law 3215/2006 explicitly states that a piece of land of 850 square meters in the Botanikos area is granted by the state for the construction of a mosque and other facilities. Ownership of the mosque will belong to the Greek State. An imam will be appointed for a two-year renewable term and paid by the Ministry of Education and Religious Affairs. After a plea for annulment by which the constitutionality of respective provisions was contested relating to the mosque's location, the Council of State (Judgment 2399/2014) upheld its construction as being in full compliance with the Constitution.[10]

In 2015, the then-newly elected left government passed an amendment to the existing legislation on certain technical issues related to the construction of the official mosque. This sparked furious debate, in public opinion and Parliament, especially by the far right, with the anti-Muslim MPs arguing that 'Greece will become Islamised' or that 'Muslims are against the Western way of life'.[11] At two rallies organized by opponents to the mosque's construction, there were accusations bandied of a conspiracy against Greece that has the country's Islamisation as a main goal. Finally, after years of acrimony, the mosque was inaugurated in the district of Eleonas on 7 June 2019 (EfSyn, 2019). Meanwhile, to date there has been little progress towards approving the allocation by the Greek Church in 1992 of 20 hectares of land for a Muslim cemetery at Schisto, near Athens.

The dispute over 'sharia law'

Muslim Greek citizens who are resident in Western Thrace are allowed to use sharia law as a parallel legal system for private law (ECHR, 2018: 21). Inherited from the Ottoman Empire, this practice is applied to Muslim populations under Greek jurisdiction. The treaties of Sèvres (1920) and Lausanne (1923) regulating the fate of 'minorities' in Turkey and Greece provided that they could continue to live according to their own customs. Thereafter, the Greek courts have held that sharia law must apply to all members of the Muslim community of Thrace in matters of marriage, divorce, and succession. The law gives muftis judicial power to rule on disputes between Muslims concerning inheritance and family matters (Law 2345/1920).[12]

In the meantime, an interesting case examined by the European Court of Human Rights (ECtHR) (*MollaSali v. Greece*) raised serious concerns about the application by the Greek courts of Islamic religious (Sharia) law to a dispute concerning inheritance rights over the estate of the late husband of Ms MollaSali, a Greek national and member of the Muslim minority.[13] On 19 December 2018, the ECtHR ruled that Greece violated the European Convention on Human Rights by applying Sharia to an inheritance case in 2014 in which a widow lost three-fourths of her inheritance after family members requested a Sharia ruling on the matter without her consent. The Court ruled that the compulsory application of sharia law on Muslims was discriminatory compared to a non-Muslim Greek testator.

Greece, however, anticipated this decision by voting to limit the powers of Islamic courts and making the use of sharia law and the mufti jurisdiction optional through a law of 15 January 2018. Parliament thus changed a century-old law that gave Islamic courts priority over family law matters among the Muslim minority in Western Thrace. From now on, Greek civil law will apply in cases where all parties do not agree to the settling of a dispute in religious court. Specifically, the regulatory framework on sharia law[14] refers to the provisions of the Civil Code, except if the interested parties sign a notarized declaration of property upon death, containing exclusively the expressive will of the testator to subject his succession under sharia law.

The 'judicial authority' of muftis

As a rule, muftis in Greece have never been elected by the people; they are nominated by the Greek authorities, a practice contested by the Turkish state, and also by a part of the minority population. Since 1990 there have been five muftis in Thrace, three of whom were appointed by the Greek State and two elected by the minority but not recognized by the

Greek authorities, which has given rise to disputes and led the European Court of Human Rights to find violations of Article 9 of the Convention (ECHR, 2018: 21).

Again, the recently introduced presidential decree (PD52/2019) on the appointment of muftis and their 'authority' in Komotini, Didymoteicho, and Xanthi drew the ire of the Turkish Muslim community, which claimed the decree takes away the community's rights to elect their own clerics. Among its provisions are the use of the Greek language in mufti offices and the assignment of muftis and their staff by the Ministry of Education, both of which are viewed as restricting the rights of muftis. The Turkish Ministry of Foreign Affairs issued a statement on 21 June 2019 calling the presidential decree an 'aggravation' of Greek 'violations' of Muslim minority rights that 'disregards the rights of the Turkish minority in Greece guaranteed by the Lausanne Peace Treaty also on the basis of reciprocity'.[15] The Greek foreign ministry responded that the decree improves the work of muftis who maintain judicial powers and provides guarantees for the parties resorting to the muftis (Kathimerini, 2019a).

Similarly, the administration of wakfs has been another thorny issue. Since the 1967 military coup, members of all wakfs' boards in Greece have been appointed by the Greek authorities. Law 3647/2018 on wakfs foundations applied to Western Thrace allows the election of board members. However, some members of the Muslim minority continued to criticize the appointment by the government of members entrusted to oversee the wakfs' endowments, real estate, and charitable funds, arguing that the Muslim minority in Thrace should elect these members.

Education and religious affairs

According to Article 16, paragraph 2, of Constitution, education is a key mission of the state and aims at the development of national and religious consciousness. It is in this spirit that the Greek education system includes ecclesiastical education. The primary task of ecclesiastical schools (junior high schools and lyceums) is to educate and adequately prepare students with the values of the Orthodox faith and Christianity. As from the academic year 2007/2008, Higher Ecclesiastical Schools operate as Higher Ecclesiastical Academies, equivalent to higher education institutions (Law 3432/2006).

The Ministry of Education and Religious Affairs is responsible for supervising religious education and administrative issues related to governance of religions in Greece. The organizational structure includes the General Secretariat for Religious Affairs, which is divided in two directorates: the Directorate of Religion Administration and the Directorate of Religion Education and Inter-religion Relations whose competencies cover the issues of religious education and inter-religion relations, while the activities of the Department of Muslim Affairs evolve around the issues of the Muslim minority of Thrace. The purpose of the General Secretariat for Religious Affairs (Presidential Decree 18/2018) is the supervision of the religious education system and the connection of religion and culture with the simultaneous promotion of action against intolerance and in favour of inter-religious relationships.

Greek Orthodox religious education at the primary and secondary school levels is included in the curriculum. School textbooks focus mainly on Greek Orthodox teachings; however, they also include some basic information on some other 'known' religions. Students may be exempted from religion class upon request, but parents of students registered as Greek Orthodox in school records must declare that the students are not Greek Orthodox believers in order to receive the exemption.

This issue has caused serious debate, the outcome of which is illustrated in another case that has appealed to the ECtHR, namely, *Papageorgiou and Others v. Greece* (no. 4762/18 and

6140/18). The applicants, who are students living on two small Aegean islands, complain that the compulsory religious education violates Articles 8 and 14, and 9 and 14 in combination because the exemption from religion class stigmatizes the student and the student's parents as it makes public the fact that they are not followers of the 'dominant religion'. The applicants also complain that the students are deprived of hours of classes because of their religious and philosophical convictions. The very same religious education being questioned by *Papageorgiou and others* as a violation of their freedom of thought, conscience, and religion (Article 9 of the ECtHR) was ruled by the Council of State – in a case raised by Archbishop Serafim of Piraeus – as in violation of the Constitution for being insufficiently confessional in nature. The Council of State, in its 20 September 2019 plenary session, deemed the changes to religious education introduced by the previous government as unconstitutional. According to its judgement (1749–1752/2019) the previous government's reforms did not aspire to the development of students' Orthodox Christian consciences and did not comprise a comprehensive teaching of the dogmas, traditions, and moral values of the Orthodox Christian Church (Kampouris, 2019).

The Orthodox Church's involvement with the religious education in public schools is regulated by the relevant law that provides the church the right to deem whether what is taught at school is doctrinally correct. Recently, the curriculum of religion courses has been subject to revisions at all levels. The revision process started in 2011, and in 2014 was ready for a pilot implementation in secondary schools, while in 2016 it formally replaced the previous religion curriculum. The Orthodox Church strongly opposed the new religion curriculum. This crisis escalated when a bishop, along with a group of theologians and two parents, filed an injunction against this new programme with the Council of State, claiming that the new material proselytizes the children and threatens their religious identity. The first decision of the Council of State ruled against the implementation of the new religion curriculum, considering it unconstitutional and contrary to the ECtHR (U.S. Department of State, 2019b: 1). In the meantime, the association of Greek atheists, with the support of the Hellenic Foundation for European and Foreign Policy (ELIAMEP), filed an appeal to the Council of State seeking a different process of exemption from the religion lesson because the latter is exclusively based on Orthodox dogma.

Although there are no purely (private) religious schools in Greece, certain foreign-owned private schools and individual churches may teach optional religion classes on their premises and which students may attend on a voluntary basis. The law provides for optional Islamic religious instruction in public schools in Thrace for the recognized Muslim minority and optional Catholic religious instruction in public schools on the islands of Tinos and Syros. The government operates secular Greek-Turkish bilingual schools and two Islamic religious schools in Thrace. According to the regulatory framework for religious education (Article 36),[16] instead of teaching the Quran in the local mosques, for the first time it is provided for Islamic religion teachers to teach the Quran in public primary and secondary schools in Thrace to students who are members of the Muslim minority exempted from the course of Religious Education (U.S. Department of State, 2019a: 7). This provision is already implemented in other regions, such as the islands of Tinos and Syros, where Catholic students may instead attend a class taught by Catholic priests or theologians hired by the Greek State.

All Islamic religion teachers must be Greek citizens and members of the Muslim minority, holders of a degree on Islamic studies of a tertiary school of Theology (in Greece or abroad). The positions of Islamic religion teachers are allocated to each muftiate by decision of the Minister of Education and Religious Affairs after obtaining the opinion of the Special Committee[17] and of the local mufti.[18]

Since 1997, there has been a quota system (5 percent) for entrance to Greek universities of students from Muslim minority of Western Thrace and the Dodecanese. Likewise, 2 percent of students entering the national fire brigade school and academy are required to be from the Muslim minority in Thrace (U.S. Department of State, 2019a: 7).

Another important development in the area of higher education was the introduction in 2016 of a new undergraduate programme in Islamic Studies at the Theological School of the Aristotle University of Thessaloniki.[19]

Concluding remarks

The Greek Orthodox Church has long had an influential role in Greek public life, and a large number of Greeks see national identity and religion as inextricably linked, and this, in turn, has diachronically defined their national project of 'ethnos'. It is not a coincidence that heads of the Orthodox Church take for granted their authority to address a speech on political and diplomatic issues such as the 'Macedonia name issue', denoting that they feel comfortable to speak about the nation.

In fact, until 30 years ago, Greece was considered largely a mono-ethnic, mono-cultural, and mono-religious country, thus a paradigm of a hard core 'nation-state'. During the last three decades, the country has had to familiarize with and make space for the cultural, ethnic, and religious diversity which has been extended in three demographic units/levels: native population, 'Old Islam', and 'New Islam'.

The historic context related to the governance of 'Old Islam' along with the management of the religious diversity related to 'New Islam' remain the most important challenges for Greek society and its polity. On the one hand, the evidence discussed extensively in this chapter affirms the religious diversity in relation to 'New Islam', while, on the other, the long-persisting thorny issues between Greece and Turkey on 'Old Islam', appears indeed to have been met with strong opposition by public opinion. Apparently, this is partly related to geopolitics and national identity, hence linking the religious aspects of Islam with the question of national security and bilateral relations between Turkey and Greece.

It should be acknowledged, however, that the overall Greek policy and legal framework towards the religious minorities has been substantially reformed on the basis of liberal principles and human rights standards, recognizing as such the equality of individuals before the law regardless of their religious and ethnic affiliation. However, the meaning of tolerance towards religious and cultural diversity is still perceived as minimal liberal tolerance, meaning that there is no pro-active accommodation of the *de facto* cultural, religious, ethnic, and linguistic diversity (Triandafyllidou and Kouki, 2012: 3). In terms of governance of religious diversity, despite the recent reforms, the central state policy appears fragmented and thus far we have just had bits and pieces of policies that are not reflected in laws, but rather in the non-application of laws. While the legal context has been modernized, the mentality and public attitude have not been modernized in the same way.

Notes

1 These figures were quoted by a theologian in her capacity as an adviser to the office of the Secretary General of Religion Affairs, and a journalist who is a spokesperson of a Muslim association based in Athens, in their respective interviews.
2 Available from: http://www.catheclesia.gr/hellas/index.php/catholic-church-in-greece

3 There is a Jewish Kindergarten and a Primary School operating as a private school that belongs to the Jewish Community of Athens. For more information see: https://www.jewishmuseum.gr/en/the-jewish-school-of-athens/
4 Available from: https://www.minedu.gov.gr/publications/docs2014/141210_Law_4301_2014_Organization_legal_form_religious_communities_organizations_Greece.pdf
5 Constitution of Greece, Article 13. According to Law 1363/1938 (Metaxas law) proselytism is considered a criminal offence. The European Commission against Racism and Intolerance (ECRI) in its 2009 Report suggested the criminal law provision banning proselytism should be repealed. For more information see: https://rm.coe.int/fourth-report-on-greece/16808b5793
6 For more information see: https://www.minedu.gov.gr/publications/docs2017/EGYKLIOS_ANEGERSHS.pdf
7 Available from: https://www.minedu.gov.gr/publications/docs2016/270716_Circular_Update.pdf
8 Available from: https://www.kodiko.gr/nomologia/document_navigation/154207/nomos-3512-2006
9 Available from: https://www.kodiko.gr/nomologia/document_navigation/62759/nomos-4014-2011
10 Available from: https://www.minedu.gov.gr/publications/docs2015/Council_of_State_decision_on_Mosque.pdf
11 Parliament Proceedings, 24 June 2015, Session ΞΒ [62], p. 71
12 For more information see: https://www.viadiplomacy.gr/tag/nomou-2345-1920/
13 A 67-year-old widow, Hatijah Molla Salli, from the city of Komotini in Western Thrace filed a complaint against Greece over an inheritance dispute with her late husband's sisters. Salli won an appeal in the Greek secular justice system, but the Supreme Court in 2013 ruled that only a mufti had the power to resolve Muslim inheritance issues.
14 Official Gazette of the Hellenic Republic, January 15, 2018 Issue A' Amendment of Article 5 of Legislative Act of December 24, 1990 'On Muslim Clerics' (A' 11) ratified by the Sole Article of Law 1920/1991 (A' 11).
15 For more see http://www.mfa.gov.tr/sc_-43_-muftulukler-hk-yunanistan-cbsk-kararnamesi-hk-sc.en.mfa
16 Law 4115/2013. Available at: https://www.minedu.gov.gr/publications/docs2016/13-01-13_L.4115_2013_art._53_Islamic_religion_teachers.pdf
17 The selection of Islamic religion teachers is made by a Committee of five members consisting of: (a) the local mufti, (b) an official of the Ministry of Education, (c) a university faculty member specialized in Islamic studies, (d) a distinguished Muslim theologian, and (e) a distinguished Muslim theologian proposed by the local Mufti.
18 The cost of the remuneration of Islamic religion teachers shall be borne by the budget of the Ministry of Education.
19 See: https://www.theo.auth.gr/en/islamic-studies

References

Anagnostopoulos, A. N. (2017). *Orthodoxy and Islam. Theology and Muslim-Christian Relations in Modern Greece and Turkey*. Abingdon, Oxon and New York, NY: Routledge, an imprint of the Taylor & Francis Group.

AMNA (Athens-Macedonian News Agency). (2018, November 6). PM Tsipras, Archbishop Ieronymos reach agreement on management of church assets. Available at: https://www.amna.gr/en/article/307844/PM-Tsipras--Archbishop-Ieronymos-reach-agreement-on-management-of-church-assets. Accessed 18 February 2020.

Baltsiotis, L. (2011). The Muslim chams of Northwestern Greece. *European Journal of Turkish Studies*, 12: 1–31.

ECHR (European Court of Human Rights). (2018, December 19). Case of Molla Sali v. Greece, 32 Judgment, STRASBOURG. Available at: https://hudoc.echr.coe.int/eng#{%22itemid%22:[%22002-12267%22]}. Accessed 12 March 2019.

EfSyN (Efimerida ton Syntakton). (2019, June 8). Athens finally got a mosque [in Greek]. Available at: https://www.efsyn.gr/ellada/koinonia/198982_epiteloys-i-athina-apektise-tzami. Accessed 20 February 2020.

Fokas, E. (2012). 'Eastern' orthodoxy and 'Western' secularisation in contemporary Europe (with special reference to the case of Greece). *Religion, State and Society*, 40(3–4): 395–414.

Gemi, E. (2018). *Housing and Spatial Segregation of Migrants in Greece* [in Greek]. Athens: Papazisis Publishing.

Halikiopoulou, D. (2011). *Patterns of Secularization: Church, State and Nation in Greece and the Republic of Ireland*. Farnham, UK: Ashgate.

Hatziprokopiou, P. & Evergeti, V. (2014). Negotiating Muslim identity and diversity in Greek urban spaces. *Social & Cultural Geography*, 15(6): 603–626.

Kampouris, N. (2019, September 20). Previous SYRIZA Government's reforms to religious education ruled unconstitutional. *GreekReporter.com*, 20 September. Available at: https://greece.greekreporter.com/2019/09/20/previous-syriza-governments-reforms-to-religious-education-ruled-unconstitutional/. Accessed 18 February 2020.

Kathimerini. (2019a, June 22). Greece rejects Turkish claims over Muftis in Thrace. Available at: http://www.ekathimerini.com/241828/article/ekathimerini/news/greece-rejects-turkish-claims-over-muftis-in-thrace.Accessed 18 February 2020.

Kathimerini. (2019b, July 16). Mitsotakis tells Ieronymos gov't will halt changes to church-state relations. Available at: http://www.ekathimerini.com/242633/article/ekathimerini/news/mitsotakis-tells-ieronymos-govt-will-halt-changes-to-church-state-relations. Accessed 18 February 2020.

KIS (Central Board of Jewish Communities in Greece). (2019). Available at:https://kis.gr/en/index.php?option=com_content&view=article&id=411&Itemid=74. Accessed 24 February 2020.

MIP (Ministry of Immigration Policy). (2019). Statistics 2019. Available at: http://www.immigration.gov.gr. Accessed 24 February 2020.

Pew Research Center. (2018).Eastern and Western Europeans differ on importance of religion, views of minorities, and key social issues. Available at: https://www.pewforum.org/2018/10/29/eastern-and-western-europeans-differ-on-importance-of-religion-views-of-minorities-and-key-social-issues/.Accessed 24 February 2020.

Reuters. (2018, November 6). Greece to take clergy off its payroll in deal with Orthodox Church. Available at: https://www.reuters.com/article/us-greece-church/greece-to-take-clergy-off-its-payroll-in-deal-with-orthodox-church-idUSKCN1NB2QG.Accessed 24 February 2020.

RVRN (Racist Violence Recording Network). (2019). Annual report 2018. Available at: https://www.unhcr.org/gr/wp-content/uploads/sites/10/2019/04/RVRN_report_2018gr.pdf. Accessed 24 February 2020.

Skoulariki, A. (2010). Old and new mosques in Greece: a new debate haunted by history. In S. Allievi (ed.), *Mosques in Europe: Why a Solution Has Become a Problem* (pp. 300–318). NEF Network of European Foundations. London: Alliance Publishing Trust.

The Catholic Church in Greece. (2019).Available at: http://www.cathecclesia.gr/hellas/index.php/-catholic-church-in-greece. Accessed 24 February 2020.

To Vima. (2019, February 14). Constitutional review: Article 3 on State-Church relations passed [in Greek]. Available at: https://www.tovima.gr/2019/02/14/politics/ektos-syntagmatikis-anatheorisis-to-arthro-3/. Accessed 24 February 2020.

Tsitselikis, K. (2012). *Old and New Islam in Greece from Historical Minorities to Immigrant Newcomers*. Leiden: Brill/Nijhoff.

Triandafyllidou, A. & Kouki, H. (2012). *Tolerance and Cultural Diversity Discourses and Practices in Greece*. Deliverable 5.1 Country Synthesis Report, Accept Pluralism Research Project. European University Institute. Available at: http://cadmus.eui.eu/bitstream/handle/1814/23261/ACCEPT_WP5_2012-25_Country-synthesis-report_Greece.pdf?sequence=3&isAllowed=y. Accessed 24 February 2020.

Turkish Ministry of Foreign Affairs, QA-43. (2019, June 21).Statement of the spokesperson of the ministry of foreign affairs, Mr. Hami Aksoy. In *Response to a Question Regarding the Recent Presidential Decree in Greece Concerning Muftis*. Available at: http://www.mfa.gov.tr/sc_-43_-muftulukler-hk-yunanistan-cbsk-kararnamesi-hk-sc.en.mfa. Accessed 24 February 2020.

U.S. Department of State. (2019a). *Greece 2018 Human Rights Report*. Available at:https://www.state.gov/wp-content/uploads/2019/03/GREECE-2018-HUMAN-RIGHTS-REPORT.pdf. Accessed 24 February 2020.

U.S. Department of State. (2019b). *Greece 2018 International Religious Freedom Report*. Available at:https://www.state.gov/wp-content/uploads/2019/05/GREECE-2018-INTERNATIONAL-RELIGIOUS-FREEDOM-REPORT.pdf. Accessed 24 February 2020.

Part III
Central Eastern Europe and Russia

9

Hungary

Religion as the government's political tool

Dániel Vékony

Introduction

The complex issue of religious governance has become a hot topic in Hungary in recent years. The government was widely criticized by its international partners for both its introduction of new legislation on religions and its adoption of a new Fundamental Law (constitution) since coming to power in 2010.

This chapter argues that the government uses religion and related legislation to control and exploit certain religious groups for political purposes, treating traditional religious communities and some further Christian denominations as partners. As a result, numerous social functions customarily offered by the government have been outsourced to these communities.

At the opposite end of the spectrum, other communities, especially Muslims, often feel under pressure because the hostile narrative on Muslims and Islam is linked to the topic of migration with negative connotations. In the government's narrative, Islam and Muslims are presented as a threat to the physical and ontological security of Hungarians. In this process, the government positions itself as the guarantor of society's security. Additionally, the government positions itself and the country as the contemporary guardians of Europe from migration and Muslims who represent a security threat for the country and the continent as a whole – a rhetoric that increasingly resonates not only domestically but also at a wider European level.

Historical context

Hungary's geographical location places it at a crossroads, in more than one sense: the area of Historical Hungary lay at the border of Byzantine and Roman Christianity. The founding of the historic Hungarian kingdom is linked to the adoption of Roman Christianity at the end of the tenth century. It was a conscious political decision of the Árpád dynasty to adopt the Roman branch of Christianity instead of the Byzantine. This aligned the country with the Western part of the European continent throughout the centuries. As a result, Christianity constitutes a strong element in national identity. Even though Hungary was a Christian kingdom from the start of its statehood, numerous other ethnic and religious groups also lived in its territory. Beside Jews, there was a tangible Muslim community living in the Hungarian kingdom from the tenth century to the thirteenth. These Muslims helped run the feudal Hungarian state; they were coin minters, tax collectors, and served as guardians of the southern border territories. It was due to the pressure from Rome that Hungarian kings gradually forced these communities to either assimilate or leave the Kingdom (Pap et al., 2014).

Protestantism reached Hungary in the sixteenth century and enjoyed great popularity at the time. Although during Ottoman rule, the nobility stepped up against Protestant denominations, these movements enjoyed the same position as the Roman Catholic Church under the territories ruled by the Ottomans. Thanks to charismatic preachers, Calvinism became widespread, followed by the Lutheran denomination (Horváth, 2011). During the one-and-a-half-centuries of Ottoman occupation, both Protestantism and Judaism were tolerated and thrived in the conquered and vassal territories. By the end of the sixteenth century, the majority of the population became followers of one of the Protestant churches (Molnár, 1999).

Ottoman rule brought much destruction to the territory of the kingdom of Hungary. The 150 years of Turkish occupation is still remembered as the most tragic period of Hungarian history. In the mainstream collective memory narrative (Misztal, 2003; Vékony, 2019:7–8), Hungary acted as a protector of Christian Europe. However, as European countries were not able to unite in their fight against the Muslim Ottoman empire, the country was taken over by the Muslim invaders.[1]

Today, Islam is still considered as alien to Hungarian culture. Memories of Muslim presence during the early centuries of Hungarian history have been erased from the collective memory narrative of Hungarians. However, the tragedy of the Ottoman occupation is still a reference point. Correspondingly, Hungary's image as a protector of Christian Europe and the image of ungrateful European countries in the face of this threat have been rediscovered as a historic symbol for the contemporary Hungarian collective memory narrative (Vékony, 2019:7–8).

After the Ottomans' ouster, Islam was not tolerated in the Habsburg-dominated Hungarian state. Protestantism and Judaism were also put under pressure. Protestantism has become a symbol for resistance against the Habsburg rule in Hungary. During Ottoman rule, Calvinism became the state religion in Transylvania, although this did not occur in the Ottoman- or Habsburg-dominated territories of Hungary. With the eviction of the Ottomans, Protestant churches could not secure legal privileges from the Catholic Habsburg rulers. Gradually, Catholicism became the dominant religion again (Molnár, 1999).

By the World War I, Hungary had become a multi-ethnic and multi-faith country as part of the Austro-Hungarian empire. The increasingly nationalist Hungarian elite regarded both Hungary's ethnic minorities and the governing Habsburgs as threats to the Hungarian nation (Paksa, 2012). The breakup of the multicultural Historic Hungarian state into separate states after the World War I left Hungarian society traumatized (Romsics, 2010). The moral of the story for many Hungarians was that when alien ethnic groups settle in the country, this is likely to lead to the country's break-up. Ethnic homogeneity is thus regarded as a means of ensuring unity since heterogeneity is linked past trauma.

Csepeli and Örkény note that the strong Islamophobic attitude shaped by Hungarian history offers the broader context for the more pronounced racist and xenophobic tendencies in Hungary compared to other European countries (2017, 98–99). The fact that Muslim communities are very small in number can also be an explanation for this high degree of negative attitudes towards Islam and Muslims. As Muslims are largely absent from everyday life, they can be regarded as the invisible threat, an image further aggravated by the media (ibid., 101).

The ethno-religious composition of contemporary Hungary

Hungary is regarded today as a homogenous country, with only small groups of ethnic and religious minorities. There are a few ethnic minorities, of mainly neighbouring countries, such as Croatians, Germans, Romanians, Serbs, Slovaks, and so on. Most of these groups traditionally follow some creed of Christianity with a state recognition. The largest ethnic minority group is the Roma (or Gypsy) community. The 2011 census recorded 316,000 individuals belonging to this group. However, according to some estimates, the population could range from 620,000 to 876,000 (Pénzes et al., 2018). One reason for such a wide discrepancy is that many members of the Roma community face regular discrimination. During 2008 and 2009 a small group of radical individuals belonging to a Hungarian far-right underground cell committed a series of killings against Roma people; they were caught and sentenced to life imprisonment in 2016 (Népszava, 2016).

However, as the migration narrative gained spotlight in recent years, the anti-Roma rhetoric has lost some ground. Still, as the socio-economic challenges for this community still exist, the resurfacing of anti-Roma rhetoric would not be surprising in the future..

As far as religious groups are concerned, the latest census taken by the Hungarian Central Statistical Office (n.d.), still shows Roman Catholics as the largest religious group, comprising 39 per cent of the population (Table 9.1). The second largest group are the Calvinists (11 per cent), followed by smaller communities such as Lutherans, Methodists, and some neo-Protestant groups. 0.1 per cent of the respondents declared their belonging to Judaism and the figure is the same (0.1 per cent) for Islam too. However, it is very likely that many followers of these faiths choose not to reveal their religious affiliation, given that religious affiliation was not a mandatory question on the census. More realistic estimates put the number of Jews between 58,936 and 110,679 (Kovács and Barna, 2018); the Muslim population was estimated at 32,618 in 2010 (Sulok, 2010).

Table 9.1 Breakdown of religious affiliation in Hungary based on the 2011 census

Roman Catholics	39%
Calvinists	11.6%
Lutheran	2.2%
Other religions	1.8%
Non-religious	18.2%
Undeclared	27.2%

Source: Hungarian Central Statistical Office (n.d.).

More than 45 per cent of the population either declared that they do not belong to a religious community or did not belong to one of the religious groups listed on the census questionnaire. This further supports the claim that people who are members of smaller religious groups are concealing their religious identity (Hungarian Central Statistical Office, n.d.).

Taxpayers in Hungary may choose to offer 1 per cent of their payable income tax to a religious community. This makes it possible to estimate the number of followers of certain religious communities from another aspect. If we look at the number of people who offered this 1 per cent, the list is somewhat different. This biggest group is still the Catholic community, followed by the Calvinist and Lutheran churches, with the fourth-largest group being the Hungarian Society for Krishna Consciousness and the Hit Gyülekezete (Community of the Faith) right behind (Hungarian Tax and Customs Administration, 2019). This latter community is the most important neo-Protestant, born-again Christian community in Hungary. Like many born-again Christian communities in the US, they are pro-Israel and often openly anti-Muslim in their rhetoric.

To recap, Catholicism is still the biggest religious community in the country, followed by some traditional communities, but other religious groups are also present. The Jewish community is relatively large, compared to other Jewish communities in other Central European countries. The Muslim community is rather small and the members of these latter two groups may also conceal their identity in official statistics. What is also striking is the high number of those who declare that they do not belong to any religion: Hungary, it seems, is becoming more and more post-Christian, which is characteristic of other countries in the region.

Islam was practically non-existent during much of the Cold War period. From the 1970s onwards, Muslims students from so-called friendly or progressive[2] countries came to Hungary to study at institutions of higher education as Hungary sought to expand its export market in the Middle East and the government offered generous scholarship programmes to a number of so-called friendly or progressive Muslim majority countries. These Muslim students started to organize themselves along religious lines in the 1980s. The government wanted to control this dynamic, thus the Association of Muslim Students was formed with active government intervention. From these dynamics, the Hungarian Islamic Community was founded in 1988 with State consent (Sulok, 2010; Csicsmann and Vékony, 2011). The government decided to grant recognition to Islam and the Muslim community on its own terms. This also enabled the government to keep the goodwill of 'friendly' Islamic countries in the Middle East that were important export markets for Hungary (Békés and Vékony, 2018). Thus, Islam's recognition in Hungary did not only signal acceptance of a new social reality in the country but that foreign policy and economic objectives also played a role.

Contemporary governance of religion in Hungary

The year 2010 was a watershed moment in Hungarian politics that also affected the relationship between the State and various religious groups as a new Constitution – the Fundamental Law of Hungary – was adopted in 2011 and amended in 2013 (Government of Hungary, n.d.).

Drawing on the ideas of Ádám and Bozóki (2016), Rogers Brubaker argues that in this new legal and political framework Prime Minister Viktor 'Orbán's Christianism is entirely secular; it functions as a marker of identity rather than as a sign of religious practice or belief' (2017, 1208). According to this logic, religion is used to bring a sacral legitimacy to a government policy that is organized along secular power dynamics.

However, the new Constitution creates an ambiguous situation. On the one hand, Article VII, par 3, separates church from state, declaring that 'religious communities shall operate separately' and that they '…shall be autonomous'. It also emphasizes individuals' freedom of thought and choice of religion. On the other hand, Article VII, par 4, states that 'the State and religious communities may cooperate to achieve community goals. At the request of a religious community, the National Assembly shall decide on such cooperation. The religious communities participating in such cooperation shall operate as established churches.[3] The State shall provide specific privileges to established churches with regard to their participation in the fulfilment of tasks that serve to achieve community goals'.

As we can see, the new Constitution enabled the State to enter into a closer relationship with certain religious communities, blurring the line between church and state. It delegated the power of approving such cooperation to the legislative branch of power. As such, it is up to elected politicians to decide which religious community will be allowed to establish a closer relationship with the government. This makes relations between church and state essentially a political issue. In order to better understand this, one must take a closer look at the latest Law on Churches adopted by the Fidesz-dominated government.

After the introduction of the new Fundamental Law, the government decided to rewrite the regulation on religious communities too. Before the new law, registration of religious communities was a rather simple process conducted by Hungary's civil courts. This resulted in a mushrooming of churches in the country; indeed, at one point there were more than 300 registered churches in Hungary – which is a very high number compared to other countries in Europe at the time.[4] One reason for this was the fact that the being recognized as a church gave communities a tax-free status. The government argued that these so-called business churches should no longer be recognized as religious communities. Moreover, communities that may pose a security risk to society should also have their recognition cancelled (Antalóczy, 2013, 29, 31).

The new law shifted the right to recognize religious communities as churches from the judicial branch to the legislative. To be recognized, religious communities would now require a two-thirds vote in Parliament, based on the government's recommendation. The measure drew international criticism, which led to its further amendment returning authority to register religious communities to the judiciary (U.S. Department of State, 2017).

The current version of the law recognizes religious communities on four levels (Government of Hungary, 2018, par 4). Religious communities can create a religious association (*vallási egyesület*). These religious associations must be registered at a Budapest civil court in order to gain legal personality. Besides this first basic level of recognition, the latest amendment of the Law on Churches creates three further levels of church recognition (Government of Hungary, 2011, 2018, par 4, 8) (Table 9.2).

Table 9.2 Levels of recognition of churches and religious communities

Non-church recognition	*Religious association (vallási egyesület)*
Basic church recognition	'Registered' church (*nyilvántartásba vett egyház*)
Intermediate church recognition	'Listed' (*bejegyzett egyház*)
Highest level of church recognition	'Established' church (*bevett egyház*)

Source: The table is based on Government of Hungary (2018).

'Registered' churches (*nyilvántartásba vett egyház*) need to meet certain conditions to be inscribed on a 'secondary' level, for instance, proof that they have operated as a religious association for five years, or recognition in another country for at least 100 years, or at least 1,000 registered members with a legal residence in Hungary (Government of Hungary, 2018, par 5).

The 'listed' church (*bejegyzett egyház*) is the next level of recognition. Here conditions are stricter; these organizations need to be registered as a religious association for at least 20 years (or as a registered church for at least 15 years) (Government of Hungary, 2018, par 5).

'Established' church (*bevett egyház*) is the highest level of recognition. Established churches enter into a cooperation agreement (*együttműködési megállapodás*) with the state. Churches can request such a cooperation agreement from the minister responsible for churches. Churches that have previously been granted the established status still can apply for a cooperation agreement within this new framework. If the minister approves the request, the agreement needs parliamentary approval. These cooperation agreements allow churches to run schools and other social and educational institutions as well as to receive financial support from the state. Churches in general are allowed to offer religious instruction in state-sponsored schools, provide chaplaincy services in prisons and other state institutions, and receive funding for these activities (Government of Hungary, 2018, par 5). However, operating entire institutions such as schools is a privilege reserved for churches that have been granted the precious cooperation agreements and become established churches.

In this complex regulatory framework, the state's neutrality vis-á-vis religious communities is questionable. It is true that almost any community can apply for the status of a religious association. These groups will be able to apply for higher status as they acquire members, financial supporters (that is, proof that they are able to sustain themselves), and after a certain period of time has passed from their registration (ibid.). However, this system makes it very hard for new religious communities to reach a higher status of recognition in a short period of time. This means that younger communities do not enjoy the same privileges as older, well-established communities. Furthermore, it is the government that decides with which religious community it is willing to cooperate in certain social and educational domains. The state treats a number of churches (mostly from the group of established churches) differently. They receive financial support for their charitable activities. They are allowed to run primary and secondary schools, as well as receive additional financial support for this activity (Domschizt, 2019). Given that which religious communities enjoy this closer communication is at the government's discretion, there are a number of privileged churches that receive far more generous support than others.

In short, even though the Constitution declares the separation of church and state, relations between church and state are not characterized by neutrality. The favoured communities are mostly (but not only) Christian communities with an historic heritage or significant number of followers. Neutrality of the state towards religious communities is not mentioned in the text of the Law of Churches. Indeed, the historic role of Christianity is recognized by a special status vis-á-vis the state, which is also mirrored in the Preamble of the Fundamental Law. The text notes that the first king of Hungary 'Saint Stephen built the Hungarian State on solid ground and made our country a part of Christian Europe one thousand years ago' (Government of Hungary, n.d., 2).

The document also states that the Hungarian people 'are proud that our people has over the centuries defended Europe in a series of struggles' (ibid.) and emphasizes 'the role of Christianity in preserving nationhood' (ibid.). From these excerpts, it becomes clear that due to its historic heritage, Christianity enjoys a *primus inter pares* status among religions in the country. As a result, Brubaker's idea mentioned earlier is questionable. As we will see later, Christianity is utilized and internalized by the governing elite to support their political agenda. However, the close and intense relations between certain churches and the state places the government's secular Christianism (Brubaker, 2017, 1208) under question. The idea of moderate secularism can be considered as more appropriate to describe this institutional setup (Modood, 2017). However, Modood emphasizes the mutual autonomy of churches and state in this model, where there is no one-sided control from either of the parties. What we see in the current Hungarian situation is an asymmetric interdependence, where the state enjoys more room for manoeuvre.

As far as Muslim communities are concerned, besides the Hungarian Islamic Community (Magyar Iszlám Közösség, henceforth, MIK) founded with state consent towards the end of the communist era (Sulok, 2010; Csicsmann and Vékony, 2011), the Organisation of Muslims in Hungary (Magyarországi Muszlimok Egyháza, henceforth MME) was registered in 2000, followed by the founding of the Islamic Church in 2003.

When the new legislation was introduced in 2011, only two of these organizations (the MIK and the MME) applied for a church status. Together, they created the Hungarian Islamic Council and, as a result, both groups received state recognition as members of the Hungarian Islamic Council. After the Law on Churches was amended, both the MIK and the MME were granted the highest level of recognition, that is, the status of established churches. This type of recognition would suggest the state's intent to enter into a closer relation with these organizations, as it has done with a number of Christian and Jewish communities favoured by the government, yet unlike many of their Christian and Jewish counterparts, the MIK and MME have not been given the chance to run their own denominational schools[5] nor are they treated as partners in social programmes.

The situation of Muslims has deteriorated since the migrant and refugee crisis in 2015. The government decided to link migration and Islam and place the issue in a security framework (Buzan et al., 1998). Government-sponsored media campaigns against migration and migrants were organized. This was complemented by radical narratives on Muslims and Islam in media outlets close to the government. This narrative – which was adopted from far-right movements in Western Europe – paints a negative, essentialist picture of Muslims and Islam. In this narrative, immigrants, who are mainly Muslims, are described as potential criminals with radical world views who are not willing and not able to integrate. Hungary, in this narrative, is described as the protector of Europe. The image of Western European societies is also negative, casting them as having left their Christian heritage and as a result sleepwalking to a dark and potentially violent future where national identities will be lost due to migration (Vidra, 2017; Krekó et al., 2019). Europe is painted as an ungrateful ally that does not want to help Hungary protect the continent from an invasion of migrants with a mainly Muslim background. This narrative is very easy to affiliate with its close links to the elements of Hungarian collective memory mentioned earlier. By taking on a narrative that is simultaneously anti-Islam and anti-West, the government can position itself as the guarantor of not only physical security, but of ontological security as well (Giddens, 1991).

What this shows is that Islam and Muslims are once again used for political purposes by the government. During the 1980s, they were used for achieving economic and foreign policy goals; in recent years, the issue is used mainly in domestic politics; however, the governing party also tries to capitalize on this narrative in its foreign policy endeavours.

Concluding remarks

Religious governance went through fundamental changes in the past ten years. The new Basic Law and the Law on Churches created a new framework for religious groups in Hungary. The new Constitution separates the state from churches. However, this separation does not mean that the state plays a neutral role vis-á-vis religious groups. The role of Christianity is recognized in the Basic Law as part of Hungarian heritage and identity. This gives Christianity – especially traditional Christian churches such as Catholicism, Calvinism, and Lutheranism – a higher status among religions.

The state also has a multi-level system of recognition for religious communities. Although registering a religious organization as a religious association is a simple task – which can be completed in a civil court – the state also created three further levels of church recognition. This means that churches seeking to run their own schools and other institutions must enter into a special cooperation agreement with the government and have themselves recognized as established churches, the highest level of recognition that also enables them to receive state funding.

Being an established church suggests the ability to forge such a closer relationship with the government, but this is not always the case. Even though two Muslim churches have the status of recognized churches, they still do not receive public funding for opening their own schools or similar projects. This can be attributed to the government's negative narrative with regard to Islam and Muslims that is linked to migration and set in a security framework. Although Hungary has historical links to Islam, this religion and its followers are often still treated as aliens to Hungarian society.

To sum up, religion is a highly political issue in contemporary Hungary despite the fact that society is becoming increasingly detached from religion. Still, the government often uses religion to further its political objectives. One good example is Islam: putting Islam and migration in a security narrative since 2015 has enabled to government to frame itself as a guardian of Hungarian society and Europe in both domestic and international politics.

Notes

1 In trying to contain Ottoman expansion, in the fifteenth and sixteenth centuries Hungary repeatedly asked for help from other European states, but the help never came. A good example of this is the tolling of the church bells, which was first ordered by Callixtus III in 1456. The pope wanted European countries to send armies to help the Hungarian troops fighting the Ottomans. As countries decided not to send troops, the pope ordered the tolling of the bells as a symbolic gesture. The tolling of the bells at noon is still broadcast by Hungarian state radio and TV every day. This trauma is still present in Hungarian folklore, literature, and other parts of national cultural heritage (Tarján, n.d.).
2 These were countries that had closer relations with the Soviet bloc during the Cold War, such as Afghanistan, Iraq, Syria, and South Yemen.
3 Currently there are 32 established churches in Hungary. For the complete list, see Ministry for Human Resources (n.d.).
4 One very good example is the Noé for the Life Community (*Noé az Életért Közösség*), which was a religious organization created by the Hungarian Noé Animal Shelter organization (Szőnyi, 2011).
5 Yet there are a number of schools run by Muslim communities, but they are directly related to Turkish and Lybian communities and not to one of the state-recognized Islamic Churches (Vékony, forthcoming).

References

Ádám, Zoltán, & Bozóki, András. (2016). State and faith: Right-wing populism and nationalized religion in Hungary. *Intersections* 2(1): 98–122.
Antalóczy, Péter. (2013). Az Alaptörvény és az egyházakra vonatkozó legújabb szabályozás dimenziói [The Basic Law and the newest dimensions of legislation concerning churches]. *Jog, Állam, Politika* 4(3): 23–38.
Békés, Csaba, & Vékony, Dániel. (2018). Unfulfilled promised lands: Missed potentials in relations between Hungary and the countries of the Middle East, 1953–75. In Philip Muehlenbeck & Natalia Telepneva (eds), *Warsaw Pact Intervention in the Third World: Aid and Influence in the Cold War* (pp. 271–297). London & New York: IB Tauris.
Buzan, Barry, Wæver, Ole, & de Wilde, Jaap. (1998). *Security: A New Framework for Analysis*. Boulder & London: Lynne Rienner Publishers.
Brubaker, Rogers. (2017). Between nationalism and civilizationism: The European populist moment in comparative perspective. *Ethnic and Racial Studies* 40(8): 1191–1226.
Csepeli, György, & Örkény, Antal. (2017). *Nemzet és Migráció* [Nation and Migration]. Budapest: Eötvös Loránt Tudomány Egyetem – TáTK.
Csicsmann, László, & Vékony, Dániel. (2011). Muslims in Hungary: A bridge between east and west? In Jarsolav Bures (ed.), *Muslims in Visegrad* (pp. 53–67). Prague: Institute of International Relations Prague.

Domschizt, Mátyás. (2019). *Négyszer többet költ a kormány az egyházi iskolában tanulókra, mint az állami diákokra* [The state spand four times as much on students learining in schools run by churches than on students in state-run schools]. index.hu. May 08. Available at: https://index.hu/gazdasag/2019/05/08/negyszer_tobb_penz_forras_egyhazi_iskolak_allami_koltsegvetes_tanulok_diak_roma_cigany_szegregacio_elkulonites/. Accessed 06/10/2019.

Giddens, Anthony. (1991). *Modernity and Self-Identity: Self and Society in the Late Modern Age.* Cambridge: Polity Press.

Government of Hungary. (n.d.). The new fundamental law of Hungary. kormany.hu. Available at: https://www.kormany.hu/download/e/02/00000/The%20New%20Fundamental%20Law%20of%20Hungary.pdf. Accessed 02/05/2020.

Government of Hungary. (2011). *2011. évi CLXXV. törvény az egyesülési jogról, a közhasznú jogállásról, valamint a civil szervezetek működéséről és támogatásáról* [CLXXV 2011 Law on association, public benefit status, and the operation and support of non-governmental organizations]. Net Jogtár. Available at: https://net.jogtar.hu/jogszabaly?docid=a1100175.tv. Accessed 02/15/2020.

Government of Hungary. (2018). *2018. évi CXXXII. törvény A lelkiismereti és vallásszabadság jogáról, valamint az egyházak, vallásfelekezetek és vallási közösségek jogállásáról szóló 2011. évi CCVI. törvény módosításáról* [The right to freedom of conscience and religion, and the churches, on the status of religious and religious communities CCVI 2011 amending the Act]. Magyar Közlöny, December 21.

Horváth, Attila. (2011). A vallásszabadság és az egyházjog története Magyarországon az államalapítástól a II. világháborúig. [The history of religious freedom and religious law from the founding of the state until World War II]. *Hét Hárs* 10(3–4): 12–20.

Hungarian Central Statistical Office. (n.d.). *Népszámlálás - Vallás, felekezet* [Census – Religion, denomination]. Available at: http://www.ksh.hu/nepszamlalas/tablak_vallas. Accessed 06/08/2019.

Hungarian Tax and Customs Administration. (2019). *Egyházak, kiemelt költségvetési előirányzatok* [Churches and other major bugdetary appropriations]. June 08. Available at: https://www.nav.gov.hu/nav/szja1_1/kimutatasok_elszamolasok/egyhazak_kiemelt_koltsegvetesi_eloiranyzatok/Kozlemeny_a_2017__ren20180111.html. Accessed 02/15/2020.

Kovács, András, & Barna, Ildikó. (2018). *Zsidók és zsidóság Magyarországon 2017-ben* [Jews and Jewry in Hungary]. Budapest: Szombat.

Krekó, Péter, Hunyadi, Bulcsú, & Szicherle, Patrik. (2019). *Anti-Muslim Populism in Hungary: From the Margins to the Mainstream.* Working Paper. Washington, DC: Brookings Institute.

Ministry for Human Resources. (n.d.). *Egyházi Nyílvántartó rendszer 1.0* [Church record system 1.0]. Available at: https://egyhaz.emmi.gov.hu. Accessed 06/10/2019.

Misztal, Barbara A. (2003). *Theories of Social Remembering.* Maidenhead: Open University Press.

Modood, Tariq. (2017). Multiculturalizing secularism. In Phil Zuckerman & John R. Shook (eds), *The Oxford Handbook of Secularism* (pp. 1–20). Oxford: Oxford University Press.

Molnár, Antal. (1999). Church history. In *Kereszt és félhold : A török kor Magyarországon (1526–1699)* [Cross and Cresent: The Ottoman Epoch in Hungary (1526–1699)]. Budapest: Enciklopédia Humana Egyesület. Available at: https://mek.oszk.hu/01800/01885/html/index5.html. Accessed 01/20/2018.

Népszava. (2016, January 12). Jogerős életfogytiglan a romagyilkosságok elkövetőinek [Life inprisonment for the prepetrators of the Roma murders]. Available at: https://nepszava.hu/1082093_jogeros-eletfogytiglan-a-romagyilkossagok-elkovetoinek. Accessed 06/10/2019.

Paksa, Rudolf. (2012). *A magyar szélsőjobboldal története* [History of the Hungarian Far-Right]. Budapest: Jaffa Kiadó.

Pap, Norbert, Reményi, Péter, Császár, Zsuzsa M., & Végh, Andor. (2014). Islam and the Hungarians. *Mitteilungen der Österreichischen Geographischen Gessellschaft* 156(1): 191–220.

Pénzes, János, Tátrai, Patrik, & Pásztor, István Zoltán. (2018). A roma népesség területi megoszlásának változása Magyarországon az elmúlt évtizedekben [Changes in the spatial distribution of the roma population in Hungary during the last decades]. *Területi Statisztika* (KSH) 58(1): 3–26.

Romsics, Ignác. (2010). *Magyarország története a XX. században* [History of Hungary in the 20th Century]. Budapest: Osiris kiadó.

Sulok, Sultan. (2010). *Muslim Minority in Hungary.* Warsaw Symposium on the Muslim minorities in Eastern and Central Europe, 8–10 December 2010. Budapest: Organisation of Muslims in Hungary, pp. 1–10.

Szőnyi, Szilárd. (2011). *Isten állatkertje: Az ötven legkétesebb magyarországi egyház* [God's Zoo: The 50 Most Controversial Hungarian Churches]. válasz.hu. 02 09. Available at: http://valasz.hu/vilag/isten-allatkertje-35171. Accessed 02/15/2020.

Tarján, Tamás M. (n.d.). 1456. június 29. | *III. Callixtus pápa elrendeli a „déli harangszót"* [29th June 1456, Callixtus III orders the "noon bell tolling"]. Rubiconline. Available at: http://www.rubicon.hu/magyar/oldalak/1456_junius_29_iii_callixtus_papa_elrendeli_a_deli_harangszot. Accessed 01/20/2020.

U.S. Department of State. (2017). *2016 Report on International Religious Freedom: Hungary.* Available at: https://www.state.gov/reports/2016-report-on-international-religious-freedom/hungary/. Accessed 06/09/2018.

Vékony, Dániel. (2019). *Country Report: Hungary.* GREASE 10. Available at: http://grease.eui.eu/wp-content/uploads/sites/8/2019/10/WP2-Mapping_Hungary-report_Daniel-Vekony-tcm2.pdf. Accessed 10/31/2019.

Vékony, Dániel. (forthcoming). Hungary. In Egdunas Racius (ed.), *Yearbook of Muslims in Europe 2020.* Leiden: Brill.

Vidra, Zsuzsanna. (2017). *Dominant Islamophobic Narratives: Hungary.* Working Paper. Budapest: Center for Policy Studies – Central European University. Available at: https://cps.ceu.edu/sites/cps.ceu.edu/files/attachment/publication/2923/cps-working-paper-countering-islamophobia-dominant-islamophobic-narratives-hungary-2017_0.pdf. Accessed 01/15/2020.

10
Lithuania
The predicament of the segregation of religions

Egdūnas Račius

Introduction

Though the period of Lithuania's current independence is comparatively short – it became independent in 1991, following the breakup of the USSR – it was rather a restoration of its statehood than the beginning, as Lithuania had been an independent state from 1918 to 1940. Soon after regaining independence, Lithuania embarked on the course towards Euro-Atlantic integration, which culminated in its accession to both the EU and NATO in 2004. Lithuania's legal system, including governance of religion, is, thus, permeated by EU standards, which it had to adhere to in order to join the bloc.

The peculiarity, at least in the broader European context, of the Lithuanian regime of the governance of religious diversity lies particularly in the formal distinction between three or even four levels of recognition of religious collectivities and their organizations operating in the country. Lithuania has a special category, that of 'traditional' religious communities and Churches, which *inter alia* includes Sunni Muslims, while all other branches of Islam fall under other categories. Two other non-Christian 'traditional' religious communities are Judaist and Karaite. As such, 'traditional' religious communities, through their organizations, have exceptional rights to build temples and own property, expect tax exemptions, teach their religion to children in public schools, and seek assistance from the state for their projects. Furthermore, individual religious rights (dietary, clothing, feast days, and similar) of members of 'traditional' religious communities are not only formally guaranteed but are to be secured in practice.

The chapter shows what complications arise from the current legal system of religious diversity governance in Lithuania, which, as a country, starts *inter alia* being affected by arrival of revivalist and other 'non-traditional' forms of religiosity within religions officially recognized as 'traditional'. For instance, the appearance of the Chabad Lubavich community, which has never existed in Lithuanian territory, has challenged the notion of what the contents of Judaism (recognized as a 'traditional' faith in the country) is: the state did recognize Chabad Lubavich as 'traditional' even when the autochthonous Judaist community protested against this. Likewise, registration by the state of a revivalist-leaning Muslim religious organization as 'traditional' contrary to an explicit protest by an established Muslim religious organization run by autochthonous Tatars puts into question the hitherto cosy understanding that 'traditional' Islam in Lithuania is Tatar-professed Islam. This chapter argues that with the changing Lithuanian religious landscape – and not only in relation to such 'traditional' religions as Judaism, Islam, and Karaism (which, with the dwindling numbers of its followers, is dying out) – the current system of religion's governance is not only outdated but also not sustainable and needs to be thoroughly overhauled to come more in line with the evolving social reality.

Current ethno-confessional composition of the population and challenges arising from it

Ethnic Lithuanians comprise the overwhelming majority of the country's inhabitants: according to the latest population census, in 2011, they are over 84 per cent of three-million-strong nation (Department of Statistics, 2013: 7); the second largest ethnic community, Poles, comprise 6.6 per cent, with a third ethnic group, Russians, comprising 5.8 per cent. Belarusians and Ukrainians make up 1.2 and 0.5 per cent respectively. People of all other ethnicities found in Lithuania are less than 2 per cent of the population. Though the last population census was conducted a decade ago, the country's ethnic make-up probably has not changed much as there is virtually no immigration to Lithuania of either asylum seekers or economic migrants (Table 10.1).

Current data attest to the fact that there has been little immigration to independent Lithuania: as of 1 January 2019, there were just 58,000 foreigners residing in Lithuania, comprising just little over 2 per cent of total population. The biggest national group are Ukrainian nationals – around 17,000 (Delfi.lt, 2019). Other large groups are also nationals of neighbouring countries: some 12,500 Russians and over 12,000 Belarusians. Citizens of these three Slavic Orthodox majority countries comprise some 85 per cent of all foreigners living in Lithuania. The largest group of EU member state citizens are from Latvia (1,100), Germany, and Poland (more than 700 from each). However, around 60 per cent of foreigners reside in the country on a temporary basis, mainly through employment contracts.

Immigrants from outside Europe are a negligent share of the population. Those hailing from Muslim majority regions in Asia and Africa may total 1,000 but they come from a plethora of countries with none dominating. Lithuania has been a transit country for both economic migrants and political refugees, with only a few requesting asylum. For instance, in 2018, only 279 asylum requests were filed: 74 by Tajiks, 39 by Russians, 34 by Iraqis, and 30 by Syrians. The rate of asylum approval has been traditionally low with only a handful receiving conventional refugee status. But even those granted asylum tend to leave Lithuania for another (Western) European country.

According to the latest population census, nominally, some 83 per cent of Lithuania's population are of Christian cultural background, with Roman Catholics (predominantly ethnic Lithuanians and Poles) making up over 77 per cent and Russian Orthodox (primarily Russians,

Table 10.1 Main ethnic groups in Lithuania (percentage)

Lithuanians	84.2
Poles	6.6
Russians	5.8
Belarusians	1.2

Source: Compiled by the author based on the population census results.

Table 10.2 Faith groups in Lithuania (percentage)

Roman Catholics	77.2
Orthodox	4.1
Old believers	0.8
Other religions	1.7
Non-religious	6.1
Undeclared	10.1

Source: Compiled by the author based on the population census results.

Belarusians, and Ukrainians) over 4 per cent. Around 6 per cent of the population self-identify as 'non-religious'. Members of non-Christian religious communities (chiefly, Muslim, Buddhist, Judaist, Karaite, Krishna consciousness) total less than 0.5 per cent. According to census figures, in 2011 there were 2,727 Sunni Muslims in Lithuania, representing a mere 0.1 per cent of the population. Shia Muslims – largely Azeris, who came to Lithuania in the Soviet period – number fewer than 300. The share of people of Muslim background in Lithuania is one of the lowest in all of Europe (Račius, 2018: 3–4) (Table 10.2).

Irrespective of religious identity, many Lithuanians do not hold such essential Abrahamic religious beliefs as belief in life after death, Hell and Heaven; or if they do hold 'religious' beliefs, those often tend to be non-Christian, such as the evil eye or reincarnation (Pew Research Center, 2017). In any case, most Lithuanians, as numerous surveys reveal, do not attend religious services (Manchin, 2004).

In view of this ethno-confessional composition of the Lithuanian population, Lithuania may be seen as one of the most culturally homogenous nations in Europe and described as a rather secular post-socialist society of Western Christian cultural heritage. Therefore, culturally internally, there are hardly any tensions or cleavages that could threaten its socio-political stability. Nonetheless, as a recent survey revealed, almost 36 per cent of Lithuanians would not want to have a Muslim neighbour (Institute for Ethnic Studies, 2019) even though few have ever met a Muslim. This high response of people who dislike or are distrustful of Muslims results primarily from negative reporting in the media (national, Western, and Russian) of Islam and Muslims (Baliūnaitė, 2018; Dikšaitė, 2015). Indeed, these numbers temporarily spike after every news report of a terrorist attack in Europe.

The presence of the ethnic Polish minority, which is concentrated in the south-east along the border with Belarus, while generally not viewed as problematic is nonetheless perceived by some nationalistically inclined ethnic Lithuanians as a potential danger to the integrity of the Lithuanian state. With Polish governments expressing concern for the well-being and rights of ethnic Poles in Lithuania – which in the past caused bilateral relations between the two countries to sour (Burant & Zubek, 1993: 370; The Economist, 2012; Radio Poland, 2011), ethnic Polish citizens of Lithuania are sometimes suspected by ethnic Lithuanians of, if not harbouring irredentist feelings, then collective unwillingness to fully identify with the Lithuanian state. But with practically all Poles nominally Roman Catholic, there is no difference in their religious identity from the majority of ethnic Lithuanians.

Historical background of state-organized religion relations

Lithuania, or rather what then was the Grand Duchy of Lithuania, which at its peak in the fifteenth and sixteenth centuries stretched from the Baltic Sea all the way to the Black Sea, had been multi-confessional since its founding in the thirteenth century. While its leaders and ethnic Lithuanians remained pagan until the end of the fourteenth century, Lithuania already hosted both Roman Catholic (mainly merchants and other settlers from Western Europe) and Orthodox (local Slavs) populations. By the sixteenth century, its confessional composition had diversified further to include, besides various Christian confessional groups, such non-Christian religious communities as Judaists, Karaites, and Muslims.

The appearance of the first Muslims and Karaites on Lithuanian territory dates back to the fourteenth century when the first migrants – political refugees – from the Golden Horde (and later, the Crimean Khanate) came to the then-Grand Duchy of Lithuania. They were soon joined by new arrivals, consisting chiefly of mercenaries hired by Lithuanian grand dukes, more refugees, and prisoners of war who, once freed, chose to stay. The immigrants, the majority of whom were recently Islamized Turkic speakers (Tatars) but also Turkic-speaking Karaites, settled mainly in the north-western parts of the Duchy, usually in village communities around the capital Vilnius.

The Grand Dukes granted the Muslim and Karaite elite the nobility rank and gave tracts of land to be used as fiefs that later became their personal possession. Neither Muslims nor Karaites of the Grand Duchy of Lithuania were ever forced to abandon their faith either through coerced conversion or because of artificially created obstacles in practising their religion (such as bans, prohibitions, segregationist decrees, and so on.). It is believed that mosques on the then-territory of the Grand Duchy were being built as early as the late fourteenth or early fifteenth century (Kričinskis, 1993: 158). In the times of the Republic of Two Nations (that is until its final partition in 1795) there may have been up to two dozen mosques (Kričinskis, 1993: 161), with adjacent cemeteries as a rule.

Though the first Jews may have come to live on the territory of the Grand Duchy of Lithuania as early as the thirteenth century, their immigration and permanent settlement took place between the fourteenth and the fifteenth centuries. Jews were officially treated as free persons, something that arguably facilitated their communities' growth and prosperity. Unlike Muslim Tatars and Karaims, whose communities throughout the history of Lithuania remained miniscule, the Jewish population grew exponentially to reach hundreds of thousands.

Although Roman Catholicism by then had become the dominant confession, the Statutes (that is, the Constitutions of the time) of the Grand Duchy of Lithuania, and particularly the Second (1566) and the Third (1588), established equality among Christian confessions and also confirmed the *de facto* existence of wide-ranging civic rights for the nobility of minority ethno-confessional groups (such as Muslims and Karaites), although, admittedly, these fell short of full citizens' rights. This allowed minority religious groups to continue practising their faith publicly, own and build temples and other religious-purpose buildings, as well as have their own cemeteries, educational establishments, and the like.

For over a century (between 1795 and 1916), when Lithuania was under Russian imperial rule, the tsarist regime pursued the policy of Russification of the local population, which was endorsed by the Russian Orthodox Church. Both the imperial regime and the Russian Orthodox Church saw the Roman Catholic Church as an enemy and its Catholic flock (Lithuanians, Poles, and some Latvians were the empire's only Catholic subjects) as a disloyal population. Though practising Catholicism was never banned in Lithuania under tsarist rule, the clergy and other Catholic Church personnel had a hard time under the tsars and the Catholic Church's property was frequently confiscated by the authorities and either turned into Orthodox churches or razed. Minority religious groups – including Muslims, Karaites, and Judaists – fared better than Catholics.

During its brief 20-year stint of independence between the world wars (1918–1940), Lithuania sought to grant religious rights to all major religious groups. Though the Roman

Catholic Church, as the religious organization representing the overwhelming majority of the population, clearly held a privileged position, *inter alia*, granted to it by the Concordat of 1927, other religious groups, including such non-Christian ones like Jews (some 7 per cent of the country's population) and miniscule Karaite and Muslim communities, exercised their religious rights unhindered. Curiously enough, the Muslim community, which in inter-war Lithuania numbered just 1,000 – most Muslims of the former Grand Duchy of Lithuania at the time lived in Polish-controlled territories, including Vilnius – was lucky enough to have the state pay for construction of its mosque in the interim capital Kaunas, and the state also provided modest salaries for Muslim imams.

The Second World War ushered in almost complete obliteration of the Jewish population and also heavily affected Tatar and Karaim communities, all of whom lost most of their religious property, institutions, and infrastructure. The Soviet period (1944–1990) in Lithuania, as elsewhere in the USSR, was marked by the regime's atheistic stance, which was debilitating and detrimental to all religious groups in the country. But once again, it was the Catholics and their Church that were singled out as the biggest enemies of the communist state. In the first decade of Soviet rule numerous churches were closed, with many demolished and their priests deported to Siberia, imprisoned, and often killed. However, in subsequent decades the persecution of Catholic activists eased, but official atheistic anti-religious position and rhetoric persisted and religious people continued to feel discriminated against on religious grounds. The Catholic Church at that time took upon itself the role of the preserver and protector of the double identity of Lithuanian-Catholics; some of the clergy as well as clandestine monks and nuns participated in peaceful resistance to the communist regime – activity for which they often paid for with their freedom. Apart from the Roman Catholic and Orthodox Churches, no other religious group managed to preserve its integrity or organizational structure during the Soviet period.

Though Lithuania did not become truly sovereign until 1991, even before declaring its independence a year earlier, the lot of believers had improved significantly in the last years of Soviet rule when the central administration in Moscow practically abandoned all restrictions on religious freedom. Already in 1989, numerous Christian and non-Christian religious organizations were revived or established for the first time in the still-Soviet Lithuania. The process of restoration of full religious freedoms and rights was then continued with the country's independence.

Current institutional structure for governing religion and religious diversity

The current institutional structure for governing religious diversity in Lithuania is to be found in, and is based on, two legal acts – the Constitution of the Republic of Lithuania (adopted in 1992) and the Law on Religious Communities and Associations (passed in 1995). Additionally, a number of other laws (for instance, the law on restitution of communal property) regulate relations between the state and religious collectivities. Although there have been numerous amendments to both primary pieces of legislation, they have not profoundly changed the original foundation of the institutional structure for governing religious diversity in the country. There have also been – so far unsuccessful – attempts by the Ministry of Justice to profoundly change the Law on Religious Communities and Associations. The draft law prepared by the ministry and which proposes to overhaul the typology of religious collectivities and reconsider privileges accorded to some of them by the state, however, has been shelved by Parliament, allegedly because of fierce opposition from the Catholic Church to any changes to the current regime of governance of religion.

The country's foundational law, the Constitution, besides guaranteeing in a number of its articles religious freedom to the country's inhabitants, makes an explicit distinction in Article 43 between what it refers to as 'traditional' and merely 'registered' 'churches'[1] and religious organizations, while, however, remaining silent on which ones fall under which category and generally does not establish the difference between them (Seimas of the Republic of Lithuania, 1992). The ambivalence in the Constitution regarding which religions or faith communities are to be recognized as 'traditional' was rectified by a *lex specialis*, namely, the Law on Religious Communities and Associations. Article 5 of the Law states: 'The State shall recognise nine traditional religious communities and associations existing in Lithuania, which comprise a part of Lithuania's historical, spiritual and social heritage: Roman Catholic, Greek Catholic, Evangelical Lutheran, Evangelical Reformed, Russian Orthodox, Old Believer, Judaist, Sunni Muslim and Karaite' (Seimas of the Republic of Lithuania, 1995). All of these faith communities have a presence in Lithuania that exceeds 300 years. These are the top-tier religious communities, which, as the law establishes, are accorded a range of privileges not available to the religious collectivities and their organizations of lower rank.

Among the rights and privileges granted to 'traditional' faith communities are: the right to build temples and own communal property; tax exemptions on property and a range of economic activities regarded as religious or religion-related, like production and sale of religious items; the right to teach their religion to children of community members in public schools, establish confessional schools, and seek assistance from the state for their projects. Individually, members of 'traditional' faith communities have certain dietary and clothing rights, the right to paid days off work during their religious feasts, and their religious wedding ceremonies are recognized and registered by the state as official.

The Law on Religious Communities and Associations also talks about 'state-recognized' religious communities and associations, but refers to them in generic terms, without naming a single one. Achieving state recognition is the highest level that 'non-traditional' religious collectivities may hope for, as the scope of rights and privileges (the main two of which are the right to confessional teaching in public schools and recognition of religious wedding by the state) is also very wide and second only to the 'traditional' religious collectivities. Only those faith communities who can provide documented evidence of having been present in Lithuania for more than 25 years may apply for such status. At present, four Christian communities of Protestant denominations are 'state-recognized' in Lithuania.

A third category of religious communities and associations, not referred to in the Constitution, is also discernible in the Law: religious communities and associations which are neither 'traditional' nor 'state-recognized'. In the Law on Religious Communities and Associations, they are referred to in the context of application for the status of 'state-recognized' and approximate the Constitutional 'registered' religious collectivities but none are mentioned by name (Seimas of the Republic of Lithuania, 1995). There are almost 200 such religious organizations in Lithuania.

Article 43 of the Constitution declares that there is no state religion in Lithuania; thus, all of the traditional religious communities named in the Law on Religious Communities and Associations are officially equal, both vis-à-vis the state and among themselves. Non-Christian religious communities such as Karaites, Judaists, and Sunni Muslims, with their share in the country's population hovering around or less than 0.1 per cent, have the same rights as the Roman Catholic community, or 77 per cent in the latest census in 2011 (Department of Statistics, 2013: 5).

In practice, however, the numerically dominant Roman Catholic Church gets preferential treatment from the state and public institutions. For instance, the Roman Catholic Church has its representative on the Council of the national TV and radio broadcaster (LRT), and Roman Catholic priests serve in state institutions (Armed Forces, Border Police) as salaried chaplains and are otherwise routinely invited to consecrate and bless state property (groundbreaking ceremonies, new police cars) and perform rituals at military events (blessing unit flags).

However, the very separation of 'traditional' religious communities from others raises the question of equality between the former and the latter. Article 3 of the Law on Religious Communities and Associations assures that 'All individuals, regardless of religion they profess, their religious convictions or their relationship with religion, shall be equal before the law. It shall be prohibited to, directly or indirectly, restrict their rights and freedoms, or to apply privileges' (Seimas of the Republic of Lithuania, 1995). Nonetheless, building on the constitutional distinction between religious communities in Article 43 of the Constitution, Articles 10 and 11 of the Law on Religious Communities and Associations establish a clear distinction between the two categories of religious communities and associations, not least with respect to the status and rights of their legal persons (Seimas of the Republic of Lithuania, 1995). So, for instance, Article 14 of the Law on Religious Communities and Associations clearly prioritizes 'traditional' religious communities over 'non-traditional' ones by stipulating that

> Educational and training establishments of traditional religious communities and associations providing general education of the national standard shall be funded and maintained in accordance with the procedure established by the Government or an institution authorised by it, allocating the same amount of the budget funds as allocated to state or municipal educational establishments of the corresponding type (level).
> *(Seimas of the Republic of Lithuania, 1995)*

The inequality between religious communities has become evident in the practical application of the Law on Religious Communities and Associations in various fields. As an example, for the past two decades, the traditional religious communities have received, through their legal persons, annual payments from the state. The sum of these payments is divided proportionally based on the number of believers recorded by the Department of Statistics. The Roman Catholic Church receives the largest share, with the Orthodox Church being a distant second, and the remaining seven traditional religious communities receiving negligible amounts. It is not the amount that matters here but the fact that since 1997 the state, through successive governments, has distributed such payments exclusively to traditional religious communities even though there is no legal basis for that – no law requires the government to financially support any religious community in this manner. The 'traditional' religious communities may use these funds at their own discretion and are not required to report back to the state on how the funds were spent. As a result, numerous Christian and non-Christian religious communities (among them non-Sunni Muslims like Shias and Ahmadis), though registered, received no monies from the state, regardless of their size.

The *de facto* legally unequal status of religious communities of different categories discernible in both the Constitution and the Law on Religious Communities and Associations, as well as a plethora of subsequent laws stemming from it, was challenged at the turn of the century by a group of MPs who approached the Constitutional Court for an explanation. The Court, on two occasions, in 2000 and 2007, endorsed the status quo promulgated in the Constitution (Constitutional Court of the Republic of Lithuania, 2000, 2007). In its 2000 decision, the Court ruled that

the provision of Paragraph 1 of Article 43 of the Constitution providing for the presence of traditional Lithuanian churches and religious organisations is the constitutional basis upon which a different status of traditional churches and organisations may be established if compared with other churches and religious organisations. This means that, without limiting the rights guaranteed for all churches and religious organisations, additional rights for traditional churches and religious organisations may also be ensured by law which are not enjoyed by the churches and organisations which are not traditional.
(Constitutional Court of the Republic of Lithuania, 2000)

In 2007, explaining its own ruling of 2000, the Court stated that this is possible because

certain rights, which are not enjoyed by other churches and religious organisations recognised by the state, are established to the churches and religious organisations traditional in Lithuania specifically on the constitutional basis that these churches and religious organisations are traditional in Lithuania, and if any other (non-traditional in Lithuania) church or religious organisation is recognised by the state, in itself this does not provide grounds to establish such rights to them, to which churches and religious organisations traditional in Lithuania are entitled because they are traditional in Lithuania.
(Constitutional Court of the Republic of Lithuania, 2007)

The Law on Religious Communities and Associations foresees that religious communities may operate without formal registration. However, if they want to become 'state-recognized' religious communities, that is, to be recognized as 'being a part of Lithuania's historical, spiritual and social heritage', they must first formally register with the Ministry of Justice and become 'state-registered' legal persons. Twenty-five years after their first registration, they may apply for the status of 'state recognized religious community' (Seimas of the Republic of Lithuania, 1995). But the Law on Religious Communities and Associations also stipulates that an applicant community needs to have a 'back[ing] by society' and the 'instruction and rites thereof are not contrary to laws and morality' (Seimas of the Republic of Lithuania, 1995). In the case of rejection, they may reapply after a period of ten years (Seimas of the Republic of Lithuania, 1995). However, 'state recognition (…) may be withdrawn, if a respective church or religious organisation recognised by the state loses its support in society or its teaching and practices become contradictory to laws or public morals' (Ruškytė, 2008: 175).

Such legal stipulations have several repercussions. First, they rank religious collectivities operating (or wishing to operate) in the country in a rather discriminatory manner. Second, they make it difficult for some to move up the ranking ladder as the legal condition to 'have a backing by society' is too fluid and may be manipulated by interested parties, foremost politicians (in this case, MPs), who decide which religious communities are to be promoted to a higher rank.

Concluding remarks

Although Lithuanian society is, on the one hand, rather secular and, on the other, composed of people professing numerous faiths, the regime of governance of religious diversity in the country favours those religious communities that had been historically institutionalized by treating them as 'traditional'. Besides a number of Christian denominations, Judaist, Karaite, and Sunni Muslim communities have been assigned to this category. The Roman Catholic

Church, representing the overwhelming majority of the country's believers, though officially not 'more equal among equals', in practice receives markedly more favourable treatment from the state than any other 'traditional' faith community. Moreover, the law inadvertently puts any newly emergent religious collectivities at a disadvantage. Thus, in practice, faith communities and their representative organizations form a sort of pyramid, with the towering Roman Catholic Church at the top as representative of a 'traditional' faith community par excellence, followed by other 'traditional' faith communities, with 'state-recognized' communities next, and all others, registered and not, at the bottom.

There is, however, an inherent flaw in the very concept of 'traditional' religious collectivities, since aside from the unitary Roman Catholic Church, the others do not have uniform religious authority. Thus, splits in original religious organizations representing those faith communities inevitably led to questions of whether there may be more than one religious organization representing the same 'traditional' religious community and whether changes and evolution in their religious doctrine may render them not 'traditional'. Both Judaism and Islam are good examples of this. But of all the 'traditional' religious communities, it is the (Sunni) Muslims that appear to be least compatible with the present system of religious governance in Lithuania. Institutionalization of Islam through the Religious Communities Law is counterproductive as it fails to recognize the wider social reality – the multiplicity of parallel (and even rival) forms of Islamic religiosity that claim to be truly 'traditional'.

While, as indicated above, there have been attempts to change the legal *status quo* by overhauling the Law on Religious Communities and Associations, these attempts so far have been inconclusive. Thus, to this day, the Lithuanian case of the regime of governance of religion with its entrenched distinction between 'traditional' and non-traditional 'churches' and religious organizations, though it may seem unique in some respects, is representative, if not symptomatic, of a cluster of post-communist Eastern European states that have similar regimes, and particularly those that include Muslim (but also Judaist) collectivities in the category of 'traditional' religious communities or organizations. As shown by the Lithuanian case, such regimes of governance of religion are very problematic, if not counterproductive, in general, to say the least; application of the label and status of 'traditional' religious organization to Muslim religious collectivities, due to rapid diversification of forms of Islamic (or other religions') religiosity found in most of post-communist Europe, makes it altogether untenable.

Some Eastern European countries have already experienced splits and rivalries in their Muslim communities that have led to both the fragmentation of the domestic Islamic religious scene as well as claims and counterclaims (and attached political manipulations) of being representative of true, if not 'traditional', forms of Islamic religiosity. Thus, it becomes increasingly difficult to define what 'traditional' Islam (and, for that matter, Judaism or any other religion) means and who represents it, obscuring the very dichotomous paradigm of 'traditional'/ 'non-traditional' religious communities and their organizations.

The Lithuanian case may prove an exception, but, as such, it inevitably faces future changes in its regime of governance of religion. One may only hope these changes take place sooner rather than later.

Note

1 The term 'church' used in the Constitution is to be understood as a generic term synonymous to 'formalized religious hierarchy'.

References

Baliūnaitė, Ilona. (2018). *Media as Fear Creator: The Expression of Islamophobia in Lithuanian Online News Media* [Unpublished MA thesis]. Vilnius Gediminas Technical University [in Lithuanian].

Burant, Stephen R. & Zubek, Voytek. (1993). Eastern Europe's old memories and new realities: Resurrecting the Polish-lithuanian Union. *East European Politics and Societies* 7 (2), 370–393.

Constitutional Court of the Republic of Lithuania. (2000, June 13). *Ruling on the Compliance of Item 5 of Article 1, Paragraphs 3 and 4 of Article 10, Paragraph 1 of Article 15, Article 20, Item 2 of Article 21, Paragraph 2 of Article 32, Paragraphs 2, 3 and 4 of Article 34, Items 2 and 5 of Article 35, Item 2 of Article 37 and Items 2 and 3 of Article 38 of the Republic of Lithuania's Law on Education with the Constitution of the Republic of Lithuania*. Available at: http://www.lrkt.lt/en/court-acts/search/170/ta1161/content. Accessed 09/27/2019.

Constitutional Court of the Republic of Lithuania. (2007, December 6). *Decision on Construing the Provisions of a Constitutional Court Ruling Related with the Status of the Churches and Religious Organisations that Are Traditional in Lithuania*. Available at: http://www.lrkt.lt/en/court-acts/search/170/ta1375/content. Accessed 09/27/2019.

Delfi.lt. (2019, January 18). Ukrainians become the largest foreign community in Lithuania. Media Briefing. Available at: https://en.delfi.lt/politics/ukrainians-become-the-largest-foreign-community-in-lithuania.d?id=80145005. Accessed 09/27/2019.

Department of Statistics. (2013). *Gyventojai pagal tautybę, gimtąją kalbą ir tikybą* [Inhabitants by Ethnicity, Mother Tongue and Faith, in Lithuanian]. Vilnius: Statistics Lithuania. Available at: https://osp.stat.gov.lt/documents/10180/217110/Gyv_kalba_tikyba.pdf/1d9dac9a-3d45-4798-93f5-941fed00503f. Accessed 09/27/2019.

Dikšaitė, Rimgailė. (2015). Transformations of the Arab image in the Lithuanian Press [in Lithuanian]. *Politikos mokslų almanachas* 17, 57–89.

Institute for Ethnic Studies. (2019). Lithuanian public opinion survey shows negative attitudes toward refugees. Muslims. Available at: http://www.ces.lt/wp-content/uploads/2010/02/Visuomen%C4%97s-nuostatos-apklausos-rezultatai_20191.pdf. Accessed 09/27/2019.

Kričinskis, Stanislovas. (1993). *Lietuvos totoriai*. Vilnius: Mokslo ir enciklopedijų leidykla [in Lithuanian].

Manchin, Robert. (2004). Religion in Europe: Trust not filling the pews. Gallup. Available at: https://news.gallup.com/poll/13117/religion-europe-trust-filling-pews.aspx. Accessed 09/27/2019.

Pew Research Center. (2017). *Two-thirds of Greeks, Latvians Say They Believe in the Evil Eye*. Available at: https://www.pewforum.org/2017/05/10/religious-beliefs/pf-05-10-2017_ce-europe-03-00/. Accessed 09/27/2019.

Račius, E. (2018). *Muslims in Eastern Europe*. Edinburgh: Edinburgh University Press.

Radio Poland. (2011, March 2). *Current Disputes Must Not Spoil Bilateral Relations, Says Komorowski*. Available at: https://www.polskieradio.pl/395/8112/Search?q=Current%20disputes%20must%20not%20spoil%20bilateral%20relations,%20says%20Komorowski. Accessed 09/27/2019.

Ruškytė, Ramutė. (2008). Legal aspects of religious freedom. In Drago Čepar & Blaž Ivanc (eds), *Legal Aspects of Religious Freedom: International Conference* (pp. 148–198). Ljubljana: Office of the Government of the Republic of Slovenia for Religious Communities.

Seimas of the Republic of Lithuania. (1992). *Constitution of the Republic of Lithuania*. Available at: http://www3.lrs.lt/home/Konstitucija/Constitution.htm. Accessed 09/27/2019.

Seimas of the Republic of Lithuania. (1995). *Law on Religious Communities and Associations of the Republic of Lithuania*. Available at: https://e-seimas.lrs.lt/portal/legalAct/lt/TAD/TAIS.385299?jfwid=16j6tpgu6w. Accessed 09/27/2019.

The Economist. (2012, March 10). Bad blood: Polish-Lithuanian ties are ancient but increasingly acrimonious. Print edition, Europe. Available at: https://www.economist.com/europe/2012/03/10/bad-blood. Accessed 09/27/2019.

11
Slovakia
Fear of new religious minorities

Egdūnas Račius

Introduction

Slovakia as a modern sovereign nation state is rather young – it became independent in 1993 after a peaceful split of Czechoslovakia into two independent states – the Czech Republic and the Slovak Republic.[1] Almost from the first day of independence, Slovakia has pursued the goals of Euro-Atlantic integration, which culminated in its accession to both the EU and NATO in 2004. Slovakia's legal system, including governance of religion, is, thus, permeated by the EU standards though it retains some features of the former Czechoslovakia.

The uniqueness of the Slovak regime's governance of religion among democratic states of Europe lies particularly in its strict (one might say, stringent) rules of registration for religious collectivities. This has led to Slovakia being one of the few European states where Muslims do not have a registered Muslim religious organization and are thus forced to operate (including religious rituals and other activities) through NGOs. Legislation governing religion has also prevented other minority faith communities (particularly those new to the country) from registering their religious organizations. Having no religious organizations, these faith communities have been effectively marginalized in the religious landscape as they are not allowed to build temples or own property, nor can they expect tax exemptions or that their clergy's salaries be paid by the state or teach their religion to children in public schools or seek any assistance from the state. Furthermore, their individual religious rights (dietary, clothing, feast days, and similar), though officially guaranteed, in practice are not secured.

Although there are a number of faith communities that are legally deprived of the right to have a religious organization, it is widely believed that the draconian legislation was designed to prevent followers of Islam from institutionalizing their religion in the country as both the country's political elite and the population are decidedly Islamophobic (*Islamophobia*, 2018). And all this against the backdrop of the reality where people of Muslim background number just 5,000 and no signs of Muslim religious radicalization have ever been reported. Although officially it is not so, in practical terms, the current stance, through both rhetoric and policies, of the Slovak governments vis-à-vis Islam and Muslims is markedly negative, making Slovakia, along with Czech Republic, if not unique, then still exceptional in the EU context. Slovakia, along with the other Višegrad Four countries of central Europe – namely, Hungary,

Czech Republic, and Poland – is among the European countries where securitization, both institutional and informal, of Islam has reached unprecedented levels (Račius, 2020).

Another aspect that makes Slovakia distinctive in the European context is the fact that in the 2016 parliamentary elections an extreme far-right political party, Kotleba – People's Party Our Slovakia (*Kotleba – Ľudová strana Naše Slovensko*) won more than 8 per cent of the vote and entered Parliament for the first time. Since then, the party has been increasingly gaining in popularity; in recent polls (December 2019), its support was around 12 per cent, with the ruling party polling between 18 and 19 per cent. Earlier, in the European Parliament elections on 25 May 2019, Kotleba won more than 12 per cent of vote (European Parliament, 2019). The party is at the same time nationalist and populist, which translates into its promotion of what it calls 'traditional Slovak values and way of living' as opposed to EU-promoted values and ways of living purportedly led by immigrants and particularly Muslims (Rafa, 2015).

This chapter unveils how stigmatization, securitization, and even demonization of the country's Muslim population are enshrined in the current regime of religious diversity governance and how, promoted by political elite and media alike, it has affected relations between the Muslim community, on the one hand, and the state and wider society, on the other. The case of the Muslim religious community in Slovakia may serve as a blueprint for analysis of other unregistered minority religious collectivities in the country.

Current composition of the population and challenges arising from it

Both ethnically and confessionally, Slovakia is rather diverse: while ethnic Slovaks make up almost 81 per cent of the roughly 5.5-million-strong nation (Table 11.1), ethnic Hungarians are 8.5 per cent with a third ethnic group, the Roma, possibly comprising 9 or 10 per cent, although the official census data put them at just 2 per cent. Based on interviews with Slovak experts conducted by the author in Bratislava in May 2019, it is widely believed in Slovakia that of the more than 382,000 (or, 7 per cent of the population) people who chose not to disclose their ethnic identity, many, if not most, are in fact of Roma ethnicity; likewise, some Roma may have identified themselves as either ethnic Slovaks or Hungarians. All in all, Slovakia's Roma population may number 500,000 and exceed the number of ethnic Hungarians. All other ethnic groups comprise less than 1 per cent each.

As there has been little immigration to independent Slovakia, the biggest national group of immigrants are Ukrainians (as of 2019, over 20 per cent of the 121,000 foreigners in the country) (IOM, 2019). Nationals of EU member states make up almost half of the foreigners living in Slovakia. According to the International Organization for Migration, immigrants from Asian

Table 11.1 Main ethnic groups in Slovakia (percentage)

Slovaks	80.7
Hungarians	8.5
Romani	2.0 (9–10)
Ruthenians	0.6

Source: Statistical Office of the Slovak Republic. (n.d.).
Table 10: Population by nationality – 2011, 2001, 1991.
Available at: https://slovak.statistics.sk/wps/wcm/connect/-bd447dc5-c417-48d6-89e1-0a2d60053cf6/Table_10_Population_by_nationality_2011_2001_1991.
pdf?MOD=AJPERES&CVID=kojGfKx&CVID=kojGfKx.
Accessed 09/13/2019.

countries (mainly Vietnam, China, South Korea, and Thailand) in 2019 totalled just 7 per cent (less than 9,000) of the country's foreign population. Although Slovakia is not a primary destination country for migrants, it has been a transit country because of its geographic location. Migrant numbers, however, have fallen substantially since Slovakia (as well as neighbours Poland and Hungary) joined the EU, thus becoming an EU frontier state, resulting in significantly enhanced border control with Ukraine. In 2018, there were fewer than 3,000 migrants crossing into the country illegally, and in 2019 their number is reported to have fallen to below 1,000 (Francelová, 2019). In 2018, just 178 applications for asylum were submitted, mostly by citizens of Afghanistan, Iraq, Yemen, and Azerbaijan; Slovakia granted asylum to only five individuals in 2018. In the nearly three decades since independence, Slovakia has received some 59,000 applications for asylum, of which it granted 854, while another 746 persons were given subsidiary protection (IOM, 2019). Overall, foreigners, including nationals of EU member states, comprise some 2.2 per cent of the population – one of the lowest percentages in the EU.

According to the latest population census figures, three-quarters of Slovakia's population are of Christian cultural background, although only one-third of believers attend services monthly (Starr, 2019), while over 13 per cent self-identify as 'non-religious' (Table 11.2). Nominally, Roman Catholics comprise the majority of Slovakia's population (62 per cent, a 7 per cent decline in the decade since the previous census), followed by the Evangelical Church of the Augsburg Confession, nearly 6 per cent; Greek Catholics, less than 4 per cent; the Reformed Christian Church, less than 2 per cent; and Orthodox, around 1 per cent. Members of all other (Christian and non-Christian) religious communities total slightly over 1 per cent. As indicated above, there are an estimated 5,000 people of Muslim background living in Slovakia (Pew Research Center, 2017), a mere 0.09 per cent of the population. This is one of the lowest percentages of Muslims in all of post-communist East and Central Europe (Račius, 2018). Incidentally, Slovakia is the only country in Europe that does not have a single mosque (for prayers, Muslims use spaces at their NGO premises).

In view of this ethno-confessional composition of the Slovak population, Slovakia may be seen as one of the most culturally homogenous nations in Europe and described as a rather secular post-socialist society of Western Christian cultural heritage. Therefore, ethno-confessionally, there are hardly any tensions or cleavages that could threaten its socio-political stability. Nonetheless, as a recent survey revealed, over 54 per cent of Slovaks would not want to have a Muslim as neighbour (Institute for Sociology, 2017).

Socio-economically, however, Slovakia is not so homogenous, with ethnic Roma occupying the lowest rung of socio-economic stratification. Many Roma (whose largest

Table 11.2 Religious affiliation of Slovak population (percentage)

Roman Catholic Church	62.0
Evangelical Church of Augsburg confession	5.9
Greek Catholic Church	3.8
Christian Reformed Church	1.8
Orthodox Church	0.9
No religion	13.4
Not specified	10.6

Source: Statistical Office of the Slovak Republic. (n.d.). Table 14: Population by religion – 2011, 2001, 1991. Available at: https://slovak.statistics.sk/wps/wcm/connect/87ee3f0c-54fd-4647-b083-67c399e68bfb/Table_14_Population_by_religion_2011_2001_1991.pdf?MOD=AJPERES&CVID=kojGgO

concentration is in the eastern part of the country) live in conditions of poverty and have little education and high rates of unemployment (EU Agency for Fundamental Rights, 2014). Finally, Roma are generally viewed by ethnic Slovaks with contempt bordering on racism and thus experience constant social discrimination (Lake, 2013; Machlica, 2019). Roma are seen by the Slovak majority as the least desirable neighbours – over 62 per cent of respondents in a recent survey did not want Roma living next to them (Institute for Sociology, 2017). Roma have until recently been the primary targets of far-right and nationalist groups, which have engaged in hate crimes and violent acts against them. There are reports that even government policies sometimes discriminate against Roma (Amnesty International, 2013). This is not exclusive to Slovakia – neighbouring countries (Hungary, Serbia, Romania) all record similar attitudes.

The presence of a Hungarian minority – which is concentrated in the south, along the border with Hungary – generally is not viewed as problematic. Nonetheless, it is perceived by some nationalistically inclined ethnic Slovaks as a potential danger to the integrity of the Slovak state. With revisionist voices and the Hungarian government's expressed concern for the wellbeing and rights of ethnic Hungarians in Slovakia – something that has soured bilateral relations between the two countries in the past (Adam, 2008; EarthTimes.org, 2008; Der Spiegel, 2009; Rousek & Gulyas, 2010; BBC, 2010; Than & Santa, 2010) – ethnic Hungarian citizens of Slovakia are sometimes suspected by ethnic Slovaks of harbouring irredentist feelings. Thus, far-right and nationalist groups have been particularly wary of the ethnic Hungarian population in Slovakia. However, with the majority of both Slovaks and Hungarians historically having been Catholic, there are no religious cleavages or tensions to be found in the relations between these two ethnic groups (and their respective states).

Historical background of state-organized religion relations

Before independence and for almost 70 years – with a short break during the Second World War when it was what some observers call a satellite clero-fascist state of Nazi Germany – Slovakia was part of a joint Czech and Slovak state, which itself was born out of ruins of the Austro-Hungarian Empire. Prior to the collapse of the Austro-Hungarian state, Slovak lands were in the Hungarian part of the Empire. Although initially a primarily Western Christian state, Austro-Hungary gradually became a multi-confessional country with Orthodox Christian, Jewish, and Muslim minorities (particularly after the occupation of 1878 and subsequent annexation of Bosnia in 1908). All major confessions were recognized by the state and centrally controlled. Islam was officially recognized in the Austrian part by an imperial decree known as *Islamgesetz* in 1912, followed by official recognition by the Hungarian Parliament in 1916. The Empire facilitated the founding of a Muslim religious organization, which was meant to become independent of the Ottoman Shaykh al-Islam based in Istanbul and was modelled after Christian Churches with a hierarchical ecclesiastical-bureaucratic structure (Hafez & Dautović, 2019). Its head was appointed by the Kaiser from among the candidates submitted by the Muslim religious organization. These formal recognitions and founding of a Muslim religious organization based in distant Sarajevo, in Bosnia, however, did not have any effect on Slovakia, as there were no Muslim collectivities on its territories at the time.

In the inter-war period, religious freedoms of adherents of recognized religions were generally respected in the Czechoslovak Republic, even though the Roman Catholic Church was preeminent. As there was a nascent Muslim community of converts and expatriates in the Czech part of the country, Muslims unsuccessfully sought to register their religious organization in the capital, Prague. It was finally registered in the years of the Second World

War by the Nazi occupation authorities. However, as Slovakia was at the time a nominally separate state, this registration did not extend to its territory. In the end, as the leaders of the war-time Muslim community had been accused of having (and, indeed, appear to have) collaborated with the Nazis, their organization was banned in the newly reconstituted post-war Czechoslovakia and its leadership was prosecuted (Mendel, 1998: 127–141).

With the communist takeover in 1948, as elsewhere in the communist-ruled Eastern Europe, the religious life of practically all faith communities was made very difficult and only the major Christian denominations managed to continue it (Kaplan, 1986). Catholic and other Christian Churches adapted to the political reality and even tactically collaborated with the communist regime. As there were virtually no Muslims (or indeed any non-Christians other than Jews) or Muslim organizations during communist rule, it is not possible to talk about state-Islam relations in that period.

Current institutional structure for governing religion and religious diversity

After the communist regime's collapse in 1989 but still under the joint state, religious rights for Slovaks were restored, particularly through the Law on Religious Freedom and the Legal Status of Churches and Religious Organizations of 1991, which superseded a 1949 communist-era law on religions, and communities were once again allowed to publicly engage in religious rituals. New religious communities started forming and sought to register their organizations. The Law was then inherited by independent Slovakia, which introduced several amendments. These include a 2007 amendment establishing the required minimum number of members 'who have residential address in the territory of the Slovak Republic and who are Slovak citizens' (Art. 11) of the religious community seeking to register their religious organization as 20,000.

Thus, governance of religion in today's Slovakia stems from its Constitution, the constitutional Bill of Basic Rights and Freedoms, and the Law on Religious Freedom and the Legal Status of Churches and Religious Organizations. The registration of churches and religious societies is further governed by the Law on Religious Freedom and the Legal Status of Churches and Religious Organizations, and the Law on the Registration of Churches and Religious Organizations.

As may be expected of a European state that is an EU member, the Constitution of Slovakia (Art. 24) unequivocally guarantees religious freedom:

> 1. Freedom of thought, conscience, religion and belief shall be guaranteed. This right shall include the right to change religion or belief and the right to refrain from a religious affiliation. Everyone shall have the right to express his or her mind publicly. 2. Everyone shall have the right to manifest freely his or her religion or belief either alone or in association with others, privately or publicly, in worship, religious acts, maintaining ceremonies or to participate in teaching. 3. Churches and ecclesiastical communities shall administer their own affairs themselves; in particular, they shall establish their bodies, appoint clericals, provide for theological education and establish religious orders and other clerical institutions independent from the state authorities.

The Law on Religious Freedom and the Legal Status of Churches and Religious Organizations (Art. 1) re-confirms these constitutional provisions, establishing the mutual autonomy between the state and religious collectivities and their organizations.

The regime of governance of religion in Slovakia operates on a one-tier principle – all registered religious organizations are treated as equal before the law – i.e. there is no distinction between 'traditional' or 'historical' religious communities and others (Art. 4.2) – but that the state 'recognizes only those churches and religious societies that are registered' (Art. 4.4). The Roman Catholic Church, however, has a privileged status, as Slovakia signed a Concordat with the Holy See in 2000. Similar agreements were signed in 2002 between the state and a dozen registered Christian religious organizations (Churches) representing the country's Christian minorities.

The government institution charged with supervising relations between the state and religious organizations is the Ministry of Culture. In the 1990s, the then-Minister of Culture, Ivan Hudec, established a separate institution to supervise relations between the state and religious organizations. It was, however, abolished in 2011 by the then-Minister, Daniel Krajcer, and since then the task has been charged to a ministry department.

In 2016, in the wake of the so-called European refugee crisis, the Law on Religious Freedom and the Legal Status of Churches and Religious Organizations was amended for the first time in ten years. Though the President vetoed it, arguing that the amendments curtailed religious freedoms and rights, his veto was overturned and the amendments passed by a two-thirds majority in Parliament in 2017 (The Slovak Spectator, 2017). The most symbolic amendment raised the minimum number of members for the registration of a religious organization from 20,000 to 50,000 members who are Slovak citizens permanently residing in Slovakia. Such a requirement is arguably the tightest in Europe and effectively kills the chances of any new faith communities to institutionalize their religion in Slovakia. The minor faith communities are thus forced to register according to the 1990 Law on Civic Associations (which, incidentally, explicitly states that the Law does not cover religious collectivities (Section 1, Point 1c)) (International Labour Organisation, 1990) and operate as NGOs. This effectively strips them of many of rights accorded to registered religious organizations, including the right to build and own temples and other properties, establish institutions of religious education, provide pastoral care, and lobby for religious feasts and diet- or clothing-related rights. The amendments' passage has been widely seen as placing a restraint on Muslims so that they do not form a religious organization and institutionalize Islam in the country. Some observers have even labelled the process in the law's amendment as the 'criminalization of Islam in Slovakia' (Werleman, 2018).

As of early 2020, there were 18 registered Churches and religious societies (*cirkvi a náboženské spoločnosti*) in Slovakia, of which only two were of non-Christian nature – those of Judaists and Bahais. Judaism is an historical religion in Slovakia – with Jews settling in the territory of present-day Slovakia as early as the eleventh century. Before the Second World War, there was a sizeable Jewish community whose numbers were sometimes cited as high as 137,000. War atrocities reduced that figure to just 24,000 and the Jewish community in Slovakia has continued to decline in numbers since then; according to the latest census, there were just 631 Jews living in Slovakia. However, in the same census, the number of those belonging to Jewish Religious Communities was 1,999.

Bahaism is a recent appearance in Slovakia. Nonetheless, Bahais, whose overwhelming majority are ethnic Slovaks (and citizens), succeeded in attaining registration of their religious organization in 2007, after collecting 28,000 signatures of supporters (the then-applicable legislation required 20,000 signatures), most of whom may have been relatives or friends of 'true' believers but not necessarily members of the group (Bahai World News Service, 2007). Similarly, another tiny religious community, the Church of Jesus Christ of the Latter-day Saints, commonly known as Mormons, also managed to garner the support of over 20,000

Slovaks to gain official registration in 2006. Their number in the census, however, was significantly smaller: 972.

These two cases of non-traditional religious collectivities garnering sufficient support by the Slovak population to enable them to register should, however, be seen as exceptional, as no other religious collectivity has since repeated their success (or indeed tried to). With the number of required full members raised to 50,000 and in the atmosphere of rising securitization of religion and overall cultural primordialism, it is unlikely that a newly forming religious collectivity, no matter how seemingly innocent and non-threatening, might expect to achieve official registration by the state.

It is worth noting that the Atheist Church of Non-Believers also sought official registration in 2006 and even produced the required 20,000 signatures. The Ministry of Culture, however, rejected its application on the basis that the group was a not a religious collectivity (Hall et al., n.d.).

In 2001, the then-chief of the secret service, Vladimír Mitro, reportedly 'described religious sects as among the major threats to national security' (Hall et al., n.d.); however, religious radicalization among members of non-Christian faith communities has not been observed in Slovakia. Nonetheless, the Slovak Information Service claims to have 'dealt with efforts of harmful sectarian groupings and pseudo-religious communities to acquire new members, infiltrate the education system, make financial profit and psychologically manipulate their membership' (2017). The Church of Scientology and similar non-registered groups usually fall under the category of 'harmful sectarian groupings', but followers of certain forms of Islamic religiosity, like Salafis and Wahhabis, are also sometimes included.

Slovak intelligence services admit that there is practically no threat of terrorism (understood as stemming solely from jihadis) to the country. For instance, in its annual report for 2017, the Slovak Information Service admitted that they 'did not acquire any intelligence suggesting a real threat to the country or its interests abroad' (2017). However, at the same time, they consider that 'the threat level had a mild tendency to rise particularly as a result of the number of completed/thwarted individual violent attacks that had been perpetrated largely by jihadists in some European countries' (ibid.).

Despite the fact that there have been no instances of Muslim religious radicalization in Slovakia, since (and, practically, prior to) the start of the so-called European refugee crisis and the formation of the Islamic State of Iraq and Syria, Islam and Muslims have been increasingly vilified and securitized at both the social and political levels. Slovakia initially agreed to accept several hundred refugees within the framework of the EU refugee distribution quota system but very soon decided not to take them in, arguing that accepting refugees presumed to be chiefly of Muslim background would increase the country's vulnerability and decrease its national security (Migration Policy Centre, n.d.). Robert Fico, the Prime Minister at the time, made numerous negative remarks and statements about migrants, whom he identified with Muslims. For instance, in November 2015, after the terrorist attacks in Paris, Fico publicly stated that the Slovak government was 'monitoring every single Muslim currently present in the territory of Slovakia' (Colborne, 2017); he has also said, in 2016, that 'Islam has no place in Slovakia' (ibid.) and that he firmly stood by his objective to prevent 'emergence of a united Muslim community in Slovakia' (ibid.).

Numerous pronouncements by politicians, both mainstream and populist-nationalist like Kotleba, and practical activities by groups and individuals recorded in reports on Islamophobia in Slovakia, attest to the fact that Muslims as a faith group have been targeted at all levels of state and society as the religious (but also cultural) out-group par excellence. The current legislation regulating the regime of governance of religion, though harmful to a plethora of other religious collectivities, is widely seen, both inside and outside Slovakia, as primarily targeted at Muslims in a move to prevent them from institutionalizing in the country; it is also seen as aimed at limiting their religious activities as much as possible and thus making Slovakia unattractive to believing Muslim immigrants. That the situation has become so untenable is illustrated by the fact that even a well-integrated long-time resident of Slovakia, the leader and imam of one of the larger informal Muslim congregations in the capital city Bratislava, chose to move abroad with his family.

Concluding remarks

Though Slovak society is, on the one hand, rather secular and, on the other, composed of people professing numerous faiths, the regime of governance of religion in the country favours religious communities that had been institutionalized historically. The legislation ultimately prevents any newly emergent religious collectivities from institutionalizing unless they pass a high threshold of 50,000 citizen-members. While the rationale behind such a high minimum is to prevent pseudo-religious groupings ('dangerous sects' and business enterprises) from obtaining recognition by the state as religious organizations, there have been no instances of religious radicalization on the side of new religious communities. Ultimately, the regime of governance of religion in the country is widely perceived to be focussed to a great extent on Muslims, who have become a sort of scapegoat.

Slovakia's stringent rules for registration of religious organizations are arguably the strictest in all of Europe, however several neighbouring countries – foremost, Hungary and Czech Republic – also have very strict rules for registration of religious organizations on their territories. In these countries the wave of Islamophobia, both institutionalized and social, is also unprecedented and matches that found in Slovakia. Therefore, Slovakia, rather than being an isolated or unique case, needs to be studied within the context of social, political, and legal developments in the entire region of Central Europe comprising the so-called Višegrad 4: Poland, Czech Republic, Slovakia, and Hungary. In all of them, similar socio-political processes (such as the ascent of populist-nationalist political forces to power) produce analogous shifts in the legislation governing religion. As a rule, these shifts are in the direction of a segregationist approach towards and more control over religious collectivities. Thus, Slovakia, like other Višegrad countries, is to be watched with concern that the proclaimed values of the EU, among them freedoms and rights related to religion, are being supplanted by those stemming from a narrow primordialist populist-nationalist mind-set.

Note

1 Admittedly, there was a short-lived period of a semi-independent Slovak state that was closely allied to Nazi Germany around the Second World War. For more, see Ward (2013).

References

Adam, Christopher. (2008). Slovakia rejects Hungarian suggestions to tackle discrimination. *Canadian Hungarian Journal*, 12–06. Available at: http://kanadaihirlap.com/2008/12/03/slovakia-rejects-hungarian-suggestions-to-tackle-discrimination/. Accessed 09/13/2019.

Amnesty International. (2013). Slovak authorities in breach of obligations to Romani school children. Available at: https://www.amnesty.org/en/latest/news/2013/09/slovak-authorities-breach-obligations-romani-school-children/. Accessed 09/13/2019.

Bahai World News Service. (2007, May 13). Government of Slovakia recognizes the Baha'i Faith. Available at: https://news.bahai.org/story/531/. Accessed 09/13/2019.

Bayrakli, Enes & Hafez, Farid (eds.). (2018). European Islamophobia Report. *Islamophobia Europe* [online]. Available at: http://www.islamophobiaeurope.com/wp-content/uploads/2019/09/EIR_2018.pdf. Accessed 02/23/2020.

BBC. (2010, May 26). Slovaks retaliate over Hungarian citizenship law. Available at: https://www.bbc.com/news/10166610. Accessed 09/13/2019.

Colborne, Michael. (2017). Muslims: Slovakia's least wanted. *BlogAktiv.eu*, August 25. Available at: https://guests.blogactiv.eu/2017/08/25/muslims-slovakias-least-wanted/. Accessed 09/13/2019.

Der Spiegel. (2009, August 25). Slovakia and Hungary 'dangerously close to playing with fire'. Available at: https://www.spiegel.de/international/europe/the-world-from-berlin-slovakia-and-hungary-dangerously-close-to-playing-with-fire-a-644853.html. Accessed 09/13/2019.

EarthTimes.org. (2008). Slovak, Hungarian presidents blame tension on radicals. December 6. www.earthtimes.org. Accessed 09/13/2019.

EU Agency for Fundamental Rights. (2014). Poverty and employment: The situation of Roma in 11 EU Member States. Available at: https://fra.europa.eu/sites/default/files/fra-2014-roma-survey-employment_en.pdf. Accessed 09/13/2019.

European Parliament. (2019). European election results. Available at: https://election-results.eu/national-results/slovakia/2019-2024/. Accessed 09/13/2019.

Francelová, Nina Hrabovská. (2019). Life on the Slovak-Ukrainian border: Buried migrants, dead border guards'. *Slovak Spectator*, November 29. Available at: https://spectator.sme.sk/c/22271519/migration-on-the-slovak-ukrainian-border.html. Accessed 01/09/2020.

Hafez, Farid & Dautović, Rijad. (2019). *Die Islamische Glaubensgemeinschaft in Österreich. 1909–1979–2019- Beiträge zu einem neuen Blick auf ihre Geschichte und Entwicklung* [in German]. Vienna: New Academic Press.

Hall, Dorota, Goldberger, Goran, Grešková, Lucia, & Smoczyński, Rafal. (n.d.). *Societal Reactions to New Religious Movements*. Paper drafted within the REVACERN project, New Forms of Traditions and New Religious Movements *subarea*.

Institute for Sociology of the Slovak Academy of Science. (2017). Our European values. Available at: http://www.sociologia.sav.sk/cms/uploaded/2786_attach_EVS_2017_SR_TK_SU_SAV_181217.pdf. Accessed 09/13/2019.

International Labour Organisation. (1990). Citizens Civil Law Associations Act No. 83/1990 of March 27, 1990 Available at: https://www.ilo.org/dyn/natlex/docs/ELECTRONIC/99932/119583/F-255803203/SVK99932%20Eng.pdf. Accessed 09/13/2019.

International Organization for Migration (IOM). (2019). Migration in Slovakia, April 5. https://www.iom.sk/en/migration/migration-in-slovakia.html. Accessed 09/13/2019.

Kaplan, Karel. (1986). Church and state in Czechoslovakia from 1948 to 1956, parts I-III, *Religion in Communist Lands* 14(1–3): 59–72, 180–193, 273–282.

Lake, Aaron. (2013). The New Roma Ghettos. *Vice*, December 25. Available at: https://www.vice.com/en_us/article/wdpmdm/the-new-roma-ghettos-000519-v20n4. Accessed 09/13/2019.

Machlica, Gabriel. (2019). The social exclusion of Roma in the Slovak Republic calls for immediate policy action. *OECD Ecoscope*, February 5. Available at: https://oecdecoscope.blog/2019/02/05/the-social-exclusion-of-roma-in-the-slovak-republic-calls-for-immediate-policy-action/. Accessed 09/13/2019.

Mendel, Miloš. (1998). The islamic Religious Community in Bohemia and Moravia (1934-1945), *Archív orientální* [Quarterly Journal of African and Asian Studies] 66(2): 127–141.

Migration Policy Centre. (n.d.). *Slovakia*. www.migrationpolicycentre.eu. Accessed 09/13/2019.

Pew Research Center. (2017). Europe's growing Muslim population. Available at: http://www.pewforum.org/2017/11/29/europes-growing-muslim-population/. Accessed 09/13/2019.

Račius, Egdūnas. (2018). *Muslims in Eastern Europe*. Edinburgh: Edinburgh University Press.

Račius, Egdūnas. (2020). *Islam in post-Communist Eastern Europe: Between Churchification and Securitization*. Leiden and Boston: Brill.

Rafa, Tomas. (2015). Slovak far right nationalists and hooligans against refugees and Islam. *New Nationalism*, July 10. Available at: http://your-art.sk/?p=2819. Accessed 09/13/2019.

Rousek, Leos & Gulyas, Veronika. (2010). Hungary Eases Citizenship Rules, Irks Slovakia'. *The Wall Street Journal*, May 27. Available at: https://www.wsj.com/articles/SB10001424052748704032704575268431789961338?mod=WSJ_latestheadlines, Accessed 09/13/2019.

Slovak Information Service. (2017). Annual report. Available at: http://www.sis.gov.sk/for-you/sis-annual-report.html. Accessed 09/13/2019.

Starr, Kelsey Jo. (2019). Once the same nation, the Czech Republic and Slovakia look very different religiously. *Pew Research Center*, January 2. Available at: https://www.pewresearch.org/fact-tank/2019/01/02/once-the-same-nation-the-czech-republic-and-slovakia-look-very-different-religiously/. Accessed 09/13/2019.

Statistical Office of the Slovak Republic. (n.d.). Table 10: Population by nationality - 2011, 2001, 1991. Available at: https://slovak.statistics.sk/wps/wcm/connect/bd447dc5-c417-48d6-89e1-0a2d60053cf6/Table_10_Population_by_nationality_2011_2001_1991.pdf?MOD=AJPERES&CVID=kojGfKx&CVID=kojGfKx. Accessed 09/13/2019.

Than, Krisztina & Santa, Martin. (2010). Hungary citizenship law triggers row with Slovakia. *Reuters*, May 25. Available at: https://www.reuters.com/article/us-hungary-citizenship-slovakia/hungary-citizenship-law-triggers-row-with-slovakia-idUSTRE64O32220100525. Accessed 09/13/2019.

The Slovak Spectator. (2017, February 1). Registration of churches to become stricter. Available at: https://spectator.sme.sk/c/20448220/registration-of-churches-to-become-stricter.html. Accessed 09/13/2019.

Ward, James Mace. (2013). *Priest, Politician, Collaborator: Jozef Tiso and the Making of Fascist Slovakia*. Ithaca: Cornell University Press.

Werleman, C. J. (2018). Slovakia's deplorable move to criminalise Islam. *The New Arab*, September 18. Available at: https://www.alaraby.co.uk/english/comment/2018/9/18/slovakias-deplorable-move-to-criminalise-islam. Accessed 09/13/2019.

12

Russia

Governance of religion – what, how, and why

Marat Iliyasov

Introduction

The great Russian poet Fiodor Tyutchev described Russia as 'baffling to the mind' and 'not subject to the common measure'. These oft-cited words are especially useful when a topic being examined is particularly complicated to explain, which is partly the case with religious governance. The difficulty here is in determining the ability of both society and state to accommodate seemingly incompatible and contradictory attitudes, decisions, and policies. Indeed, even the fact that in the lifespan of a single generation the country has completed a full turn from suppressing religion and clergy to incorporating them into state politics is rife with contradictions. This chapter seeks to address some. It aims to outline the current relationship between the state and religion, to explain the state's unequal attitude towards different religions, and to analyse the legal basis of religious governance and consider its effectiveness. To this end, the study presents the country's ethno-religious composition, offers an overview of the history of the relationship between state and church, and presents the laws regulating religious affairs. It also identifies the factors that influenced the design of the current legal foundation of religious governance. The context of multiculturalism, the special state-Orthodox Church relationship, and popular reaction to the governance of religion is present even if not always explicit in the text.

The chapter proceeds as follows: the first part offers a general overview of Russia's ethno-religious composition today. It presents some statistical information regarding the number of believers and expert estimates of active religious practice. The second part explores the historical background of religious governance and identifies some factors that determine the current relationship between the state and religion. The section also delves into the transformations of the Russian state and analyses how these changes are reflected in religious governance. It also looks at the process of religious revival after decades of state suppression and examines further developments in the state-religion interaction. The last section considers the factors that shaped the country's legislative initiatives regarding religious governance. It observes the most significant trends and the practices that were and still are present in the country. The research identifies and presents inherent problems with the legislation and

Marat Iliyasov

juridical practices. The chapter concludes by emphasising the need for further work in improving the legislative basis and research of religious governance in Russia.

Current ethno-religious composition

Outlining the ethnoreligious composition of the Russian Federation is somewhat problematic. It cannot be very precise for at least five reasons. First, it can be based only on the last official census of the Russian Federation, which was conducted a decade ago, in 2010.[1] The demographic trends in the country suggest that the Muslim population has increased since then, whereas the size of the non-Muslim population has contracted (Iliyasov, 2019). Second, the census does not register people's religious affiliation. This can be extrapolated from the information on ethnicity, which is not in reality accurate: as it is known, religious identity is not always inherited with ethnicity. Moreover, the dominance of the atheist ideology in the comparatively recent past significantly reduced the numbers of believers in all ethnic groups. Third, the census does not include the population of the Crimea (over two million people) annexed by Russia in 2014, a significant part of which is Muslim. The fourth problem derives from the issue of who can be considered a believer: everyone who declares their religious belonging or those who strictly adhere to all the commands of a religion. Finally, there is a huge variety of practised religions. Some scholars claim that up to 70 religious denominations are currently practised in Russia (Leksin, 2009). Even though these religious groups are quite small, the total of the believers can still constitute a significant number. Unfortunately, the scope of this chapter does not allow for the presentation of all beliefs that are present in Russia.

These obstacles limit the possibility of the accurate calculation of the believers in the Russian Federation. Therefore, Table 12.1 provides only approximate figures based on the religious belonging determined by ethnicity.

The issue of the accuracy of the data presented in Table 12.1 with regard to the ethnoreligious composition of the Russian Federation has concerned researchers for some time. One of the most credible and respectful research groups in Russia, the Levada Centre, tried to find more accurate figures of believers through a survey conducted in 2012, whose results are presented in Table 12.2.

Table 12.2 shows religious affiliation as a percentage of the population. The table presents people's religious belonging based on their self-identification. However, the accuracy of this data is also doubtful. First, the demographic situation in the country has changed since 2011. If the 'Muslim' ethnic groups were steadily growing, the 'Christian' population was decreasing (Iliyasov, 2019). Some people might have migrated from one religious (or atheist) group to another. Furthermore, deeper investigation conducted by other researchers revealed a huge disparity between the declared religious identity and actual practice. For instance, Kuropatkina (2014) claims that almost half of Russia's population is not religious at all. According to data collected and analysed by Zagvozdina (2012), among those who identify as Russian Orthodox, nearly one-third (29 per cent) visit churches only for formal occasions such as weddings, funerals, or baptisms, or when 'they feel like doing so'; 24 per cent do not visit church at all. Furthermore, only 11 per cent follow religious services or participate in them, while only 7 per cent regularly confess – the practice, which makes a person a true believer, according to Orthodox priests. Kuropatkina (2014), in turn, claims that the number of 'true believers' is even smaller; even though attending mass is not a significant indicator of religiosity in the Orthodox tradition, she refers to the fact that no more than 3 per cent of self-declared Orthodox Christians regularly attend church services.

Table 12.1 The largest ethnic groups of the Russian Federation and their 'ethnic religions'

O – Orthodox Christians MS – Muslims Sunni MSh – Muslims Shiites AC – Apostolic Church T – Traditional (Pagan) B – Buddhism	Millions (of people)		Percentage of respondents who indicated ethnic background	
	2002 г.	2010 г.	2002 г.	2010 г.
All	145.17	142.86		
Those who indicated their ethnic background	143.71	137.23	100.0	100.0
Russians (O)	115.89	111.02	80.64	80.90
Tatars (MS)	5.55	5.31	3.87	3.87
Ukrainians (O)	2.94	1.93	2.05	1.41
Bashkirs (MS)	1.67	1.58	1.16	1.15
Chuvash (O/MS)	1.64	1.44	1.14	1.05
Chechens (MS)	1.36	1.43	0.95	1.04
Armenians (AC)	1.13	1.18	0.79	0.86
Avars (MS)	0.81	0.91	0.57	0.66
Mordva (O/T)	0.84	0.74	0.59	0.54
Kazakhs (MS)	0.65	0.65	0.46	0.47
Azeries (MSh/MS)	0.62	0.60	0.43	0.44
Dargins (MS)	0.51	0.59	0.35	0.43
Udmurts (O/T)	0.64	0.55	0.44	0.40
Mari (O/T)	0.60	0.55	0.42	0.40
Ossetians (O/MS)	0.51	0.53	0.36	0.39
Belorossians (O)	0.81	0.52	0.56	0.38
Kabardans (MS)	0.52	0.52	0.36	0.38
Kumyks (MS)	0.42	0.50	0.29	0.37
Yakuts (T/O/MS)	0.44	0.48	0.31	0.35
Lezgins (MS)	0.41	0.47	0.29	0.35
Buryats (B/T/O)	0.45	0.46	0.31	0.34
Ingush (MS)	0.41	0.44	0.29	0.32
Others	4.85	4.81	3.40	3.51
Those, who did not indicate ethnic identity	1.46	5.63		

Source: Compiled by the author based on 2002, 2010 census; http://www.demoscope.ru/weekly/2011/0491/perep01.php; http://www.demoscope.ru/weekly/ssp/rus_nac_02.php

She notes that a similar situation can be observed among the followers of most of other religions too. The smallest disparity between declared religious affiliation and observation of religious practice is observed among the followers of Judaism, the Apostolic Church, and Sunni Islam.[2] The latter, being the second largest religion in Russia, is most prevalent in the eastern area of the North Caucasus (five republics highlighted in the lower left corner of Figure 12.1), where most of the population not only declare but also follow religious prescriptions.

The salience of religious identity in the North Caucasus is probably linked to a comparatively recent confrontational history of the region with Russia and the domination of local

Table 12.2 Religious identity of the Russia's inhabitants as declared (2011)

Religion	Percentage of the population (%)
Orthodox Christianity	69
Atheism	22
Islam	5
Catholicism	<1
Protestantism	<1
Judaism	<1
Buddhism	<1
Hinduism	<1
Other	1
Cannot answer	4

Source: Religious groups in Russia, http://www.demoscope.ru/weekly/2011/0477/opros01.php

Figure 12.1 'Muslim' regions in the Russian Federation.
Source: Research Service "Sreda" http://sreda.org

ethnic groups over the non-Muslim population. Indeed, unlike Tatarstan and Bashkortostan (two regions also highlighted in Figure 12.1), the North Caucasus region became part of the Russian Empire only in 1861 and since that time has had a turbulent history of confrontation with Russia (see Figure 12.2). Moreover, non-Russian ethnic groups in the eastern and central parts of the North Caucasus constitute the overwhelming majority (ranging from 70 per cent in Kabardino-Balkaria to 96 per cent in Chechnya).[3] Such an ethnic composition implies societal pressure, which translates into gradual Islamisation even of those who were less religious due to the harsh Soviet policies of religious discrimination and even outright atheisation. As is known, collectivism is embedded in the lifestyle of the North Caucasian ethnic groups. Individuals consider themselves as part of a group/community/ethnicity and

Figure 12.2 The North Caucasus.
Source: http://www.islamicworld.it/wp/the-anxiety-of-russian-muftiates-and-their-political-religious-role/
Note: The populations of Dagestan, Chechnya, Ingushetia, Kabardino-Balkaria, and Karachay-Cherkessia are predominantly Muslim.

'the group as a continuation of oneself' (Pavlova & Semenova, 2018). Values such as respect of the elderly, family, relatives, and even unrelated people further restrain individual choices. Hence, an individual often feels pressured to behave in a socially 'appropriate' manner. Observation of religious rites and commands would be an example of such behaviour.

To sum up, it is difficult to have a precise image of Russia's ethno-religious composition. The approximate statistics supported by the scholarly analysis (Aleinikova & Burianov, 2015; Krzhevov, 2011; Leksin, 2009) show that the two biggest religions in Russia are Orthodox Christianity and Sunni Islam. Followers of these religions (as well as of other smaller religions) have had historically a complex relationship, which was further complicated by the strict religious governance of the Soviet regime and the dominance of the Russian Orthodox Church before and after communist rule. The latter aspects are explored further in the historical overview of the relationship between the state and religion in Russia.

Religion and the state: the history of interaction

Some of the Russian Principalities became Orthodox Christian in 988. Since that time, the established Russian Orthodox Church has played a very important role in the political life in the territory known today as the former Soviet Union. For a very long period, the church shared and competed for power with the state (first with some Russian principalities and then with the Russian Empire), whose dominance was eventually established in the eighteenth century. Nevertheless, the church preserved its importance, which was reflected in the clergy's role in state affairs (Isaev, 2010). Therefore, the model of the relationship between church and the state until the beginning of the twentieth century can be identified as clericalism, which is understood as the church's attempt to play a dominant role in society (Katin, 2015). Indeed, despite having lost its monopoly over education and the power to legitimise the monarchical rule, the church still possessed considerable assets and influence and could not be disregarded by political leaders.

As in many other countries, the separation of the state and religion in Russia was a long and sometimes painful process that lasted for several centuries. The state rightly considered the church as a rival and tried to restrict its domain by taking over functions that were not directly related to religion. The church's leaders resisted the state's advance and sought to preserve the exceptional position and the power accumulated during Mongol rule over the Russian principalities from 1280 to 1448. Such accumulation of wealth and power became possible due to the tolerant (religion-wise) policies of the Golden Horde (Isaev, 2010). However, the increased significance and political sovereignty of the Moscow principality in the fifteenth century changed the *status quo*. Religious leaders were no longer more (or equally) powerful than state authorities but could still challenge them. This rivalry between the state and the church for dominance continued until the eighteenth century, when it was ended by the reforms of Peter the Great who established state control over the church (Andreeva, 2001). Since that time, Russian monarchs rather enjoyed unconditional support of the Church in exchange for allowing it to be 'totalitarian', to some extent, in the religious affairs of the society (Furman, 1989). The state supported the church's efforts to convert non-Orthodox believers and marginalise non-institutionalised groups such as Old Believers (ibid.).

The church's influence was not curtailed only because of the threat it posed regarding its dominance of the state. At the start of the sixteenth century, the Grand Moscow Principality was expanding to the west, east, and south as it transformed into the Russian Empire. This expansion significantly increased the presence of other religious groups in the country, among them Muslims, Protestants, Catholics, Buddhists. At first, the state followed the Russian Orthodox Church's dictum and regarded other religious groups as the subject of baptism or annihilation. However, this attitude led to continuous rebellions and violent clashes with the newly conquered nations. This, eventually, forced the state to reconsider its approach. Contrary to the Church's will, the state began implementing more tolerant and flexible policies, incorporating the clergy of different faiths and the elites of the newly conquered nations. This change paid off – both (clergy and elites) became conduits of Russian Imperial policies to the respective local populations. Even though the newly integrated clergy of other religious groups (non-Orthodox Christians, Muslims, Buddhists) did not receive the same privileges as the Russian Orthodox Church, the latter still regarded its positions as threatened and advocated for the forceful Christianisation of the incorporated nations (ibid.).

The Russian Orthodox Church retained its privileged position up until the end of the Russian Empire. The 1917 coup that brought the Bolsheviks to power also changed the 'symphony' between the state and the church.[4] The negative position of Patriarch Tikhon (the head of the Church at that time) regarding the coup and the Bolsheviks in general opened an ideological confrontation. The Bolsheviks labelled the Orthodox clergy a 'class enemy' and introduced repressive measures that later shaped the state's anti-religious policy and eventual attempt for the complete eradication of religion.

A turn away from such an antagonistic attitude towards religion occurred in the middle of the Second World War when the state was at its weakest. Josef Stalin, the Russian leader at that time, recognised the failure of the anti-religious policies and decided to use religion's power in mobilising the population for the war (Isaev, 2010). However, the partial restitution of nationalised church property and the reestablishment of believers' religious rights were initiated in 1943 and ended in the late 1950s. Nikita Khrushchev, Stalin's successor as General Secretary of the Communist party, returned to the anti-religious policies, which aimed at gradually suppressing religion until it withered away (Leksin, 2009). The practical measures against religion and the clergy, however, now took a different form. Instead of the direct repression so common in the 1930s, the state established tighter control over priests, believers, and the population in general through the state secret service (KGB) and created special councils for religious affairs. The latter were responsible for disseminating ideological propaganda, exposing 'the lies of religion', censoring sermons and religious literature, designing religion-related laws and regulations, gathering statistical data on believers and religious institutions, and closing 'non-attended' churches (Sebentsov, 2010; Soskovets, 2008). Supervising education was another important function given these councils; no one could become a clergyman without a council's approval (Soskovets, 2008). The councils were partly successful in achieving their goals, but this policy failed to eradicate religion.

The political changes and liberalisation initiated in 1985 by the last leader of the USSR, Mikhail Gorbachev, created conditions for religion's revival. This was triggered by the millennial celebration of Russia's baptism in 1988. Since then, the number of religious organisations, churches, mosques, synagogues, shrines, parishes, and temples grew quickly: in 1985 there were only 6,806 Orthodox organisations in the country; five years later their number had reached 10,380 (Hvostova, 2008). Islam in the North Caucasus demonstrated even faster growth: the number of mosques there grew from a mere 47 to 431 during the same period (Pokalova, 2017).

The state had to react to such a significant social change – and it did by issuing a law 'On the freedom of religious beliefs' in 1990 (Leksin, 2009). The law was so liberal that it allowed practically any religious organisation or group to settle in the country and preach freely. This, according to Mitrokhin (2002: 54–55), turned Russia into an 'El Dorado desired by all kind of religious organizations', including ones forbidden in the US and Europe (Yakhyaev & Kamyshova, 2013). It must be said that the guest religious organisations were quite successful in settling in Russia and spreading their beliefs for two reasons. The first was the shattered reputation of the home-grown religious authorities who had discredited themselves by collaborating with the KGB.[5] The second was the lack of religious knowledge, which was especially exploited by some branches of radical Islam (for example, Salafism). The success factor of these groups was clearly identified by the former Mufti of Tatarstan Ildus Faisov who stated that 'every Arab at that time was perceived by the Soviet Muslims as the Prophet Muhammad' (Souleimanov, 2015).

This situation prompted security concerns and the Russian Federation reacted by adopting other less liberal and more restrictive laws that (with some amendment) regulate the relationship between the state and religion today. The law 'On the non-commercial organizations' (N7-F3 adopted in 1996) and the law 'On the freedom of conscience and religious associations' (N125-F3 adopted in 1997)[6] serve as examples of such a restrictive legislation. On the one hand, they halted the spread of ideologies imported from abroad but on the other, they became a potential source of religious discrimination and consequently probable conflict. Furthermore, Law N125-F3 in its Preamble emphasises the special role of Orthodox Christianity in 'the country's history and culture'.[7] This was also perceived as an emphasis of the privileged position of the Russian Orthodox Church vis-à-vis other religions and thus provoked the dissatisfaction of other religious groups (Kanevsky, 2002).

Moreover, the Russian Orthodox Church's privileged position can be seen through its involvement in state affairs and participation in international and domestic politics as well as through the funding it receives from the state and through the special relationship with the political leadership. For instance, the blessing of the new Russian military ships and weaponry or the soldiers departing for the mission has already become normalised as a practice in Russia. Furthermore, Yakhyaev and Kamyshova (2013) emphasise that unlike the leaders of the Russian Orthodox Church, the heads of other religious groups do not have a direct phone line to the President of the Russian Federation. Adding to this, it can be mentioned that Patriarch Kirill is a frequent guest of all official events in the Kremlin. In turn, the state leadership can also be often seen participating in religious ceremonies of the Orthodox Church. Moreover, it should be noted that Orthodox priests receive a salary from the state budget and that the Orthodox Church has the right to claim airtime on national television. Furthermore, as Yakhyaev and Kamyshova (2013) rightly point out, officials' active contacts with Orthodox clergy can be regarded as violating Article 4.4 of the law 'On the freedom of conscience and religious associations', which restricts the promotion of religions by state officials. All these facts encourage Russian scholars to regard the relationship between the Russian Orthodox Church and the state as exclusive and to evaluate the current state of affairs as a gradual clericalisation of the country (Isaev, 2010). This has raised concern among Russia's intellectual elite. Leksin (2009) refers to the 'letter of ten' in which ten members of the Russian Academy of Science expressed their dissatisfaction with the state's clericalisation and the contradictions between Russian law and adherence to it. Similar concerns are present among the representatives of other religions who feel like second-rate citizens due to the privileged position of the Russian Orthodox Church.

Indeed, other religions do not enjoy the same privileges as Orthodox Christianity. The state leadership, even if it emphasises the importance of Islam, still does not shape the relationship with it in the same way as the Orthodox Church. This attitude stems from several reasons. First, Orthodox Christianity is considered the state-founding religion. Second, its followers comprise the majority of the population. Third, historically, it provides a background for the country's ideology and self-identity, which makes Russia a stand-alone country between the East and the West. Fourth, Orthodox Christianity is widespread throughout the country, whereas other religions are rather concentrated in the regions (see Figure 12.1). Fifth, other religions are considered potentially more 'dangerous' than Orthodox Christianity. The latter explains the passage of discriminatory legislation (or the discriminatory application of laws) and regulations towards some religions (Yakhyaev & Kamyshova, 2013). This discrimination is also clear from the identification of some religions as 'traditional' and others not – a designation stated in the Preamble to the law 'On the freedom of conscience and religious associations' (Biriukov, 2008).

To sum up, the relationship between the state and religion has taken different forms and shapes and, over time, can be described as rivalry for power, a 'symphony' of mutual support, or a direct confrontation. These relationships to some extent were determined by the state's strength: when it was weak, it was more inclined to rely on the Orthodox Church in official affairs, even though this could provoke a rivalry for power; when the state was strong, it was keen to suppress or control religion. Today, the state is officially secular. However, in practice, the Orthodox Church plays a very important and intrusive role in state affairs and society. This role exceeds the boundaries of a majority religion usually in a secular state. The place that the Orthodox Church occupies in Russia leads to the identification of two problematic aspects in the relationship between the state and religion. First, the historically predetermined inequality among religious groups has been re-established and is supported by the political leadership. This results in grievances and dissatisfaction among the non-Orthodox population. Second, it is the spread of the politically active religious ideologies and Russia's defensive reaction to them in a form of discriminatory legislation and its arbitrary application. The latter burgeoned in the 1990s in the North Caucasus and requires a more detailed analysis, which is provided in the next part.

Religious governance and Islam

As previously noted, Islam is the second largest religion in the Russian Federation. This fact is often repeated by the state leadership in Muslim religious forums in Russia and abroad.[8] However, acknowledging this fact does not enhance the relationship between Islam and the state in Russia. The complexity of the relationship is determined by the state's favouritism towards Orthodox Christianity, a history of aggressive integration of some Muslim ethnic groups, and the global war on terrorism that sometimes translates into anti-Islamism. In constructing the state's relationship with believers, Russian officials draw a clear line between institutionalised and non-institutionalised religions especially to followers of Islam. The institutionalised Muslims are considered loyal citizens of the state, whereas the non-institutionalised represent a potential threat. The roots of this distinction are found in the early 1990s, when the new Russian Federation reborn from the Soviet Union started shaping its relationship with religions.

With respect to Islam, the state was less successful in imposing control over all Muslim groups. Seeking to implement this goal, in 1994 the state established the Spiritual Administration of Muslims of the Central-European region. The organisation was meant to be an umbrella for all branches of Islam. However, this was not the case. Although today this institution, known as the Spiritual Administration of Russian Muslims Russia [further Spiritual Administration], unites more than 120 religious organisations,[9] many believers disregard its authority.

The limited success of the state's initiative is due to several factors, some of which are discussed above. Among them, the close connection between the leaders of the Spiritual Administration and state officials, low-level religious education, non-inclusivity of the institution, and the tarnished reputation of the Islamic clergy due to its collaboration with the state's secret services. These facts re-created the problem that had also existed in the Soviet Union. A large share of Russian Muslims does not want to belong to, or even be associated with, institutionalised Islam. Many prefer to follow 'pure' Islam and end up joining its main alternative branch – Salafism. The latter is often synonymised with terrorism in Russia (and especially in the North Caucasus). This creates a situation in which many non-institutionalised Muslims are regarded as a threat to the state (Dagestan interview, 2019).

This negative state attitude – which was exacerbated by Russia's history, complex relations with ethnic minorities, separatism in the North Caucasus, and global trends – brought into being the laws 'On countering the extremist activities' (N114-F3, 2002) and 'On countering terrorism' (N 35-F3, 2006). Both the text of this legislation and its implementation became the subject of harsh and partly justified criticism.

Indeed, one can easily identify two main problems with these laws. First, when drafted and passed, these laws implicitly targeted Salafi Muslims of the North Caucasus – the region where most of Russia's Muslim population is concentrated. This state's attitude automatically labels both laws as 'anti-Islamic' in the eyes of the believers. Second, the lack of clear definition of the key terms 'extremism' and 'terrorism' created room for the laws' misinterpretation and, consequently, their arbitrary application. The latter is also particularly acute in the North Caucasus. Local authorities, who are empowered to implement anti-terrorist and anti-extremist measures, are entitled to complement federal laws with supplemental regulations. This is often done in such a way that fuels further tensions between non-institutionalised Muslims and the state. A good illustration of this is a perception of the legal situation that is present in the North Caucasus.

> Who is an extremist in Russia today? An extremist is the one who was assigned this label to. It is up to *siloviki*, the law enforcers to make one an extremist if they want to. The reasons might be different. Maybe they did not like what you have written on your Facebook page, or maybe they just need to show the result and want another star on their epaulets. Either case, no one has guarantee that tomorrow he will not appear on the list of the wanted. Of course, people are upset with this situation and having in mind the Caucasian 'hot blood', it is possible to understand why the youth are taking up arms so willingly. (Dagestan interview, 2019)

The interviewee was referring to the juridically enforced situation in Dagestan, where the law enforcement officers created a special list of people who are the targets of 'prophylactic' actions. As such, they are subject to restrictions, constant monitoring, and possible repression; they cannot leave the republic while others avoid contact with them out of fear that they too may end up on the 'prophylactic' list. The consequences of 'being on the list', according to the same informant, encouraged some youth to join the armed resistance 'before the police get them' (Dagestan interview, 2019).

Similar 'prophylactic' legal measures are employed in other republics of the North Caucasus too. As confirmed by my informants, suspects, their relatives, or even random individuals today can easily become victims of law enforcement. Abductions, torture, or even killings are not that uncommon in the North Caucasus (Yarlykapov, 2018). For instance, according to the Novaya Gazeta and Human Rights Centre Memorial, in January 2017 alone the Chechen police executed 27 people without any due process (Sokirianskaia, 2019). The statistics of previous years are even more dire, and the situation cannot improve significantly because – as Starodubovskaia & Kazenin (2014) point out – people do not have any protection mechanism from this kind of state repression. This persecution is sometimes publicly sanctioned by the leadership of the local republics. For instance, the head of the Chechen Republic, Ramzan Kadyrov, publicly declared that Salafists ('the Satans' in Kadyrov's words) do not have a place in Chechnya and 'should be killed'. This was reiterated by a Kadyrov's close associate, a deputy minister of Chechnya's Ministry of the Interior, Apti Alaudinov, on Grozny TV. In the address to his subordinates, he stated: 'I swear by the Quran, if there is any little resemblance with Wahhabis ... I personally told – hack them down. Who you can imprison – imprison, if you have a chance to put something into the pocket [meaning drugs or weapons] and press charges afterward – do it. Do whatever you want, kill whoever you want' (Malashenko, 2014).

Unlike in Chechnya, Dagestan's authorities were slightly more willing and persistent in seeking a dialogue with the Salafis. There was a brief period in 2010–2012, when by the order of the republic's then-president Magomedsalam Magomedov, the authorities stopped repressing Salafi Muslims and their businesses, which led to a temporary easing in the standoff between law enforcement and Islamic radicals. Later, the police returned to previous repressive methods and this eventually pushed the Salafis back underground. Less harsh policies have been adopted by the governments of Kabardino-Balkaria and Ingushetia, where the governments invest in rehabilitation programmes (Sokirianskaia, 2019). The authorities of the Volga Muslim republics of Tatarstan and Bashkortostan are even more tolerant towards Salafism. As one of my interviewees indicated, 'Salafis are not excluded from the religious life of the republics and play a significant role in it' (Kazan interview, 2018).

The analysed examples illustrate the complex relationship between the state and Islam. The control over the religion that the state seeks to exert over believers brought some Russian Muslims under the umbrella of institutionalised Islam, whereas all other Muslims fell into a category of potential threat and often become a target of law enforcement authorities. The confrontational relationship between the state and non-institutionalised Muslims is especially obvious in the North Caucasus. The regional authorities and law enforcement construct their relationships with non-institutionalised Muslims on the anti-terrorist and anti-extremist laws instead of on the laws ensuring freedom of conscious (discussed earlier).

Concluding remarks

The relationship between the state and religion has a long and complex history in Russia and its legacy can still be felt in the country. On the one hand, modern Russia inherited a very secular society from its state-predecessor, the Soviet Union; on the other, the Soviet Union's anti-religion policies provoked an opposing reaction and made it possible for religion's revival. Moreover, the pre-Bolshevik history of state-religion relations determined the exclusive position of the Orthodox Church in today's Russia. The Church was an important institution that helped the state implement its policies and mobilise the population whenever necessary. The mobilising power of religion was realised and used even during the atheist rule of the communists, thus supporting the thesis of the reverse dependency between state power and the position of religion.

The turbulent events of the 1990s brought religion back to the political foreground and consolidated the privileged position of the Russian Orthodox Church. Despite the grievances of other (less privileged) religious groups and the contravention of the country's secular status, state officials support the status quo for several reasons. First, unlike other religious groups (except for pre-Christian), Orthodox Christianity has been established in the country for the longest period. Second, it contributed to the Russian state- and identity-building. Third, it is considered as a religion most loyal to the state. According to critics, this signifies the shift from authoritarian secularism to clericalism (Leksin, 2009), with the domination of the Orthodox Church; other religions have to be satisfied with a secondary or even tertiary role.

Furthermore, the State's attitude often associates non-institutionalised religious groups as a threat, thus making followers a subject of official persecution. Those who belong to non-institutionalised Islam are in a particularly precarious position due to three main factors: the political stance of some branches of Islam that spread in the Russian Federation after the collapse of the Soviet Union; the nationalism of the 1990s that evolved into Islamism or was hijacked by Islamists; and, the global war against terrorism, which is often linked to Islam. All these factors facilitated Russia's turn towards autocracy in religious governance. The latter, after a liberal interim period in the early 1990s, was established with the help of institutionalised religions and particularly the Orthodox Church.

Appendix 1 Religious maps of Russia

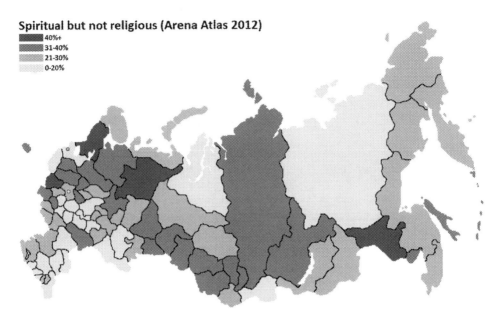

Russia: governance of religion

Islam (Arena Atlas 2012)
- 31-60%+
- 5-30%
- 1-5%
- 0-1%

Buddhism (Arena Atlas 2012)
- 30-60%+
- 5-20%
- ~1%
- 0-1%

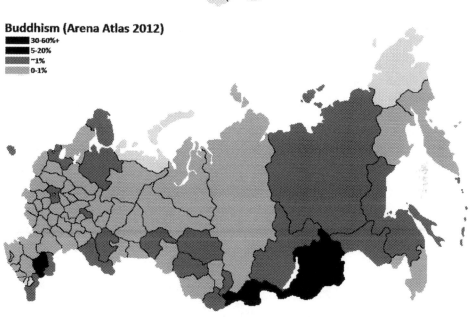

Notes

1 The next census will be held in 2021.
2 For a better understanding of the situation, see 'Atlas of Religions in Russia' (2012) available online http://sreda.org/arena. Accessed 16/01/2020 and Appendix 1, Religious maps of Russia.
3 Tatarstan is roughly 53.2 per cent ethnic Tatars, while ethnic Bashkirs comprise 29.5 per cent of Bashkortostan's population. The ethnic Muslim population in Bashkortostan is roughly 55 per cent because of a significant number of Tatars living in the republic. See Census 2010 available online https://www.gks.ru/free_doc/new_site/perepis2010/croc/perepis_itogi1612.htm. Accessed 16/01/2020.
4 The harmonious relationship between the state and church in literature is often called 'symphony' (Kudryashova & Mchedlova, 2008).
5 According to Starodubovskaia and Kazenin (2014), state support to Sufi Islam continues to discredit it in the eyes of believers even today. The youth see the institutionalised religion as part of the corrupt and unjust system and this spurs the popularity of other, often politically charged, branches of Islam. A similar situation can be observed in the case of Orthodox Christianity, which is the main benefactor of state support in Russia today.
6 Both laws have been amended several times, but the chapter refers only to the active articles of these laws.
7 This acknowledgment established a special relationship between the State and the Russian Orthodox Church, which, according to many, violates the principle of secularism established in Article 14 of the Constitution (Kanevsky, 2002; Leksin, 2009; Stepakova, 2011).
8 Putin nazval Islam 'yarkim elementom Rossiyskogo kul'turnogo koda' 22/10/2013. Newsru media agency Available on https://www.newsru.com/religy/22oct2013/ufa.html Accessed 08/02/2020. See also 'Putin nazval islam neot'emlemoi chast'yu religioznoi zhizni Rossii'. 30/08/2012. Delfi News agency. Available on https://rus.delfi.ee/daily/abroad/putin-nazval-islam-neotemlemoj-chastyu-religioznoj-zhizni-rossii?id=64895248. Accessed 08/02/2020.
9 Official website of the Spiritual Administration of Russia's Muslims http://dumrf.ru/common/org. Accessed 08/02/2020.

References

Aleinikova, S., and S. Buryanov. (2015). *Svetskoe gosudarstvo v voprosah I otvetah: kratko, dostupno I aktualno.* Moscow: Fund Zdravoyslie.
Andreeva, L. (2001). Khristianstvo I vlast v Rossii I na zapade: comparativnyyi analiz. *Obshestvennye nauki I sovremennost,* 11(4), 85–102.
Biriukov, V. (2008). Sistemnyi analis gosudarstvennoi politiki Rossii v otnoshenii netraditsionnyh religioznyh organizatsiy: istoriya voprosa, sovremennoe sostoyanie I tendentsiya razvitiya. *Izvestiya gosudarstvennogo pedagogicheskogo universiteta im Gertsena,* 29(65), 42–50.
Furman, D. (1989). *Religia, ateism i perestroika. Na puti k svobode sovesti.* Moscow: Progress, 7–18.
Hvostova, G. (2008). Religioznaia situatsiya v SSSR nakanune prinyatiya zakona 'O svobode sovesti i religioznyh organizatsiyah'. *Izvestiia Samarskogo nauchnogo tsentra RAN,* 10(4): 1162–1167.
Iliyasov, M. (2019). Chechen demographic growth as a reaction to conflict: the views of chechens. *Europe-Asia Studies,* 71(10)1705–1733.
Isaev, A. (2010). Rol i mesto Russkoi Pravoslavnoi Tserkvi v razvitii gosudarstva: istoriya i sovremennost. *Srednerusskiy vestnik obshchestvennyh nauk,* 1(14), 138–148.
Kanevsky, K. (2002). Religioznyi renessans v Rossii: Problemy gosudarstvenno-konfessionalnyh otnosheniy. *Rossiyskaya Yustitsiia,* 11(2), 62–65.
Katin, V. (2015). Tipologiya vzaimootnosheniy tserkvi I gosudarstva. Izvestiya irkutskogo gosudarstvennogo universisteta. *Politologiya. Religovedenie,* 13(1), 181–185.
Krzhevov, V. (2011). Vzaimootnosheniya gosudarstva i tserkvi v sovremennoi Rossii. *Filosofskie nauki,* 53(2), 26–42.
Kudryashova, M., and E. Mchedlova. (2008). Religiya i politika v sovremennom Rossiyskom obshestve. *Vestnik Moskovskogo Universiteta,* 12(4): 23–30.
Kuropatkina, O. (2014). Rol religii v natsiestroitelstve sovremennoi Rossii. *Kontury globalnyh transformatsiy: politika, ekonomika, pravo,* 7(1 (33)): 26–38.

Leksin, V. (2009). Rossia kak svetskoe gosudarstvo: religioznye ob'edineniia v sekuliarnom obshchestve. *Mir Rossii. Sociologia. Ethnologia*, 18(2), 141–171.

Mitrokhin, L. (2002). O printsipe svobody sovesti. In Mchedlov, M. (ed.), *O sotsialnoi kontseptsii russkogo pravoslaviia. социальной концепции русского православия.* Moscow: Respublika, 41–67.

Pavlova, O., and F. Semenova. (2018). Tsennostnye orientatsii musulmanskoi molodezhi Severo-Zapadnogo Kavkaza. Minbar. *Islamic Studies*, 11(2):361–374.

Pokalova, E. (2017). The North Caucasus: from mass mobilization to international terrorism. *Small Wars & Insurgencies*, 28(3): 609–628.

Sebentsov, A. (2010). Vzaimootnoshenia gosudarstva I religii v Rossii v nachale XXI veka. *Tsennosti I smysly*, 4(7): 5–26.

Sokirianskaia, E. (2019). Mozhno li predotvratit novye volny radikalizatsii na Severnom Kavkaze? Radikalizatsia i ee profilaktika v Chechne, Insushetii, Dagestane i Kabardino-Balkarii. Centr Analiza i predotvrashcheniya konfliktov. Report.

Soskovets, L. (2008). Sovety po delam religiy kak provodniki gosudarstvennoi politiki v otnoshenii tserkvi. *Izvestiia Tomskogo politekhnicheskogo universiteta*, 312(6): 162–167.

Souleimanov, R. (2015). Religioznoe vliyanie islamskih stran vostoka na musulman Tatarstana v post-Sovetskiy period. *Musulmanskii Mir*, 71(3), 40–56.

Stepakova, I. (2011). Sovremennoe Rossiyskoe gosudarstvo i RPTs: osobennosti i perspektivy vzaimootnosheniy. *Politicheskaia ekspertiza. POLITEKS*, 7(3), 265–282.

Yakhyaev, M., and E. Kamyshova. (2013). Vlast I religiya v sovremennoy Rossii: metamorfozy vzaimodeistviya. *Islamovedenie*, 15(1), 6–19.

Yarlykapov, A. (2018). Islam and Muslim Youth of the North Caucasus. In A. Yarlykapov (ed.), *Islam and Muslim Youth in Central Asia and the Caucasus*. Special Edition for the 4th session of the Islamic Conference of Youth and Sports Ministers. Baku: Azerbaijan, 158–189.

Interviews

Interview with an expert, Kazan 23/03/2019.
Interview with an expert, Dagestan 15/01/2019

Media and online resources

Delfi News Agency. (2012, August 30). Putin nazval islam neot'emlemoi chast'yu religioznoi zhizni Rossii. 30/08/2012. Available at: https://rus.delfi.ee/daily/abroad/putin-nazval-islam-neotemlemoj-chastyu-religioznoj-zhizni-rossii?id=64895248. Accessed 08/02/20.

Malashenko, A. (2014). Rossiiskie musulmane v mezhdunarodnom kontekste. Rossiia v globalnoi politike. Available at: https://globalaffairs.ru/number/Rossiiskie-musulmane-v-mezhdunarodnom-kontekste---17204. Accessed 13/04/2019.

Newsru Media. (2013, October 22). Putin nazval Islam 'yarkim elementom Rossiyskogo kul'turnogo koda'. Available at: https://www.newsru.com/religy/22oct2013/ufa.html. Accessed 8/02/20.

Ob itogah Vserossiyskoi perepisi naseleniya 2010 goda. *Demoscope*. Available at: http://www.demoscope.ru/weekly/2011/0491/perep01.php. Accessed 23/04/2019.

Official website of the Spiritual Administration of Russia's Muslims. http://dumrf.ru/common/org. Accessed 08/02/2020.

Starodubovskaia, I., and K. Kazenin. (2014). Severnyi Kavkaz: quo vadis? *Seryi Zhurnal*. Available at: http://kopomko.com/doklad-severnyiy-kavkaz-quo-vadis-kuda-idesh/. Accessed 14/04/2019.

The Telegraph. (2015, May 7). Fifteen years of Vladimir Putin: in quotes. Available at: https://www.telegraph.co.uk/news/worldnews/vladimir-putin/11588182/Fifteen-years-of-Vladimir-Putin-in-quotes.html. (Accessed 12/09/2019).

Vserossiyskaya perepis' naseleniya 2002 goda. Natsionalnyi sostav naseleniya po regionam Rossii. Demoscope. Available at: http://www.demoscope.ru/weekly/ssp/rus_nac_02.php. (Accessed 23/04/2019).

Zagvozdina, D. (/2012, December 17). V Rossii bolshe musulman. *Novaia Gazeta*. Available at: https://www.gazeta.ru/social/2012/12/17/4894681.shtml. Accessed 02/06/2019.

Part IV
South-Eastern Europe

13

Bulgaria

Strong cultural legacies, weak institutions, and political instrumentalisation of religion

Mila Mancheva

Introduction

Since its foundation as a modern national state in 1878, Bulgaria emerged as a multi-confessional secular state with proclaimed freedom of religious beliefs. With respect to the historical context, Orthodox Christianity, as the religion of the majority of Bulgaria's population, constituted an important aspect of Bulgarian cultural and national identity, while the largest minority religion, Islam, has been perceived as the 'other' within the construct of the Bulgarian national idea. With the exception of the communist period, when Bulgarian society was subjected to a process of forced secularisation, the relationship between state and religion has been dominated by two-way autonomy, with the government exerting moderate control over the country's denominations and Orthodox Christianity being designated as dominant faith.

This chapter is structured in four sections. The first and the second discuss the main factors conditioning religious diversity governance in Bulgaria, namely, the ethno-confessional structure of the country's population, the attendant socio-economic characteristics, and the levels of religiosity among the country's population. The third section discusses the socio-political processes in motion that shaped state-religion relations and the governance of religious diversity in historical perspective. Finally, the fourth section discusses the present-day framework of state-religion relations and the legal and regulatory frameworks for religious diversity governance in the country.

Demography and socio-economic factors conditioning religious diversity governance

Population composition and challenges arising from it

As of 2018, Bulgaria's population is 7,000,039 persons. The country displays negative population growth since the 1980s. In particular, between 2017 and 2018, the population decline was 0.7 per cent (-49,995 persons) and was the outcome of both negative natural growth and emigration (NSI, 2018: 15). With regard to the rural/urban divisions, during a good part of

Mila Mancheva

Figure 13.1 Map of Bulgaria.
Source: *Encyclopaedia Britannica*, Inc. Available in: Carter, F W. Bulgaria. 2020. Bulgaria. Britanica.com. Available at: https://www.britannica.com/place/Bulgaria

the twentieth century the country's population was predominantly rural (see Figure 13.1.). The trend changed in the 1970s as a result of the policy of accelerated urbanisation and industrialisation conducted by the then-communist government. The share of the urban population reached 58 per cent in 1975 and 72.5 per cent in 2011 (NSI, 2011a: 10). The population is ageing, with the share of those aged 65 and above in 2018 being 21.3 per cent and those aged 15 and under being 14.4 per cent (NSI, 2018: 15–16). In 2018, the gender division favoured females (51.5 per cent); still, males prevailed in the population up to 53 years of age while the share of females was higher among the elderly (NSI, 2018: 15).

The ethnic and religious composition of Bulgaria's population is diverse and can be discussed based on the results from the last census conducted in 2011. The majority of the population are ethnic Bulgarians (84.8 per cent), with Turks being the largest ethnic minority (8.8 per cent), followed by Roma (4.9 per cent). The Turkish and the Roma communities are historic minorities formed during the centuries of Ottoman domination between the fourteenth and nineteenth centuries. Smaller ethnic minorities such as Armenians, Aromanians, Jews, and Vlachs comprise 0.7 per cent of the total population, as shown in Table 13.1.

When it comes to religious affiliation, the majority of those who responded to the question about religion in the 2011 national census professes Orthodox Christianity (76 per cent); Muslims

Table 13.1 Population of Bulgaria by ethnicity in 2011

Ethnic affiliation	Number	Share (%)
Total population	7,364,570	100
Bulgarians	5,664,624	84.8
Turks	588,318	8.8
Roma	325,343	4.9
Other	44,304	0.7
Not declared	53,391	0.8

Source: National Statistical Institute, National Census Results 2011. Definitive data: 23–24.

Table 13.2 Population of Bulgaria by denomination in 2011

Denomination	Number	Share of those who responded to the question of religious affiliation (%)	Share of the total population (%)
Total population	7,364,570		100
Those who did not respond to the question	1,606,260		21.8
Those who responded to the question of religious affiliation	5,758,310	100	78.2
Eastern Orthodox	4,374,135	76	59.4
Muslim	577,139	10	7.8
Catholic	48,954	0.8	Less than 1
Protestant	64,476	1.1	Less than 1
Other denominations (Jewish, Armenian, other)	11,444	0.2	1.5
Not self-identified	409,898	7.1	5.5
No denomination ('I don't have')	272,264	4.7	3.7

Source: National Statistical Institute, National Census Results 2011. Volume 1 Population, Book 2. Demographic and Social characteristics of the population, 2–11: 34–35.

(10 per cent) are the largest religious minority. There are a number of other religious denominations that comprise very small communities: Protestants (1.1 per cent), Catholics, including Uniates (0.8 per cent), Armenian-Gregorians (0.03 per cent), and Jews (0.01 per cent). The religious structure of the country's total population involves 59 per cent Eastern Orthodox Christians, 8.8 per cent Muslims, and less than 2 per cent professing other denominations (Catholic, Protestant, Jewish, etc.); 31 per cent of census respondents either did not reply to the question of religion, did not self-identify in religious terms, or declared that they have no denomination, as shown in Table 13.2.[1]

While the overwhelming majority of ethnic Bulgarians (87 per cent) and ethnic Turks (88 per cent) who responded to the question about religion profess Orthodox Christianity and Islam, respectively, this is not the case with ethnic Roma people who share different religious affiliations, including Orthodox Christianity, Evangelism, and Islam. The division in religious affiliations and mother tongues (Romani or Turkish) among the Roma tend to reflect different ethnic self-identifications (see Table 13.3.), respectively Bulgarian for those professing Eastern Orthodoxy, Catholicism or Protestantism and Turkish for those professing

Table 13.3 Distribution of religious affiliations among self-identifying Roma[2]

East-Orthodox Christians	84,867	36.60%
Muslims	42,201	18.30%
Protestants	23,289	10.10%
No religion	30,491	13.22%
Not stated	49,491	21.46%

Source: Data in Table 13.3 is based on 2011 Census results, cited in: Evstatiev,S., P. Makariev and D. Kalkandjieva (2015) Christianity, Islam, and Human Rights in Bulgaria, in: Ziebertz Hans-Georg, G. Cripic (eds.) Religion and Human Rights. An International Perspective, Springer: 1–17.

Table 13.4 Newly registered third-country nationals, by year

	2012	2013	2014	2015	2016	2017	2018
TCN	5,003	12,265	15,671	13,066	10,677	11,888	12,452

Source: NSI. Data provided upon request on 31 May, 2019.

Islam (Benovska-Sabkova & Altanov, 2009; Slavkova, 2004: 17). A note should be made that processes of conversions from one religion to another within the Roma community are not uncommon.

Islam is the religion of a number of old historic minorities: Turks, Bulgarian-speaking Muslims, and Roma. The community of Bulgarian-speaking Muslims was formed during the Ottoman domination when, under various circumstances, they converted from Christianity to Islam. Members of this community today self-identify in three different ways. Some of them declare themselves Bulgarians, others as Turks, and a third group self-identify as Pomaks. All of them are Muslims, with Bulgarian being their mother tongue.[3] The majority of Muslims in Bulgaria are Hanafi Sunni (95 per cent, or 546,004 persons) followed by a small Shia community (4.75 per cent or 27,407 persons). The country hosts a small Alevi/Kizlibashi/Bektasji community that evolved during Ottoman rule out of old heterodox orders. This community, however, appears to be a silent and invisible minority as they are not given proper option to self-identify in the national censuses.[4] Both the Sunni and the minority of Shia (as per census denomination) profess traditional Islam, which has been developed under the influence of the Ottoman Empire and during centuries of interaction with majority Christian populations. This Islamic tradition is different from interpretations and practices of Islam across other continents and was termed 'Balkan Islam' by one of the leading scholars in the field, Alexandre Popovic (1986).

Bulgaria hosts a small immigrant community. As of December 2017, the number of third-country nationals with long-term or permanent residence in Bulgaria was 31,578 persons. The top five countries of origin for third-country nationals in Bulgaria were Turkey (13,034 persons), Russia (4,721), North Macedonia (3,208), Ukraine (2,757), and Serbia (1,095) (see Table 13.4).[5]

When it comes to refugees, between 1993 and 2018 a total of 85,537 asylum applications were registered and 25,156 persons were granted international protection. About 68 per cent of the asylum seekers arrived in the country in the period 2013–2016 (58,034 persons) (SAR, 2019). The three top countries of origin since 2013 appear to be Syria, Iraq, and Afghanistan. Refugees are predominantly Muslims. Available research, which is still scarce, reveals that there is little religious interaction between Muslim immigrants and historic

Table 13.5 Education levels by ethnicity (percentage)

	High university education (%)	Secondary education (%)	Basic education (%)	Have never attended school (%)
Ethnic Bulgarians	23	47.5	20	0.4
Ethnic Turkish	5	26	43	3.6
Roma	0.3	6.8	35.3	9.4

Source: National Statistical Institute. Census and dwellings fund in 2011. Volume 1 Population, Book 2. Demographic and Social characteristics of the population, 2–11: 194–209.

Muslim minorities in Bulgaria (Troeva & Mancheva, 2011). Little is known at the academic level about the religiosity and religious practices of immigrant and refugee communities in the country.

Economic and cultural factors relating to population composition

The social and economic status of Bulgaria's Muslim minorities (Turks, Bulgarian-speaking Muslims, and Roma) is lower than that of the Orthodox Christians (the majority of whom are ethnic Bulgarians). In the post-communist period and in the context of a country-wide economic crisis, the Muslim minority communities such as Turks, Roma, and Bulgarian-speaking Muslims were hit the hardest. They were continuously displaying higher levels of unemployment and had poorer access to healthcare and public education.

Statistical data from 2011 (census results) reveal that the Roma and Turkish ethnic communities share lower levels of employment and educational attainment than members of the majority Bulgarian ethnic communities.

The ethnic differences in employment and unemployment among the economically active population are stark, with employment rates of 19.4 per cent for the Roma, 33.7 for the Turks, and 46.9 for the Bulgarians and unemployment rates of 19.3 per cent for the Roma, 11.7 for the Turks, and 6.6 for the Bulgarians (NSI, 2011c: 56), as shown in Table 13.5.

Levels of religiosity

It should be noted that religiosity in the canonical sense has not been high in Bulgarian society, from both the historical and contemporary perspectives. Experts in the field usually prefer definitions such as 'traditional Christianity' and 'traditional Islam' to the type of religiousness often characterised as a mixture of pagan beliefs and practices covered by a thin layer of official religion (Zheljazkova et al., 1994). Many of those who declared themselves Eastern Orthodox or Muslim in the 2011 census are not practising believers and many are not baptised. This is the outcome of high levels of secularisation among both Orthodox Christians and Muslims, on the one hand, and of the tradition of perceiving religion as a component of one's ethnic or cultural identity, on the other.[6] This trend is demonstrated in the results of both quantitative and qualitative studies.

According to the 2008 European Value Survey for Bulgaria (Karamelska, 2009), 73.3 per cent of Bulgarians declare affiliation to a particular denomination (58.6 per cent with Orthodox Christianity and 12.8 per cent with Islam) but only 55.2 per cent identify as religious. Still, 49 per cent do not affiliate themselves with the monotheist idea of 'One God' but express belief in the existence of 'a Spirit or Force'. When it comes to practising religion, 4.4 per cent participate in religious services weekly, 9.2 per cent monthly, and 45.5 per cent take part only on religious holidays. One-fourth of respondents declared that they never attend religious services. At the same time, the majority of Christian Orthodox Bulgarians believe that religious rituals should be performed at birth (63 per cent), marriage (68 per cent), and death (73 per cent) – an illustration of the appropriation of the ritualistic side of religion. However, only 4 per cent of Bulgarians declare themselves as atheists. This trend seems confirmed by the findings of a qualitative study of religious values conducted in 2011[7] that demonstrates low levels of individual religiosity, absence of basic canonical literacy among parish members, and the utilisation of religion for everyday purposes, often at the level of superstition (visits to the church only on religious holidays for luck and good health).

Both the 2008 and 2011 studies point to low theological competences of those Bulgarians who declare themselves Orthodox Christian, nominal practising of religious faith, and high aptitude to the cultural significance of religion for the majority of Bulgarian citizens. The main factors contributing to this reality highlighted by the studies include the absence of systematic catechisation of the population; the lack of a comprehensive concept for religious education on the part of the Orthodox Church; the absence of a tradition of introducing religion to children within the family; the encapsulation and passivity of the Orthodox Church and its weak presence in the social sphere with respect to marginalised groups and groups in need, as well as the weak relationship between clergy and parish members; and last but not least, the impact of the forced atheist propaganda during the communist regime (1944–1989) (Garvanova & Shapkalova, 2018).

A more recent national representative study of religiosity among Muslims in Bulgaria conducted in 2016[8] with 1,200 respondents reveals a clearly manifested religious identity, respect for certain religious norms, yet low rather than high religiosity at the deeper level. While 86 per cent of the Muslim respondents declared that religion plays an important role in their lives, 41 per cent reported that they don't go to the mosque and only 54 per cent reported praying; 20 per cent identified as deeply religious and 8.8 per cent said they prayed five times a day.

An indirect indication of the relatively high levels of secularisation in Bulgarian society could be found in the comparison of census results between 1992 and 2011, which demonstrate decreasing shares of the Orthodox Christian (by 9.7 per cent) and the Muslim (by 3.1 per cent) population, as shown in Table 13.6. This decline seems to correspond to some extent with the observed increase in the share of people who have not declared religious affiliation in the national censuses (from 0.1 per cent in 1992 to 7.1 per cent in 2011) (NSI, 2011b: 132).

The decrease could be the result of lower levels of affiliation with religion for some members of Bulgarian society (that is, secularisation) or due to unwillingness on the part of some Muslims to affiliate themselves officially with Islam due to a public atmosphere of prejudice

Table 13.6 Population of Bulgaria by denomination: 1992, 2001, 2011

Denomination	1992	2001	2011
Total population	7,274,592	7,928,901	7,364,570
Eastern Orthodox (%)	85.7	82.6	76
Muslim (%)	13.1	12.2	10
Not self-identified (%)	0.1	3.9	7.1

Source: National Statistical Institute. Census and dwellings fund in 2011. Volume 1 Population, Book 2. Demographic and Social characteristics of the population, 2–11: 124–127.

and suspicion towards this denomination. It should be noted that 21.8 per cent of census respondents in 2011 did not answer the question of religious affiliation. The fact that their majority belong to young age groups and live in the country's three biggest cities (Sofia, Plovdiv, and Varna) suggests that this is likely an indication of secularisation.

State-religion relations and religious diversity governance in historical perspective

State-religion relations

Since its establishment as the official state religion of the medieval Bulgarian state in 885, Orthodox Christianity has had a significant influence on the formation and development of Bulgarian cultural identity. In the seventeenth century, the process of development of national consciousness was intertwined with the struggle of Bulgarians for liberation from the Ottoman Empire. In this context Orthodox Christianity attained the role of important identity marker around which the modern Bulgarian national identity was constructed (Garvanova & Shapkalova, 2018). With the establishment of the independent national Bulgarian state in 1878, the Bulgarian Orthodox Church (BOC) was one of the important actors engaged in constructing the new state and national identity based on Bulgarian ethnicity and Orthodox Christianity. In the Constitution of 1879, Orthodox Christianity was defined as the 'dominating faith in the Bulgarian principality' (Chapter 9, Article 37). According to D. Kalkanjieva, a leading scholar of the history of the Bulgarian Orthodox Church, the 1979 Constitution confirms *de facto* the role of the exarchate as a guardian of the national unity of Bulgarians (2014). The Constitution also postulated that religious faith could not be the basis to avoid compliance with state laws (Chapter 9, Articles 41).

Church-state relations in the period until the Second World War were marked by a stronger role on the part of the state.[9] According to the Constitution, the country's denominations were to be supervised by the corresponding minister (Chapter 9, Article 42). A trend evolved towards direct interference on the part of the state in financial and internal church matters. The trend was reinforced through the eparchial statute from 1883 which allowed the participation of state power in the church government, in particular when it came to its property (Daskalov, 2005: 445).[10]

During the socialist period (1944–1989) the relationship between state and church changed abruptly; Bulgarian society was subjected to a process of forced secularisation. BOC assumed a subordinate position with regard to the state and came to be viewed as an ideological enemy of the new regime. In essence, BOC lost its autonomy and active public presence in the context of state-promoted atheism that dominated all aspects of social and public life, including education and culture (Kalkandjieva, 2002). While freedom of religion and religious rites were guaranteed in the two socialist Constitutions of 1947 and 1971, which also proclaimed the separation of church and state (Constitution of People's Republic of Bulgaria, 1947: Art. 53, 1971), aggressive control and interference on the part of the state in religious matters was imposed by the Denominations Act (Law on Denominations in Bulgaria, 1949). Some of the strict state restrictions imposed by the Denominations Act involved the requirement of approval of denominations' statutes by the Minister of Foreign Affairs (Art. 6); the dependence of representatives of the clergy on the same Minister, who had the authority to fire them if they were considered to be abusing state laws or public order (Art. 12), the submission of the finances of all denominations to the control of state financial institutions just like any other public organisation (Art. 13). In addition, all denominations fell under the law on nationalisation and agricultural lands, thus losing their main source of income. The state compensated this loss by introducing annual state subsidies that were effectively used to further subordinate the denominations to state power.

Governing religious diversity

Throughout the twentieth century state policy towards the traditional Muslim minorities in Bulgaria was highly inconsistent with periods of free and liberal expression of traditional religion, alternating with periods of repression and assimilation attempts. According to the 1879 Constitution, all religions other than Orthodox Christianity of both Bulgarian citizens and foreigners residing in the country enjoyed freedom of profession under the condition that they did not abuse the country's laws (Chapter 9, Article 40). They were to be organised according to their respective statutes.

In the period prior to the Second World War, the Islamic denomination was constituted through the 'Statute for the spiritual leadership of the Muslims in the Kingdom of Bulgaria' of 1919. The head of the community was the Chief Mufti, with regional muftis directly elected by Muslims. Between 1880 and 1934, the attitude towards Islam was comparatively liberal. One stark exception was the campaign for forced conversion of Bulgarian-speaking Muslims conducted by the Bulgarian Orthodox Church in 2012–2013 and in the context of the Balkan Wars (Georgiev and Trifonov, 1995). After Bulgaria's defeat, the converted population returned to their Islamic faith and rituals with the approval of the Bulgarian government. The overall state policy towards Muslim communities until 1944 was one of isolation and economic, educational, and social marginalisation. It was compounded by support for the preservation of communities' conservative religiosity as a safeguard to Kemalist influences for secularisation and modernisation which were seen as a vehicle for the emancipation and political self-organisation of these communities.

After 1945, minority denominations were subjected to the same strict regulations imposed on the Orthodox Church, including stark administrative interference in denominational matters. In addition, a process of repression against clergymen of all denominations was begun, which took more severe forms after 1947 (Peteva, 2003: 38). The harshest anti-religious attacks were directed against the non-Orthodox Christian communities that comprised some 100,000 believers. A show trial of 15 Protestant Pastors in 1949 destroyed the leadership of the main Protestant churches. Between 1951 and 1953 the Roman Catholic and the Greek Catholic Churches were incapacitated, their priests, nuns, and many laymen tortured and prosecuted in a series of trials (Kalkandjieva, 2014). With respect to Islam, the main goal of the communist regime was to integrate Muslims in the 'unitary socialist nation'. Islamic practices and traditions were subject to pressures from two sides. On the one hand, religion in general was officially persecuted as incompatible with socialist ideology and values; on the other, Islam was seen as a basis for maintaining an identity different from the Bulgarian one. The communist state policy of forced assimilation used different methods, starting with shutting Muslim newspapers and schools in the late 1950s and reaching as far as conducting several assimilation campaigns against Bulgarian-speaking Muslims and Turks during the late 1960s, 1970s, and 1980s. Muslim names were forcibly changed, religious practices and customs were persecuted, and traditional Muslim clothing was prohibited (Gruev & Kalionski, 2008).

Current institutional structure for governing religion and religious diversity

According to the current Constitution of 1991, Bulgaria is established as a secular state respecting freedom of denominations (Art. 13.1) and proclaiming separation between religion and state (Art. 13.2). With respect to religious diversity it proclaims the principles of non-discrimination (Art. 6.2), freedom of choice of denomination and of religious or atheist beliefs (Art. 37.1).[11] The state is mandated to assist in the maintenance of tolerance and respect among believers of different denominations as well as between believers and non-believers (Art. 37.1). The Constitution also stipulates that religious institutions and beliefs shall not be used to political ends (Art. 13.4) and that freedom of denominations cannot be used against national security, the public order, or against the rights and freedoms of other citizens (Art. 37.2). While the Constitution proclaims religious pluralism, it also declares Eastern Orthodox Christianity as the traditional religion in the Republic of Bulgaria (Art. 13.3). The differentiation between the majority religion and the other denominations is reinforced through the Denominations Act, which distinguishes Orthodox Christianity as the 'traditional denomination' in the Republic of Bulgaria, with the Orthodox Church legally established by the Law itself (Art. 10.2).

All other denominations in Bulgaria are to be legally established based on registration at the Sofia City Court along the Civil Procedure Code (Denominations Act, Article 15.1). In addition, registration by the Sofia City Court could be aided by expert opinion of the Directorate of Denominations at the Council of Ministers upon request (Art. 16). Some of the main denominational rights established by the Act include: foundation of religious communities; establishment of prayer houses, temples, and monasteries; performance of religious rights; conduct of religious education in a language of choice; establishment of humanitarian institutions; publishing of religious publications; gathering financial donations from persons and institutions; use of language other than Bulgarian in religious sermons according to the traditions of the respective religious community (Art. 5 and 6). In addition, all denominations are eligible for state budget subsidies with amounts calculated based on the number of believers as per registration in the national censuses (Art 28).

The state body designated to coordinate the relationship between the executive power and the denominations is the Directorate of Denominations at the Council of Ministers (DDCM) (Art. 35). DDCM is the agency exerting control over the implementation of the Denominations Act (Art. 35.1), assisting the implementation of state policy for maintenance of tolerance and respect among the different denominations (Art. 35.2), providing expert positions as foreseen per the Act (Art. 25.4), and preparing proposals for annual state budget subsidy distribution among the different denominations (Art. 35.9). In addition, DDCM maintains the public register of all prayer homes, temples, and monasteries (Art. 12.3) based on information provided annually by each denomination (Art. 12.2). DDCM is also mandated to issue requests for closure of registered denominations to the Sofia City Court (Art. 20a.3).

Institutional organisation of the country's denominations

In the post-socialist period, developments related to the Bulgarian Orthodox Church were influenced by the communist legacy. Between 1992 and 2002, the Orthodox Church appeared divided into two Synods with the dispute between them being strongly influenced by political actors – the United Democratic Forces (UDF) supporting the Alternative Synod and the Bulgarian Socialist Party supporting the old Synod. The so-called Alternative Synod was established in 1992 by some synod members after the UDF acting government claimed that the then-acting Patriarch Maxim had been elected by the communist party. The accusation was compounded by the Directorate of Religious Affairs' denouncement of Maxim's election in March 1992. An essential aspect of this dispute involved the restoration of church properties nationalised by the communist regime. The restoration of church property followed the trajectories of political power. When UDF was in government, restorations were transferred to the Alternative Synod; when the Bulgarian Socialist party (BSP) was in power, they were directed to Maxim's Synod. The dispute was addressed by the new Denominations Act of 2002 which defined Maxim's Synod as the only legitimate successor to the historical Bulgarian Orthodox Church (Art. 10.1–2; Transitory and Final Provisions, para. 3) (Kalkandjieva, 2006: 35–36). The issue was finally resolved in 2004 by the intervention of the Chief Prosecutor, who ordered the confiscation of Alternative Synod churches and property and their transfer to the Holy Synod of Patriarch Maxim.

The structure of the Islamic denomination in Bulgaria is governed by its internal statute (Treaty of Muslim Denomination, 2011) and attendant regulations for the functioning of its main bodies (Statute of Organization and Practice of the Chief Mufti and the Structures of the Muslim Denomination, 2011; Statute of Organization and Practice of the Higher Muslim Council of Muslim Denomination in the Republic of Bulgaria, 2011; Statute of Practice of Clergy, 2011). The National Muslim Conference (NMC) approves changes in the Denomination statutes as well as the election of the Chief Mufti and the chairman and members of the Senior Muslim Council (SMC). The NMC is convened by the SMC at least once every five years. It consists of *ex-officio* and elected delegates (one representative of each and any of the Muslim Board of Trustees in Bulgaria – 1,225 in 2011). SMC is composed of 31 members, is elected by the NMC, and acts as the highest administrative body of the Muslim denomination with authority to convene Muslim Conferences for the election of the Chief Mufti, his deputies, and the chairman of the SMC. The SMC elects the deputy muftis and the regional muftis, and issues decisions in all financial and organisational matters of the denomination. The Chief Muftiate is the institution in charge of administering and exercising control over the Islamic denomination in the country and of representing it before third parties. The Chief Muftiate represents all Muslims in Bulgaria, regardless of their ethnicity and the branch of Islam to which they belong. Thus its power does extend not only over the Sunni from the Hanafi school (the majority), but also over those Muslims who identify as Shia (who have representatives in the SMC).[12] In 2019 the Chief Muftiate included 20 regional muftiates in towns with large Muslim communities and administered 1,154 mosques and *masjids* (prayer homes) (Chief Mufti, n.d.).

The state subsidy to the Muslim denomination has been traditionally low and insufficient to cover the denominational needs of the Muslim community, amounting to 180,000 levs in 2011 and 360,000 levs in 2014 (US Department of State, 2012, 2013, 2014, 2015). In 2017, of the five million levs allocated from the national budget for the construction and maintenance of religious facilities and related expenses, 3.37 million were directed to BOC, 360,000 to the Chief Muftiate, and 50,000 each to the Catholic Church, the Armenian Apostolic Orthodox Church (AAOC), and the Jewish community (US Department of State, 2018:1). That reality prompted, to a certain extent, the openness of the Chief Muftiate to foreign funds coming either through bilateral agreements (from Turkey and Iran) or through donations from other Muslim states.

In the post-communist period, the Muslim leadership appeared deeply divided by struggles for control over the Chief Muftiate. This division was fostered by factors similar to those that split the Orthodox Synod into two rival entities. The struggles within the Muslim religious leadership were manipulated by political parties among which the Movement for Rights and Freedoms (MRF)[13] played an active role. The control over the Chief Muftiate and the resources it managed translated into political capital and provided opportunities for consolidation of the Muslim/Turkish vote. As a result, since the early 1990s two Senior Muslim Councils have existed, each backed by a different political party and electing two different Chief

Muftis. In essence, the Muslim Conference majority disputed the legitimacy of the Chief Muftiate headed by Nedjim Gendjev and elected in the last years of the communist regime. The conflicts between the two factions of the Muslim denomination persisted until 2011 and served to weaken the authority of the institution as the spiritual leader of Muslims in Bulgaria.

Concluding remarks

The model of state-religion relations in Bulgaria is one of a two-way autonomy involving separation of church and state. The Constitution acknowledges freedom of belief and religious pluralism, maintaining, however, a dominant place of the majority 'traditional' religion, that of Orthodox Christianity. While the majority of Bulgaria's population (both Christian and Muslim) is highly secularised, religion has a strong influence as it constitutes an important component of cultural identity for the majority of Bulgarian citizens. At the same time the relationship between the (mainly Orthodox Christian) clergy and parish members is weak due to clergy's aloofness and passivity and the absence of the population's systematic catechisation. Another important factor to account for when discussing state-religion relations is the weakness of the main religious institutions (the Orthodox Synod and the Chief Muftiate) in the context of the communist legacy and post-communist political rivalries. It is within this context that, to date, religion in Bulgaria appears easily manipulated by political actors and has a weak hold over the country's population in the canonical sense.

Notes

1. The official estimate of the religious structure of the population by the National Statistical Institute is based on the number of the persons who responded to the question of religious affiliation (NSI, 2011a: 12). Therefore, the estimates regarding religious structure of the whole population are made by the author based on the official census data.
2. Data in table 3 is based on 2011 Census results, cited in: Evstatiev et al. (2015).
3. To pay respect to the differentiating ways in which members of this community self-identify, the term chosen to denote them in this report is Bulgarian-speaking Muslims. For a detailed account of the representation of Bulgarian-speaking Muslims in the demographic statistics, see Ivanov (2012).
4. The only available Islamic denomination different from Sunni in the national census is that of Shia. In effect many of the Alevi/Kizlibashi/Bektasji identify as Shia to distinguish themselves from the Sunni Muslims.
5. National Statistical Institute, data provided upon request on 31 May 2019.
6. The instruction for collecting data under the 2011 Census, defines 'religious affiliation' as the 'historically determined belonging of an individual or his/her parents and forefathers to a particular group with specific religious views'.
7. The study involved interviews with 110 clergymen (93 per cent of whom were members of the Christian Orthodox Church) and a survey of 175 students (Nazarska, 2015).
8. Information based on press release: general results from the research on 'Attitudes of Muslims in Bulgaria – 2016'. The study was conducted by Alpha Research and New Bulgarian University.
9. One historical factor that accounts for this reality is the model of the Constantinople Patriarchy of the Byzantine Empire inherited by the Bulgarian Orthodox Church and which is characterised by persistent political interweaving between state and church with the state dominating this relationship. On the historical genesis and meaning of the term 'symphony' denominating the nature of church-state relations in the Orthodox world, see Kalkandjieva, 2011.
10. It should be stated that the close relations of church and state in Bulgaria were no exception from Orthodox-dominated countries in Europe where the phenomenon of autocephaly (referring to the status of a hierarchical Christian Church whose head bishop does not report to any higher-ranking bishop) was the major reason for the international decentralisation of Orthodoxy and the close relations of church with not only the state but also the nation (Kalkandjieva, 2011).

11 These provisions are confirmed in the Denominations Act (2002), which guarantees the equality, freedom, and autonomy of different religions and forbids state interference in their matters (Article 4.1-4). Still, some articles of the present Denominations Act concerning registration (Art. 16), closure (Art. 20a.3), and subsidy proposals (Art. 35.9) provide the potential for political interference in denominational matters.

12 Shia is the only available Islamic denomination other than Sunni on the national census card. For this purpose many Muslims who are Alevi (also called Kizilbashi/ Bektashi) tend to identify themselves in national censuses as Shia. The internal division of Muslims into Sunni and Alevi was never officially recognised by the modern Bulgarian state and all Muslims have always been dominated by the Chief Mufti's Office, which is Sunni.

13 The Movement for Rights and Freedoms (MRF) was established in 1990 as a political party of the Turkish and Muslim populations in Bulgaria. MRF's stable political base helped it evolve into an important factor in Bulgarian political life whose support was often key to the promotion of political decisions. In 2003 the party obtained executive power for the first time as a member of the coalition government at the time. Since then its influence at the executive level of governance has grown considerably.

References

Benovska-Sabkova, M. & Altanov, V. (2009). Evangelical Conversion among the Roma in Bulgaria. *Nouvelles identités rom en Europe centrale & orientale*: 133–168.

Chief Mufti, Regional Muftis, Republic of Bulgaria. (n.d.). Muslim Denomination. Chief Mufti. [in Bulgarian] Available at: https://www.grandmufti.bg/bg/glavno menyu rm.html.

Constitution of People's Republic of Bulgaria. (1947, 1971, 1991). National Assembly of the Republic of Bulgaria. Available at: https://www.academia.edu/6830294/CONSTITUTION_the_Peoples_Republic_of_Bulgaria_from_12_06_1947_Chapter_I_Peoples_Republic_of_Bulgaria: 1-17

Daskalov, R. (2005). *Bulgarian Society 1878–1939, Vol. 2, Population. Society. Culture*. Sofia: Guttenberg.

Evstatiev, S., Makariev, P. & Kalkandjieva, D. (2015). Christianity, Islam, and Human Rights in Bulgaria. In H.-G. Ziebertz & G. GordanČrpić (eds), *Religion and Human Rights an International Perspective* (pp. 1–17). Switzerland: Springer International Publishing.

Garvanova, M. & Shapkalova, S. (2018). Is there a crisis among traditional religious communities in Bulgaria? In G. Nazarska, M. Garvanova, & S. Shapkalova (eds), *Sustaining the Non-material Cultural Heritage: Religious Values in Contemporary Bulgaria* (pp. 75–88). Sofia: IPHS, Bulgarian Academy of Sciences.

Georgiev, V. & Trifonov, St. (1995). *Christening of Bulgarian Muslims 1912–1913*. Sofia: Academic Publishing Marin Drinov.

Gruev, A. & Kalionski, A. (2008). *The Revival Process. Muslim Communities and the Communist Regime*. Sofia: Ciela.

Ivanov, M. (2012). Pomaks according to the Bulgarian ethno-demographic statistics. *Naselenie*, 2012 (1–2): 163–197.

Kalkandjieva, D. (2002). *Bulgarian Orthodox Church and 'the People's Democracy' (1944–1953)*. Silistra: Demos Foundation.

Kalkandjieva, D. (2006). *The Consent of State and the Blessing of Church: A Case Study on the New Bulgarian Denominations Act*. The Romanian Journal of Political Sciences. Romania: Romanian Academic Society: 101–114.

Kalkandjieva, D. (2011). A comparative analysis on Church-State relations in Eastern Orthodoxy: Concepts, models and principles. *Journal of Church and State*, 53(4): 571–614.

Kalkandjieva, D. (2014). The Bulgarian Orthodox Church at the crossroads: Between nationalism and pluralism. In A. Krawchuk & T. Bremer (eds), *Eastern Orthodox Encounters of Identity and Otherness* (pp. 47–68). New York: Palgrave Macmillan.

Karamelska, T. (2009). Attitudes toward religion in Bulgaria according to the EVS (2008). *Christianity and Culture*, 4: 28–35.

Law on Denominations in Bulgaria. (1949). [in Bulgarian]. Available at: http://santokiriko.blog.bg/politika/2015/02/09/zakon-za-izpovedaniiata-1949g.1336990.

National Statistical Institute. (2011a). Census 2011. Definitive data. https://www.nsi.bg/en

National Statistical Institute. (2011b). Census and dwellings fund in 2011. Volume 1 Population, Book 2. Demographic and Social characteristics of the population, pp. 2–11 [in Bulgarian]. Available at: http://www.nsi.bg/census2011/pagebg2.php?p2=175&sp2=218

National Statistical Institute. (2011c). Census and dwellings fund in 2011. Volume 1 Population, Book 3. Economic characteristics of the population [in Bulgarian]. Available at: http://www.nsi.bg/census2011/pagebg2.php?p2=175&sp2=218

National Statistical Institute. (2018). Population and demographic processes in 2018 [in Bulgarian]. Available at: https://www.nsi.bg/sites/default/files/files/publications/DMGR2018.pdf.

Nazarska, G. (2015). Research of religious values in contemporary Bulgaria. In R. Krikoriyan, K. Slavcheva, & St. Penov (eds), *Values, Paradigms and Challenges in Inter-religious Relations* (pp. 68–80). Sofia: National Council of Religions in Bulgaria & Institute for Interreligious and Ethnic-Cultural Dialogue and Bulgarian Academy of Science.

Peteva, J. (2003). Church and state in Bulgaria. In S. Ferrari & C. W. Durham (eds), *Law and Religion in Post-Communist Europe*. Leuven, Belgium: Peeters: 37–56.

Popovic, A. (1986). L'islam balkanique. *Les musulmans du sud-est européen dans la période ottomane, Berlin & Wiesbaden*. Wiesbaden Harrassowitz: Balkanologische Veröffentlichungen.

Religious Denominations Act of Bulgaria. (2002). [in Bulgarian]. Available at: www.lex.bg

Slavkova, M. (2004). The 'Turkish Gypsies' in Bulgaria and their new religious identity. In D. Todorović (ed.), *Evangelization, Conversion, Proselytism* (pp. 87–100). Niš: Punta.

State Agency for Refugees. (2019). Information on persons requesting international protection and number of decisions for the time period 01.01.1993-30.04.2019 [in Bulgarian]. Available at: https://aref.government.bg/bg/node/238.

Statute of Organization and Practice of the Chief Mufti and the Structures of the Muslim denomination. (2011). [in Bulgarian]. Available at: http://www.grandmufti.bg/bg/za-nas/normativni-dokumenti/880-pravilnitzi.html.

Statute of Organization and Practice of the Higher Muslim Council of Muslim Denomination in the republic of Bulgaria. (2011). [in Bulgarian]. Available at: http://www.grandmufti.bg/bg/za-nas/normativni-dokumenti/880-pravilnitzi.html.

Statute of Practice of Clergy (vayz, imam-habib, muesin). (2011). [in Bulgarian]. Available at: http://www.grandmufti.bg/bg/za-nas/normativni-dokumenti/880-pravilnitzi.html.

Treaty of Muslim Denomination. (2011). [in Bulgarian]. Available at: http://www.grandmufti.bg/bg/za-nas/normativni-dokumenti/881-ustavi.html.

Troeva, E. & Mancheva, M. (2011). Migration, religion and gender: Female Muslim immigrants in Bulgaria. In Marko Hajdinjak (ed), *Migrations, Gender, and Intercultural Interactions in Bulgaria* (pp. 155–192). Sofia: International Center for Minority Studies and Intercultural Relations.

US Department of State. (2011–2016). *International Religious Freedom Reports for Bulgaria*. Available at: https://bg.usembassy.gov/our-relationship/official-reports/

Zheljazkova, A. L., Nielsen, J. S. & Kepell, J. (eds), (1994). *Relations of Compatibility and Incompatibility between Christians and Muslims in Bulgaria*. Sofia: International Centre for Minority Studies and Intercultural Relations Foundation.

14

Albania
Legacy of shared culture and history for religious tolerance

Liliya Yakova and Leda Kuneva

Introduction

The role of religion and its governing in Albania have developed throughout centuries of interchanging governance models, foreign intervention and occupation, isolationist regimes, and international influence. Numerous dichotomous pairs – colonialism and postcolonialism, authoritarianism and democracy, theocracy and secularism – have served to chisel the relationship between state, religion and society from the very conception of the Albanian identity to the current twenty-first-century state of affairs. Hence, the chapter at hand examines the *modus vivendi* of this relationship. The following five thematic aspects regarding the state-religion relationship in Albania are addressed: (1) legal and regulatory framework, (2) historical and socio-political factors, (3) socio-demographic factors, (4) economic factors, and (5) cultural factors.

Legal and regulatory framework

The relationship between state and religion was initially reflected in the replacement of the communist atheist agenda with an inclusionary narrative by the first pluralist parliament in 1991. This change included the stipulation of the right of thought, conscience, and belief; the respect for religious freedoms and their exercise; and the right to freedom of expression individually and collectively. Experts, however, argue that these symbolic first steps in the recognition of religious freedoms lacked the necessary legal formalisation – a process that lasted almost a decade (Elbasani & Puto, 2017: 59). The 1998 Constitution serves to depict this formalisation process and includes several key articles delineating the existence and exercise of religious belief in Albania under the conditions of Albanian-style *laïcité*: the mutually independent and neutral, yet cooperative relationship between the state and the religious communities (Elbasani & Puto, 2017). In simple terms, the Constitution, as illustrated via the Articles highlighted in Table 14.1, demonstrates a deliberate political will in establishing a liberal and tolerant position in line with progressive European values.

Table 14.1 Constitutional provisions on the issue of religion, religious freedoms, state-religion relations, and religious governance

Provision	Article number
'religious coexistence, and coexistence with, and understanding of Albanians for, minorities are the basis of this state, which has the duty of respecting and protecting them' (p. 1)	Article 3
Political parties which instigate racial, religious and ethnic hatred are prohibited by law	Article 9
'In the Republic of Albania there is no official religion' (p. 2)	Article 10
'The state is neutral on questions of belief and conscience and guarantees the freedom of their expression in public life' (p. 2)	Article 10
'State recognizes the equality of religious communities' (p. 2)	Article 10
'The state and the religious communities mutually respect the independence of one another and work together for the good of each and all' (p. 2)	Article 10
'Relations between the state and religious communities are regulated on the basis of agreements entered between their representative and the Council of Ministers' (p. 2)	Article 10
'Religious communities are juridical persons. They have independence in the administration of their properties according to their principles, rules and canons, to the extent that interests of third parties are not infringed' (p. 2)	Article 10
No one can be discriminated against on the basis of religion	Article 18
People have the right to freely express their religious belonging	Article 20
'Freedom of conscience and religion is guaranteed' (p. 5)	Article 24
'Everyone is free to choose or to change his religion or beliefs, as well as to express them individually or collectively, in public or private life, through cult, education, practices or the performance of rituals' (p. 5)	Article 24
'No one may be compelled or prohibited to take part in a religious community or its practices or to make his beliefs or faith public' (p. 5)	Article 24

Source: OSCE-Albania, 1998.

The first formal governmental body to deal with religious matters was the State Secretariat (or State Commissariat) founded in 1992 (Elbasani & Puto, 2017: 59), which was replaced by the currently operational State Committee on Cults (SCC) in 1999 (Kulla, 2007: 38–40) under the Ministry of Social Welfare and Youth (OHCHR, 2017). The SCC is chaired by a 'neutral civil servant, representing the state' (Elbasani & Puto, 2017: 62) and is responsible for managing the relations between the state and the religious groups, for safeguarding the right to freedom of religion and its expression, the promotion of interreligious harmony and peaceful coexistence, and for overseeing the integrity of the agreements between the state and the recognised religious communities (OHCHR, 2017). The SCC also has the capacity to assist and advise in drafting laws and regulations, as well as in developing religious teaching curricula (Dyrmishi, 2016).

With regard to the legal recognition of religious groups, the state does not explicitly require their registration and the process is not formalised in a separate legal provision specifically for religious groups. Rather, the Law on Non-Profit Organisations (Law 8788, 2001) is interpreted to include religious associations. The registration under Law 8788 (which grants juridical personhood) could be followed by contracting an agreement between a representative of the religious group and the Council of Ministers – which is then ratified by Parliament. The religious group is thereby granted legal personhood and deemed a 'community'. The agreements between the state and the religious communities are usually bilateral and codify formal provisions in areas such as recognition and restitution of property lost during communist rule, tax exemptions, property management, and self-administration of funds, among others (US Department of State, 2018: 3). The bilateral agreements must always be concluded with respect to the Constitution and may vary from community to community (OHCHR, 2017). The Office of the United Nations High Commissioner for Human Rights' (OHCHR) 2017 preliminary findings on Albania, however, point to the fact there is no legislation defining what constitutes a 'community', and to date only five denominations have been recognised as religious 'communities'[1] – the Sunni Muslim, Bektashis, Orthodox Christians, Catholics, and Evangelists, of which the first four are classified as 'traditional religious communities'. Although numerous other groups have attempted to gain the same level of recognition, the Council of Ministers has not approved any further claims.

Other important aspects of state-religion relations in Albania concern the funding of religious communities, their right to freedom of religion and religious expression, and the management of religious property and places of worship. With regard to funding, only four of the five religious communities (Evangelists excluded) receive government support regulated under the Law on the Financing of Religious Communities (Law 10140) passed May 2009. Before its approval, state financing of religious communities was prohibited (OHCHR, 2017). Law 10221 harmonised Albanian legislation with EU directives on freedom of religion and religious expression and establishes a separate institutional body to process and rule on discrimination complaints – the Office of the Commissioner for Protection from Discrimination. As for management of religious property and places of worship, the Albanian Agency for Treatment of Property (ATP) is charged by law to process claims by the religious communities about confiscated or otherwise lost properties during the communist period, while the Agency for the Legalization, Urbanization, and Integration of Informal Construction (ALUIZNI) is responsible for the legalisation of unofficial churches, mosques, and *tekkes* (Bektashi places of worship). Inefficiencies in the legalisation and registration procedures for places of worship, especially for the so-called *para-jamaats* (illegal mosques), are highlighted as increasingly problematic in the broader discussion of national security and radicalisation concerns (AIIS, 2015; OSF, 2016).

In addition to national legislation, Albania has signed and ratified the nine core international human rights treaties (ratification years in parentheses): International Convention on the Elimination of All Forms of Racial Discrimination (1994), International Covenant on Civil and Political Rights (1991; OP2-DP-2007), International Covenant on Economic, Social and Cultural Rights (1991), Convention on the Elimination of All Forms of Discrimination against Women (1994), Convention Against Torture and Other Cruel, Inhuman or Degrading Treatment or Punishment (1994; OP-2003), Convention on the Rights of the Child (1992; OP-AC- and OP-SC-2008), International Convention on the Protection of the Rights of All Migrant Workers and Members of Their Families (2007), International Convention for the Protection of All Persons from Enforced Disappearance (2007), and Convention on the Rights of Persons with Disabilities (2013). The bulk of those treaties contain provisions as to the right to freedom of religion and religious expression. Albania is also a member of the UN, NATO, the Council of Europe, and a signatory of the European Charter of Human Rights,

Historical and socio-political factors

The history of Albania is key to the establishment of the current relationship between state and religion. There is a broad consensus among scholars that the Albanian ethnos can be traced back to the ancient Illyrians, with influence from the Greek colonists, the Roman

Empire, and Slavic expansion campaigns. In a contentious and strategic position, the present-day territory of Albania fell under the rule and occupation of many states and was under the control of different religious organisations. In the thirteenth century a feudal system with Albanian princes at the top of the social structure was established. Upon this background of interchanging foreign influences, religions, and socio-economic modes of organisation, the structure that remained throughout the centuries was the clan (*fis*) system, or as Lopasic (1992) delineates it, a tribal patrilineal system of blood and kin ties unaffected by religion, economic rearrangements, or foreign penetration, that lies at the very basis of Albanian identity (Zhelyazkova, 2000; Gjuraj, 2013: 91).

During the fourteenth and fifteenth centuries, the predominantly Christian Orthodox territories of Albania faced the growing threat of the Ottoman Empire. An important figure for that period is George Kastrioti-Skanderbeg, who was appointed by the Ottomans as *sanjak-bey* (military and administrative commander) of Debar and saw an opportunity to organise a resistance and bring together the Albanian princes in a League. Skanderbeg led several successful military operations against the Sultan even though he served the Ottomans. It is notable, however, that the power of kinship and family interests took the upper hand, and by 1457 the League was abandoned by the princes, some of whom joined the Ottomans for fear of losing their authority and possessions. After Skanderbeg's death in 1468, the Ottomans began a laborious establishment of control over the Albanian territories. The Islamisation of the population began with the influx of Anatolian settlers and the construction of administrative buildings and military garrisons, while local aristocracy and feudal clans started converting to Islam for purely economic reasons – to preserve their lands and positions of privilege. Islamisation of the lower classes began in the urban areas, where Christians and Jews owned tangible riches which they did not wish to relinquish. This practical nature of the religious conversion allowed the continued existence of the clan mode of organisation, customary law, and the ideological order of the *Kanun of Lek* and the *Code of Skanderbeg* (customary systems). Customary law did not clash with, but superseded, sharia law and created a dual system whereby converted Albanians were formally Muslim, but *de facto* followed their previous moral affiliation and traditional practices. Rural and mountainous populations, on the other hand, were often isolated from Islamisation currents and continued observing their pre-existing moral system unhindered. It could thus be concluded that religious ideologies and beliefs never became an intrinsic part of Albanian identity during Ottoman rule (Gjuraj, 2013).

The rise of nationalist narratives in Albania was slowed by the persistence of traditional differences between the sub-groups of Albanian society, particularly between the South and the North (Tosks and Gegs), which, despite their overwhelmingly homogenous faith (70 per cent of ethnic Albanians were Muslim by the late nineteenth century), experienced clashes in culture, language, and historical origin. Thus, Albanian Renaissance ideology entailed both the devising of a strong unifying notion (the civil religion – Albanianism) and the employment of 'othering' vis-à-vis the Turks to avoid the equating of Albanian Muslims with Asiatic Turks (Elbasani & Puto, 2017: 56). The period immediately preceding the fall of the Ottoman Empire in 1912 was characterised by a plethora of rebellions, which is seen as evidence of the nationalist maturity of ethnic Albanians (Zhelyazkova, 2000). In 1913, the Great Powers recognised Albania as independent, and in 1914 the German prince Wied was enthroned in Albania (ibid.).

The 1922 Constitution codified secularism, state neutrality in religious matters, and freedom of religion. Secularism was further established under Zog (1924–1928), who employed stricter controls on religion, but co-opted religious communities in achieving state goals.

After his self-proclamation as King of Albania, Islamic courts lost their competences and the Albanian Muslim Community lost political and legal authority (Elbasani & Puto, 2017: 57–58). The curtailment of the Albanian Muslim Community's higher comparative authority followed Zog's objective of equality among religions (Gjuraj, 2013: 96–97). In 1939, however, Albania was assimilated under Italian control, and resentment over the occupation led to the formation of the Communist Party in 1941 (Zhelyazkova, 2000).

The communist regime in Albania held power from 1944 to 1990, with Enver Hoxha at its head. From the onset, Hoxha's government sought to curtail the rights of religious communities, dismantle their administrative autonomy, terminate their services, confiscate their land and properties, dissolve religious education, and implement censorship on their publications (Zhelyazkova, 2000; Elbasani & Puto, 2017). During the 1950s, religious officials were obliged to declare loyalty to the Party, while acting clerics were subjected to arrest and conviction (Gjuraj, 2013: 98).

The process of democratisation in Albania after 1990 provided an opportunity to include different societal sub-groups (Gjuraj, 2013: 102). Importantly, the lack of legislation in this area allowed the quick expansion of religious freedoms. The first Parliament of 1991 asserted governmental respect for religious freedoms, while the 1992 Democratic Party (DP) government stood behind the freedom of thought, consciousness, and religion as a fundamental right, along with the freedom to change and express religious beliefs. The DP also established strong ties with the Albanian Muslim Community and granted it a chair position at the State Secretariat. This also led to the founding of Kultura Islame (KI), an organisation linking the DP, the Albanian Muslim Community, and foreign Islamic charities with the goal of reviving Islam in Albania. The role of Islamic donors and Albania's membership in the Organisation of Islamic Conference (OIC)[2] during this initial period were appreciated by the government, which could not secure financial aid from the West (Elbasani & Puto, 2017: 59–60). But loose regulation and the intensive utilisation of foreign sources of funding proved unstable in the long-term, especially with the decline of DP popularity in 1997, when the Socialist Party (SP) won the elections. The SP, in cooperation with European anti-terrorist agencies and the FBI, led a campaign to investigate the threat of Islamic 'charities' that undertook illegal activities related to terrorism, closed such organisations, and prosecuted persons linked to terrorist activities. An important development was the codification and formalisation of the ties between the state and the religious communities as an Albanian-style *laïcité* via the 1998 Constitution.

Socio-demographic factors

According to the latest Albanian national census in 2011, the population can be defined as generally homogenous (with notable exceptions) in terms of ethnicity and language (Gjuraj, 2013: 90), but less so in terms of faith. With a population of over 2.8 million people (>3 million according to the CIA Factbook, 2019), the vast majority (82.58 per cent) identify as ethnic Albanians, followed by 0.87 per cent as ethnic Greeks, 0.2 per cent as Macedonians, 0.3 per cent as Aromanians and Roma each, and around 0.1 per cent as having Montenegrin and Egyptian ethnicity. In linguistic terms, almost 2.8 million persons cite Albanian as their mother tongue, with seven other languages – Greek, Macedonian, Romani, Turkish, among them – cited by roughly 2 per cent of the population. The statistical differences are more pronounced in terms of religious belief, with the majority (56.7 per cent) being of Muslim (Sunni) faith, and minority religious communities of 10.03 per cent Roman Catholic, 6.75 per cent Orthodox Christian, 2.09 per cent Bektashi, and 0.14 per cent Evangelists. It is noteworthy that around 8 per cent of the population either do not affiliate with one of the given religious denominations or follow any faith (Botimi, 2012).

A 2018 survey by the Institute for Democracy and Mediation (IDM) with a nationally representative sample sheds light on Albanian society's views and perceptions on religion. Respondents were overwhelmingly likely to take up their parents' religious affiliation (some 93.5 per cent identified with the religious beliefs of one or both parents). In terms of practising religion, the data reveal that only 19.2 per cent perform religious rites and abide by religious rules on a regular basis, 31.8 per cent do so on most occasions, while the remaining 48 per cent are either non-practising believers or are non-believers. Also, 23.9 per cent of the respondents never engage in prayer – some 3 per cent more than those who pray every day. The data also show that respondents' social circles are more likely to be constituted of people of different religions than solely persons of the same religion, while 21.1 per cent are equally close to both believers in different religions and atheists. In terms of social perceptions of religious harmony, 92.8 per cent assessed the current state of religious tolerance as high or very high. Additionally, most Albanians are likely to support or at least accept inter-religious marriages, while only 4.7 per cent would object to that under any circumstances.

Keeping in mind both the socio-demographic indicators, as presented in the 2011 census report, and the recent data published by IDM, the mode of interaction among the different religious communities could be predefined as cooperative and tolerance-based by society itself. As the Albanian public is cohesive in national, ethnic, and linguistic terms while exhibiting a high percentage of religiosity, with a well-established sense of tolerance towards others and a demonstrated desire to embrace interreligious harmony, it is evident that there is a strong societal drive for formalising religious coexistence.

Despite the overall *modus vivendi* of religious communities within Albania, as characterised by tolerance and interreligious harmony, a couple of socio-demographic aspects remain problematic for the governing of religion and religion-related phenomena.

The first problematic aspect relates to, on the one hand, the societal support for equality among the different religious communities, and, on the other, the claims from the Evangelist community (VUSH) that they do not enjoy the same treatment as their Sunni Muslim, Bektashi, Catholic, and Orthodox counterparts. Under the agreement between the state and VUSH there is no explicit mentioning of financial support, yet the SCC has committed in writing to providing such to the Evangelical community. Furthermore, VUSH has reported difficulties in property acquisition for worship sites and has been critical of the inadequate engagement of the state and the media with the Evangelical community (US Department of State, 2018: 2–7). The OHCHR pays more attention to the issue of ethnic minorities, such as the Macedonians, who have failed to gain government recognition for the Macedonian Orthodox Church. The issue of the curtailed rights to freedom of religion or belief of Roma and Egyptian communities is also touched upon, but hardly engaged with (2017).

Another aspect in the nexus between society and religion lies in the role of the social sphere in the proliferation of radical religious ideas. The 2018 IDM survey pointed out that as many as 93.5 per cent of respondents 'inherit' the religious belief of their parents – key evidence that the family is a main driver in the practising of religion. In addition, Qirjazi and Shehu (2018) admit that 'enabling social networks' built upon trust can be highly influential among vulnerable groups – the marginalised, the poor, youth. These networks can create a cycle of dependency by providing both a sense of belonging as well as tangible goods such as food, money, and shelter (Qirjazi & Shehu, 2018: 19). Such dynamics have been instrumental in the religious radicalisation processes that have marked Albania in the recent past.

Economic factors

The 2019 Economic Reform Programme (ERP) assessment for Albania by the European Commission (EC) focusses on the main improvements and challenges in the economic realm. Albania reached a GDP growth of 4.2 per cent in 2018 and has reduced its public debt, while achieving a gradual increase in GDP per capita. The EC assessment reports positive developments in the labour market as well – an improved labour force participation rate, lower unemployment rates, and higher employment rates. Such progress continued into the second quarter of 2019 (INSTAT, 2019). Across sectors such as education for employment, business environment, social welfare, R&D, trade and investment, among others, there have been notable improvements, yet inherent problems persist.

Key challenges pertain to the issues of unemployment, inactivity, labour discouragement, inadequate public services, inequality, the 'grey' economy, to name a few. There is agreement among experts that Albanian youth remain a vulnerable group in the labour market. World Bank statistics from 2007 to 2015[3] exhibit an unstable trend of change for the NEET indicator (that is, the share of youth not in education, employment, or training as a percentage of the youth population), with the NEET rate rising to 32.8 per cent in 2015. The EC assessment, on the other hand, demonstrates a positive trend in this aspect with the 2019 NEET rate falling to just above 23 per cent for the 15–29 age group. It does, however, remain quite high for the 24–29 age group at 37.7 per cent. Against the backdrop of these data, the challenge of undeclared work and the consequential lack of access to employment rights and social and health insurance are still not exhaustively addressed by the Albanian State Labour Inspectorate (EC, 2019: 17). Absence of publicly available poverty data hampers efforts to engage with risk groups such as the unemployed, the unskilled, or rural populations, as well as ethnic minorities such as the Roma and the Egyptians. In relation to equality of income and opportunities, the EC classifies rural populations as particularly vulnerable due to the higher poverty scores for rural regions, the limited availability of education, training, and employment services in rural regions, the manifestly lower pensions, and social marginalisation (EC, 2019: 17–20).

Against this backdrop, consideration ought to be paid to the relationship between society, the economy, and religious governance. The Albanian Institute of Statistics (INSTAT) offers no comprehensive reports on government expenditures with regard to religion and religious governance. No reports are available from the State Committee on Cults (SCC) either. The only freely available indication of such can be accessed through KNOEMA – a statistical web tool.[4] KNOEMA's data (not verified, however) point out that the general government expenditure on recreation, culture, and religion (for a lack of a more specific category) for 2018 stands at 0.45 per cent of GDP, marking an increase of 0.04 per cent over its 2017 value. In more precise terms, the 2018 US Department of State religious freedom report on Albania cites the fact that the Catholic, Orthodox, Sunni Muslim, and Bektashi communities together have received some $1.02 million in local currency for 2018, or roughly 0.007 per cent of GDP.[5]

The 2018 Institute for Democracy and Mediation's (IDM) nationally representative survey includes questions that provide several indicators for the interconnectedness between religion and the economy. The first such indicator is related to the possibility of discrimination in receiving socio-economic development opportunities due to one's religious affiliation – a statement with which only 12.8 per cent of respondents agree. The report points out that the majority of respondents who agree with this statement come from underdeveloped areas in Albania. Another indicator pertains to people's belief that religious groups offer economic and material privileges in return for one practising their religion. This proposition is supported by about 30 per cent of respondents, with higher percentages of support among residents of smaller municipalities and some underdeveloped areas. The question about whether one would refuse a lawful job or economic earning due to one's religious rules is answered in the affirmative by 33.1 per cent and in the negative by 51.2 per cent, while regular practitioners of religion showed higher scores of agreement and younger persons exhibited the lowest levels of agreement across the board (IDM, 2018).

Economic issues both in the ties between the state and the religious communities and in society itself pose challenges for the governance of religion. Important issues here include: (1) the long-term effects of the pre-2009 lack of governmental commitments to the financing of religious communities (Kagioglidis, 2009; IDM, 2018); (2) the lack of transparency in the reporting of state activities and expenditure towards governing religion (Kulla, 2007); and (3) the adverse repercussions of inefficient economic policies when it comes to economically vulnerable groups (IDM, 2018; Vurmo, 2018), which have led to perceptions that religious organisations and charities are means of securing income (OSF, 2016; Elbasani & Puto, 2017).

With respect to the challenge of the lack of governmental funding for religious organisations prior to 2009, it is crucial to consider the historical background of the prohibition on state financing for religious activities, as described earlier in the section on history. A pressing issue during the 1990s was the proliferation of mosques constructed by foreign entities, which could easily be controlled by their financing parties, outside the reach of both the Albanian Muslim Community (AMC) and the state (Elbasani & Puto, 2017: 59). The lacking formal relationship between the government and the religious communities and the legislative voids allowed for an influx of '"advisors", observers and religious groups who came to recruit for their faiths' (Youngs, 1997: 5). Arab foundations pushed forward ideas of 'pure' Islamic values through the construction of mosques, schools, and centres for Islamic theology, provision of scholarships for students to pursue studies abroad, and offering of Quran courses (Elbasani & Puto, 2017: 60). At present there are still mosques and groups offering interpretations of the Quran that fall outside the reach of the AMC and the state (AIIS, 2015). Vurmo, in turn, comments on the fact that government officials and civil society representatives classify religious believers of both illegal and formerly illegal (recently put under AMC authority) mosques, where alternative interpretations of religion still take place (2018: 21), as being vulnerable to radicalisation.

The second problematic aspect is the difficulty in, or even impossibility of, obtaining official data related to the economic aspects of religious governance in Albania. The predecessor of the State Committee on Cults (SCC), the State Secretariat, and the religious communities had no obligation to report their funding and expenditure (Kulla, 2007: 38–40). Nowadays, the SCC also does not issue public reports on its economic activities or those of the religious communities.

The third problematic area has received vast attention by both public policy experts and academics. The IDM 2018 study ranks economic reasons on the second place of factors for religious radicalisation. Vurmo also admits that economic reasons, poverty, unemployment, economic disillusionment, and the lack of social services are all factors for the turn to alternative interpretations of Islam (2018: 17–18). The 2011 World Bank brief on governance in Albania points out that gaps exist between laws and policies on paper and in practice, in both the economic and financial spheres as well as other areas of governance (World Bank, 2011: 8), which reflects the insufficient engagement of the government in building up the policy framework for vulnerable groups, such as NEET youth, the unemployed, and rural populations. What generally occurs in the case of such legislative and policy voids in Albania is the entanglement of alternative sources of support, funds, and opportunities (IDM, 2018:

50–53). In such circumstances, foreign charitable foundations and faith-based organisations have been engaged in providing goods such as food, clothes and shelter, health services, emotional support, and education to at-risk groups (IDM, 2018: 50). Kagioglidis notes that such organisations have provided students from vulnerable groups with the opportunity to study at Islamic universities abroad (2007: 25–26). Opportunities for steady income and family support are offered by religious, sometimes radical, organisations while young people, men in particular, and the unemployed are likely to condone participation in illegal economic activities offered by such organisations for the sake of survival (IDM, 2018: 54–56).

Cultural factors

Albania is characterised by values and perceptions that have persisted throughout several centuries with few changes. Traditions and customs are the basis of the particular organisational model of Albania's society – the kinship system. Thus, Albanian social harmony is based upon a national identity stemming from tradition, language, and culture, and is not negatively influenced by the differences in religious belief of the citizens (Davies, 2014: 191). This idea of a national identity arising as a result of unitary cultural practices across time is key for developing a sufficient understanding of the way culture impacts social perceptions of religious harmony and coexistence. Further cultural factors such as levels of education, levels of religiosity, and inter-gender differences are also capable of informing both the positive interactions between culture and religion as well as the challenges to religious governance in terms of problematic cultural aspects such as the effect of the lack of knowledge and education for the comprehension of religious narratives.

In terms of religious values, most Albanians have shared attitudes about religion. A nationally representative 2018 UNDP study of religious tolerance in Albania found broad agreement among respondents that all religions distil into the same system of values (61.2 per cent agree with this statement), while 72.5 per cent said that religions have similar moral teachings. The majority of respondents – 63.1 per cent – also disagreed with the statement that there is only one true religion (UNDP, 2018: 38). There was overwhelming agreement that national feelings and secularism promote religious tolerance, that religious leaders are important agents for religious tolerance, and that the state's non-interference in religious questions is a positive aspect (supported by over 80 per cent) (UNDP, 2018: 46). A viable causal link between culture and religious tolerance has been identified in the survey: the dominance of national traditions over religious ones is seen as one of the most important factors enabling interreligious acceptance in Albania (UNDP, 2018: 49). Finally, the survey results highlight that Albanian society is accepting of members of other religious groups in a variety of positions, such as politicians, teachers, supervisors, and in-laws (UNDP, 2018: 56). Against this backdrop, experts argue that the high regard for common culture and tradition among the different religious communities (in the sense of exchanging and mutual practising of religious rites) is a key aspect of social resilience and countering radical or fundamentalist religious narratives (Qirjazi & Shehu, 2018).

As religious leaders have been identified as prominent carriers of religious tolerance in society (UNDP, 2018: 46; IDM, 2018: 103–104) and thus stand at the joining point between culture and religion, it is crucial that their role for the governance of religion is examined. According to the 2018 UNDP survey, respondents are highly likely to believe that local-level clerics and leaders promote religious coexistence and tolerance, while the data from the 2018 IDM survey rank senior religious leaders (members of the SCC) and clerics among the top three most important actors in preventing alternative narratives of Islam, as they formally and bindingly scrutinise and approve the meanings of religious texts and doctrines, and devise counter narratives (UNDP, 2018: 46; IDM, 2018: 114). The preparedness – in terms of knowledge and skill sets to implement counter narratives and oppose extreme interpretations of religious texts – of clerics at all levels, but especially local-level clerics who tend to be in tighter-knit relations with their communities and thus enjoy higher credence, is also believed to be a significant resilience factor against violent extremism in Albania (IDM, 2018: 115). However, as explored further below, the same survey denotes that the potential of clerics to act as a barrier to radical interpretations of religious narratives is hampered by the lack of training in countering VE offered to them (2018: 104–105). It is important to emphasise the fact that religious leaders and clerics do not operate separately from the state clerics – the agreements between the state and the religious communities are signed via legal representatives (US Department of State, 2018). High-level religious leaders also comprise the Interreligious Council in Albania (US Department of State, 2018: 1). In that sense, the religious leaders and clerics are in a mediatory position not only between culture and religion, but also between their religious communities and the state.

From the quantitative data in the IDM and UNDP surveys conducted in 2018, it could be concluded that Albanian culture and the long-standing supra-narrative of the kinship (*fis*) system (not to be confused with more common for the nation-state sensibilities such as the sense of fraternity or brotherhood) act as a unifying factor among the religious communities and as a mark of trust in the particular relationship between the state and the religious communities (Albanian-type *laïcité*, as categorised by Elbasani & Puto, 2017). As explored in the section on history, the *fis* system forms the basis of Albanian socio-cultural identity and could serve as a potent counterweight to the potentially divisive power of religion due to its conflation of cultural, national, and social traditions, beyond differences of religious affiliation (Zhelyazkova, 2000; Gjuraj, 2013). This, however, should not be taken to equate a lack of problematic areas in the nexus between culture, religion, and governance. With respect to this interrelation, certain challenges persist in the country: the risk factor of low education for the promotion of religious understanding; the often-perceived lack of preparedness of religious clerics; and, the gender dynamics in the religious sphere.

The question of religious and general formal education persists in all spheres of social existence. The 2018 IDM study emphasises the statistical links between education and religious tolerance: respondents with advanced levels of education (university and post-graduate) exhibit higher acceptance of interreligious marriages (over 80 per cent) than respondents with either no or only primary education (between 60 and 70 per cent) (IDM, 2018: 43). Education and awareness are also crucial in understanding the precursors for diverging into alternative, often radical, conceptions of religion, Islam in particular. Low education levels are considered the predominant factor for religious radicalisation in the 2018 IDM study. Insufficient or 'wrong' religious education, disinformation, and propaganda could become causes of engaging in radical activities. Religious leaders have long recognised the threat of the 'misinterpretation of the mission of Islam' and have identified the encouragement of awareness and education on religious issues as a primary step in addressing this challenge (Qirjazi & Shehu, 2018: 15–18). Thus, it becomes clear that the challenge of education is a question of cooperation not only between society and the religious communities – the latter being in charge of delivering religious education and training – but also cooperation with the state, in particular the Ministry of Education, which is in charge of approving the religious teaching programmes of schools (Dyrmishi, 2016).

The second issue also pertains to education, yet in a more constrained aspect: the education and preparedness of religious clerics. According to the 2018 IDM study, some 23.2 per cent of respondents strongly disagree with the statement that clerics have adequate religious education (IDM, 2018: 104–105). The study's authors, nonetheless, hold the opinion that local-level religious clerics must have sufficient influence and capacity to promote resilience against alternative interpretations of religion, radicalisation, and extremist ideologies (IDM, 2018: 105). Furthermore, incapable clerics are ranked among the top eight factors enabling religious radicalisation (IDM, 2018: 113).

The third and final challenge in the relationship between culture and religion stems from the gender dynamics in present-day Albanian society. This aspect is far less explored compared to the issue of education, yet the UNDP and IDM surveys both allow for some conclusions to be drawn. The first concerns the differences in interreligious tolerance by gender: men are three times more likely to blame other religions for the weak economy in Albania; the same correlation exists for those who agreed that people of other religions are to blame for high rates of crime (UNDP, 2018: 59–60). Women were less likely to label the Albanian state as 'unfair' (44 per cent) than men (50.9 per cent) (IDM, 2018: 63). The IDM survey, however, found no statistical divergence between genders on questions of religious tolerance, denouncement of religious extremism, and propagation of radical interpretations of religion (2018: 32, 82, 99). However, as is the case in the socio-demographic and economic spheres, young men and women remain a vulnerable group in terms of being drawn into contact with religious groups that offer both tangible and intangible support (IDM, 2018: 53). Due to factors such as low education level, unemployment, exclusion, and marginality, the youth as 'early phase religious believers' (Vurmo, 2018: 21), regardless of gender, are in need of long-term policy measures in welfare and radicalisation prevention – both from the Albanian state and from local communities and religious leaders in cooperation.

Concluding remarks

The current relationship between state and religion in Albania is defined by a national legal and policy framework for religious governance that reflects the international responsibilities the Albanian state has taken up since the fall of the communist regime and the tendency to favour the structured, albeit thematically broad, codification of rights and obligations of and towards religious groups and communities under specific laws or bilateral agreements. The state-religion-society nexus has been examined in its historical context, whereby the Albanian identity remains as it had developed through the ages from fragmented domestic governance to oppressive regimes. The importance of the kinship system as a unifying factor and as a driver of resilience towards religion-based intolerance and enmity has found high praise in the analyses of numerous experts, as included in this chapter. One of the ground-setting conclusions is related to the malleability of the relationship between the state and religion, shaped by political modes of governance, constitutional orders, state leaders, foreign interventions, and, most importantly, society itself.

The legal and historical overviews brought about the need to examine a spectrum of socio-demographic, economic, and cultural aspects that serve to inform the past, present, and potential future policy measures on part of the Albanian state for the governance of religion and religious diversity. Observable is the conflation of the public and the private spheres in the area of religious governance: the differential treatment by the state towards the religious communities, the lack of state funding for the communities prior to the passage of Law 10140 in 2009, and the absence of transparency in state reporting of religion-related expenditure. On the other side of the coin, private-sphere phenomena such as the evolution/dissolution of social networks and family ties coupled with the problematics of low educational status, unemployment, poverty, and marginalisation permeate the state-religion nexus of Albania. Hence, the main take-away of this analysis lies in the need for constant re-evaluation and re-estimation of the spectrum of tangible and intangible factors that come into play on the three sides of the state-religion-society relationship.

Notes

1 The agreements between the Albanian state and the religious communities were signed during the 2000s: with the Catholic Church in 2005, with the Albanian Muslim Community in 2009, with the Orthodox Church in 2009, with the Bektashi Community in 2009, and with the VUSH (Evangelists) in 2011.
2 The Organisation of [the] Islamic Conference, a.k.a. the Organisation of Islamic Cooperation, is an international association of states (some dub it the second largest international organisation after the UN), currently comprised of 57 members. There has been a fair amount of controversy around the OIC about its stance on radical Islamic movements, the Palestinian question, and human rights violations by its member states. The OIC also allows unlimited voluntary donations, which is critiqued for enabling rich states to push forward their own political agendas. More information on the OIC can be accessed here: https://www.oic-oci.org/page/?p_id=52&p_ref=26&lan=en
3 The latest available data on the webpage of the World Bank for Albania are for 2015.
4 KNOEMA is a source of compiled global data that uses some 1,200 primary sources such as the ILO, UNICEF, WHO, public census data from different countries, etc. The enterprise has been known to collaborate with governments in developing national statistical agencies. It has also worked with the EC's Joint Research Centre and the African Development Bank. More about KNOEMA's data is available here: https://insights.knoema.com/our-data/
5 As INSTAT has not published publicly available figures for Albania's GDP, the value used for share calculation is sourced from the statistics of the World Bank.

References

AIIS. (2015). *Assessment of Risks on National Security/the Capacity of State and Society to React: Violent Extremism and Religious Radicalization in Albania*. Aiis-albania.org. [online] Available at: https://www.aiis-albania.org/?q=node/368. Accessed 30 April 2020.
Botimi, D. (2012). *Population and Housing Census 2011*. INSTAT. [online] Available at: http://www.instat.gov.al/media/3058/main_results__population_and_housing_census_2011.pdf. Accessed 08 November 2019.
CIA Factbook. (2019). *The World Factbook–Albania*. [online] Available at: https://www.cia.gov/library/publications/the-world-factbook/geos/al.html. Accessed 08 November 2019.
Convention against Torture and Other Cruel, Inhuman or Degrading Treatment or Punishment (CAT) (1984). (Resolution 39/46), Opened for Signature 10 December 1984, Entered into Force 26 June 1987. [online] Available at: https://www.ohchr.org/EN/ProfessionalInterest/Pages/CAT.aspx. Accessed 08 November 2019.
Convention on the Elimination of All Forms of Discrimination against Women (CEDAW) (1979). (Resolution 34/180), Opened for Signature 18 December 1979, Entered into Force 3 September 1981. [online] Available at: https://www.ohchr.org/EN/ProfessionalInterest/Pages/CEDAW.aspx. Accessed 08 November 2019.
Convention on the Rights of the Child (CRC) (1989). (Resolution 44/25), Opened for Signature 20 November 1989, Entered into Force 2 September 1990. [online] Available at: https://www.ohchr.org/en/professionalinterest/pages/crc.aspx. Accessed 08 November 2019. Accessed 08 November 2019.
Convention on the Rights of Persons with Disabilities (CRPD) (2007). (Resolution 61/106), Opened for Signature 30 March 2007, Entered into Force 03 May 2008. [online] Available at: https://www.ohchr.org/en/hrbodies/crpd/pages/conventionrightspersonswithdisabilities.aspx. Accessed 08 November 2019.
Davies, L. (2014). One size does not fit all: complexity, religion, secularism and education. *Asia Pacific Journal of Education*, 34(2): 184–199.

Dyrmishi, A. (2016). *Radicalisation and Religious Governance in Albania.* Tirane, Albania: The Center for the Study of Democracy and Governance.

Elbasani, A. & Puto, A. (2017). Albanian-style laïcité: A Model for a Multi-religious European Home? *Journal of Balkan and Near Eastern Studies,* 19(1): 53–69.

European Commission. (2019). *Commission Staff Working Document: Economic Reform Programme of Albania (2019–2021) Commission Assessment.* [online] Available at: https://data.consilium.europa.eu/doc/document/ST-8543-2019-INIT/en/pdf. Accessed 08 November 2019.

Gjuraj, T. (2013). The inter-religious tolerance of the Albanian multi-religious society. Facts and misconceptions. *European Scientific Journal.* [online] Available at: https://eujournal.org/index.php/esj/article/view/969/1000. Accessed 11 November 2019.

IDM. (2018). *Violent Extremism in Albania: A National Assessment of Drivers, Forms and Threats.* Idmalbania.org. [online] Available at: http://idmalbania.org/download/5328. Accessed 11 November 2019.

INSTAT. (2019). *Quarterly Labour Force Survey–2019 Q2.* [online] Available at: http://www.instat.gov.al/media/3058/main_results__population_and_housing_census_2011.pdf. Accessed 08 November 2019.

International Convention on the Elimination of All Forms of Racial Discrimination (ICERD) (1965). (Resolution 2106(XX)), Opened for Signature 21 December 1965, Entered into Force 4 January 1969. [online] Available at: https://www.ohchr.org/en/professionalinterest/pages/cerd.aspx. Accessed 08 November 2019.

International Convention on the Protection of the Rights of All Migrant Workers and Members of Their Families (CMW) (1990). (Resolution 45/158), Opened for Signature 18 December 1990, Entered into Force 1 July 2003. [online] Available at: https://www.ohchr.org/en/professionalinterest/pages/cmw.aspx. Accessed 08 November 2019.

International Convention for the Protection of All Persons from Enforced Disappearance (CED) (2006). (Resolution 61/177), Opened for Signature 20 December 2006, Entered into Force 23 December 2010. [online] Available at: https://www.ohchr.org/en/hrbodies/ced/pages/conventionced.aspx. Accessed 08 November 2019.

International Covenant on Civil and Political Rights (ICCPR) (1966). (Resolution 2200A (XXI)), Opened for Signature 16 December 1966, Entered into Force 23 March 1976. [online] Available at: https://www.ohchr.org/en/professionalinterest/pages/ccpr.aspx. Accessed 08 November 2019.

International Covenant on Economic, Social and Cultural Rights (ICESCR) (1966). (Resolution 2200A (XXI)), Opened for Signature 16 December 1966, Entered into Force 3 January 1976. [online] Available at: https://www.ohchr.org/en/professionalinterest/pages/cescr.aspx. Accessed 08 November 2019.

Kagioglidis, I. (2009). 'Religious Education and the Prevention of Islamic Radicalisation: Albania, Britain, France and the Former Yugoslav Republic of Macedonia', PhD thesis, Naval Postgraduate School, viewed 08 November 2019.

KNOEMA. (2019). *General Government Expenditure on Recreation, Culture and Religion in Albania.* [online] Available at: https://knoema.com/IMFCOFOG2017/government-finance-statistics-gfs-expenditure-by-function-of-government-cofog?country=1000010-albania. Accessed 08 November 2019.

Kulla, I. (2007). State-religion relations in transition Albania. In J. Pettifer & M. Nazarko (eds), *Strengthening Religious Tolerance for a Secure Civil Society in Albania and the Southern Balkans* (pp. 38–41). Amsterdam: IOS Press.

Lopasic, A. (1992). Cultural values of the Albanians in the Diaspora. In T. Winnifrith (ed.), *Perspectives on Albania* (pp. 89–105). Basingstoke: Macmillan.

OHCHR. (2017). *Preliminary Findings of Country Visit to Albania by Ahmed Shaheed, Special Rapporteur on Freedom of Religion or Belief.* Tirana, Press Statement. [online] Available at: https://www.ohchr.org/en/NewsEvents/Pages/DisplayNews.aspx?NewsID=21627&LangID=E. Accessed 09 November 2019.

OSCE-Albania. (1998). *1998 Constitution of the Republic of Albania.* Osce.org. [online] Available at: https://www.osce.org/albania/41888?download=true. Accessed 08 November 2019.

OSF. (2016). *Dealing with Returning Foreign Fighters.* [online] Available at: https://dgap.org/sites/default/files/article_downloads/open_society_foundation_dealing_with_returning_foreign_fighters.pdf. Accessed 09 November 2019.

Qirjazi, R. & Shehu, R. (2018). *Community Perspectives on Preventing Violent Extremism in Albania. Country Case Study 4.* Berlin/Tirana: Berghof Foundation and Institute for Democracy and Mediation.

US Department of State. (2018). *Albania 2018 International Religious Freedom Report.* [online] Available at: https://www.state.gov/wp-content/uploads/2019/05/ALBANIA-2018-INTERNATIONAL-RELIGIOUS-FREEDOM-REPORT.pdf. Accessed 08 November 2019.

UNDP. (2018). *Religious Tolerance in Albania.* [online] Available at: https://www.undp.org/content/dam/albania/docs/religious%20tolerance%20albania.pdf. Accessed 11 November 2019.

Vurmo, G. (2018). *Extremism Research Forum–Albania Report.* London: Foreign and Commonwealth Office.

World Bank. (2011). *Report No. 62518-AL, Governance in Albania; A Way Forward for Competitiveness, Growth, and European Integration.* A World Bank Issue Brief. Poverty Reduction and Economic Management Unit Europe and Central Asia Region.

Youngs, A. (1997). Religion and Society in Present Day Albania. Institute for European Studies: *Working Paper* 97(3).

Zhelyazkova, A. (2000). *Albanian Identities.* International Centre for Minority Studies and Intercultural Relations (IMIR). [online] Available at: http://pdc.ceu.hu/archive/00003852/01/Albanian_Identities.pdf. Accessed 09 November 2019.

15

Bosnia and Herzegovina

Persisting ethno-religious divide

Gergana Tzvetkova and Rosalina Todorova

Introduction

Through the centuries, and especially in the last decade of the twentieth, Bosnia and Herzegovina's tumultuous history has left a mark on the role of religion and its interaction with national identity, the economy, culture, and the development of state-religion relations. Once part of the Ottoman and Habsburg empires and the socialist Yugoslav federation, Bosnia and Herzegovina (BiH) is now a multi-ethnic state established by the power of the international Dayton Agreement signed in 1995. During and after the 1990s war, religion has increasingly coalesced with ethnicity to form three distinctive national identities – Muslim Bosniak, Orthodox Serb, and Catholic Croat. While international intervention, culminating in the Dayton accord, succeeded in ending the Bosnian War, it also cemented certain ethno-religious divisions and created a complex and often clumsy governance and administration set-up. This inevitably hinders decision- and policy-making, slows down reconciliation and trust-building, and jeopardises the country's prospects for NATO and EU accession.

The first section of this chapter focusses on the legal and regulatory framework, encompassing major laws and policies regulating religious matters and state-religion relations. The second section is dedicated to those historical and socio-political factors that influenced the country's current regional and global position the most. The third section concentrates on key socio-demographic features, such as population composition and demographic profile. The fourth section focusses on economic factors, especially unemployment rates and economic inequalities. Lastly, we turn to cultural factors, namely, the state of the education system, levels of religiosity, and gender issues.

Legal and regulatory framework

BiH was established as a sovereign state with the December 1995 Dayton Agreement, which ended the Bosnian War (1992–1995). Signed by BiH, Croatia, and Yugoslavia and witnessed by the European Union (EU), France, Germany, Russia, the United Kingdom (UK), and the United States (US), the agreement stipulated that the independent state of BiH is composed of two parts, the largely Serb-populated Republika Srpska (RS) and the Croat-Bosniak

Federation of Bosnia and Herzegovina (FBiH). The district of Brčko is a self-governing administrative unit in north-eastern BiH. Annex 4 to the Dayton Agreement includes the Constitution of the new state, but each of the two constituent entities has a Constitution of its own as well.

Article II/3(g) and 4 of the Constitution of BiH and Part II, Article 2 of the Constitution of FBiH proclaim freedom of religion and prohibit discrimination on religious grounds. Freedom of religion is established in collective and individual terms by the Constitution of FBiH (Part II, Art. 2) and in collective terms in the Constitution of RS (Art. 28). The Constitution of BiH also stipulates that '[n]o person shall be deprived of Bosnia and Herzegovina or Entity citizenship on any ground such as sex, race, color, language, religion, political or other opinion, national or social origin, association with a national minority, property, birth or other status' (Art. 7, (b)). The constitutions of the two constituent entities reiterate the principle of religious freedom, but RS's Constitution specifically links the Orthodox Church to a particular ethnic group – the Serbs (Art. 28).

BiH promotes a model of separation of state and religion including the principle of equality of all religious communities. State-religion relations are regulated by the Law on Freedom of Religion and the Legal Status of Religious Communities and Churches (hereto referred to as the Law). Article 1 recognises the multi-confessional character of BiH and proclaims the equal rights of all religious communities. The Law establishes the autonomy of religious communities – they enjoy the right to self-administration and to appoint their own personnel (Art. 11, 1–3). It proclaims a clear separation between the religious communities and the state (Art. 14), forbidding any interference on the part of the state in religious affairs (Art. 14, 2) and stipulating that religious laws and doctrines have no civil-legal effect (Art. 11, 1). In terms of religious diversity governance, the state is not allowed to accord state church or state religion status to any religious community (Art. 14, 1) and no church may obtain any special privileges from the state (Art. 14, 3). The state may provide material assistance, but this should be done without discrimination on any grounds (Art. 14, 4).

When it comes to legalising religious communities, the Law delineates three types of religious organisations, subject to different registration procedures. The first type encompasses four major religious communities, designated as legal personalities – the Islamic Community, the Serbian Orthodox Church, the Catholic Church, and the Jewish Community. The second type includes those religious communities registered before the enactment of the 2004 Law (Art. 8, 2). The third type involves newly formed churches and religious communities that need to register according to Art. 18, 4 of the Law.

While the Law prohibits favouring one religious community over another, Ahmet Alibašić and Nedim Begović (2017: 27) argue that this often happens locally due to the nature of the BiH system of governance, which allocates substantial powers to local authorities. Privileges to the community that makes up the majority in the respective administrative unit might include funding, construction permits for religious sites, or, as in the case of RS, a formal distinct status for the Serbian Orthodox Church (ibid.). At the same time, in Bosnian-controlled areas, there are many religious buildings erected without official controls, while Christian ones await formal approval for years (Institute on Religion and Public Policy, 2006). The law was criticised for violating the Organization for Security and Co-operation in Europe (OSCE) standards by requiring a high registration threshold (300 members) to apply for recognition of a new church or religious community (ibid.).

The Law was authored by the Interreligious Council of BiH comprising representatives of the traditional religious communities (Islamic, Serbian Orthodox, Catholic, and Jewish). Established in 1997, the Council aims to serve as a forum for inter-religious dialogue, promote religious tolerance, and support projects for social reconciliation and civil society building. It cooperates with state institutions to investigate and prosecute desecrations of holy sites and attacks on the property and person of religious figures.

Although the Council has been praised as an important symbolic step towards reconciliation, it is often criticised for not being active enough in its peace-building efforts (Clark, 2010b: 676–677). The dissociation of national and local levels presents an issue – even when dialogue unfolds centrally, it rarely happens locally (ibid.: 677). Despite positive statements by religious leaders and actions by faith-based activists, the power of religion in BiH to inspire tolerance and peace is not sufficiently exploited – this would require severing the still-existing link between organised religion, ethno-nationalism, and political structures (Perica, 2014). To a large extent, this link was if not forged, then reinforced, during the 1990s war. It often affects the different groups' attitudes and predispositions towards major international actors.

Historical and socio-political factors

Currently, BiH is a multinational and multi-religious federation of three constituent peoples, where religious identities strongly overlap with ethnic ones – Muslim Bosniaks, Orthodox Serbs, and Catholic Croats. Its territory has been part of many empires, kingdoms, and federations governed by various types of regimes. To a different extent, these legacies have affected or have been manipulated to affect the way the 1990s Bosnian War was started, fought, and brought to an end. Peace, however, did not bring easy solutions, reconciliation, and restoration. More than 20 years after the war's end, BiH is described as a 'laboratory' for 'state-structures which will manage ethnic relations' (Keil & Perry, 2015: 463), where the 'political landscape is polarized along ethnic lines' (ODIHR, 2018: 2) and in general as a country with 'one of the most complex and unwieldy political systems' in Europe and beyond (Bieber, 2018: 63).

Before the Ottoman conquest of Bosnia, the rivalry for religious influence over the local population was mainly between the dualistic sect of Pataria/Bogomils, Catholicism, and Orthodox Christianity (Zhelyazkova, 2001: 6). The Ottoman conquest ushered in the quick advance of Islam in the country. Towards the end of the seventeenth century, the number of Christians had diminished significantly (due to conversions, blood tax[1]). In the late eighteenth and early nineteenth century, the Muslim population in BiH decreased in numbers due to epidemics and military recruitment. In the nineteenth century, Serbs and Croats began searching for evidence that Muslims in BiH were mostly of Croatian (Catholic) and Serbian (Orthodox) descent. During Ottoman times, many Jewish people arrived from Spain and settled permanently in these territories.

During Austro-Hungarian domination (1878–1919), Catholicism was informally privileged and both Catholic and Orthodox communities benefited from favourable political conditions and significant state subsidies (Eldarov in Zhelyazkova, 2001: 83). Islam was separated from the state as Sharia courts were modernised and integrated into the Habsburg legal system. However, these tendencies and processes also contributed to the spatial and cultural isolation of the Muslim community.

Formally, the Kingdom of Yugoslavia (1918–1941), which followed Austro-Hungarian rule, promoted the equality of religious communities. Informally, however, Orthodox Christianity was favoured as the Kingdom was essentially an extension of the pre-war Serbian kingdom and the Serbs dominated the administration and the army (Bieber, 2006: 8). The interwar period saw the consolidation of the national identities of Serbs, Croats, and

Slovenes. The Bosnian Muslim community was sidelined in this process and, hence, remained largely undetermined (Bougarel, 2017: 37).

The Second World War (1939–1945) saw the crumbling of the Kingdom of Yugoslavia amidst a clash of radical ideologies – the fascist and Nazi-allied Ustasha led by Ante Pavelić, originating in Croatia, and the nationalist and anti-Axis Chetnicks, commanded by Draža Mihailović, originating in Serbia. In 1942, the Young Muslims movement was founded in BiH and its supporters developed an avid interest in pan-Islamism. Suppressed memories and unquenched fears related to the Second World War period would resurface during the 1990s wars.

Before the 1990s, another regime change took place in BiH, with the establishment of the Social Federal Republic of Yugoslavia (1945–1992[2]). Despite the proclaimed areligious nature of communism, religious communities in BiH were largely allowed to operate to secure support for the new authorities (Bieber, 2006: 10). In 1968, the Muslim nation was officially recognised. Although recognition improved Muslim representation in party and republican institutions, the administration, and especially the Ministry of Interior, remained dominated by Serbs (ibid.: 11). Hence, recognition exacerbated a feeling of discomfort among Muslim politicians and intellectuals – on the one hand, Yugoslavism was suppressing the Muslim identity; on the other, Yugoslav federal structures were protecting them from Serbian and Croatian nationalist aspirations (Bougarel, 2017: 87). In the 1960s, a pan-Islamist current reappeared amidst the Islamic community.

In the 1980s, the consolidation of ethno-religious identities, the crumbling personality cult of Tito triggered by his death, the rise of aggressive Serb nationalism, the growing desires for independence of the constituent republics, and the manipulation of history for political purposes fuelled nationalist agendas that soon created deep rifts between Serbs, Croats, and Bosniaks. In 1992, the Socialist Federal Republic of Yugoslavia dissolved into its successor states and the Yugoslav wars continued for ten years (1991–2001). The Bosnian War (1992–1995) deepened the ethno-religious divisions within Bosnian society and posed the challenge of accommodating religious freedom and inter-religious balance in post-war Bosnia. These divisions materialised after the war. While before the war the settlement patterns of the three main groups were largely mixed, the end of the hostilities brought 'territorialization of ethnicity', along with nearly 200,000 killed and half of the population displaced (Bieber, 2006: 3).

As the war was fought over ethno-religious lines and symbols, the post-war reconstruction of BiH involved the reconceptualisation of the state relationship with its various ethno-religious communities, as well as among the communities themselves. However, this process was hindered by the frequent institutional gridlocks, inherent in the Dayton institutional system, and the difficult local implementation of decisions taken at federal level.

The Dayton Peace Agreement ended the violence in the country. However, it established an ethno-centric system, which actually deepened ethno-religious rifts and encouraged the ethnicisation of politics. For example, BiH's tripartite presidency is formed by representatives of the three constituent nations – a Bosniak and a Croat elected from FBiH and a Serb elected from RS. These representatives rotate to chair the presidency during a single term. This means – and was recognised as discriminatory by the European Court of Human Rights – that a Bosniak from RS or a person identifying as belonging to a group different from the three constituent nations cannot run for president. Soeren Keil and Valery Perry (2015: 466) argue that in BiH, the mixture of strict ethnic power-sharing and autonomy in a decentralised federal structure does not seem to work, even in the presence of the High Representative for BiH[3] (ibid.).

This set-up's inflexibility affects not only BiH's internal politics, but also its foreign policy and the way it is perceived by international actors. BiH is a state contested both internally – by a significant part of its own population – and externally, primarily by neighbouring Serbia, which continuously stimulates secessionist aspirations of Bosnian Serbs (Džankić & Keil, 2019: 183–184). Consensus on foreign policy in BiH is difficult and usually extends to non-contentious issues; while EU membership is mostly supported, NATO membership is problematic due to Russian and Serbian influence on RS elites (Huskić, 2014: 134–137). Furthermore, in contrast to FBiH, RS is very active in foreign policy, but its actions are often contrary to the foreign policy direction adopted by BiH (ibid.: 129). Lastly, the foreign policy vacuum left by state institutions opens room for intervention by non-state actors, notably religious organisations, which still participate vigorously in BiH's foreign policy (ibid.: 130).

Last but not least, BiH's place on the world stage has changed. Initially, the US was involved with the country, but after the beginning of the financial crisis in 2007, it moved on to other foreign policy priorities. Since 2013, the EU has put a break on its enlargement process and in late 2019, France called for changes in the procedures for joining the EU and remaining a member. BiH is still only a Potential Candidate for EU membership with serious issues to address in the field of good governance, rule of law, electoral and constitutional reforms, fight against corruption, and peaceful reconciliation.

Socio-demographic factors

The 2013 census – the first after the war's end – was organised by the Central Census Bureau of BiH and supported by the EU.[4] According to its results, the population of BiH is 3,531,159 persons: 2,219,220 living in the FBiH, 1,228,423 in RS, and 83,516 in the Brčko District (See Figure 15. 1).[5]

The distribution by ethnic/national affiliation is as shown in Table 15.1.

Table 15.1 Population of BiH by ethnic/national affiliation, Census Results 2013[6]

Ethnicity↓	Federation BiH	RS	Brčko	TOTAL BiH (numbers)	Total BiH (%)
Bosniak	1,562,372	171,839	17,411	1,769,592	50.11
Croat	497,883	29,645	8,859	544,780	15.43
Serb	56,550	1,001,299	14,023	1,086,733	30.78
Other	79,838	15,324	695	96,539	2.73
Not declared	18,344	8,189	213	27,055	0.77
No answer	4,233	2,127	49	6,460	0.18
TOTAL BiH				3,531,159	

Source: Agency for Statistics of BiH (2016: 54).

According to a 2018 estimate, the population growth rate is negative: −0.17 per cent, as the birth rate is 8.7 births/1,000 population (2018 est.) and the death rate is 10.1 deaths/1,000 population (CIA, 2019).

Bosnia and Herzegovina: ethno-religious divide

Figure 15.1 Map of Bosnia and Herzegovina.
Source: Map No. 3729 Rev. 6, March 2007, UNITED NATIONS.

Recent data show that the median age in the country is 42.5–40.9 years for men and 43.9 years for women. In terms of age structure, similarly to elsewhere in Europe, the population in BiH is ageing, as approximately 30 per cent is older than 55 years (ibid.) and the number of women (1,798,889) is slightly higher than that of men (1,732,270) (BHAS, 2016: 25). In terms of urbanisation, data from 2019 indicates that 48.6 per cent of the population lives in urban settlements, while the northern and central areas of the country are the most densely populated (CIA, 2019).

181

Population composition in terms of religious affiliation shows that Islam is the predominant religion in BiH (50.70 per cent), followed by Orthodox Christianity (30.75 per cent) and Catholicism (15.2 per cent). The majority of Orthodox Christians (92 per cent) live in RS, while the majority of Muslims (88 per cent) live in FBiH. When we look at data combining religious affiliation and ethnicity, the compact ethno-religious identities become clearly delineated: Muslim Bosniaks, Orthodox Serbs, and Catholic Croats (See Table 15.2).

Table 15.2 Population of BiH according to ethnicity and religious affiliation[7]

Area	Ethnicity→ Religion↓	Bosniak	Croat	Serb
Federation of BiH				
	Islamic	**1,533,650**	1,313	60
	Catholic	1,106	**484,173**	232
	Orthodox	992	245	**51,965**
Republika Srpska				
	Islamic	**169,144**	53	32
	Catholic	148	**26,662**	236
	Orthodox	175	888	**992,743**
Brčko District				
	Islamic	**35,044**	9	-
	Catholic	24	**16,856**	14
	Orthodox	15	39	**28,564**
Bosnia and Herzegovina total				
	Islamic	**1,737,838**	1,375	92
	Catholic	1,278	**527,651**	482
	Orthodox	1,182	1,172	**1,073,272**

Source: Agency for Statistics of BiH (2016: 68–81).

According to a 2019 survey (IRI, 2019: 152), a total of 73 per cent respond that they observe religious practices and rules either 'somewhat less strictly' or 'much less strictly', while only 4 per cent respond that they do so 'much more strictly' and 17 per cent 'somewhat more strictly'. Only 14 per cent identify as 'very religious' in comparison to 44 per cent as 'somewhat religious' and 33 per cent 'not very religious', thus confirming the overall moderate levels of religiosity in the country.

BiH does not have a large immigrant community, although the number of issued visas has risen from 12,107 in 2013 to 28,751 in 2017 and the number of individuals with temporary residences from 8,838 in 2013 to 11,372 in 2017 (Ministry of Security of Bosnia and Herzegovina, 2018: 28). Around two million BiH natives reside abroad, the highest number in Croatia, followed by Serbia and Germany.

Economic factors

Understandably, the 1990s war significantly affected the socio-economic environment and the prospects for economic development in the country. Bieber (2006: 35) notes that 'the lack of foreign investment and the massive destruction of the economy through the war has resulted in persistently low wages and high unemployment'. The war created new economic elites, enriched largely through criminal activities, and impoverished the pre-war middle class – phenomena that 'dramatically changed the social structure of society and caused the emergence of stark social differentiation' (ibid.).

In October 2018, the number of registered unemployed in BiH was 441,672 (BHAS, 2018: 1). Almost 90 per cent were long-term unemployed (European Commission, 2019: 17). Indicative of the seriousness of the issue are the results of a 2019 poll: more than 40 per cent in all age groups consider unemployment the biggest problem facing the country. Even more alarmingly, this response is given by 44 per cent of interviewees between 18 and 35 years of age and by 31 per cent of those with bachelor/master/doctoral degrees.

Insufficient education is the largest obstacle to overcoming economic inequality (World Bank, 2015: 4), while a further contributing factor is the 'brain drain' (TRTWorld, 2019). The latter could be partially explained by the persistently low average gross monthly salary – around 1,400 BAM or 700 euro. Young people, especially well-educated ones, tend to seek employment abroad, including in former-Yugoslav countries which joined the EU – Slovenia and Croatia. The disparities between wages in the constituent entities are negligible.

However, economic indicators available at state level are distorted by the large grey sector. The labour force is discouraged from participating in the formal labour market by the high tax wedge, which disproportionately affects low-wage workers. The social services are not able to sufficiently address the needs of the most disadvantaged. As main care givers, women are among the most affected and especially susceptible to unemployment. According to the European Commission (2019: 17), 'although social expenditure is comparatively high, means-tested social assistance does not cover basic living needs'. Geopolitical disturbances at home and abroad, as well as the economic crisis of 2009, have contributed to the rise of poverty levels in the country.

The lack of economic and political acumen in fiscal planning, further aggravated by the lack of adequate statistical underpinning in support of political and economic action, negatively influences the BiH's economic prospects (European Commission, 2019: 3). The country's economic outlook has been strongly affected by the segregated multi-layered administrative system (ibid.). Its existence is detrimental to attracting foreign investments, to repairing the economy, and to the emergence and sustainability of businesses. The fragmentation of the economic sphere and the inefficiency of the legislative system and the public administration harm BiH's competitiveness in the international market and dim the prospects for EU membership in the foreseeable future.

Education, media, and culture

To an extent, Bosnia's education system institutionalises and fosters existing divisions among ethno-religious groups through (1) mono-ethnic schools, (2) bussing to these schools, (3) the unique educational arrangement 'two-schools-under-one-roof', and (4) the continuing ethnicisation of school curricula.

At the national level, the fairly broad Framework Law of Primary and Secondary Education in BiH guarantees the right to quality education (including religious education) regardless of religious, ethnic, or cultural belonging and prioritises human rights, solidarity, religious freedom (freedom of religion and freedom of religious expression), and protection of diversity. According to Article 9, '[h]aving in mind diversities of beliefs/convictions within BiH, pupils shall attend religious classes only if latter match their beliefs or beliefs of their parents … Students who do not wish to attend religious education classes shall not in any way be disadvantaged compared to other students'. Art. 56 stipulates that the law's implementation will be supervised by the Ministry of Civil Affairs, which is responsible, among other things, for education and science at the state level.

The situation is more complicated at the constituent entities' level as RS has its own Ministry of Education that formulates educational laws and policies and has the authority to create new schools in RS. The FBiH consists of ten cantons, each of them with its own education ministry. Furthermore, among the departments of the government of Brčko District, there is a Department for Education. Therefore, there are 12 institutions responsible for education in the country that act quite independently from one another, designing and implementing their own rules, policies, curricula, and educational content in the language of the ethno-religious majority.

Both mono-ethnic schools and the 'two-schools-under-one-roof' practice have been condemned as discriminatory by the UN Committee on the Rights of the Child, the UN Committee on the Elimination of Racial Discrimination, the European Parliament, the Council of Europe, and OSCE (2018: 14–15). Mono-ethnic schools not only continue to exist, but new ones are opened in multi-ethnic regions as students from other settlements are bussed to and from the school each day. As its name suggests, the 'two-schools-under-one-roof' system creates a segregated environment where children from different ethnic groups attend classes in separated sections of the same building, study under different curricula and textbooks, and have almost no opportunity for mixing and interacting. Each of the schools under one roof[8] has its own administration, parent and student councils, student clubs, etc. (UNGA, 2014: 10). In some schools, students study in the same building, but one of the ethnic groups attends classes in the morning and the other in the afternoon. Interestingly, in theory students can choose which school to enrol in, but in reality there are numerous obstacles to doing so (OSCE, 2018: 15).

Religious classes are offered in both primary and secondary schools in every constituent entity, but are not mandatory. In RS primary schools, religious education is optional, but once selected, becomes mandatory from second until ninth grade, as parents can choose among Orthodox Christianity, Catholic Christianity, or Islam as the religion their child will study (Lakic, 2018).[9] Alarmingly, through the years there have been reports of 'soft measures punishments' – such as being ridiculed or ostracised – against students who choose not to take religious classes (Bureau of Democracy, Human Rights, and Labour, 2009: 4). No Jewish religious classes are offered at either primary or secondary level (ibid.). This is another manifestation of the trend noticed at the level of political representation: Roma, Jewish, and other smaller minorities are disadvantaged in comparison to the three constituent peoples.

Despite ongoing debates about the context of religious textbooks, religious classes are not the most ideologically charged in the BiH school curriculum. When it comes to 'national subjects' (history, literature, and language), consensus is hardest to achieve and this is especially valid for the 'two-schools-under-one-roof' system. After the war, BiH textbooks followed a trend observed in all former-Yugoslav countries – i.e. to paint an ethnocentric picture with national history at the centre that does not allow for perspectives of others and sometimes even creates negative images of the other (Koren, 2002: 194). Even after the adoption of guidelines for writing and evaluating textbooks by the BiH education ministries, history books are still found to feature an ethno-national bias. The teaching of literature is utilised by nationalistic ideologies to build opposing narratives which affect students' perceptions (UNGA, 2014: 15). Political will for change is missing – and there are politicians who exacerbate the problem. In 2019, RS authorities announced that as from the following school year, high-school history textbooks will be 'harmonised with Serbia, sharing the same standpoints on the 1992–95 war' (Lakic, 2019).

Some positive developments can be observed too. Firstly, disciplines like civic education, democracy and human rights education, life skills and attitudes were introduced in the 2000s (Clark, 2010a: 353). Occasionally, there have also been student protests demanding the abolition of segregated school systems. In Mostar and Sarajevo, there are integrated gymnasia where classes are offered in all three official languages. However, the number of such schools remains low and integration minimal. The Brčko district system sets a good example for an integrated school system, where students of different ethno-religious backgrounds are allowed to attend classes together and express themselves in their own language, while teachers are allowed to incorporate both Latin and Cyrillic spellings in their teaching approaches (UNGA, 2014: 25).

Public service media in BiH has also suffered from ethnically and religiously inspired strife. In 2017 it faced collapse due to insufficient funding. Again, the issues resulted from the regulative framework that delegated funding decisions and overall broadcasting and media legislation to the two entities, which have been unable to work together to harmonise media laws in RS with those in FBiH (European Federation of Journalists, 2017). Furthermore, many Bosnian Croats do not feel represented by either one of the two entity-level public broadcasters – Radio-Television of the FBiH (RT FBiH) and Radio-Television of RS (RTRS) – and have refused to pay subscription fees (Freedom of the Press, 2015). These developments have led to insufficient public access to media services and, inevitably, to low-quality service. Most of the privately owned media outlets are divided along ethnic lines and broadcast politically and ideologically charged content (ibid.). Freedom of expression in BiH is limited by political pressure, and journalists investigating instances of ethno-religious propaganda are often threatened.

The 1990s war left its mark on cultural life as well. In 2014, it was reported that the future of major cultural Yugoslav-era institutions was uncertain as they were not accepted by all political actors. The National Museum had to close in 2012 but reopened in 2015 (Jukic, 2015). Furthermore, RS has established its own 'mirror institutions' such as the Peoples and University Library of RS, the Library for the Blind and Visually Disabled, the Kinoteka in Pale, and the Museum of Contemporary Art (UNGA, 2014: 4) Another serious issue was the destruction of historical monuments and sites of cultural significance during the conflict and the subsequent attempts for reconstruction. Here again, one can notice a familiar trend – the Commission entrusted with preservation and reconstruction has significant powers and is active, but its cooperation with the two entity-level institutes for protection of monuments insufficient and their objectives often diverge (ibid.: 17–18).

The legal dimensions of cultural inequality in BiH are particularly visible when it comes to Muslim Bosnian women's freedom of religion and freedom of religious expression. Although valid for the entire population of BiH, the 2016 ban on religious symbols (Toe, 2016b) for employees in judicial institutions disproportionately affects female members of the Muslim faith. Furthermore, it was ratified despite overwhelming opposition from Muslim religious leaders in the country (Toe, 2016a). Official bans on religious dress practices have been controversial and widely discussed since the 1950 ban on face veils (Mesarič, 2013: 7). Veiling is (and was) a practice exclusively relevant to Muslim women in rural areas (ibid:13).

Therefore, the objects of culturally restrictive legislation perfectly mimic the structure of economic inequality, still valid in BiH to this day with elderly, low-educated women from rural areas at the bottom of the structure (World Bank, 2015: 33–34).

The education system in BiH not only exemplifies, but also perpetuates the attempts to produce and preserve ethno-religious-national separation in an already geographically fragmented territory. The physical separation of representatives of the once-warring parties might have been beneficial in the immediate wake of the 1990s war (although such an argument must be questioned and further explored) but it certainly cannot remain a permanent arrangement. Communication between different ethno-religious groups for the purpose of fostering greater tolerance and respect, instead of segregation, should be the norm. The ability to participate in the country's cultural life is hindered by the politicisation of many related issues, like the existence of historical sites and monuments and bans on religious attire.

Concluding remarks

The rift between ethno-religious groups that opened during the 1990s war and the inability to overcome it due to the specific arrangement of the post-Dayton system and the lack of political will has had a negative influence on all aspects of life in BiH. The tangled web of relationships between different ethno religious groups created out of dynamic historical processes has been manipulated for political purposes. This has led to clear-cut divisions between these communities and their gradual but steady detachment from one another.

Complex intertwinement of ethnicity, religion, and nationality is characteristic of all BiH demographic, institutional, administrative, and identity structures. These three markers of identity have been explicated, redefined, and reaffirmed throughout the state's turbulent history. This currently translates into segmented educational, cultural, and economic systems and a dysfunctional political system and inter-ethnoreligious intolerance. Religious affiliation is inseparable from the ethno-national association at both individual and structural levels. Addressing issues of religion requires examining and understanding concomitant phenomena related to ethnicity and nationality.

The persisting mistrust among BiH's constituent ethno-national communities and the inadequacy of reconciliation and state-building processes have affected BiH's economic and political development. It remains a marginalised state in Europe, whose prospects for a quick accession to the EU are growing slim. Religion is still frequently used to exacerbate separation and inequality. Religious organisations, often under the influence of foreign actors, meddle in and hamper efficient public and foreign policy-making. BiH's political elite and society need to overcome the consequences of the 1990s war. This, however, is conditional upon a reform of the current constitutional and administrative set-up and the implementation of policies and initiatives that encourage intra-religious and intra-ethnic dialogue, confidence-building, and cooperation.

Notes

1 The practice called *devshirme* involved the taking by military officers of Christian boys from the provinces of the Ottoman Empire to be raised to serve the state.
2 From 1945 to 1963, Federal People's Republic of Yugoslavia; from 1963 to 1992, Socialist Federal Republic of Yugoslavia.
3 The post of the High Representative for BiH and the Office of the High Representative were established after the signing of the Dayton Peace Agreement to oversee the implementation of its civilian

aspects. The NATO-led Implementation Force (IFOR) has been tasked with implementing the military aspects of the agreement.

4 The results were released in 2016 because of a dispute between the statistical agencies of Federation of BiH and RS. RS opposed the inclusion in the census of the 'non-permanent Bosnian residents – those who were absent for 12 months prior to or after the census' (Toe, 2016c). According to Eurostat, the methodology used by the Bosnian statistical agency complies with international recommendations.

5 The Brčko District is formally part of both entities, RS and FBiH, but is in fact a neutral, self-governing administrative unit.

6 Note the formulation 'ethnicity/national affiliation'. It fails to take into account that a person of Croat ethnicity could identify their national affiliation as Bosnian.

7 This table summarises the Census results only with respect to the three main ethnicities and the three main religions. The number in boldface reflects the composition of the biggest ethno-religious groups in BiH, thus identifying the communities where declared ethnicity and religious affiliation intersect.

8 According to a November 2018 OSCE report, there are 23 locations/cases of primary schools and 5 locations/cases of secondary schools in the Federation of BiH where the 'two-schools-under-one-roof' system is still in place.

9 In April 2018 it was reported that Milorad Dodik, the current Serb member of the Bosnian presidency, announced that religious education will become mandatory in high schools in RS. It is also worth noting that in all Catholic-majority Cantons in the Federation, religious classes can be replaced with ethics classes (Bureau of Democracy, Human Rights, and Labour, 2019).

References

Agency for Statistics of Bosnia and Herzegovina (BHAS). (2016). *Census of Population, Households, and Dwellings in Bosnia and Herzegovina, 2013. Final Results*. [online] Available at: http://www.popis2013.ba/popis2013/doc/Popis2013prvoIzdanje.pdf.

Agency for Statistics of Bosnia and Herzegovina (BHAS). (2018). *Demography and Social Statistics. Persons in Paid Employment by Activity. August 2018*. Sarajevo. [online] Available at: http://www.bhas.ba/saopstenja/2018/LAB_02_2018_09_0_BS.pdf.

Alibašić, A. & Begović, N. (2017). Reframing the relations between state and religion in post-war Bosnia: Learning to be free! *Journal of Balkan and Near Eastern Studies*, 19(1): 19–34. DOI: 10.1080/19448953.2016.1201987.

Bieber, F. (2006). *Post-war Bosnia Ethnicity, Inequality and Public Sector Governance*. Hampshire and New York: Palgrave Macmillan.

Bieber, F. (2018). *The Rise of Authoritarianism in the Western Balkans*. Cham, Switzerland: Palgrave Macmillan.

Bougarel, X. (2017). *Islam and Nationhood in Bosnia and Herzegovina Surviving Empires* (C. Mobley, Trans.). London and New York: Bloomsbury Academic.

Bureau of Democracy, Human Rights, and Labour. (2009). *Bosnia and Herzegovina 2009 International Freedom Report. Executive Summary*. United States Department of State. [online] Available at: https://www.justice.gov/sites/default/files/eoir/legacy/2013/06/10/Bosnia and Herzegovina_2.pdf

Bureau of Democracy, Human Rights, and Labour. (2019). *Bosnia and Herzegovina 2018 International Freedom Report. Executive Summary*. United States Department of State. [online] Available at: https://www.state.gov/wp-content/uploads/2019/05/BOSNIA-AND-HERZEGOVINA-2018-INTERNATIONAL-RELIGIOUS-FREEDOM-REPORT.pdf

CIA. (2019). *The World Factbook. Bosnia and Herzegovina*. [online] Available at: https://www.cia.gov/library/publications/the-world-factbook/geos/bk.html

Clark, J.N. (2010a). Education in Bosnia-Hercegovina: The case for root-and-branch reform. *Journal of Human Rights*, 9(3): 344–362.

Clark, J.N. (2010b). Religions and reconciliation in Bosnia and Herzegovina: Are religious actors doing enough? *Europe-Asia Studies*, 62(4):671–694. DOI: 10.1080/09668130037370190.

Džankić, J. & Keil, S. (2019). The Europeanisation of the contested states: Comparing Bosnia and Herzegovina, Macedonia and Montenegro. In J. Džankić, S. Keil & M. Kmezić (eds.), *The Europeanization of the Western Balkans* (pp. 181–206). Cham, Switzerland: Palgrave Macmillan.

Eldarov, S. (2001). History of the orthodox and catholic Churches in Bosnia and Herzegovina. In A. Zhelyazkova (ed.), *The Curious Case of Bosnia* [in Bulgarian] (pp. 1–327). Sofia: IMIR

European Commission. (2019). *Commission Staff Working Document Economic Reform Programme of Bosnia and Herzegovina (2019–2021) Commission Assessment.* Brussels. [online] Available at: https://ec.europa.eu/neighbourhood-enlargement/sites/near/files/bosnia_and_herzegovina_2019-2021_erp.pdf.

European Federation of Journalists. (2017). *Safe and Reform Public Service in Bosnia and Herzegovina.* European Journalists. [online] Available at: https://europeanjournalists.org/blog/2017/06/16/safe-and-reform-public-service-media-in-bosnia-and-herzegovina/.

Framework Law on primary and secondary education in Bosnia and Herzegovina/ I–General provisions. (2003). Bosnia and Herzegovina. [online] Available at: https://aposo.gov.ba/sadrzaj/uploads/Framework-Law.pdf.: 1–18.

Freedom of the Press. (2015). *Bosnia and Herzegovina.* Freedom House. [online] Available at: https://freedomhouse.org/report/freedom-press/2015/bosnia-and-herzegovina

Huskić, A. (2014). Complex system, complex foreign policy: The foreign policy of Bosnia and Herzegovina. In S. Keil & B. Stahl (eds.), *The Foreign Policies of Post-Yugoslav States* (pp. 122–143). Hampshire and New York: Palgrave Macmillan.

Institute on Religion and Public Policy. (2006). *Bosnia and Herzegovina.* [online] Available at: https://www.osce.org/odihr/21531?download=true.

International Republican Institute. (2019). *Bosnia and Herzegovina: Public Opinion on Foreign Influence and Violent Extremism.* [online] Available at: https://www.iri.org/sites/default/files/2019_bih_national_poll_with_ea_edits_1.pdf.

Jukic, M.E. (2015). *Bosnia Museum Re-opens After Three-Year Wait.* Balkan Insight. [online] Available at: https://balkaninsight.com/2015/09/16/bosnia-national-museum-re-opens-after-three-years-09-15-2015/.

Keil, S. & Perry, V. (2015). Introduction: Bosnia and Herzegovina 20 years after Dayton. *International Peacekeeping*, 22(5): 463–470. DOI: 10.1080/13533312.2015.1100614.

Koren, S. (2002). Yugoslavia: a look in the broken mirror. Who is the 'other'? In C. Kolouri (ed.), *CLIO in the Balkans: The Politics of History Education* (pp. 193–194). Thessaloniki: Center for Democracy and Reconciliation in Southeast Europe.

Lakic, M. (2018). Bosnian Serbs to Introduce Mandatory Religious Education. *Balkan Insight.* [online] Available at: https://balkaninsight.com/2018/04/12/bosnian-serbs-mull-for-mandatory-religion-classes-04-11-2018/.

Lakic, M. (2019). Bosnian Serb Schoolbooks to Teach Same War History as Serbia. *Balkan Insight.* [online] Available at: https://balkaninsight.com/2019/07/22/bosnian-serb-schoolbooks-to-teach-same-war-history-as-serbia/.

Mesarič, A. (2013). Wearing hijab in Sarajevo: Dress practices and the Islamic revival in post-war Bosnia-Herzegovina. *Anthropological Journal of European Cultures*, 22(2): 12–34.

Ministry of Security of Bosnia and Herzegovina. (2018). *Bosnia and Herzegovina Migration Profile.* [online] Available at: http://www.msb.gov.ba/PDF/MIGRACIONI%20PROFIL_2017_%20ENG_FINAL.pdf.

National Assembly of the Republic of Srpska. (1996). *The Constitution of the Republic of Srpska.* Official Gazette of the Republic of Srpska No. 21/92 – consolidated version, 28/94, 8/96, 13/96, 15/96, 16/96, 21/96, 21/02, 26/02, 30/02, 31/02, 69/02, 31/03, 98/03, 115/05, 117/05,48/11. [online] Available at: https://www.narodnaskupstinars.net/sites/default/files/upload/dokumenti/ustav/eng/USTAV-RS_English.pdf.: 1–39.

ODIHR. (2018). *Election Observation Mission, Bosnia and Herzegovina, General Elections.* 7 October 2018. [online] Available at: https://www.osce.org/odihr/elections/bih/397043?download=true.

Official Gazette of Bosnia and Herzegovina. (2004). *Freedom of Religion and Legal Status of Churches and Religious Organisations in Bosnia and Herzegovina*, No 5/04. [online] Available at: http://host.uniroma3.it/progetti/cedir/cedir/Lex-doc/Bos_l-2004a.pdf.

Official Gazette of Bosnia and Herzegovina. (2009). *Law on Prohibition of Discrimination*, no 59/09. BiH Law on Prohibition of Discrimination BiH Official Gazette No. 59/09, published on 28 July 2009 Entered into force on 5 August 2009. [online] Available at: https://arsbih.gov.ba/wp-content/uploads/2014/02/002-Anti-Discrimination-Law-.pdf.: 1–15.

Organization for Security and Co-operation in Europe (OSCE). (2018). *'Two Schools Under One Roof': The Most Visible Example of Discrimination in Education in Bosnia and Herzegovina.* [online] Available at: https://www.osce.org/mission-to-bosnia-and-herzegovina/404990?download=true.

Perica, V. (2014). *Religion in the Balkan Wars.* Oxford Handbooks Online. [online] Available at: https://www.oxfordhandbooks.com/view/10.1093/oxfordhb/9780199935420.001.0001/oxfordhb-9780199935420-e-37.

Refworld. (1994). *Constitution of the Federation of Bosnia and Herzegovina. 18 March 1994.* Reference: BIH-040. "Official Gazette" of the Federation of Bosnia and Herzegovina, 1/94, 13/97, 16/02, 22/02, 52/02, 60/02, 18/03, 63/03. [online] Available at: https://www.refworld.org/docid/3ae6b56e4.html.: 1–35.

Toe, R. (2016a). Bosnian Judiciary to consider hijab ban. *Balkan Insight.* [online] Available at: https://balkaninsight.com/2016/01/26/bosnian-judicial-authorities-challenge-right-to-wear-hijab-01-25-2016/.

Toe, R. (2016b). Hijab ban in court angers Bosnian Muslims. *Balkan Insight.* [online] Available at: https://balkaninsight.com/2016/02/11/high-judicial-and-prosecutorial-council-confirms-hijab-ban-02-10-2016/.

Toe, R. (2016c). Bosnia to publish census without Serb agreement. *Balkan Insight.* [online] Available at: https://balkaninsight.com/2016/06/30/bosnia-to-release-long-awaited-census-results-on-thursday-06-29-2016/.

TRTWorld. (2019). *Massive Brain Drain Threatens Bosnia's Labour Force.* [online] Available at: https://www.trtworld.com/europe/massive-brain-drain-threatens-bosnia-s-labour-force-25503.

United Nations General Assembly (UNGA). (2014). *Report of the Special Rapporteur in the field of cultural rights, Farida Shaheed, Addendum Mission to Bosnia and Herzegovina.* 13–24 May 2013. [online] Available at: https://digitallibrary.un.org/record/767041?ln=en.

United Nations, Bosnia and Herzegovina, Map No. 3729 Rev.6, March 2007, UNITED NATIONS [online] Available at: https://www.un.org/Depts/Cartographic/map/profile/bosnia.pdf.

US Department of State. (2019). *2018 Report on International Religious Freedom: Bosnia and Herzegovina.* [online] Available at: https://www.state.gov/wp-content/uploads/2019/05/BOSNIA-AND-HERZEGOVINA-2018-INTERNATIONAL-RELIGIOUS-FREEDOM-REPORT.pdf.: 1–10.

World Bank. (2015). *Poverty and Inequality in Bosnia and Herzegovina 2007–2011.* Agency for Statistics of BiH, FBiH Institute for Statistics, RS FBiH Institute for Statistics. Available at: http://documents.worldbank.org/curated/en/228531467999134102/pdf/97643-REVISED-P132666-P152786-Box393190B-BiH-Poverty-and-Inequality-in-BiH.pdf

Zhelyazkova, A. (ed.). (2001). *The Curious Case of Bosnia* [in Bulgarian]. Sofia: IMIR.

Part V
The MENA region

16
Turkey
Whither secularism?

Haldun Gülalp

Introduction

Turkey is widely considered to be a pioneering example of secularism in a Muslim-majority nation. According to Ernest Gellner (1997: 236), for example, Islam is an exception among religions because it cannot be secularized, and Turkey is 'the exception within the exception'. Because of this seemingly unlikely combination of Islam and secularism, much controversy and mythmaking have accompanied scholarly analyses of the Turkish experience. Whether as an expression of appreciation or regret, there has nevertheless been a general agreement around the view that Mustafa Kemal (Atatürk) and his associates, that is, the Kemalist leadership of the Republic of Turkey, embarked on a course of state-led, top-down modernization and secularization that aimed to transform this Muslim nation into a Westernized, secular entity, albeit with only limited success. This conception of Muslim society versus the 'authoritarian secularism' of Kemalist Turkey has led to perceiving the rise to power of the Justice and Development Party (AKP, in its Turkish acronym) as a 'democratizing' force (Kandiyoti, 2012). As the AKP's democratic credentials, after years in power, have been extensively criticized in the literature, here I approach the subject matter from a different angle and question whether Turkey's model of state-religion relations has really ever been an example of secularism, let alone 'oppressive' (Yavuz, 2003) or 'assertive' (Kuru, 2009) secularism.

The Constitution indeed describes the state as 'secular' ('*laik*'), but Sunni Islam is practically the official religion of the state, for Turkish national identity is closely tied to Islam and the religious bureaucracy is part of the state structure. Although the creation of the republic is often taken as a break in Turkey's history of religious affairs, there are in fact significant continuities between the Ottoman and republican periods in terms of both political culture and state structure (Deringil, 1993; Meeker, 2002; Gülalp, 2005; Bottoni, 2007). This is true whether we consider the *secularization* of society as a modernization process or the institution of *secularism* as a normative political principle. By the former, I mean the process whereby 'the social significance of religion diminishes' through economic, social, and institutional differentiation and rationalization (Wallis & Bruce, 1992: 8–9), while the latter refers to the principle that aims to guarantee citizens the right to freedom of 'conscience and religion' as spelled out in international human rights documents (Universal Declaration of Human

Rights, Article 18; European Convention on Human Rights, Article 9), which includes the freedom of 'atheists, agnostics, sceptics and the unconcerned', as noted in European Court of Human Rights (ECtHR) judgements. It is useful to distinguish between these two concepts because in both the Ottoman Empire and the Turkish Republic, the *secularization* of the economy, social life, and institutions of the state proceeded to a greater extent than the establishment of *secularism* as a political principle, despite serious efforts in that direction.

Islam defines the nation

Unlike early modern European state-building, bent on cleansing populations along religious lines in order to create 'national' homogeneity (Marx, 2003), the Ottoman Empire (OE), although an Islamic empire, had a religiously diverse population. A religious community (called '*millet*') could include different ethnic and linguistic groups, and residents of different regions of the empire. While the Muslim population was at the top of the hierarchy, the imperial state nonetheless granted each *millet* some form of autonomy in their internal legal, judicial, as well cultural and educational affairs, and each was represented by a leader whose position was incorporated into the central administration of the empire (Braude & Lewis, 1982; Barkey, 2008). During the nineteenth century, as new norms of equal citizenship were being instituted in the OE, the term '*millet*' began to acquire its current meaning in the Turkish language, that is, 'nation' (Karpat, 1982). Although the *millet* system was significantly circumscribed in the last decades of the OE and formally disappeared with the creation of the Turkish Republic, there are still remnants of it both in the formal structures of the state and in popular notions of nationhood.

The Turkish nation was created by the expulsion of non-Muslims from the territory defined as Turkey during the course of the First World War (1914–1918) and the subsequent War of National Liberation (1919–1922). The remaining small non-Muslim communities were given 'minority' status and brought under protection (and granted some small measure of autonomy) by the Lausanne Treaty, which secured Turkey's independence and laid the foundation for the declaration of the Republic on 29 October 1923. Turkish nationalism had mutually contradictory sources. It unsuccessfully attempted to synthesize Islamism, Turkism, and territorial nationalism, although as a legacy of the Ottoman *millet* system, religion retained its centrality in Turkish national identity (Cagaptay, 2006). Kurds, for example, as non-Turkish-speaking Muslims, were considered capable of assimilation into the Turkish nation, but non-Muslims were always assumed to be inassimilable and fundamentally alien. The hope and expectation was that they would leave the country, as they indeed did during political crises involving coordinated attacks on their lives and property in the 1940s, 1950s, and early 1960s. In short, minority and non-Muslim have been (and still are) identical in Turkish national consciousness. Non-Muslim citizens of Turkey are not considered Turkish; they remain as 'step-citizens' of the Republic, with significantly curtailed citizenship rights (Ekmekcioglu, 2014).

Today, Turkey's population of roughly 82 million is officially regarded as being 99.9 per cent Muslim. On the one hand, this figure represents the miniscule proportions of the remaining communities of officially recognized religious minorities (identified by the Turkish government as the Greek Orthodox, Armenians, and Jews), that number only in the thousands. On the other hand, this nominal characterization does not reflect the demographic reality, for many of those listed as Muslim do not necessarily practise. Besides, there are several other religious groups, such as Syriacs, Roman Catholics, Protestants, Bahais, Jehovah's Witnesses, and others, that have *de facto*, but legally insecure, presence. Moreover, none of the groups listed above has legal personality. Finally, the most serious violation of non-recognition concerns the Alevis, considering the size of the community (at least 15 million) and its deep historical roots in Turkish society. The Alevi faith is officially declared to be a 'heretic' sect of Islam and their places of worship are not recognized despite several judgements in their favour from both the ECtHR and high courts within Turkey in recent years.

The Islamic identity of the new Turkish state was evident in its first Constitution, adopted by the National Assembly in April 1924. Article 1 defined the state as a Republic, and Article 2 defined the religion of the state as Islam. The clause that defined the religion of the state was removed in 1928 and subsequently replaced by a clause that defined the state as 'secular' (*laik*) in 1937. While the characterization of the state as 'secular' has remained in the Constitution to this day, the same cannot be said about actual structure of the state and its policies, as we see below. In terms of both popular cultural assumptions and state policy, then, the Turkish nation is primarily imagined as a (Sunni) Muslim entity. This religious core of national identity seems to defy the secularism of the state enshrined in the Constitution and uncritically accepted in established historiography.

State regulation of religion

In Western/Christian societies, secularism is often conceptualized as a mode of relationship between *church* and *state*, that is, between clerical and temporal authority, arranged in a variety of forms, such as strict separation, mutual autonomy, institutional cooperation, and so on. None of these concepts are relevant to the Ottoman-Turkish experience as clerical authority has never had a corporate existence independent of the state. The religious establishment in the OE was incorporated into the state structure, dominated by the sultan. Although doctrinally there is no clerical hierarchy in Islam, as no intermediary should go between God and the faithful, there was just such a bureaucracy as part of the Ottoman state. But this bureaucracy did not have any real independent power because the sultan was also the *Caliph*, and the religious establishment only exercised authority in his name. The *Şeyhülislam*, as the head of the religious hierarchy, was the government's chief jurist, whose advice the sultan would seek on legal and political matters, but he was directly appointed and deposed by the sultan (İnalcık, 1989).

When Istanbul came under British occupation at the end of the First World War, paralysing the Ottoman government, the nationalists led by Mustafa Kemal formed a parallel government in Ankara waging the Liberation War. In 1920, the Ankara government created the Ministry of Sharia and Pious Foundations in place of the office of the *Şeyhülislam*, which was based in occupied Istanbul. After the Liberation War was won and the Republic founded, among the new institutions created in 1924 was the Directorate of Religious Affairs (DRA) attached to the prime ministry, which took the place of the Ministry of Sharia and Pious Foundations. The DRA formally resembled the Ottoman institution of *Şeyhülislam* insofar as each was part of the respective state structure. But the substantive difference between them illustrates the character of Kemalism's project of 'secularism'. While the *Şeyhülislam* would issue religious opinions regarding matters of state and law, war and peace, and so on, as the sultans formally sought their political and legal advice, the republican regime, attempting to turn faith solely into a private and personal matter, restricted the role of DRA to issuing opinions on the daily affairs of the average believer.

Some argue that the Kemalist regime created the DRA specifically in order to dominate religious affairs and even suppress religiosity in society. According to Hakan Yavuz (2000: 29), for example, 'In order to subordinate religion to the political establishment, as was done in the Communist Eastern bloc, the new Kemalist Republic created its own version of Islam by establishing the Directorate of Religious Affairs' (see also Gözaydın, 2009; Kadıoğlu, 2010). But this interpretation is unfounded. In fact, the creation of this institution had 'liberal' origins, intended precisely to separate religion from politics. At the time that the law was passed, the government structure included both the chief of staff of the military and the head of the religious institution as members of the cabinet. Mustafa Kemal had already made clear his views on the role of the military in civilian politics (Volkan and Itzkowitz, 1984: 66–7). In a single bill of law, both seats were removed from the cabinet and reduced to the level of departments of the prime ministry, on grounds that neither military nor religious affairs leaders should be involved in politics or political decision-making (Genç, 2005). Addressing the National Assembly about this bill, Mustafa Kemal declared, 'it is indispensable to liberate the religion of Islam, within which we have been living peacefully and happily with devotion, from the customary ways in which it has been a means of politics' (quoted in Akan, 2017: 139). The parliamentary debate on what to call this department's affairs concluded that the term 'religion' (*din*) in the original proposal was inappropriate, and the decision was made to call it 'piety' (*diyanet*). The difference is significant, for the objectives of the department were described in terms of helping pious citizens with questions about their private affairs regarding religious practice and no more than that. The intention was the privatization of religion and its separation from politics.

The privatization of religion was not a new idea. An early precedent existed in a statement attributed to Sultan Mahmut II (1808–1839), who said that he wishes to see religious differences between his subjects only when they have entered their mosques, synagogues, and churches (Akçura, 1904: 20). Likewise, in his famous speech of 1927, Mustafa Kemal Atatürk described his conception of secularism as follows: 'A government that has various religious communities among its citizens and is responsible for treating individuals from every religion in a just and equitable manner, and for providing justice in its courts equally to subjects and foreigners alike, is obligated to respect the freedom of religion and thought' (Atatürk, 1927: 523). He went on to indicate that secularism meant bringing sovereignty down from the heavens to the people and that those who pursued politics by reference to religion were opposed to both popular sovereignty and the freedom of religion. Yet, while this ideal of 'privatization' continued to exist, its aim to create equal citizenship was never successfully achieved.

The modernizing and secularizing 'reforms' of the OE had begun in the early nineteenth century, were deepened during the *Tanzimat* (Reorganization) period, proclaimed in 1839, and culminated in the Constitution of 1876. The *Tanzimat* reforms pointed towards the building of a modern state in place of the patrimonial empire. Drawing the outlines of a constitutional monarchy, the reforms aimed to bring the *millet* system to an end by making each individual, *qua* individual, equal before the law and independent of the communal hierarchy, thus turning imperial subjects into citizens. The 1876 Constitution was promulgated by Sultan Abdülhamit II (1876–1909) and then shelved within a year or so, though he continued with the modernizing (and secularizing) reforms of the state. An autocratic pan-Islamist, he went on to build a rational bureaucracy, expand mass schooling, the postal service, railways, and so on, while at the same time he legitimized his power through Islamist ideology (Deringil, 1998). Many of the bureaucratic institutions of Republican Turkey were founded during his reign.

As the OE was integrated into global capitalism, the judicial system had to be secularized. In the classical *millet* system there was judicial plurality because Jews and Christians had their own courts outside of the Islamic justice system. Additionally, there was another parallel justice system applicable to foreign traders, which was arranged through 'capitulations' granted to the governments of their home countries. In dealings with them, an impersonal and written ('Weberian') legal system prevailed, as opposed to the '*kadi* justice' of Islamic law. As these capitulations began to cover non-Muslim Ottoman citizens as well, because foreign powers could also bring them under their protection in business dealings, Muslim traders fell into a disadvantage. Consequently, the state was forced to create a system of 'secular and heavily western-influenced commercial courts in Istanbul and Cairo in the 1850s' (Kuran, 2011: 208). A similar secularization trend also prevailed in the education system in the mid-nineteenth century. The needs of the bureaucracy and the military to adapt to the pressures of modernization, trying to catch up with Western European states, necessitated the introduction of secular curricula and methods of education, which developed alongside the traditional religious education dominated by the Islamic *ulema* (Ortaylı, 1983). But these secularizing moves did not change the organizational structure of state-religion relations in the OE.

During the early years of the Republic, the government continued with the measures started in the Ottoman period to further rationalize and secularize the legal, judicial, and educational systems. The dual structures in the form of parallel Islamic and secular institutions, still in existence as inherited by the Republic, were finally eliminated and unified. The Law of Unification of Education was passed in March 1924, on the same day that the DRA was created. All religious schools run by the defunct Ministry of Sharia were closed and responsibility for all education, including the religious, was transferred to the jurisdiction of the Ministry of Education. A month later, in April, Islamic courts were closed and the judicial system was unified under the Ministry of Justice. But this unification did not mean that the legal system was unified. Religious laws continued to exist along with the secular. In 1926, a set of new laws was passed that were mostly adopted from European codes taken as models. The most important of these for our purposes was the Civil Code, which replaced the Islamic family and personal status law. In the preparatory stage before the passing of this law, the leaders of the non-Muslim communities were invited (some would say, pressured) to relinquish their right to have their own family laws granted to them by the Lausanne Treaty, which they did, so that when the law was adopted it became universally valid for all citizens (Oran, 2003).

Usually counted among the republican regime's 'secularizing' measures is the abolition of the *Caliphate*, which incidentally took place on the same day as the creation of the DRA and hence considered to be somehow related to it, as if one institution took the place of the other. But as we saw, the DRA took the place of the Ministry of Sharia, which, in turn, had taken the place of the Ottoman office of the *Şeyhülislam*. The abolition of the *Caliphate* was an altogether different matter. When the nationalist struggle ended in victory in the fall of 1922, European powers invited both the Ottoman government based in occupied Istanbul and the nationalist government based in Ankara to commence peace talks at Lausanne. In response, the National Assembly in Ankara met on 1 November 1922 to separate the *Caliphate* from the *Sultanate* and to abolish the *Sultanate*, in effect dissolving the Ottoman Empire for good. The Ottoman sultan at the time (Vahdettin) then sought refuge with the British and fled the country, and his cousin (Abdülmecit II) was named the new *Caliph* by the National Assembly. Two years later, in 1924, the newly declared Republic passed a law that abolished the seat of the *Caliphate* with the justification that the caliphate is intrinsic to the meaning and concept of government and republic, and therefore cannot exist as a distinct centre of power (Genç, 2005: 35). The same law banished the Ottoman dynasty from Turkey, sending Abdülmecit and his family into exile.

Paradoxically, however, these measures did not involve the building of *secularism* in accordance with the normative principles of equality and freedom. Islamic influence was presumably removed from political and public affairs, but Islam still remained as part of the state establishment and identity. Herein lay the internal contradiction of the Kemalist project. As Kandiyoti (2012: 516) remarks, 'the blows that Kemalism dealt to the symbols and institutions of Islam … must not be conflated or confused with a transition to a civic concept of citizenship that positions the state in an equidistant relationship to all its ethnically and religiously diverse citizenry'. The question is: how do we account for this?

Secularization of social life in the early republican period

As no religious organization such as the Catholic Church existed independent of the state, the Kemalists did not have to struggle against, or reach a mode of accommodation with, the clergy *per se*, because the clergy was already in the employ of the state. But one could perhaps imagine 'mutual autonomy' between state and religion in this context in terms of the state leaving religious organization to the forces of civil society without any direct intervention or regulation, and abandoning such actions as licensing mosques and putting the clergy on government payroll, and so on. This might be preferable, because, after all, the (Sunni) Muslim clergy's salary comes out of the taxes of *all* citizens, whether Muslim or not, or whether religious or not. Could (or should) not the Kemalists have gone further and completely separated state and religion in this sense, and relieved itself and the non-Muslim and non-religious citizens of the burden?

Perhaps they could, except that they tended to see unchecked religious associations as a political threat or, worse, as simply dangerous, considering the impressionability of the 'illiterate and uneducated masses'. The way they saw it, their struggle was not against the clergy, but against those 'civil society' forces that might use the religious sentiments of the masses to politically undermine the republican regime. In this struggle, they saw the clergy on their side, as the project was *not* to suppress Islam, as has sometimes been claimed, but to build what they considered a 'proper' and 'enlightened' conception of Islam (Azak, 2010). The division that has historically existed between secularists and Islamists in Turkey, then, has not been between lay political leaders and the clergy, but between the secularists and Islamists that could be found both within the clergy and among the political leaders. The 'proper' Islam imagined by the Kemalists was free of the elements of 'folk' Islam, such as 'superstitious' beliefs and local 'sheiks' who could manipulate the religiosity of the masses.

In 1925, the regime was challenged by a serious uprising in the Kurdish-populated southeast, led by Sheikh Said, an influential and revered head of the Naqshbandi order. Said publicly condemned the Kemalists for destroying religion and incited rebellion to end the 'blasphemy'. Researchers note that although the objective was to create an independent Kurdistan, or at least gain some form of autonomy, religious language was used to motivate followers into rebellion (Bruinessen, 1992; Tunçay, 1981; Olson, 1989). In addition, the British had a longstanding interest and involvement in Kurdish nationalism, and although there was no direct evidence of British involvement in the Sheikh Said rebellion, as far as the government was concerned the Kurds were in alliance with the British and were serving a sinister imperialist plan to divide up the country that the nationalists had fought so hard to save from occupation. The rebellion broke out in February; Said was captured and executed in April. The incident led the regime to envisage an intimate connection between the Kurdish and Islamic threats to its own stability and prompted it to accelerate its move towards further emphasis on secularization and Turkish nationalism.

In March 1925, soon after the beginning of the rebellion, the Law for the Maintenance of Order (*Takrir-i Sükun Kanunu*) was passed, giving the government extraordinary powers. In June 1925 the regime closed down the opposition party in the Parliament, the Progressive Republican Party, because of its alleged Islamist leanings (Ahmad, 1993: 57–60). In November 1925, the Law for Dervish Lodges (*Tekke ve Zaviyeler Kanunu*) was passed, banning *sufi* brotherhoods and other grassroots religious groupings because they were seen as potential sources of political trouble. In March 1926, a new Penal Code was adopted, including an article that banned 'the utilization of religion or religious sentiment or things considered sacred by religion for inciting people to violate the security of the state or to form associations to this effect' and 'the founding of political associations based on religious ideas and sentiments'. The same code also included several articles protecting the 'freedom of religion', by banning any publications 'denigrating any of the religions recognized by the state' and any acts 'that prevented religious worship' or 'damaged religious sites or objects'.

The Law for the Maintenance of Order remained in effect until 1929. Along with the introduction of the Civil Code and the Penal Code, the infamous 'Hat Law' (of 1925), often associated with the regime's 'secularizing' efforts, was introduced in this period. Headgear regulation had a precedent in the OE. In the classical period, 'clothes, and particularly headgear, were important markers of ethnic, religious, and other communal identities as well as of social class and rank' (Yılmaz, 2013: 22–23). In 1829, the modernist Sultan Mahmut II had proclaimed the fez, an inauthentic item, as the national headgear to represent the equality of Ottoman citizens before the state through a uniform appearance (Bottoni, 2007: 181). The objective of the Hat Law was the same; but it also expressed the desire to simulate the outward appearance of what at the time was considered to be 'civilized', considering that the Europeans associated the fez with Ottoman tradition and backwardness (Yılmaz, 2013: 29). No dress code was promulgated for women, but those who were using the face veil and *çarşaf* (similar to the Iranian *chador*) were *encouraged* to remove them and wear headscarves and overcoats instead. For the regime, this was a step in the legal and political emancipation of Turkish women; more steps would be taken later. Removing the face veil was necessary for women's active presence and participation in the public sphere (Adak, 2014). Yet another novelty introduced in this timeframe was the Latin alphabet in place of the Arabic script used to write Turkish during the Ottoman Empire.

These measures that 'secularized' social life have often been described as top-down impositions rejected by the society with predominantly Muslim sensibilities, whereas in fact they were not planned in advance and forced in a blueprint (Clayer, 2015). Anti-veiling campaigns, for example, 'were shaped by discussions, negotiations and concessions at the local level' (Adak, 2014: 60). Often local elites, such as newspaper writers and editors, prominent members of local associations and professional organizations, rather than state administrators, took the lead in these campaigns. Women themselves, who wanted to take their place in society as equal to men, were also active in anti-veiling efforts. Many of these measures met with mixed reactions, giving 'a much more complicated picture than either total compliance or total resistance' (Yılmaz, 2013: 74).

During the 1930s, the government attempted to shift the conception of national identity from Islam to Turkishness, defined ambiguously with reference to both race and territory. But despite these efforts and the introduction of 'secularism' into the Constitution (1937), by the time that Atatürk died in 1938 and his close associate İsmet İnönü took over as President and head of the ruling Republican People's Party (RPP), founded by Mustafa Kemal in 1923, national identity was still Muslim and appealing to it still an effective method of winning political support. Through all this, moreover, the religious bureaucracy (DRA) remained as part of the state structure. Complete separation never took place, although the significance of the DRA declined through the 1930s. Its budget and functions were already limited as it was primarily concerned with the administration of mosques and their personnel, with further limitation in 1931, when this particular function was transferred to the Directorate of Pious Foundations, also part of the government bureaucracy. The DRA was then only directly responsible for the appointment of local *mufti*s (Islamic scholars). But this decline phase did not last very long. At the end of the Second World War, only several years after secularism entered the Turkish Constitution, state policies on religion experienced yet another shift, this time in the opposite direction.

Post-war trends

At the end of the Second World War, Turkey was recruited by the US for the anti-Soviet front, and the RPP government was encouraged (or perhaps pressured) to re-introduce multi-party democracy and expand the infrastructure for religion. Turkey's religious identity would be a useful ideology in the context of the Cold War to reinforce national solidarity against the 'foreign' influences of socialism and communism. The ruling RPP and the Democrat Party (DP), the most important among those (opposition) parties formed in the immediate postwar period, were in full agreement on this policy of emphasizing Turkey's religious identity (Akan, 2017). The DP was an offshoot of the RPP, seriously challenged it in the elections of 1946, and brought it down from office in the 1950 elections. Already before the DP's ascent to power, and partly under the pressure of competition from the DP, the RPP government took steps between 1946 and 1950 to widen the space for religion. The administration of all mosques was returned to the DRA, and its size and budget were increased. A number of schools were opened for religious education, notably *Imam-Hatip* Schools, designed to train preachers and prayer leaders employed by the DRA (Akşit, 1991), along with a Faculty of Theology at Ankara University. Regardless, the DP won the 1950 elections and further expanded the space for religious language in public and political life.

With the DP in power, the nuance regarding the question of separating religion from politics became more evident, as the leaders of the RPP criticized the behaviour of the DP politicians by underlining the distinction between 'the exploitation of religion' and the 'religiosity of the citizens' (Azak, 2010: 130). But while critical of the DP's use of religion in political discourse, implying that one could be both Muslim and secular at the same time, they were also wary of an institutional design that would leave religious affairs to the forces of civil society, and hence still in favour of keeping the DRA within the state structure.

After the military coup of 1960 that overthrew the DP government, the DRA actually found its way into the Constitution for the first time. The expansion of its infrastructure reached a new threshold following the 1980 coup, with the military's adoption of the so-called Turkish-Islamic Synthesis (Çetinsaya, 1999) as official ideology. While only a brief mention of the DRA may be found in the 1961 Constitution, Article 136 of the 1982 Constitution assigned a specific role to it in an internally contradictory formulation: the DRA 'shall exercise its duties ... in accordance with the principles of secularism, ... aiming at national solidarity and integrity'. In other words, national solidarity and integrity were important goals for the military as a bulwark against socialist and communist ideologies, and Islam was found to be a convenient identity to unite around (Akan, 2017). The further expansion of the religious infrastructure within the state gave the Islamist movements an unprecedented fertile ground for political mobilization in the 1980s.

The end of the Cold War, however, created a temporary confusion and setback for the expanding Islamic influence, as Turkey's geo-strategic position as a member of NATO led to a new form of assignment. In 1995, NATO formally shifted its attention from the now-extinct Soviet bloc to the rise of Islamist movements around the world, with Turkey as the 'centrepiece' of US policy and pursuit of interests in the Middle East. Now that the communist threat was replaced by the threat of Islamic 'fundamentalism', Turkey was urged by NATO (and the Western community of nations more generally) to take a firmer position domestically to prevent the development of Islamism (Gülalp, 1996). This configuration, combined with the electoral success of the Islamist *Welfare Party* in 1995, resulted in yet another military intervention in 1997, which, by contrast to the 1980 coup, imposed limitations on religious expression in the public sphere. The *Welfare*-led coalition government was forced to resign, and the following year the Constitutional Court ruled for the closure of this party for violating the principle of secularism. This closure was upheld by the ECtHR, in a section judgement in 2001 and Grand Chamber in 2003. An attempt to create another political party to replace *Welfare* also ended in similar closure in 2001. The ban in Turkish universities (and certain other institutions) on the use of the headscarf as a symbol of Islamic identity was implemented particularly in this timeframe. Similar bans were imposed in a number of other European countries, and these bans were also upheld by the European Court.

This policy soon gave way to an alternative concept, however. In the post-9/11 context, 'moderate Islam' was contrasted with 'radical Islam' and promoted to counter the threat of 'terrorism'. The AKP was founded in 2001 and conceived as a role model of 'moderate Islam' that Turkey could offer to the Muslim world. Initially claiming a project of correcting the alleged past 'injustices' of Kemalist secularism and describing its own ideology as 'conservative democracy', and welcomed by the West, the AKP swept to power in 2002 and has remained in office to this day. But, cautious at first and speaking the language of democratization, the AKP gradually turned authoritarian and began to Islamize the state and society as it more securely entrenched itself in power (Özbudun, 2014; Kaya, 2015; Esen and Gumuscu, 2016; Somer, 2019). It did so, as we see below, by taking advantage of those instruments at the state's disposal, which are presumed to be associated with Kemalist secularism (Gülalp, 2017).

Deepening Islamization

The AKP government's Islamization policy was best expressed by Recep Tayyip Erdoğan, President of Turkey and leader of the ruling AKP, in his address to the Religious Council of Turkey, on 28 November 2019: 'According to our faith, religion is not restricted to certain spaces and times. Islam is a set of rules and prohibitions that embrace all aspects of our lives. ... We have been commanded to live as Muslims ... No one can deny these tenets, because a Muslim is obligated to adapt his life to the essence of his religion and not the religion to his conditions of existence. ... Even if it may be hard for us, we will place the rules of our religion at the centre of our lives and not the requirements of our time' (*T24*, 2019b).

This policy has impacted nearly all areas of social and political life. In foreign affairs, for example, the government has been pursuing a 'neo-Ottomanist' programme, building on Muslim Brotherhood networks, leading to a loss of allies and a tendency to resort to military hard power in the region instead of diplomatic soft power. Domestically, intervention in people's lifestyles, primarily in the form of restricting the consumption of alcohol through exorbitant taxation and a policy of limiting times and zones of alcohol sale and consumption, has led to a violation of citizens' right to privacy and freedom of choice. Blatant discrimination on the basis of religious identity or degree of religiosity, including in public employment, has been rampant. Several other issues – which may at first be seen as unrelated to Islamism as they may appear in other regimes as well – including crony capitalism, corruption, and economic mismanagement, the routine practice of prosecuting academics, students, and journalists critical of the government's actions, and the rapid decline in the status of women, are all in fact the outcome of the attempted authoritarian imposition of an Islamist regime (Negrón-Gonzales, 2016; Esen & Gumuscu, 2018; Özpek & Park, 2019; Arat & Pamuk, 2019).

Islamization policies pursued through the institutions that presumably serve state 'secularism' are particularly evident in the expanded functions of the DRA and in the changes in the educational system. The DRA, which had continued to grow in size and extend its reach in the 1980s during the hegemony of the ideology of 'Turkish-Islamic Synthesis', turned into a powerful and prominent institution under AKP rule (Gözaydın, 2009). The DRA's functions were diversified in this period, and its budget and personnel grew inordinately. A law passed in 2010 vastly expanded the DRA's scope of activities, conferring to the organization a wide range of responsibilities in the realm of social and cultural life, such as keeping values and morals alive and educating the people in the ways of Islam as regards the economy, gender relations, and so on (Adak, 2015; Akan, 2017; Mutluer, 2018). The long list of duties enumerated in Article 6 of this law include 'offering legal advice' on the laws, statutes, and regulations prepared by the administration, apparently bringing the DRA closer to the position of the office of the *Şeyhülislam*, as in the OE. Clearly, this reverses the role of the DRA as originally envisaged by the Kemalists, whose aim was to move towards secularism.

In 2012, the AKP government's plan to 'raise pious generations' was revealed, leading to a radical overhaul of the entire educational infrastructure (Cengiz, 2014; Kandiyoti & Emanet, 2017; Karapehlivan, 2019). Religious instruction began to occupy a greater part of the curriculum at all levels; and, more specifically, *Imam-Hatip* Schools began to turn into a mainstream venue for secondary education for both boys *and* girls so that in recent years both their number and share in the public budget multiplied. The number of *Imam-Hatip* high schools rose fourfold, from 450 (in 2002–2003) to 854 (in 2013–2014) and to 1,623 (in 2018–2019). The total number of *Imam-Hatip* middle and high schools (the former had been previously closed but then reopened by the AKP government in 2012) went from 2,215 (in 2013–2014) to 5,017 (in 2018–2019), housing over one million pupils. As of 2019, the budget per pupil for these schools was nearly twice the average for other schools. Despite all this, however, the success rate of *Imam-Hatip* graduates in university entrance exams has been the lowest among all types of high schools, with such diversion of resources towards them risking a decline in the overall level of education (SODEV, 2019). Similar tendencies have prevailed at the university level, particularly after the massive purge of academics in 2016–2017.

The objective of this orientation in education is not hard to fathom and has indeed been clearly expressed. A pamphlet prepared by the DRA and distributed free of charge in early 2019 expounded on the inverse relationship between secular education and religiosity, suggesting that higher levels of education encouraged 'individualism and freedom' and discouraged 'belief and worship'. The Director himself repeated the same observation later in the year, in his address to the meeting of the Religious Council of Turkey, and noted the growing 'popularity' of the assumption that scientific advances will 'transform or completely displace religions' and lead to 'new threats toward belief' (*T24*, 2019a). The threat that 'secular education' poses to the government is not illusory. There is indeed an inverse relationship between the level of education and the level of religiosity, and, likewise, the electoral support for the AKP is in an inverse relationship with the level of education, but in direct correlation with the level of religiosity (KONDA, 2019).

Paradoxically, however, these efforts to 'raise pious generations' has been a self-defeating process. Those youths from the secularist upper and middle classes, whose families could afford to send them abroad for better education, have begun to leave the country. Those youths from the conservative lower classes, whose families have been the power base of the AKP, may be unable to leave, but they have begun to turn away from religion. There is currently a decline in religiosity and rise in deism and atheism that is alarming the AKP government and its religious establishment (Azak, 2018; Hurtas, 2019).

Concluding remarks

The Constitution of Turkey formally endorses the freedom of conscience, religious belief, and worship, and prohibits discrimination based on religious grounds. It also prohibits the exploitation of religion or religious feelings for political ends or for regulating state affairs. Still, the nearly complete (imagined) homogeneity of the population around the Muslim identity, combined with the secular foundation of the republic, has led to a perennial tension between the secularists and Islamists throughout Turkish political history and to an ongoing debate on the proper place of religion in public and political life. While Islamists, and recently some 'liberals' and 'multiculturalists', have demanded a greater role for religion in public and political affairs, the secularists have argued that religion needs to be kept private and that politics should not be based on religious precepts. The outcome of this debate has varied, depending on the relative room for manoeuvre that the politically powerful group has had. Some historical periods, such as the 1990s, witnessed restrictions on public religious expression, such as the wearing of Islamic headscarves by female university students, whereas in the 2000s, there has been a rapid expansion in the religious infrastructure and the use of religious language in politics and state affairs. The institutional structure inherited from the OE, incorporating the religious establishment into the state, far from being an apparatus of 'oppressive secularism' readily allows for the use of religious language for political mobilization and offers a natural advantage to Islamist political forces and movements. It is therefore ironic that Islamists should complain of 'secularism' for restricting the freedom of religion, because if any mention is to be made of limitations on this freedom, they certainly apply to non-Muslim and non-Sunni groups.

References

Adak, Sevgi. (2014). Anti-Veiling Campaigns and Local Elites in Turkey in the 1930s. In Stephanie Cronin (ed.), *Anti-Veiling Campaigns in the Muslim World*. London: Routledge, 59–85.
Adak, Sevgi. (2015). 'Yeni' Türkiye'nin 'Yeni' Diyaneti. *Birikim*, 139, 78–85.
Ahmad, Feroz. (1993). *The Making of Modern Turkey*. London: Routledge.
Akan, Murat. (2017). *Politics of Secularism: Religion, Diversity, and Institutional Change in France and Turkey*. New York: Columbia University Press.
Akçura, Yusuf. ([1904] 1987). *Üç Tarz-ı Siyaset*. Ankara: Türk Tarih Kurumu.
Akşit, Bahattin. (1991). Islamic Education in Turkey: Medrese Reform in Late Ottoman Times and Imam-Hatip Schools in the Republic. In Richard Tapper (ed.), *Islam in Modern Turkey: Religion, Politics and Literature in a Secular State*. London: I.B. Tauris, 145–170.
Arat, Yeşim & Pamuk, Şevket. (2019). *Turkey between Democracy and Authoritarianism*. Cambridge: Cambridge University Press.
Atatürk, Mustafa Kemal. ([1927] 1963). *Nutuk*. Ankara: Türk Dil Kurumu.
Azak, Umut. (2010). *Islam and Secularism in Turkey: Kemalism, Religion and the Nation State*. London: I.B. Tauris.
Azak, Umut. (2018). Secularism and Atheism in the Turkish Public Sphere. *Turkish Policy Quarterly*, 16(4), 57–73.

Barkey, Karen. (2008). *Empire of Difference: The Ottomans in Comparative Perspective*. Cambridge: Cambridge University Press.
Bottoni, Rossella. (2007). The Origins of Secularism in Turkey. *Ecclesiastical Law Journal*, 9(2), 175–186.
Braude, Benjamin & Lewis, Bernard (eds). (1982). *Christians and Jews in the Ottoman Empire*. New York: Holmes and Meier.
Bruinessen, Martin van. (1992). *Agha, Shaikh and State*. London: Zed Books.
Cagaptay, Soner. (2006). Passage to Turkishness: Immigration and Religion in Modern Turkey. In Haldun Gülalp (ed.), *Citizenship and Ethnic Conflict: Challenging the Nation-State*. London: Routledge, 61–82.
Cengiz, Orhan Kemal. (2014, June 26). Erdogan's Reforms Meant to Educate 'Pious Generation'. *Al-Monitor*.
Çetinsaya, Gökhan. (1999). Rethinking Nationalism and Islam: Some Preliminary Notes on the Roots of 'Turkish-Islamic Synthesis' in Modern Turkish Political Thought. *The Muslim World*, 89(3/4), 350–376.
Clayer, Nathalie. (2015). An Imposed or a Negotiated *Laiklik*? In Marc Aymes, Benjamin Gourisse, & Elise Massicard (eds), *Order and Compromise: Government Practices in Turkey from the Late Ottoman Empire to the Early 21st Century*. Leiden: Brill, 97–120.
Deringil, Selim. (1993). The Ottoman Origins of Kemalist Nationalism. *European History Quarterly*, 23(2), 165–191.
Deringil, Selim. (1998). *The Well-Protected Domains: Ideology and the Legitimation of Power in the Ottoman Empire, 1876–1909*. London: I.B.Tauris.
Ekmekcioglu, Lerna. (2014). Republic of Paradox: The League of Nations Minority Protection Regime and the New Turkey's Step-Citizens. *International Journal of Middle East Studies*, 46(4), 657–679.
Esen, Berk & Gumuscu, Sebnem. (2016). Rising Competitive Authoritarianism in Turkey. *Third World Quarterly*, 37(9), 1581–1606.
Esen, Berk & Gumuscu, Sebnem. (2018). Building a Competitive Authoritarian Regime: State–Business Relations in the AKP's Turkey. *Journal of Balkan and Near Eastern Studies*, 20(4), 349–372.
Gellner, Ernest. (1997). The Turkish Option in Comparative Perspective. In Sibel Bozdoğan and Reşat Kasaba (eds), *Rethinking Modernity and National Identity in Turkey*. Seattle: University of Washington Press, 233–244.
Genç, Reşat, (ed.). (2005). *Türkiye'yi Laikleştiren Yasalar: 3 Mart 1924 Tarihli Meclis Müzakereleri ve Kararları*. Ankara: Atatürk Araştırma Merkezi.
Gözaydın, İştar. (2009). *Diyanet: Türkiye Cumhuriyeti'nde Dinin Tanzimi*. İstanbul: İletişim Yayınları.
Gülalp, Haldun. (1996). Islamism and Kurdish Nationalism: Rival Adversaries of Kemalism in Turkey. In Tamara Sonn (ed.), *Islam and the Question of Minorities*. Atlanta: Scholars Press, 93–109.
Gülalp, Haldun. (2005). Enlightenment by Fiat: Secularization and Democracy in Turkey. *Middle Eastern Studies*, 41(3), 351–372.
Gülalp, Haldun. (2017). Secularism as a Double-Edged Sword? State Regulation of Religion in Turkey. In Anna Triandafyllidou & Tariq Modood (eds), *The Problem of Religious Diversity: European Challenges, Asian Approaches*. University of Edinburgh Press, 273–296.
Hurtas, Sibel. (2019, January 9). Turks Losing Trust in Religion Under AKP. *Al-Monitor*.
İnalcık, Halil. (1989). *The Ottoman Empire, The Classical Age*. New Rochelle, NY: Orpheus Publishing.
Kadıoğlu, Ayşe. (2010). The Pathologies of Turkish Republican Laicism. *Philosophy and Social Criticism*, 36(3–4), 489–504.
Kandiyoti, Deniz. (2012). The Travails of the Secular: Puzzle and Paradox in Turkey. *Economy and Society*, 41(4), 513–531.
Kandiyoti, Deniz & Emanet, Zühre. (2017). Education as Battleground: The Capture of Minds in Turkey. *Globalizations*, 14(6), 1–8.
Karapehlivan, Funda. (2019). Constructing a 'New Turkey' through Education: An Overview of the Education Policies in Turkey under the AKP Rule," Available at: https://tr.boell.org/en/2019/10/01/constructing-new-turkey-through-education.
Karpat, Kemal. (1982). Millets and Nationality: The Roots of Incongruity of Nation and State in the Post-Ottoman Era. In Benjamin Braude & Bernard Lewis (eds), *Christians and Jews in the Ottoman Empire*, vol.1. New York: Holmes and Meier, 141–169.
Kaya, Ayhan. (2015). Islamisation of Turkey under the AKP Rule: Empowering Family, Faith and Charity. *South European Society and Politics*, 20(1), 47–69.

KONDA. (2019). 23 Haziran 2019 Sandık Analizi ve Seçmen Profilleri. Available at: https://konda.com.tr/wp-content/uploads/2019/07/23Haziran2019_Istanbul_Sandik_Analizi.pdf.

Kuran, Timur. (2011). *The Long Divergence: How Islamic Law Held Back the Middle East.* Princeton, NJ: Princeton University Press.

Kuru, Ahmet. (2009). *Secularism and State Policies Toward Religion: The United States, France, and Turkey.* New York: Cambridge University Press.

Marx, Anthony. (2003). *Faith in Nation: Exclusionary Origins of Nationalism.* Oxford: Oxford University Press.

Meeker, Michael. (2002). *A Nation of Empire: The Ottoman Legacy of Turkish Modernity.* Berkeley and Los Angeles: University of California Press.

Mutluer, Nil. (2018). *Diyanet's Role in Building the 'Yeni (New) Milli' in the AKP Era. European Journal of Turkish Studies,* 27, 1–24.

Negrón-Gonzales, Melinda. (2016). The Feminist Movement during the AKP Era in Turkey: Challenges and Opportunities. *Middle Eastern Studies,* 52(2), 198–214.

Olson, Robert. (1989). *The Emergence of Kurdish Nationalism and the Sheikh Said Rebellion, 1880–1925.* Austin: University of Texas Press.

Oran, Baskın. (2003). Lozan'da Azınlıkların Korunması. *Toplumsal Tarih,* 115, 72–77.

Ortaylı, İlber. (1983). *İmparatorluğun En Uzun Yüzyılı.* İstanbul: Hil Yayınları.

Özbudun, Ergun. (2014). AKP at the Crossroads: Erdoğan's Majoritarian Drift. *South European Society and Politics,* 19(2), 155–167.

Özpek, Burak Bilgehan & Park, Bill (eds). (2019). *Islamism, Populism and Turkish Foreign Policy.* London: Routledge.

SODEV. (2019). Türkiye'de Eğitim: İmam Hatipleşme, Beklentiler ve Memnuniyet Araştırması Raporu. Available at: http://sodev.org.tr/ERapor.pdf.

Somer, Murat. (2019). Turkey: The Slippery Slope from Reformist to Revolutionary Polarization and Democratic Breakdown. *The Annals of the American Academy of Political and Social Science,* 681(1), 42–61.

T24 (2019a, November 28). 6. Din Şûrası. Available at: https://t24.com.tr/haber/6-din-surasi-bilimin-dinin-yerini-alacagi-kabulu-inanca-yonelik-yeni-tehditler-ortaya-cikariyor, 850044.

T24 (2019b, November 28). Erdoğan, Available at: https://t24.com.tr/haber/erdogan-6-din-surasi-kapanis-programi-nda-konusuyor, 849989.

Tunçay, Mete. (1981). *Türkiye Cumhuriyeti'nde Tek Parti Yönetiminin Kurulması (1923–1931).* Ankara: Yurt Yayınları.

Volkan, Vamık D. & Itzkowitz, Norman. (1984). *The Immortal Atatürk: A Psychobiography.* Chicago, IL: The University of Chicago Press.

Wallis, Roy & Bruce, Steve. (1992). Secularization: The Orthodox Model. In Steve Bruce (ed.), *Religion and Modernization.* Oxford: Clarendon Press, 8–30.

Yavuz, Hakan. (2000). Cleansing Islam from the Public Sphere. *Journal of International Affairs,* 54(1), 21–42.

Yavuz, Hakan. (2003). *Islamic Political Identity in Turkey.* London: Oxford University Press.

Yılmaz, Hale. (2013). *Becoming Turkish: Nationalist Reforms and Cultural Negotiations in Early Republican Turkey, 1923–1945.* Syracuse, NY: Syracuse University Press.

17

Lebanon

Confessionalism and the problem of divided loyalties

Yüksel Taşkın

Introduction

It is possible to offer two contradictory interpretations of Lebanese political and social life from nineteenth-century Ottoman times to the post-independence era. Negative and even catastrophic readings generally portray the country on the brink of collapse or dysfunction due to the intense polarization among different sects. The unending involvement of regional and global actors is also considered to be a further element of de-stabilization. Lebanon is also argued to have failed to develop a binding national identity vis-á-vis these challenges. Accordingly, the confessional system which has been improvised as a temporary solution within the framework of consociationalism has itself turned out to be a prevailing problem by sliding into a suffocating cage of sectarianism. It was believed to be 'temporary' since the 1926 Lebanese Constitution was also inspired from the French model of *laïcité* as a universal ideal.

However, there are cautious optimists, too. Some commentators draw attention to 'the vitality of Lebanese political life, the multiplicity of its actors and the variety of its topics from women's rights to election laws … that displays a capacity for continuous adaptation. The actors' "path of resilience" (their capacity to face the many dangers threatening the country)' (Di Peri & Meier, 2017) should be taken seriously to arrive at a more nuanced understanding of the country beyond the repetitive analyses of failure.

I contend that Lebanon offers an interesting case of continuous efforts of adaptation in the middle of seemingly insurmountable challenges posed by extremely politicized and polarized religious diversity with domestic and regional variables. The country has legitimate political actors playing within the parameters of a national-political field. Despite the existence of prolonged and fundamental crises, this political class seems to either defer their problems to an uncertain future or provide short term solutions working, at least, until the outbreak of the next crisis.

Especially after the Civil War (1975–1990) and under the shadow of Syrian domination (1990–2005), the rival Lebanese political elites have managed to work within an institutional framework defined as consociationalism which was inherited from before the war. Consociationalism is a model of consociational democracy, which is employed in countries that have a variety of different segmental groups along social, political, ethnic, linguistic, and racial lines as well as by religion or by region/nationality. In other words, it is a form of power-sharing among various segmental groups in order to maintain political stability and civil order and to avoid the outbreak of civil violence (Lijphart, 1977). Confessionalism is a sub-category of consociationalism, where the main lines of divisions take place around religion (Reinkowski & Saadeh, 2006).

In scholarly research on religious diversity governance, the two models that are typically put forward when talking about European approaches to religiosity are France's *laïcité,* or radical secularism characterized by its refusal to acknowledge and accommodate religious diversity in the public space, and Britain's moderate or 'multiculturalised secularism' (Modood, 2019: Ch. 8). In this regard, the Lebanese confessionalism does not fit into either model. On the contrary, there is no recognition of a secular state authority as guarantee of religious and non-religious freedoms. As Makdisi argues, (in Lebanon) 'the modern state was established as liberal and (putatively) democratic, but not secular' (1996: 3). Furthermore, Lebanon presents a unique case as its confessional system, the weak state capacity, and the existence of powerful armed militias as a result of continuous geo-political challenges.

The Lebanese confessionalism can be considered as an improvised form of the Ottoman *millet* system based on a hierarchy of religions. While the Sunni Muslim population was at the top of the hierarchy, the Ottoman imperial state granted each *millet* some form of autonomy in their internal legal, judicial, as well as cultural and educational affairs and each was represented by a leader whose position was incorporated into the central administration of the empire (Barkey, 2008).

There is an ongoing and intense political and intellectual debate in Lebanon on whether the confessional system is a working solution or source of enduring political, cultural, and economic problems. While some defend the viability of Lebanese confessionalism and blame external causes for the ultimate breakdown of the political system in 1975, others contend that Lebanon's peculiar corporate power-sharing model hardens sectarian identities, invites systemic deadlock, precludes the emergence of cross-sectarian modes of political mobilization, and, ultimately, leads to cyclical domestic crises that invite external interventions (Salloukh, 2015).

This is the reason why those supporters of a secular or post-sectarian Lebanon tend to blame the persistence of Lebanese confessionalism and related sectarianism for the failure of emergence of a sense of trans-sectarian inclusive citizenship as well as the interest-based rather than identity-based political affiliations (Clark & Salloukh, 2013; Kingston, 2013). Those critics of the confessional system argue that the Lebanese remain unequal sectarian subjects compartmentalized in self-managed communities rather than citizens with inalienable rights.

It is important to note that there are various efforts and calls for a post-sectarian Lebanon. In fact, during the Arab uprisings, the Lebanese protesters adopted the slogan of the Tunisian and Egyptian uprisings, 'the people want to topple the regime', but changed it slightly to 'the people want to topple the sectarian regime' (Di Peri & Meier, 2017: 2).

Will these struggles for post-sectarian Lebanon manage to create conditions for a secular Lebanon or lead to some improvements in the otherwise resilient confessional structure in a regional environment eroding the bases for inter-confessional trust? In fact, the relevant question for the proposed study is whether the confessional system of power-sharing could adapt itself to the new challenges emerging in the aftermath of the Arab uprising, especially with the outbreak of the Syrian Civil War and its conclusion with the Assad regime's victory.

All the risks and challenges that Lebanon is facing today seem to have exacerbated the historically existing animosities, especially among the religious communities. Indeed, Lebanon experienced several serious challenges since the late nineteenth century, which involved the risk of turning the country into a failed state and failed national-political community as well. Nevertheless, it managed to survive primarily because of its elites' willingness to remain and work within the framework of confessionalism and consociational democracy. Even though all communities pose harsh criticisms towards this system of power-sharing, they do not leave the table and tend to be creative in bringing novel elements into the system to cope with the pressing new and old challenges.

Apparently, this 'temporary solution' of confessionalism seems to have survived and developed its own history and reality. This adaptability would further prolong its life in the future simply because the defence of non-sectarian alternatives does not attract the religio-political elites who occupy a disproportionally advantageous position in the Lebanese confessionalism. This is the reason why, rather than expecting a radical rupture towards, for instance, a secular restructuring of the system, one can anticipate further improvements and improvisations in the existing system of power-sharing.

However, the significant question here is whether these improvements and improvisations would gradually prepare the societal conditions for a future move towards a secular partition of power. In this regard, it would be meaningful to analyse the long history of the struggles for civil law and civil marriage in Lebanon. It can be argued that this seemingly micro-arena of struggle highlights many complexities, including the powers and weaknesses of the confessional system. Therefore, a brief history of these related struggles will be introduced in the next section as the mirror of weaknesses and strengths of the confessional system.

To offer some modest anticipations for these questions, we need to introduce the main pillars of the confessional system and the changes that it has undergone in relation to the unending political crises.

Current composition of the population and challenges arising from it

Despite the fact that no population census has been held in Lebanon since 1932 due to a fragile political balance between the Christian and Muslim populations, some projections estimate the total population as approximately 6,861,464 in 2019 (World Population Review, 2019). While the Christian population was estimated at around 34.9 per cent in 2011, Sunni and Shia Muslims were each considered to comprise 29.3 per cent of the population. According to the last official census held in 1932, the total population of Lebanon was only 786,000. In 1932, different Christian sects comprised 51.3 per cent of the population, while Muslim groups made up 48.8 per cent (Table 17.1).

There seems to be a drastic decline in the Christian population vis-á-vis the Muslims in Lebanon. Among the 1.5 million people that left the country, especially during and after the Civil War, Christians constituted a clear majority. This process that I consider as part of an ongoing de-Christianization in the Middle East and Africa (MENA) in general could be expected to have significant outcomes for the future of the confessional system in Lebanon as it further erodes the basis of power-sharing. Besides, the call for a post-sectarian Lebanon tends to intimidate the Christians in general as they are afraid of losing existing guarantees secured by the confessional system. They fear that the dismantling of the existing confessionalism without building a truly secular alternative would make them a fragile minority vis-á-vis an expanding Muslim majority.

After civil war broke out in Syria in 2011, nearly one million Syrian refugees – which roughly comprise one-quarter of the total population of Lebanon – have arrived in the country. This enormous refugee influx has considerably de-stabilized the country's demography,

Table 17.1 Percentage of Christian and Muslim Sects: 1913–2011

Year	1913	1932	1975	2011
Christians Maronite	58.3	28.8	23	19.3
Greek Orthodox	12.6	9.8	7	6.7
Greek Catholic	7.7	5.9	5	4.3
Other	0.8	6.8	5	4.2
Total Percentage	79.4	51.3	40	34.9
Muslims Shi'a	5.6	19.6	27	29.3
Sunni	3.5	22.4	26	29.3
Druze	11.4	6.8	7	5.4
Total Percentage	20.5	48.8	60	65.1
Total Population	414,963	786,000	2.5 M.	4.8 M.

Source: Salloukh et al. (2015).[1]

economy, and politics. Today approximately 400,000 Palestinian refugees (mostly Sunni) live in camps in the south of Lebanon, in areas originally home to Shia Muslims.

Economic and cultural factors that relate to the population composition

One of the key issues facing Lebanon is the economic and social impact of the Syrian crisis. The Syrian crisis has already hit a fragile Lebanese economy. The country continues to face several long-term structural weaknesses that predate the Syria crisis such as weak infrastructure, poor service delivery, institutionalized corruption, and bureaucratic inertia. The debt-to-GDP ratio was expected to persist in an unsustainable path, at 151 per cent by end-2018 – the third highest in the world (Lebanon Economic Monitor, 2018).

The Syrian Civil War cut off one of Lebanon's major markets and a transport corridor through the Levant. Syrian refugees have heightened social tensions and competition for low-skill jobs and public services, considerably straining Lebanon's public finances. The crisis is expected to worsen poverty incidence among Lebanese citizens as well as widen income inequality. According to an overview by the World Bank,

> it is estimated that as a result of the Syrian crisis, some 200,000 additional Lebanese have been pushed into poverty, adding to the erstwhile 1 million poor. An additional 250,000 to 300,000 Lebanese citizens are estimated to have become unemployed, most of them unskilled youth.
>
> *(World Bank in Lebanon, 2019)*

Bearing in mind the Palestinian refugee influx's de-stabilizing effects on Lebanese domestic politics in the second half of the twentieth century, it is not difficult to anticipate that Syrian refugees will continue to be one of the crucial political issues for the immediate future. The Syrian refugees have also brought their politicized sectarian identities, distrust, and fears emanating from their 'others'. They also sparked apprehension among the Lebanese who felt marginalized as either members of the already fragile Lebanese nation or members of a religious community with their own historical repertoire of fears and threats supposedly coming from other religious communities.

The overwhelming majority of Syrian refugees are Sunni and this may alter the sectarian proportions of the Lebanese confessional system. Dionigi argues that

> most political groups claiming to represent the Christian Lebanese community interpret this as a risk for the integrity of the national identity of Lebanon. It is not a coincidence that Christian political leaders have been the most vociferous promoters of the restrictive policies towards Syrian presence and its protraction. Similar to the previous cases, then, religious identity plays a role in the prospect of managing Syrian presence in Lebanon in the long term, because it impacts on the status quo of its confessional politics.
>
> *Dionigi (2017: 141)*

State-religion relations and religious diversity governance

State-religion relations in historical perspective

Before dealing with the new and persistent challenges that confessionalism is facing especially after the Syrian Civil War, we need to provide an outline of the crucial steps in the emergence of this system within the framework of historical developments.

For many centuries the Ottomans ruled Lebanon through powerful Druze families, with semi-autonomous Druze and Maronite regions. In the mid-nineteenth century, growing rivalry between Druze and Maronites resulted in brutal conflict between the two communities in the Mount Lebanon region. After a series of bloody battles during the 1860s in which thousands of Christians were killed, the Maronites gained an autonomous status under the protection of European powers.

The Ottoman authorities attempted to bring order in Mount Lebanon by creating a balance of power around the institution of *Mutasarrifiyya* between the Maronite and Druze communities (Traboulsi, 2009: 41–52).

> The Mutasarrifiyya system – under the protection of the European powers and following the '*Règlement Organique*' (1861), a form of communitarian division promoted by the Great Powers to pacify the Mount Lebanon area – brought the communities into politics and transformed civilian and religious institutions into political actors, which politicized collective identities by labelling them as 'Maronites', 'Druzes', or 'Sunnis.'
>
> *Di Peri and Meier (2017)*

Lebanon remained nominally under Ottoman control until the breakup of the Ottoman Empire after the First World War. Following the war, France was given the mandate of the area now comprised of Lebanon and Syria by the League of Nations. Under the auspices of the French mandate, a Constitution was written in 1926, while the 1932 census was realized to serve as a point of reference for the confessional partition of power over subsequent decades.

The 1926 Constitution further attributed confessionalism a privileged place in private and public life. To cite some examples, Article 9 obliges the state 'to render homage' to God, 'to respect all religions and sects and guarantee the freedom to hold religious rites under its protection', and to respect each sect's 'personal status laws and their religious welfare'. Article 10 buttressed this constitutional defence of sectarian autonomy by guaranteeing that education should not 'contravene the dignity of any religion or sect' and by granting each confessional group the right to operate its own private schools. Despite claiming to reflect the French system of *laïcité*, the 1926 Constitution recognized the need of continuing the

Ottoman-initiated confessional system. In this regard, it reflected a contradictory embrace of the French secular model and a practice based on the improvisation of Ottoman *millet* system in the form of confessionalism.

The Constitution created a parliamentary regime coupled with proportional representation along confessional lines, with a Christian president and a Sunni Muslim prime minister. However, it is ironic to remember that, according to the Article 95, this proportional sharing of state offices between the main confessions was to be temporary; it was anticipated that a Lebanese national identity would strengthen over time.

On 13 March 1936, the French High Commissioner Damien de Martel promulgated Decree No. 60 L.R. The Decree recognized 18 official sects in Lebanon – 12 Christian, five Muslim, and one Jewish – and their right to create and manage their own religious courts and to follow their own personal status and family laws (Di Peri & Meier, 2017). The officially recognized sects possessing their own personal status laws are the Maronite, Melkite, Armenian Catholic, Syriac Catholic, Roman Catholic, Chaldean, Greek Orthodox, Armenian Orthodox, Syriac Orthodox, Nestorian, Protestant, Sunni, Shia, Jafari, Druze, and Jewish sects. The 'Alawis, Ismailis, and Orthodox Copts are recognized by the state but do not have their own personal status laws and follow, respectively, the personal status laws of the Jafari and Orthodox laws.

The next, and perhaps more, crucial step towards confessionalism came with the 1943 National Pact when independence officially arrived. This unwritten pact between the Maronite and Sunni leaders was a supplement to the 1926 Constitution and carried equal weight. The pact asserted that neither Christians nor Muslims would seek foreign protection: not Christians from the West, nor Muslims from the East.

The National Pact distributed executive, legislative, and judicial powers based on a corporate confessional power-sharing arrangement. The power-sharing was based on the 1932 census – the last official census for political reasons explained below – and accordingly affixed a 5:6 ratio of Muslims to Christians in the state bureaucracy. It reserved the presidency to the Maronites. The Constitution deposited in the presidency substantial executive prerogatives, elevating it to the single most powerful office in the pre-Civil War state. The post of prime minister was given to the Sunni community while the Speaker of Parliament was to be elected by the Shia community.

As Table 17.1 clearly illustrates, this was a system biased towards the Christian population and also disproportionally empowered the president. However, demographic and political realities and developments that fuelled the Civil War made it imperative to work out another deal: the Ta'if Accord (1989).

Following the Second World War, Lebanon was hailed as one of the most stable countries of the region. Until the 1960s the National Pact seemed to have channelled existing conflicts into political avenues rather than violence, as the competing communities had a stake in national stability (Traboulsi, 2009: 100–128). The rise of Nasser's pan-Arabism had also de-stabilized Lebanese politics by reviving old tension in the new forms. In fact, during the Cold War, the initial rivalry between Lebanism and Arabism had gained a new character between pro-Western Christian Maronites and pro-Nasser Arabists.

The Palestinian refugee influx intensified in the 1970s and Palestinians' increasing assertiveness in Lebanese politics posed serious threats to the confessional system shaped around the 1943 National Pact. Christians set up armed militias against what they saw as an attempt by the Palestinian Liberation Organization (PLO) to seize Lebanon. In this strained climate, the Sunni groups attempted to use the PLO's presence as leverage to increase their status in the government. These groups also split into armed factions, competing among one another and against Christians.

In order to avoid a PLO takeover in Lebanon, Syria entered the conflict in 1976 and this led to the division of Lebanon into zones controlled by Syria, the PLO, and Maronite militias. The spiral of violence involved the minority Shia population as well, which set up its own militia, Amal, in the late 1970s. Inspired from the Iranian revolution in 1979, some Shia militants created a more religious militia named 'Hizbullah' (The Party of God). During the Israeli invasion of 1982, Hizbullah became the main resistance movement against the Israeli occupation of south Lebanon.

Syria assumed the leadership in bringing an end to the Civil War with the Ta'if Accord (1989). As a result of the war, at least 100,000 Lebanese were dead, tens of thousands had emigrated abroad, and an estimated 900,000 civilians were internally displaced.

Current institutional structure for governing religion and religious diversity

The Ta'if, also known as the Document of National Reconciliation, was more than a political settlement between warring parties; it was rather a constitutional remaking of the sectarian order under the supervision of regional and international mediators. In fact, the regulations introduced by the Ta'if Accord were also integrated into Lebanon's Constitution in 1990.

The outbreak in 1975 of the Civil War underscored the failure of the 1943 National Pact to manage the inherent contradictions of Lebanon's confessional politics, which were also exacerbated by domestic and external contests. Mirroring the domestic and regional balance of power, Ta'if shifted the balance of executive power away from the Maronite president, placing it instead in the Council of Ministers' collective capacity. The Council of Ministers, which is made up of a grand coalition of sects, became the real custodian of executive authority. The constitutional supremacy of the Maronites was finally and formally abolished and replaced by what has been called the rule of 'three presidents' or the Troika. In this new arrangement, the Maronite President of the Republic, the Sunni Prime Minister, and the Shia Speaker of the House were all placed at the same level of power. According to the new Constitution, none of the three leaders is able to unseat either of the other two (Reinkowski & Saadeh, 2006: 102).

This naturally empowered the Sunni prime minister's office, which now became an institution independent of the once all-powerful presidency. The Ta'if Accord also embodied the political and military rise of the Shia community and Syria's position as the post-war umpire of Lebanese affairs (Salloukh et al., 2015). The Ta'if Accord applied the principle of equitable confessional division of seats to Parliament and all other primary posts throughout state institutions. As Table 17.2 shows, Muslims and Christians are now represented equally in Parliament:

Table 17.2 Sectarian composition of post-Taif Parliament

Christians	Seats	Muslims	Seats
Maronites	34	Shia	27
Greek Orthodox	14	Sunnis	27
Greek Catholic	8	Druze	8
Armenian Orthodox	5	'Alawi	2
Armenian Catholic	1	—	—
Protestants	1	—	—
Christian Minorities	1	—	
Total Christians	64	Total Muslims	64

Source: Salloukh et al. (2015).

There is irony in the fact that the 1920 Constitution, 1943 National Pact, and Ta'if Accord (hence the 1990 Constitution) all committed to the abolition of confessionalism as a 'temporary solution'. The Ta'if Accord and 1990 Constitution went further, envisioning an institution to be installed by Parliament that would consider ways to achieve deconfessionalization (Reinkowski & Saadeh, 2006: 103). However, entrusting the religio-political elites – who have a vested interest in the confessional life – with the task of abolishing the life source of their existence is quite contradictory.

Even the confessional system's most ardent religious critics have made invaluable gains from it that they may not easily give up. Beyond material concerns, there are some minority sects that are wary of any significant change in the current system as they are afraid of losing what they have. Despite their unhappiness with the current confessional system, this fear makes them reluctant *status quoists*.

Moreover, not all proponents of de-confessionalization defend complete secularization. According to Reinkowski and Saadeh, there are roughly two different groups here.

> The first group ... argues for a political deconfessionalization, as is also stipulated in the Ta'if Accord. Deconfessionalization would thus concern only matters in the national political arena, while personal status law would be left to the rule of the respective confessional groups. The major objection to the idea of 'political' deconfessionalization, however, is that the proposed separation between a confessional and a non-confessional zone would not work. Laws and institutions in the confessional realm would easily breed a sectarian culture in all other areas of the body politic. Hence, the second group... advocates a complete secularization of the political system and society.
>
> *Reinkowski and Saadeh (2006: 104)*

Perhaps difficulties faced by supporters of civil law and civil marriage since independence can offer some ideas about the entrenched nature of the confessionalism in Lebanon. Indeed, one of the most significant struggles in Lebanon is related to the calls for a civil law and civil marriage independent of religious authorities. In fact, the 1926 Constitution envisioned the separation of state and religion in line with the French notion of *laïcité* and the introduction of a secular civil law as well. Yet religious authorities fiercely opposed any steps towards the realization of this goal as a direct infringement on their authorities and, on many occasions, forced the state to retreat. The emerging practice further empowered sectarian autonomy in family matters and education as well.

In the end, only citizens who did not belong to any of the 18 state-recognized sects, such as the Bahais, were allowed civil marriage in Lebanon. The 2 April 1951 law relegated all personal status matters to sectarian courts. It also stipulated that all sects should submit their personal status laws to the Lebanese state for ratification. However, most sects did not and continued to manage them autonomously.

These practices encouraged intra-sectarian marriages and hindered intermarriages among different sects, forcing citizens to be dependent on their respective sectarian institutions for personal status matters. As there is no alternative civil personal status law, there is no option outside the sectarian identities. Conversion to another sect was recognized within the logic of confessionalism, yet there was no lay option outside the religious authorities empowered by the confessional structure.

Consequently, in the Lebanese political system rights and entitlements have been allocated according to an individual's confessional affiliation; personal status laws, as well as the institutions through which these laws are applied, have been under the exclusive control of the religious authorities of Lebanon's officially recognized confessional groups. The main problems here are the denial of citizenship and caging of individuals inside sectarian identities. Despite several attempts to introduce civil law, a secular alternative has not emerged due to apparent state inefficacy and the unwillingness of religio-political elites.

Yet those struggles to overcome the impositions of sectarianism have also made significant legal and political gains. In 2007, Talal El-Husseini started an initiative to remove the religious denomination from registry records based on Article 11 of Decree No. 60 L.R., which states that any citizen who has reached legal age and does not suffer from any mental disability may exit or embrace a state-recognized sect and change her or his personal status (Salloukh et al., 2015: 36). Some others followed El-Husseini's precedent, and in 2009 the Ministry of Interior and Municipalities accepted applications where the section identifying a citizen's sectarian affiliation had been left blank, thus allowing for citizens to claim themselves outside the sectarian affiliation.

Another common practice against the sectarian straitjacket is to marry abroad in a civil ceremony and register in a foreign country's civil law. When a married couple adheres to another country's civil law, Lebanese civil courts must adjudicate marriage-related matters in line with the rules of the foreign country's civil law. This is an increasingly popular practice for bypassing sectarian imposition. In fact, some Christians opt for it to escape restrictions on divorce imposed by their individual sects.

Finally, Kholoud Succariyeh and Nidal Darwish were the first couple in Lebanon to have a civil marriage. Following El-Husseini's precedent, the couple deleted their sectarian affiliations and requested to register their civil marriage in the Lebanese civil courts (Merhi, 2012). Their marriage touched off a heated debate because it directly challenged the sectarian monopoly in marriage matters. Some prominent members of the political establishment such as Saad al-Hariri, Michel Aun, and then-President Michel Suleiman expressed their support for adopting a civil marriage law. The Council of Maronite Bishops argued that religious and civil marriages may coexist, while the Higher Islamic Shia Council and Hizbullah denounced civil marriage, as did the Sunni Mufti Mohammad Rashid Qabbani (Salloukh et al., 2015: 38).

Despite significant *de facto* gains realized by those willing to opt for non-sectarian and citizenship-based alternatives, there is still no recognition of an optional or compulsory civil personal status law. In fact, the sectarian elite seem to be determined to impede access to a basic civic right. Nevertheless, these legal and political struggles have significantly weakened the hegemony of the sectarian system.

Recent political challenges to the Lebanese Confessionalism

Although the Ta'if Accord ended the Civil War, Lebanon has remained an insecure and occasionally violent place. Hizbullah's prominent place on the national scene, the continued influence of Syria and Iran, emergence of a Saudi-US-supported political bloc, the frustrations of Christian sects due to their increasing sense of loss of power, and Israel's demonstrated willingness to intervene militarily continue to complicate domestic tensions. All these tensions have also prepared a fertile ground for religious radicalization. Yet the eruption of the Syrian Civil War in 2011 was perhaps the most severe crisis that Lebanon has faced since the end of its Civil War in 1990.

The Ta'if Accord also recognized the growing Syrian domination (1990–2005) in Lebanon which also significantly changed the *de facto* and *de jure* balance of power between Christians and Muslims in the latter's favour. Maronite-dominated Lebanon gave way to

Muslim-dominated Lebanon during the Syrian domination. Since then the country has been locked in a fierce Sunni-Shia power struggle over control of the post-Syrian Lebanese state. Within this context, Christians have felt increasingly marginalized and resented Syrian suzerainty – and Sunni Muslim domination in particular. Syrian domination indirectly contributed to the empowerment of the confessional system since Syrian authorities found it easier to rule with divide-and-rule tactics by playing off Muslims against Christians.

In the 1990s Sunni Lebanese felt themselves as the most powerful and optimistic group, especially under the leadership of Prime Minister Refik Hariri. Indeed, 'Harirism' as a moderate socio-political phenomenon turned out to be the most significant bastion against the calls for Sunni radicalism. Yet in the aftermath of Hariri's assassination in 2005, Sunnism inexorably started to face an erosion regarding its weight in Lebanese politics. The new status of the Sunni community in Lebanon became one of political, social, and economic marginalization vis-á-vis the unexpected rise of Shia community under the flagship of Hizbullah.

The domestic, regional, and international struggle for Syria effectively divided the Lebanese between proponents and opponents of regime change in Damascus along a Sunni-Shia fault line. With Hizbullah's increasing involvement in the Syrian Civil War, regional Sunni-Shia rivalry, spearheaded by Saudi Arabia and Iran, has inevitably fostered a destabilizing effect on the Lebanese politics.

The Sunni community's fear of 'Syrian-Iranian tutelage' over Lebanon as well as the prevailing notion of the 'Sunnis as victims of Shia power' seems to have empowered the legitimacy of radical Sunni groups. For instance, the Shia image of Hizbullah, progressively built up as a foe as the group responsible for the Sunnis' disempowerment and vulnerability, largely contributed to shaping Sunni radicalism's claim of defending the Sunnis' pride and honour in Lebanon.

Just as Sunnis fear what they consider Shia radicalization, Shia Lebanese are also increasingly intimidated by what they perceive as 'the Sunni Salafism' and its domestic ramifications. The fear of Daesh and other *takfiri* groups[2] is seen as the factor welding many Shia men and women to Hizbullah, which does not seem to face recruitment problems for its military operations in the war in Syria.

Concluding remarks

Compared to the authoritarian regimes of the MENA, Lebanon possesses significant advantages from the existence of a tradition of parliamentary democracy. But this political system is strictly defined in line with sectarian identities, and the religio-political elites are extremely exclusionary. Despite these inherent problems, the Lebanese political system could survive and adapt itself to the strained conditions. This adaptive power seems to be the most significant asset as a potential mechanism for solving the problems discussed in this chapter.

Yet despite legitimate calls for a post-sectarian or secular Lebanon, the weak state capacity inherent in the confessional system, political crises exacerbated by geographical uncertainties, and the exclusionary nature of the religio-political elites make any step towards reform almost impossible in the short- and medium-term.

The creative and dynamic initiatives in the area of civil law and civil marriage, however, can further contribute to the ongoing legal gains. There is emerging an active civil society in defence of a trans-sectarian inclusive citizenship as well as interest-based rather than identity-based political affiliations. Empowerment of trans-sectarian interactions could also contribute to the elimination of the trust problem among the different sectors of Lebanon compartmentalized in their communities.

Notes

1 It should be noted that that last population census held in 1932 was the basis of the power-sharing in 1943. Since then no census has been held due to the fragile nature of the political balance among different confessions. These numbers, except 2017, were compiled by the authors of Salloukh et al., *Politics of Sectarianism in Post-War Lebanon*. For 1913 figures, see Ghassan Salamé, Al-Mujtama' wal-Dawla fil-Mashriq al-'Arabi (Beirut: Markaz Dirasat al-Wihda al-'Arabiya, 1987), p. 103. For 1932 and 1975, see Helena Cobban, The Making of Modern Lebanon (London: Hutchinson, 1985), p. 16. For 2011, see "Min Ayna Yabda' Ilgha' al-Nizam al-Ta'ifi fi Lubnan," al-Safir, 2 June 2011.
2 *Takfiri*: Pronouncement that someone is a non-believer (*kafir*) and no longer Muslim. Takfir is used in the modern era for sanctioning violence against leaders of Islamic states who are deemed insufficiently religious. Source: Oxford Islamic Studies Online, http://www.oxfordislamicstudies.com/article/opr/t125/e2319

References

Barkey, Karen. (2008). *Empire of Difference: The Ottomans in Comparative Perspective*. New York: Cambridge University Press.
Clark, Janine & Salloukh, Bassel F. (2013). Elite Strategies, Civil Society and Sectarian Identities in Post-War Lebanon. *International Journal of Middle East Studies* 45, 731–749.
Cobban, Helena. (1985). *The Making of Modern Lebanon*. London: Hutchinson.
Di Peri, Rosita & Meier, Daniel (eds). (2017). *Lebanon Facing the Arab Uprisings: Constraints and Adaptation*. London: Palgrave Macmillan.
Dionigi, Filippo. (2017). Statehood and Refugees: Patterns of Integration and Segregation of Refugee Populations in Lebanon from a Comparative Perspective. *Middle East Law and Governance* 9, 113–146.
Kingston, Paul. (2013). *Reproducing Sectarianism: Advocacy Networks and the Politics of Civil Society in Post-War Lebanon*. New York: The State University of New York.
Lebanon Economic Monitor. (2018, Fall). Available at: https://www.worldbank.org/en/country/lebanon/publication/lebanon-economic-monitor-fall-2018.
Lijphart, Arendt. (1977). *Democracy in Plural Societies*. New Haven: Yale University.
Makdisi, Ussama. (1996). Reconstructing the Nation-State: The Modernity of Sectarianism in Lebanon. Middle East Report 200 (July/September), 23–26.
Merhi, Zeinab. (2012, October 8). *Civil Marriage in Lebanon: The Time Is Now*. Beirut: al-Akhbar.
"Min Ayna Yabda' Ilgha' al-Nizam al-Ta'ifi fi Lubnan," al-Safir, 2 June 2011, Beirut.
Modood, Tariq. (2019). *Essays on Secularism and Multiculturalism*. London: ECPR and Rowman and Littlefield.
Reinkowski, Maurus & Saadeh, Sofia. (2006). A Nation Divided: Lebanese Confessionalism. In Haldun Gülalp (ed.), *Citizenship and Ethnic Conflict: Challenging the Nation-State*. London: Routledge.
Salamé, Ghassan. (1987). *Al-Mujtama' wal-Dawla fil-Mashriq al-'Arabi*. Beirut: Markaz Dirasat al-Wihda al-'Arabiya.
Salloukh, Bassel F., et al. (2015). *The Politics of Sectarianism in the Post-War Lebanon*. London: Pluto Press.
Traboulsi, Fawwaz. (2009). *A History of Modern Lebanon*. London: Pluto Press.
World Bank in Lebanon. (2019). Available at: https://www.worldbank.org/en/country/lebanon/overview (Last updated April).
World Population Review. (2019). Available at: http://worldpopulationreview.com.

18

Egypt

Religious diversity in an age of securitisation

H.A. Hellyer

Introduction

The Arab Republic of Egypt overlaps the two continents of Africa and Asia, sitting at the heart of the Arab world and the wider Middle East, and at a point bordering the Mediterranean Sea that brings together many languages, religions, and ethnicities. The most populous Arab country and third most populous on the African continent, Egypt's historical heritage is traced back to the sixth millennium before Christ, spawning a vast academic literature around its Classical period.

Modern Egypt was founded a century ago when it emerged as a nominally independent monarchy, and then an Arab republic following the military coup led by Gamal Abdel Nasser. Its cultural impact on the rest of the Arab world – and further beyond via the presence of the Azhari religious establishment – should not be underestimated.

As a country with a population of 108 million (Diwan, Houry & Sayigh 2020) and a history stretching so far back, Egypt naturally has a long, multi-layered, and rich history of religious diversity (Pérez-Accino, 2019). But modern Egypt's religious landscape is far less layered compared to its past.

Sunni Muslims make up about 90 per cent of Egypt's population, while the remaining 10 per cent are Christians (El-Gergawi, 2016). The Coptic Orthodox Church accounts for 90 per cent of Egypt's Christians, while the rest include Anglican, Episcopalian, and other Protestant denominations; Jehovah's Witnesses; Mormons; Greek and Syrian Orthodox; and Armenian Apostolic. The country also has Bahai,[1] Shia Muslim, and Jewish communities, as well as small atheist and agnostic populations. Judaism remains recognised but only a handful of its Egyptian followers remain in the country (El-Gergawi, 2016). However, there are no reliable estimates or figures for these smaller groups.

Below, Egypt's history in context is elaborated upon in relation to religious diversity, from early in its modern history until the present day. Egypt's regulatory framework, as well as the role of the law and other state apparatuses, is then explored in relation to the same.

H.A. Hellyer

Historical overview

Modern Egypt saw a deeply multi-religious society at the turn of the twentieth century and was then occupied by the British Empire from 1882 to 1956, when the last British troops departed. Until the 1940s, one could speak quite commonly of Egyptians from various ethnic and religious groupings; Christians, Jews, Muslims; Latins, Bedouins, Greeks, and so forth. During that period, followers of different faiths lived equally in relative harmony, each contributing significantly to the country's rich cultural, economic, and political arenas. Monarchic Egypt was home to influential and largely independent Islamic and Coptic religious institutions as well as a sizeable Jewish community, with relatively liberal laws, tolerant and diverse social decorum and a chaotic, but comparatively free political atmosphere allowing these religions to co-exist peacefully.

However, following the establishment of Israel in British-mandated Palestine in 1948, a range of sentiments abounded in Egypt, among both officialdom and the public. Perceived notions that Israel received support from Egyptian Copts and Jews, which coincided with public debate about national identity following the collapse of the Ottomans in 1924 amidst colonial divide-and-rule policies, culminated in tensions between Muslim and non-Muslim Egyptians. Soaring nationalistic sentiment and resulting measures led to the forced departure from their motherland of many members of historically non-Arab communities such as Jewish-Egyptians, Greek-Egyptians, and Latin-Egyptians.

In 1952, a military coup led by the Free Officers Movement, whose members had varying religious affiliations and visions, ended the Egyptian monarchy. The country's three-star flag resembling its diverse population was replaced with one symbolising the Arab nationalist identity that now overpowered all others. With the new Egyptian state preoccupied with transitioning from a monarchy to a republic and eliminating its internal rivals as well as expelling the British presence from Egypt, little attention was paid to relations between religious communities and rather focussed on each grouping individually.

Even though the state claimed to be a neutral protector of Egypt's three main religious communities – the Muslims, Christians, and Jews – its security agencies and political elite problematised Jews for alleged ties to Israel. The new military authorities restricted civil liberties and political freedoms and thus began to co-opt Muslims, Christians, and non-religious public figures, movements, and institutions – a process that was used by subsequent regimes to settle scores against rival political entities. For instance, Gamal Abdul-Nasser, who became president in 1954, waged a war against certain Islamist movements, particularly the Muslim Brotherhood, with inflammatory nationalistic sentiments and communist rhetoric. Nasser's successor, Anwar El Sadat, who came to power in 1970, empowered the same Islamist groups – particularly the Muslim Brotherhood – to curtail the Nasserist political trend and leftists as he opened the country's market and led it down the path of more neo-liberal capitalism. Over the course of the following decades, the Egyptian state reduced the space for independent religious institutions in a bid to engage in a culture war against oppositional Islamist groups; this, in turn, may well have led to the undermining of credibility of those institutions in Egypt and increased the influence of self-taught, and self-proclaimed, religious leaders.

Abdel-Nasser's conflict with Islamist movements, especially the Muslim Brotherhood, began in 1954, when an attempt on the life of the country's new ruler was attributed to them. A period of crackdown, which began in 1956, ended with the execution of their founder, Hassan al-Banna, and the arrest and imprisonment of many of his followers.

Since rising to the helm, late President Sadat appeared more aligned with finding some common cause with oppositional centrist Islamist movements and willing to amplify a more publicly religious identity. His 1971 constitutional amendments made Islam a main source of legislation, presumably to win over conservative support, and this has since been maintained, including in the current Constitution, which was passed in 2014 and amended in 2019. Like earlier constitutions, it acknowledges the three Abrahamic religions, and its third article states that Judaism and Christianity are the sources of legislation for personal status law for their adherents.

With time, relations between religious communities grew more sensitive domestically. In the 1970s, this developed into an issue of international concern as the extremist Islamist crisis began to surface. Many Islamists who were imprisoned and tortured under Nasser's regime became radicalised in jail. They were then released by Sadat into an Egyptian society that was increasingly importing austere purist Salafi interpretations of Islam from oil-rich Arabian Gulf countries where thousands of mostly low-skilled labourers migrated for work. The labourers, who generally received low levels of religious education in Egypt, were influenced significantly by their time in the Gulf.

New rounds of securitisation in the 1980s and 1990s followed Sadat's assassination in 1981 by extremists for making peace with Israel in 1973. Stories of mistreatment in Egypt's detention centres helped both the Brotherhood and Salafi groups like Ansar al-Sunna and al-Gama'a al-Islamiyaa gain some sympathy in Egyptian society. This paved the way to the current charged atmosphere of mistrust from which Egypt suffers. Asef Bayat argues:

> The major difference lay in the fact that Egypt began to develop a fairly powerful Islamist movement since the presidency of Anwar Sadat who paid lip service to the rising 'Islamic Associations' in the universities as a way to undermine the Nasserist nationalists and communists as he was drawing close to the West. These Islamic Associations grew and, in the process, got radicalized by the 1980s during (President Hosni) Mubarak's rule, turning into the insurgent al-Gama'a al-Islamiyya and al-Jihad. Together with the powerful Muslim Brotherhood, who had maintained their non-violent strategy, and other emerging groups, Egypt experienced a strong 'Islamic mode' during the 1990s and early 2000s. Egypt's Islamism developed basically outside and even in opposition to al-Azhar or the institution of the ulema.
>
> *Gokmen (2016)*

When the revolutionary uprising in 2011 took place, an environment of political freedom and openness occurred for the first time in decades. On the one hand, this allowed for extensive media freedom, and religious and ideologically based media outlets sprouted at unprecedented rates. On the other hand, it unleashed a populist rhetoric with hues of intolerance, sectarianism, and austerity that became more visible in certain parts of the pro-Islamist public sphere, along with developments in terms of extremism which shall be discussed later in this chapter (see the section 'Law and the judiciary').

In this environment of freedom, the Muslim Brotherhood – which had been a banned political group for most of its existence since 1924, owing to its being identified as an extremist group at different times by the political and military establishment – was allowed to partake freely in the political sphere, joined by the nascent but significantly popular Salafi political players. The Brotherhood scored pluralities in the elections following the 2011 revolt, winning a plurality in Parliament and reaching the presidency for the first time. Salafi political parties achieved electoral yields that were remarkable for new political players. This new political dominance of these types of Islamists alarmed religious minorities and non-Muslim

Brotherhood and non-Salafi politicians in the country. This anxiety was shared by many who were not supportive of growing Muslim Brotherhood and Salafi political influence, whose fear for their own religious and civil liberties were heightened by anti-Islamist, or anti-change, media outlets.

This deep polarisation ultimately led to the 2013 army-led ousting of the Muslim Brotherhood's president Mohamed Morsi following widespread protests. Morsi's arrest along with thousands of other party leaders and supporters in an ongoing crackdown was harshly criticised by local and international human rights organisations. Laws were passed criminalising any association with the movement – which was designated a terrorist group – and anyclaimed connected ideologies. Pro-army media outlets published a variety of accusations alongside vilification campaigns against its sympathisers. However, most supporters of much of the Salafi political trend escaped the same harsh fate, although they have also seen their political involvement marginalised.

The forced dispersal of pro-Morsi sit-ins, resulting in a substantial loss of life of protesters, triggered a string of attacks on churches by angry Brotherhood sympathisers who perceived Christians as key supporters of the Army's move to overthrow then-president Morsi. It also sparked a rise and intensification in terrorist attacks that has killed hundreds of policemen, army personnel, and civilians since 2013. This rise in violence was then instrumentalised by the authorities to justify their clampdown on dissent as part of their 'war on terror', including other types of opposition groups who were accused of belonging to the outlawed Muslim Brotherhood, which previously they had clearly opposed.

Regulatory framework

The Egyptian state's approach to religious diversity since 1952 has been and continues to be reactionary and largely dormant. This means that the state usually only acts in order to contain an outburst of violence or periodically issues perfunctory reassurances that all Egyptians are seen as equal rather than adopting and enforcing consistent policies that protect equality on the ground.

As such, the regime maintains that Article 64 of the Constitution – which states that 'freedom of religion is absolute' – continues to provide sufficient guarantees for Egyptians to practise and hold other non-Abrahamic belief. At the same time, those falling outside of the three Abrahamic religions – for instance, atheists, Bahais, and agnostics – continue to be largely unacknowledged by the state and its laws.

Article 64 has also not removed bureaucratic limitations, some of which date back to the Ottoman-era, restraining Copts' ability to build places of worship, for example (Abouelenein & Abdellah, 2016). Until 2016, a 1934 interior ministry law had been in place forbidding construction of churches near schools or railway stations (Mazel, 2016). In 2016, Coptic leaders praised the partial lifting of some of its restrictions, such as the requirement to obtain permission from security agencies before building churches. The 2016 law does, however, maintain the authorities' right to choose the size of the church based on the number of Christians in its area. This is a calculation that is difficult to assess since the government does not accept independent tallies of Christians by church leaders nor does it count them itself (Abouelenein & Abdellah, 2016).

Other constitutional articles that do provide more protections, such as Article 65 that guarantees freedom of expression, are constrained by the vaguely worded Penal Code Articles 98 (f), 160, and 161 (Barsoum, 2016). Even though the constitution's legal authority overrides the Penal Code, these statutes are routinely employed by authorities to prosecute people for their expressed views (ibid.). Since 2011, there have been at least 63 such cases, and in 2017 the US Commission on International Religious Freedom ranked Egypt sixth globally for blasphemy laws (The Economist, 2017).

Even when there are no penal or civil codes obstructing the application of liberal constitutional provisions like Article 53 that criminalises religion-based discrimination, the state does not apply them consistently across the board. For example, it is difficult for Muslims to change their religion status on their national ID, although it is possible for Christians to change theirs to Islam. The Bahais were, according to press reports, able to come close to getting recognition on their national ID; after suing the government, in 2009 they managed to achieve the right to replace their religious identification with a dash (-) (Human Rights Watch, 2009).

Outside civil rights matters, Article 2, which states that the principles of the Sharia are the principal source of legislation, has had little impact on Egyptian laws, whose French origins (in terms of civil law) are a relic of France's nineteenth-century occupation. It is important to note that Article 2 acts as a restraining mechanism in terms of legal precedent, rather than an active positive law-making mechanism that then results in further legislation one way or another.

There are, however, signs that the state's approach to governing relations between religious communities may change or become more proactive in the near- or medium-term. President Sisi has been attending Christmas mass celebrations since 2016, sending an objectively small, but rare and significant message of inclusion to the public as he is the first Egyptian president to do so (Xinhua, 2018). At the same time, the increase in prosecutions of perceived insults to religion signalled to many a change of state's policy of indifference towards non-conformists that was present prior to the rise of Islamist radicalisation (Darwish, 2015).

Law and the judiciary

Egypt witnessed an unprecedented legislative expansion after June 2013 to consolidate the authorities' priorities vis-à-vis Egypt's version of the 'war on terror' and also contain all perceived threats to the regime from the January 2011 uprising. A number of these measures indirectly impact upon governing diversity, in terms of combating what the state assesses as extremism.

Beyond the civilian judiciary system, military courts have also been pivotal in prosecuting suspects of terrorism charged with targeting army facilities or members of the armed forces, including conscripts. Imposing a state of emergency and the enactment of the emergency law, particularly in North Sinai and following the bombing of Saint Mark's Coptic Orthodox Cathedral in Alexandria in April 2017, has helped the regime reproduce the Courts of State Security, characterised by their hasty trials and unappealable sentences.

Furthermore, Law 25 of 2018 ushered in the creation of the Supreme Council for Combating Extremism, whose task is to develop counter-terrorism strategies at the national and regional levels. This has included drafting developmental schemes for marginalised regions and compiling educational curricula to serve these goals. Security apparatuses dominate the Council, which is characterised by a lack of transparency in its deliberations and decisions that allows for little to be known of its composition, role, and real impact. The General Intelligence Directorate, Military Intelligence, the National Security Agency (formerly State Security), and the Administrative Control Authority – which is directly controlled by the president – are all represented on this council.

Religious institutions

The Ministry of Endowments (MoE) plays a particularly active role by virtue of its authority over mosques. Its primary focus is dismantling potential channels of communication between the public and organisations of extremist Islamism and less radical groups that can take place through mosques and their facilities. These measures also have a bearing on governing religious diversity, as the MoE's efforts to further the state narrative introduce additional ways through which the state controls religious expression.

As such, Law 51 of 2014 stipulates that religious sermons must be authorised by imams of Al-Azhar and delivered only by those appointed by the MoE. Temporary permits issued for imams to deliver sermons allow for the continuous monitoring of their compliance to such regulations.

Informal prayer halls, or smaller mosques known as '*zawaya*', were brought under the MoE's supervision by Decree No. 64 of 2014. Since 2013, the ministry has reportedly shut down nearly 20,000 *zawaya*.

The MoE also undertook initiatives to safeguard youth from being recruited by extremists. Examples include the 'Schools of Knowledge' initiative launched in 2017 that involves imams teaching religious curricula to the public in schools operating in major mosques.

Similarly, many female preachers have been reportedly appointed to track women, who account for the majority of donations made to support extremist groups and political religious groups that oppose the state. A ban on financial activity by non-government entities in mosques has also been imposed by MoE decree.

Al-Azhar, the world's pre-eminent seat of religious learning for Sunni Muslims, is also active. One of its vital instruments is al-Azhar's 'Observatory to Combat Extremism' with its social media platforms, which spread its interpretation of Islam in 12 languages. It also tracks terrorist operations and discourses in various countries, as well as engages in studies related to them.

As for its role at home, al-Azhar's efforts include representatives holding communal instructional sessions within local communities that largely target university students nationwide. This invariably is likely to buttress an Egyptian national identity that is respectful of religious diversity in the country, particularly vis-à-vis Christian communities.

That said, a significant contribution by al-Azhar is its collective set of amendments to the institution's learning curricula after 2013. The objective was to revise and eliminate excerpts of the curricula that were deemed too outdated and at odds with modern times. These updated curricula are reportedly subject to assessment every three years. However, if the changes are not done carefully, this may actually lead to graduates being unable to properly contextualise classical texts, which will leave those open to misinterpretation by extremists.

Finally, Dar al-Ifta' ('House of Religious Verdicts') is another government institution that launched its own media-focussed Monitoring Observatory to examine radical views, including sectarianism, and refute them on social media.

Here, it is pertinent to describe 'sectarianism', which is described by Ussama Makdisi (2000) as a culture. In the culture of sectarianism, religion-based fault lines between social categories that were once unnoticed or dormant jolt to life, or erupt, under governances that contribute to the construction of sociodemographic categories based on religious differences, remapping people, redistributing wealth and power, and emphasising divisions.

The extent to which these three institutions influence people's acceptance of religious diversity and tolerance towards other religious communities remains unclear. Similarly, their outreach among youth and other social groups cannot be accurately assessed in a definitive manner. However, it is likely that their efforts on the ground are limited in impact because of the multi-layered gaps separating them from the average citizen and their day to day problems.

On the other hand, the Coptic Church has always had a much stronger impact and outreach among Egypt's Coptic Christian community as a minority community indelibly affected by this institution. The historic institution has long maintained a monopoly over the voice of Egypt's largest religious minority and a degree of institutional independence, which it secured by maintaining a close relationship with the regime (Fahmi, 2014). For instance, the church refused to apply a Supreme Court ruling in 2010 to allow the remarriage of Copts who were divorced by the judiciary, on the basis that it clashed with the Bible's teachings.[2]

The church's political involvement and its monopoly in representing the Copts began to change in the final years of Mubarak's rule. Driven by frustration at the state's lack of action to stop discrimination or secure equality among Egyptians of all faiths, many Coptic youths rejected the church's submissiveness to the state and broke from its grip to join young opposition movements, beginning a journey of political activism that drew more of Coptic community. The shift in the church's political involvement was sharpest during Morsi's one-year tenure, which saw the church openly supporting his unseating by the army.

Morsi's overthrow contributed to a dangerous schism in Egyptian society as many of his supporters began deeply resenting those sectors of society opposed to Morsi, particularly Christians, who reportedly had participated – alongside most other sectors of Egyptian society – in mass protests against Morsi's rule in the lead-up to the overthrow and whom his supporters blamed for the state violence that ensued. As previously noted, in the wake of his overthrow, Morsi's supporters attacked some 220 churches and Christian properties across Egypt following the August 2013 mass killings at Raba'a al-Adawiya and al-Nahda. Egyptians on both sides of the conflict, with help and instigation from relentless propaganda from state-controlled and pro-Muslim Brotherhood media, came to see each other as existential opponents intent on destroying each other (Coleman, 2012).

Since 2013, what are left of Egypt's different political groups exist in name only, are thoroughly of the government, or have seen their activity severely curtailed, while mutual feelings of animosity and distrust continue unabated between significant portions of Egypt's religious communities. As previously indicated, incidents of communal violence against Christians have been on the rise in Upper Egypt, while substantial adherents to Sufi orders are harassed by Islamist extremists in North Sinai and elsewhere.

Securitisation and diversity

Terrorist groups like the so-called 'Islamic State of Iraq and Syria' [ISIS] and their supporters have targeted Christians in different parts of the country, causing many deaths despite a massive counter-terrorism effort by the state. This intense security crackdown potentially contributed to the country's vulnerability to extremist narratives and has directly impinged on the societal governance of religious communities and diversity. For instance, the state and its bodies co-opted numbers of community forces in the border provinces, where terrorist groups are mostly based. There, the state reached an understanding with area tribes to facilitate the arrest of wanted terrorists who rely on logistical support from locals.

Furthermore, nearly a decade later, authorities still hold mosques in a strict framework, closing unlicensed ones and outlawing non-state-sanctioned Friday sermons on the pretext of fighting terrorism. As ties between Muslims and Christians soured in different localities, interfaith discourse and counter-extremism strategies have been state-led. Moreover, the continuing suppression and restriction of political activity has taken a great toll on civil society, shutting down NGOs and stifling political parties critical of the state. As such, attempts to bridge differences between the various religious communities are overshadowed by securitisation, with state policy driven by the crackdown on rising extremism. According to some analysts, securitising the issue of religious diversity reflects the lack of a genuine political will to undertake legal and social reforms that guarantee all citizens equal civil and religious rights, or at least consider it as an overriding concern in the ongoing campaign to combat extremism and terrorism (Ibrahim, 2015).

This securitisation is particularly evident in the state's handling of recurring sectarian disputes, especially in provinces of Upper Egypt where sectarian mobs clash with their Coptic neighbours and often attack their properties. These are often seen as 'conflicts over the practice of religious rituals, conflicts over consensual sexual and emotional relationships, conflicts relating to the expression of opinion on religious issues, conflicts resulting from community disputes, conflicts arising from political differences and finally, conflicts resulting from the exploitation of Copts as a minority group, such as kidnappings or financial blackmail' (ibid.: 5). Sectarian clashes are reportedly regularly minimised by different state officials as isolated cases are influenced by 'foreign actors' and only taken seriously when resulting in terrorist attacks (Kaldas, 2019). Typically, the disputants are brought together by 'customary reconciliation councils' whose composition varies depending on the reason behind the dispute and where it took place, but often include politicians, community leaders, and security personnel (Ibrahim, 2015: 16). The outcomes of these arbitration councils are also seen as varied and inconsistent, which deepens sectarian divisions more than it reconciles the disputants. As the Egyptian Initiative for Personal Rights report notes: 'the desire to impose rapid calm and the fear of escalating violence casts a shadow over the decisions of customary sessions'; moreover, they, 'tend to favour the stronger party at the expense of the weaker one, i.e. the Christian party in most instances' (ibid.: 44).

In late 2018, Egyptian President Abdel-Fattah El Sisi announced the formation of a committee to combat sectarianism in Egypt (State Information Service, 2018). The announcement was welcomed as progress away as its function would shift authorities away from the extra-judicial reconciliation councils whose members are often untrained to conduct such tasks, and are of an overwhelming Muslim majority, rather than engaging more widely with Christian citizens at this level of leadership and coordination.

This agency's formation continues the tradition of the state's securitisation of this issue as it consists of members of the Armed Forces, military intelligence, general intelligence, the Administrative Control Authority, and the National Security Agency. The agency is chaired by the president's advisor on security and anti-terrorism affairs, who currently is the interior minister (Kaldas, 2019). The committee does not include representatives of either the judiciary or legislature, nor does it include any experts in human or civil rights. This makes it difficult for it to conduct a neutral, legal dialogue that could lead to reforms. Most noticeably, its membership lacks widespread representation of the religious minorities that it is tasked to protect (ibid.). Overall, this committee reflects the security-based view that dominates the handling of Egypt's Coptic community and other religious groupings.

Concluding remarks

In many ways, the state's official narrative on governing religious diversity has promoted a respect for an Egyptian national identity that values minority communities, specifically Christian ones.

At the same time, many of its strategies are overshadowed by a focus on securitisation that curtails effective strategies that would benefit from involving more substantial societal engagement.

As noted, approximately 90 per cent of Egyptians are Sunni Muslims and the vast majority of the remaining population are followers of Coptic Orthodox Christianity. This, combined with the fact that Egypt has been run by a strongly military-influenced Nasserite republican model since 1952, limits public discussion on such a sensitive issue as religious diversity, except in the modes that the state supports. The exception was the period between the 2011 uprising and the end of the democratic experiment in 2013 when Egyptian activists interested in religious diversity issues experienced an opening for such discussions. Society cannot sufficiently address bigotry and sectarianism effectively when doing so may be perceived as challenging public order. At present, this is the space that civil society actors find themselves within, and thus limit their activity, preferring to avoid scenarios where they might find themselves crossing lines that the state finds problematic.

The credibility of the roles of religious institutions was also skewed by their relations with the state. This likely diminished their legitimacy as trusted bodies capable of delivering independent and unbiased views on religion to Muslims and others more generally. State-approved efforts on their part have often been perceived as unlikely to resonate with the masses. While the Ministry of Islamic Endowments and Dar al-Ifta', as fully integrated state entities, have become subordinate to state narratives, Al-Azhar continues to vie for independence, which is only met by more tension with the state more widely. It is thus difficult to gauge these institutions' impact on the ground.

Ironically, actors who engaged in violence in 1980s and 1990s, like al-Gamaa al-Islamiyya and Al-Jihad, previously had more of a counter-radicalisation impact. Their earlier experience and revised stance vis-à-vis modern 'jihadi' narratives as a concept possibly worked in their favour. This history of 'jihadism' enables factions like the Salafi Call and Al-Gamaa Al-Islamiyya to engage in intellectual debates with Salafi jihadists on modern discussions on jihad as a concept, as well as on relations with state and society. However, the credibility of these groups among hard-line, yet more centrist, Islamists was impacted by their political positions post-2013.

As such, one might note that the regulatory framework that currently exists in Egypt via the judiciary, religious institutions, and the overall securitisation of diversity, makes it clear that there is much work to be done. Egypt has many resources to draw on in terms of effectively tackling sectarianism and highlighting the plurality that it historically has enjoyed and benefited from. However, against the current climate, that potential is not likely to be met without a significant amount of reform.

Notes

1 The Bahais are an offshoot of Shia Islam – the religion dates back to the nineteenth century. It is not recognised as a part of Shia Islam by Shia Muslims, nor do Bahais consider themselves as such.
2 'The decision of the Holy Synod regarding the subject of the second marriage for divorcees, against the religion's teachings', 9 June 2010, https://st-takla.org/News/Holy-Synod-Statements/2010-06-09__Regarding-Second-Marriage-01.html

References

Abouelenein, Ahmed & Abdellah Mohamed. (2016, August 30). *Egyptian Parliament Approves Long-awaited Church Building Law*. Reuters. Available at: https://www.reuters.com/article/us-egypt-politics-religion/egyptian-parliament-approves-long-awaited-church-building-law-idUSKCN1152KK.

Ahmed, Nouran S. (2019). Toward understanding violence and revising counter-violence policies in southern Mediterranean. *Euromesco*, April. Available at: https://is.gd/wJCITU.

Al-Mishtawy, Mohamed. (2014, October 18). Arrested by the Interior Ministry and Dumped in the garbage: Mischievous Sayed [in Arabic]. *Masr Al-Arabia*. Available at: https://is.gd/YShNq1.

Arij. (n.d.). Made in Prison [in Arabic]. Available at: https://arij.net/made_in_prison/.

Awad, Mokhtar & Hashem, Mostafa. (2015). *Egypt's Escalating Islamist Insurgency*. Paper. Carnegie Middle East Centre. Available at: https://is.gd/qVZM6I.

Ayyash, Abdelrahman. (2019). *Strong Organization, Weak Ideology*. Arab Reform for Initiative. Available at: https://is.gd/34SxEH.

Barsoum, Marina. (2016, May 15). Egypt's anti-blasphemy law: Defence of religion or tool for persecution? *Ahram Online*. Available at: english.ahram.org.eg/NewsContent/1/151/216896/Egypt/Features/Egypts-antiblasphemy-law-Defence-of-religion-or-to.aspx.

Birdsall, Nancy. (1999). *Putting Education to Work in Egypt*. Paper. Carnegie Endowment Center for International Peace. Available at: https://carnegieendowment.org/1999/08/25/putting-education-to-work-in-egypt-pub-685%20Car.

Byers, Bryan D. & Jones, James A. (2007). The impact of the terrorist attacks of 9/11 on anti-Islamic hate crime. *Journal of Ethnicity in Criminal Justice*, 5(1): 43–56.

Central Agency for Public Mobilization and Statistics. (n.d.). Percentage of those unable to afford the cost of obtaining food only (cost of survival). *Graph* [in Arabic]. Available at: https://www.capmas.gov.eg/Pages/IndicatorsPage.aspx?Ind_id=1121.

Coleman, Jasmine. (2012, January 21). Egypt election results show firm win for Islamists. *The Guardian*. Available at: https://www.theguardian.com/world/2012/jan/21/egypt-election-clear-islamist-victory.

Darwish, Passant. (2015, January 15). Egypt's 'war on atheism'. *Ahram Online*. Available at: english.ahram.org.eg/NewsContent/1/151/120204/Egypt/Features/Egypts-war-on-atheism.aspx.

Diwan, Ishac, Houry, Nadim & Sayigh, Yazid (2020). Egypt After the Coronavirus. *Arab Reform Initiative*. Available at: https://www.arab-reform.net/publication/egypt-after-the-coronavirus-back-to-square-one/.

Drevon, Jerome. (2016). Embracing Salafi Jihadism in Egypt and mobilizing in the Syrian Jihad. *Middle East Critique*, 25(4): 321–339, 9–10.

El-Gergawi, Sherry. (2016, February 7). Egypt military restoring churches destroyed following Morsi's ouster. *Ahram Online*. Available at: english.ahram.org.eg/News/185985.aspx.

El-Raggal, Ali. (2018). Islamist movement Hazemon. *Effervescent Egypt: Venues for Mobilization and the Interrupted Legacy of 2011* [in Arabic]. Arab Forum for Initiative. Available at: https://archives.arab-reform.net/ar/node/1222.

Fahmi, Georges. (2014, December 18). *The Coptic Church and Politics in Egypt*. Carnegie Middle East Centre. Available at: https://carnegie-mec.org/2014/12/18/coptic-church-and-politics-in-egypt-pub-57563.

Gokmen, Ozgur. (2016, April 30). Five years after the Arab uprisings: An interview with Asef Bayat. *Jadaliyya*. Available at: https://www.jadaliyya.com/Details/33222.

Hamama, Mohamed. (2015, December 22). The hidden world of militant 'special committees'. *Mada Masr* [in Arabic]. Available at: https://is.gd/5ucWoU

Hamama, Mohamed. (2016, October 4). Interior ministry policy inks the end of the Qualitative Committees' Engineer. *Mada Masr* [in Arabic]. Available at: https://is.gd/zORpss.

Human Rights Watch. (2009). *Egypt: Decree Ends ID Bias Against Baha'is*. Available at: https://www.hrw.org/news/2009/04/15/egypt-decree-ends-id-bias-against-bahais.

Ibrahim, Ishak. (2015, June). *According to Which Customs the Role of Customary Reconciliation Sessions in Sectarian Incidents and the Responsibility of the State*. Egyptian Initiative for Personal Rights, p. 8.

Kaldas, Timothy E. (2019). *Egypt's Sectarian Committee to Combat Sectarianism*. The Tahrir Institute for Middle East Policy.

Kamel, Kamel & Arafa, Ahmed. (2015, August 24). MB denounces its religious committee and claims it did not call for using force against security. *Youm7* [in Arabic]. Available at: https://is.gd/vLYQxP.

Lacroix, S. & Shalata, A.Z. (2016). The rise of revolutionary salafism in Post-Mubarak Egypt. In B. Rougier & S. Lacroix (eds), *Egypt's Revolutions* (pp. 38–39). The Sciences Po Series in International Relations and Political Economy. New York: Palgrave Macmillan.

Makdisi, Ussama. (2000). *A Culture of Sectarianism*. Berkeley: University of California.

Manshurat. (2014, October 22). *Verdict in case publicly known as 'Madinat Nasr Cell'* [in Arabic]. Available at: https://manshurat.org/node/1289.

Mazel, Zvi. (2016, September 16). A new law aims to make building churches in Egypt easier – But will it work? *The Jerusalem Post*. Available at: https://www.jpost.com/Middle-East/A-new-law-aims-to-make-building-churches-in-Egypt-easier-but-will-it-work-466890.

Mcmanus, Allison & Green, Jake (2016). *Egypt's Mainland Terrorism Landscape*. The Tahrir Institute for Middle East Policy. Available at: https://is.gd/kCS9mj.

Pérez-Accino, José. (2019, April 19). Ancient Egypt gave rise to one of the world's oldest Christian faiths. *National Geographic*. Available at: https://on.natgeo.com/2ZNgaRF.

Rock-Singer, Aaron. (2017, January 23). Islamic media and religious change in 1970s Egypt. *MPC Journal*. Mashreq Politics & Culture. Available at: https://mpc-journal.org/blog/2017/01/23/islamic-media-and-religious-change-in-1970s-egypt/.

Roth, Kenneth. (n.d.). *Egypt: Events of 2017*. Human Rights Watch. Available at: https://www.hrw.org/world-report/2018/country-chapters/egypt.

Sayed, Ashraf. (2018, February 9). Countering terrorism is the most dangerous issue for 2018: Sisi follows the Comprehensive Military Operation in Sinai. *Veto* [in Arabic]. Available at: https://www.vetogate.com/3062805

Speri, Alice. (2014, August 12). Egypt's Rabaa Massacre of 1,000 Morsi Supporters Went 'According to Plan. *Vice News*. Available at: https://news.vice.com/en_us/article/yw4k87/egypts-rabaa-massacre-of-1000-morsi-supporters-went-according-to-plan.

State Information Service. (2018, December 31). *Sisi Issues a Decree to form Committee to Counter Sectarian Incidents*. Available at: https://sis.gov.eg/Story/136850/Sisi-issues-a-decree-to-form-committee-to-counter-sectarian-incidents?lang=en-us.

Tadros, Samuel. (2014). *Mapping Egyptian Islamism*. Hudson Institute, pp. 54–55.

Tahrir Institute for Middle East Policy. (2014a, July 22). *Jund Al-Islam*. Available at: https://is.gd/KY67z3.

Tahrir Institute for Middle East Policy. (2014b, July 22). *Ajnad Misr*. Available at: https://timep.org/esw/non-state-actors/ajnad-misr/.

Tahrir Institute for Middle East Policy. (2014c, July 23). *Wilayat Sinai*. Available at: https://timep.org/esw/non-state-actors/wilayat-sinai/.

Tahrir Institute for Middle East Policy. (2017a, March 29). *Liwaa Al-Thawra*. Available at: https://is.gd/TSrihB.

Tahrir Institute for Middle East Policy. (2017b, March 29). *Hasam*. Available at: https://is.gd/iLangP.

Tahrir Institute for Middle East Policy. (2017c, May 8). *Islamic State in Egypt*. Available at: https://is.gd/hEnWWX.

The Economist. (2017, August 13). *Ranking Countries by Their Blasphemy Laws*. Available at: https://www.economist.com/erasmus/2017/08/13/ranking-countries-by-their-blasphemy-laws?fsrc=rss.

Walsh, Declan & Youssef, Nour. (2017, October 21). Militants Kill Egyptian Security Forces in Devastating Ambush. *The New York Times*. Available at: https://www.nytimes.com/2017/10/21/world/middleeast/egypt-ambush-hasm.html.

Xinhua. (2018, January 7). *Egypt's Sisi Attends Coptic Christmas Celebration Amid Tight Security*. Available at: http://www.xinhuanet.com/english/2018-01/07/c_136877006.htm.

Zahran, Mostafa. (2018). Regional Jihad: Contemporary Jihadist movements in Egypt. In *Ma al-siyasi fi al-Islam?* (What is political in Islam?) [in Arabic]. Dar Maraya.

19
Tunisia
Governing the religious sphere after 2011

Georges Fahmi

Introduction

While Tunisia is the only Arab country (to date) undergoing a successful democratic transition, it is still faced with a number of challenges, among which: how to govern the role of religion within both the state and society in the post-2011 era, particularly with the deep wave of violent radicalization that the country has been witnessing since Ben Ali's ouster in January 2011.

Since then, religion has been freed from the control of state institutions, namely, the security services. The transitional period has henceforth opened a new space for religious actors, both moderate and radical, that were banned under the old regime to reappear on the public scene and organize in political parties, charity associations, or preaching movements. This has opened a debate among the Tunisian political elite over the question of how to regulate the religious sphere in the new republic.

The debate has revolved around how to regulate religion on the three levels of the polity: state, political society, and civil society. The state level concerns mainly the issues of the identity of the state and Sharia. At the level of political society, the main issue concerns religious parties and how they should manage the relationship between their political and religious activities. Finally, at the level of civil society, the central issue is whether religious groups should be given access to mosques or not. This debate is deeply connected to the Salafi-Jihadi challenge that the country has been facing since 2011.

The worsening of the economic and social situation of the lower and middle classes after the revolution has led to deep frustration particularly among university graduates. Ninety per cent of the youth living in the suburbs of Tunis – Douar Hicher and Ettadhamen – estimate that their situation has not changed since 2011, and 46 per cent consider it even worse than it was under Ben Ali's regime (Lamloum et al., 2015). The optimism occasioned by the revolution has quickly transformed to general disappointment among the youth, leading some of them to join the Salafi-jihadi movement in a sign of protest.

From its side, the Salafi-Jihadi movement has taken advantage of the vacuum in the post-2011 religious sphere to preach for its ideas and recruit new members with little resistance or competition from other religious actors. Hence, the debate over how religion should be regulated in post-2011 Tunisia could either reinforce the current radicalization movement or, conversely, help stop it from growing.

This chapter addresses these two interrelated questions in three main parts. The first will present an overview of religion-state relationship prior to 2011; the second will look at the debate over religion within the state, political society, and civil society after 2011; and the third will explore the links between the governance of the religious sphere and the current wave of violent radicalization.

Islam and state in Tunisia before 2011

Tunisia witnessed a process of modernization starting from the nineteenth century with its first reforming monarch, Ahmad Bey (1837–1855). Although Ahmad Bey's project aimed mainly at modernizing the Tunisian military, his reforms also reached the religious sphere, as is the case with his Act known as the *mullaqa* in 1842 organizing the recruitment of teachers and other personnel of Al-Zaytouna Mosque. This reform process continued with Mahammad Bey (1855–1859) and al-Sadiq Bey (1859–1881), and included the drafting of Tunisia's first constitutional document in 1861 that established a consultative assembly, penal court, and a court of appeals.

Khayr al-Din Pasha is widely considered Tunisia's greatest reformer. Although he served as prime minister for only four years, from 1873 to 1877, this was a period of intense reformist activities. In 1874, he issued a ministerial decree downsizing the Sharia courts so that no court would include more than one qadi and one mufti. One year later, he reorganized educational procedures at Al-Zaytouna Mosque, introducing modern subjects into its curriculum and giving the prime minister's office stronger control over its management. He also created a central bureau (*Jam'iyat al-awqaf*) to administer public endowments and founded a secondary school (Sadiqi College) to give potential civil servants an adequate background in modern subjects, including European languages. In 1876, he asserted control over the elementary Quranic schools by re-organizing teacher recruitment. In the same year he also appointed a commission to draft a comprehensive law code in harmony with the Sharia (Green, 1976).

Although his strategy aimed at shifting the relationship between Islam and state institutions, Khayr al-Din viewed the Ulama's cooperation as essential to his project's success. He involved Ulama as much as possible in his reforms. For example, the president and vice-president of the Awqaf Administration were, respectively, sheikhs; of the nine-man commission that created Sadiqi College and reorganized Al-Zaytouna Mosque, six members were Ulama themselves; and three of the four members of the commission appointed to codify Tunisian law were Ulama. As a result, when this indigenous phase of development ended with the French occupation in 1881, the Tunisian Ulama continued to enjoy traditional privileges and authority.

Under French rule, the French authorities worked to impose their control over the Ulama. The French sponsored the creation of the jami'ya al-Khaldounia in 1896 to introduce the teaching of 'modem sciences' at Al-Zaytouna. They also succeeded in subjugating to French rule the primary Quran schools, the madrasas, and Sadiqi College. However, they failed to do the same with Al-Zaytouna Mosque because of the Ulama's resistance. In the realm of jurisprudence, a number of Tunisian civil tribunals were created, further diminishing of the role of Sharia (Ghozzi, 2002).

The Ulama's strategy aimed at avoiding political confrontation with the new political authorities, while resisting only moves against their power. They thus withdrew as much as possible from the political movements of the nationalist period, resisting only when seriously threatened. The Ulama's actions sometimes gave the impression that they had entered a *modus vivendi* with the French in order to defend the status quo against the nationalists. The allegation that the Tunisian Ulama sided with the French against the nationalists largely explains the ruthlessness with which the religious leaders were stripped of their remaining functions and authority after independence (Green, 1976).

Tunisia achieved full independence from France in March 1956. In July 1957, the Tunisian republic was declared, and one of the most prominent figures of the independence struggle, Habib Bourguiba, became Tunisia's first president. During his three decades in power, Bourguiba spearheaded a process of modernization in all sectors, including religion-state relations. He understood secularism not as separation between religion and the state, but rather as placing religion under the strict control of state institutions. In Bourguiba's mind, the Ulama had failed to stand up to the French colonial power and failed to reinterpret Islam to adapt to modern realities. Hence, he adopted a number of measures in order to ensure all religious institutions in the country were dependent on, and subordinate to, the new republic's political institutions.

Bourguiba abolished the religious Sharia courts in favour of a single, unified secular judicial system. He also abolished religious endowments, both private and public, as he considered them the main source of funding for religious organizations. He issued several laws promoting women's rights such as abolishing polygamy, establishing the requirement of mutual consent before marriage, entitling women to initiate divorce proceedings, and equal division of goods after divorce, as well as forbidding husbands from unilaterally ending their marriages.

The new regime dismantled Al-Zaytouna University, which was founded in 737. The Ministry of National Education nationalized the Quranic schools, previously administrated by Al-Zaytouna Ulama. The Zaytouna college was closed down in 1957, and transformed into the faculty of theology and religious science at the University of Tunis in 1961 (Shahin, 2018: 39). Bourguiba also established a Department of Religious Affairs, which was responsible for coordinating government activity in religious affairs, appointing and training imams, and regulating religious rituals and education programmes.

Bourguiba viewed all his measures as a way of reconciling Islamic tradition with modern requirements. These policies were welcomed by some of Tunisian society as necessary steps to modernize the then-new republic. However, other Tunisians viewed Bourguiba's policies as an attempt to destroy Tunisia's Muslim identity and impose the French secular model on Tunisian society. That was the case with many of those who established the Islamist movement in the 1960s, including the movement's leader, Rachid Ghannouchi (Wolf, 2013: 561).

The regime relied on its struggle for independence in order to push for this secularization process in the 1950s. However, the situation started to shift in the 1960s as the regime faced a number of economic difficulties that impacted its political legitimacy. In order to face this legitimacy crisis, the regime relied on religious claims in order to strengthen its political legitimacy. It was Bourguiba himself who established in 1968 the National Association for the Preservation of the Quran to promote the teachings of Islam and encourage the presence of mosques in schools and factories (Dell'Aguzzo & Sigillò, 2017: 512). The regime also relaxed some of its previously implemented strict rules towards religion, for example, allowing for a space for state employees to pray. Moreover, Bourguiba reintroduced religion as a specific subject separate from civic education.

These new policies offered a conducive environment for the reappearance of Islamic forces, mostly inspired by the doctrine of the Muslim Brotherhood in Egypt, in the public sphere, first through religious activities and later as a political platform. One of the main figures of this movement is Rachid Ghannouchi. This was a gradual process as the movement shifted from religious activities and preaching to a political platform represented by the Mouvement de la tendence islamique (MTI) founded by Ghannouchi in 1981. In just a few years, this new movement managed to establish itself and compete with both the official religious institutions and the political regime. Feeling threatened, the government answered with a number of measures aimed at controlling MTI; these failed, paving the way for a bloodless coup by the then-minister of interior, Ben Ali, in November 1987 on the pretext of Bourguiba's faltering health.

In order to legitimize his new rule, Ben Ali offered a narrow political opening through a process of national reconciliation with the political opposition, including the Islamists, in the framework of the National Pact. Like his predecessor, Ben Ali sought also to use religion to legitimize his rule. He allowed for a certain degree of society's Islamization in an attempt to neutralize Islamic contestation by adopting their discourse. According to this logic, if the state itself adopts a religious discourse, Islamic forces would have no rhetorical leverage against the regime.

Ben Ali granted the leader of the Islamic movement, Rachid Ghannouchi, amnesty in 1988 and promised the Islamic movement the license for a political party. In an interview with the French newspaper *Le Monde*, Ben Ali confirmed that nothing stood in the way of recognizing the MTI, if the group abided by the laws pertaining to political parties. The Islamist movement took advantage of this new political environment to increase its political presence. The MTI rebranded itself under the name of Ennahda (renaissance) in order to be consistent within the Tunisian law banning religious political parties (Chouikha & Gobe, 2015).

As part of limited political openness, Ben Ali held slightly competitive elections in 1989 in which the Islamists were allowed to field an independent slate. However, their relatively strong showing – around 15 per cent nationwide and 30 per cent in Greater Tunis – led Ben Ali to change his approach and adopt a severe policy towards religious actors. In 1992, he banned Ennahda and went after its leadership, who ended up either jailed, in exile, or underground. (Great Britain granted Ghannouchi political asylum in 1993.)

Ben Ali's strict policies against the opposition pushed Islamic and secular parties towards a tentative rapprochement. In 2003, Ennahda together with Congress for the Republic (CPR), the Democratic Forum for Labour and Liberties known as Ettakatol, and the Progressive Democratic Party (PDP) (all of which held seats in the Constituent Assembly established after 2011) signed the Tunis Declaration of 17 June 2003. The declaration represented a compromise between Islamist and secular forces, with secularists accepting the right of Islamist groups to participate in democratic politics and Islamists agreeing that popular sovereignty, not religious texts, is the only source of legitimacy. In 2005, these four political parties went one step further and met with representatives of smaller parties and agreed on 'The 18 October Coalition for Rights and Freedoms in Tunisia' declaration after three months of negotiations. The document stressed that any future democratic state would have to be a 'civic state' and that 'there can be no compulsion in religion. This includes the right to adopt a religion or doctrine or not' (Stepan, 2012).

As for the situation of the religious sphere inside Tunisia, with Ennahda going underground in the 1990s, Salafism started to rise. Salafism generally refers to a literal and puritanical version of Islam that emphasizes following the path of the Islamic ancestors (*salaf al-salih*) in order to apply the prophetic model by the companions of the Prophet and their followers. It is often classified into two categories: scripturalist (*al-salafiyya al-'ilmiyya*) and jihadi (*al-salafiyya al-jihadiyya*). The former is generally apolitical and refuses to go against its rulers as long as they do not prevent the practice of Islam, while the latter believes in armed struggle to establish an Islamic state.

Scripturalist Salafism grew through private meetings, books, and audio-visual materials and the religious satellite channels that attracted many Tunisians striving for religious knowledge due to the 'religious desertification' under Ben Ali. These apolitical activities were loosely tolerated by the regime as Ben Ali thought Salafism could offer an apolitical alternative to Ennahda (Fahmi & Meddeb, 2015: 5).

Tunisia also witnessed the emergence of a Salafi-jihadist trend during the 1990s. This movement began to grow in the aftermath of the attacks of September 11, 2011, and the subsequent war on terrorism led by the US. Young Tunisians joined Salafi-jihadist groups in Iraq, Afghanistan, Yemen, and Somalia to resist what they saw as a Western attack on the Muslim world. Jihadists have also been active inside Tunisia. In 2002, Tunisian jihadists attacked a synagogue on the Tunisian island of Djerba. This attack led the Ben Ali regime to issue a counterterrorism law in 2003 and arrest around 2,000 people on charges of belonging to Salafi-jihadi groups.

By the end of the 2000s, and despite high unemployment and inflation rates, the lack of political freedoms, and the elite's corruption, the Ben Ali regime seemed stable and hard to challenge politically. However, a minor incident in December 2010, when a street vendor, Mohamed Bouazizi, set himself on fire to protest the police confiscation of his products, spurred a month-long popular uprising that resulted in Ben Ali's ouster and flight from the country in January 2011.

Under Article 57 of the Tunisian Constitution, in the event that the president dies, resigns, or is incapacitated, the speaker and head of Parliament – in this instance, Fouad Mebazaa – steps in as interim president. In March 2011, Mebazaa announced a new transitional plan according to which Tunisians would vote for a 'National Constituent Assembly' to draft a new Constitution. Elections were held in October 2011, with a remarkable turnout of approximately 86.1 per cent: Ennahda won 41 per cent of the vote and the Congress for the Republic (CPR) polled second with 13.4 per cent, followed by the Popular Petition with 12 per cent, and Ettakatol with 9.2 per cent. Ennahda's victory has increased fear among secular circles in Tunisian society that it might try to establish a religious rule. However, aware of these fears and their possible implications on the transition process, Ennahda decided to form a troika government with the CPR and leftist Ettakatol in which Ennahda would take the premiership, the CPR would fill the presidency, and Ettakatol would determine the chairmanship of the constituent assembly.

The debate over religion's place after 2011

The debate over the place of religion in post-2011 Tunisia has revolved around how to regulate religion at the three levels of the polity: state, political society, and civil society. The state level concerns mainly the issues of the identity of the state and the role of Sharia in the legislation process. At the level of political society, the main issue concerns religious parties, whether these should be allowed, and how they should manage the relationship between their political and religious activities. Finally, at the level of civil society, the central issue is how religious groups engage in preaching activities, and questions such as whether they should be given access to mosques or be under the strict control of state institutions as was the case under the old regime.

Tunisia: governing the religious sphere

The debate over Sharia in the constitution

During the process of drafting the new Constitution, which began in February 2012, there was considerable debate between Islamic political groups, represented by Ennahda, and secular movements, represented by the CPR and Ettakatol, over the role of Sharia in the legislative process. After winning more than 40 per cent of the seats in the Constituent Assembly, some representatives of Ennahda proposed a constitutional provision declaring Islam to be the main source of legislation. A prominent Ennahda member, Sahbi Atiq, declared that Islam should be incorporated in state institutions and not just be a slogan. The debate over this issue has raised the level of tension not only in the constituent assembly but also in society between secularists and Islamists. Representatives of Ennahda's allies – the CPR and Ettakatol – announced that Ennahda's proposal emphasizing Islam as the main source of legislation is unacceptable. After months of debate and negotiations, and as polarization reached worrying levels, Rachid Ghannouchi interfered and persuaded members of his party that there is no need to explicitly refer to Islamic Sharia in the Constitution and that it would be enough to keep the pre-existing first clause of the old Constitution which states that 'Tunisia is a free, sovereign and independent state, whose religion is Islam'.

Ennahda sources indicated that Ghannouchi approached the issue both rationally and ideationally. Rationally, Ghannouchi argued that Ennahda is unlikely to secure the two-thirds majority needed to pass the Constitution with this article as even its coalition partners are likely to vote against it. This would make it seem like the issue of Sharia has been rejected once and for all. Ideationally, Ghannouchi argued that the debate over the issue of Sharia has divided Tunisian society and might be a source of instability and chaos, which according to Sharia itself should be avoided at any cost (personal communication, Tunis, March 2019).

The case of religious parties

Tunisia has seen the establishment of religious parties during the transitional period as has been the case with Ennahda and the Salafist Reform Front Party. The establishment of religious parties has been one of the debated issues during the transitional period.

For its part, Ennahda has taken huge steps to differentiate between its political and religious activities. At its 10th general assembly held in May 2016, Ennahda successfully enacted important internal reforms, such as making a clear demarcation between its political and religious identities. After a few years of debate among Ennahda's leadership and between the leadership and its rank-and-file, the reformist voices prevailed. The assembly agreed to implement a division between the political party and the preaching activities that would practically prevent the political party leaders from also holding senior positions in religious associations or even from preaching in mosques. Even more, the assembly final statement insisted that the party no longer belongs to the category of political Islam, but rather seeks to establish a larger coalition of Muslim democrats that would include non-Islamist voices as well.

However, these changes within Ennahda came with a price that has largely gone unnoticed: it damaged Ennahda's position within the religious sphere. First, the political compromises Ennahda had to make during the constitutional drafting process in matters of Sharia damaged its image among religiously conservative youth. In an interview, a Salafi youth activist said: 'So what's Islamic about Ennahda, if they cannot even add an article about Sharia to the constitution?' (personal communication, Tunis, March 2015). Along the same line, the decision of the 2016 general assembly stating that the movement no longer belongs to the category of political Islam has also disappointed many Islamist youths.

While many people perceive Ennahda as a political party and thus assess its experience during the transitional period as a success, others perceive it as a religious movement and think it failed completely in achieving its role in upholding the principles of Islam. As Ennahda is both a political party and a religious movement, both evaluations should be taken into consideration. Ennahda's decision to focus on the political side has deprived the religious market of a strong religious player that would have balanced the presence of radical religious movements. It would have been far better if the movement had undertaken a reform of religious interpretation towards a more innovative and modernist understanding rather than dropping the religious altogether (Meddeb, 2019: 12).

The debate over the neutrality of mosques

The debate over the regulation of religion at the society level involves the issue of who has the right to preach in mosques and if this should be under the control of the state or whether religious movements should also be allowed to have access to mosques to preach their religious ideas.

After the Ben Ali regime was toppled in 2011, the security apparatus lost control over the religious sphere. Unlike Egypt, where the religious 'market' was characterized by relatively strong state religious institutions such as Al-Azhar, Egypt's oldest centre of Sunni teaching, and a strong presence of the Muslim Brotherhood and Salafi groups under the rule of Mubarak, the market in Tunisia was almost empty when the regime fell (Fahmi & Medded, 2015: 11). Moderate groups, like Ennahda, but also more radical ones, like the Salafi-Jiahdi Ansar Al-Sharia, took advantage of this religious vacuum to spread their ideas and recruit new members. Mosques turned into battlefields in which several religious players competed for control. For those players, mosques were the best channel through which they could influence or control the entire religious sphere.

From their side, state religious institutions were ill-equipped to compete with these newcomers to the religious sphere, either because they had been weakened by the policies of the old regime, as in the case of the religious university of Al-Zaytouna, or because they were delegitimized in the post-Ben Ali era as a result of their support for the old regime, as is the case with the official imams affiliated with the Ministry of Religious Affairs. For example, during the Friday prayers that followed Ben Ali's flight, Islamists, whether proponents of political Islam or Salafists, took over mosques and expelled imams appointed by the state. Estimates point to approximately half of the mosques in the country having had their imams expelled during this period (Donker, 2019: 507). Some mosques even witnessed violent clashes between political Islamists and Salafists who competed for control of the same mosque. During the months after the revolution, the Ministry of Religious Affairs lost authority over many of Tunisia's 5,000 mosques, including historic ones such as Al-Zaytouna, the Great Mosques of Kairouan, Msaken, and Sfax.

As state institutions have started to regain their strength and legitimacy, since 2013 successive ministers of religious endowments have been determined to extend the ministry's control over all mosques and imams and close all illegal mosques. The Ministry also relieved a number of unlicensed Salafi preachers from their duties, including the renowned Salafi preacher Bechir Ben Hassan, and appointed other imams affiliated to the Ministry in their place. These measures even went beyond the Salafi preachers to include religious figures close to Ennahda, including the former minister of religious affairs Noureddine Khadmi himself.

The debate over the neutrality of mosques started as part of the dialogue that took place in the transitional stage about the identity of the state and society and the relationship between religion and politics. The neutrality of mosques was one of the most intensely debated issues during the national dialogue and was included in the road map agreed upon by different political factions for resolving the 2013 political crisis. The members of the National Constituent Assembly stressed the importance of mosque neutrality in the new Constitution instituted on 26 January 2014, whose sixth chapter stipulates that the state protects religion, guarantees freedom of belief and conscience and religious practices, protects sanctities, and ensures the neutrality of mosques and places of worship away from partisan instrumentalization.

Supporters of the neutrality of mosques argue that mosques are religious spaces that should not be involved in politics and should not be used by any faction for political or electoral gains. Critics of this demand, however, argue that it is not possible in Islam to separate the religious from the political, that religious discourse cannot be confined to spiritual matters, and that imams have the right to discuss worldly affairs that concern the Muslim public.

Governing the religious sphere and challenges of violent extremism

While Tunisia is, to date, the only Arab country undergoing a successful democratic transition, it has also been home to a growing Salafi-jihadi movement since the fall of former president Zine el-Abidine Ben Ali in January 2011. This is evidenced by the number of deaths due to terrorism per year, which increased from four in 2011 to 81 in 2015. Moreover, Tunisia has been one of the top exporters of Salafi-jihadist fighters, with more than 5,500 Tunisians fighting with jihadist groups in Iraq, Libya, Mali, Syria, and Yemen, as estimated by the UN in 2015 (OHCHR, 2015).

The most organized group within the Tunisian post-2011 Salafi jihadism scene was Ansar al-Sharia. The movement was established in April 2011 as a group following the Salafi-jihadi ideology, but with a specific focus on the strict implementation of the Islamic Sharia law. However, unlike other cases, most Ansar al-Sharia leaders rejected the use of violence inside Tunisia, calling Tunisia a land for preaching, not combat. Ansar al-Sharia founder Abu Ayadh is a prime example of this trend. He insisted that violence was a trap and that the focus should be on preparing society for the rule of Islam through religious and social activities, not combat. The movement took advantage of the security vacuum the country witnessed after Ben Ali's ouster to take control over a number of mosques in order to preach its ideas and recruit new members. Their preaching and charitable activities allowed them to expand their influence in the public sphere and recruit militants in the suburbs of Tunis and the inland regions, especially Sidi Bouzid, Jendouba, Kairouan, and Kasserine, and thus to exceed a membership of 50,000, according to the movement spokesperson Bilel Chaouachi.

Nonetheless, some members of Ansar al-Sharia have indeed engaged in violence, either outside Tunisia by joining jihadi groups in Syria and Iraq or inside Tunisia by targeting security forces and secular political figures. The decision of some members to take up arms resulted in a series of attacks against the Tunisian police and the assassination of two political figures from the opposition, Chokri Belaid and Mohamed Brahmi, in February and July 2013, respectively. The assassinations put the post-revolutionary political transition process at risk because secular political forces accused Ansar al-Sharia of being behind the assassinations and the ruling Islamist party Ennahda of protecting it.

Two approaches competed within Ennahda regarding how to deal with this crisis. The first argued that by allowing Jihadi Salafists to work publicly, they would moderate their ideas through interaction with other Islamic groups and could thus be an asset to the Islamic movement in their competition against the secular forces. This position was supported by Ghannouchi, who said that Salafi-Jihadi youths remind him of himself when he was young. The second approach perceived them as a threat not only to the Tunisian political process, but also to the Islamic experience of Ennahda. This argument was made by then-Prime Minister and Ennahda secretary-general Ali Larayedh. The rise in political violence in 2013 gave the second group the legitimacy to act. In May 2013, the government refused to allow Ansar al-Sharia to hold its third annual meeting; in August, Larayedh declared Ansar al-Sharia a terrorist organization. According to his official declaration, Ansar al-Sharia was involved in the killings of Chokri Belaid and Mohamed Brahmi and other security officers. The declaration led to the arrest of more than 6,500 young Tunisians who were members of, or sympathized with, Ansar al-Sharia and prompted many other Jihadi Salafists to leave the country for Libya or Syria. These members mainly joined the self-proclaimed Islamic State (ISIS) in these two countries.

During 2014, ISIS began to establish a presence in Libya, with the largest group based in Sirte. ISIS also established a camp at Sabratha, near the Tunisian border that focussed on training Tunisian fighters. Among this group were the individuals responsible for attacks in 2015 against two prominent tourist destinations: the Bardo Museum in Tunis (where 22 civilians were killed) and the beach resort of Sousse (where 38 civilians, including 30 British tourists, were killed). Tunisians who had joined ISIS in Libya also led the armed attack on the Tunisian border town of Ben Guardane in March 2016, when a number of ISIS fighters crossed the Libyan-Tunisian border and attempted to control the city to create an Islamic emirate as in Mosul (Iraq), Raqqa (Syria), and Sirte (Libya). However, the local population of Ben Guardane resisted this invasion and supported the Tunisian security forces deployed to protect the city.

The monopolization of the religious sphere before 2011 has played an important role in fuelling the Salafi Jihadi movement in Tunisia as it left a vacuum in the religious sphere that the Salafi-jihadi movement took advantage of to preach its ideas with little resistance or competition from other religious actors. Hence, preventing violent radicalization also requires a discussion on how to manage the religious in post-2011 Tunisia.

The Tunisian state still needs to negotiate its way between the two extremes: chaos, as was the case after 2011, and tight control of the religious sphere, as was the case under Ben Ali. State institutions need to manage, but not control, the religious sphere. The Islamic religious field is characterized by a diversity of ideas and organizational structures that makes it impossible to apply uniform policies. The state's desire for control leaves some populations – particularly the youth – with no room to express their opinions and beliefs, driving them to other religious outlets.

Concluding remarks

While Tunisia is the only Arab country undergoing a successful democratic transition, it is still faced with two challenges with regard to the governance of religion in the new republic: first, how to govern the role of religion within both the state and society in the post-2011 era, and, second, how to face the deep wave of violent radicalization that the country has witnessed in the last decade. This chapter argues that these two challenges are deeply connected.

The transitional period that followed Ben Ali's ouster in January 2011 opened a new space for religious actors that were banned under the old regime to reappear on the public scene, to get organized, preach their ideas, and recruit new members. This has opened the debate among the Tunisian political elite, both religious and secular, over how to regulate the religious at the three levels of a polity – state, political society, and civil society – at a time when Tunisia has been facing a wave of violent radicalization that is much deeper than under the old regime. Tunisian secular and religious actors have made important compromises in this area; however, these measures might have a negative effect on efforts to combat violent radicalization.

At the state level, Islamic political actors, including the religiously inspired Ennahda party, have tried to avoid any discussion on Sharia out of fear of being labelled a religiously conservative movement. However, Sharia remains the key concept linking Islamic religious values to governance. By avoiding the debate over Sharia, the main political actors have allowed more conservative religious voices to monopolize the discourse in the name of Islam and Sharia, as is the case with Salafi groups.

At the political society level, religious parties such as the Ennahda movement don't need to completely give up their religious role, but rather to draw an institutional differentiation between the political party and the religious movement. Although Ennahda's 10th general assembly agreed in May 2016 to separate the political party from preaching activities, the movement still needs to find the right balance between the religious and the political, as most of its cadres went to the political branch and ignored the religious one.

At the society level, the different governments during the transitional period have been trying to regain control over the religious sphere. Some of the religious figures expressed their fear that these measures might put the religious sphere under the strict control of the state, as it was under Ben Ali, and thus will not stop violent radicalization but might reinforce it as it delegitimizes preachers and makes them look like mouthpieces of the state, and paradoxically allows for the emergence of a parallel marketplace of religious ideas that could create breeding grounds for violent religious movements.

References

Chouikha, L. & Gobe, É. (2015). *Histoire de la Tunisie depuis l'indépendance*. Paris: La Découverte.
Dell'Aguzzo, L. & Sigillò, E. (2017). Political Legitimacy and Variations in State-religion Relations in Tunisia. *The Journal of North African Studies*, 22(4): 511–535.
Donker, T. H. (2019). The Sacred as Secular: State Control and Mosques Neutrality in Post-Revolutionary Tunisia. *Politics and Religion*, 12(3): 501–523.
Fahmi, G. & Meddeb, H. (2015). *Market for jihad*. Beirut: Carnegie Middle East Center.
Ghozzi, K. (2002). The Study of Resilience and Decay in Ulema Groups: Tunisia and Iran as an Example. *Sociology of Religion*, 63(3): 317.
Green, A. (1976). Political Attitudes and Activities of the Ulama in the Liberal Age: Tunisia as an Exceptional Case. *International Journal of Middle East Studies*, 7(2): 209–241.
Lamloum, Olfa, et al. (2015). Experiences and Perceptions of Young People in Tunisia: The Case of Douar Hicher and Ettadhamen. *International Alert*.
Meddeb, H. (2019). *Ennahda's Uneasy Exit from Political Islam*. Beirut: Carnegie Middle East Center.
OHCHR. (2015). *Foreign Fighters: Urgent Measures Needed to Stop Flow from Tunisia-UN Expert Group Warns*. Tunis/Geneva. Available at: https://www.ohchr.org/EN/NewsEvents/Pages/DisplayNews.aspx?NewsID=16223&LangID=E. Accessed April 2020.
Shahin, E. (2018). *Political Ascent: Contemporary Islamic Movements in North Africa*. New York: Routledge.
Stepan, A. (2012). Tunisia's Transition and the Twin Tolerations. *Journal of Democracy*, 23(2): 89–103.
Wolf, A. (2013). An Islamist 'Renaissance'? Religion and Politics in Post-Revolutionary Tunisia. *The Journal of North African Studies*, 18(4): 560–573.

20
Morocco
Governing religious diversity

Mehdi Lahlou and Mounir Zouiten

Introduction

Morocco, a country of some 36 million people, is located in the north-west of Africa, 14 kilometres across the sea from Spain. Its population is presented as almost totally Muslim: 99 per cent of Morocco's inhabitants are considered Muslim. But this stratification is, in fact, only statistical. In reality, the census does not include any question about religion or whether respondents engage in religious practice. Nor has there ever been a survey on this issue to determine the share of the population that is Muslim, non-Muslim, practising, non-practising, Sunni or Shia, and so on.

Morocco's recent history – especially since the 1970s – has been marked by two developments: one makes it similar to the rest of the MENA region, from Algeria to Iraq, passing by Tunisia, Libya, Egypt, or Jordan; the other renders it a sort of exception within the Arab world.

The first is aptly summarized in the following paragraph from a text by Rachid Ouaissa (2018): 'Religion in the MENA region has been strikingly reconfigured since mid-1980s and certainly since the so-called Arab Spring that began in 2010–2011. The failure of postcolonial development models, and their associated pan-Arab and nationalist narratives, allowed an Islamic discourse to gain a foothold among broad sections of Arab societies. Islamic movements have increasingly become gathering points for frustrated and marginalised sections of society, as well as growing pious Arab middle classes … Indeed, in many Arab countries, the adoption of structural adjustment programmes dictated by the International Monetary Fund and the World Bank has allowed Islamic movements to assume control of social welfare functions'.

As for the second point, Morocco is generally considered as a democracy (Guigou, 2012; Pollock, 2013) among the countries of the Arab world, with a 'multi-party system', local and national elections, and a functioning parliament since the early 1960s, even if it had never had any significant power. The fact is that the real power is held by the King ('Malik or Sultan', in literal Arabic) who is not subject to election and considered, albeit not by the Constitution, as a sacred person who can't be the object of any criticism or held politically responsible despite being the Chief Commander of the Army, the head of the Ministers Council, the head of the Justice Authority, and the head of National Security Council.

Another manifestation of this 'Moroccan exception' is illustrated by the form and consequences of the Arab Spring demonstrations which were initiated and spearheaded in Morocco in early 2011 by the 'February 20' movement.

This movement – supported by the radical socialist opposition parties (represented by all the socialist movements except the USFP, *Union Socialiste des Forces Populaires*) as well as many human rights associations and associations of unemployed persons – lead a series of important protests in almost 150 cities, especially in Rabat, the capital, and major urban centres such as Casablanca, Fès, and Tangiers.

As in other Arab countries, the protestors' main demands were for political reforms: combatting corruption; independence of the justice system; separating the head of state's role in politics from religious affairs; a Constitution of a civil state; reducing the social gap within the Moroccan population and less social injustice; removal of some regime symbols represented by friends of the King and other persons very close to him.

But, contrary to what happened in Tunisia and Egypt, where street protests sought the ouster of, respectively, Ben Ali and Hosni Mubarak, protesters in Morocco did not seek Mohamed VI's removal from office but rather expressed a desire for deep-rooted reform, justice, more jobs, dignity, less corruption, and less gender inequality. This was one of the most important differences vis-à-vis the protests that sparked revolutions in the rest of the Arab countries.

Another difference with regard to Islamist movements, including radical factions, is the long history of the Moroccan political system. Indeed, the monarchy is very old and rooted in historical legitimacy, with a strong religious respect for the king/sultan/roi at its foundations. The King is, according to the constitution, '*Amir al-Mu'minin*' (Leader of the Faithful), even if some Moroccan jurists and intellectuals question this notion of 'commandery of believers'. This is the case with the lawyer Abderrahim Berrada who considers that the latter 'has never been defined by the constitution which contenting itself with stating, for the most part, that the king is the guarantor of the sustainability of Islam' (Berrada, 2019).

The king is also considered by some of the population as the 'Representative of God on earth'; in the same sense, he is a 'Sharif', or descendant of the prophet. No other Arab or Muslim head of state is imbued with these qualities.

These factors may explain why the middle and poorer classes – who are generally conservative, and in the latter case, less educated – did not join the protests and why some Islamist movements even supported the King and condemned the protests. This is particularly the case with the Party for Justice and Development (PJD) – the counterpart in Morocco of the Tunisian *Ennahda* movement and Turkish Justice and Development Party (AKP) – which has been the ruling party in Rabat since the beginning of 2012. This is also the case of the 'Boutchichi' association, a very strong Sufi organization based in the eastern part of Morocco that organized a massive street demonstration against the February 20 movement and called on people to vote in favour of the new Constitution as proposed by the King in June 2011.

Thus, radical movements are directed more towards 'social deviations' and impious foreign powers than towards the Moroccan monarchy as most of these movements see the King as the 'Protector of Islam'.

The religious sphere in Morocco: which demographic background?

The Moroccan population multiplied almost three-fold between 1961 and 2019,[1] as shown in Table 20.1 hereafter, growing from 11.89 million to 35.67 million in less than three decades.

Table 20.1 Evolution of the (legal) Moroccan population by area of residence, 1960–2019 (millions)

Year	Total	Urban	Rural	Urban population (% of total)
1961	11,897	3,547	8,350	29.81
1971	15,379	5,409	9,969	35.17
1982	20,419	8,730	11,689	42.75
1994	26,073	13,407	12,665	51.42
2004	29,891	16,463	13,428	55.07
2014	33,848	20,432	13,415	60.36
2019	35,675	22,439	13,236	62.9

Source: Haut Commissariat au Plan, Rabat, Morocco. https://www.hcp.ma/Population-du-Maroc-par-annee-civile-en-milliers-et-au-milieu-de-l-annee-par-milieu-de-residence-1960-2050_a677.html

After peaking at over 2.7 per cent between 1969 and 1972, the birth rate has since declined and today is at 1.25 per cent – among the lowest in Africa. However, the overall decline in population's growth rate is related to the fact that urban population has surged by a factor of 6.32 per cent (Haut Commissariat au Plan, 2014). This means that the focus on critical issues such as housing, unemployment, security, or migratory pressure is now concentrated on the cities.

These various social deficits will have more pronounced effects in terms of political opposition and religious radicalization as the Moroccan population is comprised mainly of young people, like the populations of developing countries. Indeed, Morocco is a demographically young country with 27 per cent of the population under the age of 15; 18 per cent between the ages of 15 and 24; 42 per cent between 25 and 54 years; 7 per cent between the ages of 55 and 64; and just 6 per cent aged 65 years and older. The median age of Moroccans is just 29 years (2018 data), with a life expectancy of about 75 years.

As for the distribution of the Moroccan population according to religious belief and practices, there is no census data and there have never been any field surveys in Morocco on ethnic or religious background. The most commonly held estimates suggest that about 99 per cent of Moroccans are 'Sunni Muslims', religiously or culturally, simply because 'they are Moroccans'. Morocco's Jewish community is very old but today numbers no more than 4,000 as most Morroccan Jews migrated to Israel between 1956 and 1967. Most of the Jewish community is concentrated in Casablanca (NPR, 2015). Christians of all faiths are estimated at around 40,000, including 30,000 Roman Catholics, 10,000 Protestants, and 8,000 Moroccan Christian converts (Joseph, 2017). There is also a small community of Shia Muslim converts and Bahai, although their numbers are unknown.

This data, particularly the overwhelming majority of Muslims in the population, means that the question of the management of the religious sphere essentially concerns Islam and Muslims. As for those who are Jewish or Christian, they are respected under the Constitution in terms of their faith and religious practices. However, the various other minorities or Moroccans who do not identify as Muslims – without necessarily proclaiming this publicly – are ignored and accordingly subject to common laws, including those that are fundamentally religious, such as those relating to family, inheritance, the practice of Ramadan, or the consumption of alcohol.

In this regard, if the Moroccan Penal Code does not provide for the death penalty for apostates of Islam unlike, for example, the Kingdom of Saudi Arabia or the United Arab

Emirates, the fact remains that this freedom is only allowed to 'non-Muslim Moroccans'. This negates much of the meaning of the corresponding article.

This subject remains extremely sensitive and poses a great threat to many Moroccans. Even if voluntary conversion is not considered a crime, proselytism can be punished with a prison sentence of six months to three years. Article 220 of the Moroccan Penal Code provides for a similar penalty for 'whoever employs means of seduction in order to shake the faith of a Muslim or to convert him to another religion, either by exploiting his weakness or his needs, or by using for this purpose educational institutions, health, asylums or orphanages'.

Historical background of state-organized religion relations in Morocco

Any analysis of the politico-religious field in Morocco, and in particular the relatively late emergence of Islamist players in the Moroccan political and social sphere, must take into account the importance of the long term. We are indeed tackling a phenomenon taking place in a country that has been ruled since the sixteenth century by a dynasty claiming to be descended from the Prophet, and whose existence is based on an arbitral religious power between the different components of Moroccan society.

This dynasty was at the origin of certain 'modernization' attempts in the nineteenth century, and in 1912 accepted the French protectorate under the pressure of the colonial system. It then used this new situation to establish its legitimacy over the entire territory (as the Sultan's/King's authority was exerted only partially throughout the territory). The legacy of this past consists of a certain form of religious legitimacy, to which was added a new form of legitimacy arising from the monarchy's commitment to the nationalists.

Moroccan Islam is officially Sunni, but historical Islam is a complex and diverse religion, and has the capacity to adapt to social demand and particular context of the country.

Since independence in 1956, Morocco has shaped its own reference of a nationalized and territorialized Islam. This ideological construction, reinforced by the very early religious public policy, refers to 'Malikism' (linked to Imam Malik) as the unique rite, unlike other Arab-Muslim countries where many rites coexist.

The choice of the *Malikite* rite is not a newly made decision; it is based on a long historical process that resulted from the combined influence of the Andalusian clerics who settled in Morocco after the Reconquista and the pragmatic and rigorist Amazigh (Berber) puritanism.

As a result, the current political approach adopting a national project of 'Moroccan Islam' based on *'Malikism'* to protect it from international 'Salafism' does not come out of nowhere but is based on three historical reasons. These are: one, the Moroccan dynasty has been in power for 12 centuries when it was started by a descendant of the Prophet who came from the Levant at the request of local Berber tribes; two, the unique situation of Morocco as the only Muslim country not to have been conquered by the Ottoman empire; and, three, early relations with Europe that have had a lasting impact on the Moroccan cultural substratum and constitute a key element of this Moroccan 'exception'.

Another characteristic that defines the nature of the Moroccan monarchy and its religious legitimacy is that it holds both a dynastic and a religious legitimacy, which corresponds to what the German-born American historian Ernest Kantorowicz calls the theory of 'the two bodies of the king' (Kantorowicz, 2016). These two bodies combine the human, the divine, and the Caliph. The monarch, therefore, is not only 'chosen' by the grace of his own personal virtues, but also because he is a member of a sacred prophetic filiation that makes him different from the others. Furthermore, the concept of 'Sharifism' – that is, being a descendent of the Prophet and making of it a title of sovereignty – means that power is not just a matter of secular governance and personal qualities, but is also a matter of legitimacy and diffuse sacredness (Saghi, 2016).

Following the independence of all the Maghreb countries, the new states had to face fresh challenges to meet multiple expectations by adopting an approach that corresponds to their own historical path. For its part, Morocco has suffered little from the 'hormonal imbalances' of colonization compared to its Algerian neighbour. After independence, Morocco's monarchy – which is characterized by a complex legitimacy – was put under the stress test of the profane reality 'to connect the political power of the historical time to the prophetic power of the sacred time'.

The 1980s were decisive in the organization of the religious space in Morocco. In fact, in 1984 the public authorities initiated a reorganization and control of the religious field. Thus, in an international context marked by a return of the religious aspect – incarnated by an unprecedented event in the history of the Islamic world, namely, the Iranian revolution and the establishment of a fundamentally Shiite state that controls the entire society by imposing a total religious order – a mobilizing religious frame of reference has popped up all over the Islamic world. This religious frame of reference was determined to supplant 'militant ideologies' that marked the world in the twentieth century and replace them – first in the Arab-Muslim world, which lagged economically, socially, and democratically – with a religious order that aims to undermine the dominant political and ideological system and substitute it with a model founded on religion. Morocco did not escape this 'spectrum' that haunts the Muslim Arab world.

To better understand this unprecedented mutation, its modes of expression and its management by the Moroccan monarchy – which was anxious to remain the central producer of the political order and its values – it is appropriate, within the framework of this study, to take an inventory of the permanence of the religious question in Morocco, its modes of expression, and its supervision by the public authorities in the light of the emergence of the Islamist player in the political arena. The Dahir of 1984 (under the rule of the late Hassan II) and the Dahir of 2004 (urged by King Mohamed VI) remain the two legislative frameworks in force.

Factors determining authorities' influence on the religious sphere today

Today, in addition to the historical motives listed above, the main goals for the management, as closely as possible, of the religious sphere by the state in Morocco can be summarized as follows:

- A quest for political and social legitimacy. Thus, the preservation of the king's authority and, therefore, of the royal system's sustainability does not depend on elections, a Parliamentary vote, or any other designation's system of main responsibility for the State, but on the supposed adherence of the population's majority. In Morocco this is fundamentally linked to the belief among a large sector of society in the king's prominent religious role that responds to a strong demand for serenity and moral security in the absence of material well-being and economic and social order.
- To counter, in the field, political and labour opposition that emerged in the last three decades of the twentieth century with the Left political socialist and communist opposition, and more recently following the protests born of the Arab Spring since 2011.
- To face, since the late 1970s, both the rise in power of Shiite Islam in Morocco resulting from greater Iranian influence in the Maghreb and Middle East and the religious radicalization of a part of society fomented by external events linked to the wars in Afghanistan

and the Balkans as well as repression by Israeli security forces since 2000, in particular, against the Palestinian population in the occupied territories, Gaza, or Lebanon.
- To support Moroccan diplomacy, especially in certain sub-Saharan African countries politically close to Morocco, like Mali, Senegal, and Guinea-Conakry. At this level resides the reason for the creation of the Mohammed VI Foundation for African Scholars.[2] This foundation is based on a set of goals including 'to unify and coordinate the efforts of Muslim scholars, both in Morocco and in the rest of the African countries, to define, spread and consolidate the tolerant values of Islam, on the basis of the unity of [Islamic] doctrine'.

The institutions and means implemented for these objectives

Within the framework of the Moroccan political system, the king is the main actor in the management of religious space as he is the first beneficiary. To ensure not only his religious functions, but also his role as head of the state, the king relies, in addition to many rules and principles directly inspired (according to the conjuncture and the mood of the moment) by the Quran and the Sunnah, on the Constitution. The latter is supplemented by laws, many of which, in particular in civil and family domains, are Islamic in their essence.

As for the institutional instruments of this management, they reside in the Ministry of Habous and Islamic Affairs and the High Council of Ulema. With regard to the education system, it now represents a major pillar, notably in its traditional component, of the Islamization of Moroccan society in the direction desired by the public authorities, which also have exclusive control on the official audio-visual media, some of which are totally devoted to religious/ Islamic themes[3]; this is not without consequence on a population with an adult illiteracy rate of 32 per cent.

The king, cornerstone of the management of the religious sphere in Morocco

More than the laws and regulations, it is important to note the role of the king in religious matters with particular reference to the powers conferred on him by the Constitution, approved in July 2011 by referendum with 95 per cent of the vote (Lahlou, 2011), held in response to the Arab Spring protests that had erupted in February.

The Preamble proclaims that, as *'A sovereign Muslim State* [emphases added] attached to its national unity and to its territorial integrity, the Kingdom of Morocco intends to preserve, in its plenitude and its diversity, its one and indivisible national identity. Its unity is forged by the convergence of its Arab-Islamist, Berber and Saharan-Hassanic components, nourished and enriched by its African, Andalusian, Hebraic and Mediterranean influences. The pre-eminence accorded to *the Muslim religion* in the national reference is consistent with the attachment of the Moroccan people to the values of openness, of moderation, of tolerance and of dialog for mutual understanding between all the cultures and the civilizations of the world'.

Article 3 proclaims that 'Islam is the religion of the State, which guarantees to all the free exercise of beliefs'. At this level, it is important to emphasize that this 'free exercise of beliefs' only concerns, as already mentioned, the Jewish and Christian minorities within the Moroccan population.

The administration and management of the religious sphere falls entirely within the authority of the king, who is also, according to the Constitution, the head of the executive branch, President of the judicial authority, and commander-in-chief of the armed forces. *Thus, according to the Article 41 of the Constitution, 'The King, Prince (Commander) of the Faithful ('Amir al-Mu'minin'), sees to the respect for Islam. He is the Guarantor of the free exercise of beliefs'*

(Secrétariat général du gouvernement, 2011). He presides over the Superior Council of the Ulemas (*Conseil supérieur des Oulema*), which reviews questions submitted to it by the king. This council is the sole body authorized to make pronouncements (*se prononcer*, in French) on religious consultations (Fatwas) before they are officially approved on questions referred to it, and this on the basis of the tolerant principles, precepts, and designs of Islam.

The attributions, composition, and modalities of the Council's operation are established by Dahir (or a Royal Decree). The King exercises by Dahirs the religious prerogatives inherent to the institution of the Emirate (the Principality) of the Faithful which are conferred on him in exclusive manner by this Article. Under this umbrella, the Ministry of Habous and Islamic Affairs exercises full authority over official mosques and other religious institutions and on all religious activities and similar events in the country.

The constitution, for the proclamation of principles; the law, for the reality on the ground

The Moroccan constitution (see appendix), which fuels the official discourse regarding religiousity and Islam, seems to be directed mainly towards foreign chancelleries and public opinion in Western countries (in particular, those with which Morocco has friendly relations), while domestic laws seek to ensure the continuity of the internal religious and social public order.

This fully justifies the fact that, while the Constitution proclaims, for example, freedom of worship or equality between men and women, the Penal Code continues to be based on laws completely inspired by religion, that is, Islam. For example, the Penal Code punishes eating in public during the month of Ramadan or having (even) consensual sex outside marriage. Similarly, the Family Code still does not accept women's testimony in inheritance or marriage cases, and maintains that in this inheritance, the man's share is two times greater than the woman's share

Thus, according to the preamble of its last constitution – adopted after the beginning of Arab spring protests in Tunisia, Egypt, and Syria – within which it wished to show how opened and modern it is, the 'Kingdom of Morocco', 'with fidelity to its irreversible choice to construct a democratic State of Law, resolutely pursues the process of consolidation and of reinforcement of the institutions of a modern State, having as its bases the principles of participation, of pluralism and of good governance. It develops a society of solidarity where all enjoy security, liberty, equality of opportunities, of respect for their dignity and for social justice, within the framework of the principle of correlation between the rights and the duties of the citizenry'.

But, because Islam is considered as one of the most important foundations of the state; because the majority of the Moroccan population considers itself as Muslim; because there is a strong imbrication between the religious and political spheres in the country. Equally, because the authorities – in fact, the king as the head of the executive power – are generally considered as responsible for the economic and social problems Morocco is experiencing: of which, the poverty of a large part of the population, the high level of unemployment especially in the cities and among the young, the high level of illiteracy, etc.... Finally, because Moroccan society is increasingly conservative, socially and culturally for many reasons, including precisely poverty and illiteracy among its population, as indicated above. The religion, 'the Islam', as it's considered as one of the main important pillars of the political system in Morocco, and as a central factor of legitimization of the monarchy, is progressively rehabilitated in its most traditional values.

This rehabilitation, directed towards the domestic public opinion, reflects the strong contradiction that exists between the different principles and the multiple proclamations of freedom, democracy, and modernity formally stated in the constitution and the laws applied in all the domains which are in direct or indirect report with Islam.

In this sense, the constitution, which also fuels the official political discourse, seems to be directed more globally towards foreign chancelleries and public opinion (in Western countries, in particular, with which Morocco has friendly relations), while domestic laws seek to ensure the continuity of the internal, religious, and social public order.

This fully justifies the fact that, while the constitution proclaims freedom of worship, for example, or equality between men and women, the Moroccan Penal Code continues to be based on many laws completely founded on a strict application of Islam and Koranic law (sharia).

To illustrate this, one can, for example, cite some examples, including:

- Eating in public space: The Article 222 of the Moroccan Penal Code punishes by one to six months imprisonment and a fine of 200 to 500 dirhams, who 'is notoriously considered as muslim ostensibly eats in a public place during the time of Ramadan, without reason admitted by this religion'.
- Also, 'The Penal Code punishes the sexual relations out of wedlock (Article 490)'. 'The penalty is the imprisonment of a month to a year'.
- In terms of inheritance, women still receive half of the part of goods bequeathed by their parents received by men. And any discussion relating to this subject is still a breach of public order, because the text of the Qur'an that prescribes this asymmetry ' is clear about this matter'.
- At another level, women's testimony is not accepted in inheritance or marriage cases and also in criminal affairs.
- When it comes to marital union, and in case of mixed marriages of a Moroccan, woman or man, with a non-Morocco (i.e., a Non-Muslim), this requires a special authorization called 'Mixed marriage authorization'.

  To obtain this authorization, whether it is the case of a Moroccan man or woman wishing to marry a foreigner, a complete file, containing numerous elements, must be addressed with the secretarial office at the Family Justice Division: Among those, a Declaration of Confession in the name of the foreign bride, certified true or a certified copy of the act of conversion to Islam or any other means of proof proving her confession, or certified copy of the act of conversion to Islam or any other means of proof proving the Muslim faith of the husband.
- Concerning Wine sale and consumption: Theoretically the sale of wine (and beer) to Moroccans and its consumption by them are prohibited in Morocco. However, for various reasons, including the fiscal resources collected by the State at this occasion, these operations are generally tolerated, and the law seems to be applied only to punish public drunkenness.

But, the same operations are totally prohibited in the public space during the month of Ramadan (and also few days before and after) and at the occasion of religious feasts. This, which represents a true social hypocrisy on the part of the state, is considered as a form of 'respect for religion'.

The Ministry of Habous and Islamic Affairs

This is considered one of the most important government departments along with defence and the Ministry of the Interior. It is responsible for the effective management of the religious sphere in Morocco. As such, it ensures the control and also, very often, the construction of mosques, controls the training and the preaching of imams, oversees the actions of the Council of Ulemas, and exercises complete control over traditional education and a part of the public educational system.

The current Minister of Habous and Islamic affairs was appointed directly by the king and has held the office for almost 20 years.[4] The religious conscience of the majority of Moroccans stems from many strong beliefs, the most determining of which are the following: that religion gives meaning to life; that justice at all levels is a central value in religion; and that religion encompasses the basis of life and regulates it for both individual and community.

During a 2014 meeting of the United Nations Security Council dedicated to the fight against terrorism the minister stated: 'The case of Morocco is considered exemplary in the legitimacy of the religious ruler, for the institution of the commander of the faithful, in its symbolic and functional dimension, has its roots in Islam. This institution rests on the allegiance which is a formal contract of loyalty for the ruler's in exchange for the ruler's commitment to protect what the Islamic jurists (*fuqahā*) call the "fundamentals of religion". These include five fields, defending religion, protecting life, guarding against harmful ideologies, preserving property and defending honor and dignity. These fundamentals include guaranteeing all the rights stipulated in modern constitutions, in addition to the protection of religion' (Toufik, 2014).

The high council of Ulemas

Chaired by the king and placed under the authority of the Minister of Habous and Islamic Affairs, as indicated above, the Superior Council of Ulemas has the role of, according to the laws that established it, 'the religious scholars in a number of domains, such as implementing the fundamentals of religion, especially in mosques, the intellectual enhancement of the care-takers of religion and of the general public, which would definitely curb negative phenomenon such as terrorism. Their role in providing guidance and in directing people's behaviour also includes the dignity of the individual, the Divine Decrees and human rights in general, a role they perform in accordance with the traditions of the Sunna and the acts of the founding fathers. They exercise it within the sphere of freedom and legality, and their educational roles are in conformity with the great principle known in Islam as "enjoining good and forbidding evil". More often than not terrorism abuses this principle to disturb public life in societies and to contest the legitimacy of the ruler' (Toufik, 2014).

Traditional/Islamic religious education

Islamic education, introduced into general public education system in the mid-1970s, represented a significant change in teaching religion in Moroccan public schools. It was deliberately intended, through the political instrumentalization of Islam, to counteract the rise of secular political and ideological streams, particularly among educated youth in high schools and universities. From then on, the youth would become the privileged target of a systematic action of Islamization carried out both by the state, under the supervision of the Ministry of Habous and Islamic Affairs, and by the emerging Islamist organizations. In fact, the implementation of this policy of Islamization of youth in schools and universities started in the mid-1960s, following the demonstrations of 1965, and continued ever more significantly in the subsequent years. The goal was to eradicate secular (socialist/Marxist) ideologies in schools and universities. The government thus believed it would be able to contain youth protests which, at that time, were spearheading the opposition.

The religious policy inaugurated at that time responded to the monarchy's strategy of hegemony, which had made winning over school youth one of its main objectives. The emerging traditional Islamist forces naturally had also made Islamization of schools one of their strategic goals. The field of education has always been under pressure from their side to review educational programmes in order to Islamize its content. The traditional clerics organized in the League of Moroccan Ulemas have never ceased pressing public authorities to change the curriculum in the same way. Some political parties had also pushed for the same purpose. Istiqlal, a centre-right nationalist party of the old reformist leader Allal Al-Fassi, was one of these forces. Its officials, strongly present in positions of responsibility within the Ministry of National Education, have always worked in this direction, guided in their choice by the party's Salafist ideology and by its doctrine in the field of education. The new policy choices in the field of education during the 1970s and 1980s bolstered this trend, particularly in terms of education's Arabization. This went hand-in-hand with the Islamization of the content of the programmes, becoming more concrete as the authorities began to follow this path. The Istiqlal party could only rejoice at the turn taken by events, and has participated through the involvement of one of its main leaders, the then-Minister of National Education, in the implementation of this Arabization-Islamization of education under the combined effect of the party's religious reformism (Salafism) and the religious fundamentalism of the monarchy, which was interested mainly in its sustainability.

Within this traditional/religious system of education, as in general public education, the Ministry of Habous and Islamic Affairs plays a central role. Indeed, it completely controls five key areas, in addition to the Mohammed VI Foundation of African Ulemas, already mentioned. These include: the structures of religious education covering the Quranic education, called renovated education, of which the ministry has been in charge since 1964; and schools supposed to be traditional, which are former centres of religious learning, scattered throughout Morocco, and whose mission is to train junior clerics such as preachers, muezzins, and imams of mosques.

Radicalization of Islamic movements, a challenge for the future

Despite this constitutional, institutional, legislative, and public policy arsenal, in the late 1970s and early 1980s, Morocco saw a rise in conservatism and radicalization of an increasingly visible segment of its younger population in connection with a set of international events and parallel to domestic economic, social, and political developments.

Among the external events, it is possible to mention all those for whom Moroccans, as Arabs and Muslims, have a very strong sensitivity. These include the conflict in Afghanistan from the 1970s through the present. The war in Afghanistan against the former USSR was initially seen as a war between Islam and communism; from 2001 onwards, with the American intervention in this same country, the Afghan wars will be seen as a confrontation between the West, represented by the US, and Islam.

The Bosnian War, which lasted from 1992 until 1995 and led to the deaths of around 100,000 civilians and soldiers, among which at least 25,000 Bosnian Muslims, is another such event. Within this war, the massacre in Srebrenica in July 1995 and its 8,372 dead, all Bosnian civilians, had an immense impact in the Arab-Muslim world, including Morocco.

To the effects of these wars, one must add the consequences on Arab (and Muslim) public opinion of the *Intifidas*/Uprises of 1987 and 2000 in the occupied Palestinian territories, as well as the wars in Iraq (from 2003) and in Syria (from 2011).

These external events were amplified inside Morocco (as in several Arab-Muslim countries) by socio-economic and political developments, sensitising a large segment of the population, and especially young people, to the arguments made by supporters of 'Political Islam', for whom all Muslims' sufferings stem from their distance from the 'true values of Islam' and in the Westerners' hatred of them. Among those elements, it is possible to quote some, which are of economic and social nature such as a widespread poverty and a great imbalance in the distribution of national wealth, youth unemployment, high levels of illiteracy, and an inadequate public health system. All these elements are summarized in the human development index (HDI), as published annually by the United Nations Development Program. According to the latest report, Morocco's HDI value for 2018 is 0.676, putting the country in the medium human development category – or 121 out of 189 countries and territories ranked (UNDP, 2019).

Others qualitative, intangible, cultural, and political influences include schools' failure or the progressive weakening of 'traditional' political parties, including left-wing parties.

All this led first – during the 1980s and 1990s – to the strengthening of radical Islamist currents, under the influence of trends related to Saudi 'Wahhabism' or to the Muslim Brothers 'brotherhood'. At this level, it is important to note the rise in power, with the Moroccan authorities, of the political weight of the Kingdom of Saudi Arabia, which has become a major donor to Morocco – like many other Arab and African countries, and later some European countries – since the external debt crisis of 1982/1983 (Sardar, 2014).[5] Subsequently, young Moroccans became involved in or committed numerous terrorist actions in Europe and in Morocco, and hundreds joined the war fields in the Middle East, especially after 2011.

In Europe, Moroccans (migrants or children of migrants) became involved, particularly, in the train attacks in Madrid (11 March 2004) where the blasts killed 191 people and wounded 1,841[6] or in the Paris attacks (13 November 2015) that killed 130 people and wounded hundreds more[7] or in the Brussels Airport and Metro attacks (22 April 2016), when 32 people were killed and many more injured[8] or in the Barcelona and Cambrils attacks (17–18 August 2017), where a driver, within a group of 12 Jihadists, killed 16 people and injured more than 100.[9]

Concluding remarks

All the elements presented above – which will be elaborated upon in other papers within the GREASE project – and many others indicate that a large number of Moroccans, young people in particular, have become radicalized over the past 30–35 years, and have initiated violent actions – both in Morocco and abroad – over the last decades.

This has happened, and will likely happen again, despite:

- the role of 'Commander of the believers' devolved by the Constitution to the King;
- the entire legislative arsenal tending to 'protect' Moroccan society against religious radicalization;
- the political discourse seeking to accredit the idea of a moderate and open Moroccan Islam on its international humanist environment;
- the control exercised by the Ministry of Habous and Islamic Affairs – a real state within the state – on the majority of mosques in the country and on large parts of the education system;
- political (and often financial) control over public and private media.

However, if the reality of the ground on the radicalization front does not seem to correspond to what the Moroccan rulers want – or, let's say, to what they are wishing – is because powerful factors are still acting within Moroccan society (leaving aside external factors here). At this level, it is possible to mention:

- the strengthening of conservative currents within society, in cities as well as in rural areas, in relation to the reforms introduced in the Moroccan education system since the 1970s. This has also been shaped by the penetration, since the 1990s, of Arab satellite television, easily accessible to illiterate women as well as to the most disadvantaged social strata, as it's one of their very few entertainment sources;
- the socio-economic situation, as presented succinctly above, marked by high unemployment levels among young people (and graduates in particular), greater precariousness of a large part of the population, as well as difficulties in accessing basic public services such as school, health, water, and sanitation;
- the high level of illiteracy among the population and the fact that the official and private media play no role in the education of society and its possible openness to the principles and universal human values;
- the difficulties of organization and expression in (normal) political parties and also the impossibility of controlling the economic or political decisions engaging society. This gives rise to a fatalistic approach in many people, especially the poorest, who rely on God to solve their problems. Hence the great influence of the slogan 'Islam is the solution' often heard during protests organized by Islamist currents.

All this indicates that, even if the management of public space by the state seems to please large Moroccan social categories, which ultimately consider that Morocco is in a better economic situation than most African countries or that it enjoys greater stability and security than a large number of Arab countries, the threat of religious radicalization remains.

And in fact, the question of the management of the religious sphere in Morocco today largely concerns the problem of radicalization. With freedom of worship and exercise of their rites granted by the Constitution to the Moroccan Jewish and Christian minorities, the only minorities who remain in search of recognition are Moroccans who have changed their religion or the Shias. The latter could eventually be granted certain rights in relation to their religious beliefs, thanks in particular to the work of the National Council for Human Rights which acts under the umbrella of the Constitution and to which the king often seems to listen.

Notes

1 The data for 1961 are a reverse projection based on the results of the general population and housing censuses of 1961, 1971, 1982, 1994, 2004, and 2014. After 2014, the figures are projections based on the results of the 2014 census.
2 This was decided under a Royal Decree on 24 June 2015 and is chaired by the King Mohammed VI.
3 On 16 June 2004 in Rabat, the king launched the Mohammed VI television channel, Assadissa (the Sixth), to broadcast the Quran. This channel, inaugurated a year after the terrorist attacks perpetrated of May 2003 in Casablanca, aims to 'thwart extremists who damage the image of Islam' and follows the same logic as the 'Quranic Radio Mohammed VI', which had been launched in 2003, with the objective of 'reflecting the orientations of Morocco in the religious field and carrying a message of tolerance and openness inspired by the Coran and Sunnah'.
http://www.habous.gov.ma/fr/annonce-et-activit%C3%A9s-minist%C3%A8re/3006-lancement-de-la-cha%C3%AEne-mohammed-vi-du-saint-coran-assadissa.html.

4 The minister, Ahmed Toufiq, has been in office since 7 November 2002. Parallel to his ministerial duties, he was appointed by King Mohammed VI on 2 April 2010 as chairman of the 'Hassan II Mosque Foundation' in Casablanca and on 13 July 2015 as deputy chairman of the Mohammed VI Foundation of African Ulemas.
5 'The beginning of Islam's fifteenth century, it was being suggested in Muslim intellectual circles, would herald the return of Islam as a force in world affairs and as a power in Muslim societies. The Saudis would be in the driving seat, ready to fuel the resurgence with their petrodollars. Mecca might have failed to hold an Islamic Summit, but it had now become the capital of Muslim conferences. In 1976, the city was host to the First International Conference on Islamic Economics, which established the newly emerging discipline of "Islamic economics" and later led to the formation of a host of Islamic banks, financial institutions and Islamic economics departments in universities throughout the world. 17 The following year, the city was welcoming the delegates to the First World Conference on Muslim Education. 18 This led directly to the formation of an Islamic Academy in Cambridge, UK, and generated an international debate on how higher education could be infused with Islam'. Z. Sardar, 'Mecca, the sacred city'. pp. 297/298.
6 https://www.bbc.com/news/av/world-europe-14666717/2004-madrid-train-attacks
7 https://www.bbc.com/news/world-europe-48784476
8 https://www.bbc.com/news/world-europe-35869985
9 https://www.bbc.com/news/world-europe-40964242

References

Berrada, A. (2019). *Plaidoirie pour un Maroc laïque*. Rabat: Tarik Editions
Guigou, J.L. (2012). Le nouveau monde méditerranéen (The new Mediterranean World). Paris: Editions Descartes et Cie.
Haut Commissariat au Plan. (2014). *Résultats du recensement général de la population*. Available at: https://www.hcp.ma/downloads/RGPH-2014_t17441.html
Joseph, M. (2017, January 5). Morocco's Christian converts pray in hiding. La Croix International. Available at: https://international.la-croix.com/news/moroccos-christian-converts-pray-in-hiding/4445.
Kantorowicz, E-H. (2016). *The King's Two Bodies: A Study in Medieval Political Theology*. Editions Paperback.
Lahlou, M. & Zouiten, M. (2019). Morocco: Country Report. GREASE Project. European University Institute. Available at: http://grease.eui.eu/wp-content/uploads/sites/8/2019/11/Morocco-report.pdf.
Lahlou, M. (2011). *Maroc: Un grand pas vers le passé*. Review [online]. Politis.fr. Available at: https://www.politis.fr/articles/2011/07/maroc-un-grand-pas-vers-le-passe-14843/.
Ouaissa, R. (2018). Religion. In Jörg Gertel & Ralf Hexel (eds), *Coping with Uncertainty: Youth in the Middle East and North Africa* (pp. 80–96). London: Saqi Books.
Pollock, D. (2013). A Moroccan Exception?. Journal of International Security Affairs. Fall-Winter. Available at: https://www.washingtoninstitute.org/policy-analysis/view/a-moroccan-exception/
PBS. (2015, July 29*). In Morocco, Muslims and Jews study side-by-side but for how long?* NewsHour. Available at: https://www.pbs.org/ NewsHour / world / morocco-muslims-jews-study-side-side
Saghi, O. (2016). *Comprendre la monarchie* marocaine. Paris: Editions La Croisée des Chemins.
Sardar, Z. (2014). *Mecca, the sacred city*. Bloomsbury Publishing Plc. Available at: file:///C:/Users/21266/AppData/Local/Temp/Mecca%20The%20Sacred%20City%20by%20Ziauddin%20Sardar%20(z-lib.org).epub.pdf
Secrétariat Général du Gouvernement. Royaume du Maroc. *La Constitution 2011*. Available at: http://www.sgg.gov.ma.
Toufik, A. (2016, February 4). *The Experience of the Kingdom of Morocco in the Fight Against Terrorism*. Intervention by Minister of Habous and Islamic Affairs, Ahmed Toufiq, September 30, 2014, New York [in French]. Available at: *http://www.habous.gov.ma/fr/documents-de-la-rencontre/3141-%C2%AB-l%E2%80%99exp%C3%A9rience-du-royaume-du-maroc-pour-lutter-contre-le-terrorisme%C2%BB-new-york, -30-septembre, -2014-intervention-mr-ahmed-toufiq.html.*
UNDP. (2019). *Inequalities in Human Development in the 21st Century. Briefing Note for Countries on the 2019 Human Development Report, Morocco*. Human Development Report. New York: UNDP.

Appendix
Main articles of the Moroccan Constitution relating to Islam (author's translation)

Preamble

With fidelity to its irreversible choice to construct a democratic State of Law, the Kingdom of Morocco resolutely pursues the process of consolidation and of reinforcement of the institutions of a modern State, having as its bases the principles of participation, of pluralism and of good governance. It develops a society of solidarity where all enjoy security, liberty, equality of opportunities, of respect for their dignity and for social justice, within the framework of the principle of correlation between the rights and the duties of the citizenry.

A sovereign Muslim State, attached to its national unity and to its territorial integrity, the Kingdom of Morocco intends to preserve, in its plentitude and its diversity, its one and indivisible national identity. Its unity is forged by the convergence of its Arab-Islamist, Berber [amazighe] and Saharan-Hassanic [saharo-hassanie] components, nourished and enriched by its African, Andalusian, Hebraic and Mediterranean influences [affluents]. The preeminence accorded to the Muslim religion in the national reference is consistent with [va de pair] the attachment of the Moroccan people to the values of openness, of moderation, of tolerance and of dialog for mutual understanding between all the cultures and the civilizations of the world.

Article 1

Morocco is a constitutional, democratic, parliamentary and social Monarchy. The constitutional regime of the Kingdom is founded on the separation, the balance and the collaboration of the powers, as well as on participative democracy of [the] citizen, and the principles of good governance and of the correlation between the responsibility for and the rendering of accounts. The Nation relies for its collective life on the federative constants [constantes federatrices], on the occurrence of moderate Muslim religion, [on] the national unity of its multiple components [affluents], [on] the constitutional monarchy and [on] democratic choice.

Article 3

Islam is the religion of the State, which guarantees to all the free exercise of beliefs.

Article 41

The King, Commander of the Faithful [Amir Al Mouminine], sees to the respect for Islam. He is the Guarantor of the free exercise of beliefs [cultes]. He presides over the Superior Council of the Ulema [Conseil superieur des Oulema], charged with the study of questions that He submits to it. The Council is the sole instance enabled [habilitee] to comment [prononcer] on the religious consultations (Fatwas) before being officially agreed to, on the questions to which it has been referred [saisi] and this, on the basis of the tolerant principles, precepts and designs of Islam.

The attributions, the composition and the modalities of functioning of the Council are established by Dahir [Royal Decree]. The King exercises by Dahirs the religious prerogatives inherent in the institution of the Emirate of the Faithful [Imarat Al Mouminine] which are conferred on him in exclusive manner by this Article.

Part VI
South and Southeast Asia and the Asia Pacific

21
India
The challenge of being plural and multicultural

Gurpreet Mahajan

Introduction

The political leaders of independent India were extremely conscious of the country's religious diversity and wanted the two largest communities – Hindus and Muslims – to live together in the newly constituted democracy. Even though many people responded to the Partition of the country and the ensuing communal attacks by campaigning for a 'Hindu' India, the Constituent Assembly, engaged in framing the Constitution, moved in a different direction. The most influential leaders, from Nehru to Patel and from Rajendra Prasad to Ambedkar, affirmed the vision of a plural India.

Until 2007, India was the only country in South Asia[1] whose Constitution did not bestow a special status on any religion. The leadership that guided the struggle for independence firmly believed that the establishment of a state religion invariably accords priority and preference to that religion. Irrespective of the extent of religious liberty that is given to other religions, it puts in place not just a symbolic hierarchy but a real one. Valuing religious diversity, in their view, required not just freedom of religion for all but a framework that announced the equality of all.

This was a bold and imaginative way of thinking about religious diversity. In some significant ways it was different from the liberal secular framework that prevailed in other, more stable and older democracies at that time. It was premised on the belief that living with diversity required something more than granting the same basic rights to all citizens. Accordingly, it instituted formal measures for recognition of diversity and supplemented these with several informal measures of accommodation (Mahajan, 2013: 97–126).

However, the strain of inter-community conflict, wars with neighbouring countries, the contemporary global context of religious radicalization and terrorism, pressures generated by the neo-liberal economy, and the logic of competitive electoral politics have led to the consolidation of the Right (in the form of religious-cultural majoritarianism) in India. There is a new dimension being added to the picture of a plural and diverse India, where the majority community is demanding due recognition of its cultural and material concerns. In a democracy, the political and cultural history of the nation is continuously being rearticulated, reshaped, and contested. The work of citizens, civil society, and other political actors is therefore never finished; they must continuously create a public consciousness that affirms the Constitutional values.

The Constitution had created a framework that could check the threat of cultural assimilation that minorities face. However, day-to-day engagement with issues of accommodation required political judgement: how should conflict between competing community claims be dealt with? Whom should the government listen to in a community? These issues had to be assessed each time. The Constitution laid down the principle of equality for all, but it was for the government of the day to take the appropriate decision. With hindsight one can see the mistakes that the latter made and learn from that experience so that we can avoid the same pitfalls in the future.

India's journey, despite the mixed bag of successes and failures, is an important reminder that the everyday life of a person is, to some extent, shaped by religion and group affiliation. The experience of the group affects and influences how individuals act in the social and political arena. In a plural society, such embedded persons bring diversity of habits and practices into the public domain. The presence of such differences need not raise anxiety and trepidation. What should matter is that cultures, within which people give meaning to their lives, do not become stagnant and static. India's experience with legal and institutional pluralism and the space it accorded to communities to manage their own affairs provides many insights the challenges that governance of religious diversity presents – the mistakes we might make and the rewards we might receive when we even make the gesture of accommodating religious diversity.

Religious diversity: population composition and emerging issues

Religious and cultural diversity is not a new feature of Indian society. It is not a consequence of recent migrations or globalization. People of different religions have lived in India for centuries, so diversity is a given fact of social life. The first census after independence (1951) registered that almost 84 per cent of the total population were Hindus; of the remaining population, about 10 per cent were Muslims, 2.3 per cent Christians, 1.89 per cent Sikhs, 0.74 per cent Buddhists, 0.46 per cent Jains, and all others 0.43 per cent. The 2011 census revealed that the percentage of minorities has increased, and this itself is significant. Hindus constituted 79.80 per cent of the population, Muslims 14.3 per cent, Christians 2.30 per cent, Sikhs 1.72 per cent, Buddhists 0.72 per cent, Jains 0.37 per cent, with all 'other religions' totalling 0.66 per cent; 0.24 per cent declined to state their religion. With a total population of over 1.2 billion (1,210,569,573), India has the largest population of Hindus in the world. Also, by some estimates, 11.1 per cent of the world's Muslim population lives in India according to the 2015 data. This means that after Indonesia, India had the largest population of Muslims living in any country[2] (Diamant, 2019). Although in terms of percentage, Christians constitute a mere 2.3 per cent of the population, in absolute numbers there are more than 20 million Christians living in India (see Table 21.1). Thus, the nature and range of diversity is enormous, even when we do not take into account any of the numerous tribal religious forms and practices.[3]

Although Hindus constitute almost 80 per cent of the population, this number is created through the census exercise, which places a number of sects and denominations within this religion. People identify their religion as 'Kabir panth', 'Brahma kumari', and 'Sanatan dharm' (to name a few), and the office of the Census Commissioner classifies them as Hindu. For this reason, many scholars maintain that India has only innumerable, diverse minorities; even the so-called majority is, in actuality, a conglomeration of different groups with different beliefs and practices, and it is the homogenizing drive of the modern, legal discourse that has coalesced them into one category.

Table 21.1 Population by religious affiliation

Religion	2001 (%)	Numbers	2011 (%)	Numbers
Hindus	80.5	827,578,868	79.80	966,257,353
Muslims	13.4	138 188,240	14.23	172,245,158
Christians	2.3	24,080,016	2.30	27,819,588
Sikhs	1.9	19,215,730	1.72	20,833,116
Buddhists	0.8	7,955,207	0.72	8,442,972
Jains	0.4	4,225,053	0.37	4,451,753
Other Religions	0.6	6,639,626	0.66	7,937,734
*Not stated	0.1		0.24	2,867,303
Total		1,028,610,328		1,210,569,573

Source: Census of India, 2011 and 2001, Ministry of Home Affairs, Government of India.
*Category introduced in 2011 census.

A feature that has attracted considerable attention, particularly from the religious Right, is that the percentage of Hindus has been steadily declining while the Muslim population has grown over time. In 2011, for the first time, the Hindu population dipped below 80 per cent and the percentage of Sikhs also decreased. The fact that estimates had projected a further increase in the Muslim population has been used to create 'paranoia' in the majority, with leaders of some Hindu organizations calling it a 'population jihad' that will make India an Islamic state (PTI, 2015; see also Singh, 2015; Joshi et al., 2003).

However, these conclusions have been challenged and many experts point out that the Muslim population grew at a slower rate than it had in the previous decade (Rukmini & Singh, 2015). Yet representations based on existing population size continue to circulate in many forums.

An analysis of the 2011 census shows that among the major religious communities, Muslims have the lowest literacy rates[4]; the gap between male and female literacy levels is also the largest among Muslims.[5] Muslims also had the lowest work participation rate, 32.6 per cent, with Sikhs and Jains having marginally higher work participation rates of 36.3 and 35.5 per cent, respectively. Although women from all communities, had a lower work participation rate, it was strikingly low for Muslim women at just 14.1 per cent. In 2014–2015, the recruitment of minorities in government jobs, public banks, and public sector undertakings was a meagre 8.57 per cent.[6] Data for the private sector is not available, but in the case of Sikhs and Muslims, the majority are self-employed (Jodhka, 2010). This means that larger shares of these communities do not have the social security net that is available to those working in government and public sector jobs.

Muslims are not a homogeneous population and differences exist along lines of occupation and region (Robinson, 2007). In Kerala, where they comprise almost one-quarter of the population, the literacy level and economic status of Muslims is far better than in Assam where they are present in higher numbers. In West Bengal, under the Left government there were no communal riots yet large sections of the community remained economically weak and lived in districts with poor infrastructure. It is difficult to explain these trends. While some studies identify poverty as the primary cause of their backwardness, others point to cultural reasons. Neither takes into account the fact that many Muslims were engaged in traditional occupations that became unsustainable with technological advancement. In some cases, fears about personal safety compelled them to leave the places where they had lived and worked for years. All these elements have contributed to their marginalization.

However, the narrative of development is a complex one. In India, Muslim women have lower levels of literacy and few among them enter the work force, but the infant mortality rate is lower in this community when compared to other communities. Even more significantly, among all religious groups, Muslims have the most favourable sex ratio. Despite the higher incidence of poverty, life expectancy among Muslims is marginally above the national average.[7]

In 2006, when the Sachar Committee Report[8] revealed that Muslims lagged in major development indicators, the Congress-led UPA government initiated a number of policies to rectify the situation – from scholarships and programmes for advancing the educational and skill levels to making credit available through public sector banks. The findings of the Sachar Committee, however, gave an opportunity to the Right to claim that other political parties were merely 'pseudo-secular'[9] (Jafferlot, 1993), that they engaged in identity politics[10] and neglected the 'development' concerns of the community members. Muslims, in their view, needed economic betterment and this required greater integration and uniformity. The Left-leaning voices, on the other hand, argued that the myth of 'minority appeasement' had been exposed: Muslims were a neglected minority and no government had made any effort to benefit and improve their lives.

There has been a demand to recognize caste-like distinctions within the Muslims, so that they can receive the benefits available under the reservation policy to Scheduled Castes (Sikand, 2003). Although this specific demand has not been accepted by the central government, segments of the Muslim population that are identified as socially and economically backward are included in the list of Other Backward Classes (OBCs) and are eligible for reservation quotas.

Although the question of the Muslim minority has gained centrality, other religious minorities also have pressing concerns that need to be addressed by state and community. The Parsi population is diminishing at a fast rate and this is a matter of considerable anxiety (Unisa et al., 2008). The Sikhs have complained of neglect in post-independence India and experienced a phase of militancy in the 1980s (see Singh, 1995). Despite having a higher literacy rate, they have a highly adverse sex ratio. The Jains have an even higher literacy rate among men and women, but the work participation rate of Jain women remains low. The effect of these parameters has yet to be studied carefully, but all communities face social challenges. More significantly, while economic betterment remains an important concern, religious and identity-related issues such as recognition for their practices and places of worship also rank high on the agenda of religious communities.

India is a deeply diverse society; besides religion, differences exist along caste lines. Diversities of language and cultures are equally pivotal, and each of these produces different vulnerabilities. For instance, while Hindus are doing better than Muslims in almost all indicators, the lower castes (those categorized as Scheduled Castes) remain among the most marginalized sections of society. Similarly, Hindus may be a religious majority, but Tamil-speaking Hindus became a linguistic minority in Bengal. Caste, religion, and language thus yield different sets of minorities, and addressing the concerns of one does not necessarily provide benefits to the others.

Governance of religious diversity

The constitutional framework

After a long, sustained movement, India gained independence from British rule in 1947, but independence came with the grief of Partition. A section of the Muslim leadership, led by

M.A. Jinnah, had demanded a separate homeland for the Muslim population in the region. Pakistan was created ostensibly to meet that demand. The population 'transfer' that followed the Partition saw unprecedented communal violence: an estimated 1.5 million people lost their lives and another 5 million were displaced. In this context, the question of religion, and the anxieties of the religious minorities, particularly Muslims who had stayed on in India, were uppermost in the mind of the Constituent Assembly. Members spent considerable time deliberating on such questions as what should be the place of religion in society, what should be the relationship between state and religion, and what rights should be given to religious communities, particularly the minorities, in independent India.

Eventually the framework that was devised did not adhere *fully* to the available paradigm of liberal secularism. It accepted some aspects of that framework: most notably, it did not subordinate state to religious authority (Modood, 2019; Modood & Sealy, 2019). It accepted the 'no-establishment' principle (that is, the state was to have no religion of its own), gave equal rights (including religious liberty) to all citizens, and affirmed that no religious education would be provided in any educational institution 'wholly maintained out of State funds' (Article 28[1]).

However, it did not rest with this liberal secular framework. It recognized that minorities, particularly religious minorities, had anxieties and demands that required supplementary provisions. To address their concerns, the Constituent Assembly rearticulated the public-private distinction: in the political (public arena), all persons were treated as undifferentiated citizens, but in the cultural and religious domain (private sphere) the population was seen as heterogeneous and citizens were differentiated on the basis of their community membership. In other words, in the political domain all had the same rights and no community had separate representation. Hence, no distinction was made along community lines here (Mahajan, 2011: 1–50).

In the cultural domain some distinction was made between the majority and the minorities. While all persons were granted 'freedom of conscience' and the right to 'profess, propagate and practice' their religion (Article 25),[11] for matters relating to family (marriage, divorce, inheritance), all persons were to be governed by the personal laws of their community. Thus, a form of legal pluralism was accepted in the culture-religious domain.

Two provisions were included to protect the rights of the minorities. First, they could establish educational institutions to impart the 'education of their choice' (Article 30 [1]). Second, they were given the right to conserve their distinct language, culture, and script (Article 29). Minority educational institutions could receive funds from the state, although there was no injunction relating to the extent of support they were to receive. This flexibility also meant that the minorities had a choice: they could seek state support or be self-funded. Needless to say, a greater degree of autonomy accrued to the latter (Mahajan, 1998).

The framework that was devised for the governance of religion and religious diversity had three key elements. First, a system of legal pluralism (members of a particular community were to be governed by the personal laws of that community). Second, recognition of community institutions, with the latter having considerable autonomy to regulate their religious affairs. Some community institutions like Sikh Gurudwara Prabandhak Committee (set up under the Sikh Gurudwara Act 1925) already existed and governed the functioning of their religious places of worship. In 1964, following the provisions of the Waqf Act 1954, the Central Waqf Council was established to manage their trust properties and places of worship. In 1972, the All India Muslim Personal Law Board was set up to deal with matters relating to community personal laws. These bodies are formally recognized and officially viewed as the organizations responsible for the administration and regulation of the religious and cultural affairs of their respective communities. Third, a plural network of community educational and charitable institutions, some of which are exclusively for the community, while others are open to the rest of society.

This was a complex system of religious governance. While it gave the right to religion to everyone, it operated in a majority-minority framework. That is, after giving equal rights to all persons, it saw individuals as belonging to different communities – the Hindu majority or other minority communities. It considered the possibility of the cultural majority becoming a political majority and provided safeguards to shield minorities from the threat of cultural assimilation.

The formal framework for the governance of religious diversity was in practice accompanied by a slew of informal measures. For instance, major religious festivals or events from all religions were included in the list of public holidays, and national symbols were chosen that were acceptable to most communities or perceived as being inclusive (Parekh, 2015). A deliberate effort was also made to have members from all communities in the highest decision-making bodies (the central cabinet) and other prestigious public positions. These informal gestures were symbolic but formed an integral part of the accommodation of religious diversity in India, particularly public perception of it.

Contextual paradoxes

This was a plural and multicultural framework of accommodation. It implicitly accepted that a liberal state might embody the cultural orientation of the majority; hence, it put in place some checks. Were they enough? Did this framework resolve issues relating to religion and religious practices in the public sphere? Did it ensure peaceful co-existence of diverse communities? Could it protect and nurture diversity?

The Indian framework has been reasonably successful in accommodating religious diversity in the public arena. Different dress codes, food habits, rituals, and practices are readily accepted and highly visible in the market, workplace, educational institutions, and government offices. The presence of minority educational institutions has meant that parents who want to give a religious-cultural education to their children can do so; they can send their children to minority educational institutions, and this has taken pressure off the state. Rarely, if ever, are demands made upon government schools for a separate prayer room or other facilities for the observance of religious practices and rituals. In short, issues of the kind that have dominated European discourses on secularism over the last two or three decades have been nearly absent in India.

Religious places of worship are seen side-by-side (or back-to-back) everywhere, and the air resounds with sounds of different prayers and chants. From the sound and activity, most people can identify a religion. Whether they visit different places of worship or not, people can decipher religious differences. This learning has emerged from the visibility of different religions in the public domain as schools (or non-minority public and private schools) do not provide religious education.

Religion, in both its spiritual and ritualistic form, plays an important role in the life of individuals as well as society. Thus, claims relating to religious practices and observances are taken seriously and, in normal circumstances, an effort is made to accommodate them. More importantly, religion-inspired practices do not generate anxiety. Seeing someone in a veil or a turban, or a woman singing on stage with a *ghunghat* (partially covered face) does not raise alarm bells in the liberal mind. Nobody asks for these practices to be banned. In this sense, matters of religion are treated differently; they mark an exception.

However, in a society where religion and accompanying ideas of what is sacred are so pervasive, religion remains a volatile subject. This trigger can be pressed anytime for purely instrumental reasons: to woo one community or marginalize another. Therefore, in India, we have two extreme situations: on the one hand, an enormous degree of religious and cultural diversity and, on the other, conflicts around religious issues. In other words, co-existence of difference does not always translate into absence of conflict. One can create formal space for accommodation of diversity, but after that, trust between communities has to be nurtured assiduously by the government and civil society. In a locality where a temple and a mosque are placed close together, conflict can suddenly erupt over the volume of the loudspeaker that relays the morning prayers. Small disputes of this kind can flare into communal conflict. In such precarious situations the response of the local administration, civil society actions, and inter-community initiatives can make a crucial difference. If local administration remains indifferent or if some party members mobilize for stopping the use of loudspeaker at dawn, the situation can easily spark inter-community conflict.

The Constitution created a complex structure for accommodating diversity, but this can yield the desired result only when trust between communities is carefully nurtured. Some governments have tried to generate trust by according due recognition to different communities in the history of the nation and through symbolic gestures of accommodation – for instance, declaring an additional state holiday for a religious festival, hosting celebratory gatherings on such occasions, providing assistance to minority institutions, and reaching out to different communities.

While governments and political parties express their goodwill towards a community through such informal gestures, different communities also vie for the support of the elected representatives. The emerging dynamics, on the one hand, produces reliance on political patronage that fosters competitive communitarianism, and on the other, helps build links between political parties and religious community leadership. The latter enables minorities to develop a stake in the democratic system; they can receive support from political parties and make their voice count. Even if the demands of a community are not accepted fully, having sympathetic voices on their side helps ward off the sense of alienation that can otherwise grip minorities.

In India, informal gestures of accommodation have played a critical role in nurturing a sense of being counted and treated as equal. To many these may seem symbolic measures that are not required by a strict reading of the Constitution, nevertheless when governments do away with these practices or diminish the space for such informal accommodation, it triggers anxiety among the minorities. Eventually it is not just the formal provisions or representation that sustains the multicultural fabric: the narrative of pluralism has to be cultivated continuously by a positive affirmation of respect towards different communities.

State-religion relationship

In contemporary times, most secular democracies grapple with the two fundamental questions relating to state-religion relationship. First, whether religion should enter the public domain – for instance, should public officials be allowed to display or wear visible religious symbols and participate in religious practices. Second, whether the state should deal with religious issues by adopting a hands-off policy or by intervening to determine what is permissible.

Immediately after independence, India grappled with questions of this nature. When the issue of reconstructing the Somnath temple arose, Jawaharlal Nehru (India's first prime minister) argued that the Constitution disallowed the use of public money for religious purposes. He also maintained that state officials should not publicly participate in religious ceremonies. However, many in his cabinet – as well as the President, Dr. Rajendra Prasad – disagreed. Although the temple was constructed by a private trust, the President accepted the invitation to be part of the installation ceremony at the reconstructed Somnath Temple (Gopal, 1979: 155).

Since that initial moment, divergent views continue to prevail on this subject. Secularists express alarm when elected representatives display personal religious beliefs in public, such as when Ministers start their work by performing ceremonial religious worship in full glare of the cameras. However, few object when officials visit different places of worship as a gesture of respect to all communities.

India steered away from the accepted liberal secular framework and permitted greater mingling of state and religion. The state often acts to ensure that communities can perform their religious practices without external hindrances. For instance, it routinely makes arrangements for pilgrims who come for a holy dip in the Ganges on the occasion of *Kumbh* or when a community holds a religious procession in a city. There are innumerable occasions when the state is administratively involved in the performance of religious practices.

The more challenging question, however, is: should the state legislate to protect the religious practice of a community? If the cow is sacred for the Hindus, should the state legislate to ban the slaughter of cows? Similarly, if a community regards their place of worship to be sacred, should the state restrict the sale of meat and alcohol around the temple complex?

The Constitution did not endorse a 'hands-off' policy, but it did not give any clear directions on how matters of this nature should be settled. As a consequence, the decision rests with the government or the political leadership of the day and we have no clear policy on this. In fact, governments in different regions at different times have responded to these questions in varied ways. For instance, in the 1960s, Congress governments in some states banned the slaughter of cows, but many others did not follow the same path.[12]

In a situation of deep diversity, there can be a conflict between the religious practices of two communities, as well as dissenting voices seeking change in the existing religious-social practices. In cases involving both these issues (resolving conflicts and effecting change), the burden has fallen disproportionately upon the judiciary. When conflicts emerge between practices, the Supreme Court applies what it calls the 'essential practice' test. It interprets religion to determine if the said practice is an essential part of that religion (Mahajan, 1998; Sen, 2010): for example, whether slaughtering a cow on Eid is an essential part of the religious practice in Islam. Instead of leaving matters of religion to the community or religious leadership, it determines matters of religious belief and practice. Similarly, when disputes arise around the ownership of a particular site of religious worship, it is the Supreme Court that is often asked to adjudicate. When a group seeks recognition as a separate and new religion, it is the Supreme Court that decides whether a particular system of beliefs constitutes a separate religion or merely a sect or denomination of another religion.

Although the judiciary has interceded to decide what constitutes a religion and an essential practice within a religion, the governments have, by and large, been reluctant to intervene in religious practices[13] even when these clash with the principle of gender equality or personal autonomy. In fact, in 1985 when the Supreme Court ruled in favour of Shah Bano's petition seeking maintenance for herself and her children, the Congress government stood with the community leaders that rejected the verdict. The following year the government passed the Muslim Women's Protection of Divorce Act 1986 that restricted Muslim women from seeking judicial intervention for maintenance. More recently, when the Supreme Court declared the practice of prohibiting women of a certain age from worshipping at the Lord Ayyappa Shrine, many political parties as well as members of the ruling party sought a review of the decision.

On questions of religious practices, state institutions often speak in different voice. While this may appear to be messy and evasive, it has provided space that vulnerable sections can use to express their voice and seek change in the existing practices.

Consolidation of the right

Paradoxically, when India gained Independence and polarization along community lines was very sharp, the Right-wing majoritarian sentiments did not receive wide support. In the first general election, the Jan Sangh (the party associated with this position) received a meagre 3 per cent of the vote; of the 812 candidates it fielded for the Lok Sabha, State Assemblies, and electoral colleges, 536 lost their deposit (ECI, 1955). In the 1990s voter support for the Bhartiya Janata Party (BJP, which emerged in the 1980s and occupied the ideological space vacated by the Jan Sangh) rose to 20 per cent. In 2019 this figure further increased to 37.4 per cent and the party secured 303 of the 542 seats in the Lower Chamber. This consolidation from the 1990s to the present has occurred against the backdrop of a major shift in economic policy – namely, greater liberalization and privatization. A similar trend can be seen in many other parts of the world, indicating that the larger context of a crisis-ridden neo-liberal economy is significant.

Nevertheless, in a democracy there is always a local flavour and content through which popular support is won. In India, the Partition, subsequent wars with Pakistan, political turmoil in Kashmir valley, and recurrent terror attacks have made national security concerns paramount. The Right has owned this agenda more stridently and supported a muscular nationalism that should correct the wrongs done to the Hindus. By constructing a narrative around 'invasions' by Mughal rulers, oppression of Hindus in the past, and terrorist attacks by members of various Islamic groups in contemporary India, it has cast a shadow over the Muslim presence. To many, Muslims appear as a 'hostile other'. Although the finger is pointed at the 'external other', there is always some slippage in the popular imagination shaped by identity politics.

In the emerging polarization between 'us' and 'them', the Right has focussed considerably on the 'us' component. Extolling the virtues of Hinduism as a tolerant and peaceful religion – something that had been a part of the narrative of the plural idea – it has successfully glorified the Hindu past and claimed the moral high ground for the community.

Two other elements are added to this narrative. The first is that the majority has been wronged and treated unfairly: past governments have tried to 'appease' the Muslim minority in various ways – from granting subsidies for the Haj pilgrimage, holding Iftar parties (on the occasion of Id-Ul-Fitr), or not reforming the Muslim personal law (despite demands from the women in the community). The second is that, as a minority, Hindus suffer discrimination in the neighbouring countries: in India, the Muslim minority enjoys a better status and as statistics show, their numbers have been steadily increasing. In effect this signals that the Hindus are neglected in India and discriminated against in the region.

To rectify these wrongs, the BJP has usurped aspects of the liberal agenda to demand the formulation of a Uniform Civil Code and eliminate community-based personal laws. Since the Muslim personal law alone has not been reformed to ensure greater gender equality, this would effect changes in those laws and simultaneously question the rationale for community/group differentiation.

India put in place a constitutional framework to accommodate diversity. That remains more or less in place, but it is the everyday, informal modes of accommodation that are under stress. There is greater visibility and space for the majority culture and religion; renaming of streets and public places is just one instance of this. However, the structural spaces that were provided for minorities continue to exist.

Concluding remarks

When cultural plurality exists in society, it is bound to spill into the public domain. Restricting visible diversity to the private sphere places minorities under stress. It invariably tends to enhance their marginalization. In Quebec, for instance, insensitivity to the cultural codes of minority communities resulted in Orthodox Jews and Muslims not using the benefits provided by the state-run health care facilities; elsewhere, public intolerance of the dress requirements resulted in women being restricted to community-dominated spaces. In other words, even the pursuit of development goals requires an environment that is sensitive to the cultural orientation and needs of minorities.

The political leadership that shaped the thinking of independent, democratic India understood this. They created a constitutional framework that recognized and accommodated religious diversity. Formal legal measures gave visibility to difference and space for minorities to continue with their way of life. This made minority cultures more secure and confident of resisting pressures of assimilation. However, making cultures secure did not make individual members of these communities secure. Repeated incidents of communal violence revealed that the task of ensuring basic citizenship rights for all remained unrealized (Krishna, 1985).

The experience of India shows that neither the realization of individual rights nor accommodation of diversity is by itself enough. Both these ends need to be pursued side-by-side. Instead of seeing them as alternatives from which we must choose one or the other, they must be seen as parallel concerns that should co-exist. When diversity is accommodated, the state and community need to ensure that basic right of equality is protected for the vulnerable groups in a community and inter-community conflict is swiftly curbed and dealt with. When basic rights are protected for all individuals, one needs also to ensure that the dominant majority culture does not disadvantage or shrink opportunities for minorities; that minorities have the space to live in accordance with their way of life and pass their cultural heritage to the next generation. Democracies need this twin sensibility in the modern world.

Notes

1 Previously, Nepal was identified as a Hindu kingdom, but the new Constitution declared it a secular state.
2 In 2009, Pew Research Center estimates showed that India had the third-largest population of Muslims (see, https://www.pewresearch.org/wp-content/uploads/sites/7/2009/10/Muslimpopulation.pdf). However, their estimates suggest that it now has the second-largest population of Muslims living in a country, with a total population of 194,810,000; and by 2050 this number is projected to increase to 333,090,000, making it the country with the highest Muslim population in the world (see, https://www.pewresearch.org/fact-tank/2019/04/01/the-countries-with-the-10-largest-christian-populations-and-the-10-largest-muslim-populations/).
3 India has more than 500 tribes. While some have assimilated into other major religions (Hinduism, Christianity), many continue with their own distinct religious and cultural world views. In fact, increasing numbers among them are asking for recognition of 'tribal religion' as a category in the census itself.

4 Between 2001 and 2011, literacy rates rose among all communities, but Muslims, above the age of seven, still had a higher percentage of illiteracy compared to other religious communities. The comparative figures for illiteracy in this age group were – Muslims 42.7 per cent, Hindus 36.4 per cent, Sikhs 32.5 per cent, Buddhists 28.17 per cent, and Christians 25.7 per cent. See, PTI Report, 2016.
5 In all religious communities, the literacy rate among women is lower than for men of their community; this gap is smallest among the Jain community.
6 Press Information Bureau, Government of India, Ministry of Foreign Affairs, 26 July 2016 (17.06 IST). Available at: http://pib.nic.in/newsite/mbErel.aspx?relid=147820
7 *Social, Economic and Educational Status of the Muslims in India: A Report*, Prime Minister's High Level Committee, Cabinet Secretariat, Delhi: Government of India, 2006, pp. 37–38 (also known as the Sachar Committee Report). Religious and cultural differences are often invoked to explain this; see, Bhalotra et al. (2009).
8 The Commission was set up by the Congress-led UPA government in 2015.
9 A term used by the BJP to describe the actions of Congress and other parties favouring minorities.
10 That is, played up cultural differences and appeased the religious leadership.
11 Going beyond freedom of belief and worship, this gave all persons fairly extensive religious liberty. Indeed, several women and liberal-minded members were concerned that the right to observe one's religious practices would disadvantage women. Nevertheless, this concession was made for religious communities; to accommodate liberal concerns, a sub-clause was inserted that allowed the state to legislate for the welfare of women.
12 Political discretion of this sort has given religious community leaders an important role in public affairs. When religious demands of this nature won the support of the government, it strengthened their influence over their community members, and legitimized their claim to speak on behalf of the community.
13 The notable exception being caste-based discrimination involving segregation, exclusion, and stigmatization of some groups. Drawing upon the struggles for equality in pre-independence India, the Constitution abolished the practice of untouchability and the state subsequently legislated to open temples to all castes.

References

Bhalotra, Sonia, R, Valente, Christine, & Van Soest, Arthur. (2009, February). The Puzzle of Muslim Advantage in Child Survival in India. *IZA Discussion Paper 4009*.
Diamant, Jeff. (2019). *The Countries with the 10 Largest Christian Populations and the 10 Largest Muslim Populations*. Pew Research Centre. Available at: https://www.pewresearch.org/fact-tank/2019/04/01/the-countries-with-the-10-largest-christian-populations-and-the-10-largest-muslim-populations/
ECI (Election Commission of India). (1955). *Report of the First General Elections, 1951–52*, Volume I. New Delhi: GOI.
Gopal, Sarvepalli. (1979). *Jawaharlal Nehru - A Biography*, Volume 2. London: Jonathan Cape.
Jafferlot, Christophe. (1993). *The Hindu Nationalist Movement and Indian Politics*. London: Hurst & Co.
Jodhka, Surinder S. (2010). Sikhs Today: Development, Disparity and Difference. In G. Mahajan & S. S. Jodhka (eds), *Religion, Community and Development: Changing Contours of Politics and Policy in India* (pp. 173–202). New Delhi: Routledge.
Joshi, A. P., Srinivas, M. D., & Bajaj, J. K. (2003). *Religious Demography of India*. Chennai: Centre for Policy Studies. Available at: https://www.cpsindia.org/dl/religious/ppt-eng.pdf
Krishna, Gopal. (1985). Communal Violence in India: A Study of Communal Disturbance in Delhi. *Economic and Political Weekly*, 20(3): 117–131.
Mahajan, Gurpreet. (1988). *Identities and Rights: Aspects of Liberal Democracy in India*. Delhi: Oxford University Press.
Mahajan, Gurpreet. (ed.). (2011). *Accommodating Diversity: Ideas and Institutional Practices*. Delhi: Oxford University Press.
Mahajan, Gurpreet. (2013). *India: Political Ideas and the Making of a Democratic Discourse*. London: Zed Books.
Modood, Tariq. (2019). *Essays on Secularism and Multiculturalism*. London: Rowman & Littlefield International.

Modood, Tariq & Sealy, Thomas. (2019). *Secularism and the Governance of Religious Diversity.* Concept Paper, GREASE. Available at: http://grease.eui.eu/wp-content/uploads/sites/8/2019/05/GREASE_D1.1_Modood-Sealy_Final1.pdf.

Parekh, Bhikhu. (2015). *Debating Indian Politics: Essays on Indian Political Discourse.* Delhi: Oxford University Press.

Press Information Bureau, Government of India, Ministry of Foreign Affairs. (2016, July 26). 17.06 IST. Available at: pib.nic.in/new site/mbErel.apsx?relid=147820.

PTI. (2015, September 3). Hindutva Leaders Seek Curbs on Muslims Over Population Growth (updated January 22, 2018). *Business Line.* Available at: https://www.thehindubusinessline.com/news/national/hindutva-leaders-seek-curbs-on-muslims-over-population-growth/article7611780.ece.

PTI Report. (2016, September 1). Muslims Least, Jains Most Literate: Census (updated September 22). *The Hindu.* Available at: http://www.thehindu.com/news/national/Muslims-least-jains-most-literate-Census/article14615996.ec.

Robinson, Rowena. (2007). Indian Muslims: The Varied Dimensions of Marginality. *Economic and Political Weekly,* 42(10): 839–843.

Rukmini, S. & Singh, Vijaita. (2015, August 25). Muslim Population Growth Slows (updated February 13, 2017). *The Hindu.* Available at: http://www.thehindu.com/news/national/Muslim-population-growth-slows/article10336665.ece.

Sen, Ronojoy. (2010). *Articles of Faith: Religion, Secularism and the Indian Supreme Court.* Delhi: Oxford University Press.

Sikand, Yoginder. (2003). Islam, Social Stratification and Empowerment of Muslim OBCs. *Economic and Political Weekly,* 38/46, 4898–4901.

Singh, Dipti. (2015, August 29). Rising Muslim Population a Worry, says Praveen Togadia. *Indian Express.*

Singh, Gurharpal. (1995). The Punjab Crisis Since 1984: A Reassessment. *Ethnic and Racial Studies,* 18(3): 476–493.

Social, Economic and Educational Status of the Muslims in India: A Report. (2006). Prime Minister's High Level Committee, Cabinet Secretariat. Delhi: Government of India.

Unisa, Sayeed, Bhagat, R. B., Roy, T. K., & Upadhyay, R. B. (2008). Demographic Transition or Demographic Trepidation? The Case of Parsis in India. *Economic and Political Weekly,* 43(1): 61–65. Available at: https://www.jstor.org/stable/40276446

22

Indonesia

A complex experience of religious diversity governance

Pradana Boy Zulian and Hasnan Bachtiar

Introduction

The experiences of every society and polity in dealing with diversity and plurality are unique. Social context, political dynamics, and cultural aspects are among the factors determining the singularity of those experiences. Indonesia is not an exception. The scholarship on Indonesia describes this in different ways, but nuances notwithstanding, there is general acknowledgment of a positive attitude towards religious diversity in the past that continues in the country's modern history. However, this does not mean that the Indonesian experience has always been a success story as the governance of religious diversity has been a dialectical process in both its pre-modern and modern history.

This chapter will examine the nature and practice of religious diversity governance in post-independence Indonesia. The first part provides a brief historical overview and basic facts about religious diversity and religious groups, including the relationship between them and how they form the nucleus of Indonesia's religious diversity. Next, the chapter deals with the normative basis of religious diversity governance and how it is used as a framework for maintaining religious diversity. The chapter's final part looks at the empirical situation and dynamics of religious diversity governance so that the normative basis discussed can be compared with empirical evidence.

It should be emphasised from the outset that although religious diversity governance in Indonesia formally comes under state affairs, the contribution of civil society groups in enriching and enhancing it cannot be overlooked. On this basis, the role of civil society will also be presented and analysed. This is due to the fact that religious life in Indonesia has not only determined the nature of religion in the country but has also defined the nature of the relationship between the state and religion, religion and society, and society and the state.

Historical context

Comparing the Western and the Asian contexts of religious diversity and pluralism, scholars like Bernard Adeney-Risakotta (2015) and Anthony Reid (2015) are convinced that Western and Asian experiences are distinctive. Adeney-Risakotta (2015: 22–23), for instance, relates the Indonesian experience to two key facts about Indonesia: it has the fourth largest population in the world and hosts the largest Muslim community; and, it is one of the world's most diverse countries, both religiously and culturally. As a result of these two facts, Indonesia has long experienced diversity – an experience Adeney-Risakotta (ibid.) roots in the country's ancient history.

In a similar vein, Reid (2015) praises the practice of religious pluralism in Asia, including in Indonesia, viewing it as a model for religious pluralism in a global context in which diverse ritual practices live peacefully co-existent. More specifically, Reid refers back to the syncretic amalgamation of Islamisation[1] in the region, which parallels what Risakotta identifies as Indonesia's ancient history of dealing with diversity. 'Syncretic' refers to Islam's ability to adapt to local traditions without losing its basic values. Inevitably, this syncretic nature distinguishes the Islamisation process in Indonesia, or Nusantara in general, from other regions such as in Arab world and Indian subcontinent where conquests were involved more in the Islamisation process. (Before independence, Nusantara referred to a geographic entity that embraced the present-day countries of Indonesia, Malaysia, Singapore, Brunei Darussalam, Thailand, and the Philippines. In the nation-states period, its definition changed slightly, and while the peoples of Malaysia, Singapore, Brunei Darussalam, Thailand, and Philippines still consider themselves part of Nusantara, Indonesians, in general, view the term as referring exclusively to Indonesia, both geographically and culturally.)

As syncretism is one entry point of the Islamisation process in Indonesia, cooperation and, later, domination among religious traditions took place. As evidence, Reid furthermore notes that the most sacred sites at the centre of Hinduism-Buddhism education and meditation peacefully accepted Sufis as fellow truth-seekers, and those centres were even gradually dominated by Sufis (2015: 48–51). Diverging slightly from these scholars' views on Islam as a religion followed by majority of Indonesians, a prominent Indonesian scholar, the late Dawam Rahardjo (2010: 234) argued that in modern times, Muslims in Indonesia are generally exclusive, at least on a discursive level. However, Rahardjo too acknowledged that Indonesian society has its way of dealing with multiculturalism or diversity which he dubbed 'stratified cultural geology' (Rahardjo, 2010: 235). Quoting Dennis Lombard, Rahardjo identified some aspects of cultural geology such as the indigenous culture of Nusantara as well as Hinduism, Islam, Catholicism, Christianity, modernity, secularism, and agnosticism that shaped the popular subconscious subsequently manifested in the national credo of *Bhinneka Tunggal Ika*, or unity in diversity.

Diversity of religion

As a modern nation-state, Indonesia is formed through a long process. Once scattered as independent kingdoms in many parts of the archipelago, it was known as Hindia Belanda or Netherlands East Indies after the coming of Dutch in the region. Dutch colonisation in Indonesia, which was initially motivated by economic purposes due to the richness of Indonesian natural resources, had turned into political activities that also included the politics of religious life. This situation was then followed by struggles for independence from the Hindia Belanda side. Furthermore, the Dutch colonisation sparked the nationalist movements among Netherlands East Indies leaders and the emergence of nationalist movements aimed at gaining Indonesia's freedom, such as Sarikat Indonesia and Budi Utomo.

The Declaration of Independence in 1945 by Sukarno and Hatta, the then-first president and vice president of Indonesia, marked a new phase of Indonesia as an independent nation-state. However, as a newly founded polity one of the most important challenges was formulating state philosophy where all groups living in Indonesian society are accommodated, including diversity of religious groups. As we will show in the following sections, this issue sparked debate in many meetings of the committee for formulating the Constitution and state philosophy. Through long processes of discussion, the final version of Indonesian state philosophy expressed a more inclusive formulation that granted the same positions and status to all religions in Indonesia under the national Constitution.

As an implementation of the state philosophy, the national Constitution guarantees diversity of religion in Indonesia, which formally acknowledges six religions: Islam, Christianity (Protestantism and Catholicism), Hinduism, Buddhism, and Confucianism. Among these, Islam is the religion of the majority. Indonesian Statistical Agency data for 2018 shows Muslims number 237 million, or 87.18 per cent of the population; Protestants represent 6.9 per cent of the population, Catholics 2.9 per cent, Hindus 1.69 per cent, Buddhists 0.72 per cent, and followers of Confucianism 0.05 per cent. For the purpose of this study, however, I will analyse religious diversity through the case of Islam to demonstrate the huge tradition of diversity even within a single religion.

Islam and its internal divisions

As the religion with the largest following, Islam in Indonesia is not a single entity. Although Muslims fundamentally follow the same basic creeds and tenets, there are many nuances and differences in its practice. As in other parts of the world, this adds to the complexity of Islam, which cannot be understood as monolithic entity or in a single way. Scholars thus diverge in their descriptions of categories and typologies of Islam in Indonesia.

Defining ideology in academic terms is not an easy task. Ideological division in this context refers to major denominations of Islam that emerge as variations of Islam's understanding that later spread beyond the boundaries of its origin as it was adopted by Muslims around the world. Within this broader framework, there are three ideological trends in Indonesia, namely, Sunni, Shiite, and Ahmadiyah. Most Indonesian Muslims follow Sunnism.

Aside than Sunnism, Shiism is also present in Indonesian religious life. Jalaluddin Rakhmat, a leader of Indonesian Shia, informed that the arrival of Shiism in the Indonesian archipelago took place in three phases. This is supported by other authors such as Hendropriyono (2009) and Tim Ahlul Bait Indonesia (2012). According to Jalaluddin Rakhmat, the first phase coincided with the first wave of Islam's spread to Nusantara. Although the evidence for this theory is inconclusive, its basis is that Persia, the homeland of the Shiism, was one of the countries from where Islam in Nusantara originated. The next phase took place in the 1980s and the post-Iranian revolution era. The ascendance of the Iranian revolution against the Shah's regime boosted the spread of Shiite teachings around the Muslim world. Indonesia was no exception. Later, in the last days of Suharto's administration, Rakhmat described Shiism as an Islamic ideology that attracted followers mainly from intellectual circles. This claim is based on his conviction that Shiism is an Islamic ideology that 'offers a revolutionary type of thinking and strong critique against social injustice' (Zulian, 2018). In the last phase, Shiism's spread in Indonesia took a more conventional form, that is, through Shiite jurisprudence which differs significantly from Sunnism (Zulkifli, 2004). It is important to note, aside from its differences with Sunnism, within Shiism itself, dissension in religious thought and orientations are common (Atjeh, 1977).

Ahmadiyah is also present in Indonesia. Although recently Ahmadiyah has been controversial among Indonesian Muslims to the extent that its adherents are subject to social discrimination, it is as old as established Islamic organisations in the country such as Muhammadiyah and Nahdlatul Ulama' (NU), founded in 1912 and 1926 respectively. Ahmadiyah reached Indonesia as early as pre-independence, although historians dispute the precise date. There are two groups of Ahmadiyah: Qadiani and Lahore. Both exist in Indonesia using different labels. Qadiani is called Jemaat Ahmadiyah Indonesia (JAI), while the Lahore group is known as Gerakan Ahmadiyah Indonesia (GAI). JAI believes that Ahmadiyah came to Indonesia around 1925 through the efforts of Rahmat Ali from India who disseminated Ahmadiyah teachings in Tapaktuan on the western coast of Aceh. In one of my interviews while researching Ahmadiyah, an Ahmadi leader in Tasikmalaya, West Java, informed that although Rahmat Ali's teachings attracted some locals, many rejected them.[2] Ali's arrival was followed by other Ahmadi missionaries from India and Pakistan. He later left Aceh for Java sometime in 1931. In Jakarta, he successfully attracted other followers. Subsequently, the Ahmadiyah board in Jakarta was established in 1932 with only 27 members (Zainal, 2007: 267–294). Ahmadiyah is recognised by Indonesian law. It was granted the status of a social organisation and institution in 1953 by the Ministry of Justice of the Republic and the Directorate of the Relations of Political Institutions (75/D.I./VI/2003) (Yogaswara, 2008: 82).

From the perspective of orientations, Indonesian Islam can be understood in terms of modernist, traditionalist, and revivalist groups – and all three can basically be understood in reference to Islamic organisation. Some scholars have also described other orientations of Islam in Indonesia as mystical Islam (Endraswara, 2006; Mulkhan, 1999; Simon, 2004), cultural Islam, formalistic (*sharia*-oriented) Islam, and political Islam. Formalistic Islam usually emphasises the observance of Islamic obligations as what is written in Sharia sources and ulama's interpretations of them. In the history of Islamisation in Nusantara, this formalistic Islam is often referred to as *Wali Songo* (the nine saints). However, many others categorise the Wali Songo under cultural Islam since it used local tradition as the medium for spreading Islam. However, overall, I believe that the Wali Songo are the guardians of the formalistic type of Islam (see Mulkhan, 1999).

Indonesian Islam is also distinguished by numerous religious orientations that have characterised various social movements which developed during the colonial period, especially at the dawn of twentieth century. This period witnessed the emergence of diverse Islamic movements that attempted to respond to and confront the socio-economic mire of Muslims under the impact of Dutch imperialism. Using religion as a major source of their struggle against the imperial power, movements such as Jamiat al-Khair, Muhammadiyah, al-Irsyad, and *Persatuan Islam*, among many others, were established. Some attempted to redress social conditions by embarking on theological purification of religious beliefs that they perceived as having been corrupted and responsible for society's decline. It was in this context that some of these groups attacked the syncretic nature of Muslim society in Indonesia as a major factor for this degeneration. A leading Indonesian Muslim intellectual, the late Nurcholish Madjid, argued that tensions among Islamic movements were common during the colonial period; in the political arena, he wrote, there were Islamic organisations that followed non-cooperative paths such as al-Irsyad and those opting for a cooperative path such as Muhammadiyah (1992: 161). Some organisations like Muhammadiyah and al-Irsyad were open to modern elements of Dutch education, while others rejected them and strove instead to strengthen the 'original' system of Indonesian education, including the *madrasa* and *pesantren* systems (ibid.).

Other orientations found in Indonesian Islam are mystical and cultural Islam. Both are often discussed in contradiction to *sharia*-oriented Islam since they are seen as representing more heterodox versions of Islam while *Sharia* emphasises religion's legal and orthodox outlook (Kuntowijoyo, 2001: 233). However, although the first and second types of religious practice might be seen as less authentic expressions of Islam, it cannot be denied that their emergence is indicative of Islam's ability to adapt to and accommodate local elements, cultures, and traditions. This syncretic Islam is, in a way, what Merle Ricklefs refers to as 'mystical synthesis' or a kind of 'reconciliation of Javanese and Islamic identities, beliefs, and style' (2006, 2012: 7); that is, that with this hybrid and blended identity, being Javanese also means being Muslim. In other words, mystic synthesis suggests that Muslims are religiously pious while maintaining local elements in beliefs and practices derived from pre-Islamic religious beliefs and culture. This kind of synthesis is popularly known as *Islam Kejawen* in Indonesian terminology (Endraswara, 2006) or, in Kuntowijoyo's understanding, as *Jawaisme* (2001: 230).

Given the central position that local culture has played in Islamising Java, and Indonesia in general (Purwadi, 2004), it is understandable that local cultural elements are inseparable from Islamic practices and teachings. In Moeslim Abdurrahman's view, Islam or being Muslim cannot be reduced to a single or static meaning since their meanings are dynamically conditioned by socio-historical factors (Abdurrahman, 2006: x). In a similar vein, Reza Aslan contends that cultural elements are determinant in the formation of religious interpretations (2005: xix). Consequently, Indonesian Islam(s) can also be identified by analysing the cultural aspects within the practice of Islamic beliefs. It is this cultural consciousness that partly led anthropologist Clifford Geertz to portray Indonesian Muslims in terms of *abangan*, *santri*, and *priyayi* (1960). Although several scholars have criticised this classification, it is relevant in portraying Islam's cultural richness in Indonesia and the dialectical relationship of Islam and cultures.

Turning to the formalistic or *sharia*-oriented form of Islam, it has been argued that while *fiqh* (Islamic jurisprudence) forms a central aspect of Islamic teachings based on the two most fundamental Islamic sources of law, the Quran and *Sunna*, overemphasising law as central to religious life and expressions is a major form of religiosity in this characterisation of Indonesian Islam. Generally, the majority of Indonesian Muslims are legally affiliated to the Shafii school of law within the Sunni denomination (Abdurrahman, 2012; Ali, 1990: 76–80; Azizy, 2003; Effendy, 2010; Nahdlatul Ulama, 2011). However, the assumption that Indonesian Islam is identical to the Shafii school is an over-simplification. Although the majority of Indonesian Muslims belong to the Shafii school of jurisprudence, there are also those who are affiliated with the Hanafi, Maliki, and Hanbali schools. The existence of these different religious schools within the Sunni tradition has enriched the variety of religious beliefs and practices of Muslims in Indonesia. Of the many differences between these schools, the primary is in *fiqh* or the legal interpretations of two basic sources of Islam, the Quran and *Sunna*. In Islamic legal terms, these differences occur at the level of *furū'* (branches) and not in terms of *uṣūl* (basic principles).

Even within the same Sunni denomination, Indonesian Muslim scholars differ in their interpretations of specific legal issues. Inheritance law offers an example. It is generally accepted, as stipulated in the Quran, that daughters are entitled to half of what is accorded to sons from their parents' inheritance. However, many Indonesian Muslims no longer practise this based on sociological considerations. Hence, the late Munawir Sjadzali, who served as Minister of Religious Affairs during Suharto's reign, had proposed a new understanding of inheritance law using the ratio of 1:1 and not 1:2 as generally accepted (Nafis, 1995). This opinion reflects the thought of the late legal scholar Hazairin, a former law professor at the University of Indonesia, who argued that the common understanding of inheritance law following patrilineal lineage is an Arabic norm that is incompatible with Indonesian values and proposed instead a bilateral principle of inheritance that is seen as more contextually rooted (1982; Hamid, 2007).

Apart from the diversity within Sunni Islam manifested in different *fiqh* schools as well as diversity within each of them, the non-monolithic face of Indonesian Islam is also evident in the existence of other Muslim religious minorities, not excluding the Shia. Diversity of Islam in Indonesia has been further enriched by the co-existence of these groups within the predominantly Sunni Muslim community. Shia, which emerged in the early course of Islamic political history, had developed its own doctrines, teachings, rites, and methods of interpretation of the Quran, *Sunna*, and certain major important historical facts. It is these differences that are often highlighted as the root cause of tensions between Sunni and Shia (al-Musawi, 1983; Habsyi, 1991; Habsyi and Naqvi, 1991; Shihab, 2007; Sidogiri, 2008).

Minority religions

All other official religious groups in Indonesia together represent just a small percentage of the total population, with Christian denominations comprising two-thirds of this minority. Many of the smaller groups are also fragmented into sects, ideologies, and institutions. The indigenous religions are the oldest; religions such as Kapitayan, Sunda Wiwitan, Musi, Aluk Tolodo, Arat Sabulungan, Marapu, Masade, Pelebegu, Pemena, Tolotang, Wor, and others predate Hinduism and Buddhism throughout the Nusantara region (Subagya, 1981) and certainly since before the Common Era. Archaeological sites such as Gunung Padang and Batu Panjang, among others, attest to the ancient existence of these religions.

Today, however, they are labelled by the State as non-mainstream or *aliran kepercayaan* (indigenous beliefs). Consequently, adherents to such beliefs are identified as indigenous believers (*penganut kepercayaan*) on their national ID cards – a bureaucratic practice that blurs diversity at this level by classifying them under a single grouping. And while all *penganut kepercayaan* believers total just 0.50 per cent of the population, these religions are spread across the region, especially in remote areas where there is little contact with Muslims, although tensions and conflicts with Muslims sometimes flared (Djatikusumah, 2011: 365–374).

Two old religions originating from Chino-Indo civilisations, Hinduism and Buddhism, evolved in the region during rise and fall of the ancient Nusantara Kingdoms such as Salakanegara, Kutai Kertanegara, Tarumanegara, Sriwijaya, Singosari, and Majapahit. Since the start of the Common Era, around 600 CE, both were transmitted via the lines of either religious or political diplomacy as well as trade, emerging as the dominant religions in the period of pre-European colonialism that handed down rich traditions and wisdoms. However, their dominance gradually declined under colonialism and they slid into the minority.

Institutionally, the modern Hindu in Indonesia has been categorised as either *Parisada Hindu Dharma Indonesia,* the national organisation of Hinduism in the country, or various living Hinduisms. *Parisada Hindu Dharma Indonesia* was established in 1984 by Gedong Bagus Oka, while the latter has followed certain local traditions in each area of Indonesia, for example, as Hindu Kaharingan in Borneo, Hindu Jawa in Jawa, Hindu Toraja in Sulawesi, Parmalim in Sumatera, and Boda Suku Sasak in Lombo and the West Nusa Tenggara. Meanwhile, Bali is the country's most identifiable centre of Hinduism and is known for its thousands of Hindu temples.

Buddhism in the region also shows great diversity. This has been determined by spiritual schools such as Mahayana, Vajrayana, and Theravada. Mahayana consists of two groups, namely, Buddha Mahayana and Tridharma. While the former depicts a combination between Zen and Sukhavati (Chinese Buddhism), the latter has been strongly influenced by Taoism and Konghucu.

Vajrayana is also known as Tantrayana. In the 1950s, a group of Tantrayana, Kasogatan, was established. Three decades later, a school of Tantrayana, Zenfo Zong, emerged through the establishment of the Yayasan Satya Dharma Surya Indonesia. Both institutions were merged in 1988 as Perwakilan Umat Buddha Indonesia. This merged group changed its name into Majelis Agama Buddha Tantrayana Kasogatan Indonesia in 1994 and again, in 2001, to Majelis Agama Buddha Tantrayana Zhenfo Zong Kasogatan Indonesia.

The last Hindu group is Theravada. It originated from Wat Bovoranives, Thailand. In 1972, Theravada split into groups affiliated, respectively, with Thailand and Indonesia. In 1974, both groups were merged and named Maha Sangha Agung Indonesia. However, two years later, some monks of the Maha Sangha Agung Indonesia established their own institution called Sangha Theravada Indonesia.

Followers of Hinduism and Buddhism are recognised by their respective religions on national identity cards. Additionally, as officially acknowledged religions, the Ministry of Religious Affairs oversees administrative issues of concern to believers and provides rules as well as facilities for both religions.

Christians are Indonesia's second largest religious group, comprising nearly 10 per cent of the population; roughly one-third of Indonesia's Christians are Catholic, and the rest are Protestant. By some accounts, Christianity spread to Nusantara in the seventh century by Catholic priests from southern India. It was begun by the establishment of the St Thomas Church in Tapanuli. In the sixteenth century, Catholicism was brought by Portugal (Alfonso de Albuquerque in a mission of the spice trade) in Maluku and its missionary, Antonio Galvao. It was then spread to Ambon, Halmahera, Ternate, and Tidore by a Spanish Jesuit priest, namely, Franciscus Xaverius.

In 1596, Cornelis de Houtman had led the trade mission of the Compagnie van Verre in the region and one year later, his job was followed by Jacob van Neck, van Heemskerck, and van Waerwijck. One of their ships had sailed to Maluku in order to establish the trade centre. When Vereenigde Oostindische Compagnie (VOC) had begun its mission, at the same time, the Protestants of Netherlands took over the Catholic's roles in the eastern part of Nusantara. Accordingly, in 1605 the first Protestant Church, De Protestantsche Kerk in Nederlandsch-Indie was established. The church's influence was vast, embracing other places such as Minahasa, East Nusa Tenggara, Sumbawa, Jawa, and Sumatera.

The Catholic Church in Indonesia is neither various nor fragmented. It tends to show its unity in the blessed hand of the Pope of Rome. Protestantism, however, is totally different. Due to the significant influence of the Protestant Reformism, its churches fall into three categories: the racially based churches, denominational churches, and non-denominational churches. The first is represented by Gereja Kristen Jawi Wetan, Gereja Kristen Jawa, Huria Kristen Batak Protestan, Gereja Toraja, Gereja Masehi Injili di Minahasa, Gereja Kalimantan Evangelis, Banua Niha Keriso Protestan, and many others. Examples of the second include Gereja Reformasi, Gereja Lutheran, Gereja Injili, Gereja Methodis, Gereja Menonit, Gereja Pentakosta, and Gereja Baptis. The non-denominational group includes, among others, Gereja Yesus Sejati, Gereja Kristus di Indonesia, and Gereja Masehi Advent Hari Ketujuh.

Both Catholicism and Protestantism are officially recognised by the state and thus appear as such on followers' national identification cards. Administrative matters regarding the respective religions – for instance, registration of marriages – have been facilitated by the Ministry of Religious Affairs. In dealing with the issue of religious harmony and diversity, their representatives have joined the Forum Kerukunan Umat Beragama (FKUB), an interreligious forum supported by the state.

Another minority religion is Konghucu. Although Chinese culture has a long history in Nusantara, Konghucu has had its own institutionally, beginning in 1883, when Boen Tjhiang Soe (Wen Chang Ci) established the Konghucu temple Gredja Boen Bio (De kerk van Confucius) in Surabaya; in 1966, the name was changed to Gabungan Perhimpunan Agama Konghucu Se-Indonesia and therefore, Majelis Tinggi Agama Konghucu Indonesia.

The Konghucu community's existence in Indonesia has been challenging. In the 1980s, the government signed the Rule of Minister of Home Affairs No. 477/74054/BA.01.2 that officially recognised Islam, Protestantism, Catholicism, Hinduism, and Buddhism. This prompted concern among Konghucu believers. In the post-reform era, the Constitution was amended to reflect Indonesia's ratification of the Universal Declaration of Human Rights. Consequently, in 2000, the Rule of 1990 that discriminated against Konghucu was overturned by the higher court as a violation of the Constitution. Konghucu believers now have the right to register their religion on national ID cards and actively participate in the interreligious FKUB forum.

The dynamics of religious diversity governance

Post-independence Indonesia is mostly understood in three periods: the Old Order (1945–1968), New Order (1966–1998), and Reform Era (1998 to the present). The New Order marked a new development in terms of intra-religious as well as inter-religious relationships, showing a marked tendency to limit the participation and expressions of Islam in the public sphere. For instance, in 1985–1986, all Islamic organisations in Indonesia had to adopt *Pancasila* as their sole philosophical basis, or *asas tunggal*. As Douglas E. Ramage asserted, Islam 'as a political movement is not officially allowed to present an ideological alternative to *Pancasila*' (Ramage, 2010: 40; Jurdi, 2010: 278–282). In the last quarter of the New Order regime, the strong manifestations of religious revivalism were evident. In the words of Azyumardi Azra, during this period, despite President Suharto's attempts to introduce certain kinds of Javaism known as *Aliran Kejawen*, the tendency of *santrinisasi* outweighed this (2009).

Following the collapse of the New Order regime, diverse Islamic groups with varying religious orientations come to the fore, ranging from conservatism to those espousing liberal views. The most striking development has been the emergence of politically radical and fundamentalist Islamic movements such as *Front Pembela Islam* (FPI), Jamaah Islamiyah, Salafi Jihadist, and those represented by *Partai Keadilan Sejahtera* (PKS) and *Hizbut Tahrir Indonesia* (HTI). The emergence of these radical groups in Indonesia is intertwined with political repression during the New Order period. One of the most visible consequences of this movement is the growth and strengthening of support for enforcing Islamic morality in the public sphere.

These groups are generally hostile to any type of contemporary discourse that they perceive as Western constructs such as democracy, gender equality, and pluralism. Democracy, for example, is seen as an un-Islamic system based on the conviction that it grants sovereignty to the people, while in their Islamic conception of power, God is the sovereign and *sharia* is law that encodes this sovereignty (Yunanto, 2003). This type of Islam also shows the same uncompromising attitude towards discourse on religious pluralism. Elements within this group argue that Islam is not compatible with the idea of religious pluralism (Husaini, 2005, 2006; Thaha, 2005).

At the other end, competing Muslim groups have also emerged to promote agendas that are radically different from the Islamist groups. They are active in the discourse on religious pluralism and critical of dominant views that undermine or attack pluralism and liberalism.

For example, within the circles of Nahdlatul Ulama'an, the Islamic organisation most-identified as traditional Islam, a number of supporters of pluralism have come to the fore, be it individually or institutionally. Masdar Farid Mas'udi, Ulil Abshar-Abdalla, Zuhairi Misrawi, Guntur Romli, and Moqsith Ghazali are among the many individuals known as strong supporters of pluralism and who actively write articles, essays, and books aimed at influencing the public in this direction. *Lembaga Kajian Islam dan Sosial* (LKIS) in Yogyakarta, *Jaringan Islam Liberal* (JIL), and the Wahid Institute in Jakarta are a few examples of groups in this camp. A similar development is also seen in the case with Muhammadiyah; in early 2000, Muhammadiyah saw the rise of *Jaringan Intelektual Muda Muhammadiyah* (JIMM) and *Pusat Studi Agama dan Peradaban* (PSAP), which strongly articulate and advocate for the promotion of tolerance, pluralism, and democracy within the movement.

The above reveals that religious diversity has been an integral feature of Indonesian Islam. At the sociological level, this diversity is manifested in competing ideas and endeavours to realise the ideals, principles, and teachings of Islam. The types of religious orientations that feature in the diversity of group thought are strongly conditioned by specific social and historical contexts. Given the plurality of religious groups and thought, essentialist pronouncements of religious authorities demonising Muslims based on differences in their understanding of Islam appear to betray the hard truth of diversity of religious thought and experience in Indonesia, with serious repercussions on the lives of those affected.

Religious diversity governance

An important feature of religious life in Indonesia shaping this uniqueness is the claim that Indonesia is neither a state of religion nor a secular state, thus fundamentally adopting a consensus between the two. The former refers to the fact that Indonesia is a state which is not exclusively governed and based on a certain religion's law; in the latter, 'secular' does not carry the meaning of separation between religion and state but rather connotes being anti-religion. Historically, in the period of pre-independence, the republic's founding fathers debated the model that the Indonesian state would adopt. On the one hand, Muslim leaders such as Muhammad Natsir, Kahar Muzakkir, and Wahid Hasyim aspired for Indonesia to be an Islamic state or a state based on Islamic law. On the other, nationalist leaders like Sukarno viewed the secular state as a suitable model. Tension between these two orientations was inevitable. This, however, could be resolved when a middle path was proposed as a solution. Both sides eventually compromised by not insisting on the two diametrically opposed positions; Indonesia would not be a religion-based state as it was not only Muslims who were struggling for independence of Indonesia, while at the same time Indonesia is religiously thus could not be a secular state (Mahfud, 2019).

The late Munawir Sjadzali, the long-serving Minister of Religious Affairs during Suharto's administration (1983–1993), explained that Indonesia is not a religion-based state – which he described as having an official religion, laws whose source is the scripture of an official religion, and, in which state power is held by religious leaders. Sjadzali believed that all three conditions cannot be found in the Indonesian case. The fact that Islam is the religion with the widest following in the country cannot be presented as evidence that Islam is the state's religion. In terms of law, Indonesia does not take any scripture as its source, although some laws may be inspired by the scripture of many religions allowed in Indonesia. And lastly, no religious leader in Indonesia is the holder of state power. At the same time, Indonesia is not a secular state as politics and affairs of the state are not completely separate from any religious affairs; the government is present in the religious lives of citizens without being too deeply involved in personal religious affairs, but rather to govern and improve the quality of religious life (Sjadzali, 1993: 80–85).

Pancasila: a crystallisation of diversity

Nonetheless, the government regulates religious diversity and life in the country. In this context, the term 'secular' here also comes with its specific meaning. While governance is not based on certain religious principles exclusively, at the same time, it is mandatory for all Indonesian citizens to profess a religion of their preference. Consequently, it is not surprising that atheism is not formally recognised in Indonesia.

As Indonesia does not identify itself as either religious or secular, its state philosophy is often presented as an alternative to this binary. This state philosophy is called *Pancasila*, which literally means five principles or fundamentals. The first principle is *'Ketuhanan Yang Maha Esa'*, which can generally be translated as the unity of God. This serves, first and foremost, as a national principle regarding religious diversity. The phrase 'unity of God', at the same time, signifies the primacy of professing a religion, obligation to embrace one of the country's six recognised religions, and also guarantees that the government will protect citizens' religious preferences provided they are in compliance with the state's principles.

As noted by Syafii Maarif (2006), it was obvious that although *Pancasila* is seen as a uniting factor and point of convergence of various religions in Indonesia, it is facing challenges from Muslim leaders. M. Natsir from the Masyumi Party and Ahmad Zaini of Nahdlatul Ulama' are among those criticising *Pancasila* as an abstract and neutral concept that can be understood in very relative ways depending on the interpretation framework (ibid.: 147). Furthermore, both leaders dispute *Pancasila*'s religious or Islamic content: Natsir described it as vague or merely as 'pure concept' and secular – that is, anti-religion, or *la-diniyah*; Zaini, meanwhile, described *Pancasila* as a beautiful slogan but devoid of meaning.

Muslim leader Roeslan Abdulgani and Christian leader Arnold Mononutu defended *Pancasila* against these criticisms that it lacked religious values. Abdulgani revealed that India perceived the Pakistani state founded after independence as modelled on an ancient medieval state because it uses religion as its basis, arguing that if categorisation was that simple, European countries like Ireland, Sweden, Norway, Denmark, Switzerland, and Greece are not modern states as their constitutions clearly mention religion (Abdulgani, n.d.: 36). With regard to secular and theocratic states, he further quoted Sukarno and the Pakistani intellectual Kemal A Faruki, who said that if secular means all worldly affairs, then Islam is a secular religion as it pays attention and sets guidelines on issues of state and worldly life (Abdulgani, n.d.: 37). On theocracy, Abdulgani quoted Sukarno:

> There is no theocracy in Islam, although Islam is a religion. Theocracy is usually defined as the government run by religious leaders. In Catholic churches we see the hierarchy of priest … There is no such a system in Islam. Islam requires direct relationship of God and human beings without any mediation of priest and religious leader. For this reason, theocracy is not known in Islam.
>
> *(p. 37)*

Abdulgani quoted Sukarno to rebut certain Muslim leaders' criticisms of *Pancasila* and at the same time affirm that Indonesia is not a state of religion in the sense of theocracy as understood by Sukarno, but is also not a secular state in the sense of *Negara dimana kekuasannja melulu ditudjukan kepada keduniawiaan* (h. 37). Abdulgani also quoted George Mc T Kahin who called *Pancasila* a 'matured social philosophy' and the most optimal example of a combination of Western democracy, Islamic modernism, and Marxism with rural democracy and genuine communism (p. 47). In other words, Abdulgani is convinced that it is impossible to separate *Pancasila* from Islamic teachings.

Some Christian leaders also followed Abdulgani's line. Arnold Mononutu, for instance, viewed *Pancasila* as a manifestation and culmination of Christian values (Maarif, 2006: 153). He further argued that *Pancasila* is completely compatible with the Bible. As an example, in the first principle of *Pancasila* on belief in God, Mononutu argued: 'Pancasila is a form of logical philosophy, it is religious and monistic, which Christian can accept as a state philosophy of the Republic of Indonesia'; moreover, '…the most important is that Pancasila is a common ground of all groups who believe in the God, regardless the difference of Prophet of those respective groups' (ibid.) In the same vein, Mgr. Soegijapranata, a Catholic thinker, argued that *Pancasila* reflects God's order (Abdulgani, n.d.: 43).

The Catholic philosopher N. Driyarkara (1980) also expressed his agreement on *Pancasila*'s compatibility with Catholic teachings and proposing the concept of love and passion: '…the principle of *Pancasila* on belief in God cannot be separated from other principles'. The integrality of those principles, according to Driyarkara, is due to human beings' most basic nature; human existence cannot be separated from love and passion – love of fellow human beings and love of God as the Creator of human beings:

> if we deeply grasp Pancasila principle on belief in God, it will be obvious that Pancasila can actually be crystallized into only 'Ekasila' (One Principle). It is humanity, social justice, love to people, and nationhood. All these values are actually expressions of one single principle: Love and Passion. Now, it become more obvious that love is basically love to God.
>
> Therefore, it is evident that Pancasila is law of nature. As it is law of nature, it is not only for us. But, we may be proud that in our country that law of nature is first principle to be formulated as State Philosophy.
>
> *(ibid.: 48)*

The fact that some Christian leaders saw *Pancasila* as compatible with Christian values and doctrines only added to critics' conviction that *Pancasila* really is neutral (Maarif, 2006: 154) – in other words, it does not bear any religious values, especially not those of Islam. Interestingly, though, some Muslim leaders' attitudes to *Pancasila* shifted. M. Natsir initially viewed Pancasila in a positive light, as reflected in his remarks on Pakistan, where he mentioned *Pancasila* as a moral, spiritual, and ethical basis for Indonesia.

Nevertheless, at a practical level, the governance of religious diversity leaves many fundamental questions unanswered. Freedom of religion, the protection of minority rights, and the tyranny of the majority are among many important issues that remain unresolved in the context of religious diversity in contemporary Indonesia.

This last statement may raise a question: how do people know whether someone is atheist or religious? As religious preference or orientation is something very private, how does it come to the attention of the state? In the Indonesian context, a citizen's religious affiliation is automatically public as it is recorded on the national identity card, *Kartu Tanda Penduduk*, or KTP. Thus, a citizen may be refused a KTP if they refuse to fill in their religious affiliation.

In addition to the state's governance philosophy, the Constitution also stipulates how religion operates within Indonesian society. Article 29, par. 2 iterates: 'The state guarantees the freedom of its citizens to profess religion of their preference and to perform rituals based on their religions and beliefs'. It is obvious from this Article that the State of Indonesia grants its citizens freedom to embrace any religion and guarantees to protect the exercise of the respective religion's rituals. Implementation of this principle means that all religions can build houses of worship. But since people of different faiths live side by side in the community, their construction often creates tensions – which a decree issued jointly in 2006 by the Minister of Interior and Minister of Religious Affairs aimed to address.

Another important element of religious diversity governance in Indonesia is the establishment of a Ministry of Religious Affairs. For many countries, it may seem peculiar that religious affairs are regulated by the government as many believe that religious activities are in the private sphere of citizens' lives. As the majority of Indonesian citizens are Muslims, this Ministry deals mostly with administering Muslims' religious life. However, departments were also created proportionally within it for all other religions.

Public holidays also offer a glimpse at religious diversity governance. In Indonesia, these include religious observances. For Muslims, the feasts of Idul Fithri and Idul Adha are considered public holidays. The same situation applies for Christians with regard to Good Friday and Christmas Day. The Indonesian government also respects the holy days of Hindus, Buddhists, and followers of Confucianism as national holidays for all Indonesian citizens.

These normative contexts, however, are not always in accordance with empirical evidence. Discriminatory treatment of minority groups in Indonesia, for followers of religions other than Islam and non-mainstream Muslim groups, poses a serious challenge and sets a bad precedent for the management of religious diversity. For example, Dawam Rahardjo (2010: xi) severely criticised the government for its failure to provide protection for the Ahmadiyah community. He contended that the verbal promotion of pluralism and tolerance by the government will not bring any benefits if at the same time it does not take firm action on ideologically based torture and discrimination against minorities such as Ahmadi communities. In this context, Rahardjo saw the government as having failed to defend *Pancasila* in the form of guaranteeing freedom of belief for all people.

Basuki Tjahaya Purnama might also be considered another case of blatant discrimination. Purnama was the Chinese-Christian governor of Jakarta who filled Jokowi's position after he became president in 2014. In May 2017, Ahok, as he is popularly known, was charged with blasphemy and sentenced to two years in prison after opponents in the 2016 gubernatorial election claimed he had committed the crime of insulting Islam during a campaign rally. He was accused of wrongly interpreting the Quran surah Al-Maidah verse 51, 'O you who have believed, do not take the Jews and Christians as allies. They are, in fact, allies of one another. And whoever is an ally to them among you, then indeed, he is one of them. Indeed, Allah guides not the wrongdoing people'. Ahok had argued that his opponents repeatedly used this verse as a smear campaign against him and that he had told supporters that 'You all have been deceived by Muslim politicians using the Al-Maidah 51'. Obviously, what he had expressed was disagreement with any political instrumentalisation of religion, but this created a backlash of Islamist populism as millions of Muslims came out to protest against Ahok's manoeuvre.

The Ahok case highlights two critical problems. The first is the evident discrimination stemming from the racial, ethnic, and religious issues. The second is that Indonesian criminal law (*Kitab Undang-Undang Hukum Pidana*, KUHP), especially its articles on blasphemy, remains problematic. Anyone who is in a minority in terms of issues potentially risks being attacked in any political process in the name of majoritarianism. In addition, although the Constitution has completely affirmed the essentials of international human rights law, the blasphemy law seems to contradict this. In another words, the blasphemy law has opened a space of discrimination primarily to the different views on religion. The law could become an instrument for violating the right to freedom of religion or belief. Furthermore, the state has faced a serious challenge with regard to legal harmonisation, emphasising that its laws (*undang-undang*) should be in line with the Constitution as the highest legal instrument (*Undang-Undang Dasar*).

Concluding remarks

To conclude discussion of this chapter, some important points can be reiterated. First, from a normative perspective, the governance of religious diversity in Indonesia has been well reflected in the Constitution and formal regulation issued by the state. The formulation of the state philosophy *Pancasila,* which outlines an inclusive formulation for the existence and observance of all religions officially acknowledged by state, is one of the best practices of religious diversity governance that Indonesia can present. Since state philosophy is fully abstract in nature and functions as an umbrella for other lower and more practical laws and rules, many other laws and rules regarding diversity of religion in Indonesian are issued. Still, one other point of Indonesia's uniqueness regarding governance of religious diversity is its declaration as 'not a secular state nor a state based solely on one certain religion', which theoretically guarantee the equality of position of all religions before the state.

Second, although normative formulations are convincingly inclusive, the practices of religious diversity are not always in line with that theoretical basis. Generally, in the last decade, the incidence of intolerance has remained high. In 2011, there were 185 cases reported; in 2012 these fell to 110 but then more than doubled in 2013, to reach 245. According to a report from the Wahid Institute, in the period 2014–2017, the number of cases reported annually has remained over 200. While those involved in these incidents are members of the Muslim majority, hardliners, and the state apparatus, the victims are minority groups and communities, for example, Ahmadis, Shiites, Christians, and local indigenous believers. The attacks include 'sweeping raids on places considered contrary to sharia law, attacking on houses of worship of other faiths, demonstrations against groups perceived as tarnishing the sanctity of Islam, and being active in groups that explicitly work to impose sharia law' (Wahid Foundation, 2017: 10).

Above all, however, there remains the question of how these normative rules are implemented, but this is beyond the scope of this chapter.

Notes

1 The history of Islamisation in Nusantara is not a simple process. In terms of origin, scholars in Indonesia are familiar with four versions, namely: Arab, Persian, Indian, and Chinese. The debate, then, is not limited to versions but also modes, motives, and orientations. Being aware of this situation, I consciously do not deal with the too complicated nature of Islamisation in the whole region, but take the Javanese case as an example. So, by Islamisation here, I refer to a wider context.
2 Interview with Dodi Kurniawan, Tasikmalaya, 26 May 2013.

References

Abdulgani, Roeslan. (n.d.). *Resapkan dan Amalkan Pantjasila.* Jakarta: B.P. Prapantja.
Abdurrahman, Asjmuni. (2012). *Manhaj Tarjih Muhammadiyah: Metodologi dan Aplikasi.* Yogyakarta: Pustaka Pelajar.
Abdurrahman, Moeslim. (2006). Bangkitnya Spiritual: Islamisasi dengan Damai. In Ahmad Syafii Mufid (ed.), *Tangklukan, Abangan dan Tarekat: Kebangkitan Agama di Jawa (Foreword).* Jakarta: Yayasan Obor Indonesia.

Adeney-Risakotta, Bernard. (2015). Pendahuluan: Mengelola Keragaman. In Bernard Adeney-Risakotta (ed.), *Mengelola Keragaman di Indonesia: Agama dan Isu-isu Globalisasi, Kekerasan, Gender, dan Bencana di Indonesia* (pp. 19–43). Bandung: Mizan.
Ahlul Bait Indoensia, Tim. (2012). *Buku Putih Mazhab Syiah Menurut Para Ulamanya yang Muktabar*. Jakarta: Dewan Pengurus Pusat Ahlul Bait Indonesia.
Ali, H.A. Mukti. (1990). *Ijtihad dalam Pandangan Muhammad Abduh, Ahmad Dahlan, dan Muhammad Iqbal*. Jakarta: Bulan Bintang.
al-Musawi, Syarafuddin. (1983). *Dialog Sunnah-Syi'ah*. Bandung: Mizan.
Aslan, Reza. (2005). *No God But God: The Origins, Evolution and Future of Islam*. New York: Random House.
Atjeh, Abubakar. (1977). *Aliran Syi'ah di Nusantara*. Jakarta: Islamic Research Institute.
Azizy, A. Qodry. (2003). *Reformasi Bermazhab: Sebuah Ikhtiar Menuju Ijtihad Saintifik-Modern*. Jakarta: Teraju.
Azra, Azyumardi. (2009). Foreword. In Bambang Pranowo (ed.), *Memahami Islam Jawa*. Jakarta: INSEP & Pustaka Alvabet.
Djatikusumah, P. (2011). Posisi Penghayat Kepercayaan dalam Masyarakat Plural di Indonesia. In Elza Peldi Taher (ed.), *Merayakan Kebebasan Beragama: Bunga Rampai Menyambut 70 Tahun Djohan Effendi* (pp. 365–374). Jakarta: Democracy Project.
Driyarkara, N. (1980). *Driyakara tentang Negara dan Bangsa*. Yogyakarta: Penerbitan Yayasan Kanisius.
Effendy, Djohan. (2010). *Pembaruan Tanpa Membongkar Tradisi: Wacana Keagamaan di Kalangan Genrasi Muda NU Masa Kepemimpinan Gus Dur*. Jakarta: Penerbit Buku Kompas.
Endraswara, Suwardi. (2006). *Mistik Kejawen: Sinkretisme, Simbolisme dan Sufisme dalam Budaya Spiritual Jawa*. Yogyakarta: Narasi.
Geertz, Clifford. (1960). *The Religion of Java*. Chicago: The University of Chicago.
Habsyi, al-Husin. (1991). *Sunnah Syi'ah dalam Dialog: Antara Mahasiswa UGM dan UII Yogya dengan Ustadz Husein al-Habsyi*. Solo: Yayasan Ats-Tsaqalain.
Habsyi, al-Husin & Naqvi, Abulhasan Ali. (1991). *Sunnah-Syi'ah dalam Ukhuwah Islamiyah*. Malang: Yayasan al-Kautsar.
Hamid, Abdul Ghoni. (2007). Kewarisan dalam Perspektif Hazairin. *Jurnal Studi Agama dan Masyarakat*, 4(1): 29–67.
Hazairin. (1982). *Hukum Kewarisan Bilateral Menurut al-Qur'an dan Hadits*. Jakarta: Tintamas.
Hendropriyono, A.M. (2009). *Terorisme: Fundamentalis Kristen, Yahudi, Islam*. Jakarta: Penerbit Kompas.
Husaini, Adian. (2005). *Pluralisme Agama Haram: Fatwa MUI yang Tegas dan Tidak Kontroversial*. Jakarta: Pustaka al-Kautsar.
Husaini, Adian. (2006). *Pluralisme Agama: Parasit bagi Agama-agama: Pandangan Katolik, Protestan, Hindu, dan Islam*. Jakarta: Dewan Dakwah Islamiyah Indonesia.
Jurdi, Syarifuddin. (2010). *1 Abad Muhammadiyah: Gagasan Pembaruan Sosial Keagamaan*. Jakarta: Kompas.
Kuntowijoyo. (2001). *Muslim Tanpa Masjid: Esai-Esai Agama, Budaya dan Politik dalam Bingkai Strukturalisme Transendental*. Bandung: Mizan.
Maarif, Ahmad Syafii. (2006). *Islam dan Pancasila sebagai Dasar Negara: Studi tentang Perdebatan dalam Konstituante*. Jakarta: LP3ES.
Madjid, Nurcholish. (1992). *Islam, Doktrin dan Peradaban*. Jakarta: Yayasan Wakaf Paramadina.
Mahfud, M. D. (2019, June 10). Indonesia Bukan Negara Agama dan Bukan Negara Sekuler. https://-www.republika.co.id/berita/dunia-islam/islam-nusantara/19/01/10/pl49ek320-mafhud-md-indonesia-bukan-negara-agama-dan-bukan-sekuler.
Mulkhan, Abdul Munir. (1999). *Syekh Siti Jenar: Pergumulan Islam-Jawa*. Yogyakarta: Bentang.
Nafis, M. Wahyuni (ed.). (1995). *Kontekstualisasi Ajaran Islam: 70 Tahun Prof. Dr. H. Munawir Syadzali*. Jakarta: IPHI dan Paramadina.
Nahdlatul Ulama, P.B. (2011). *Solusi Problematika Aktual Hukum Islam: Keputusan Muktamar, Munas dan Konbes Nahdlatul Ulama' (1926–2010)*. Jakarta & Surabaya: LTN PBNU and Khalista.
Purwadi. (2004). *Dakwah Sunan Kalijaga: Penyebaran Ajaran Islam di Jawa Berbasis Kultural*. Yogyakarta: Pustaka Pelajar.
Rahardjo, M. Dawam. (2010). *Merayakan Kemajemukan, Kebebasan dan Kebangsaan*. Jakarta: Penerbit Kencana.
Ramage, Douglas E. (2010). *Politics in Indonesia: Democracy, Islam, and the Ideology of Tolerance*. London: Routledge.

Reid, Anthony. (2015). Pluralisme Agama Sebagai Tradisi Asia. In Bernard Adeney-Risakotta, (ed.), *Mengelola Keragaman di Indonesia: Agama dan Isu-isu Globalisasi, Kekerasan, Gender, dan Bencana di Indonesia* (pp. 45–58). Bandung: Mizan.

Ricklefs, M.C. (2006). *Mystic Synthesis in Java: A History of Islamisation from Fourteenth to the Early Eighteenth Centuries*. Norwalk: EastBridge.

Ricklefs, M.C. (2012). *Islamisation and Its Opponents in Java: A Political, Social, Cultural and Religious History, c. 1930 to the Present*. Singapore: NUS Press.

Shihab, M. Quraish. (2007). *Sunnah-Syi'ah Bergandengan Tangan: Mungkinkah?* Jakarta: Lentera Hati.

Sidogiri, Tim Penulis Buku. (2008). *Mungkinkah Sunnah-Syiah dalam Ukhuwah?: Jawaban atas Buku Dr. Quraish Shihab, Sunni-Syiah Bergandengan Tangan! Mungkinkah?* Pasuruan: Pustaka Sidogiri.

Simon, Hasanu. (2004). *Misteri Syekh Siti Jenar: Peran Wali Songo dalam Mengislamkan Tanah Jawa*. Yogyakarta: Pustaka Pelajar.

Sjadzali, Munawir. (1993). *Islam Realitas Baru dan Orientasi Masa Depan*. Jakarta: UI Press.

Subagya, Rachmat. (1981). *Agama Asli Indonesia*. Jakarta: Sinar Harapan dan Yayasan Cipta Loka Caraka.

Thaha, Anis Malik. (2005). *Tren Pluralisme Agama: Tinjauan Kritis*. Jakarta: Penerbit Perspektif.

The Wahid Foundation. (2017). *Laporan Tahunan Kemerdekaan Beragama/Berkeyakinan (KBB) di Indonesia 2017*. Jakarta: The Wahid Foundation.

Yogaswara, A. (2008). *Heboh Ahmadiyah: Mengapa Ahmadiyah Tidak Langsung Dibubarkan?* Yogyakarta: Narasi.

Yunanto, S. (ed.). (2003). *Militant Islamic Movements in Indonesia and South-East Asia*. Jakarta: Freiderich-Ebert-Stiftung.

Zainal, Abidin E.P. (2007). *Syarif Ahmad Saitama Lubis: Dari Ahmadiyah untuk Bangsa*. Yogyakarta: Logung Pustaka.

Zulian, Pradana Boy. (2018). *Fatwa in Indonesia: An Analysis of Dominant Legal Ideas and Modes of Thought of Fatwa-Making Agencies and Their Implications in the Post-New Order Period*. Amsterdam: Amsterdam University Press.

Zulkifli. (2009). *The Struggle of the Shi'is in Indonesia* [Doctoral dissertation]. Leiden University.

23
Malaysia
A secular constitution under siege?

Zawawi Ibrahim and Imran Mohd Rasid

Introduction

Religion and ethnicity have been crucial components in Malaysian political discourse and modes of governmentality. Much of this is due to the long historical process, including colonialism, that fostered the dynamic transformation of race relations and religious identity in the formation of politico-legal structures in the Malay world and the post-colonial Malaysian nation-state. This chapter discusses the intimate link between the state and religion in Malaysia from the pre-colonial period to the present. It also reviews the current constitutional framework, religious demographics, and political competition as well as the emerging trends and challenges that Malaysia faces in the governance and management of religious diversity and social order.

Historical overview of state–religion relations

Throughout the course of Malay history, the amalgamation of religions and cultural norms has been fundamental to the arrangement of social and political order. Before colonial rule and the eventual formation of independent Malaya (and later Malaysia) as a modern nation-state in 1957, polities were based on laws and systems that were deeply religious in nature. Prior to the spread of Islam, Malay polities followed customs that were influenced to a very significant extent by a fusion of Hindu and Buddhist concepts. Since the first millennium CE, the region was subjected to various foreign ideas and cultures as well as concepts of statecraft, divine authority, and rulership, especially those from Indian traditions. This is not to say that the indigenous communities did not develop a set of their own ideas through a process of cultural adaptation and hybridisation involving selectivity and proactiveness based on local agency. Historians describe this process of translation of religious ideas and culture into the modes of governance in the Malay world through a concept of 'local initiative' (van Leur, 1955) or 'localisation' and 'relocalisation' (Wolters, 1999). Religious ideas such as the notion of *devarāja* (god-king), observance of the *Dharmaśāstra* (the sacred law of Hinduism based on ancient Sanskrit texts) and specifically the codification of *Mānava-Dharmaśāstra* (Laws of Manu) at the state or even local level, are visible in the articulation of the mode of governance in the Malay world before the advent of Islam in the region.

Broadly speaking, Islam was brought to the Malay world by Arab and Indian missionaries and traders, especially from the twelfth century onwards. Subsequently, after Parameswara, the first ruler of the Melaka sultanate (r.1402–1414), accepted Islam and married a princess of the Sumatran Muslim polity of Pasai, Islam spread more rapidly throughout the Malay world. As a result, Sharia or Islamic law began to be incorporated into the pre-existing state and customary law (*adat*). In time, legal documents were compiled and written as codes of law (*undang-undang*) and legal digests (*risalah*). These are among the most valuable indigenous sources on the Malay world since the rules designed to regulate life offer insights into the expected standards of behaviour and also into what went wrong.

The *Undang-undang Melaka* (Melaka Laws, also known as *Hukum Qānūn Melaka*) is the most important and best known Malay legal code, with the core of the text being a series of regulations issued by Sultan Muhammad Syah (r.1424–1444) and expanded by Sultan Muzaffar Syah (r.1445–1458) (Liaw, 2007: 87, 2013: 415). Manuscripts of the *Undang-undang Melaka* are often hybrid compilations containing a number of different parts, most commonly the *Undang-undang Melaka* proper relating to the law of the land and the *Undang-undang laut* on maritime law. The entire corpus of the canon fuses Islamic principles and jurisprudence and customary law, with the former being the regulative principle for the latter. It dealt with the regulation of commercial matters both on land and sea, marriage, and rules of evidence. The criminal section the *Undang-undang Melaka* regulated relations between individuals and the state. It set the ethical codes and punishments for various offences or transgressions, including *hudud* (punishments under Sharia) and disobedience to the ruler. In a similar vein, the *Undang-undang Pahang* (Pahang Laws) was composed in the late sixteenth and early seventeenth centuries, and drew on the earlier *Undang-undang Melaka*, while the *Undang-undang Kedah* (Kedah Laws) dates from *c.*1650 onwards. Altogether, over 50 legal manuscripts are known, many containing local variants of the code from Aceh, Patani, Johor, and elsewhere in the Malay world.

The existence of these legal codes and the pre-eminence of such laws gradually changed the politico-legal structures of the Malay states so that by 1908 the colonial administrator R.J. Wilkinson was able to write: 'There can be no doubt that Moslem law would have ended by becoming the law of Malaya had not British law stepped in to check it' (cited in Roff, 1998: 211). The relationship between the legal precepts derived from Islam and the common law tradition that arrived with colonialism has created a complicated nexus of competing jurisprudence that remains salient to this day.

The arrival of British rule in the Malay world certainly disrupted the politico-legal order that had been put in place by the sultans and aristocracy over several centuries. The British incursion into the Malay peninsula was piecemeal. Under the auspices of the East India Company, and answerable directly to the colonial government of Bengal in India, the port cities of Penang, Singapore, and Melaka were amalgamated as the Straits Settlements in 1826 and then ruled as Crown colonies from 1867 onwards. Legal provisions here derived directly from the Indian Penal Code. By contrast, the traditional Malay states came under British rule through a series of treaties. The Federated Malay States (FMS) – Selangor, Perak, Negeri Sembilan, and Pahang – were established by the British government in 1895, while the Unfederated Malay States of Johor, Kedah, Kelantan, Perlis, and Terengganu were drawn into a kind of 'protected' status in the early twentieth century.

One of the most crucial moments of early colonialism was the signing of Anglo-Perak Pangkor Treaty of 1874, which legitimised British rule and relegated the sultan to a ceremonial role as protector of Islam and Malay custom while ceding political and economic control. The treaty specified that a British resident's advice 'must be asked and acted upon on all questions other than those touching Malay religion and custom' (Means, 1969: 274; Ahmad Fauzi, 2009: 158). This arrangement lay the grounds for the eventual establishment of the FMS and the gradual introduction of English-style legal provisions, courts, and judges. As a result, Islamic law came to be regarded as secondary and only applicable to Muslims in limited matters relating to the family and inheritance or in some aspects of religious transgressions. According to M.B. Hooker (1983: 173), 'The only substantive Muslim principle dealt with were "offences against religion", i.e. attendance at mosque for prayers, fasting, teaching religion without authority, and unlawful proximity'. Here Islamic laws were relegated to the realm of personal law, while English laws were to be applied to the 'non-privatised' areas of life. With these legal restrictions placed upon the juridical powers of the sultans, a secular conception of a separation between religion and state hitherto alien to the Malay worldview and practice began to take its logical course.

In order to administer Muslim affairs, Islam was bureaucratised. At the apex of the religious hierarchy of each state was the Majlis Agama Islam dan Adat Istiadat (Council of Islamic Religion and Malay Customs), comprising the sultans, the aristocratic elites, and religious advisers (Maznah, 2016: 63). The formation of these councils marked a new arrangement in terms of religious governance in the Malay world. Their effects persist to today.

> The Majlis personified a newly found alliance between the Sultans, the aristocratic elite and a nascent religious bureaucracy linked to colonial officialdom. Shari'ah courts were instituted, but their verdicts could be overridden by civil and magistrate courts. Religious personnel such as muftis, district qadis and imams were made public servants dependent on state payroll. Thus was born an official class of 'ulama' (religious scholars) who were increasingly divorced from the masses, over whom they had been granted authoritarian policing powers.
>
> *Ahmad Fauzi (2009: 160)*

In 1957, 11 of the 13 British colonial entities in the region – two of the Crown colonies and nine Malay states – attained independence and signed a Constitution governing a newly independent Federation of Malaya that would eventually culminate in the formation of Malaysia in 1963. Islam was made the 'religion of the federation'. But this constitutional assertion imposes no limits on the legislative power of Parliament, as the intention in making Islam the official religion of the federation was primarily ceremonial (Shad, 2005: 265).

At the state level, traditional rulers retained their positions as the heads of Islam. The king (Yang di-Pertuan Agong) – the constitutional monarch who in Malaysia's unique system is elected as the head of the federation on a rotating basis every five years – continued to be the head of Islam in his own state as well as in other states that have no traditional rulers: Melaka, Penang, the Federal Territories, Sabah, and Sarawak. Article 8(2) of the Federal Constitution guarantees 'there shall be no discrimination against citizens on the ground only of religion, race, descent, place of birth or gender in any law or in the appointment to any office or employment under a public authority' (Federal Constitution, 2010: 23). This means that no provisions in the Constitution can restrict the appointment of non-Muslims as the prime minister, chief ministers, ministers, or federal high officials. Article 11 also stipulates that 'Every person has the right to profess and practise his religion...', while every religious group has the right '(a) to manage its own religious affairs; (b) to establish and maintain institutions for religious or charitable purposes; and (c) to acquire and own property and hold and administer it in accordance with law' (ibid.: 25–26). Yet in practice, freedom of religion is subject to several important constraints. The propagation of any religious doctrine or belief among

Muslims may be controlled or restricted by state law. Non-Muslim missionary activities are often subject to strict regulation or even prohibition under the same laws.

Current constitutional and legal framework

Malaysia's history of encompassing long-established Islamic jurisprudence and colonial-era laws has clearly influenced the provisions of the Federal Constitution, the most authoritative document of the legal system. The principles and provisions that are enshrined in it are mostly inspired by the incorporation of these two historical legacies: pre-colonial Islamic laws and traditional customs, and the colonial administrative system introduced during British rule (Aishah, 1993: 3–4). It was during the colonial period that secularisation – understood primarily in terms of enforced separation between religion and the state – became more pronounced. A succession of legal, administrative, and educational reforms based on English law followed in both the Straits Settlements and Malay states. As a consequence, these laws effectively displaced Islamic law from its premier position in colonial governance (Sharifah & Rajasingham, 2001: 25).

The political settlement established at independence was based on the Westminster parliamentary model, together with the arrangements for federalism and constitutional monarchy. Although the word 'secular' is not mentioned in the Federal Constitution, it is clear, as affirmed by the parties involved in the drafting process, that the new state should embrace secularism as the governing principle by assuming a separation between state and religion. Tunku Abdul Rahman, leader of the Alliance coalition and later the first prime minister of independent Malaya, had assured the other members of the working committee who reviewed the draft prepared by the British-appointed Reid Commission that the whole exercise was undertaken on the understanding that the resultant federation would be a secular state (Fernando, 2006: 259–260, 265–270).

It is worth noting that Article 3(1) declares that while 'Islam is the religion of the Federation' other religions may be practised in peace and harmony in any part of the country – a proclamation that arguably was not intended to alter the state's secular nature (Federal Constitution, 2010: 19). Historical evidence based on the Reid Commission report, the legislative white paper, and all the primary constitutional documents clearly suggests that this provision was primarily intended to have symbolic and ceremonial significance and that the state envisioned by the Constitution's framers would be secular (Shad, 2005: 265; Fernando, 2006: 250, 262; Zawawi & Ahmad Fauzi, 2017: 172). Barely a year after independence, due to the confusion stemming from this provision, Tunku Abdul Rahman was called upon to clarify the matter during the debate in the legislative council. He insisted: 'I would like to make it clear that this country is not an Islamic State as it is generally understood, we merely provide that Islam shall be the official religion of the federation' (Abdul Rahman, 1977: 246). This view was later affirmed by serving chief justices' statements and judgements qualifying that the meaning of Islam's formal status merely pertained to rituals and ceremonies on official occasions rather than as a triumph over the primacy of the secular legislative framework (Mohamed Suffian, 1962: 8–11; Ahmad Ibrahim, 1985: 213–216). The passage of time has, however, blurred the initial intentions of the Constitution's framers, with some recent scholarly works and judicial decisions starting to challenge the secular basis of the state.[1]

The system stipulated in the Constitution mostly follows the plural legal provisions the British established during the colonial era. It adopts a court system familiar to those of common law jurisdictions, as well as incorporating distinct characteristics in the form of sharia courts and two separate high courts for Peninsular Malaysia and the Borneo states (Sabah and

Sarawak). The Malay rulers retain their positions as heads of Islam in their respective states and are responsible for overseeing the sharia courts and appointing judges based on the recommendations of state Islamic religious departments and councils that manage the operation of the courts (Federal Constitution, 2010: 20). With respect to Islamic matters, each state is given the constitutional right to identify an interpretation of Islamic laws that is applicable to Muslims within its territory. Each state is also given the right to establish courts to adjudicate disputes involving Muslims within a set range of areas as listed in the ninth schedule, state list of the Constitution:

> Islamic law and personal and family law of persons professing the religion of Islam, including the Islamic law relating to succession, testate and intestate, betrothal, marriage, divorce, dower, maintenance, adoption, legitimacy, guardianship, gifts, partitions and non-charitable trusts; Wakafs and the definition and regulation of charitable and religious endowments, institutions, trusts, charities, and charitable institutions operating wholly within the State; Malay customs; Zakat, Fitrah and Baitulmal or similar Islamic religious revenue, mosques or any Islamic public places of worship, creation and punishment of offences by persons professing the religion of Islam against precepts of that religion, except in regard to matters included in the Federal List; the constitution, organization and procedure of Syariah Courts, which shall have jurisdiction only over persons professing the religion of Islam and in respect only of any of the matters included in this paragraph, but shall not have jurisdiction in respect of offences except in so far as conferred by federal law; the control of propagating doctrines and beliefs among persons professing the religion of Islam; the determination of matters of Islamic law and doctrine and Malay custom.
>
> *Federal Constitution (2010: 198)*

This provision allows for each state to have the freedom to enact its own interpretation of Islamic law and establish its own state Islamic courts to adjudicate disputes. In recent decades, a series of constitutional amendments has given sharia courts increased autonomy to adjudicate disputes arising under Islamic law. States have begun to aggressively interpret the scope of their powers to regulate the affairs of Muslims located within their boundaries, resulting in an increased volume of Islamic legislation passed by individual states (Farid, 2014: 92).

Of late, a new trend has emerged involving court cases that invoke the constitutional rights to religious freedom. They have raised pertinent questions as to the boundaries of religious freedom for both Muslims and non-Muslims and the legal remit of sharia courts. The growing trend of Malaysian-style 'sharia-isation' – understood here as the institutionalisation of Sharia-based values, norms, and categories in the discourse and practice of the country's legal corpus – while being attached to the larger secular judicial framework as sanctioned by the Federal Constitution, has raised concerns over the practice of secularism in Malaysia (Zawawi & Ahmad Fauzi, 2017: 184). Beneath these tensions is the creeping narrative that Malaysia has *always* been an Islamic state and that the alleged 'ambiguity' of the Constitution must be interpreted in ways that prioritise Islamic principles above all else (Zulkifli, Interview, April 2019). For instance, the 2001 high court ruling in *Lina Joy v Majlis Agama Islam Wilayah & Anor* adopted the controversial view that

> Article 3(4) does not have the effect of reinforcing the status of the Federation as a secular state … Malaysia is not purely a secular state like India or Singapore but is a hybrid between the secular state and the theocratic state. The constitution of this hybrid model

accord [*sic*] official or preferential status to Islam but does not create a theocratic state like Saudi Arabia or Iran … Article 3(1) has a far wider and meaningful purpose than a mere fixation of the official religion.

Faiza Tamby Chik (2004: 128)

Judge Faiza Tamby Chik's verdict opened the floodgates for a flurry of rulings that broaden the interpretation of Article 3(1) to the extent that serious doubts have been raised about Malaysia's secular status. Many of the proponents of this view argue that the Federal Constitution does not explicitly declare Malaysia an Islamic state, yet the fact that it positively authorises the setting up and management of Islamic institutions and the enactment of Islamic by-laws by state assemblies is proof that Malaysia cannot be categorised as a secular state either (Zulkifli, Interview, April 2019; Zamihan, Interview, April 2019).

The question as to whether Malaysia was, is, or should be an Islamic or secular state is a legal question as much as it is a political one. The position held by government institutions on this question has great legal and political implications for society writ large (Whiting, 2010: 7). This is partly because the 'legality of state action is determined by reference to the Federal Constitution, so the secular – or religious – identity of the state directly shapes judicial interpretation of the constitution and answers to the question of what kinds of laws may lawfully be enacted' (ibid.: 8). As a result, much state-sponsored Islamisation has been conducted in an increasingly intolerant, authoritarian, and chauvinist manner to the extent that it directly challenges the existing constitutional rights and freedoms (that is, freedom of religion, expression, and association) that are granted to citizens. These include the banning of books, prosecution of individuals or groups for their involvement in practising 'deviant teachings', raiding private premises to enforce Sharia for such 'violations' as indecent dress, alcohol consumption, or *khalwat* (close proximity to a non-family member of the opposite sex).

With respect to freedom of religion, Article 11 of the Constitution declares that 'Every person has the right to profess and practise his religion' (Federal Constitution, 2010: 25). Yet in reality, freedom of religion is subject to several important constraints affecting both Muslims and non-Muslims. For example, state law prohibits not only non-Muslims from propagating their beliefs to Muslims, but also restricts any views or teachings by Muslims that are deemed heretical or a deviation from orthodox Sunni theology and jurisprudence. Restrictions on religious expression in public and non-public spaces have also been amplified over the years, including regulations of publications, dress codes, social media, blasphemy, and the intention to establish an interfaith commission (Mohd Sani et al., 2010: 9).

Religious demographics and governance of religious diversity

According to the Department of Statistics Malaysia (2018), Malaysia's estimated population in 2018 was 32.4 million, a 1.1 per cent growth over the previous year. The most recent census figures from 2010 indicate that 61.3 per cent of the population are Muslim, 19.8 per cent Buddhist, 9.2 per cent Christian, 6.3 per cent Hindu, while a small number practise Confucianism, Taoism, or other traditional Chinese folk religions. Other minority religious groups include animists, Sikhs, and Bahai communities. The number of self-described atheists is unknown as the topic is very sensitive and rarely studied. A 2015 global survey by WIN-Gallup International found that 3 per cent of Malaysian respondents were 'convinced atheists' and another 20 per cent described themselves as 'not a religious person' (Gallup International, 2015). Despite having no laws that restrict atheists from professing their position, many atheist groups or individuals have been put under immense pressure by the authorities. For example, a casual meeting of 20 people organised by the Malaysian chapter of the international group Atheist Republic in 2017 triggered an uproar and threats of violence from some Muslims. Asyraf Wajdi Dusuki, a minister in the government of Najib Razak (in office 2009–2018) with responsibility for Islamic affairs, demanded an investigation to determine whether any Muslims were involved in the meeting; another minister, Shahidan Kassim, said such groups went against the Federal Constitution and suggested 'forced education' for those involved (Higginbottom, 2017). The gathering also drew considerable ire online, including calls for the 'apostates' to be arrested and threats to behead the meeting's organiser (*Straits Times*, 2017). The authorities justified a hard-line response under the first principles of the *Rukun Negara* (National Principles) that every citizen is expected to believe in God (Zulkifli, Interview, April 2019). These uncompromising responses continued under the leadership of Mujahid Yusof Rawa, the minister of religious affairs of Mahathir Mohamad's short-lived second administration (2018–2020) and are likely to be maintained under the new government of Muhyiddin Yassin (2020–), as discussed below.

As a society known for its supposed multireligious and multiracial attributes, racial and religious characteristics tend to be conflated in the realms of politics, cultural expressions, and everyday social norms. The Muslim population is made up of mostly ethnic Malays, who account for approximately 55 per cent of the population. Article 160 of the Federal Constitution states that all ethnic Malays are Muslim (Federal Constitution, 2010: 151). As noted, only Sunni Islam is recognised, while the Shafi school of thought provides the legal basis for jurisprudence. Other forms of Islam, especially Shiism, are deemed illegal and subject to action by religious authorities. Some even regard Shiism as a religion that promotes violence and must be prosecuted on grounds of national security (Abu Hafiz, Interview, April 2019; Zamihan, Interview, April 2019; Zulkifli, Interview, April 2019).

After Islam, Buddhism is the second largest religion, and its history in the Malay world stretches far back before the period of Islamisation in the fifteenth century. Buddhism, and specifically the Mahayana tradition, is mainly practised by ethnic Chinese. In reality, most Chinese follow a combination of Buddhism, Taoism, Confucianism, and folk religion but when pressed to specify their faith, identify themselves as Buddhist (Tan, 1983: 217–219; Jnawali, 2009: 31).

The Christian communities mainly comprise non-Malay Bumiputeras: of the total Christian population, 64 per cent are Bumiputera, 27.3 per cent Chinese, 6.6 per cent Indian, and 1.8 per cent are various other nationalities (Loh, 2006). Two-thirds of Christians live in the East Malaysian states of Sabah and Sarawak. The major denominations include Anglicans, Baptists, Brethren, non-denominational churches, independent Charismatic churches, Lutherans, Methodists, Presbyterians, and Roman Catholics. Catholics make up the largest denomination, with 41.3 per cent of the total Christian population, due to their longer history of missionary work among the indigenes in the region compared to Protestants (Roxborogh, 1992: 54–55; Department of Statistics Malaysia, 2010). Despite the large number of Bumiputera Christians, in much academic research Malaysian Christianity has been closely associated with the metropolitan English-speaking urban Chinese and Indian middle class (Wong & Ngu, 2014: 262–263).

Hinduism is the fourth largest religion; 86 per cent of the Hindu population is ethnically Indian (Department of Statistics Malaysia, 2010). Many Hindus worship major deities such as Ganesha, Murugan, Krishna, Rama, and the goddess Mariamman, while some others pray to guardian deities like Muneeswarar, Muniyandi, Kaliamman, and Madurai Veeran and establish small shrines at residences, the borders of estates, or workplaces (Subramaniam, 2014: 20).

Given Malaysia's diverse religious and cultural background, it is understandable that successive governments have dedicated considerable time and resources to developing policies and programmes to manage religious diversity. The formulation of the mode of religious governance is predicated upon the spirit and principles of the *Rukun Negara*, which was formulated in 1970 to serve as the foundation of harmony and unity among the various ethnic and religious groups. The *Rukun Negara* calls for all citizens to be sensitive to and respectful of the concerns of other religious communities as well as to embrace 'a liberal approach towards her rich and varied cultural traditions'.

In terms of administration, the federal government of Muhyiddin Yassin that came to power in March 2020 has a ministerial position for religious affairs in the Prime Minister's Department and a newly formed Ministry of National Unity. While it is too early to predict the policy direction the new government might pursue, over the course of the previous decade successive administrations had conducted a range of activities and programmes to improve relations between the country's religious communities. For example, the administration of Najib Razak agreed to the formation of a special cabinet committee in 2010 to 'assist the government in its continuous efforts to promoting interreligious and inter-ethic understanding, harmony and social stability in Malaysia'. The committee was perceived as a framework for managing religious and cultural polarities that had increased in the previous years (Ahmad Fauzi, 2007; Ahmad Munawar & Wan Kamal, 2012). In October 2018, the Mahathir administration built on earlier initiatives when the National Unity Consultative Council released a Blueprint that had resulted from a series of unity dialogues in 2015. This was followed by roundtable conferences held nationwide to obtain feedback from stakeholders on the state of racial and religious unity in the country. The Blueprint outlined nine goals and 16 key recommendations, many of which gave special attention to improving the state of interreligious interaction within society (Malay Mail, 2018). In the event, neither of the two national harmony bills that had been mooted by the government came to pass, and commentators were left to rue a lost opportunity (*Aliran*, 2019).

New trends, old challenges

Over the past two years, Malaysia has undergone what can only be described as an unprecedented period of political turmoil. The general election of May 2018 saw the defeat of the Barisan Nasional coalition that had been in power for 61 years, a result that was predicted by almost no one. The new government, led by the veteran leader Mahathir Mohamad, was formed from a new coalition, Pakatan Harapan (Alliance of Hope), cobbled together from an assortment of political parties only in 2015. Though taken by surprise, many analysts and commentators eagerly celebrated this upset and expressed their hopes for what the government itself dubbed a 'New Malaysia' (*Malaysia Baru*). This slogan meant different things to different constituencies, including a desire to cleanse Malaysian politics of the notorious levels of rent-seeking and corruption. More broadly, there was also hope that the new government, more visibly multiracial and multicultural in its membership, might usher in a transformation in the country's race relations discourse. In any event, these hopes were badly misplaced.

Instead, during the first few months of the new government, a series of events took place that suggested a further hardening of racialised and religion-driven politics among significant sections of the majority Malay Muslim population. For example, just weeks after the government's proposal to recognise the Unified Examination Certificate (a system administered by private independent Chinese schools), there was a demonstration numbering several thousands to defend the status of 'Malay Muslim rights' under the banner of *Himpunan Kebangkitan Ummah* (Ummah Awakening Gathering) at the historic Padang Sultan Sulaiman in Kuala Lumpur. The defeated prime minister, Najib Razak, was quick to politicise and stoke this resentment: 'Muslims and Malays are concerned by what is happening in our country after [the] May 9 [general election], where the status and future of Islam and the position of the Malays is being threatened' (Mohd Iskandar, 2018). The mass rally clearly reflected a siege mentality and insecurity among Malay Muslims, who felt their interests were facing multiple 'threats' from so-called minorities. Their targets were many and included, at different junctures, the LBGT community, Chinese-language education groups, Hindu pressure groups, Shia Muslims, and so-called 'liberal' Muslims.

A few months later, on 8 December 2018, another mass demonstration of 60,000 gathered near Dataran Merdeka in central Kuala Lumpur to protest against the Pakatan Harapan government's plans to ratify the International Convention on the Elimination of All Forms of Racial Discrimination (ICERD), the core United Nations third-generation human rights instrument. Leaders of Parti Islam Se-Malaysia (PAS, Malaysian Islamic Party), the former dominant party United Malays National Organisation (UMNO), and conservative groups claimed that ratification of the convention would strip away Malay privileges and threaten Islam's position as the official religion of the state (New Straits Times, 2018). Both incidents suggest a re-emergence of a notably conservative trend in Malay Muslim nationalism – a convergence of ethnonationalism and religious nationalism that have always had a presence in Malay politics and, by extension, Malaysian politics (Ahmad Fauzi, 2016, 2018).

Historically, ethnonationalism – captured in more recent times by the idea of defending Malay supremacy (*ketuanan Melayu*) – has long been a leading strand of UMNO politics and policies. From the pre-independence period, with the mobilisation of the Malay masses against British-sponsored Malayan Union proposals in the late 1940s, to the formulation of the New Economic Policy and its articulation as a form of ethnic affirmative action in the 1970s, to the attempt to create a Malay capitalist class in the 1990s, UMNO unabashedly championed particular forms of Malay ethnonationalism. Meanwhile, religious nationalism was represented by the broad-based PAS, which has had an increasingly conservative interpretation of Islam as its main ideology. For most of the 1980s to 2010s, both UMNO (in government for the entire period) and PAS increasingly competed in an 'Islamisation race' – ratcheting up religiosity and piety as pillars of their politics – in order to maintain political legitimacy and vie for Malay electoral support.

The outcome of the 2018 general election helped change the balance of power between the two parties. UMNO lost its pre-eminence and was put into opposition for the first time alongside PAS. In effect, the two strands of Malay Muslim nationalism no longer competed against each other. Initially, the parties cooperated informally, and this proved remarkably successful. As seen from the protests and demonstrations described earlier, a tacit UMNO–PAS agreement proved very adept at mobilising Malay Muslims to press the government into reversing its policies. The anti-ICERD rally of 2018 was led by UMNO and PAS political leaders and civil society groups who argued that ratifying the convention would mean that Islam's role as enshrined in the Constitution would be curtailed and the sanctity of the institution of the Malay rulers would be jeopardised (Norshahril, 2019: 5). In a similar vein, they successfully scuppered the government's plans to ratify the Rome Statute of the International Criminal Court. As many predicted, UMNO and PAS signed an agreement on 14 September 2019, a so-called National Consensus Charter, formalising their cooperation and forming a powerful Malay Islamic bloc that threatened the Pakatan Harapan government's influence over its Malay support base. It ended decades of open competition and even hostility between the two parties.

The rising force of Malay Muslim nationalism thus posed a challenge for the Pakatan Harapan government's efforts to determine and navigate the narrative of Islam in the country. One prominent political analyst, Mohammed Nawab Osman, observed:

> What we are seeing [in the post-election period] is the amplification of the Islamisation drive that is quite different with the one experienced in the 1980s and 1990s. Earlier, the Islamisation was a clear-cut top-down approach. But as the anti-ICERD rally and a similar pattern shared by the anti-Ahok rally in Indonesia, have shown, there are now numerous forms of Islamisation at work: top-down, bottom-up, and sideways. This means that the newly elected Pakatan Harapan government will have a tougher time to dictate the Islamic narrative in Malaysia, let alone to reform it.
>
> Mohammed Nawab, Interview (April 2019)

As noted in the above, this phenomenon represented a challenge for the Pakatan Harapan government in carrying out the reforms it promised before the election. The government's response was unedifying, if not surprising: it resorted to all too familiar racial and religious rhetoric in its political programmes to win back the ebbing support of Malay communities in both rural and urban areas.

Another clear-cut example of this fierce competition for Malay Muslim support was the Malay Dignity Congress held on 6 October 2019. It was organised by four public universities and drew 5,000 Malay participants from *both* ruling and opposition parties, and was another indicator of growing anxiety in society – whether this was well founded on not. The hope for a more nuanced approach to race relations and religious dialogue seemed as distant as it had ever been. The tenor of many speeches was incendiary. Delegates made hostile allegations against the non-Malays, with some even calling for Malaysia to be exclusively for Malays. Cluster resolutions resulting from the conference included demands for: (1) the top positions in the government to be only filled by Malay Muslims; (2) the government to prevent the Human Rights Commission of Malaysia (Suhakam), the Bar Council, 'liberal' non-governmental organisations, and other similar bodies from intervening in Islamic affairs under the guise of human rights; and (3) the government to take tough action against those who challenge Islam as the federal religion (Muthiah & Tan, 2019). Conference participants included Prime Minister Mahathir Mohamad, the deputy president of the Parti Keadilan Rakyat Azmin Ali, the Amanah president Mohamad Sabu, and Bersatu's Syed Saddiq (all government ministers), as well as the PAS president Abdul Hadi Awang, the UMNO secretary general Annuar Musa, and former minister Khairy Jamaluddin (all prominent opposition leaders). The involvement of government ministers in such a racially charged event can be read as part of a desperate attempt to regain the support of the Malay community in the wake of the backlash expressed in the protest rallies.

Another example of the pressure from newly assertive opposition forces that the Pakatan Harapan government struggled to deal with was how its minister of religious affairs, Mujahid Yusof Rawa, had difficulty in translating his '*Rahmatan Lil Alamin*' (Blessing for All Creations) agenda into practice. Known by many as a figure who represents an inclusive and progressive strand of Islam, Mujahid seemed to revert to a more conservative direction under the impact of popular protests. In a BBC interview, Mujahid emphasised the need for Malaysia to endorse a 'new narrative' of 'compassionate Islam'. But when pressed further, he struggled to come up with a concrete programme that would actually deliver this vision

(BBC, 2019). He even went so far as to express his support for Zakir Naik – arguably one of the most extreme Wahhabi ideologues in the world today who is currently residing in Malaysia – by calling his preaching 'inspiring' (Lipi, 2019), when only a few months earlier he was reported as saying that Zakir Naik's combative style of propagating Islam was 'not suitable for Malaysia' (*The Star*, 2018). He also denounced LGBT groups and civil rights organisations for 'the misuse of the democratic space to defend things that are wrong in the religion of Islam' by participating in an International Women's Day march (Lim, 2019). He also announced the formation of a special unit under his ministry to monitor insults against the Prophet and Islam, and proposed new legislation, a Religious and Racial Hatred Act, to 'protect' Islam and other religions against slurs and insults (Hidir, 2018). There were many other examples of the ministry using its extensive powers under sharia law to clamp down on what it perceived as dissent and deviance.

If this conservative turn under the self-proclaimed reformist and inclusive Pakatan Harapan government was not worrying enough, recent political developments in Malaysia are likely to exacerbate this trend. In February and March 2018, the Pakatan Harapan government was brought down through the wholesale defection of some of its constituent parties and individual MPs to the opposition, which then had the parliamentary numbers to form a new coalition, Perikatan Nasional (National Alliance), with Muhyiddin Yassin as the new prime minister. The political manoeuvring has brought UMNO back to power and, for the first time since the 1970s, PAS is represented in the cabinet. Despite claims that the new government will work towards 'national unity' and 'reconciliation', it is very clear that forces that support a combination of Malay supremacy and religious conservatism hold the upper hand, even if it is too early to predict the future trajectory of an extremely volatile political system.

Concluding remarks

Since Malaysia's founding as an independent nation-state, many have argued that it was established to be a secular state as guaranteed by the Federal Constitution. Even though there were always voices that demanded greater prominence for Islam as the 'state religion', these did not find sufficient political leverage in a period when successive governments prioritised nation-building and developmentalism. However, in recent decades, proponents who interpret Islam as the religion of the federation and push for an enlargement of the judicial powers given to states and the sharia courts have found greater political purchase. Much of this can be explained by an increasing congruence of ethnonationalism and religious nationalism, partly expressed in political competition between UMNO and PAS, but it is a phenomenon that is now seemingly mainstreamed into political discourse, policymaking, and electioneering. In sum, the secular basis of the federation has been weakened and the forces of Islamisation that tentatively emerged in the 1970s have become more prominent.

Both the Pakatan Harapan political coalition that ruled briefly from 2018 to 2020 and the newly installed Perikatan Nasional government seek to instrumentalise the language of religious politics, with some having staked their political legitimacy and electoral fortunes on the promise to deliver 'Islamic governance'. This further retreat into the politics of religion and race – which normalises intolerant and divisive views in society – has disrupted earlier piecemeal initiatives to combat violent extremism, which were perhaps only ever half-hearted. A very real risk is an escalation of intolerant radical ideas into the mainstream. For the present and future of Malaysia, this phenomenon poses the greatest challenge for the country to maintain its sense of balanced governance over religious diversity and to curb the rise of potentially violent extremism in society.

Note

1 In interviews conducted with several prominent individuals in the government, all take the view that Malaysia has always been an Islamic state and not a secular one. Many interviewees feel that Article 3 of the Constitution must be read together with many policies and initiatives that have favoured Islam and Muslims since independence. They insist that such favouritism towards Islam must continue to be defended for Malaysia to remain an Islamic state. See Abu Hafiz Salleh Hudin, Interview, 10 April 2019; Zamihan Mat Zin, Interview, 12 April 2019; Zulkifli Mohamad Al-Bakri, Interview, 24 April 2019.

References

Abdul Rahman Putra al-Haj, Tunku. (1977). *Looking Back: Monday Musings and Memories*. Kuala Lumpur: Pustaka Antara.
Ahmad Fauzi Abdul Hamid. (2007). *Islam and Violence in Malaysia*. Working Paper Series No. 123. Singapore: S. Rajaratnam School of International Studies, Nanyang Technological University.
Ahmad Fauzi Abdul Hamid. (2009). Implementing Islamic law within a modern constitutional framework: Challenges and problems in contemporary Malaysia. *Islamic Studies*, 48(2): 157–187.
Ahmad Fauzi Abdul Hamid. (2016). *The Extensive Salafization of Malaysian Islam*. Trends in Southeast Asia Monograph Series, No. 9. Singapore: Institute of Southeast Asian Studies.
Ahmad Fauzi Abdul Hamid. (2018). Shifting trends of Islamism and Islamist practices in Malaysia, 1957–2017. Southeast Asian Studies: Special issue. *Divides and Dissent: Malaysian Politics 60 Years after Merdeka*, 7(3): 363–390.
Ahmad Ibrahim. (1985). The position of Islam in the constitution of Malaysia. In Ahmad Ibrahim, Sharon Siddique, & Yasmin Hussain (comp.), *Readings on Islam in Southeast Asia* (pp. 213–220). Singapore: Institute of Southeast Asian Studies.
Ahmad Munawar Ismail & Wan Kamal Mujani. (2012). Themes and issues in research on interfaith and inter-religious dialogue in Malaysia. *Advances in Natural and Applied Sciences*, 6(6): 1001–1009.
Aishah Bidin. (1993). The historical and traditional features of the Malaysian constitution. *Jebat: Malaysian Journal of History, Politics and Strategic Studies*, 21: 3–20.
Aliran. (2019, May 1). Call for more discussion, mutual consultation towards national harmony.
BBC. (2019, November 13). HARDTalk: Mujahid Yusof Rawa. Available at: www.bbc.co.uk/programmes/m000btg1.
Department of Statistics Malaysia. (2010). Population and housing census. Available at: https://www.statistics.gov.my/censusatlas/images/ReligionEN.pdf.
Department of Statistics Malaysia. (2018, July 31). Press release: Current population estimates, Malaysia, 2017–2018. Available at: https://www.dosm.gov.my/v1/index.php?r=column/pdfPrev&id=c1pqTnFjb29HSnNYNUpiTmNWZHArdz09.
Faiza Tamby Chik J. (2004). Lina Joy v Majlis Agama Islam Wilayah & Anor: High Court (Kuala Lumpur)—Originating Summons No R2-24-30 of 2000 Faiza Tamby Chik J 18 April 2001. *Malayan Law Journal*, 2: 119–144.
Farid S. Shuaib. (2014). The Islamic legal system in Malaysia. *Pacific Rim Law & Policy Journal*, 21(1): 85–113.
Federal Constitution. (2010). Malaysia. Available at: http://www.agc.gov.my/agcportal/uploads/files/Publications/FC/Federal%20Consti%20(BI%20text).pdf.
Fernando, Joseph M. (2006). The position of Islam in the constitution of Malaysia. *Journal of Southeast Asian Studies*, 37(2): 249–266.
Gallup International. (2015, June 8). Losing our religion? Two thirds of people still claim to be religious. Available at: https://www.gallup-international.bg/en/33531/losing-our-religion-two-thirds-of-people-still-claim-to-be-religious/.
Hidir Reduan. (2018, July 24). Religious and Racial Hatred Act in the pipeline. *New Straits Times*.
Higginbottom, Justin. (2017, August 22). Intolerance rising: atheists at risk in Malaysia. *The Diplomat*.
Hooker, M.B. (1983). Muhammadan law and Islamic law. In M.B. Hooker (ed.), *Islam in Southeast Asia* (pp. 160–182). Leiden: E.J. Brill.
Jnawali, Damodar. (2009). Buddhism and global peace: Perspectives on cultural geography. *The Third Pole: Journal of Geography Education*, 5–7: 28–36.
Liaw Yock Fang. (2007). Naskah Undang-Undang Melaka: Suatu tinjauan. *Sari*, 25: 85–94.

Liaw Yock Fang. (2013). *A History of Classical Malay Literature*. Singapore: Institute of Southeast Asian Studies.

Lim, Ida. (2019, March 9). Mujahid shocked Women's Day march was used to promote LGBT. *Malay Mail*.

Lipi, Emma. (2019, March 13). Mujahid Rawa meets Zakir Naik, calls his preaching work 'inspiring'. *The Star*.

Loh Kok Wah, Francis. (2006). Christians in Malaysia: Understanding their socio-economic context [Unpublished ms.].

Malay Mail. (2018, October 14). NUCC Blueprint released for public comment.

Maznah Mohamad. (2016). Policing and protecting women: Some aspects of Malay-Islamic law-making under British colonialism. *Kajian Malaysia*, 34(1): 59–78.

Means, Gordon P. (1969). The role of Islam in the political development of Malaysia. *Comparative Politics*, 1(2): 264–284.

Mohamed Suffian Hashim. (1962). The relationship between Islam and the state in Malaya. *Intisari*, 1(1): 7–21.

Mohd Iskandar Ibrahim. (2018, July 28). Najib: Himpunan Kebangkitan Ummah gathering proof that people are unhappy with PH govt. *New Straits Times*.

Mohd Sani Mohd Azizuddin & Dian Diana Abdul Hamed Shah. (2010). Freedom of religious expression in Malaysia. *Paper at the Third International Conference on International Studies*, Kuala Lumpur, 1–2 December 2010.

Muthiah Wani & Tarrence Tan. (2019, October 6). Resolutions on five areas presented at Malay Dignity Congress, but PM says not all will be met. *The Star*.

New Straits Times. (2018, November 24). Why Malaysia backpedalled on ICERD ratification.

Norshahril Saat. (2019). The UMNO-PAS unity charter and its impact. *Perspective*, No. 83, ISEAS Yusof Ishak Institute.

Roff, William R. (1998). Patterns of Islamization in Malaysia, 1890s–1990s: Exemplars, institutions, and vectors. *Journal of Islamic Studies*, 9(2): 210–228.

Roxborogh, John. (1992). Early nineteenth-century foundations of Christianity in Malaya: Churches and missions in Penang, Melaka and Singapore from 1786–1842. *Asian Journal of Theology*, 6(1): 54–72.

Shad Saleem Faruqi. (2005). The Malaysian constitution, the Islamic state and hudud laws. In K.S. Nathan & Mohammad Hashim Kamali (eds), *Islam in Southeast Asia: Political, Social and Strategic Challenges for the 21st Century* (pp. 256–277). Singapore: Institute for Southeast Asian Studies.

Sharifah Suhanan Syed Ahmad & Roy Rajasingham. (2001). *The Malaysian Legal System, Legal Practice & Legal Education*. Tokyo: Institute of Developing Economies, IDE Asian Law Series No. 4.

Straits Times. (2017, August 8). Atheist Republic members need to be tracked down, says Malaysian cabinet minister.

Subramaniam, Manimaran. (2014). An evolving trend in religious practices amongst Malaysian Hindus: A case study of shrines within the residence compound of Hindus, a new phenomenon? *Journal of Indian Culture and Civilization*, 1: 1–8.

Tan Chee-Beng. (1983). Chinese religion in Malaysia: A general view. *Asian Folklore Studies*, 42(2): 217–252.

The Star. (2018, September 24). Zakir Naik's combative style of spreading Islam not suitable for Malaysia, says Mujahid Rawa.

van Leur, J.C. (1955). *Indonesian Trade and Society: Essays in Asian Social and Economic History*. The Hague: W. van Hoeve.

Whiting, Amanda J. (2010). Secularism, the Islamic state and the Malaysian legal profession. *Asian Journal of Comparative Law*, 5(1): 1–34.

Wolters, O.W. (1999). *History, Culture, and Region in Southeast Asian Perspectives*. Ithaca, NY: Southeast Asia Program Publications, Cornell University.

Wong, Diana & Ngu Ik Tien. (2014). A 'double alienation': The vernacular Chinese church in Malaysia. *Asian Journal of Social Science*, 42(3): 262–290.

Zawawi Ibrahim & Ahmad Fauzi Abdul Hamid. (2017). Governance of religious diversity in Malaysia: Islam in a secular state or secularism in an Islamic state. In Anna Triandafyllidou & Tariq Modood (eds), *The Problem of Religious Diversity: European Challenges, Asian Approaches* (pp. 169–203). Edinburgh: University of Edinburgh Press.

Interviews

Abu Hafiz Salleh Hudin, Exco member of Bersatu Youth, 10 April 2019.
Mohammed Nawab Osman, Assistant professor, S. Rajaratnam School of International Studies (Singapore), 3 April 2019.
Zamihan Mat Zin, Officer-cum-spiritual adviser for the rehabilitation programme, Jabatan Kemajuan Islam Malaysia (JAKIM, Department of Islamic Development Malaysia), 12 April 2019.
Zulkifli Mohamad Al-Bakri, Federal Territory mufti, 24 April 2019.

24

Australia

Diversity, neutrality, and exceptionalism

Michele Grossman, Vivian Gerrand and Anna Halafoff

Introduction

Australia's European history as a nation began as a distant colonial outpost of the British Empire in the eighteenth century. This colonial history is reflected in part by its historical development as a Christian-majority nation over which hangs the long shadow of systematic dispossession, displacement, and denial of the continent's indigenous Aboriginal and Torres Strait Islander peoples, whose occupation of, and spiritual and cultural heritage grounded in, their relationship to Australian land has continued unbroken for at least 65,000 years. At the time of invasion by Europeans, who declared Australia '*terra nullius*', or empty of 'settled' peoples who could claim prior sovereignty over the land under British law, there were over 250 Indigenous language groups across the continental mainland, the island of Tasmania, and the Torres Strait Islands (AIATSIS, 2019).

Australia has a current population of just over 25 million people from a wide variety of ethnic and cultural backgrounds speaking over 300 different languages in the home (ABS, 2017a). The country has, especially since the post-Second World War era, enjoyed a global reputation as one of the world's most successful pluralist and multicultural nations.

However, this is a relatively recent development in the nation's history since the advent of White European settlement (Bouma, 1995). Australia's experience of and approach to embracing and managing religious and cultural pluralism has always been inseparable from its variable policy stances on migration and cultural diversity, whether opposed to such diversity – as was the case from 1901 until the 1950s – or in favour of it from the 1950s onwards during the post-war reconstruction period. In 2016, the latest year to provide national Census data, almost 30 per cent of Australians were born overseas; this figure increases to 49 per cent when counting both Australians born overseas and those with one or both parents born overseas (ABS, 2019).

Australia's Christian majority status has historically been composed of Protestants and Roman Catholics of various denominations. While the landscape of Christianity, as with religion more broadly, has diversified significantly since Europeans first colonised Australia, the early Australian settlement period was dominated by Anglicanism through the Church of England. Catholicism, on the other hand, was associated by the ruling powers of Australian colonies as backward, unenlightened, and allied with Irish sedition and rebellion transported to the colonies along with Irish Catholic convicts, setting the stage for decades of politically inflected sectarian conflict in Australian institutions and society (Chavura et al., 2019).

While religious and cultural diversity has been present since the earliest days of European settlement, the Australian gold rush period in the 1850s brought a diverse range of people from other ethnic and faith backgrounds to Australia who stayed on to resettle afterwards, including significant numbers of Chinese migrants from Buddhist, Taoist, and Confucian belief systems, as well as Sikhs and Hindus who worked not only on the goldfields but in the cotton and sugar industries, along with Japanese pearl divers (Bouma & Halafoff, 2017; Croucher, 1989). Muslim and Hindu South Asian, Central Asian, and Middle Eastern cameleers (who were often mistakenly lumped together as 'Afghans' or 'Ghans') also began arriving around the same time as outback pastoralism accelerated in climatic regions where camels provided more adaptable transport than horses. Muslim cameleers were involved in establishing Islam in Australia in the nineteenth century, beginning with mosques in South Australia and Western Australia (Jones & Kenny, 2010).

In 1901, Australia became a nation and member of the British Commonwealth following the federation of the previously self-governing colonies of New South Wales, Victoria, Queensland, Tasmania, South Australia, and Western Australia. At the same time, the newly formed state enshrined the Immigration Restriction Act 1901, popularly known as the 'White Australia Policy', which privileged British migrants over non-British settlers and explicitly discouraged Chinese, Japanese, and Pacific Islander migration and settlement. In part, the White Australia policy was driven by nativist labour unions who agitated against the undermining of 'white' European jobs and economic well-being by an uncontrolled influx of cheaper labour (Markey, 2004). The White Australia policy began to weaken in the 1950s and was finally abolished in full in 1973.

Since the 1970s, Australia has actively cultivated first a multicultural and then a multifaith policy framework at both Commonwealth and State/Territory levels, which has become intrinsic to concepts of Australian national identity. Today, after the 52 per cent of Australians identifying with one or another Christian denomination, the next two largest religions in Australia are Islam (2.6 per cent) and Buddhism (2.4 per cent). Just under one-third (30 per cent) of the population identify with 'no religion', and other faiths comprise less than 10 per cent of the population, with Muslim Australians at 2.6 per cent, Buddhists 2.4 per cent, Hindus 1.9 per cent, Sikhs 0.5 per cent, and Jews .04 per cent. The fastest growing religions in Australia in the 2016 Census data compared to the 2011 Census are Sikhism (74 per cent increase), Hinduism (60 per cent increase), and no religion (48 per cent increase) (ABS, 2017b).

However, these policy frameworks have never remained entirely uncontested either politically or socially. As Koleth (2010) has observed, while since the terrorist attacks of 9/11 in particular, contemporary 'concern about the global threat of terrorism and the challenges of ensuring social cohesion in societies characterised by ethno-cultural diversity' in Australia has increased, its origins lie in longer-running debates and fluctuations in Australian approaches to ethno-cultural diversity that have 'shift[ed] in emphasis from assimilation and integration to multiculturalism, and, in recent times, a return to assimilation and integration'.

These fluctuations have, alongside discourses on terrorism and the advent of heightened mobility and displacement for Muslim-background populations seeking refuge in countries around the world, focussed increasingly on the role of religion as a proxy for broader issues around the role of ethno-cultural diversity. This has been particularly evident in terms of prospects for social integration and social discord, largely in relation to the alignment of Islam and Muslims within Australian society and communities. The discussion that follows

Table 24.1 Religion in Australia: 2016 Census data summary

Religious affiliation	Population ('000)	Population (%)
Christian		
Catholic	5,291.8	22.6
Anglican	3,101.2	13.3
Other Christian	3,808.6	16.3
Total	12,201.5	52.1
Other religions		
Islam	604.2	2.6
Buddhism	563.7	2.4
Hinduism	440.3	1.9
Sikhism	125.9	0.5
Judaism	91.0	0.4
Other	95.7	0.4
Total	1,920.8	8.2
No religion[a]	7,040.7	30.1
Australia[b]	23,401.9	100

Source: Australian Bureau of Statistics (2017b).
a No religion includes secular and other spiritual beliefs.
b As religion was an optional question, the total for Australia will not equal the sum of the items above it.

will elaborate on some of the tensions, debates, and impacts that have emerged in modern Australia by offering analysis of three contemporary flashpoints in Australia's governance of religious diversity. These are: (1) education, religion, and the state; (2) discrimination and bias towards religious minorities, and (3) reviewing and legislating religious freedoms.

Education, religion, and the state

Australia is a secular country, but 'secular' here should not be interpreted to mean non- or anti-religious. Instead, Australian secularism has been most persistently defined by the doctrine of liberal separationalism (Chavura et al., 2019) or what Modood and Sealy (2019) term 'open secularism', reflected in the stance of the Australian Constitution's prohibitions on interference in the free exercise of any religion. There is no official national religion, and the Australian Constitution (Section 116) prohibits the enacting of laws that establish or set up any religious body or organisation.[1]

The way in which the Australian Constitution treats religious freedom has for many decades operated on the principle that religious beliefs and practices are voluntary and private matters for its citizens, and that people should be free to choose to exercise or indeed to refrain from exercising any religious beliefs or practices, as long as these do not interfere with the human rights or freedoms of others or with the laws of the nation. Thus, secularisation in Australia has not historically meant the rejection of religion by the state (Chavura et al., 2019; Jupp, 2009b); rather, it has transformed the relationship between the state and religion into one of managing religious influence and principles in relation to a range of social and political structures and reforms. The doctrine of liberal separationalism has persisted and was perhaps influenced by earlier periods of volatile religious sectarianism between Protestants and Catholics (ibid.: 254).

In fact, the Catholic-Protestant sectarian conflict characterising pre-Federation Australia may have actually advanced the cause of religious pluralism by helping to dismantle the funding of denominationally based education in the nineteenth century (Chavura et al., 2019: 255). Yet in modern times, the relationship between religion and education in Australia has become a periodic flashpoint in how the separationalist doctrine between the state and religion has been interpreted at various points in Australian political and social life.

Public primary and secondary education systems (and in some cases post-secondary non-university awards) are legislated and primarily funded by States and Territories, with the Commonwealth contributing only about one-quarter of schools' funding across the country (Hanrahan, 2018). This contributes in part to broader tensions between Commonwealth and State or Territory legislation concerning the intersection between religious freedom and other human rights, about which we say more below.

However, the historical legacy of government decisions to begin funding private religious schools in the 1960s following the near collapse of the Catholic independent schools system, with a significant boost to the ways in which this occurs devised under the Howard Coalition Government 1996–2007 (Buckingham, 2010), has meant that the Commonwealth continues to contribute significant funding to private religious schools. This has reversed the trend beginning in the late nineteenth century, when Victoria was the first state to pass the Education Act 1872. This Act mandated the provision of free, compulsory and secular education through public state-funded schools, becoming one of the first jurisdictions in the world to do so. By 1908, all Australian states had adopted similar mechanisms (Macintyre, 1991). From 1988 to 2006, significant growth in non-government religious school attendance occurred, driven partly by changes in government policy and partly by Australia's altering demographics, resulting in 19 per cent growth in the total proportion of Australian students enrolled in independent schools affiliated with various religions, and 15 per cent growth in the Catholic independent education system (Buckingham, 2010: 4).

In addition, some States and Territories have also funded religious instruction in public government schools at various points, a source of enduring controversy for over a century (Halafoff, 2012). The provision of religious instruction has also persisted in schools as an adjunct to official state school curricula, with Christian and Jewish volunteers providing Special Religious Instruction (SRI) in government schools, and expanding SRI provision to Buddhist, Sikh, Bahai, Hindu, and Muslim instruction at the turn of the twenty-first century (Halafoff, 2012, 2015).

However, SRI has proved highly controversial in some states. In Victoria, for example, controversy erupted in 2014 over the delivery of SRI classes by the Christian group Access Ministries, the only religious group funded by the Victorian Government to deliver SRI and chaplaincy within public schools (Percy, 2014). Non-religious parents raised concerns that their children were either automatically opted-in to Christian SRI classes or, when they chose to opt out of such classes, did not have access to meaningful educational activities as an alternative. Others complained about the proselytising content of Access Ministries resources for students, with numerous issues raised concerning this (Halafoff, 2012, 2015; Karp, 2018a).

Victorian requirements for school chaplains were challenged in 2018 on the basis that they harmed religious freedom by stating that applicants for school chaplains be connected to an organised religious group, which violated the non-religious role of pastoral care chaplaincy as defined by the Australian High Court (Karp, 2018b). Similar concerns persist in NSW and Queensland by parents and scholars regarding Christian Religious Education (RE) in state schools, although Christian providers do not receive state funding for their programmes in these states (Byrne, 2014; Maddox, 2014). In response to these debates, the Victorian State

Government removed SRI from the curriculum altogether in 2016 in order to 'make way for new content on world histories, cultures, faiths and ethics' (Cook & Jacks, 2015), with dedicated content embedded in its curriculum on 'Learning about worldviews and religions' from Foundation to Year 10 (Halafoff, 2016).

These controversies reveal abiding tensions between promoting respect for and understanding of cultural pluralism, on the one hand, and objections to the support of religious instruction by the state based on principles of secularism, on the other (Crittenden, 1988). They have produced abiding debates among Australian educationalists and commentators, including concerns that limiting religious schools could drive them into more marginalised and less accountable social spaces (Buckingham, 2010: 24).

Religious exceptionalism and human rights

The ambiguous boundaries between religion and the state in relation to education and the role of government funding and curriculum content are underpinned structurally by the distribution of legislative responsibilities across federal-state relations. In Australia's federated system, the Commonwealth's stance on non-interference in religious freedom has left States and Territories free to legislate on various religious matters. This includes the freedom to both prescribe and proscribe various religious institutions, practices, or values or to impede religious freedoms. In practice, however, States and Territories have largely adhered to the principle of non-interference established by the Constitution. Accordingly, the Commonwealth continues to balance its limited scope of powers against the greater freedom of States and Territories to legislate on religious matters, as correspondingly narrow interpretations regarding religious protections at the Commonwealth level by the Australian High Court have shown over time (Religious Freedom Review Expert Panel, 2018: 36).

Amendments to tighten State and Territory freedoms to prescribe religious laws or inhibit religious freedoms were proposed in 1944 (the Australian Post-War Reconstruction and Democratic Rights Referendum) and again in 1988 (the 1988 Australian Referendum) but were unsuccessful. The absence of positive Constitutional protection for religious rights and freedoms has periodically led some, including the Australian Human Rights and Equal Opportunity Commission in 1998, to see the protection of rights to religious freedoms as relatively weak in comparison to similar countries (Meyerson, 2009: 529). This argument holds that while there may be a Constitutional guarantee of non-establishment and free exercise of religion, it merely restricts the rights of the Commonwealth to conduct the first or interfere in the second, rather than actively asserting and protecting the religious freedom and anti-discrimination rights of citizens (Meyerson, 2009).

These issues, along with other Australian political debates about marriage equality, free speech pertaining to religious beliefs, and protections both for and against discrimination on religious grounds led to the Commonwealth Government's commissioning of a Religious Freedom Review, which published its final report in May 2018. The purpose of the Religious Freedom Review was to 'examine and report on whether Australian law (Commonwealth, State and Territory) adequately protects the human right to freedom of religion' (Religious Freedom Review Expert Panel, 2018: iii). The Review's scope included considering the intersections between the enjoyment of the freedom of religion and other human rights.

The impetus for the Review points to the complex landscape of religious freedoms and protections in Australia. Religion itself is not a protected attribute under existing Commonwealth anti-discrimination acts. This has occasioned significant disquiet among members of Australian religious minority groups who have long claimed experiences and accounts of discrimination in relation to religious identity and sought greater legislative protection for religion as a result.

However, the Review also responded to the arguments of a variety of religious groups who claimed that their religious freedoms – in particular, to the 'right to discriminate' based on religious beliefs – were increasingly limited or proscribed by legislation that treated other identity attributes (for example, sexual or gender identity) as protected under anti-discrimination legislation, despite a range of existing exemptions based on religious beliefs at both Commonwealth and State levels.

These tensions came to a head during the national referendum on marriage equality in 2017, which saw 61 per cent of those Australians who participated register their support for the passage of the Marriage Equality Act in 2017, enabling two people of the same sex to marry with the same legal recognition, rights, and responsibilities as heterosexual unions. However, opponents of the bill argued that it would harm gender education, religious freedom, and freedom of speech (Karp, 2017). These debates ultimately spearheaded the decision by government to commission the Religious Freedom Review.

Indeed, the governance of religion in Australia must manage the complex intersection of a range of other legal and governance frameworks relating to discrimination, vilification, education, marriage equality, free speech, equal opportunity, and human rights.[2] Here we summarise the chief variations in these categories across the various States and Territories. The State of Victoria and the Australian Capital Territory (ACT) each provide human rights charters that protect 'freedom of thought, conscience, religion and belief' (*Charter of Human Rights and Responsibilities Act 2006* [Vic]; *Human Rights Act 2004 [ACT]*). Discrimination based on religion is protected through various anti-discrimination acts in the ACT, New South Wales, the Northern Territory, Queensland and Tasmania and through the *Equal Opportunity Act 1984 (SA)* in South Australia and Western Australia (*Equal Opportunity Act 1984* [WA]).

Anti-vilification legislation based on religion obtains in either anti-discrimination, racial, and religious tolerance, and/or criminal code acts in Victoria, Tasmania, Queensland, New South Wales, and the ACT, but not in the Northern Territory, South Australia, or Western Australia. Provisions for exemptions on the basis of religious belief from some or all of (a) special religious education in schools, (b) sex education in schools, and (c) classes in schools exist in all States and Territories, with Western Australia, New South Wales, and the Northern Territory providing exemptions for all three through respective Education Acts. The wide variation in how protected attributes based on religious conviction, belief, activity, or opinion are applied in areas like housing, goods and services, clubs and associations, and sports across different States and Territories provides some sense of how important such instruments are in guaranteeing – or not – freedom to participate in local Australian community life.

The Religious Freedom Review Expert Panel made 20 recommendations addressing these variations and other issues. Fifteen of those have been accepted by the Commonwealth Government directly or in principle, with the remaining five reserved for further consideration and consultation (Australian Government, 2018). In its response to the Review's findings and recommendations, the Australian Government acknowledged the central importance of linking religious freedom to broader questions of human rights, including Australia's status for nearly 40 years as a signatory to the *International Covenant on Civil and Political Rights (1966)*.[3] In line with the Review's emphasis on respecting Australia's cultural, ethnic and religious diversity, it also commits the Commonwealth to commissioning data collection and analysis on issues relating to bias, harassment, intimidation, discrimination, and threats of violence linked to a person's faith, as well as 'restrictions on the ability of people to educate their children in a manner consistent with their faith' and 'the extent to which religious diversity (as distinct from cultural diversity) is accepted and promoted in Australian society' (Australian Government, 2018: 14).

The substance of the five recommendations reserved for further consideration by the Australian Government focus in particular on rights and exemptions in relation to religious freedom in employment and education contexts. These reservations may have been influenced by three factors: first, the potential for contradicting other enshrined rights such as the *Fair Work Act* and the *Sex Discrimination Act* that have become cornerstones of Australia's human rights framework; second, because of intensive lobbying for the continuation or strengthening of various exemptions based on religion by religious educational and other employer groups, and third, because of the potential for conflict between different tiers of government in Australia's federated system.

Arising from the Religious Freedom Review, a suite of three interrelated draft Parliamentary Bills (the Religious Discrimination Bill 2019 [Cth], the Religious Discrimination [Consequential Amendments] Bill 2019 [Cth], and the Human Rights Legislation Amendment [Freedom of Religion] Bill 2019 [Cth]) were circulated for public consultation in late 2019 and at the time of writing are still in development, with over 6,000 public submissions received by early October 2019 (https://www.ag.gov.au/Consultations/Pages/religious-freedom-bills.aspx).

Bias and discrimination against religious minorities

Despite Australia's decades-long history of multicultural and, more recently, multifaith policy frameworks, bias and discrimination against religious minorities has accelerated in recent times, reflecting broader trends of polarisation and social conflict that have both local and transnational antecedents. Some of these conflicts have revolved around the conflation of concerns about population growth with the phenomena of both skilled and humanitarian immigration (Cave & Kwai, 2019), while others have been spurred by a resurgence of right-wing rhetoric relating to cultural others, which has increasingly dominated the public sphere (Lewis et al., 2019).

For example, places of worship are largely uncontroversial in Australian everyday life outside of common concerns relating to increased levels of noise and traffic congestion. The exception to this is the presence of Islamic mosques and Jewish synagogues, both of which have seen recent increases in targeted hate crimes; a 2019 analysis of police records found that the vast majority of hate crimes in New South Wales are based on religion or race or both, with religious bias crimes against Muslims (73 per cent) and Jews (14 per cent) appearing in police records of incidents from 2013 to 2016 (Mason, 2019).

Other incidents around Australia include Islamophobic protests against the building of new mosques, public and online harassment of identifiably Muslim community members, and anti-Semitic harassment, vandalism, and threats directed at people and properties connected to Jewish synagogues and communities. In 2014, bitter and violent protests erupted in Bendigo, a major population centre about two hours outside Melbourne, when proposals were submitted to build the regional city's first mosque (*ABC News*, 2014; Rudner, 2017). Existing Australian mosques have also been targeted by protests and harassment, including the Parramatta, NSW, mosque where in 2015 a 15-year-old boy prayed before shooting dead a NSW Police civilian employee in an Islamic State-inspired attack. Islamic sectarian attacks against mosques have also occurred, with recent convictions against two Sunni extremists (linked to Islamic State in a separate legal case) who twice attempted to burn down a Shia mosque in Melbourne in 2015 and again in 2016 (Percy, 2019).

The Executive Council of Australian Jewry (ECAJ) in its 2018 annual report on anti-Semitism in Australia documented 366 anti-Semitic incidents, reflecting an overall 'increase of 59 per cent over the previous 12-month period'. From 2017 to 2018, this included 'increases in harassment, vandalism, threats by email, telephone and posters/stickers, [but] a decrease in graffiti and postal mail', along with a stable number of reported assaults. The ECAJ 2018 report identified both extremist fringe and more mainstream far-right groups as influential in the rise of anti-Semitic harassment, vandalism, and threats, concluding that:

> Although Australia remains a stable, vibrant and tolerant democracy… as the political far right increasingly becomes emboldened and more active, and as far right groups publicly denigrate, demonise and incite violence against Jews, it is incumbent upon political and other leaders to demonstrate that antisemitism, and all forms of racism, is not acceptable in Australia.
>
> *Nathan (2018: 8)*

Attitudes towards Muslims in Australia are 'not uniform' and have varied over time. Since 9/11 in particular, however, their place in Australian society 'has been increasingly questioned' (Akbarzadeh, 2016) as part of the broader discourses mobilised around the 'war on terror' that seek to link Islam with terrorism in fundamental ways. Yet the response of Australian Muslims to this has overall been one more characterised by resilience than by disaffection (Dunn et al., 2015). Having said that, the sense of belonging and religious and cultural freedoms experienced by Muslim communities are to a significant extent mediated and curtailed by experiences of racism, discrimination, and negative or sensationalised media discourses that contribute to Islamophobia in Australia. This produces contradictory discourses so that 'on the one hand Muslims are seen as not "fitting into" Australia [and] on the other they are prevented from belonging through racism' (Dunn et al., 2015: 39).

As a result, many Australian Muslims have felt their communities to be under siege and have experienced a reduced sense of national belonging (Briskman, 2015; Bull & Rane, 2019; Murphy et al., 2015). The exploitation of Islamophobia for political gain – particularly as the public tenor of Australian political debate has deteriorated – has also contributed to this phenomenon. For example, in 2011, the then-Liberal Party Senator Cory Bernardi publicly declared Islam as a religion to be a 'totalitarian, political and religious ideology' with Muslims 'continually trying to change our laws' (Akbarzadeh, 2016). The One Nation Party, which originally entered Parliament in 1997 under leader Pauline Hanson on a platform warning that Australia was 'in danger of being swamped by Asians', subsequently re-birthed 20 years later with an explicitly anti-Islam platform (Patel, 2016) alongside the continuation of broader assertions that multiculturalism poses a major threat to the foundations of Australian culture, identity, and shared values. In 2018, the maiden speech delivered by Senator Fraser Anning, a former One Nation Party member who became an independent, advocated for a 'final solution' to Muslim immigration that elicited immediate bipartisan condemnation for its overt referencing of Nazism (Collett, 2018).

This has been accompanied by documented rises in hate speech and hate incidents directed at Muslims (Iner, 2019), largely on social media but also in the physical world, creating disturbing echo chambers and permissiveness for violence that justify and amplify Islamophobic discourse. These findings have, in turn, brought into sharp focus the issue of Australia's unsuccessful efforts to weaken hate speech laws in 2014 and again in 2017 through proposing to amend Section 18C of the Australian Racial Discrimination Act (Mao, 2019), a position now abandoned following the Christchurch massacre.

Despite these challenges, Australian Muslim communities continue to show high levels of belief in 'Islam's compatibility with Australian norms and Muslims' support for diversity', despite experiences of Islamophobia, 'is revelatory of resilience' (Dunn et al., 2015: 39). These experiences have translated on the whole into wariness but not disaffection, and Dunn et al. (ibid.) found that Australia's 'values of diversity and multiculturalism' continue to 'give hope to Australian Muslims' in their dispositions and everyday lives.

Concluding remarks

Australia's approach to the governance of religious diversity is marked by several key features. These include a historically dominant Anglo-Christian public sphere arising from Australia's past as a British colony that has had to come to terms over time with both its intra-Christian diversity and a host of other faith systems as the country's multicultural policies and social realities began to accelerate in the twentieth century. This has occurred in the context of a continuing absence of recognition and reckoning with the nation's pre-European religious past in ways that are both meaningful and connotative of dignity and respect for complex Indigenous religious and spiritual belief systems.

Australia continues to redefine its historical relationship to 'moderate secularism' (Modood & Sealy, 2019) based on a doctrine of liberal separationalism (Chavura et al., 2019) in the context of recent debates that have created social and policy tensions between 'multiple secularisms', on the one hand, in which religion and secularism mutually constitute and engage with each other (Modood & Sealy, 2019: 15), and the backlash from Australian 'new hardliners', with their antipathy towards multicultural immigration and accommodation of minority religions, on the other (ibid.). The processes of 'non-othering' (Jansen, 2014) in relation to multifaith diversity remain unfinished business in the Australian context.

Australia's transition towards the governance of religion within a pro-diversity framework may be largely characterised as having begun with a historical commitment to 'open secularism' (Modood & Sealy, 2019: 16) that has shifted gradually towards the multiculturalisation of 'moderate secularism' (ibid.: 21), particularly in relation to state-based practices of inclusivity and the abandonment of 'difference blindness' (ibid.). Three of the four principles adumbrated by Modood and Sealy (2019) for open secularism – the moral equality of persons, freedom of conscience and religion, and the separation of church and state – continue, to a large degree, to shape the contemporary Australian landscape of state-religion relations.

However, the fourth principle – state neutrality in respect of religious and deep-seated secular convictions – is arguably more fragile and contested. Existing approaches to religious freedom in Australia are now tending towards ever-increasing demands for accommodation of exceptionalism in the context of the freedom to discriminate against others based on religious beliefs – an inconsistent position with regard to state neutrality insofar as it permits discrimination in ways that potentially infringe on the human rights of others to equality to proceed. This has significant implications for amplifying minority alienation (Modood & Sealy, 2019) not only of religious minorities, who may be increasingly marginalised by a new permissiveness towards their exclusion and rejection from public sphere institutions and practices such as education, health, and sport, but also the marginalisation of non-religious minorities, such as LGBTQI+ individuals and communities, on the basis of religious exceptionalism.

The ways in which this will influence the historical trend of Australia's trajectory towards 'diversity-friendly critiques and adaptations of secularisms' (Modood & Sealy, 2019: 27), or alternatively privilege the position of new hardliners in a regression back to a more restrictive version of moderate secularism, remains to be seen. This has implications also for the challenges faced by Australia in relation to religiously inspired or attributed radicalisation to violence.

Religious minorities in Australia have benefited both from the historical structural accommodations legislated by open secularism and increasingly from more recent moves towards policy-based inclusivity and recognition. Yet in an environment that continues to be characterised by consistent popular (and populist) associations of Islam with terrorism, by bitter debates about immigration and the 'lack of fit' between 'othered' minorities, such as Muslims, and the Australian mainstream, and by the normalising and mainstreaming of far-right anti-religious minority sentiments in both popular and party-political Australian life, there exists the potential for new contexts of conflict around religious diversity in both familiar and new guises to emerge.

Australia has a number of protective factors to draw on. These include an enduring level of comfort with multiculturalism (Markus, 2018, 2019); the evidenced contributions of diverse faith-based and multifaith community organisations to civic and cultural life; a well-developed policy infrastructure focussed on social cohesion, community resilience, and countering violent extremism (Grossman et al., 2016), and a recognition, however unevenly applied or periodically challenged, that social cohesion and the active embrace of cultural and religious diversity are hallmarks of resilience in navigating the global challenges created by social, political, and religious polarisation. However, the emergence of increased political polarisation in national public discourse, combined with the decline of social trust in both governmental and other social institutions – including those of organised religion – poses risks in Australia as it does elsewhere. Australia must remain vigilant that such risky dynamics do not overtake the protections it can currently draw upon.

Notes

1 Section 116 of the Commonwealth of Australia Constitution Act (1900) says: 'The Commonwealth shall not make any law for establishing any religion, or for imposing any religious observance, or for prohibiting the free exercise of any religion, and no religious test shall be required as a qualification for any office or public trust under the Commonwealth'. http://classic.austlii.edu.au/au/legis/cth/consol_act/coaca430/s116.html
2 A table setting out 'key protections for religious belief in Australian legislation, including anti-discrimination, anti-vilification, constitutional and human rights protections' is provided in Appendix C, Table C.1 of the *Religious Freedom Review: Report of the Expert Panel* (Religious Freedom Review Expert Panel, 2018, p. 128 ff).
3 The Australian Government specifically references Articles 18 and 2 of the *International Covenant on Civil and Political Rights* in its response to the Religious Freedom Review recommendations: 'Article 18: 1: *Everyone shall have the right to freedom of thought, conscience and religion. This right shall include freedom to have or to adopt a religion or belief of his choice, and freedom, either individually or in community with others and in public or private, to manifest his religion or belief in worship, observance, practice and teaching. 2. No one shall be subject to coercion which would impair his freedom to have or to adopt a religion or belief of his choice. 3. Freedom to manifest one's religion or beliefs may be subject only to such limitations as are prescribed by law and are necessary to protect public safety, order, health, or morals or the fundamental rights and freedoms of others. 4. The States Parties to the present Covenant undertake to have respect for the liberty of parents and, when applicable, legal guardians to ensure the religious and moral education of their children in conformity with their own convictions'.* Article 2.2 states: '*Where not already provided for by existing legislative or other measures, each State Party to the present Covenant undertakes to take the necessary steps, in accordance with its constitutional processes and with the provisions of the present Covenant, to adopt such legislative or other measures as may be necessary to give effect to the rights recognized in the present Covenant*' (Australian Government Response to Religious Freedom Review Report, December 2018).

References

ABC News. (2014, June 24). Bendigo mosque: Council approves construction despite fiery public meeting. Available at: https://www.abc.net.au/news/2014-06-19/bendigo-council-approves-mosque-despite-objections/5534634.

Akbarzadeh, S. (2016). The Muslim Question in Australia: Islamophobia and Muslim alienation. *Journal of Muslim Minority Affairs,* 36(3): 323–333.

Australian Bureau of Statistics (ABS). (2017a). *Census Reveals a Fast Changing, Culturally Diverse Nation.* Available at: https://www.abs.gov.au/ausstats/abs@.nsf/lookup/Media%20Release3.

Australian Bureau of Statistics (ABS). (2017b). *Religion in Australia: 2016 Census Data Summary 2071.0 – Census of Population and Housing: Reflecting Australia – Stories from the Census, 2016.* Available at: https://www.abs.gov.au/ausstats/abs@.nsf/Lookup/by%20Subject/2071.0~2016~Main%20Features~Religion%20Data%20Summary~70.

Australian Bureau of Statistics (ABS). (2019). *Australia's Population by Country of Birth, 3412.0.* Available at: https://www.abs.gov.au/ausstats/abs@.nsf/Latestproducts/3412.0Main%20Features22017-18.

Australian Government. (2018, December 13). *Australian Government Response to the Religious Freedom Review.* Available at: https://www.pm.gov.au/media/government-response-religious-freedom-review.

Australian Institute for Aboriginal and Torres Strait Islander Studies (AIATSIS). (2019). *Celebrating 2019, International Year of Indigenous Languages.* Available at: https://aiatsis.gov.au/explore/articles/indigenous-australian-languages.

Bouma, G. (1995). The emergence of religious plurality in Australia: A multicultural society. *Sociology of Religion,* 56(3): 285–302.

Bouma, G. D. & Halafoff, A. (2017). Australia's changing religious profile—rising Nones and Pentecostals, Declining British Protestants in superdiversity: Views from the 2016 Census. *Journal for the Academic Study of Religion,* 30(2): 129–143.

Briskman, L. (2015). The creeping blight of Islamophobia in Australia. *International Journal for Crime, Justice and Social Democracy,* 4(3): 112–121.

Buckingham, J. (2010). *The Rise of Religious Schools.* Policy Monograph 111. St Leonards, NSW: Centre for Independent Studies. Available at: https://www.cis.org.au/app/uploads/2015/07/pm111.pdf.

Bull, M. & Rane, H. (2019). Beyond Faith: Social marginalisation and the prevention of radicalisation among young Muslim Australians. *Critical Studies on Terrorism,* 12(2): 273–297.

Byrne, C. (2014). *Religion in Secular Education: What in Heaven's Name are we Teaching our Children?* Leiden: Brill.

Cave, D. & Kwai, I. (2019, April 22). Why has Australia fallen out of love with immigration? *The New York Times.* Available at: https://www.nytimes.com/2019/04/22/world/australia/immigration.html.

Chavura, S. A., Gascoigne, J., & Tregenza, I. (2019). Reason, *Religion and the Australian Polity: A Secular State?* London and New York: Routledge.

Collett, M. (2018, August 28). Final solution: Here's the Nazi history of the phrase used by Fraser Anning. *ABC News.* Available at: https://www.abc.net.au/news/2018-08-15/fraser-anning-history-of-the-nazi-phrase-final-solution/10122812.

Cook, H. & Jacks, T. (2015, August 21). Religious instruction scrapped from curriculum. *The Age.* Available at: https://www.theage.com.au/national/victoria/religious-instruction-scrapped-from-curriculum-20150820-gj425e.html.

Crittenden, B. (1988). *Parents, the State and the Right to Educate.* Melbourne: Melbourne University Press.

Croucher, P. (1989). *Buddhism in Australia: 1848–1988.* Kensington: New South Wales University Press.

Dunn, K., Atie, R., Mapedzahama, V., Ozalp, M., & Aydogan, A. F. (2015). *The Resilience and Ordinariness of Australian Muslims: Attitudes and Experiences of Muslims Report.* Sydney: Western Sydney University/Islamic Sciences and Research Academy Australia. Available at: https://www.westernsydney.edu.au/__data/assets/pdf_file/0008/988793/12441_text_challenging_racism_WEB.pdf.

Grossman, M., Peucker, M., Smith, D., & Dellal, H. (2016). *Stocktake Research Project: A Systematic Literature Review and Selective Programme Review on Social Cohesion, Community Resilience and Violent Extremism.* Melbourne: Department of Premier and Cabinet, State of Victoria. Available at: https://amf.net.au/entry/stocktake-research-report.

Halafoff, A. (2012, June 29). Time for change: A new role for religion in education. *The Conversation* [online]. Available at: https://theconversation.com/time-for-change-a-new-role-for-religion-in-education-6564.

Halafoff, A. (2015). Special Religious Instruction and worldviews education in Victoria's schools: Social inclusion, citizenship and countering extremism. *Journal of Intercultural Studies*, 36(3): 362–379.

Halafoff, A. (2016). Governance and religious diversity in Australia: Multifaith relations and religious instruction in the State of Victoria. In Andrew Dawson (ed.), *Politics and Practice of Religious Diversity: National Contexts, Global Issues* (pp. 101–117). London: Routledge.

Hanrahan, C. (2018, April 20). Here's how Australia's schools are funded – And we promise not to mention Gonski. *ABC News*. Available at: https://www.abc.net.au/news/2017-05-30/school-funding-explained-without-mentioning-gonski/8555276.

Iner, D. (ed.). (2019). *Islamophobia in Australia Report II (2017–2018)*. Sydney: Charles Sturt University and Islamic Science and Research Academy.

Jansen, Y. (2014). *Secularism, Assimilation and the Crisis of Multiculturalism: French Modernist Legacies*. Amsterdam: Amsterdam University Press.

Jones, P. & Kenny, A. (2010). *Australia's Muslim Cameleers: Pioneers of the Inland, 1860s-1930s*. Kent Town, SA: Wakefield Press.

Jupp, J. (ed.). (2009b). *The Encyclopedia of Religion in Australia*. Melbourne: Cambridge University Press.

Karp, P. (2017, August 29). Coalition for Marriage ad blitz links marriage equality to gender education. *The Guardian*. Available at: https://www.theguardian.com/australia-news/2017/aug/29/coalition-for-marriage-ad-blitz-links-marriage-equality-to-gender-education.

Karp, P. (2018a, June 1). School chaplains: Secular groups say review is proof of proselytising. *The Guardian*. Available at: https://www.theguardian.com/australia-news/2018/jun/01/school-chaplains-secular-groups-say-review-is-proof-of-proselytising.

Karp, P. (2018b, June 14). School chaplains legal challenge argues program is discriminatory. *The Guardian*. Available at: https://www.theguardian.com/australia-news/2018/jun/14/school-chaplains-legal-challenge-argues-program-is-discriminatory.

Koleth, E. (2010). *Multiculturalism: A review of Australian policy statements and recent debates in Australia and overseas*. Parliament of Australia Research Paper No. 6/2010–11. Available at: https://www.aph.gov.au/About_Parliament/Parliamentary_Departments/Parliamentary_Library/pubs/rp/rp1011/11rp06.

Lewis, J., Pond, P., & Cameron, C. (2019). Social cohesion, Twitter and far-right politics in Australia: Diversity in the democratic mediasphere. *European Journal of Cultural Studies*, 22(5–6): 958–978. DOI: 10.1177/1367549419833035.

Macintyre, S. (1991). *A Colonial Liberalism: The Life and Times of Three Victorian Visionaries*. Melbourne: Oxford University Press.

Maddox, M. (2014). *Taking God to School: The End of Australia's Egalitarian Education?* Sydney: Allen & Unwin.

Mao, F. (2019, March 20). Christchurch shooting: Australia's moment of hate speech reckoning. *BBC News*. Available at: https://www.bbc.com/news/world-australia-47620391.

Markey, R. (2004). A century of the labour movement in Australia. *Illawara Unity*, 4(1): 42–63.

Markus, A. (2018). *Mapping Social Cohesion: The Scanlon Foundation Surveys 2018*. Melbourne: Scanlon Foundation. Available at: https://scanlonfoundation.org.au/wp-content/uploads/2018/12/Social-Cohesion-2018-report-26-Nov.pdf.

Markus, A. (2019). *Mapping Social Cohesion: The Scanlon Foundation Surveys 2019*. Melbourne: Scanlon Foundation Research Institute. Available at: https://scanloninstitute.org.au/report2019.

Mason, G. (2019). A picture of bias crime in New South Wales. *Cosmpolitan Civil Societies: An Interdisciplinary Journal*, 11(1). DOI: 10.5130/ccs.v11.i1.6402.

Meyerson, D. (2009). The Protection of religious rights under Australian law. *BYU Law Review*, 3(-2009): 529–553.

Modood, T. & Sealy, T. (2019). Secularism and the Governance of Religious Diversity. (GREASE Concept Paper). Available at: http://grease.eui.eu/wp-content/uploads/sites/8/2019/05/GREASE_D1.1_Modood-Sealy_Final1.pdf.

Murphy, K., Cherney, A., & Barkworth, J. (2015). *Avoiding Community Backlash in the Fight Against Terrorism: Research Report*. Australian Research Council (Grant No. DP130100392). Australia: University of Queensland, Griffith University.

Nathan, J. (2018). *Executive Council of Australian Jewry Report on Antisemitism in Australia 2018*. Available at: http://www.ecaj.org.au/wp-content/uploads/2018/11/ECAJ-Antisemitism-Report-2018.pdf.

Patel, U. (2016, July 11). Pauline Hanson: One Nation party's resurgence after 20 years of controversy. *ABC News*. Available at: https://www.abc.net.au/news/2016-07-10/timeline-rise-of-pauline-hanson-one-nation/7583230.

Percy, K. (2014, May 30). Victoria Department of Education to overhaul religious education. *ABC News*. Available at: https://www.abc.net.au/news/2014-05-29/victoria-department-of-education-to-overhaul-religion-education/5487274.

Percy, K. (2019, May 9). Fawkner mosque arsonists were also behind Melbourne Christmas terror plot. *ABC News*. Available at: https://mobile.abc.net.au/news/2019-05-09/mosque-fire-mohamed-chaarani-moukhaiber-terrorism-guilty/11085396?pfmredir=sm.

Religious Freedom Review Expert Panel. (2018). *Religious Freedom Review: Report of the Expert Panel*. Canberra: Commonwealth of Australia. Available at: https://www.ag.gov.au/RightsAndProtections/HumanRights/Documents/religious-freedom-review-expert-panel-report-2018.pdf.

Rudner, J. (2017). *Social Cohesion in Bendigo: Understanding Community Attitudes to the Mosque in 2015*. Melbourne: Victorian Multicultural Commission.

25
Governing religious diversity across the world
Comparative insights

Anna Triandafyllidou and Tina Magazzini

Relationship between the nation and religion

Religion and religious diversity appear to be one of the toughest diversity challenges societies face today in their search for identity, equality, and cohesion in an increasingly globalised world. It has been argued that religious identity comprises one of the most important dimensions of discrimination today (Modood, 2013), and indeed religion in certain contexts appears to be a stronger identity register than national or ethnic identity and belonging. Yet, the increased mobility and (super)diversity fostered by globalisation has not seen the realisation of the predicament of the decline of the nation-state, but has rather led to the re-emergence of the nation as a relevant political community and point of reference for identification and belonging (Triandafyllidou, 2017).

In Europe, where the increasingly widespread secular values are often presented as inherently at odds with 'new' religious minorities, old paradigms of republicanism or multiculturalism seem to be in crisis, but a new 'third way' between *laïcité* and state religion that combines national and religious identity into a plural mix is struggling to emerge (Medda-Windischer, 2017; Ruiz Vieytez, 2016). In India, the approach founded on a 'deep respect for religion', in which religious and cultural diversity are acknowledged as constitutional values and where several ethnic and religious minority identities inhabit the same system of institutions, a strengthening of Hindutva in the national discourse has in recent years seen a serious deterioration of the government's capacity to peacefully manage its diverse population (Mahajan, 2017, 2020).

One question that has been present throughout the different settings, histories, and contexts analysed in this volume is whether, in accommodating religious diversity, one ought better equalise upwards (notably more religion in public life for both majorities and minorities) or equalise downwards (moving towards a more radical secularism that relegates the religious to the private sphere). What are the obstacles that different state-religion relations encounter, and can the struggle to balance freedom of religion with freedom from religion be applied – or even conceived of – similarly in different contexts?

A departing point of this book has been the need to engage in dialogue across disciplines, national contexts, and different notions about what constitutes a desirable model of state-religion relations. As noted by Modood (2019, pp. 217–218), academic dialogue rather than identity-less reasoning is relevant for multiple reasons: on the one hand, it allows for non-mainstream viewpoints, needs, and cultures to be heard. This, in turn, contributes to a growth of understanding that is genuinely novel and fosters a 'solution' or conclusion that is truly open and not the simple product of the strength of a preconceived idea, model, or theory. Finally, an academic dialogue as 'cooperation under conditions of deep diversity or "multiplicity" requires a "multilogue"' (ibid.), which is especially important in a volume combining theoretical insights about the need to protect legitimate claims of religious minorities with the existing empirical data on cultural and religious diversity.

The question of accommodating religious diversity has been at the forefront of public debate on immigration and immigrant and ethnic minority integration since the 1990s, but is posed today with renewed urgency by the re-emergence of religiously attributed violence as well as of right-wing attacks targeting religious minorities in South Asia, the MENA and Asia Pacific regions, and Europe. How can we make sense of and study the evolving role of religion(s) in contemporary societies and the relationship of religious communities to state institutions in a systematic way, allowing for comparative analysis while not losing sight of the specificities that inform each case?

The analysis in each chapter is based on a contextual approach: the socio-demographic composition of each country and its historical legacies are outlined with a view to framing the role of religion within this context and the ways in which legal and institutional structures emerged to govern religion and religious diversity – whether that was inherent in the foundations of the state or the result of later population movements. Our contextual approach, though, is not just historical but also appreciates that the law is designed to address as many situations as possible in a homogenous manner. Thus, while addressing the legal frameworks of each country, we need to acknowledge the specificities of actual practice – notably how laws, policies, and even grassroots initiatives are implemented and lived in society. In embarking on such a broad geographical scope of religious governance models, we acknowledge that not only we must recognise the diversity of religions, but also that there are different *relationships* of individuals to religions, including different ways of belonging to a religious community and not only of practising one's faith in an individualistic way.

In order to capture the diversity of constellations of different approaches while apprehending the dissonances, overlaps, and synergies between them, each chapter has followed a common structure even though flexibility was accorded to allow for highlighting aspects that are unique to each case.

A 'thick description' of nation-religion relations

We opted to organise the volume by world regions as such geographical groups of countries reflect certain similarities in shared historical legacies and approaches, even though this should not obscure the significant variation and differences that exist within those regional clusters. The Handbook has been divided into six parts: the first focusses on Western Europe, the second on Southern Europe, and the third on Central and Eastern Europe and Russia, followed by Southeastern Europe (part four). Part Five comprises studies from the Middle East and North Africa region, and Part Six gathers cases from South and Southeast Asia and the Asia Pacific.

Thinking about what we have learnt from these 23 chapters, two dimensions stand out as both descriptive and analytical. First is the relationship between nation and religion: how much is the nation identified with a given religious community and what is the level of homogeneity in terms of religion in a given country (see Tables 25.1–25.3). Second is the institutional setup with which countries manage such relationships; in other words, the different existing models of religious diversity governance (Table 25.4).

As regards the relationship between the nation and religion, and assuming that we consider the dominant discourses in each country, we distinguish between two aspects: the strength of the ties between the national community and a religion; and whether these ties related to a single religion (a religious majority community) or a set of religious communities that are recognised as part of the national community. Thus, we distinguish between strong and weak ties, and strong plural vs weak plural ties.

In the case of a strong link between the nation and a single religious community, the two are seen as nearly inseparable; religious diversity may be accommodated but is not part of the dominant national narrative. The nation is also understood as the flock in this case, the community of the faithful. Examples of such strong ties can be, for instance, Greece, Turkey, Morocco, and Egypt. In Egypt, for instance, the national ID card includes a person's religious identity, and this was also the case in Turkey until 2017 and in Greece until 2000.

A weak relationship between a single religious community and the nation means instead that religion is recognised as an historical element of the national identity, but the ties are rather weak. This would be the case of the UK, France, or Russia.

Strong plural ties, on the other hand, better reflect the situation in India, Indonesia, and Malaysia, as well as in Lebanon where religion occupies an important, indeed a dominant, position in the national narrative but a plurality of religious communities are accommodated and recognised as important for the national identity.

Finally, cases like Germany, Albania, and Australia would signal weak plural ties; notably, the national identity narratives recognise the existence of multiple faiths and related communities, but the definition of the nation is not strongly predicated on one of those or on the notion of religious diversity as a particular feature or value characterising the nation.

This typology of relations offers a thick description of the different situations in the different countries and world regions, even though some cases may be more challenging to classify than others. Typical examples of this ambiguity may be Italy or Spain where the historical and institutional relationship between the Catholic Church and the nation is strong and has been dominant for a long time, but has been receding in recent decades both because of the decrease in people's religiosity and because of religious minorities emerging as a result of immigration. Another difficult case to classify is Bulgaria where the identification between the nation and Christian Orthodoxy is strong and historically grounded, but given the communist period's suppression of religion and the size and relative importance of the Bulgarian Muslim community, we would rather position the country in the category of weak ties with a single religion rather than with neighbouring Greece, in the strong ties box.

The classification presented in Table 25.1 offers a reading grid of the variety of nation-religion relations surveyed in this volume. We have also grouped the countries per macro-region with a view to checking whether some type of nation and religion relations is characteristic of a given macro-region. Indeed what comes out after a first reading is that in Southeastern Europe, North Africa, and the Middle East it is more common for a single religion to be a strong element that defines a nation (see Gulalp, Gemi, Hellyer, Fahmi, Lahlou, and Zouiten in this volume). Such a relationship existed also in the past in Central and Eastern Europe, but 50 years of communism have loosened this link and significantly affected the level of self-identifications of those populations with historically dominant religious communities (see Vekony, Iliasov, and Racius in this volume). Having said this we witness today in

Table 25.1 Relations between the nation and religion

Relationship between religion and nation	Strong ties with a single religion	Weak ties with a single religion	Strong plural ties	Weak plural ties
Macro-regions				
Western Europe		France, United Kingdom, Belgium		Germany
Southern Europe	Greece	Italy, Spain		
Central and Eastern Europe (incl. Russia)		Russia, Hungary, Lithuania, Slovakia		
Southeastern Europe		Bulgaria	Bosnia Herzegovina	Albania
North Africa	Morocco, Tunisia, Egypt			
The Middle East	Turkey		Lebanon	
Asia Pacific				Australia
South and Southeast Asia			India, Indonesia, Malaysia	

Source: Compiled by the authors.

the region an effort from governing parties and conservative circles to bring religion back, usually for their own instrumental political ends (see Vekony, and Iliyasov in this volume).

However, there are exceptions to these cases, as, for instance, in Bosnia Herzegovina a plurality of religious communities is forcefully part of the nation's make up (see Tzvetkova and Todorova in this volume). The same is true for Lebanon (see Taskin in this volume). In Bosnia Herzegovina this plurality and the complex institutional make up that supports it is the result of the dissolution of the federal state of Yugoslavia and indeed symbolises the Balkan realities of the past where religious and ethnic mixity was the rule rather than the exception (Karakasidou, 1997; Todorova, 2009). In Lebanon, by contrast, plurality is the outcome of the historical creation of the nation as part of the process of decolonisation of the Middle East (Calfat, 2018).

Similarly we notice a certain commonality among Western European countries like Germany, the UK and Belgium, historically characterised by one or more dominant religious communities (albeit within Christianity), but where the ties between the nation and religion are nowadays weak both for historical reasons – as religious wars have marked the history of those countries (see Chapters 2, 4, and 5 by Sealy and Modood in this volume), and as a result of their post-war immigration experience and the ensuing cultural and religious diversity. In the case of Belgium, for instance, Sealy and Modood write that 'a gradual decline of religion's place in social and political life can be seen from the 1960s to the present day, with a steady decline in those identifying as Catholic, Church affiliation, involvement and attendance, and organization membership' (Chapter 2, this volume, p. 10). The case of France is more ambiguous as France is today home to the largest Muslim and largest Jewish populations in the European Union, but the dominant historical narrative is rather ambiguous on the positioning of these communities as part of the French nation. Naturally this ambiguity has to do with the concept and practice of *laïcité* and also with more complex issues about the acceptance of Islam and Judaism as properly French (see Sealy and Modood in this volume; Hafidi, 2020).

There are, though, some interesting outlier cases here like Italy and Spain where a strong identification with religion has been a part of the national consolidation process after long periods of authoritarian rule. Catholicism therefore remains deeply intertwined with national identities despite the fascist dictatorships that ended with the end of the Second World War in Italy and with Franco's death in 1975 Spain, discredited such mono-cultural and mono-religious narratives (see also Kosmin and Kysar, 2009; Triandafyllidou, 2001; and Magazzini in this volume). However, the change has been further the result of significant immigration in the post-1989 period, which has changed their demographic composition even though post-migration religious minorities (notably Muslims) are not included in dominant discourses of the nation.

South and Southeast Asia, on the other hand, show a strong similarity in their relation between the nation and religion(s) even if Indonesia, Malaysia, and India differ significantly in their demographic composition, institutional make up, and histories. They do not even share a common religious majority, as one might have argued that the importance of Islam might have dictated a strong relationship between religion and the state. On the contrary we might argue that these three countries have embraced their ethnic and religious diversity and converted it into a concept of national identity in the absence of a dominant national majority group or a dominant religion. As clearly argued by Mahajan in this volume, the traumatic partition of Pakistan from India as part of the creation of the state has marked this country's historical experience and institutional make up, emphasising both the importance of the dominant role of religion in the country's politics and the need to accommodate plurality and embrace it. Similar dynamics have been in process also in Indonesia and Malaysia, testifying both to the role of religion in nation-formation and to the plurality and mixity of the populations that find themselves within the boundaries of a single state after decolonisation (see Mahajan, Ibrahim and Rasid, Boy Zulian, and Bachtiar in this volume). These three countries also share a growing current of religious nationalism which tends to refuge their plural composition and impose a more aggressive stance towards religious minorities. Political parties play a key role in this process as they capitalise on the religious sensitivities of citizens to attract votes. While the case of India may have attracted more international attention in recent years, not least because of communal violence against Muslims, there are similar pressures in Malaysia where the governing party draws into question the secular principles of the Constitution and pushes towards the imposition of sharia (see Ibrahim and Rasid in this volume).

Discussing the role of religion and/or of religious plurality in the dominant discourses on the nation in these different countries would not be complete if we did not consider their actual demographic composition: in Tables 25.2 and 25.3 we have classified the 23 countries studied in this volume according to the size of each country's religious and non-religious minorities. Such categories are of course approximative and discretional to some extent, as data on religious affiliation is usually not included in official censuses and can be hard to come by. That being said, we believe that they are nonetheless helpful to situate and understand the context and degree of religious homogeneity, and place it in relation with the relationship between state and religion.

In Table 25.2 we distinguish between religiously homogenous countries, where religious minorities account for under 2 per cent of the total resident population; countries with moderate religious diversity, where one or more religious minorities account for 2–10 per cent of the total resident population; and, countries with significant religious diversity in their population, where minorities account for more than 10 per cent of the total population. Where relevant, we also distinguish between countries with a single religious majority community and those with two or more religious communities that have played a dominant historical role.

Comparing Table 25.1 to Tables 25.2 and 25.3, it is striking – if not paradoxical – that the level of religious homogeneity within a country is neither a sufficient nor a necessary condition for having a strong connection between the nation and a religious majority community. And similarly, the level of religious diversity is not a good predictor of a strong identification between the nation and religious plurality (what we termed above strong plural ties between nation and religion). A correlation can instead be observed between countries that have 'weak ties' between national and religious identities (Table 25.1), and the percentage of non-religious minorities in those same countries (Table 25.3).

Overall, while our 23 chapters show that demographic changes cannot be ignored and lead to changes in laws, practices, and even institutions (the role of Islam in Europe or also Australia is telling in this respect and is documented in several of our chapters, as is the increase in the non-religious sector of the total resident population), they do not always suffice for changing the national narrative. Thus, while Greece, Italy, and Spain have seen important changes in their demographic composition during the last 30 years as a result of immigration, in Italy and Spain these have been more readily (even if partly) accommodated in the national narrative compared to Greece. However, in the absence of significant demographic changes affecting the religious composition of the population, and with a significant degree of religious diversity in countries such as Turkey, we have witnessed a strengthening of the ties between religion and the nation (see Gülalpin this volume).

An interesting case is that of Australia where demographic change resulting from post-war migrations has brought religious freedom (and in particular accommodation of religious minorities' requests in education and employment contexts) centre-stage in the public

Table 25.2 Religious homogeneity of the resident population

Countries	Under 2% of religious minorities	2%–10% religious minorities	2%–10% religious minorities and more than one dominant religion	Over 10% of religious minorities	Over 10% of religious minorities and more than one dominant religion
Macro-regions					
Western Europe		France, Belgium	Germany	UK	
Southern Europe		Greece, Italy, Spain			
Central and Eastern Europe (incl. Russia)	Hungary	Lithuania		Russia, Slovakia	
Southeastern Europe		Bulgaria	Bosnia Herzegovina	Albania	
North Africa	Morocco, Tunisia			Egypt	
The Middle East			Lebanon	Turkey	
Asia Pacific		Australia			
South and Southeast Asia					India, Indonesia, Malaysia

Source: Compiled by the authors.
Note: The term religious minorities includes also minority denominations within a single religious faith.

Table 25.3 Presence of minority groups who declare themselves as non-believers, atheists, or humanists

Countries	Under 2% of non-believers	2%–10% of non-believers	10%–20% of non-believers	Over 20% of non-believers
Macro-regions				
Western Europe				UK, France, Germany, Belgium
Southern Europe		Greece		Italy, Spain
Central and Eastern Europe (incl. Russia)			Lithuania, Hungary, Slovakia, Russia	
Southeastern Europe		Bulgaria, Albania, Bosnia Herzegovina		
North Africa	Morocco, Egypt, Tunisia			
The Middle East	Turkey	Lebanon		
Asia Pacific				Australia
South and Southeast Asia	India, Indonesia, Malaysia			

Source: Compiled by the authors.
Note: This table refers to those communities or organised groups who declare themselves as humanists or atheists or non-believers. Naturally we recognise that this classification is based on imperfect data as, in many countries, religion is attributed by default and generally data available may not reflect the actual beliefs or practices of people with regard to religious matters.

debate. Linking these issues to concepts of human rights and Australian multiculturalism has been fraught with tensions as the dominant narrative has been one of benevolent non-interference of the state to religious matters (see Grossman, Gerrand and Halafoff in this volume), given also that such interference could create tensions between different tiers of government (federal and provincial level).

Combining the two dimensions presented above – notably, the level of religious diversity within the resident population of a given country and the strength of the ties between the nation and a single religious community or a plurality of communities – could be considered as a good indicator of the extent to which the accommodation of religious diversity has been a contentious issue for a given country. Contrary to the expectation that religious controversies might be more heated in those countries that see either a strong national-religious linkage, or a large religious diversity, or both, an analysis of the cases shows that even in countries with weak plural ties and a moderate level of diversity, religion has returned through the 'back door' as a contentious issue.

At the same time, we would have expected that countries with strong ties between the national identity and religious plurality and high levels of religious diversity would have smoothened the relative challenges through their institutional make-up and related laws and policies. Conscious of the importance of religious plurality for the nation and of the high stakes involved, we would have expected that countries like India or Malaysia would have worked out the relevant mechanisms and institutions ensuring representation, accommodation, and peaceful coexistence. While a system of institutional 'religious quotas' exists in the case of Lebanon, this has not been the case, for instance, in India, which has recently experienced an exacerbation of Hindu nationalism that tends to push the country towards our first column in Table 25.1 – notably towards those countries where the dominant national group identifies with a specific religion and leaves little room for diversity in the national narrative. On the other hand, it can be argued that in those countries that have included religious identities as a feature of their political system, such as Lebanon and Bosnia and Herzegovina, this has entrenched and crystallised religious segregation (see Tzvetkova and Todorova, and Taskin in this volume).

The institutional make up or the norms and policies of each country, however, are not the product of a rational calculation of costs and benefits, but rather the product of complicated histories, struggles, compromises, and oftentimes also, in the case of North African, Middle Eastern, and Asian countries the result of external interference and more specifically colonialism and post-colonial nation-building. Thus, while the tables in this chapter seek to offer an overview of the demographic and identitarian dimensions of religion and religious diversity in the countries studied, the landscape becomes increasingly complex when turning to their institutional and legal arrangements. Clear patterns are hard to find, and macro-regions do not necessarily offer meaningful clusters.

Outlining a full-fledged theory of secularism goes beyond the scope of this chapter and it is equally beyond our scope to offer a detailed legal and institutional typology of how the 23 countries under study in this volume govern their religious diversity (see also Modood and Sealy, 2019 for a fuller account). Below, though, we offer a basic typology of state-religious institutional relations and of the types of accommodation afforded to religion (whether of majorities or of minorities). Naturally these are ideal types and real country cases are more complex – and these regimes need to be nuanced. The two extreme regimes in this typology are relatively easy to define as in absolute secularism, religion is delegated to the private sphere and politics are totally free of religion. Where religion is accorded a hegemonic position, on the other hand, there is little separation between the political and the religious order. Naturally, different institutional constellations exist in our various countries but it is clear that France is the one closest to the regime of absolute secularism while Morocco or Malaysia are countries closest to a hegemony of religion.

Moderate secularism is typically the regime that prevails across the European continent and in Australia, and implies a significant level of separation between the state and religious institutions although religion remains an aspect of the public domain and there are accommodations to make room for religious faith, not just at the individual but also at the collective level. Moderate secularism is different from the strong presence of religion regime, which signals a quasi-secular arrangement where religious institutions and state are separate but a primary role is symbolically and institutionally accorded to religion as an element that can structure the public space (see also Modood and Sealy, 2019; Triandafyllidou et al., 2019).

With regard to this dimension, our book points to some very interesting variations: while in Morocco religion has a hegemonic position in politics as the King is 'Amir al-Mu'minin' (Leader of the Faithful), considered by some of the population as the "Representative of God on earth', and is also a 'Sharif', or descendant of the prophet (see Lahlou and Zouiten in this volume). Indeed, no other Arab or Muslim head of state is imbued with these qualities and the same is not true for Egypt and Tunisia. Egypt probably currently lies between moderate secularism imposed by its nationalist military authoritarian regime and a primacy of religion regime like Tunisia, where the two sets of institutions are separate but the importance of Islam is also recognised and accommodated in public and political life. Another indication here that can help us classify a country along the moderate secularism vs primacy of religion spectrum can be the existence of religious parties. This is true for the case of Tunisia (see Fahmi in this volume) but such parties are outlawed in Egypt (see Hellyer in this volume).

Table 25.4 Regimes of accommodation of religion and religious diversity

Countries	Absolute secularism	Moderate secularism	Primacy of religion	Hegemonic position of religion
Macro-regions				
Western Europe	France	UK, Germany, Belgium		
Southern Europe		Greece, Italy, Spain		
Central and Eastern Europe (incl. Russia)		Russia, Hungary, Lithuania, Slovakia		
Southeastern Europe		Bulgaria, Albania	Bosnia Herzegovina	
North Africa		Egypt	Tunisia	Morocco
The Middle East			Turkey, Lebanon	
Asia Pacific		Australia		
South and Southeast Asia			India, Indonesia	Malaysia

Source: Compiled by the authors.

Another interesting variation here is to be found between, on one hand, India – a country with an advanced system of political representation of different types of minorities (castes, tribes, and ethnic and religious communities) and strong respect for religion as an aspect of public life – and the case of Malaysia, that can best be characterised as a country where religion occupies a hegemonic position (see Ibrahim and Rasid in this volume) and the intermediate case of Indonesia where freedom of religion is acknowledged but where one must have one of the recognised religious faiths (see Boy Zulian and Bachtiar in this volume). This is particularly interesting as the regime of Indonesia does not outlaw atheism but rather does not conceive that a citizen of Indonesia is not a believer.

Delving a little further into these regimes we need also to acknowledge that among countries belonging to the moderate secularism category we may find similar norms and laws but divergent practices and degrees of accommodation. For instance, Belgium has recognised relatively early a large number of established religions including, for instance, Islam (in 1974) and Christian Orthodoxy (in 1985) – both brought to Belgium by post-war migrations – and has made necessary accommodations for the instruction of religion in schools and for the construction of worship places, even if such changes were at times not properly implemented until the early 2000s. By contrast Germany – where these two religions, and particularly Islam, are also new and the result of post-war labour migrations – has been more reluctant in practice to accommodate religious education or the construction of mosques and practice has varied a lot among the Laender. The practical difficulty of German Muslims to have Islam recognised as a public law corporation in each of the German states, as required by the law given the country's federal structure because of the country's federal structure and the specific requirements established in the law, has resulted in significant shortcomings for Muslims in Germany (like the impossibility to benefit from tax collection and other advantages accorded to religious societies established as public law corporations) (Gesley, 2017). Religious education in schools, however, has been accommodated in several Laender partly thus overcoming the lack of formally recognised status. The case of Germany may be considered as reasonably successful in accommodating post-migration Muslim minorities (see Sealy and Modood in this volume) compared to that of Italy, where starker implementation problems persist. In this country, despite constitutional provisions protecting freedom of religion, there has been strong reluctance in practice to accommodate minority religious education or the construction of mosques while Muslims in Italy cannot benefit from donations through income tax allocations.

The politics of governing religious diversity: towards greater openness or towards closure?

Historically, religion and politics, church and state have enjoyed various and often very close linkages. Nowadays, a variety of secularism models have been adopted by a number of countries, yet the entanglements of religiosity and politics are seeing a resurgence, and the issue of religious governance is often seen in problematic terms when it comes to addressing the claims and rights of religious minorities.

This situation inevitably raises important issues of both a philosophical and more broadly political and practical nature. How strict should the separation between state and religious institutions be? Can radically different cases (democracies and autocracies, for instance, or secular and non-secular states) be studied using the same concept and interpretative frameworks? What are the criteria for the comparisons we must make? And beyond the struggle for a peaceful coexistence, what can be said to constitute 'successful' religious diversity governance?

In this chapter we have looked at the compelling diversity outlined by the different cases of this book by categorising them into two dimensions, which can help us draw some linkages between the various countries and highlight their similarities and dissonances.

One dimension has to do with the relationship between religious membership and the alliance to a nation-state, which can, in turn, be declined into a) the strength of such linkages and b) the demographic composition of each country.

A second dimension, strongly intertwined with the first, is the typology of accommodation regime towards religion and religious diversity adopted by each country.

While there are neither straightforward nor causational conclusions that can be drawn between specific institutional or demographic features and religious governance models, the fact that no single dimension is determinant for the outcome is, in itself, an interesting finding. In this sense, one aspect that emerges from all the different chapters and cases is how religiosity, as any other cultural and identitarian dimension, has the potential to be politicised and instrumentalised.

As states are seeking a balancing act between forms of majority privilege and the challenges raised by new and complex religious pluralism across the world, one of the key questions about the future is how, and to what degree, the socio-economic and geopolitical influences will interact with categories of inclusion/exclusion based on religious identities.

References

Calfat, N. N. (2018). The Frailties of Lebanese Democracy: Outcomes and Limits of the Confessional Framework. *Contexto Internacional*, 40(2), 269–293.
Gesley, J. (2017, December 6). The Relationship between Church and State in Germany. *Law Library of Congress*. Retrieved from https://blogs.loc.gov/law/2017/12/the-relationship-between-church-and-state-in-germany/

Hafidi, A. (2020, March 23). France: is there such a thing as "Islamist separatism"? *OpenDemocracy*. Retrieved from https://www.opendemocracy.net/en/global-extremes/france-is-there-such-a-thing-as-islamist-separatism/

Karakasidou, A. (1997). *Fields of Wheat, Hills of Blood*. Chicago: University of Chicago Press.

Kosmin, B. A., and Kysar, A. (Eds.). (2009). *Secularism, Women and the State. The Mediterranean World in the 21st Century*. Hartford, CT: Institute for the Study of Secularism in Society and Culture.

Mahajan, G. (2017). Contextualizing Secularism: The Relationship between the State and Religion in India. In P. Losonczi and W. Van Herck (Eds.), *Secularism, Religion, and Politics: India and Europe* (pp. 36–56). New Delhi: Routledge.

Mahajan, G. (2020, February 3). In India: Secularism or multiculturalism? *OpenDemocracy*. Retrieved from https://www.opendemocracy.net/en/global-extremes/india-secularism-or-multiculturalism/

Medda-Windischer, R. (2017). Integration of New and Old Minorities: Beyond a Janus-Faced Perspective. *European Yearbook of Minority Issues Online*, 14(1), 1–36. https://doi.org/https://doi.org/10.1163/22116117_01401002

Modood, T. (2013). *Multiculturalism: A Civic Idea* (2 edition). Cambridge: Polity Press.

Modood, T. (2019). Intercultural Public Intellectual Engagement. In T. Modood (Eds.), *Essays on Secularism and Multiculturalism* (pp. 215–234). London/New York: ECPR Press.

Modood, T., and Sealy, T. (2019). *Secularism and the Governance of Religious Diversity* (No. 1). Retrieved from http://grease.eui.eu/publications/concept-papers/

Ruiz Vieytez, E. J. (2016). Cultural Traits as Defining Elements of Minority Groups. *The Age of Human Rights Journal*, (7), 6–28. DOI:10.17561/tahrj.n7.2.

Todorova, M. (2009). *Imagining the Balkans*. Oxford: Oxford University Press (updated edition).

Triandafyllidou, A. (2001). *Immigrants and National Identity in Europe*. London: Routledge.

Triandafyllidou, A. (2017). The return of the national in a mobile world. In A. Triandafyllidou (Ed.), *Multicultural Governance in a Mobile World* (pp. 19–41). Edinburgh: Edinburgh University Press.

Triandafyllidou, A., Gülalp, H., Iliyasov, M., Mahajan, G., and Račius, E. (2019). *Nation and Religion. Reflections on Europe, the MENA Region and South Asia*. Retrieved from http://grease.eui.eu/publications/concept-papers/ (No. 3).

Index

Note: Page numbers followed by "n" refer to notes.

Abdulgani, Roeslan 276
Abdul–Nasser, Gamal 218
Abdurrahman, Moeslim 271
Adeney-Risakotta, B. 267–268
Agency for the Legalization, Urbanization, and Integration of Informal Construction (ALUIZNI) 164
Ahlul Bait Indoensia, Tim 269
Ahmadiyah 269, 270
Albania, state–religion relations in 162–173; economic factors 168–170; historical and socio-political factors 164–166; Law on Non-Profit Organisations 163; Law on the Financing of Religious Communities 164; legal and regulatory framework 162–164; Ministry of Social Welfare and Youth 163; socio-demographic factors 166–167; State Committee on Cults (SCC) 163, 168, 169
Albanian Agency for Treatment of Property (ATP) 164
Albanian Muslim Community (AMC) 169, 173n1
al-Gama'a al-Islamiyaa 219, 225
Algeria, secularism in 3
Ali, Ben 231, 235, 236, 239
Ali, Rahmat 270
Ali, Rakyat Azmin 291
Al-Jihad 225
All-Party Parliamentary Group on British Muslims (APPGBM) 52
Al Qaeda 2
al-Sadiq Bey (1859–1881) 229

ALUIZNI see Agency for the Legalization, Urbanization, and Integration of Informal Construction (ALUIZNI)
Al-Zaytouna Ulama 230
Al-Zaytouna University 230
AMC see Albanian Muslim Community (AMC)
Anglicanism 17, 296
Ansar al-Sunna 219
APPGBM see All-Party Parliamentary Group on British Muslims (APPGBM)
Arab Spring 7, 239, 242
Atatürk, Mustafa Kemal 193, 195, 196, 199
ATP see Albanian Agency for Treatment of Property (ATP)
Aun, M. 24
Australia 296–305; Australian Human Rights and Equal Opportunity Commission 300; Australian Racial Discrimination Act 303; bias and discrimination against religious minorities 302–304; Charter of Human Rights and Responsibilities Act 2006 301; Commonwealth of Australia Constitution Act (1900) 305n1; Education Act 1872 299; Equal Opportunity Act 1984 301; Executive Council of Australian Jewry (ECAJ) 303; Fair Work Act 302; human rights 300–302; Human Rights Act 2004 301; Immigration Restriction Act 1901 297; International Covenant on Civil and Political Rights (1966) 301; Marriage Equality Act 2017 301; One Nation Party 303; religious education in 298–300; religious exceptionalism in 300–302;

321

Index

secularism in 5; Sex Discrimination Act 302; Special Religious Instruction (SRI) 299, 300; state–religion relations in 298–300
Ayadh, Abu 235

baptism 47, 132, 136, 137
Barmer Theologische Erklärung (Barmen Confession) 38
Bayat, A. 219
Belaid, Chokri 235
Belgium 13–22; Belgian Muslim Executive (*Exécutif des Musulmans de Belgique*, BME) 19; Centre for Equal Opportunities and Opposition to Racism 19; Council of Religions 3; Council of State 20; de-pillarization 18; devolved federalism in 16–21; economy 14; Employment Equality Directive 19; Islamic and Cultural Centre (*Centre Islamic et Culturel* [CIC]) 19; migration 15; minorities: in 19–20; National Ecumenical Commission 18; population 13–14; racial or ethnic discrimination 15–16; religion in 16–21; struggles over recognition 18–19; School–Pact–Law of 1959 17; school wars 17; socio-demographic context 13–16; trends and challenges 15–16
Bernardi, Cory 303
Big Society 53
BiH *see* Bosnia and Herzegovina (BiH)
Bosnia and Herzegovina (BiH): map of 181; state–religion relations in 176–187; economic factors 182–183; education, media, and culture 183–186; historical and socio-political factors 178–180; legal and regulatory framework 176–178; socio-demographic factors 180–182
Bosnian War 247
Bourguiba, Habib 230
Bouzekri, N. 69–70
Brahmi, Mohamed 235
Bulgaria 149–160; Bulgarian Socialist Party (BSP) 158; denominations, Institutional organisation of 157–159; Directorate of Denominations at the Council of Ministers (DDCM) 157; European Value Survey for Bulgaria (2008) 153–154; institutional structure, for religious governance/diversity 156–159; levels of religiosity 153–155; map of 150; Movement for Rights and Freedoms (MRF) 158, 160n13; National Muslim Conference (NMC) 158; population composition: challenges to 149–153; economic and cultural factors 153; religious diversity, governance of 156; Senior Muslim Council (SMC) 158; state–religion relations 155–156; United Democratic Forces (UDF) 157, 158

Catholicism: in Belgium 17–19; in France 26, 28; Roman 18; in Spain 77, 79–80, 85n9
Cesari, J. 25
Chirac, J. 31
Christianity 2; in Belgium 14; in Germany 36; in Hungary 106; Orthodox 18, 138, 149–151, 153–156, 159; socio-cultural 18
church tax (*Kirchensteuer*) 40
Cold War 201
collective consciousness 18
Compagnie van Verre 273
contemporary corporatism 39–43
Corbyn, J. 52
Crónica de los Reyes Católicos (1491– 1516) 79
Csepeli, György 102
Cymru, P. 52

Dar al-Ifta' ('House of Religious Verdicts') 222
Darwish, N. 214
Denmark 46; political secularism in 3
de-pillarization: mental 18
diversity *see individual entries*
Diyanet 19, 28
Dodik, M. 187n9
Driyarkara, N. 277
Dusuki, Asyraf Wajdi 288

Eastern Europe: secularism in 5
Economic Reform Programme 2019 (ERP) 168
EC *see* European Commission (EC)
Egypt 217–225; Free Officers Movement 218; law and the judiciary 221; Ministry of Endowments (MoE) 222; religious diversity in: historical overview of 218–220; regulatory framework 220–221; religious institutions in 222–223; secularism in 3; securitisation in 223–224
Eisenstadt, S. N. 5
El-Husseini, Talal 214
England *see* United Kingdom (UK)
Erdoğan, Recep Tayyip 201
ERP *see* Economic Reform Programme 2019 (ERP)
Europe: religious diversity in 2; secularism in 5; Western *see* Western Europe
European Commission (EC) 168
European Convention on Human Rights (ECHR) 50; Article 9, 28
European refugee crisis 126, 127

Faruki, Kemal A. 276
Al-Fassi, Allal 247
Ferrari, A. 62
Ferrari, S. 62
Finland: political secularism in 4
fiqh 272

Index

First World War/World War I (1914–1918) 27, 59, 102, 194, 195, 210
FKUB *see* Forum Kerukunan Umat Beragama (FKUB)
Forum Kerukunan Umat Beragama (FKUB) 273
France 24–32; Bureau of Religious Affairs (*Bureau des Cultes* 27; Concordat of 1801 27; *Conseil Français du Culte Musulman* (CFCM) 28; Federation National of Muslims of France (FNMF) 28; Ferry Law 27; Guermuer Law of 1977 31; Islamic Salvation Front (FIS) 30; *laïcité* 24; establishment of 26–27; and schools 30–32; struggle over 27–30; New Religious Movements (NRMs) in 28; Organic Laws of 1802–1808 26, 27; population by religious affiliation 25; radical secularism in 13; secularism in 4; socio-demographic overview 24–26; Union of Islamic Organisations of France (UIOF) 28
Franco, T. 80
freedom of religion 80–81
French Revolution 17

GAI *see* Gerakan Ahmadiyah Indonesia (GAI)
Geertz, C. 271
Gellner, E. 193
Gendjev, N. 159
Gerakan Ahmadiyah Indonesia (GAI) 270
Germany: Basic Law 42; church–state separation 37–39; contemporary corporatism 39–43; Council of the Evangelical Church in Germany (*Evangelischen Kirche in Deutschland*, EKD) 38; education in 42–43; federal corporatism 35–43; German Islam Conferences (*Deutsche Islam Konferenz*, DIK) 42; Islamic Central Institute in Berlin (*Islamisches Zentral-Institut*) 38; *Jugendweihe* 39; political secularism in 3; religious accommodations 40–42; socio-demographic overview 35–37; *Verfassungsschutz* (The Federal Office for the Protection of the Constitution – Germany's domestic security agency) 41
Ghannouchi, Rachid 231, 232, 236
Ginsborg, P. 71
Gorbachev, M. 137
GREASE project 248
Greece 88–96; Council of State 92, 95; education 94–96; Hellenic Foundation for European and Foreign Policy (ELIAMEP) 95; human geography of religion communities 89–91; legal and institutional framework, for religion and diversity 91–94; mosque controversy 92–93; muftis, judicial authority of 93–94; religious affairs in 94–96; sharia law disputes 93–94
Gunn, T. J. 26, 27

Hanson, Pauline 303
Hariri, R. 215
al-Hariri, S. 214
Harirism 215
Hassan, Bechir Ben 234
Hatta 268
HDI *see* human development index (HDI)
Hendropriyono, A.M. 269
Himpunan Kebangkitan Ummah (Ummah Awakening Gathering) 290
Hooker, M.B. 284
Houtman, Cornelis de 273
Hudec, I. 126
human development index (HDI) 248
human geography of religion communities 89–91
human rights 300–302
Hungary 101–108; ethno-religious composition 103–104; historical context of 101–102; Hungarian Islamic Community (Magyar Iszlám Közösség, MIK) 106, 107; Noé for the Life Community (*Noé Életért Közösség*) 108n4; Organisation of Muslims in Hungary (Magyarországi Muszlimok Egyháza, MME) 106, 107; religious governance in 104–107

ICERD *see* International Convention on the Elimination of All Forms of Racial Discrimination (ICERD)
IDM *see* Institute for Democracy and Mediation (IDM)
IFN *see* Inter Faith Network (IFN)
Imam-Hatip Schools 200, 202
India 255–265; All India Muslim Personal Law Board 259; Constitution of India 4; Muslim Women's Protection of Divorce Act 1986 262; population composition in 256–258; religious diversity in: consolidation of the right 263–264; constitutional framework 258–260; contextual paradoxes 260–261; emerging issues in 256–258; state–religion relationship 261–263; secularism in 4; Sikh Gurudwara Act 1925 259; Sikh Gurudwara Prabandhak Committee 259
Indonesia, religious diversity governance in 267–279; historical context 267–268; Islam 269–272; minority religions 272–274; *Pancasila* 276–279
INSTAT *see* Institute of Statistics (INSTAT)
Institute for Democracy and Mediation (IDM) 167–172
Institute of Statistics (INSTAT) 168, 173n5
institutionalisation: in Italy 66–69; in United Kingdom 52
Inter Faith Network (IFN) 52

323

Index

International Convention on the Elimination of All Forms of Racial Discrimination (ICERD) 290
Iranian Revolution of 19790 2
ISIS *see* Islamic State of Iraq and the Levant (ISIS)
Islam 1; in Belgium 19, 21, 22; in France 29; in Germany 39; in Greece 88–90, 96; in Hungary 102; in Indonesia 269–272; in Italy 68, 69; in Lithuania 112; moderate 201; radical 201; in Russia 138–140; stigmatisation of 2; in Turkey 193, 194–195
Islamic State of Iraq and the Levant (ISIS) 2, 74, 223, 236
Islamophobia: in Australia 304; in Belgium 15–16
Islamophobia: A Challenge for Us All (Runnymede Trust) 51
Italy 59–72; Albertine Statute 1848 66; Association of Italian Muslims (AMI) 72n8; Central Directorate for Religious Affairs 68; institutional framework 66–69; Italian Muslim Religious Community (Coreis) 72n8; Italian National Institute of Statistics (ISTAT) 64; Lateran Treaty 1929 68, 71, 72n5; Ministry of Interior 68; multi-tier system of legal recognition for confessions 67; National Pact 2017 69, 213; politicisation in 69–71; religious accommodation 69–71; religious diversity 69–71; state–church relations 66–69; Union of Muslim Communities and Organizations in Italy (UCOII) 72n8

JAI *see* Jemaat Ahmadiyah Indonesia (JAI)
jami'ya al-Khaldounia 229
Jaringan Intelektual Muda Muhammadiyah (JIMM) 275
Jaringan Islam Liberal (JIL) 275
Jawaharlal Nehru University 4
Jemaat Ahmadiyah Indonesia (JAI) 270
jihadism 225
JIL *see Jaringan Islam Liberal* (JIL)
JIMM *see Jaringan Intelektual Muda Muhammadiyah* (JIMM)
Jinnah, M.A. 259
Johnson, B. 52
Judaism 17, 111

Kahin, George Mc T. 276–277
Kamyshova, E. 137
Kandiyoti, D. 198
Kantorowicz, E. 241
Kartu Tanda Penduduk (KTP) 277
Kastoryano, R. 25
Kazenin, K. 144n5
Keil, S. 179

Ketuhanan Yang Maha Esa 276
Khadmi, Noureddine 234
Khan, S. 52
Khayr al-Din Pasha 229
Khrushchev, N. 136
KI *see* Kultura Islame (KI)
Kitab Undang-Undang Hukum Pidana (KUHP) 278
KNOEMA 168, 173n4
Koleth, E. 297
Krajcer, D. 126
KTP *see Kartu Tanda Penduduk* (KTP)
KUHP *see Kitab Undang-Undang Hukum Pidana* (KUHP)
Kultura Islame (KI) 166
Kuropatkina, O. 132

laicism 24, 32
laïcité 4, 24, 26–32, 59, 70, 207, 210, 309, 312; establishment of 26–27; and schools 30–32; struggle over 27–30
Larayedh, Ali 236
Lausanne Treaty (1923) 93, 94, 194
League of Nations 210
Lebanese confessionalism 207; recent political challenges to 214–215
Lebanon 206–216; Civil War (1975–1990) 206; current population composition: challenges to 208–209; economic and cultural factors of 209–210; Higher Islamic Shia Council 214; National Pact 1943 211; religious diversity governance, institutional structure for 212–214; state–religion relations, historical perspective of 210–212; Ta'if Accord (1989) 212–214
Leksin, V. 138
Lembaga Kajian Islam dan Sosial (LKIS) 275
Le Monde 231
'letter of ten,' 138
liberal intolerance 2
liberal separationalism 298, 304
Lithuania 111–119; current ethno-confessional population composition 112–113; Law on Religious Communities and Associations 115–119; religious diversity 115–118; religious governance 115–118; state-organized religion relations, historical background of 113–115
LKIS *see Lembaga Kajian Islam dan Sosial* (LKIS)
Lombard, D. 268
Lopasic, A. 165

Maarif, Syafii 276
Mahammad Bey (1855–1859) 229
Maha Sangha Agung Indonesia 273
Majelis Agama Buddha Tantrayana Kasogatan Indonesia 273
Majelis Agama Buddha Tantrayana Zhenfo Zong Kasogatan Indonesia 273

Index

Makdisi, U. 222
Malaysia 282–293; constitutional and legal framework 285–287; *Dharmaśhāstra* (the sacred law of Hinduism based on ancient Sanskrit texts) 282; Federated Malay States (FMS) 283; *Mānava-Dharmaśāstra* (Laws of Manu)) 282; religious demographics 287–289; religious diversity, governance of 287–289; trends and challenges 289–292; secularism in 4; state–religion relations, historical overview of 282–285; *Undang-undang Melaka* (Melaka Laws, *Hukum Qānūn Melaka* 283
Malikism 241
McMahon, S. 60
MENA *see* Middle East and North Africa (MENA)
Middle East and North Africa (MENA), secularism in 5
Mitrokhin, L. 137
modernity: authentic 5; multiple 5
Modood, T. 106, 298, 304, 310
Mohamad, Mahathir 288, 291
Mononutu, Arnold 276
Morocco 238–252; *'Amir al-Mu'minin'* (Leader of the Faithful) 239; Islamic movements, radicalization of 247–248; Mohammed VI Foundation of African Ulemas 247, 250n4; National Council for Human Rights 249; Party for Justice and Development (PJD) 239; religious sphere in 239–241; factors determining authorities' influence on 242–243; future challenges 247–248; management of 243–244; Ministry of Habous and Islamic affairs 245–246; Moroccan Constitution 238–240, 243–245, 249, 251–252; proclamation of principles 244–245; traditional/Islamic religious education 246–247; Ulemas, high council of 246; state-organized religion relations, historical background of 241–242; *Union Socialiste des Forces Populaires* (USFP) 239
Morsi, M. 7
Mubarak, Hosni 239
Muhammadiyah 269
multiculturalised secularism 46, 207
Muslim Brotherhood 219, 220, 230

Nahdlatul Ulama' (NU) 270
Naik, Zakir 292
nation–religion relationship 309–318
NATO 201
Natsir, M. 276, 277
Neck, Jacob van 273
Nehru, Jawaharlal 261–262
Norway, political secularism in 3
NU *see* Nahdlatul Ulama' (NU)

OE *see* Ottoman Empire (OE)
Office of the United Nations High Commissioner for Human Rights' (OHCHR) 164
OHCHR *see* Office of the United Nations High Commissioner for Human Rights' (OHCHR)
OIC *see* Organisation of Islamic Conference (OIC)
Oka, Gedong Bagus 272
Organisation of Islamic Conference (OIC) 166
Organisation of [the] Islamic Conference (Organisation of Islamic Cooperation) 173n2
Organization for Security and Co-operation in Europe (OSCE) 177
Örkény, Antal 102
OSCE *see* Organization for Security and Co-operation in Europe (OSCE)
Osman, Mohammed Nawab 291
Ottoman Empire (OE) 194, 196, 199, 203

Palestinian Liberation Organization (PLO) 211–212
Pancasila 276–279
Parisada Hindu Dharma Indonesia 272
Parti Islam Se-Malaysia (PAS, Malaysian Islamic Party) 290–292
Perikatan Nasional (National Alliance) 292
Perry, V. 179
Perwakilan Umat Buddha Indonesia 273
Pew Research Centre 62, 72n3; *Future of World Religions: Population Growth Projections, The* 1
PLO *see* Palestinian Liberation Organization (PLO)
political secularism 2–4
politicisation: in Italy 69–71
Prasad, Rajendra 262
Protestantism 17
Prussian Constitution: Article 15, 37; Article 16, 37; Article 18, 37
PSAP *see Pusat Studi Agama dan Peradaban* (PSAP)
Pusat Studi Agama dan Peradaban (PSAP) 275

Rahman, Tunku Abdul 285
Rakhmat, Jalaluddin 269
Rawa, Mujahid Yusof 291
Razak, Najib 289, 290
Reid, A. 267, 268
Reid Commission 285
Reinkowski, M. 213
religion: freedom of 80–81; penalty 48; public 53–54; reemergent 51–52; state regulation of 195–198; *see also individual entries*
religious accommodations 317; in Belgium 19–20; in Germany 40–42; in Italy 69–71; in United Kingdom 49–55
religious affiliation 18

325

Index

religious diversity: in Bulgaria 156–159; governance of 1–8; in Greece 91–94; in India 255–265; in Italy 69–71; in Lebanon 212–214; in Lithuania 115–118; politics of 318; in Slovakia 125–128; in United Kingdom 50

religious education: in Australia 298–300; in Bosnia and Herzegovina 183–186; in Germany 42–43; in Greece 94–96; in Morocco 246–247; United Kingdom 48; in United Kingdom 54

religious governance: in Bulgaria 156–159; in Hungary 104–107; in Lebanon 212–214; in Lithuania 115–118; politics of 318; in Russia 138–140; in Slovakia 125–128; in Spain 79–81; in Tunisia 235–236

religious identity 30, 95, 103, 113, 132, 133, 154, 200

religious minorities 302–304

religious pluralism 7, 157, 261

Ricklefs, Merle 271

Roman Catholicism 18

Ruiz Vieytez, E. 84, 86n18

Rushdie, S. 51

Russia 131–144; current ethno-religious composition 132–135; Islam in 138–140; religious governance 138–140; religious maps 141–143; state–religion interaction 135–138

Saadeh, S. 213
Sadat, Anwar El 218–219
Sangha Theravada Indonesia 273
Satanic Verses, The (Rushdie) 51
Schäuble, W. 42
Sealy, T. 298, 304
Second Vatican Council 80
Second World War 25, 29, 38, 46, 50, 66, 115, 124, 126, 128n1, 136, 155, 156, 179, 200, 211, 296, 312
sectarianism 222
secularism/secularisation 2–5, 26, 165–166, 193–203; anti-clerical 20, 25, 27; legal 30; moderate 4, 13; multiculturalised 46, 207; multiple 5; narrative 30; political 2–4; radical 13; rigid 4; in United Kingdom 50
securitisation: in United Kingdom 54–55
Sèvres Treaty (1920) 93
Şeyhülislam 195, 202
Sharifism 241–242
Sheikh Said 198
Shiism 269
Sisi, Abdel-Fattah El 221, 224
Sjadzali, Munawir 271, 275
Slovakia 121–128; Bill of Basic Rights and Freedoms 125; current population composition 122–124; Kotleba – People's Party Our Slovakia (*Kotleba – Ľudová strana Naše Slovensko*)122; Law on Civic Associations 1990 126; Law on Religious Freedom and the Legal Status of Churches and Religious Organizations 125, 126; religious diversity 125–128; religious governance 125–128; Slovak Information Service 127; state-organized religion relations, historical background of 124–125

Socio-demographics, trends and challenges of 60–65

Spain 74–86; Advisory Commission on Religious Freedom 82; Constitution of Cadiz 1812 79; current regulatory and constitutional framework 81–84; Islamic Commission of Spain (CIE) 76, 82, 86n16; multi-tier system of legal recognition for confessions 83; 'National Catholicism' (*Nacionalcatolicismo*) 80; Observatory of Religious Pluralism 76–78, 83, 85n4; Pluralism and Coexistence Foundation (*Fundacion Pluralismo y Convivencia*) 84; religious governance 79–81; religious trends and challenges 78–79; Royal Decree 593/2015 85n14; socio-demographic context 74–77; Spanish Centre for Sociological Research (*Centro de Investigaciones Sociologicas*, CIS) 75, 85n1; Spanish Federation of Jewish Communities 76; Spanish Federation of Religious Evangelical Entities (FEREDE) 82; Spanish Organic Law 7/1980 on Religious Freedom 81–83, 86n17; Spanish Statistical Office 77

Spanish Federation of Jewish Communities (FJCE) 82
Starodubovskaia, I. 144n5
Stasi, B. 31
Stasi Commission 1
state–church separation 25; in Germany 37–39; in Italy 66–69
state–religion relations: in Albania 162–173; in Australia 298–300; in Bosnia and Herzegovina 176–187; in Bulgaria 155–156; in India 261–263; in Lebanon 210–212; in Malaysia 282–285; regulation of 195–198; in Russia 138
Stepan, A. 3
Succariyeh, K. 214
Sukarno 268
Suleiman, M. 214
Sultan Abdülhamit II 196
Sultan Mahmut II 196
Sunnism 269
syncretism 268
Syrian Civil War 207

Ta'if Accord (1989) 212–214
Takfiri 216n2
Taylor, C. 3
TellMAMA 51

Index

Toufiq, Ahmed 250n4
'traditional' religious communities 111, 119, 126
Tunisia 228–237; debate over religion's place after 2011 232–235; neutrality of mosques 234–235; religious parties 233–234; Sharia in the constitution 233; Ennahda 233–237, 239; Islam and state before 2011 229–232; Mouvement de la tendence islamique (MTI) 231; National Association for the Preservation of the Quran 230; religious governance 235–236; Salafist Reform Front Party 233; violent extremism, challenges of 235–236
Turkey 193–203; *Caliphate*, abolition of 197; Directorate of Pious Foundations 200; Directorate of Religious Affairs (DRA) 195–197, 199–200, 202; Hat Law of 1925 199; Islam/Islamization 194–195, 201–203; Justice and Development Party (AKP) 193, 201–203, 239; Law for Dervish Lodges (*Tekke ve Zaviyeler Kanunu*) 199; Law for the Maintenance of Order (*Takrir-i Sükun Kanunu*) 199; Law of Unification of Education 197; Ministry of Education 197; post-war trends 200–201; Republican People's Party (RPP) 199, 200; secularism in 3; social life in early republican period, secularization of 198–200; state regulation of religion 195–198; Turkish-Islamic Synthesis 200; Turkish Islamic Union for Religious Affairs (DITIB) 28; Welfare Party 201
Tyutchev, F. 131

UK *see* United Kingdom (UK)
ulema 197
UMNO *see* United Malays National Organisation (UMNO)
UNDP *see* United Nations Development Program (UNDP)
Unified Examination Certificate 289–290
Unionism 17
United Kingdom (UK) 46–55; Board of Deputies of British Jews 52; British Nationality Act 1948 50; British Nationality Act 1981 50; Buddhist Society, The 52; Charities Act 2011 53; Charity Commission 53; Church of England 4, 49, 51, 53, 67, 68; Commonwealth Immigrants Act 1962 50; Department for Communities and Local Government (DCLG) 52; diversity in 50; economy 48; education 48, 54; Education Act 1944 54; Education Act 2005 54; Education Reform Act 1988 54; employment 48; Equality Act 2010 50, 54; faith 54; Hindu Council UK 52; Hindu Forum of Britain, The 52; Human Rights Act 1998 50; Immigration Act 1971 50; institutionalisation 52; Inter Faith Network (IFN) 52; Jewish Leadership Council 52; moderate secularism in 13; Muslim Council of Britain (MCB) 52, 55; National Council of Hindu Temples 52; Network of Buddhist Organisations 52; Network of Sikh Organisations 52; Office of the Chief Rabbi 52; political secularism in 4; public religion and society 53–54; religion reemergent 51–52; religious accommodations 49–55; religious census (1851) 49; secularisation 50; securitisation 54–55; Sikh Federation 52; socio-demographic overview 46–48; state–religion connexions 50–55
United Malays National Organisation (UMNO) 290, 292
United Nations Development Program (UNDP) 248
United States (US) 1
US *see* United States (US)
USSR: political secularism in 3

Vereenigde Oostindische Compagnie (VOC) 273
VOC *see* Vereenigde Oostindische Compagnie (VOC)
Volkskirche 37

Wali Songo 270
War of National Liberation (1919–1922) 194, 195
Weimar Constitution 37–38; Article 4, 40; Article 136, 37; Article 137, 37; Article 139, 40; Article 140, 39; Article 141, 39
West 1, 2; political secularism in 3; secularism in 5
Western Europe 1, 13; secularism 2
Wilkinson, R.J. 283

Yakhyaev, M. 137
Yassin, Muhyiddin 289
Yavuz, H. 195–196

Zagvozdina, D. 132
Zong, Zenfo 273

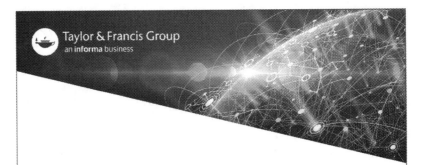

Printed in the United States
By Bookmasters